Victoria Crosses on the Western Front
The Final Advance in Picardy

October–November 1918

Victoria Crosses on the Western Front
The Final Advance in Picardy

October – November 1918

Paul Oldfield

Pen & Sword
MILITARY

First published in Great Britain in 2024 by
Pen & Sword Military
An imprint of Pen & Sword Books Limited
Yorkshire – Philadelphia

ISBN 978 1 52678 819 1

A CIP catalogue record for this book is
available from the British Library

Typeset by Mac Style
Printed in the UK by CPI Group (UK) Ltd, Croydon, CR0 4YY.

FSC www.fsc.org MIX Paper | Supporting responsible forestry FSC® C013604

Pen & Sword Books Limited incorporates the imprints of After the Battle,
Atlas, Archaeology, Aviation, Discovery, Family History, Fiction, History,
Maritime, Military, Military Classics, Politics, Select, Transport, True
Crime, Air World, Frontline Publishing, Leo Cooper, Remember When,
Seaforth Publishing, The Praetorian Press, Wharncliffe Local History,
Wharncliffe Transport, Wharncliffe True Crime and White Owl.

For a complete list of Pen & Sword titles please contact

PEN & SWORD BOOKS LIMITED
47 Church Street, Barnsley, South Yorkshire, S70 2AS, England
E-mail: enquiries@pen-and-sword.co.uk
Website: www.pen-and-sword.co.uk
or
PEN AND SWORD BOOKS
1950 Lawrence Road, Havertown, PA 19083, USA
E-mail: uspen-and-sword@casematepublishers.com
Website: www.penandswordbooks.com

Contents

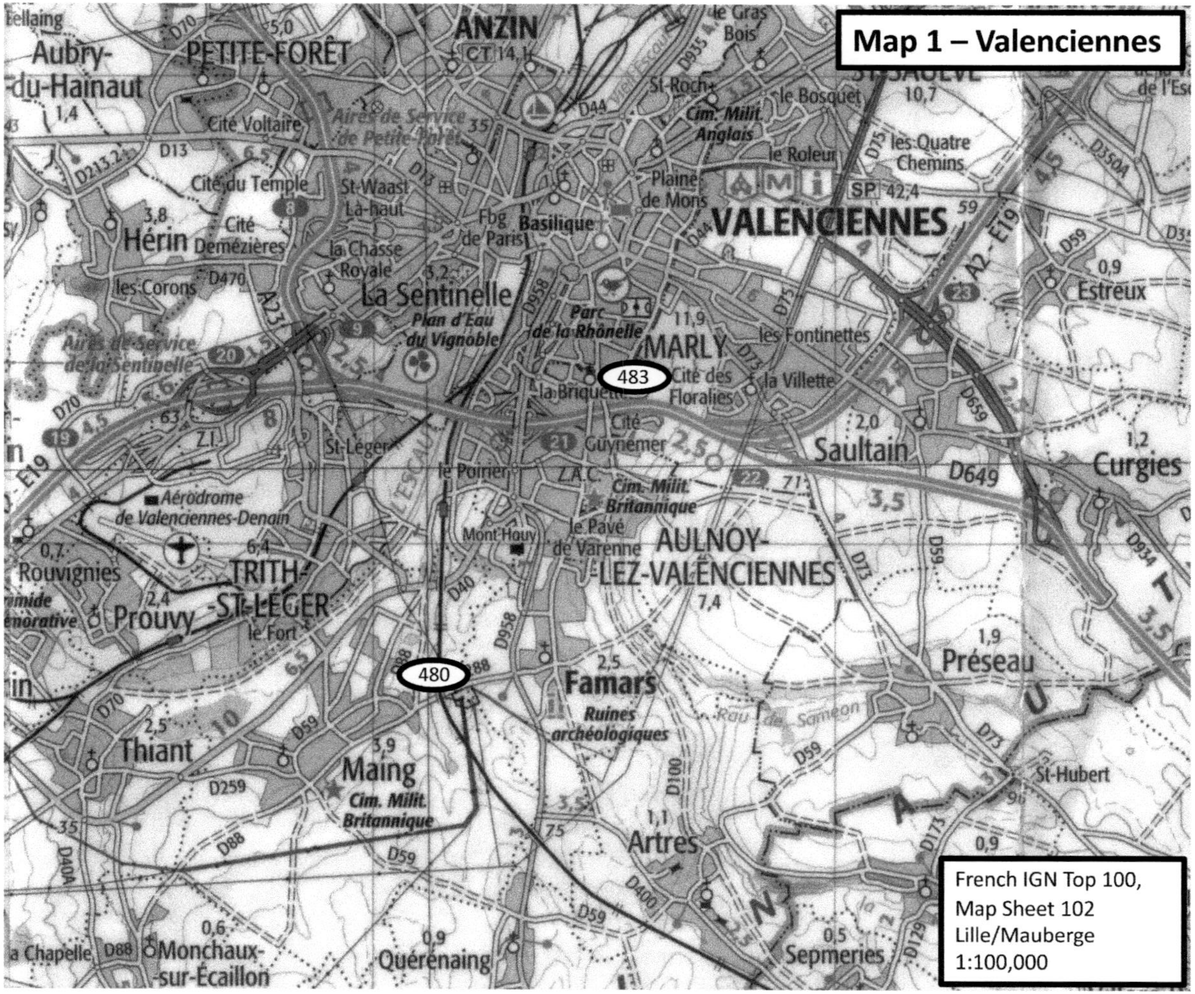

Map 1 – Valenciennes

French IGN Top 100,
Map Sheet 102
Lille/Mauberge
1:100,000

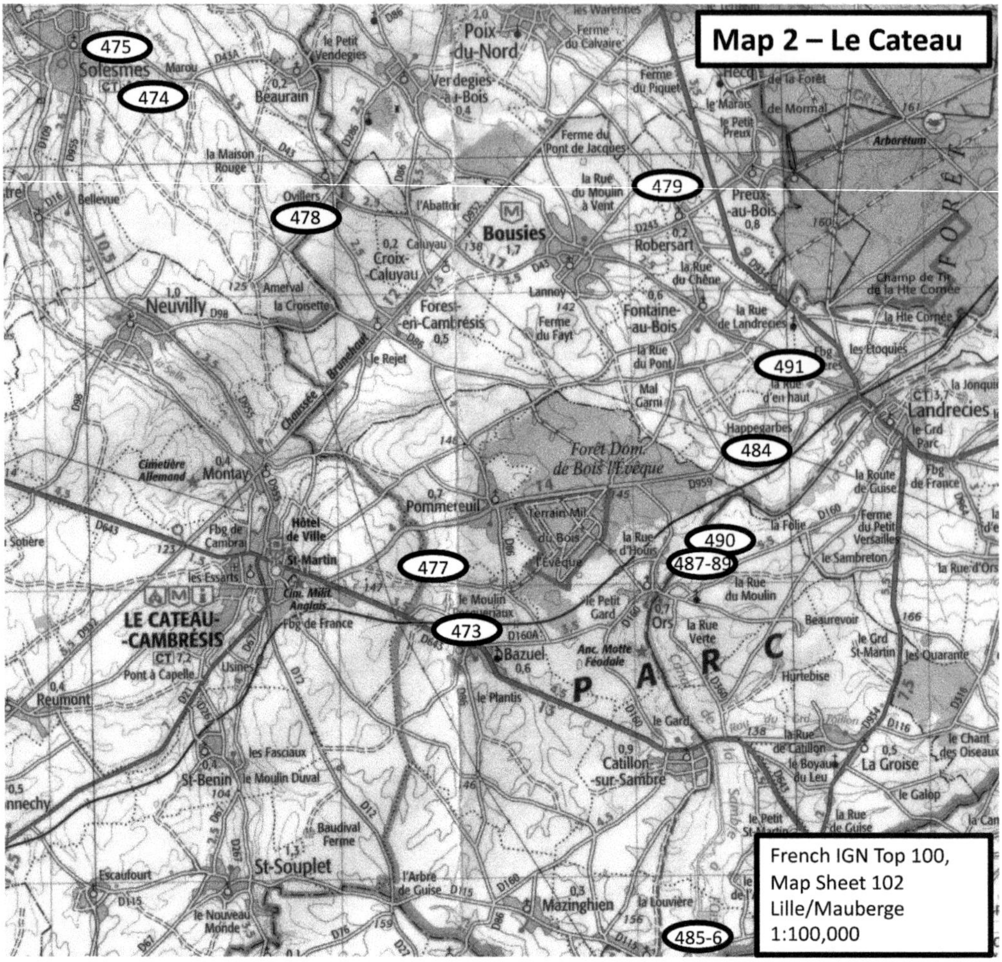

Map 2 – Le Cateau
475
474
478
479
491
484
490
487-89
477
473
485-6
Solesmes
Beaurain
Poix-du-Nord
Vendegies-au-Bois
Bousies
Robersart
Preux-au-Bois
Croix-Caluyau
Neuvilly
Fores-en-Cambrésis
Fontaine-au-Bois
Landrecies
Forêt Dom. de Bois l'Évêque
Montay
Pommereuil
LE CATEAU-CAMBRÉSIS
St-Martin
Bazuel
Ors
Reumont
Catillon-sur-Sambre
La Groise
St-Benin
St-Souplet
Escaufourt
Mazinghien
French IGN Top 100,
Map Sheet 102
Lille/Mauberge
1:100,000

Map 3 – Pont-sur-Sambre

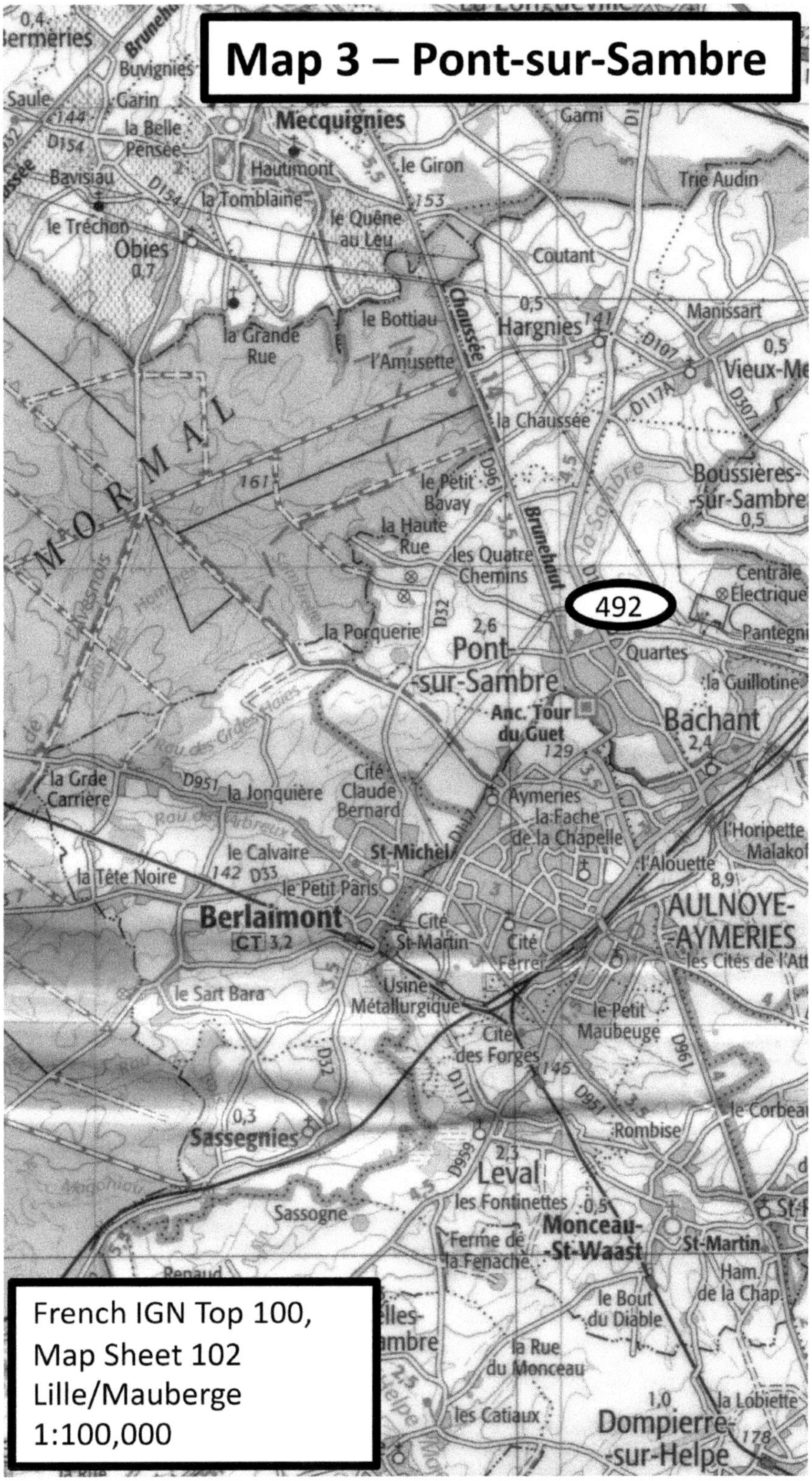

French IGN Top 100,
Map Sheet 102
Lille/Mauberge
1:100,000

Abbreviations

AB	Able Seaman
ADC	Aide-de-Camp
ADCA	Assistant Director Civil Affairs
AFS	Auxiliary Fire Service
AIF	Australian Imperial Force
AMF(L)	ACE (Allied Command Europe) Mobile Force (Land)
AMICE	Associate Member of the Institution of Civil Engineers
ANZAC	Australian & New Zealand Army Corps
ARP	Air Raid Precautions
ASC	Army Service Corps
AVC	Army Veterinary Corps
BAOR	British Army of the Rhine
BBC	British Broadcasting Corporation
BC	British Columbia
BEF	British Expeditionary Force
BM	Brigade Major
Brig Gen	Brigadier General
BSc	Bachelor of Science
Bty	Battery (artillery unit of 4–8 guns)
CA	Civil Affairs
Capt	Captain
CASC	Canadian Army Service Corps
CB	Companion of the Order of the Bath
CBE	Commander of the Order of the British Empire
CCS	Casualty Clearing Station
CEF	Canadian Expeditionary Force
CEO	Chief Executive Officer
CIGS	Chief of the Imperial General Staff
C-in-C	Commander-in-Chief
CIV	City of London Imperial Volunteers
CMG	Companion of the Order of St Michael & St George
Co	County or company
CO	Commanding Officer
Col	Colonel

Cpl	Corporal
CQMS	Company Quartermaster Sergeant
CRA	Commander Royal Artillery
CSgt	Colour Sergeant
CSM	Company Sergeant Major
Cty	Cemetery
CVO	Commander of the Royal Victorian Order
CWGC	Commonwealth War Graves Commission
DBE	Dame Commander of the Order of the British Empire
DCM	Distinguished Conduct Medal
DFC	Distinguished Flying Cross
DL	Deputy Lieutenant
DSc	Doctor of Science
DSO	Distinguished Service Order
FA	Football Association
FC	Football Club
FM	Field Marshal
FRCOG	Fellow of the Royal College of Obstetricians and Gynaecologists
FRCS	Fellow of the Royal College of Surgeons
GAF	Group of Armies in Flanders
GBE	Knight/ Dame Grand Cross of the British Empire
GC	George Cross
GCB	Knight Grand Cross of the Order of the Bath
GCMG	Knight Grand Cross of the Order of St Michael & St George
GCVO	Knight/Dame Grand Cross of the Royal Victorian Order
Gen	General
GHQ	General Headquarters
GOC	General Officer Commanding
GSO1, 2 or 3	General Staff Officer Grade 1 (Lt Col), 2 (Maj) or 3 (Capt)
HG	Home Guard
HMHS	Her/His Majesty's Hospital Ship
HMNZT	Her/His Majesty's New Zealand Transport/Troopship
HMS	Her/His Majesty's Ship
HMT	Her/His Majesty's Transport/Troopship/Hired Military Transport
HQ	Headquarters
HT	Hired Transport
ICC	Imperial Camel Corps
IRA	Irish Republican Army
IWGC	Imperial War Graves Commission
JP	Justice of the Peace
KBE	Knight Commander of the Most Excellent Order of the British
KCB	Knight Commander of the Order of the Bath
KCMG	Knight Commander of St Michael and St George

KCVO	Knight Commander of the Royal Victorian Order
Kms	Kilometres
KRRC	King's Royal Rifle Corps
KStJ	Knight of the Most Venerable Order of the Hospital of Saint John of Jerusalem
LCpl	Lance Corporal
LG	London Gazette
LMS	London, Midland and Scottish Railway
Lt	Lieutenant
Lt Col	Lieutenant Colonel
Lt Gen	Lieutenant General
Maj	Major
Maj Gen	Major General
MBE	Member of the Order of the British Empire
MC	Military Cross
MEF	Mediterranean Expeditionary Force
MGC	Machine Gun Corps
MID	Mentioned in Despatches
MiG	Mikoyan the Russian Aircraft Corporation
MM	Military Medal
MP	Member of Parliament
MS	Master of Surgery
MS	Military Secretary
MStJ	Member of the Most Venerable Order of the Hospital of Saint John of Jerusalem
MT	Motor Transport
MVO	Member of the Royal Victorian Order
NAAFI	Navy, Army & Air Force Institutes
NCO	Non-Commissioned Officer
NHS	National Health Service
NMSA	Naturopathic Medical Student Association
NZ	New Zealand
NZASC	New Zealand Army Service Corps
NZEF	New Zealand Expeditionary Force
OBE	Officer of the Order of the British Empire
OC	Officer Commanding
OIC	Officer in Charge
OStJ	Officer of the Most Venerable Order of the Hospital of Saint John of Jerusalem
OTC	Officers' Training Corps
psc	passed staff college
Pte	Private
QMS	Quartermaster Sergeant
RA	Royal Artillery

RAC	Royal Armoured Corps
RAF	Royal Air Force
RAFVR	Royal Air Force Volunteer Reserve
RAOC	Royal Army Ordnance Corps
RAP	Regimental Aid Post
RASC	Royal Army Service Corps
RD	Reserve Decoration (Royal Navy)
RE	Royal Engineers
Res	Reserve
Ret'd	Retired
RFA	Royal Field Artillery
RFC	Royal Flying Corps
RGA	Royal Garrison Artillery
RMA	Royal Military Academy
RMS	Royal Mail Ship/Steamer
RNLI	Royal National Lifeboat Institution
RNVR	Royal Naval Volunteer Reserve
RNZAMC	Royal New Zealand Army Medical Corps
RQMS	Regimental Quartermaster Sergeant
RSM	Regimental Sergeant Major
SA	South Australia
Sgt	Sergeant
SNCO	Senior non-commissioned officers
SO1, 2 or 3	Staff Officer Grade 1 (Lt Col), 2 (Maj) or 3 (Capt)
SOE	Special Operations Executive
SS	Steam Ship
TA	Territorial Army
TAVRA	Territorial Army & Volunteer Reserve Association
TD	Territorial Decoration
TF	Territorial Force
UNESCO	United Nations Educational, Scientific and Cultural Organization
UOTC	University Officers' Training Corps
USAAF	United States Army Air Force
USAF	United States Air Force
USAFR	United States Air Force Reserve
USNR	United States Navy Reserve
VAD	Voluntary Aid Detachment
VC	Victoria Cross
VRD	Royal Naval Volunteer Reserve Decoration for Officers
WAAC	Women's Army Auxiliary Corps
WAAF	Women's Auxiliary Air Force
WO1 or 2	Warrant Officer Class 1 or 2
WRNS	Women's Royal Naval Service
YMCA	Young Men's Christian Association

Introduction

The sixteenth and final book in this series covers the Final Advance in Picardy in October and November 1918. The book tells the story of seventeen Victoria Crosses.

As with previous books in the series, it is written for the battlefield visitor as well as the armchair reader. Each account provides background information to explain the broad strategic and tactical situation, before focusing on the VC action in detail. Each is supported by a map to allow a visitor to stand on, or close to, the spot and at least one photograph of the site. Detailed biographies help to understand the man behind the Cross.

As far as possible chapters and sections within them follow the titles of battles, actions and affairs as decided by the post-war Battle Nomenclature Committee. VCs are numbered chronologically 473, 474, 475 etc and, as far as possible, they are described in the same order. However, when a number of actions were fought simultaneously, the VCs are covered out of sequence on a geographical basis in accordance with the official battle nomenclature. As a result, it may appear that 476 and 481–482 are missing. However, they are covered in the previous volume.

Refer to the master maps to find the general area for each VC. If visiting the battlefields, it is advisable to purchase maps from the respective French and Belgian 'Institut Géographique National'. The French IGN Top 100 and Belgian IGN Provinciekaart at 1:100,000 scale are ideal for motoring, but 1:50,000 or 1:25,000 scale maps are necessary for more detailed work, e.g. French IGN Serie Bleue and Belgian IGN Topografische Kaart. They are obtainable from the respective IGN or through reputable map suppliers on-line.

Ranks are as used on the day. Grave references have been shortened e.g. 'Plot II, Row A, Grave 10' will appear as 'II A 10'. There are some abbreviations, many in common usage, but if unsure refer to the list provided.

I endeavour to include memorials to each VC in their biographies. However, every VC is commemorated in the VC Diary and on memorial panels at the Union Jack Club, Sandell Street, Waterloo, London. To include this in every biography would be unnecessarily repetitive.

In any work of this scale, it is almost inevitable that some errors will be included unintentionally. Every effort is made to cross-check facts. If mistakes occur, I apologise for them and urge readers to let me know so that future revisions can be made.

An extra chapter has been added to this volume exploring some themes that run throughout the series – ages, dates of birth, comparison of VCs awarded with number of casualties and a host of other factors. No particular conclusions are drawn but I hope it is of interest.

Thanks are due to too many people and organisations to mention here. They are acknowledged in 'Sources' and any omissions are my fault and not intentional. However, I again draw attention to the contribution made by fellow members of the 'Victoria Cross Database Users Group', Doug and Richard Arman, and other members who have died since work on these volumes commenced, in particular Vic Tambling, Alasdair Macintyre, Doug Porter and Alan Jordan. Without them these books would never have been completed. The work of Steve Lee and the Memorials to Valour website team has also been invaluable and their work continues.

As the series draws to a close, I must also thank the Pen & Sword team who have supported me throughout: Nigel Cave for his keen-eyed editorial comments and for pointing out the occasional missing comma; Matt Jones for suffering all the slings and arrows of the author's foibles; Mat Blurton for compiling the volumes from my drafts and Jon Wilkinson for his work on the cover graphics. Also to Katie Eaton, Lauren Burton, Heather Williams, Charlie Simpson and others for their patient assistance. To all I am most grateful.

Finally, thanks go to my family, particularly my long-suffering wife, who have put up with me locked down in the 'Fuhrerbunker' for days on end and supplied copious amounts of coffee and tea.

Paul Oldfield
Wiltshire
June 2024

Battle of the Selle

473 Sgt Horace Curtis, 2nd Battalion, The Royal Dublin Fusiliers (149th Brigade, 50th Division), Bazuel, near Le Cateau, France

18th October 1918

On 11th October Field Marshal Haig issued orders for a coordinated offensive by the Fourth, Third and First Armies to commence not before the 14th, when Second Army and the Group of Armies in Flanders were to resume their offensive to the north. Fourth Army was to make the main effort,

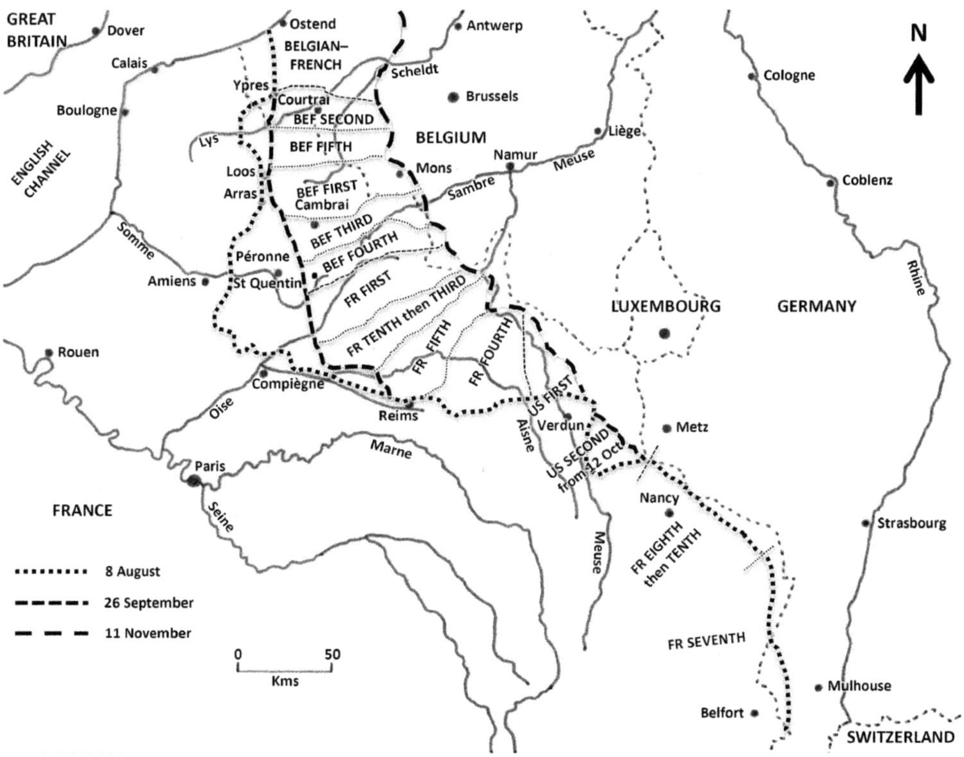

The advance of the Allied armies in the Hundred Days, as the German Army was pushed back inexorably towards its own borders.

in conjunction with the French First Army, in order to seize the line Wassigny–Le Cateau, before pressing on to the Sambre-Oise Canal. Third Army was to establish itself over the Selle, while First Army was to continue to protect the left of Third Army. The Cavalry Corps was ready to exploit towards Mons. Supply difficulties, caused by the advance outrunning its logistical support, meant that the offensive could not be launched until 17th October.

In Flanders the Second Army continued to advance in conjunction with the rest of the GAF. Roubaix, Tourcoing and Courtrai were captured and numerous crossings were made over the Lys. The right flank advanced in cooperation with Fifth Army, which began to follow up the German withdrawal on 16th October. Lille was abandoned in front of Fifth Army and by early on 20th October the whole of Second Army was over the Lys. As this phase came to an end (Battle of Courtrai) the GAF was ordered to drive on towards Brussels, with the priority being for Second Army on the right to seize crossings over the Schelde. The Battle of Courtrai is covered in the previous book in this series, *Victoria Crosses on the Western Front – The Final Advance in Flanders and Artois – September–October 1918*.

In accordance with Haig's orders Fourth Army launched the next offensive (Battle of the Selle) on 17th October, in cooperation with the French First Army. Objectives, although ambitious, were considered worthy of the risk. The troops were tired and formations were understrength, but they were in better shape than their adversaries. The Germans were expected to fight hard for the next position, the Hermann Stellung, in order to stabilise the front whilst major retirements took place in Flanders to the north and around Laon and Reims in the south. In addition, if the Hermann Stellung could be held, it would strengthen the German position in the armistice negotiations.

The Selle runs through a deep valley but in most places it is not a major obstacle, being up to one and a half metres deep and nine metres wide. However, the Germans had dammed it in places to raise the water level. There was also a railway embankment parallel with and about 300m beyond the river, which provided an excellent defensive line, in front of which were numerous machine gun posts. Because of the inundations and the enemy's positions, it was only possible to bridge the river just north of St Souplet and southeast of St Benin. The river was sufficiently narrow at St Souplet to use duckboard bridges. It was therefore decided to cross five battalions there over twelve of these bridges. At St Benin, where the river was slightly wider, it was necessary to use floating bridges, which would take about fifteen minutes to construct. Only one battalion was scheduled to cross there. The leading brigade was to cross on a three-battalion frontage, each led by a single company. Three bridging parties were formed to support these battalions, each of two officers and sixty-seven sappers and pioneers. Each group had eight bridges, four long and four short.

On the right, IX Corps, which was in contact with the French, was hampered by thick fog. Machine gun posts were overlooked and caused delays, but the objective

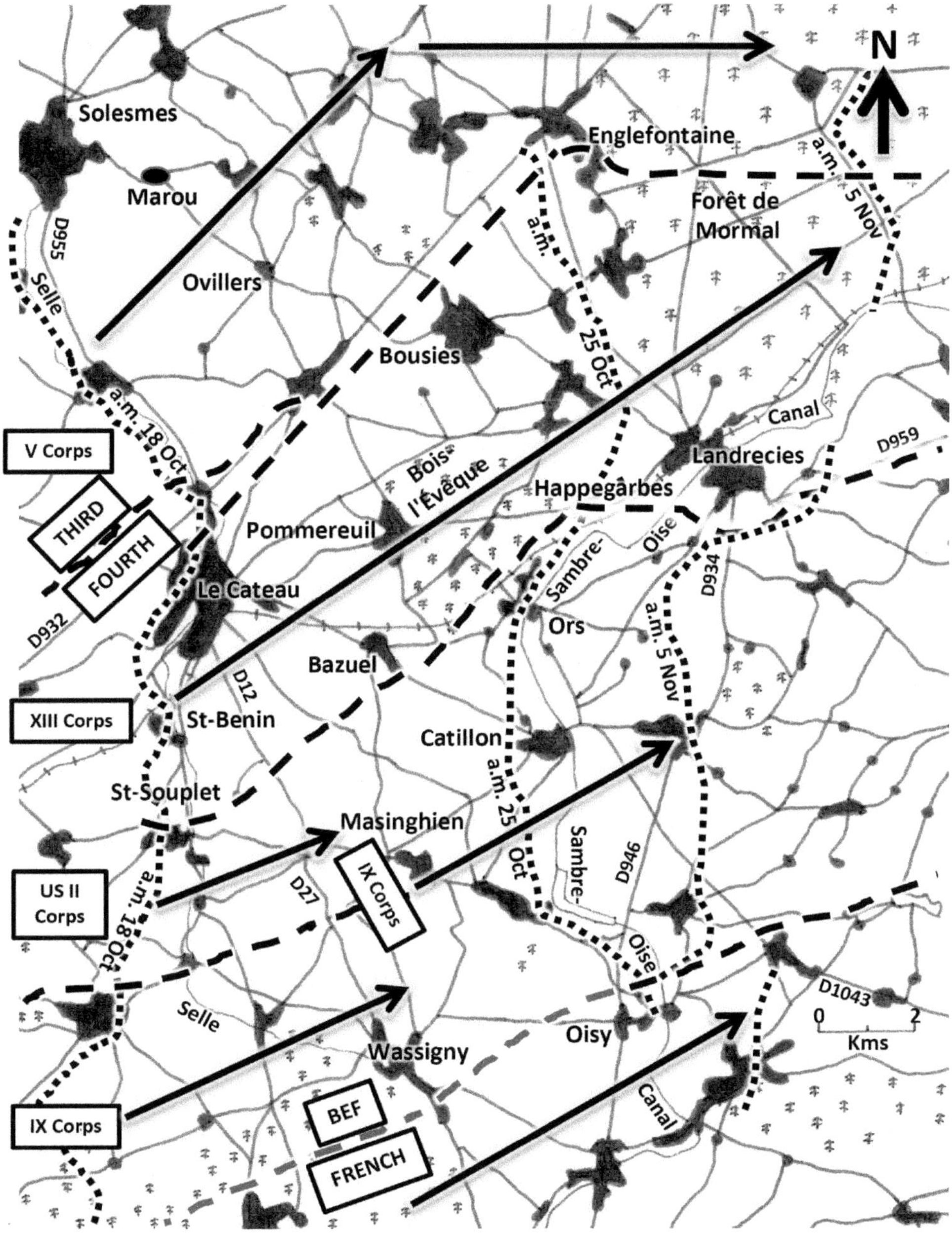

The advance of Fourth Army 18th October–5th November.

was reached in places. In others places the troops were only just short of it. In the centre the American II Corps managed to cross the Selle before encountering serious opposition. However, by the end of the day a line between the intermediate (Red Dotted Line) and first (Red Line) objectives had been gained.

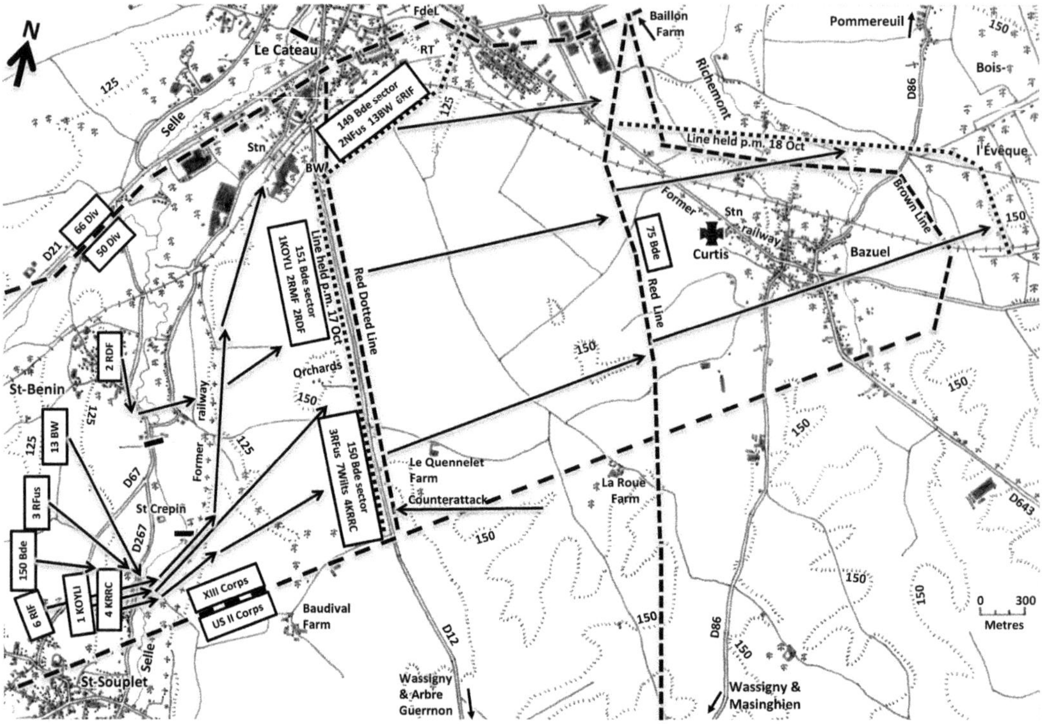

There are numerous small copses in this area, particularly around Le Cateau and Bazuel. For clarity only the most significant are shown. Three short solid lines on the Selle (two either side of St Crepin and one on the west side of Le Cateau) mark the positions of the dams. BW = brickworks, FdeL = Faubourg de Landrecies, RT = railway triangle, Stn = station. It is difficult to obtain a clear view over the ground of 75th Brigade's advance southwest of Bazuel. The former station building and course of the railway in Bazuel are still evident. From the former station, drive northwest through the village along the D643 towards Le Cateau until then road dips towards a railway bridge. Just before the railway bridge take the track on the left and drive carefully for 250m to a track junction on the right. Park here and walk up the hill to the northwest. Even from there it is difficult to see Bazuel which nestles in dead ground behind the line on trees on the eastern skyline.

The XIII Corps on the left attacked at 5.20 a.m. between St Souplet and Le Cateau. The 50th Division was on the right and 66th Division was on the left, with 25th Division in reserve. The two assault divisions also had the machine guns of 18th and 25th Divisions in support. Twelve Mark V tanks of 1st Tank Battalion were allotted to 50th Division. A change of boundaries a few days before the attack gave 50th Division a comparatively easy stretch of river to cross immediately north of St Souplet. Its operation was to unfold in three phases:

> First – 151st Brigade was to cross the Selle at 5.20 a.m. on a two-company frontage of about 550m and seize the line of the railway. The right (4th King's Royal Rifle Corps) and centre (1st King's Own Yorkshire Light Infantry)

battalions were then to move northeast onto the high ground and the intermediate objective (Red Dotted Line) along the Arbre Guernon–Le Cateau road. The left battalion (6th Royal Inniskilling Fusiliers) was to swing left to roll up the defences along the railway to the north as far as the station south of Le Cateau.

Second – 149th Brigade was to use the crossings made by 151st Brigade, except for 13th Black Watch on the left, which was to cross in the area of the demolished bridge at St Benin. The 3rd Royal Fusiliers on the right and 2nd Royal Dublin Fusiliers in the centre, were to pass through the right and centre battalions of 151st Brigade at 8.35 a.m. and capture the first objective (Red Line), the ridge about 1,800m further east. On the left, 13th Black Watch, having crossed the railway, was to turn north to reinforce 6th Inniskilling Fusiliers (151st Brigade) and move against the railway triangle, where a link was to be made with 66th Division.

Third – 150th Brigade was to pass through 149th Brigade about 11.20 a.m., when the first objective had been secured, and capture Bazuel (Brown Line), while Le Cateau was mopped up by 66th Division.

To the north, V Corps did not attack at the same time as XIII Corps and arrangements were made to mask the enemy observers on the high ground to the northeast using smoke. V Corps also agreed to distract the enemy's attention with its artillery, including firing a creeping barrage.

Despite German gas shelling and thick mist, fourteen duckboard and floating bridges were moved forward to the Selle during the night. By five minutes before zero five duckboard bridges were across the river. When the barrage of three field artillery brigades and ninety-six machine guns (50th and 100th Machine Gun Battalions MGC) opened at 5.20 a.m., the remaining bridges north of St Souplet were constructed within fifteen minutes by 446th Field Company RE and C Company, 5th Royal Irish Regiment (Pioneers). At the same time four bridges were established by 447th Field Company and two platoons of B Company of the Pioneers at St Benin.

A few minutes later, under the cover of smoke and the barrage fired by five field artillery brigades, the infantry of 151st Brigade crossed without suffering a single casualty. The 4th King's Royal Rifle Corps was the first over, followed closely by 1st King's Own Yorkshire Light Infantry and 6th Royal Inniskilling Fusiliers. The railway line and the ridge to the east were held in strength and were protected by a belt of wire in front almost thirty metres wide. By 8.45 a.m. 4th King's Royal Rifle Corps and two companies of 1st King's Own Yorkshire Light Infantry had only advanced to the western slopes of the spur east of St Crepin and the railway. The rest of 1st King's Own Yorkshire Light Infantry was in the orchards on top of the ridge east of St Benin. The 6th Royal Inniskilling Fusiliers had turned north to roll up the railway line and was encountering strong opposition amongst the station buildings.

Because of the delay 149th Brigade, which was to advance to the first objective (Red Line), became involved in the fight with 151st Brigade. On the right 3rd Royal Fusiliers crossed the railway embankment and moved up behind 4th King's Royal Rifle Corps, where it formed a defensive flank facing south, where the Americans had yet to come up in line. In the centre 2nd Royal Dublin Fusiliers supported 1st King's Own Yorkshire Light Infantry. On the left, 13th Black Watch, with two mortars attached from 149th Trench Mortar Battery, was sent north earlier than anticipated to assist 6th Royal Inniskilling Fusiliers in subduing the opposition on the railway line.

The 2nd Royal Dublin Fusiliers had to wait for 13th Black Watch, advancing northwards along the railway, to clear its front before beginning to cross the Selle at 6.35 a.m. B Company used one of the bridges and the other companies forded. Despite the thick fog, the companies were almost immediately met by heavy machine gun fire. A Company in particular suffered from flanking machine gun fire as it crossed the river. The company commander and several men were killed and a number of other officers and men were wounded. As a result, the Battalion did not reach the railway until 8.30 a.m.

By 11.00 a.m. 4th King's Royal Rifle Corps was just west of the Arbre Guernon – Le Cateau road, facing Le Quennelet (now Quenelet) Farm, and 3rd Royal Fusiliers had formed a defensive flank facing southeast. Half of 1st King's Own Yorkshire Light Infantry and 2nd Royal Dublin Fusiliers were intermingled and had been checked in the orchards on the Arbre Guernon – Le Cateau road north of 4th King's Royal Rifle Corps. Further north 6th Royal Inniskilling Fusiliers and 13th Black Watch also became mixed up as they encountered strong opposition at the station buildings south of Le Cateau.

With 149th Brigade bogged down with 151st Brigade and unable to advance on the Red Line, 150th Brigade was brought forward to carry out this task. At the same time 75th Brigade (25th Division) was allocated to 50th Division to carry out 150th Brigade's original task when the opportunity arose. In preparation for a renewal of the advance, XIII Corps' heavy artillery fired an intense bombardment for thirty minutes from 3.00 p.m. on the northern end of the station buildings and the railway triangle. However, this coincided with two strong counterattacks at the junction of 50th Division with II American Corps to the south. The 1st King's Own Yorkshire Light Infantry held but 4th King's Royal Rifle Corps and 3rd Royal Fusiliers suffered heavy casualties and were forced off the top of the ridge, as was the American 27th Division.

At 4.00 p.m. 150th Brigade was ordered to retake the lost ground and then secure the first objective. The advance was led by 7th Wiltshire and 2nd Royal Munster Fusiliers, carrying forward 4th King's Royal Rifle Corps and 3rd Royal Fusiliers with them. The first objective was secured by 4.30 p.m. Contact was established with the Americans on the right at some buildings 550m north-northeast of Bandival (now Baudival) Farm. About the same time the Germans were pushed out of Le Cateau station but held on to the brickworks.

The twelve tanks allocated to 50th Division played a part in these operations. On the day only eleven were available and these were distributed between 151st and 149th Brigades, four on each flank and three in the centre. Cribs were dropped into the Selle 275m north of the bridge on the St Souplet–Arbre Guernon road, where the river was only three metres wide and just over a metre deep. On the right one tank bogged in and developed clutch problems. However, the other three reached the intermediate objective (Red Dotted Line), cleared Le Quennelet Farm with a party of infantry and mopped up a number of machine guns between the Red Dotted and Red Lines. In the centre one crew was overcome by gas and fumes but the other two reached the objective, where they were subjected to heavy artillery and machine gun fire. One received six direct hits and caught fire. The other engaged machine guns ahead of the infantry near the brickworks until it was called back to rally with the other surviving tanks. On the left one tank broke down before reaching the river and another two bogged in. The last tank overran two machine guns, at the request of the infantry on the right flank, before moving to Le Quennelet Farm, where it was directed onto its original objective on the left. On the way a field gun was put out of action. Some Germans, who climbed on the roof of the tank, were only dislodged with difficulty. Some mortars were dealt with at the station but, finding no infantry and with the crew suffering from fumes, the tank went back along the railway and eventually rallied close to the crossing point over the Selle at St Souplet.

By the afternoon all three brigades were fully involved and the battalions were completely mixed up. The divisional commander therefore reorganised his units and gave the nearest sector to each brigade commander:

Right – HQ 150th Brigade (Brigadier-General G Rollo), with 3rd Royal Fusiliers (149th Brigade), 7th Wiltshire (150th Brigade) and 4th King's Royal Rifle Corps (151st Brigade), held the line of the Arbre Guernon–Le Cateau road from the Corps southern boundary to the orchards.

Centre – HQ 151st Brigade (Brigadier-General RE Sugden), with 1st King's Own Yorkshire Light Infantry (151st Brigade), 2nd Royal Munster Fusiliers (150th Brigade) and 2nd Royal Dublin Fusiliers (149th Brigade) continued the line to the brickworks.

Left – HQ 149th Brigade (Brigadier-General PM Robinson), with 2nd Northumberland Fusiliers (150th Brigade), 13th Black Watch (149th Brigade) and 6th Royal Inniskilling Fusiliers (151st Brigade), continued the line to the northern divisional boundary.

All three sectors established themselves firmly in their positions. At 8.00 p.m. the brickworks were taken, with one hundred prisoners, but the railway triangle was fought for all night.

North of Le Cateau, 66th Division had less distance to cover and started the main attack at 8.05 a.m., having made a feint at 5.20 a.m. It was decided to encircle Le Cateau, with 66th Division advancing around the north to nip out the railway triangle and meet up with 50th Division. Despite heavy fighting and severe flanking fire, the objective was reached but a defensive left flank with Third Army to the north was not formed until evening. Most of Le Cateau was cleared during the day, following severe fighting, and only Faubourg de Landrecies in the east was held by the Germans at nightfall.

Despite setbacks it had been a successful day for Fourth Army. All corps were over the Selle and the Hermann Stellung I position had been breached. There were no more serious obstacles to the advance until the Sambre-Oise Canal was reached. However, it would be another ten days before the French on the right drew level. Fourth Army had captured 4,500 prisoners and more than twenty guns. General Rawlinson issued orders for the advance to be pressed forward next day. The first objective was essentially the same as the Red Line on 17th October and the second was the line Wassigny–Masinghien, Bazuel and the Richemont River. Having captured that objective, divisions were to exploit as far as the Sambre-Oise Canal.

The advance by XIII Corps continued at 5.30 a.m. on the 18th under heavy shellfire. The 50th and 66th Divisions continued the attack with similar barrages to the previous day. There were no tanks available. The attack was in two phases on the right. In the first, 50th Division, still divided into three sectors, was to capture the ridge 1,800m east of the Arbre Guernon–Le Cateau road, its second objective the previous day (Red Line). In the second, at 8.30 a.m., 75th Brigade (25th Division) was attached to seize Bazuel and, if possible, a third objective, the Bazuel–Baillon Farm (northeast of Le Cateau) road.

The 50th Division's right sector was held up at first with the Americans by fire from La Roue (Roux in some accounts) Farm, but the Red Line was eventually seized. The centre sector, with 2nd Royal Munster Fusiliers and 2nd Royal Dublin Fusiliers leading and 1st King's Own Yorkshire Light Infantry in support, set off on compass bearings through the mist. They surprised the defenders, reached the first objective and took 300 prisoners. The left sector rushed the railway line, taking many prisoners and capturing a number of guns, before pressing on and seizing the railway triangle by 10.45 a.m. The battalions continued along the railway to the Le Cateau–Pommereuil road and made contact with 66th Division on the left flank.

Although all the officers were casualties, elements of a company of 2nd Royal Dublin Fusiliers surged on 1,100m beyond the first objective to reach Bazuel. **Sergeant Horace Curtis** was well ahead when his platoon came under fire from a number of machine guns, which threatened to halt the advance. He located two machine gun posts and rushed forward through their fire and the British barrage.

The site of the railway station in Bazuel, looking across the D643 from the south side towards the northeast. The railway ran towards the camera position from the opposite side of the road where there are a few prominent trees in the right distance. The line of the railway, which is still visible as a track, crossed the road at this point and then ran off to the left on the south side of the road and parallel with it. This is where Curtis attacked the train and captured the enemy party.

Having outflanked the posts, he bombed them into submission, wounding or killing both crews. His action forced four other posts to surrender with their weapons. He then led his men into Bazuel, where a train was at the station disembarking enemy troops. He shot the driver, to prevent the train from escaping, and took the whole party prisoner before the rest of his platoon joined him. Despite this outstanding success, the platoon was isolated ahead of the barrage and had to withdraw.

The 75th Brigade, with 13th Black Watch (149th Brigade) and 149th Trench Mortar Battery under command, passed through at 8.42 a.m. and established itself on the western slope of the ridge, with Bazuel at the northern end. The right flank was not in touch with the Americans, who were still held up at La Roue Farm. However, when 150th Brigade captured this post from the northeast at 3.00 p.m., the Americans were able to come up in line. The advance continued and at 5.00 p.m. Bazuel was reached, despite heavy fire from the flanks and in front. A 9.2″ gun and a complete 4.2″ howitzer battery were captured intact. A line of posts was established east and northeast of the village on the final objective.

When 75th Brigade passed through, 2nd Royal Dublin Fusiliers went into support at 11.40 a.m. At 2.00 p.m. the Battalion cleared some machine guns in houses that had been overlooked in the mist and then filled a gap on the right. This was completed by 6.00 p.m. and at 11.00 p.m., 2nd Royal Dublin Fusiliers was relieved by 198th Brigade (66th Division), having suffered 210 casualties (thirty-seven killed, 168 wounded, gassed or shell-shocked and five missing) in two days out of a trench strength of 478. In the same period, in addition to the enemy killed, the Battalion took 354 prisoners and captured nine mortars, thirty-seven machine guns and a complete battery of field guns.

The front of 50th Division was taken over by 75th Brigade at nightfall, with 13th Black Watch (149th Brigade) remaining attached. All three brigades of 50th Division then pulled back into reserve. One of the battalions, 4th King's Royal Rifle Corps (151st Brigade), numbered only one hundred riflemen and most of them had been gassed. The Division had taken 1,165 prisoners.

On the left, 66th Division completed clearing Le Cateau and moved forward to the second objective on the ridge between Le Cateau and the Richemont river. At the end of the day XIII Corps was everywhere on its objective and poised to close-up to the Sambre-Oise Canal. On Fourth Army's right flank, IX Corps swept all before it and the Americans in the centre also made their objectives. In the three days of the battle, Fourth Army took 5,139 prisoners and sixty guns.

20th October 1918

474 Pte Alfred Wilkinson, 1/5th Battalion, The Manchester Regiment (127th Brigade, 42nd Division), Marou, France

475 Sgt John Daykins, 2/4th Battalion, The York and Lancaster Regiment (187th Brigade, 62nd Division, Solesmes, France

Fourth Army continued to close up to the Hermann Position on 19th October. First Army, following the enemy retirement, was delayed in places by cratered roads and blown bridges but at the end of the day advances of almost ten kilometres had been made. The whole of First Army was then level with Third Army on the Selle. At the end of the day the southern flank of the BEF was close to the Hermann Position, but Fifth and Second Armies in the north were still sixteen kilometres away.

Unlike First Army, Third Army only had a few small bridgeheads over the Selle and the enemy matched closely the assaulting divisions in strength. Commencing the offensive with an opposed river crossing was fraught with risk. All four corps (from south to north – V, IV, IV and XVII) were ordered to attack at 2.00 a.m. on 20th October in order to establish suitable assembly positions east of the Selle. There was no preliminary bombardment to maintain surprise. It was a particularly dark night and the rain came down in torrents.

The right of V Corps formed a defensive flank and the left crossed the Selle relatively unscathed. Some stiff fighting took place on the railway but it and Neuvilly fell around 5.00 a.m. Amerval changed hands a few times during the day. On the left another attack was coordinated in the afternoon with IV Corps. Despite the setbacks, all objectives were taken.

The IV Corps planned to exclude Solesmes on its left flank until VI Corps had secured it. Both assault divisions were already on the east bank of the Selle and assembled without difficulty 125–175m beyond the river. This was possible due to the efforts of the engineers, who had placed ten bridges over the swollen river, which in no place in this area was fordable. On the right 5th Division's advance

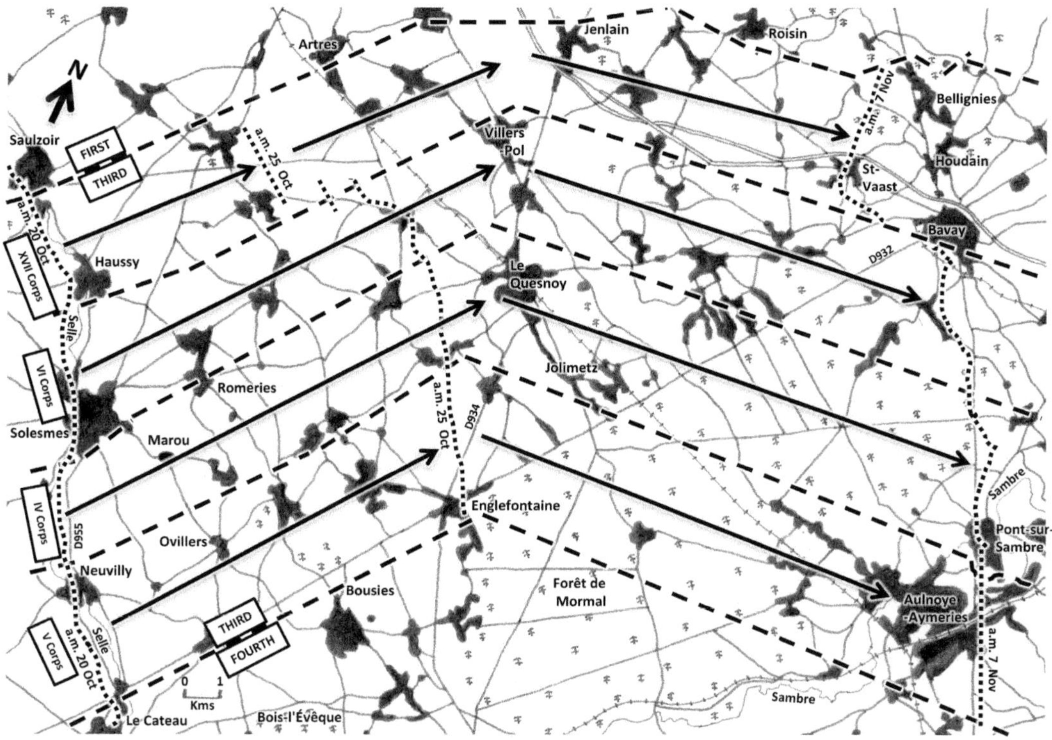

The advance of Third Army 20th October–7th November.

proceeded well until after the third objective, where resistance was not overcome until the afternoon in conjunction with V Corps.

In 42nd Division the 126th Brigade led the advance to the first two objectives (Blue and Green Lines, supported by six brigades of field artillery. On the right was 5th East Lancashire and 10th Manchester was on the left. One battalion went forward with its bandsmen, who were acting as stretcher bearers, playing the regimental march. Very heavy fighting took place for the railway (Blue Line) and it took two and a half hours to overcome the defences. The Brigade's final objective was taken by 4.40 a.m., having passed through six belts of defences. A company screened off Solesmes and made contact with 62nd Division (VI Corps) later in the morning. The 42nd Division did not have a second objective in common with 5th Division, so it was intended to go on to the third, a sunken road 1,375m from the start on the high ground.

At 4.15 a.m. 127th Brigade moved forward through heavy shelling from its assembly positions 900–1,800m west of the Selle. During the night reports were received by HQ 127th Brigade that the Selle was rising due to the heavy rain. However, despite the flooding the Brigade began crossing over the bridges that had been laid for 126th Brigade at 5.00 a.m. At 7.00 a.m. it passed through 126th

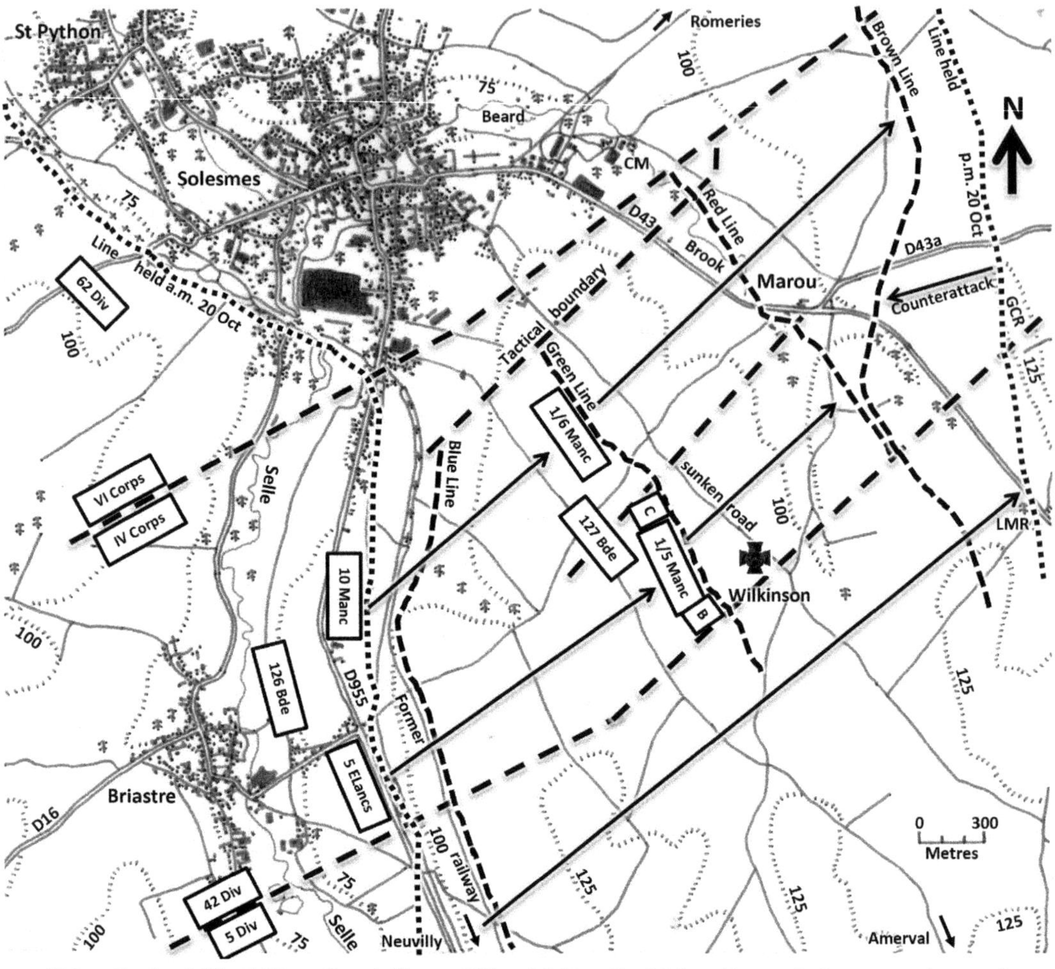

CM = Cardon Mill, GCR = Grand Champ Ridge, LMR = La Maison Rouge. Drive eastwards out of Solesmes on the D43. Pass the town cemetery of the left and after 1,600m pass through the tiny hamlet of Marou. On the left is the junction with the D43a. Carry on for 70m and turn right onto a track that leads onto the high ground topped by a series of wind turbines. Follow the track for 1,200m to a junction. Turn right and after 175m park below the first wind turbine on the left. The track you have just turned off leads on to the sunken road.

Brigade on the Green Line, led by 1/5th and 1/6th Manchester on the right and left respectively. In support was 1/7th Manchester, with a company positioned 450m behind each assault battalion to provide protection on either flank. The other two companies were the reserve. Two companies of 42nd Machine Gun Battalion provided support to the advance by firing on the final objective from behind the Green Line. B Company of the same Battalion followed 1/6th Manchester to assist in consolidating the final objective. Two mortars of 127th Light Trench Mortar

Battery also followed 1/6th Manchester, prepared to provide fire support when needed.

A very wet and misty morning made for heavy going but 1/5th Manchester reached its start line (Green Line) at 6.30 a.m. C Company, on the left, was to capture Marou in the centre of the Brigade's area and B Company, on the right, was to maintain contact with 95th Brigade (5th Division) on the right. D Company, behind C Company, was to cover any enemy advancing down the Red House (Maison Rouge) valley and push posts forward on to the ridge. A Company was in reserve. Once the objective on the ridge had been secured, the advance was to continue to the Brown Line at the sunken crossroads on top of the hill between Marou and Romeries.

From the outset 1/5th Manchester came under heavy machine gun fire from the sunken Solesmes–Amerval road, where 5th Division was temporarily checked on the right. On the left 1/6th Manchester had an easier time and quickly overcame these defences, although not without a considerable amount of fighting. The Battalion was ably supported by the Brigade Light Trench Mortar Battery. The left of the attack pressed on and cleared Marou about 8.30 a.m., where about fifty prisoners were taken at bayonet point.

B Company on the right of 1/5th Manchester was pinned down in an exposed position fifty metres short of the sunken road by machine guns to the front and right. The company commander, Lieutenant Lucas, realised that the advance could progress no further without reinforcements. Four volunteer runners were killed attempting to get back to the support company with messages requesting assistance. **Private Alfred Wilkinson** saw the four runners shot down but volunteered to try again. He covered more than 550m of exposed ground and, although numerous bullets missed him by inches, he managed to get through and help was sent forward. Wilkinson made his way back to the Company over the open ground and continued to carry out good work all day.

On the right the situation in 5th Division's area was less satisfactory. Its 95th Brigade had been unable to advance as far and this exposed 42nd Division's right flank. As a result, 1/5th Manchester's two companies on this flank were forced back to the sunken road by a counterattack, leaving posts on the high ground in front. There was very heavy enemy machine gun fire from the ridge south of Marou. However, the left leading company had reached Marou and the left support company was on the line of the Beard Brook, south of the village. Despite this success there was a considerable gap from there to the two companies on the right.

At 9.47 a.m. Brigade HQ ordered D Company, 1/7th Manchester to form a defensive right flank. Another company was pushed forward to fill the gap in the centre of 1/5th Manchester's line. About this time the CO of 1/5th Manchester, Lieutenant Colonel WF Panton, was wounded and Major Tickler MC was sent forward to take command.

From the first wind turbine looking north. Marou is in the low ground in the right middle distance. The sunken road runs away over the hill in the centre. Wilkinson raced back from close to the road in the centre across the open ground on the left to deliver his message.

By 10.30 a.m. 1/6th Manchester had reached the Marou–Cardon Mill road and was in contact with 62nd Division on the left flank. However, the Battalion was unable to press on to the Brown Line immediately due to heavy machine gun fire. At 10.47 a.m. 1/5th and 1/7th Manchester were ordered to connect the garrison in Marou with the left flank of 5th Division to the south, while 1/6th Manchester consolidated the line it had reached. At 1.00 p.m. a counterattack, that had developed against Marou from the northern end of Grand Champ Ridge, was dispersed by the artillery.

Orders arrived around 1.30 p.m. for 1/5th Manchester's to cooperate in an attack by 5th Division at 4.00 p.m. A Company advanced on the right and captured the spur south of Marou to secure the Red Line. By this time 1/5th and 1/7th Manchester were intermingled and at 5.00 p.m. orders were issued for an adjustment to the dispositions of the two battalions. At the same time it was decided to hold the line overnight with all three battalions – 1/7th on the right, 1/5th in the centre and 1/6th of the left – each distributed in depth. A battalion from 126th Brigade (1/8th Manchester) was put under command of HQ 127th Brigade and was deployed in support.

At about 5.30 p.m. 95th Brigade on the right came up in line with 127th Brigade and occupied the Brown Line. The final act of the day occurred at 9.10 p.m. when 1/6th Manchester advanced again. It reached and secured the fourth and final objective (Brown Line) north of Marou, without encountering major resistance. The enemy fled, leaving ten dead and twenty-five prisoners.

The Division suffered 509 casualties but took over 600 prisoners. The casualties for 127th Brigade were relatively light, with eight killed, 228 wounded and thirty-two missing. Of these, 129 casualties were sustained by 1/5th Manchester.

The VI Corps was still west of the Selle, which in this area was a significant obstacle, being almost two metres deep in places with a muddy bottom and steep banks. All the bridges had been destroyed and the debris of the demolished railway

bridge southwest of Solesmes formed a dam, which flooded a 900m stretch of the valley bottom. Bridging in this area was impossible. However, there was a ford at St Python in the middle of the Corps area. Solesmes on the Corps' right presented a significant problem. It was well defended but was also full of French civilians and therefore could not receive the full supporting barrage. The artillery was restricted to shrapnel. The Corps' final objective continued the line to be reached by V and IV Corps to the south.

On the right of IV Corps was 62nd Division. Its 186th Brigade, with 2/4th York & Lancaster (Hallamshires) attached from 187th Brigade, attacked Solesmes with the intention of driving through onto the high ground 1,600m to the east. The plan was to envelop the town before attempting to clear it. When the Brigade had seized its objective, including Le Pigeon Blanc Farm, 185th Brigade was to pass through and capture further objectives on the high ground. On the night of 18th/19th October, 2/4th Duke of Wellington's took over the whole of the Brigade's front. This allowed 5th Duke of Wellington's to withdraw and prepare for the attack on the 20th.

The Selle in this area was about six metres wide, up to two metres deep and had a muddy bottom throughout its length. There was one ford at St Python. Elsewhere the banks were steep and slippery. All road bridges had been demolished by the Germans and they held posts in buildings about 200m east of the river that covered most of the possible crossings. Two crossing points were selected north of Briastre and north of St Python. In addition to the existing bridges to the south, four more were to be constructed, either during the night or just before zero hour. However, on the 18th and 19th the river south of Solesmes rose as a consequence of the Germans creating a dam. Several temporary bridges were swept away and the banks were flooded. More bridges had to be constructed further south than originally intended. The barrage in 42nd Division's also area had to be modified accordingly. Four battalions were to make the attack:

On the right, where the line was already east of the Selle, 2/4th York & Lancaster was to cross north of Briastre, in 42nd Division's area, thirty minutes before zero hour, in order to reach its attack positions and avoid an assault crossing

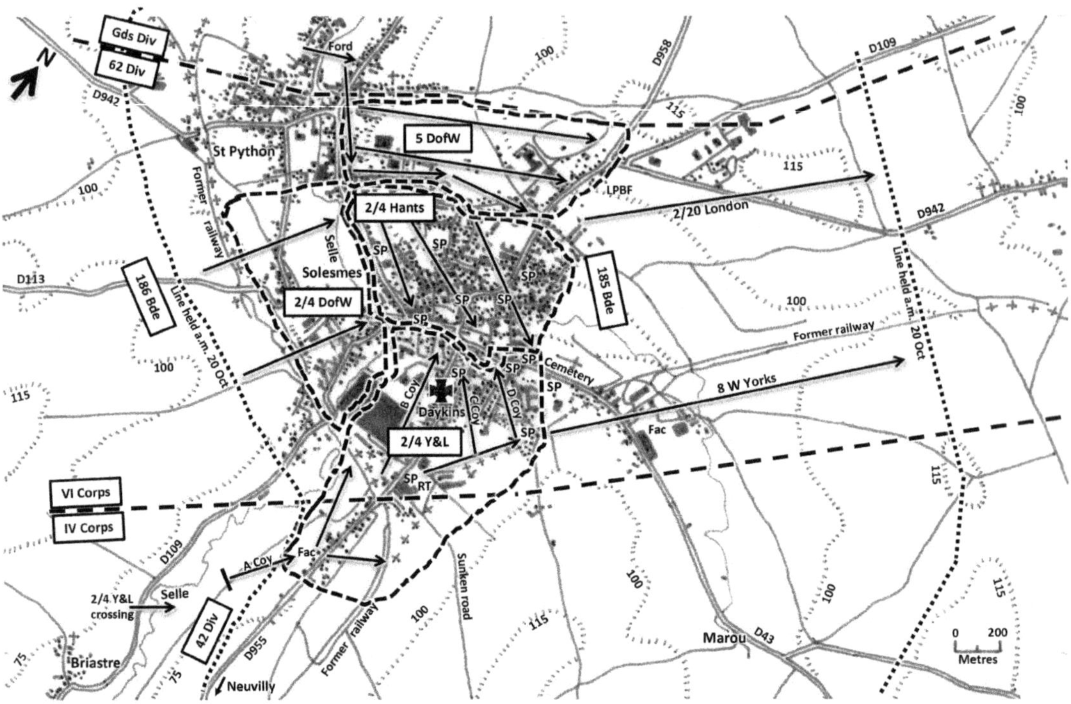

Daykins map

Fac = Factory, LPBF = Le Pigeon Blanc Farm, RT = railway triangle, SP = strongpoint. Drive into Solesmes along the D955 (Rue de l'Abbaye) from the south and park in front of the church (St Martin de Solesmes). Look back along Rue de l'Abbaye, where Daykins VC action took place.

of the river. The Battalion's first objective was the factory and railway north of it with one company. A second company was then to attack the northern arm of the railway triangle and the southern part of Solesmes. The other two companies were to advance along the railway and then turn inwards and attack Solesmes from the southeast. The risk of confusion in the town was reduced by issuing air photographs down to section level. These were studied in detail by every man to ensure that they knew their objectives.

In the centre, 2/4th Duke of Wellington's, which was holding the line, was to capture the railway in front and clear the area west of the Selle.

On the left, 5th Duke of Wellington's was to assemble in the western part of St Python and cross the river using the northern set of bridges. The eastern end of the town was to be captured by one company. Two companies were to seize the road running north-south through Le Pigeon Blanc Farm, whilst the fourth company formed a defensive flank to the south.

Finally 2/4th Hampshire was to cross the northern bridges behind 5th Duke of Wellington's and attack Solesmes from the north and meet 2/4th York & Lancaster advancing from the south.

A number of platoon strongpoints were to be established in Solesmes, with each company establishing two, one on the edge of the town and the other in the centre. A Company, 62nd Machine Gun Battalion was to assist in the consolidation of the Brigade's objective. Two sections were to cross the northern bridges behind 2/4th Hampshire and take up positions near the crossroads in the north of Solesmes and at Le Pigeon Blanc Farm. Two other sections were to cross the southern bridges behind 2/4th York & Lancaster to protect the Brigade's right flank. A creeping barrage fired by four brigades of field artillery was to cover the advance north and south of Solesmes, which was only to be swept by shrapnel. The barrage included two machine gun companies. Two medium and six light mortars were positioned on the railway and the western edge of St Python to engage specially selected targets. To facilitate recognition, white armbands were worn and the password 'Pelican' was adopted.

Although the night before the attack was very wet, it was comparatively light due to a full moon, and the battalions reached their assembly positions without difficulty. On the right, 2/4th York & Lancaster reached the Selle at 12.30 a.m. Because the river was so swollen with rain it was decided to cross immediately, rather than wait until thirty minutes before zero hour. The bridges had been completed but some men still had to wade up to their waists in places. Consequently, many men were soaked to the skin. Some casualties were caused by 42nd Division's barrage falling short on the right.

Fifteen minutes after zero, A Company advanced north-easterly on a frontage of two platoons, followed by B Company. It met a storm of machine gun fire from the factory, houses on the right along the Solesmes–Neuvilly road and the sunken road on top of the ridge east of the factory. The ground was also covered in barbed wire obstacles and numerous hedgerows. At 2.30 a.m. the barrage lifted. A Company surged through a breach in the southern wall of the factory after a machine gun had been captured in the grounds. Two sections on the right and one on the left passed around the factory to envelop the area and cut off the Germans' retreat. The factory, which was much larger than anticipated, was cleared, with twelve prisoners and two machine guns being captured. The two rear platoons of A Company swept on under heavy fire and reached the railway embankment in short rushes. More wire was encountered and a machine gun had to be silenced at the foot of the embankment. The Germans threw down grenades and continued firing machine guns from the top. The embankment was very steep but the objective was rushed after a short bayonet fight. Four more machine guns were captured and posts were established along the embankment. A patrol went on and cleared a chateau, from where the railway was being subjected to heavy fire. Another thirty-eight prisoners were taken there.

B Company took up the advance, clearing strongpoints between the Selle and the road. The two leading platoons captured the northern arm of the railway triangle and the other two platoons passed through to seize strongpoints in the town. The

Looking north, the direction in which Daykins advanced, along Rue de l'Abbaye towards the church in the centre of the town.

darkness and heavy rain made it difficult to maintain control and, on occasions, direction was lost.

In No.7 Platoon, **Sergeant John Daykins** came under fire from a machine gun on the embankment. He led his platoon to put it out of action before pressing on up the main street of Solesmes towards the church. By this time there were only twelve unwounded men remaining. Daykins made skilful use of whatever cover he could find and made good progress. Halfway along the street Daykins surprised a machine gun post that was just about to fire on them. He shot the gunner and rushed the position. About fifty metres from the church resistance stiffened again. Heavy machine gun fire and grenades seemed to come from every direction. Germans emerged from the cellars on all sides and surrounded the small party. In the ensuing hand-to-hand fighting Daykins accounted for seven of the enemy.

The ferocious response surprised the numerically superior enemy, who fled. Daykins followed, secured the final objective and set up a strongpoint. His twelve-man team had killed about twenty-five enemy and captured another thirty, without further loss to themselves. Daykins learned from a prisoner the location of a machine gun holding up the other leading B Company platoon (No.8). He impressed his men with the importance of maintaining their position and then set off alone, working his way from house to house under very heavy fire. The next thing his platoon saw was Daykins casually walking back with the machine gun over his shoulder, driving twenty-five more prisoners before him. The machine gun was incorporated into the defences. Daykins' action allowed No.8 Platoon to reach its objective and mop up a factory and the houses around it.

Nos.5 and 6 Platoons passed through and worked along the main street to set up a strongpoint. No.5 Platoon mopped up the remainder of the Company's area, assisted by an A Company platoon. Daykins' actions greatly assisted in completing the capture of the town centre ahead of schedule. The final opposition was overcome when contact was made with 2/4th Hampshire.

C Company cleared the southwest and west of the town, including a pocket in the sunken road, and established a series of strongpoints. A smoke barrage around the railway triangle covered its movement and masked the German SOS signal, so that their artillery did not respond. Machine gun fire was encountered from the direction of Solesmes church but one of the platoons captured thirty prisoners with three machine guns near the chateau. Numerous prisoners were taken and severe casualties were inflicted on the enemy during mopping up. The Company was subjected to heavy shelling all day and sustained a number of casualties. Contact with 2/4th Hampshire was made about 5.30 a.m.

D Company passed through A and B Companies and overcame opposition at the church, which was holding up the advance of C Company on the left. The platoons worked along various side streets, capturing 150 prisoners, three machine guns and a field kitchen, before setting up two strongpoints. About eighty Germans were driven into another factory, where they were captured by 8th West Yorkshire (185th Brigade). Patrols mopped up and ensured that civilians remained indoors. The success signal was launched from the cemetery on the eastern outskirts of the town at about 5.00 a.m. By 9.00 a.m. all was quiet and civilians began to move around the town again. The Battalion had been extremely fortunate, sustaining only fifty-five casualties (five killed, four missing and forty-six wounded). It had bagged 250 prisoners and twenty machine guns, in addition to killing many more Germans.

The 5th Duke of Wellington's assembled in houses in St Python west of the river by 11.00 p.m. At 1.30 a.m. the leading company crossed the Selle by the ford and 461st Field Company RE began constructing eight bridges with cork floats and trestles. Ropes and wire mats were also laid across the stream to enable men to wade, if that became necessary. Each infantry company carried five ladders to assist them in scaling the far bank. There was some sniping and inaccurate machine gun fire, but the work was carried out swiftly. By zero hour the other three companies had crossed undetected by the Germans.

The Battalion closed up to the barrage and, at zero plus three minutes, it lifted to a line about 200m further east, where it remained for twenty minutes before creeping forward to the final objective. The leading company met stiff resistance from a block of houses opposite the crossing point, but this was overcome. The company then began working southwards through the village. In the main street there was some sharp hand to hand fighting for two barricades and a machine gun post at the south-eastern end of the village, but all were overcome and St Python was secured. Many enemy were killed in this fighting and in the barrage previously.

The Battalion pressed on, dropping off posts and forming a defensive flank facing Solesmes. The two companies detailed to capture the Le Pigeon Blanc Farm road passed through and formed up behind the barrage before it moved forward again. Two platoons in each company led so far and were then leapfrogged by the rear platoons to the final objective. There was little resistance until the final objective was approached. A machine gun post at Le Pigeon Blanc Farm was taken after fifteen minutes. The objective was gained with many prisoners being taken. A company detailed to form a defensive flank met with some opposition near the southeast corner of St Python. However, it reached the crossroads in contact with the leading companies. Contact was established with the Guards Division on the left. By 4.10 a.m. all the Battalion's objectives had been taken, with few casualties, and were consolidated in depth soon afterwards.

Behind 5th Duke of Wellington's, 2/4th Hampshire reached its assembly positions in the railway cutting by 11.30 p.m. It moved up to the western edge of St Python when 5th Duke of Wellington's moved forward. The Battalion crossed the Selle at zero hour and, by 2.30 a.m., the three leading companies had formed up on the east bank without a casualty. The fourth company crossed at 3.00 a.m. to mop up the centre of the village.

The right company moved via the St Python – Solesmes road and was met with heavy small arms fire from the outskirts of Solesmes. This was overcome and thirty prisoners and two machine guns were captured. Posts were established at 4.30 and 5.15 a.m. after two more machine guns had been taken. The company area was then mopped up. The centre company skirted St Python and passed through the flank of 5th Duke of Wellington's. Heavy fire was encountered from a brick wall to the front and from the right. This enemy position was eventually turned by a flanking movement. The machine gun was captured and two posts were established by 5.30 a.m. The left company passed through 5th Duke of Wellington's and established a post by 5.30 a.m., without meeting serious opposition. However, a second platoon was met with heavy fire from machine guns and mortars, which was overcome by rifle grenades and Lewis guns before a second post was established about 5.15 a.m. The fourth company had little trouble mopping up the village centre. Five machine guns and a mortar were captured, without suffering any casualties. All objectives were taken by 7.15 a.m.

The two leading companies of 2/4th Duke of Wellington's formed up about 135m west of the railway. When the barrage came down at zero hour these companies swept forward to the railway against almost no opposition. After twenty minutes the barrage lifted again and the advance continued to the river, with almost no resistance being encountered. However, on arrival at the river there was considerable machine gun fire from the east side. Despite it eighteen prisoners with a machine gun were taken but, during consolidation, the Battalion suffered twenty casualties from enemy shelling.

The first intermediate objective having been reached, 185th Brigade passed north (2/20th London) and south (8th West Yorkshire) of Solesmes and continued the attack at 7.00 a.m. By 10.00 a.m. the final objective had been reached and a defensive right flank was held until 42nd Division to the south drew level in the afternoon. Contact was made with the Guards Division on the left, which reached all its objectives without great difficulty, and at 4.00 p.m. a counterattack was driven off. Casualties were suffered throughout the day in Solesmes and St Python due to enemy shelling. Early in the operation HQ 186th Brigade was hit by a gas shell, with all seventeen personnel becoming casualties. This interrupted communications but did not seem to affect the progress of the battalions. The total cost for 62nd Division was 452 casualties (fifty-seven killed, 380 wounded and fifteen missing). A large number of weapons was taken (seventy-one machine guns, thirteen mortars and five guns) and 699 prisoners. Including 2/4th York & Lancaster, 186th Brigade captured over 500 prisoners, forty-four machine guns and ten mortars. Total casualties were 173 (twenty-four killed, 145 wounded and four missing). At the end of the day all of Third Army's corps had achieved their objectives.

23rd October 1918

477 Pte Francis Miles, 1/5th Battalion, The Gloucestershire Regiment (75th Brigade, 25th Division), near Bois-l'Évêque, Landrecies, France

478 Lt Col Harry Greenwood, 9th Battalion, The King's (Own Yorkshire Light Infantry) (64th Brigade, 21st Division), Ovillers, France

The Fourth, Third and First Armies resumed the advance on 23rd October following a pause of two days to replenish ammunition. This next phase consisted of a right wheeling motion to bring the BEF up to, or beyond, the Hermann Position II. Although there was no continuous line of defences, the Germans had made good use of the terrain in this area. Belts of barbed wire supplemented thick hedgerows and defended posts had been constructed in depth.

On the BEF's right Fourth Army was to form a defensive flank for the main attack by Third and First Armies. This task fell to IX Corps on the right, which had three kilometres to cover to reach the Sambre Canal. It ran into considerable opposition and, although patrols reached the Canal in places, the advance through Bois-l'Évêque did not match that of XIII Corps on the left.

The XIII Corps was to maintain contact with Third Army on its left and secure the Landrecies–Englefontaine road west of the Forest of Mormal. The nature of the country was changing, with steep sided valleys and large wooded areas presenting

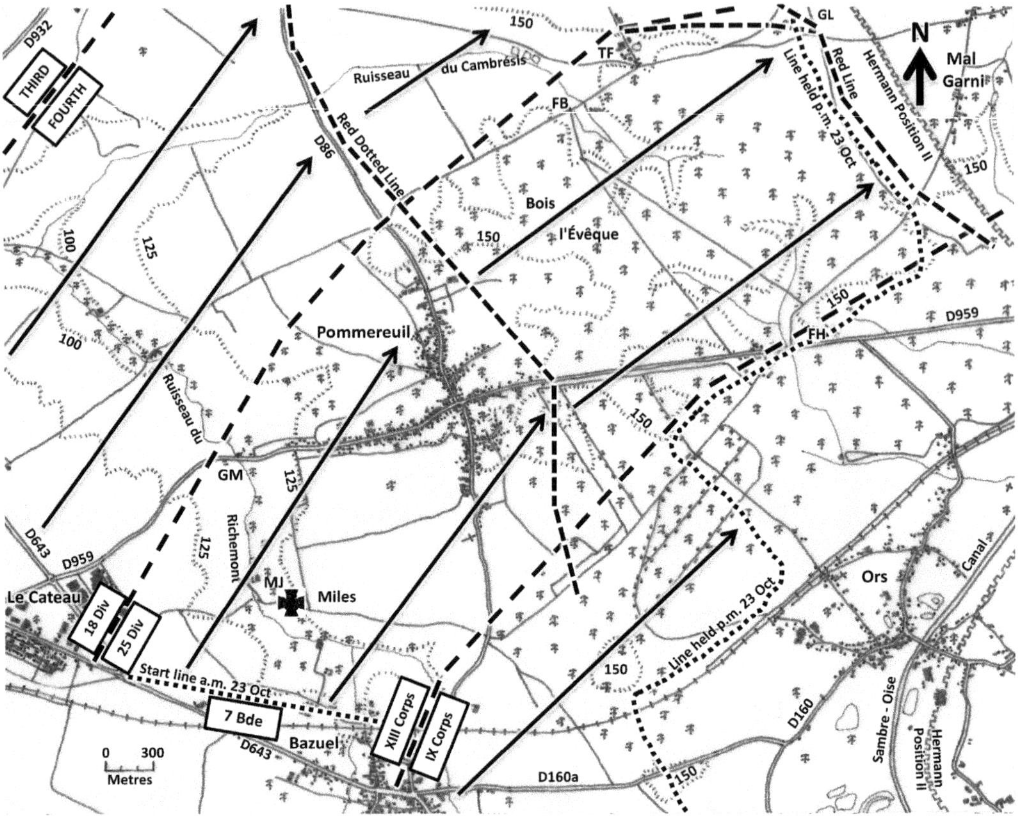

This area is covered in numerous small copses and strip woods. For the sake of clarity only the most prominent are shown. FB = Flaquet Brifaut, FH = Forester's House, GL = Green Line, GM = Garde Mill, MJ = Moulin Jacques, TF = Tilleuls Farm. Leave Le Cateau on the D959 road north-eastwards towards Pommereuil. Continue straight on at the roundabout junction with the D643 for 300m. Turn right onto a gravel track immediately after passing two large industrial buildings on the right. If you drive slowly there should be no problems. The track curves round to the left and descends into a sunken lane, possibly where Miles cleared the machine gun. Moulin Jacques can be seen through the trees at the bottom of the hill to the left of the track. Continue over the shallow ford after which is a left turn to Moulin Jacques, which is private, so carry on into another sunken section, more likely the one where Miles cleared the machine guns. After 300m there is a left turn. Stop here to look back over the way you have just travelled and the direction from which 1/5th Gloucestershire advanced. The course of the Richemont valley is clear but vegetation obscures much of the view and Moulin Jacques can be difficult to spot through the trees. Access can also be gained from the east. Leave Bazuel on the D86 road northwards towards Pommereuil. When the road reaches the south-western tip of Bois-l'Évêque on the right, turn left onto a slightly better surfaced track and follow for just over a kilometre to the same track junction mentioned above.

obstacles to movement. The ground was also very soft and, although the full moon provided plenty of light, ground mist limited visibility to fifty metres until it lifted at 9.00 a.m. Zero hour was set for 1.20 a.m.

The XIII Corps allocated 25th and 18th Divisions to make the attack, on the right and left respectively, each with a frontage of 2,300m. When both divisions had reached the first objective (Red Dotted Line), 18th Division was to encircle Bois-l'Évêque to the north, while 25th Division protected its left flank. Then both divisions would resume the advance to the remaining three objectives.

Both divisions were reinforced with extra artillery, the 25th Division receiving three Army Brigades RFA. One brigade of the divisional artillery was to move forward in close support of the infantry during the advance from the second to the third objectives. At each objective there was to be a pause before the advance continued. Prior to the start of each advance, the artillery would cease its protective fire for five minutes. It would then signal the start of the next phase with four minutes intense fire before creeping forward again.

Each division had an extra machine gun battalion to join in the barrage. Twenty-four tanks were allocated to XIII Corps, of which eight went to 25th Division. The divisions were advised that tanks and their crews could not be expected to operate on two consecutive days. Consideration had to be given to leaving half the tanks in reserve in case objectives were not taken on the first day. The two divisions in reserve, 50th and 66th, each had one brigade at one hour's notice to move in case they were needed to support the attack.

The Germans shelled the assault troops as they assembled in the railway cutting at Bazuel (also seen as Basuel). There were many casualties. Bad weather in the previous days meant that aerial reconnaissance of the enemy battery positions had not been possible. However, as the advance proceeded the effect of the enemy artillery reduced. The mist and smoke from the barrage caused considerable disruption and many troops had difficulty finding gaps in the hedgerows made by the tanks.

The 25th Division's first objective, the western edge of Bois-l'Évêque, was allocated to 7th Brigade, supported by a battalion of 75th Brigade. As 7th Brigade had a bayonet strength of only 700, it advanced with all three battalions. The 75th Brigade was then to lead to the third objective once 18th Division on the left had completed the encirclement of Bois-l'Évêque. One of its battalions was to advance along the northern edge of the Wood and establish posts to protect the right flank of 18th Division. The other battalion was to clear the northeast portion of the Wood up to the eastern edge, while 7th Brigade cleared the Wood to the south. Finally, 74th Brigade was to skirt the north of the Wood and form up behind 75th Brigade on the eastern edge, before advancing to secure the fourth and fifth objectives. Six of the tanks were lost before the operation began or ditched early on.

The leading battalion of 7th Brigade swept forward and, despite direction being lost in the mist and smoke, took Pommerueil, assisted by a tank. A gun battery was captured but a number of posts were overlooked in the Richemont valley in the mist, particularly at Jacques and Garde Mills. Consequently, the two battalions following ran into unexpected machine gun fire and it took some time to clear opposition. The advance on the left progressed well over more open ground. However, on the right 6th Division (IX Corps) encountered more difficulties and was behind. The

Moulin Jacques in the centre through the trees from the track to the southwest. The sunken track on the right is a possible location for Miles' VC action. The line of trees across the picture mark the course of the Richemont.

25th Division's first objective was reported to be secure by 7.30 a.m. and Pommereuil had been mopped up by 8.30 a.m.

An hour after zero 75th Brigade moved up led by 1/5th Gloucestershire. It formed up with three companies in line (from the right A, C and D) and B in support. After 275m the Battalion came under heavy machine gun fire from posts overlooked by 7th Brigade. It was delayed for five hours during which gruelling fighting ensued around Jacques and Garde Mills.

C Company was held up by a line of machine guns in a sunken lane at Moulin Jacques. Eventually **Private Francis Miles** made his way forward alone under heavy and continuous fire. He killed a sniper, then located a machine gun post and shot the gunner before kicking the gun over. He spotted another post ninety metres further on. Having shot the gunner, he rushed the post and eight survivors surrendered. With the main resistance overcome, he stood up and by hand signals directed the Company to take the enemy position in the rear. The attack was a complete success, with fifty-one prisoners and sixteen machine guns being taken. Without Miles' action the advance would have been more seriously delayed, jeopardising the whole operation.

Because of this action C Company was well behind and went into reserve. B Company took its place after the Battalion reached the Forester's House – Flaquet Brifaut road. Due to heavy flanking fire, B and D Companies took two hours to get into their assembly positions for the next advance to clear the Wood. Despite the thick undergrowth and resistance, the objective was reached after some hours fighting, except on the right where 6th Division (IX Corps) met stiffer opposition and was unable to keep up. A line was established at 5.00 p.m. running northeast from Forester's House to Malgarni (Mal Garni) and then roughly along the eastern edge of Bois-l'Évêque. After disengaging from stiff fighting, A Company eventually moved into support along the road running southwest from Forester's House to

Bazuel. Meanwhile 1/8th Worcestershire advanced into the north of Pommereuil and on to the northern edge of the Wood. Tilleuls Farm was taken and some howitzers were captured. A large party of enemy was seen retreating along the valley north of the Wood and, when the Battalion opened fire, 386 surrendered.

One of 74th Brigade's battalions became involved in the struggle for the Wood, the eastern edge of which was covered by fire from the Hermann Position II and thick belts of wire blocked the way. It was too late to get 74th Brigade into position to carry on the advance and the final objectives were left for the next day.

The track junction east of Moulin Jacques looking west along the sunken lane towards Moulin Jacques, which is out of sight amongst the trees in the distance.

On the left, 18th Division also reached the third objective. It was decided that both divisions should remain in these positions overnight. Despite considerable difficulties and delays, most objectives had been taken in Fourth Army's area and casualties were relatively light. The 1/5th Gloucestershire spent the night under heavy shellfire until 9.15 a.m. on the 24th, when it moved back to billets at Pommereuil.

Third Army's right had much further to advance than the left. The V Corps on the right had 8,700m to cover to reach its final objective, but the ground was uncomplicated and the mist was thinner than further south. Zero hour here was 2.00 a.m. as the right of Third Army was already ahead of the left of Fourth Army. The V Corps had five objectives – Red Dotted Line, Red Line, Green Dotted Line, Green Line and Brown Line. The 33rd and 21st Divisions, right and left respectively, made this attack, each with three tanks attached. Enemy shelling caused considerable casualties prior to zero hour. The 33rd Division reached a line a few hundred metres short of the fourth objective just before dark and the advance halted there until next morning.

The 21st Division relieved 17th Division at 10.45 p.m. on 22nd October. The attack was to be led by 64th Brigade on the right and 110th Brigade on the left. Each brigade had a section of engineers attached to construct improvised bridges, should they be needed across various streams in the area. The 62nd Brigade was in reserve until the Green Dotted Line, whereupon it was to pass through the leading brigades

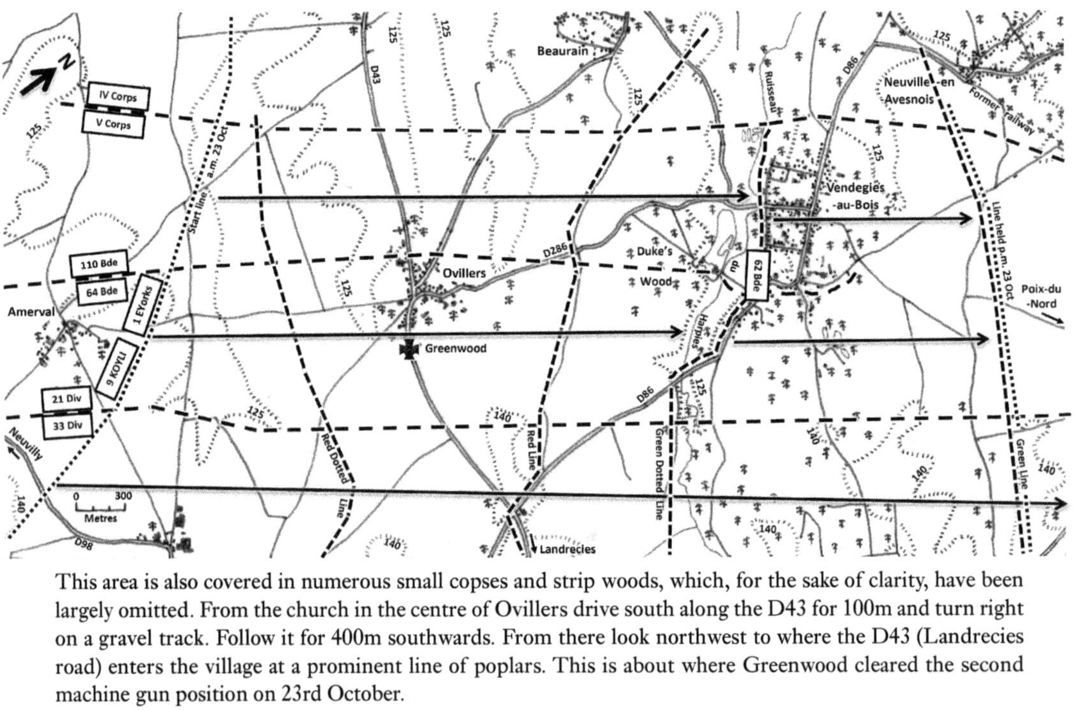

This area is also covered in numerous small copses and strip woods, which, for the sake of clarity, have been largely omitted. From the church in the centre of Ovillers drive south along the D43 for 100m and turn right on a gravel track. Follow it for 400m southwards. From there look northwest to where the D43 (Landrecies road) enters the village at a prominent line of poplars. This is about where Greenwood cleared the second machine gun position on 23rd October.

and continue through the Green Line to seize the Brown Line. The Brigade was to be followed by an engineer field company, which was to repair the road bridges over the River Selle. Two other field companies were to construct twelve strongpoints, six each in the Red and Green Lines.

One machine gun company was attached to each brigade for the advance and consolidation. Four field artillery brigades supported the advance with a creeping barrage. Two thirds of the 18 Pounders were to fire shrapnel with ten percent smoke, while the other third fired high explosive ninety metres ahead of the shrapnel barrage. The 4.5″ Howitzers and heavy artillery were to deepen the barrage in front of the 18 Pounders, paying particular attention to sunken roads and village outskirts. The 4.5″ Howitzers were to fire smoke along the line of the River Harpies during the advance from the Red Line. One and a half machine gun companies were involved in the barrage. The 62nd Brigade had 94th Brigade RFA and six mortars attached to support it when it passed through on the Green Dotted Line.

At 12.15 a.m. on the 23rd, the Germans opened a heavy bombardment on 110th Brigade's assembly areas and severe casualties were suffered. By 6.00 a.m. the Brigade had secured the Red Dotted Line. By 7.00 a.m. the lead battalion, 7th Leicestershire, had reached the sunken road north of Ovillers but, by then, was disorganised and 6th Leicestershire passed through to continue the advance under heavy machine gun fire. RAF observers at 8.00 a.m. saw troops passing through Ovillers. By 9.40 a.m. the Brigade had passed through the Red Line and was moving towards the Green Dotted Line, which was reported to have been captured at 11.00 a.m.

The 64th Brigade front was held by 15th Durham Light Infantry, while the assault battalions moved up to the railway embankment east of Neuvilly. They halted there until 11.30 p.m. on 22nd October, when they began the move to their start positions on the high ground near Amerval. The Brigade was largely unaffected by the early morning bombardment, except for some scattered gas shelling.

The advance was led by 1st East Yorkshire on the left facing Ovillers and Duke's Wood (Bois le Duc). On the right was 9th King's Own Yorkshire Light Infantry, commanded by **Lieutenant Colonel Harry Greenwood**. Each battalion had four machine guns and two mortars attached. Two tanks were to assist in clearing Ovillers by working around the edges. At zero hour the assault battalions passed through 15th Durham Light Infantry, which was to follow in support. At the Red Line two companies were to form up on the left and advance with 9th King's Own Yorkshire Light Infantry to capture the Green Dotted Line. Two companies were to follow 1st East Yorkshire and assist in mopping up Ovillers if necessary, then support the other two companies during the advance. When the Green Dotted Line had been secured, 15th Durham Light Infantry was to take it over, while the other battalions were to be prepared to form a defensive right flank or advance to the Green Line, if that became necessary.

From the gravel track south of Ovillers looking northwest. The village is on the left. The D43 runs across the centre of the picture from the line of poplars on the edge of the village left of centre. There is a light coloured field beyond the D43. Duke's Wood (Bois le Duc) is in the right distance. The second machine gun position cleared by Greenwood on 23rd October was on the D43 in the centre of this view.

The advance commenced on time and, although it was dark, there was a bright moon and the troops were spotted immediately by the German machine gunners. One machine gun on the right caused an immediate problem. It was just inside 33rd Division's area and the troops on that flank had been delayed. There was no time to await their arrival. Rapid and decisive action was required. Greenwood went ahead of his troops with a revolver and a few grenades. He outmanoeuvred the position, attacked it and killed all four crewmen. The Red Dotted Line was reported captured by HQ 64th Brigade at 4.30 a.m. but the situation in Ovillers at that time was obscure.

The advance continued until another machine gun post on the Landrecies road entrance to Ovillers was encountered. Greenwood took two runners and set off

From the D286 looking northeast, the direction of 64th Brigade's advance, towards Duke's Wood in the centre and on the right. Greenwood's battalion attacked through the right side of the wood.

to deal with this new problem. He succeeded in closing with the gun and killed the crew. At 6.00 a.m. HQ 64th Brigade reported that the enemy appeared to be holding Ovillers and 1st Wiltshire (110th Brigade) was dug in on the southwestern edge. A message received by HQ 64th Brigade timed at 7.30 a.m. reported that both battalions were 300m east of Ovillers. A message received by HQ 64th Brigade from Greenwood, timed at 7.45 a.m., reported that the Red Line had been captured and the advance was proceeding.

Following a period of reorganisation on the Red Line, 9th King's Own Yorkshire Light Infantry set off for its final objective (Green Dotted Line) when the barrage lifted at 7.08 a.m. Machine gun fire was heavy until 8.15 a.m. when it died down but scattered heavy shelling continued.

The next major feature was Duke's Wood where many machine guns had survived the artillery. The Battalion was on its own, having lost contact with flanking units. Greenwood pressed on, leaving liaison posts on the right as he proceeded. He had a fighting strength of approximately only 250 men. Closing with the Wood, the Battalion was almost surrounded by enemy machine gun posts and fire was

received from all directions. A determined counterattack, that almost succeeded in overrunning the Battalion, was halted with the enemy only thirty-five metres away.

Having beaten off the counterattack, Greenwood wasted no time and led his men in a final charge through the Wood. They reached the Green Dotted Line at 8.05 a.m. and were actually ahead of the British barrage at that stage. One hundred and fifty prisoners, eight machine guns and a field gun were captured. At 9.00 a.m. Greenwood sent a message to HQ 64th Brigade that he had personally reconnoitred the third objective and confirmed that his troops were on it. There was no contact on the right flank.

At 9.30 a.m. 62nd Brigade passed through and cleared Vendegies-au-Bois to reach the fourth objective by 2.15 p.m. Machine guns on the Poix-du-Nord ridge halted further movement and the advance was held up. When 62nd Brigade passed through, 1st East Yorkshire and 9th King's Own Yorkshire Light Infantry formed

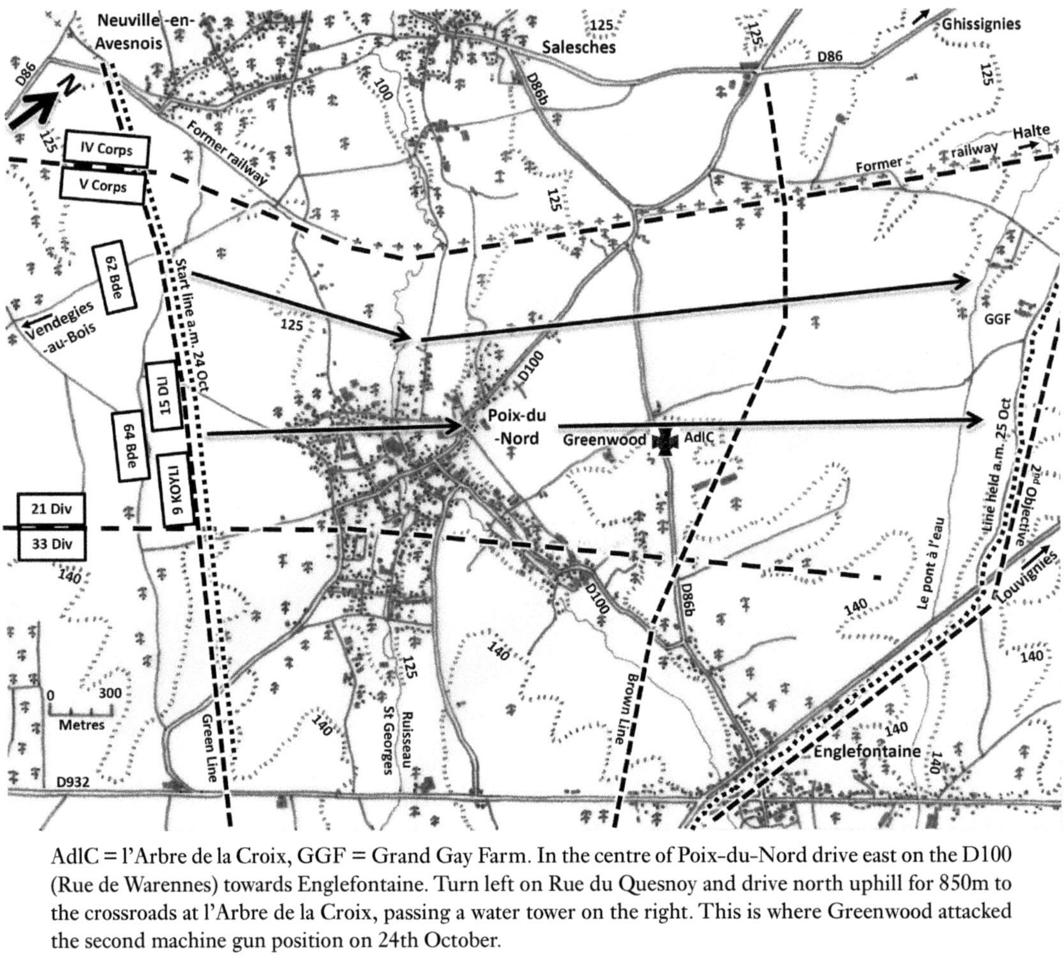

AdlC = l'Arbre de la Croix, GGF = Grand Gay Farm. In the centre of Poix-du-Nord drive east on the D100 (Rue de Warennes) towards Englefontaine. Turn left on Rue du Quesnoy and drive north uphill for 850m to the crossroads at l'Arbre de la Croix, passing a water tower on the right. This is where Greenwood attacked the second machine gun position on 24th October.

a defensive right flank facing southeast. A counterattack was repulsed at 5.45 p.m. During the day 492 prisoners entered the divisional cage.

Despite not reaching the final objective for the day, V Corps had advanced 5,600m against considerable opposition. Further north the other Corps had to carry out a more limited wheel to bring them into line with the forces to the south. Despite some setbacks Third Army was almost in the position it was required to reach. To the north First Army either stood still in preparation for a resumption of the advance next day or made relatively small advances to reach or go beyond the final objective.

At 5.00 p.m. HQ 21st Division issued a warning order that the advance was to be continued next morning. The Division advanced at 4.00 a.m. with 62nd Brigade on the left, 64th Brigade on the right and 110th Brigade in support. There were two objectives, the first being roughly the Brown Line of the previous day and the second, the sunken road running north-westwards through Grand Gay Farm to the Halte southeast of Ghissignies. The 110th Brigade would then pass through and exploit to the Jolimetz–Le Quesnoy road.

The 62nd Brigade advanced steadily against heavy artillery fire and reached the first objective by 6.00 a.m., in contact with 64th Brigade on the right. The advance continued with the railway on the left, with the intention of gaining contact with 37th Division (IV Corps) on that flank and also to attack Grand Gay Farm from the northwest.

In 64th Brigade, 9th King's Own Yorkshire Light Infantry was on the right and 15th Durham Light Infantry was on the left. The latter was held up by heavy machine gun fire from the ridge in the centre and on the left. Enemy artillery fire was extremely heavy and barbed wire also caused a delay for two hours.

Greenwood made a personal reconnaissance and found that one part of the ridge was held by only one post. He attacked it and killed the crew single handed, although they were firing at him from only twenty metres away. He then pushed A Company into the gap and turned the flank of the posts on the ridge. Resistance was overcome quickly and Poix-du-Nord was mopped up.

Greenwood led his men on. They swept away another line of machine gun posts north of Poix-du-Nord to reach the road running north-westwards from Englefontaine, through the hill at l'Arbre de la Croix, towards Salesches at 8.00 a.m. This action allowed the rest of the Brigade to take Poix-du-Nord, where many enemy were killed and 2,700 villagers were found hiding in cellars. However, HQ 64th Brigade reported that Poix-du-Nord and the first objective had fallen at 7.00 a.m.

Despite the success, 9th King's Own Yorkshire Light Infantry was well ahead of its neighbours, with both flanks in the air and it was under heavy fire from the front and right flank. The line wavered in the face of this onslaught, but Greenwood walked about calmly in front of his advanced posts in full view of the enemy and

Just south of the crossroads at l'Arbre de la Croix on Rue du Quesnoy. Greenwood's second machine gun action on 24th October was in the vicinity of the house at the crossroads just left of the centre of the picture.

encouraged the men to stick it out. L'Arbre de la Croix was held despite heavy casualties and a counterattack.

It became clear during the day that the Germans were strengthening their positions. They could not be allowed to consolidate. Another attack was launched at 4.00 p.m., by 64th Brigade on the right and 62nd Brigade on the left, with the objective of capturing the second objective, the sunken road running north-westwards through Grand Gay Farm to the Halte. Having seized this objective, patrols were to be pushed forward to the Englefontaine–Louvignies road. In this attack 9th King's Own Yorkshire Light Infantry was in support to 64th Brigade, tasked to follow the leading units, 1st East Yorkshire on the right and 15th Durham Light Infantry on the left, and form a defensive right flank facing southeast. The main attack succeeded in seizing the sunken road by 7.20 p.m. Another 213 prisoners were taken during the day.

There were no other troops on the right and 9th King's Own Yorkshire Light Infantry came under heavy fire. Despite it, Greenwood pressed on. He cleared the machine gun posts and took an objective well to the right of the Brigade's area, which was later handed over to the flanking division. With great skill he gained his objective by 6.00 p.m. and thereby secured the Division's flank. During these two days he was twice blown up by shells, hit by fragments several times and badly stunned on one occasion.

24th October 1918

479 Lt Frederick Hedges, Bedfordshire Regiment, attached 6th Battalion The Northamptonshire Regiment (54th Brigade, 18th Division), Bousies, France

Except for minor local actions on 24th October, the Second and Fifth Army areas were relatively quiet. However, Fourth, Third and First Armies spent the day

gaining the objectives that could not be reached the previous day. In Fourth Army, IX Corps pushed patrols up to the Sambre Canal and discovered that the Germans had already escaped to the east bank. The remainder of Bois-l'Évêque was cleared, except the southeast corner.

The XIII Corps had to overcome the Herman Position II in order to reach the fourth (Green Dotted Line) and fifth (Brown Line) objectives from 23rd October. Eight tanks were allocated, of which only six arrived. Immediately after zero hour at 4.00 a.m., 25th Division on the right was hit by heavy fire from the Hermann Position II as it emerged from Bois-l'Évêque in the bright moonlight. The troops surged through the wire and, after close quarter fighting, secured the fourth objective by 10.00 a.m. The advance did not get under way again until 2.00 p.m. and the final objective was secured at 6.00 p.m.

On the left of XIII Corps, 18th Division's attack on 23rd October was led by 53rd Brigade on the right and 54th Brigade on the left. They were to seize the first two objectives (Red & Red Dotted Lines), after which 55th Brigade would pass through about dawn. Six brigades of field artillery were allocated to the Division for the creeping barrage. Two machine gun battalions (18th and 100th) were part of the barrage. On the left flank 98th Brigade (33rd Division, V Corps, Third Army) was further forward than 18th Division. Consequently, its attack would only commence when 54th Brigade came up in line, planned to be forty minutes after zero.

On 20th October 54th Brigade had relieved 199th Brigade (66th Division) northeast of Le Cateau. The 2nd Bedfordshire was in the line with 11th Royal Fusiliers in support in a counterattack position, while 6th Northamptonshire was in reserve at Reumont. During the attack 2nd Bedfordshire was to capture the first objective (Red Line) and 11th Royal Fusiliers the second (Red Dotted Line), while 6th Northamptonshire was in Divisional Reserve under 55th Brigade. The main weight of the attack was to be on the left flank. The Brigade had a frontage of 625m, with its left flank parallel with and 450m southeast of the Le Cateau–Englefontaine road (D932).

The Brigade Light Trench Mortar Battery was allocated a number of point targets for a hurricane bombardment at zero hour. The Divisional Machine Gun

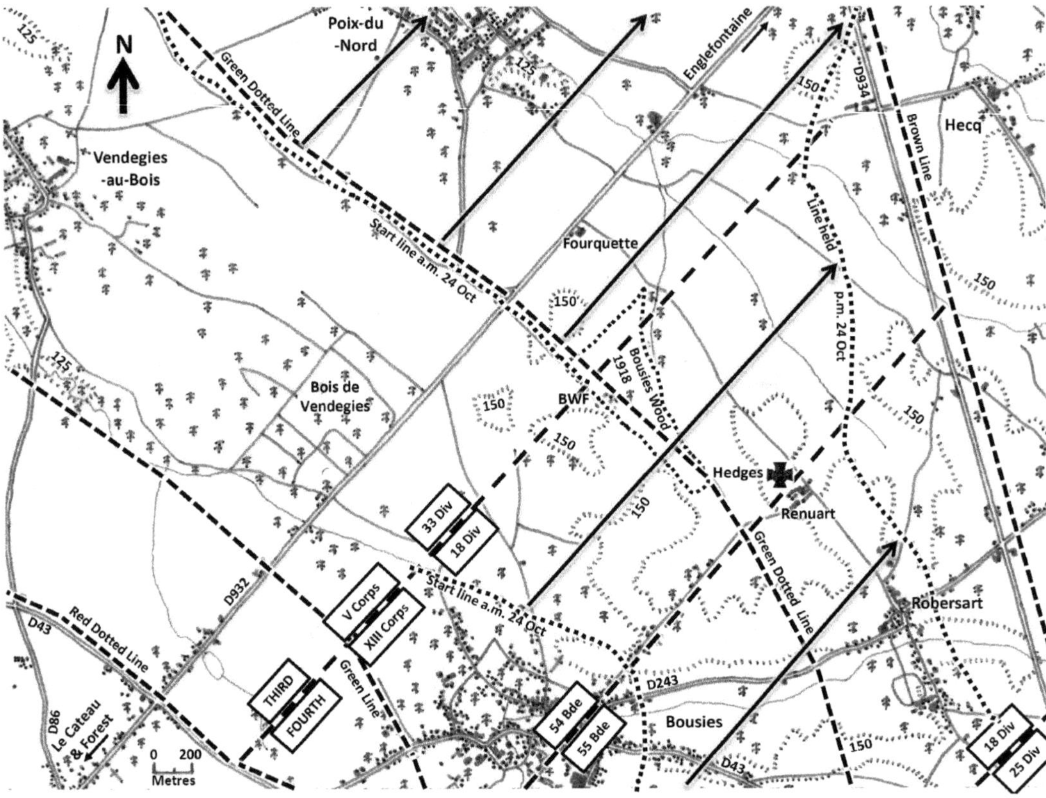

BWF = Bousies Wood Farm. When visited there was an extremely unfriendly farmer at Renuart Farm who wouldn't even allow photographs to be taken from a distance! This is unusual on the Western Front, where most landowners are generally tolerant of battlefield visitors. Because of this it is not recommended to approach the farm from the southwest from Bousies. Instead take the lane northwest out of Robersart and drive past Renuart Farm after 750m onto the slightly higher ground to the northwest to overlook the area of the Hedges VC action.

Battalion allocated 1 Section, B Company to follow the attacks on both objectives for consolidation. Two tanks of B Company, 10th Tank Battalion were to accompany the infantry but were not to be in advance of them. The tanks were given specific objectives and they were to be followed by a supply tank, carrying ammunition, water and rations. No sappers were available but light bridges were allocated to 2nd Bedfordshire to cross the Richemont River. A number of liaison posts in platoon strength were to be established with 98th Brigade as the advance progressed. On the right flank liaison posts of an NCO and three men were to be established with 53rd Brigade. Zero hour was 1.20 a.m. on the 23rd, with the aim of clearing the first two objectives by dawn, when 55th Brigade would pass through into the close country around Bousies.

Late on 22nd October 54th Brigade's battalions moved to their assembly positions on or about the railway embankment. The Germans appeared to be on edge and there was much shelling, including gas, causing a number of casualties. Heavy fighting was encountered throughout the operation amongst the skilfully sited German positions in hedgerows and orchards.

At zero hour the barrage came down well and 2nd Bedfordshire got off to a good start. A machine gun position between the start line and the barrage caused some trouble but it was dealt with. The German response was swift and caused some casualties. Opposition in three sunken lanes northeast of Richemont Hill was overcome quickly, although one post was missed and had to be dealt with by 11th Royal Fusiliers following. Because of the darkness, a number of parties lost direction and some drifted into 33rd Division's area and vice versa. Despite the problems, the advance continued steadily and many prisoners were taken. Some companies in 2nd Bedfordshire mistook a road 450m short of the objective for it.

Despite the error, 11th Royal Fusiliers passed through and continued the advance. One company moved through the outskirts of Forest and reached its objective northwest of Epinette Farm. However, with both flanks in the air, it was forced to withdraw and fell back behind a shallow ridge. There it joined the other leading company, which was digging in, believing that it had reached the objective.

At 7.30 a.m. 55th Brigade passed through led by 7th Buffs (East Kent Regiment). It went beyond the second objective about Epinette Farm, as the enemy had by then withdrawn, except for a few machine gun and mortar posts, which did not offer much resistance. By 9.00 a.m. 2nd Bedfordshire and 11th Royal Fusiliers had moved up to their original objectives to reorganise and dig in.

At 4.10 p.m. 54th Brigade was ordered to relieve 7th Buffs from the left Divisional boundary to the Fayt Farm–Renuart Farm road. At the same time 6th Northamptonshire reverted to 54th Brigade and at 4.45 p.m. was ordered to relieve 7th Buffs. At 7.30 p.m. a warning order was issued for the advance to continue next day. Orders were sent out at 1.30 a.m. on the 24th for the attack to commence at 4.00 a.m. The 55th Brigade was on the right, 54th Brigade on the left and 53rd Brigade in reserve. In 54th Brigade the lead was to be taken by 6th Northamptonshire to the Green Dotted Line, supported by 2nd Bedfordshire and 11th Royal Fusiliers, which would pass through to the final objective on the Brown Line.

The 55th Brigade met strong opposition, especially on the right. On the left 7th Queens (Royal West Surrey) got into Robersart but was driven out to just west of the village. It was not until 6.00 p.m. that the centre of Robersart was reached, and then only after 54th Brigade, on the left, had taken Renuart Farm. The Brown Line was 275m away, but it held out despite attempts to reach it at 11.00 p.m. and at dawn on the 25th.

In 54th Brigade the barrage line had already been decided and this necessitated a slight withdrawal of the line on the left. Despite this, the barrage was ragged and very short, causing a number of casualties to the leading and support battalions. At 3.15 a.m. 6th Northamptonshire reached the start line with A and B Companies in the lead. The left had to pull back 275m to avoid the British artillery dropping short. However, the attack started well and the German artillery response was light. After 450m the leading companies lay down fire to cover the advance of C and D Companies. They passed through at 4.45 a.m. and took the first objective (Green Dotted Line). C Company was held up by machine guns and wire and was forced back to the edge of Bousies Wood, where a tank gave some assistance. The barrage was lost as the Battalion became bogged down in heavy fighting amongst the thick hedges.

Soon after 5.00 a.m., the 54th Brigade support battalions went through, but they were also halted. However, a single tank managed to get behind the enemy and drove them along the Renuart Farm – la Fourquette road. At 6.20 a.m. a counterattack on the right flank against C Company, 6th Northamptonshire was repulsed with heavy losses. The 11th Royal Fusiliers also repulsed a counterattack about Bousies Wood Farm.

The support battalions passed through 6th Northamptonshire at the road running southeast from Bousies Wood Farm. The wired enemy line on the southwest side of the ridge running northwest from Renuart Farm was taken by 11th Royal Fusiliers but the Battalion was unable to cross the top of the ridge due to heavy machine gun fire from the valley beyond. The right of the attack was held up by machine guns in and around Renuart Farm. A machine gun that had survived the 55th Brigade attack on Robersart enfiladed the 54th Brigade line and made movement behind it almost impossible.

By 9.15 a.m. two companies of 11th Royal Fusiliers on the left were just short of the la Fourquette – Robersart road with the other two companies behind in support. They were in contact with 33rd Division on the left flank. Three companies of 6th Northamptonshire were about Bousies Wood, while the other company and one and a half companies of 2nd Bedfordshire were close to the German wire north of Renuart Farm. One and a half companies of 2nd Bedfordshire formed a defensive flank along the Renuart Farm – Bousies road facing southeast.

The attack then came to a halt because of the intense machine gun fire. The heavy artillery was to engage enemy positions east of the ridge running northwest of Renuart Farm, while the field artillery engaged those machine guns that had been located. There was some doubt about the location of the forward troops so the decision was taken to fire on the wired line on the west side of the ridge, which was shown on air photographs. This resulted in a number of casualties to 54th Brigade and a considerable loss of morale. Other shells fell short amongst the support companies.

It became clear that 33rd Division on the left was pressing on well and had reached Englefontaine. There was some disruption caused at HQ 54th Brigade when the commander, Brigadier General Oswald Borrett CMG DSO, was taken ill due to gas poisoning. He was replaced temporarily by Lieutenant Colonel Reginald Turner DSO, CO 6th Northamptonshire a few hours later. In the meantime,

Renuart Farm from the southwest, taken when the farmer was not looking! The hedge on the right may be the one that Hedges used as cover to advance onto the high ground.

6th Northamptonshire was ordered to extract the three companies about Bousies Wood Farm and turn the enemy position from the north at Renuart Farm. The other battalions, 11th Royal Fusiliers in the centre and 2nd Bedfordshire on the right, were to send out patrols to the front to pin the enemy down.

The other 6th Northamptonshire company on the right, C Company commanded by **Lieutenant Frederick Hedges**, was still held up in front of Renuart Farm. About 3.00 p.m. with 13974 Sergeant Fred Gibson and a Lewis gun team following some way behind, he resolved to deal with the machine guns holding up the advance. Armed only with a revolver and a cane, which he used to wave his men forward when required, he crawled up the hill under cover of a hedge. Hedges dashed out of this cover and shot the first machine gunner dead. He moved along the crest of the hillside dealing with three more posts and taking fourteen prisoners. After capturing each one he removed the feed block to ensure that the gun could not be reused. The Lewis gun section then arrived and cleared the rest of the machine guns by about 4.30 p.m. Fourteen prisoners were taken. With the resistance on the hill broken, the rest of the Battalion swept around the enemy from the north. At 5.00 p.m. 2nd Bedfordshire, in conjunction with 55th Brigade, seized Renuart Farm. One of the tanks caused chaos amongst the enemy near the Farm and blew up a dump causing heavy casualties. With the capture of these positions, the whole brigade front was able to continue the advance. By 6.00 p.m. 54th Brigade had reached a road running northwest–southeast, in places only a few hundred metres

Renuart Farm from the northwest on the Fourquette (behind camera) to Robersart road. The hedge seen in the previous photograph runs downhill on the right. This is the likely line of advance made by Hedges and his team.

short of the final objective (Brown Line), and was in touch with both flanks, but it could not get further forward.

At the end of the day Fourth Army had just about completed capturing its objectives and was well placed for what was to be the final push of the war. The bag for the two days was 1,240 prisoners and sixty-six guns. During the night 54th Brigade was relieved by 53rd Brigade. The 6th Northamptonshire was relieved by 8th Royal Berkshire and marched to Epinette Farm southwest of Bousies at 3.15 a.m. The other battalions went into billets in Bousies. Over the two days the Brigade suffered 446 casualties, including seventy-four in 6th Northamptonshire. Three hundred and fifty prisoners were taken, plus fourteen guns, six mortars, three anti-tank rifles and about one hundred machine guns.

25th October 1918

480 Lt William Bissett, 1/6th Battalion, Princess Louise's (Argyll and Sutherland Highlanders) (153rd Brigade, 51st Division), East of Maing, France

A pause in the relentless British advance followed the conclusion of the Battle of the Selle on 24th October. The troops were thoroughly exhausted, and a rest was welcomed, but Haig did not want to give the Germans time to prepare defensive positions for the winter and thereby prolong the war. He believed, contrary to many, that continuing pressure would bring about a collapse of the once powerful German army and avoid the war dragging on into 1919.

Fourth Army spent the 25th reconnoitring possible crossings points along the Sambre-Oise Canal and patrolling. Third Army tidied up a few loose ends from the previous day and, in places where the enemy had slipped away, followed up these

retirements and established outpost lines. Opposition was generally light and that night Englefontaine was seized in V Corps' area.

First Army made small adjustments on the left and in the centre, while also following up any enemy retirements. The XXII Corps on the right had the most significant action of the day, advancing towards the Rhonelle River.

By 11.00 p.m. on 22nd October 153rd Brigade had relieved 154th Brigade and assumed command of 51st Division's front, with 6th Black Watch on the right, 7th Black Watch on the left and 6th Argyll and Sutherland Highlanders in reserve at Fleury. On the right flank was 11th Brigade (4th Division) and on the left 4th Canadian Division (Canadian Corps). The Germans were holding the east bank of the River Ecaillon in strength and Thiant to the east. This made it difficult for patrols to reconnoitre bridging sites prior to an attack over the waterway. The Germans shelled Bois de l'Entrée and Grand Bois, west of the village, with gas and high explosives during the night.

Orders for the next attack by XXII Corps on 24th October were issued at 6.00 a.m. on the 23rd. There were four objectives, the Green, Blue, Brown and Brown Dotted Lines, the latter two (not shown on the map) to the east of Maing and on the high ground to the south and east of it. If possible the advance was to continue to a line of exploitation along the Valenciennes–Le Quesnoy railway. The Canadians were to provide fire support from the high ground north of the Canal de l'Escaut.

A demonstration of bridges, constructed by the sappers and fitted with cork floats and petrol tins, was given at Noyelles. However, they proved to be too heavy to be carried with ease. Once the infantry had crossed the river the engineers would re-erect and secure the bridges. Two bridges capable of taking artillery were then to be constructed at the main road through Thiant and south of the village. Three sappers per battalion were allocated to deal with land mines and booby traps.

Each forward battalion had a mobile section of field guns attached. The creeping barrage was to include machine guns and the heavy artillery was to engage various targets with delayed action fuses. One section of A Company, 51st Machine Gun Battalion was attached to each leading battalion. The other two sections were to

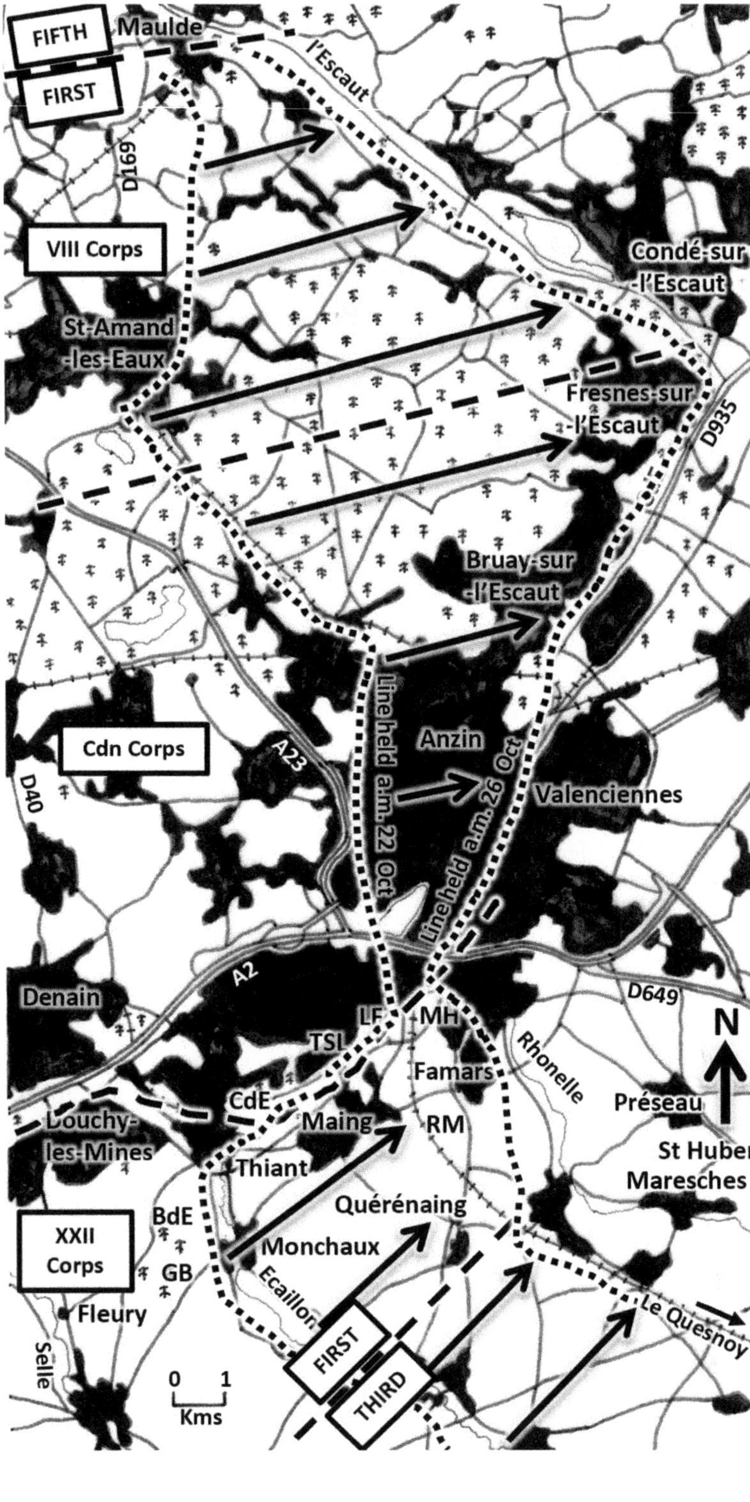

The progress of First Army 24–25th October. BdE = Bois de l'Entrée, CdE = Canal de l'Escaut, GB = Grand Bois, LF = la Fontenelle, MH = Mont Huoy, RM = Rouge Mont, TSL = Trith-St-Léger.

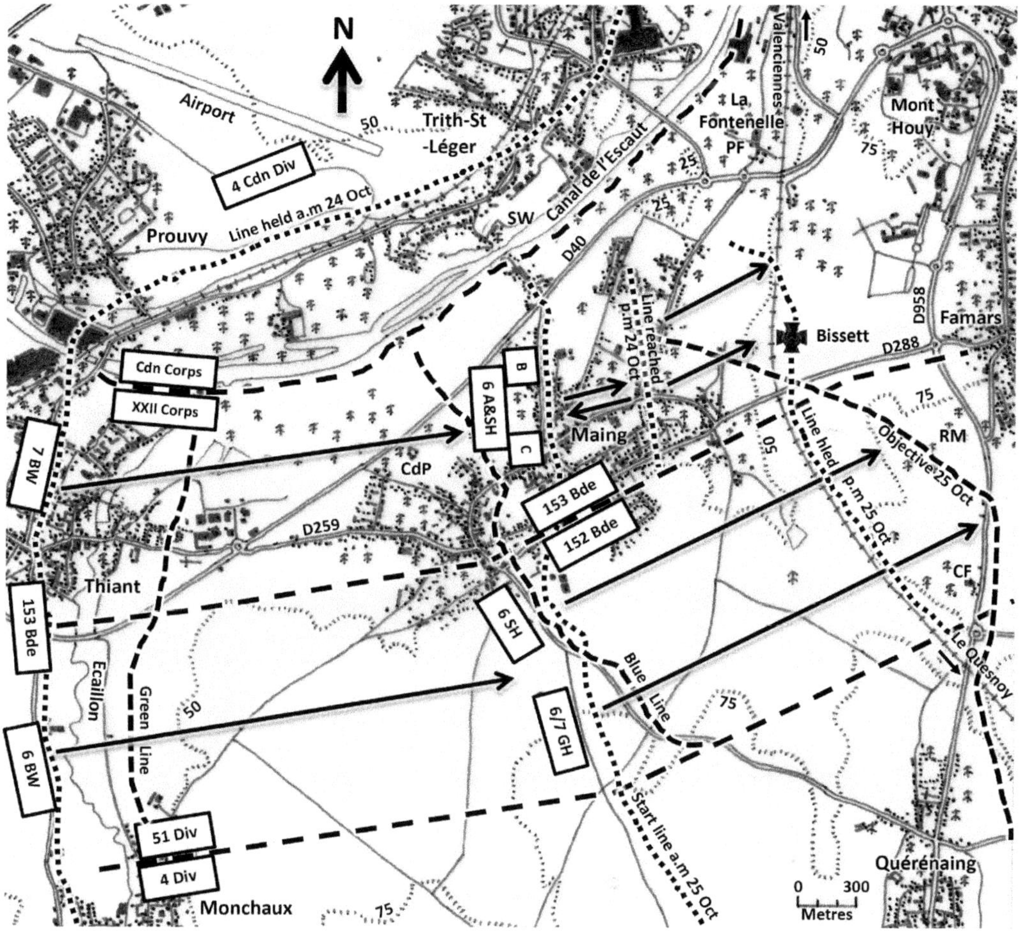

CdP = Château-des-Prés, CF = Caumont Farm, PF = Poirier Farm, RM = Rouge Mont, SW = site of steel works. Drive through Maing on the D288 eastwards towards Famars. Pass under the railway bridge and head up the hill. On the right atop the bank is a concrete wall around an electricity installation. There is space to park at the entrance and then walk back, keeping the wall on your left to look over the railway and across the road to the fields where Bissett led the charge from the railway left to right as you look at it.

take up positions around the Blue Line when the Brown Line had been captured. Each battalion had a trench mortar attached and 7th Black Watch was also allocated a German mortar.

The 153rd Brigade's left battalion, 7th Black Watch, which was also responsible for clearing along the Canal de l'Escaut, managed to position some of its bridges before zero. However, on the right 6th Black Watch's bridges had to be manhandled by the leading waves. The barrage was arranged to stand for seventy minutes on the Green Line, in order to allow the infantry sufficient time to cross the river and form up for the next phase. The battalions formed up west of the river along the Monchaux–Thiant road.

The assault troops were in position by 2.00 a.m. and the barrage fell on time at zero hour at 4.00 a.m. Ten minutes later the infantry moved forward. On the left 7th Black Watch had little difficulty crossing the river as it was narrow and partly bridged, except in the vicinity of the cemetery. On the right the river was considerably wider and both banks were thickly wired and covered by machine guns. However, with good leadership, initiative and gallantry, the companies of 6th Black Watch were able to cross. They were in time for the lifting of the barrage in front of the Green Line. One platoon swam the river.

The advance proceeded well to the next objective, the Blue Line, on the western outskirts of Maing, except at Monchaux on the right. This caused delay to 6th Black Watch, but the village was cleared and the barrage was regained. Later Monchaux was occupied by 11th Brigade. Heavy small arms fire was received from houses in the west of Maing, Château-des-Prés (now Château Payen) and the crossroads south of the village. This was overcome, although the Château held out for a considerable time, and the Blue Line was captured by 10.00 a.m. Thereafter the situation was less clear but by 3.00 p.m. a line had been established in contact with 11th Brigade on the right. The German artillery had been active throughout but, except at Thiant, it was not very intense.

Meanwhile 6th Argyll and Sutherland Highlanders had moved two companies across the river at Thiant by 11.00 a.m. One was just to the east of the village and the other to the south of it. The other two companies were in the village west of the river. The 6th Seaforth Highlanders (152nd Brigade) at Thiant came under orders of 153rd Brigade at 12.00 p.m. The attack was then halted, to be resumed

Looking north over the D288. On the left, towards Maing, is the railway bridge and in the right distance the outskirts of Famars. Bissett led his men from the railway, the line of trees and bushes running from the road on the left towards the centre of the picture, across the field towards the power lines.

next day on a two-brigade front. Beforehand 152nd Brigade relieved 6th Black Watch, which went into support, and 6th Seaforth Highlanders then reverted to 152nd Brigade. On 153rd Brigade's front, 6th Argyll and Sutherland Highlanders relieved 7th Black Watch during the night. The latter went into reserve around the railway northwest of Thiant.

The objective on 25th October was the high ground east of the railway and, if possible, to press on to secure Mont Huoy and Famars. Zero hour was 7.00 a.m. The attack was made by 12th Brigade, on the left of 4th Division, and 152nd and 153rd Brigades in 51st Division. The 12th Brigade reached its objectives, Quérénaing village and the railway beyond, with few casualties and later repulsed a counterattack on the left.

The 51st Division was to seize two objectives: the first was the high ground east of the Valenciennes–Le Quesnoy railway and the second was Famars and Mont Houy. The latter, an eighty-eight metres high feature, dominated all around it, including the southern approaches to Valenciennes, which the Canadian Corps faced. On the right 152nd Brigade deployed 6/7th Gordon Highlanders on the right and 6th Seaforth Highlanders on the left. On the left 153rd Brigade's front was covered by 6th Argyll & Sutherland Highlanders, led by C Company on the right and B Company on the left, support by D and A Companies.

Prior to the attack the troops were withdrawn to a line running north-south through Maing village, in order to establish a regular barrage line from the outset. The 152nd Brigade had a reasonable start but stiffer resistance was encountered at the railway line. However, by 11.00 a.m., 6/7th Gordon Highlanders was on the high ground at Caumont Farm and Rouge Mont. The 6th Seaforth Highlanders also reached the high ground having subdued considerable opposition. The objective was reached on the whole of 152nd Brigade's front by 2.30 p.m. The

Brigade then encountered a stronger enemy position west of Famars and there was no exploitation.

In 153rd Brigade, 6th Argyll & Sutherland Highlanders had mixed fortunes. C Company on the right was on the objective at 8.20 a.m., in contact with 152nd Brigade. In the initial assault **Lieutenant William Bissett** led his platoon with great dash and soon afterwards took command of C Company due to casualties. However, B Company on the left ran into determined opposition from the steel works just north of the Canal at the southern end of Trith-St-Léger and heavy fire from la Fontenelle, Poirier Farm and Trith-St-Léger. Trench mortars and a section of field guns were brought up to shift the enemy, who fled in panic.

Throughout the whole operation the Germans kept Maing and the railway line under heavy gas and high explosive shelling. They kept up close-range machine gun fire as the attackers attempted to consolidate their gains. Aircraft also strafed the attackers at intervals. At 4.00 p.m. the Germans counterattacked from Mont Huoy and Famars under cover of a heavy barrage. However, the British artillery response was equal to the task and caused heavy losses, as did small arms fire. The attack was stopped before it reached the new line.

During this attack Bissett realised that the Company was in danger of being cut off. Accompanied by Sergeant A Sinclair (DCM for this action), they rushed to the left flank and placed themselves with parties of machine gunners. Bissett fired his revolver at the advancing Germans and an enemy officer fired two revolver shots at him from very close range but missed. Bissett fired his last round of ammunition at the German and then threw the gun in his face. Behind, his batman, Private R McNeill (MM for this action), saw two Germans about to attack and bayoneted them both.

The Germans attacked again at 6.00 p.m. On the right of 152nd Brigade, 6/7th Gordon Highlanders was pushed back to the railway, but there it made a stand. The Germans were able to strike 6th Seaforth Highlanders in both flanks and the Battalion was also forced back to the railway.

In 153rd Brigade the left flank of C Company, 6th Argyll & Sutherland Highlanders was turned, but Bissett kept the situation under control and skilfully withdrew his men to the railway, where they were able to hold the enemy with the assistance of the field guns. Ammunition ran low when the Germans tried again around 6.00 p.m. Rather than wait for the attack to reach them, Bissett climbed on top of the railway embankment and called on C Company to follow him. They charged downhill and drove the shocked Germans back 450m with the bayonet. B Company on the left also charged and forced back the enemy. A new line was established in German trenches east of the railway, sweeping back to cross the railway south of la Fontenelle.

Bissett was wounded and gassed in this engagement. He sent two runners back, requesting reinforcements, food and ammunition. One was killed but the other made it and a small reinforcement was sent up with some ammunition. As soon as they arrived, Bissett led them forward with the remaining eleven effective men from his Company, to probe the German front line. They did not encounter any more Germans.

The front settled down for the night, in contact with the Canadians to the north, although the Germans kept up heavy artillery fire. Orders were issued for another continuation of the advance on the 26th, with the objective of seizing Famars and Mont Huoy.

The 6th Argyll & Sutherland Highlanders was relieved by 6th Black Watch and went into support east of the Ecaillon River. Only then were Bissett and his men able to seek medical attention. The Battalion took seventy-four prisoners, two anti-tanks guns, a trench mortar and ten machine guns. The Battalion's casualties for October, mainly sustained in these operations, numbered 186 (twenty-five killed, 158 wounded and three missing). It was still reasonably up to strength on 29th October, when there were thirty-eight officers and 808 other ranks.

To the north, Fifth Army remained static all day. Second Army carried out the main operations on 25th October, the Action of Ooteghem, which is covered in the previous book in this series, *Victoria Crosses on the Western Front, The Final Advance in Flanders and Artois, September–October 1918.*

Battle of Valenciennes

1st November 1918

483 Sgt Hugh Cairns, 46th Battalion (South Saskatchewan) CEF (10th Canadian Brigade, 4th Canadian Division), Valenciennes, France

In the centre of First Army, the Canadian Corps had closed up to the Escaut Canal. However, XXII Corps on the right and VIII Corps on the left were both behind. On 21st October the Army Commander, General Henry Horne, ordered bridgeheads over the Escaut to be secured where possible, but there was to be no large-scale attempt to force the waterway. While the flanking corps made their way forward, the Canadians enjoyed a short break. However, there was still much to do and, in addition to the normal commitments, large numbers of civilians had to be fed and treated at medical facilities.

Small scale attempts to get over the Canal by boat, footbridge and the debris of destroyed bridges were largely unsuccessful. It was clear that the Germans were going to make a determined stand at Valenciennes but the town could not be bombarded because of the large number of civilians there. This made it difficult to engage enemy machine gun and sniper posts overlooking the Canal, which was an

Opposite: AF = airfield, BF = brickfields, Cty = cemetery, LPS = Le Poirier Station, LT = La Targette, MS = Marly Station, SW = steelworks. Much of this area, particularly south of the A2 Autoroute, was open ground in 1918. The boundary on the left, between 10th and 12th Canadian Brigades, follows the line of the Canal as it was in 1918. North of the autoroute the Canal now follows a different line. Étang du Vignoble did not exist at the time. The Blue Line follows the course of a former railway. To visit the sites mentioned in the account of Cairns' VC action, follow the D958a (Rue Roger Salengro) northwards from the centre of Famars. After 550m there is a crossroads, with Rue Edmond Guillaume on the right. To the north are some older houses and one of these may be the one where Cairns winkled out the first machine gun from an upper floor. Continue along the D958a for just over another kilometre and turn right onto Rue du Pont d'Aulnoy. The cemetery is on the left side of this road. Having considered the second action against two machine gun posts in this area, return to the D958a and turn right to continue northwards towards Valenciennes. Cross over the autoroute and 400m beyond turn right on Rue Raux. There is a t-junction after 275m. Turn left on Route d'Aulnoy (D373). After 200m on the right amongst all the modern buildings is where the brickfields were in 1918. There is nothing much to see now. Continue for another 700m to where the railway used to cross the road at the Blue Line. On the right is Rue de la Gare, where you can park. Return to the main D373 road and turn right towards Valenciennes. The factory gate that features in the final part of Cairns' VC action is on the right after 50m.

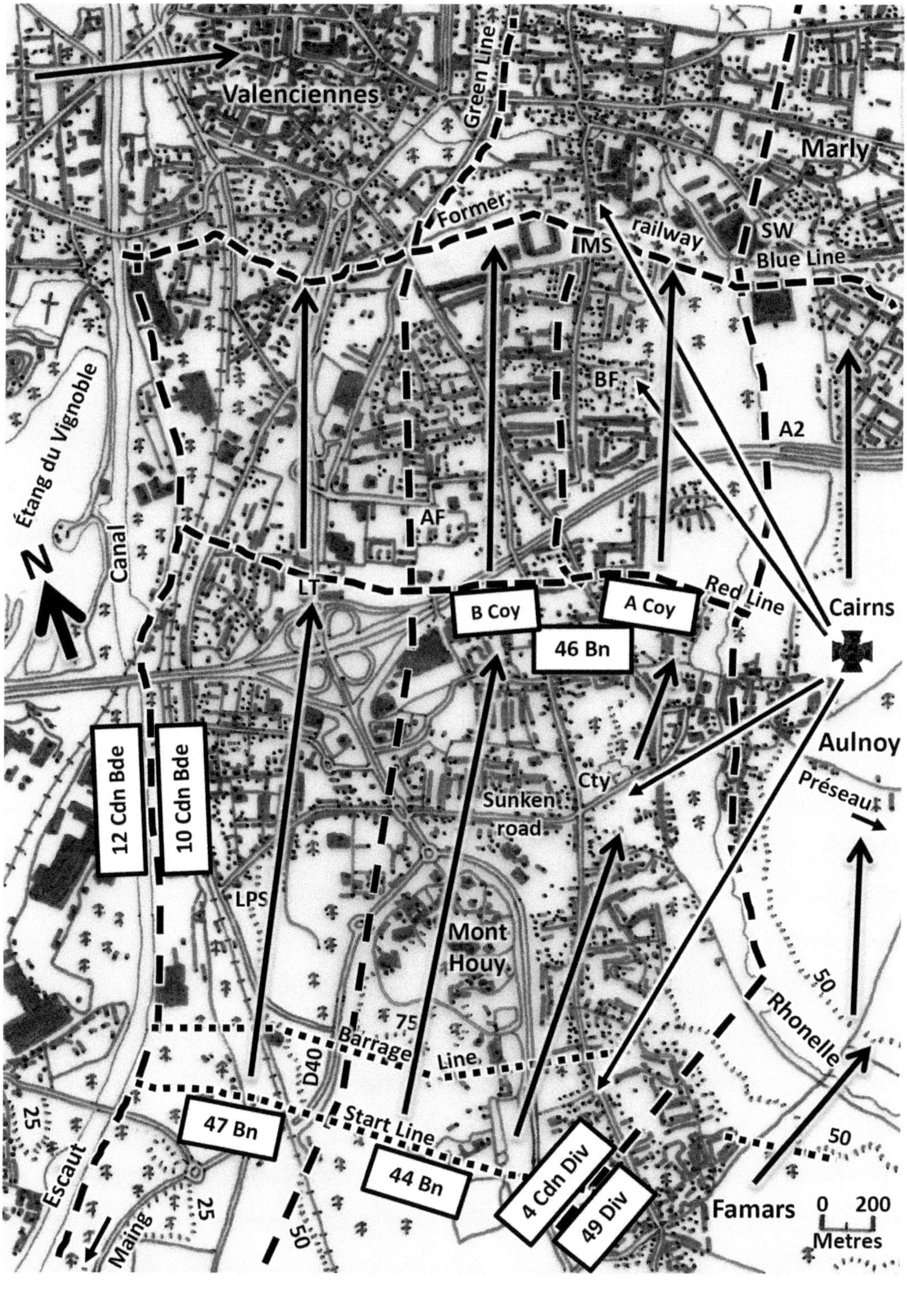
Valenciennes
Green Line
Marly
Former
railway
MS
SW
Blue Line
BF
A2
Étang du Vignoble
AF
Canal
N
LT
Red Line
B Coy
A Coy
46 Bn
Cairns
Aulnoy
Préseau
12 Cdn Bde
10 Cdn Bde
Cty
Sunken road
LPS
Mont Houy
50
Rhonelle
75
Barrage Line
D40
25
Start Line
47 Bn
44 Bn
4 Cdn Div
49 Div
50
Escaut
Maing
25
50
Famars
0 200
Metres

effective barrier wired on both banks and fortified on the east bank. Many buildings had been converted for defence with loopholes cut into the walls. The Germans had also cut gaps in the dykes and opened sluice gates, in order to flood both sides of the Canal west and southwest of Valenciennes. To the north, in the angle with the Condé-Mons Canal, the water covered many square kilometres. East of the Canal the high ground at Mont Huoy completely dominated the southern approaches to the city. Behind was a long ridge overlooking the Rhonelle, which had also been strengthened as a defensive line. There was a second line of trenches some way to the rear, although these were not as well developed as the frontline positions. The German Seventeenth Army had five understrength divisions to hold this sector, with the bulk of the strength being in the Mont Huoy area.

By the evening of 26th October 51st Division (XXII Corps) to the south had succeeded in crossing the Ecaillon and was on the outskirts of Famars, looking into the Rhonelle valley. However, attempts to advance further had been thwarted by the dominating feature of Mont Huoy and from German batteries southeast of Valenciennes.

It was clear that a frontal assault on Valenciennes, or a northern flanking movement, alone were out of the question. Mont Huoy was the key to seizing the city. First Army therefore planned a three-phase operation. In the first, XXII Corps would attack north-eastwards on 28th October to capture Monty Huoy and seize the Red Line. The 4th Canadian Division would pass through in the second phase to continue the attack between the Escaut and the Rhonelle, in order to gain the Blue Line between Préseau and the southern outskirts of Valenciennes. The third phase on 1st November would entail 4th Canadian Division capturing the high ground east of the city (Green Line), thereby outflanking it and enabling the rest of the Canadian Corps to cross the Escaut from the west.

In the first phase on 28th October, 51st Division gained Mont Houy but the Germans were determined to retain this critical position and a counterattack drove the Highlanders back to the southern slopes. Despite this setback, Le Poirier Station and Famars were taken but the line held at the end of the day was short of the Red Line.

The relief of 51st Division by 4th Canadian Division was postponed. During 29th October 51st Division fought off repeated counterattacks. That night the right of the exhausted 51st Division was relieved by 49th Division and the left by 10th Canadian Brigade. In the meantime, the overall situation had changed. Orders were issued for Fourth, Third and First Armies, in conjunction with the French First Army on the right, to resume the main offensive on 3rd November. By then it was imperative that Valenciennes had been captured in order to secure the left flank of the whole operation. To achieve this the Blue and Green Lines were to be captured in a single operation with massive artillery support. In this attack, scheduled for early on 1st November, 49th Division was on the right with 10th Canadian Brigade on the left. The latter's task was to assault Marly and Valenciennes from the south.

As the 10th advanced, 12th Canadian Brigade was to establish bridgeheads over the Escaut from the west and force its way into the city to mop up. To the north 3rd Canadian Division was also to be prepared to cross the Canal.

The presence of civilians limited the use of artillery. Only the industrial centre of Marly and its steel works came under bombardment. With its left flank so far forward the Canadian Corps was able to arrange a unique barrage on Mont Huoy. There were eight field and six heavy artillery brigades to support 10th Canadian Brigade, provided by 39th Division and 2nd, 4th and 5th Canadian Divisions. Three field brigades near Maing provided the creeping barrage, whilst the rest provided oblique, enfilade, counter-battery and point target fire. Three batteries of 4.5″ Howitzers fired an intense smoke screen to deny observation to the enemy in Valenciennes and Marly. The creeping barrage included twelve batteries of 1st and 4th Canadian Machine Gun Battalions, some of which were on the left bank of the Escaut to fire in enfilade. No.1 Company, 4th Canadian Machine Gun Battalion was with 10th Canadian Brigade, which had the honour of being the most heavily supported infantry brigade of the entire war.

On the left flank of Third Army, 61st Division (XVII Corps) was to capture Maresches and St Hubert. Thc former had been entered by 7.15 a.m. and St Hubert was taken, except for a small area about the crossroads. A counterattack pushed back the line which was re-established from the Rhonelle around the eastern edge of Maresches. Another attempt to get forward in the evening failed to make any progress.

On the right of First Army and XXII Corps, 4th Division almost reached its objective in Préseau. Counterattacks forced back the line and by the end of the day it ran 450m west of Préseau. On the left of XXII Corps, 146th Brigade (49th Division) crossed the Rhonelle and made good progress until resistance stiffened and a counterattack drove it back. However, by 10.30 a.m. the left was on the objective and the rest of the line was not far from it. At midday another counterattack developed and artillery support was requested from the Canadians on the left. Two brigades of field artillery put down a barrage 550m in front of the Blue Line. By 13.25 p.m. 146th Brigade had been driven off the Blue Line and another battalion was sent forward to re-establish the situation. At 4.00 p.m. the Germans attacked again. They were repulsed and the Brigade was able to advance to within 275m of the Blue Line.

The assembly of 4th Canadian Division took place in heavy rain showers. During the night the Germans fired some counter-preparation gas and high explosive barrages. The 10th Canadian Brigade was east of the Escaut, with 11th Canadian Brigade in support, and 12th Canadian Brigade was to the west. At 5.15 a.m. the infantry advanced behind a heavy and accurate wall of shrapnel, high explosive and machine gun fire. The German artillery retaliated promptly but its effect was quickly eroded by accurate Canadian counter-bombardment. Many Germans stunned by the barrage surrendered.

The 10th Canadian Brigade attacked west of the Rhonelle with 44th and 47th Battalions, right and left respectively, supported by 46th Battalion on the right, with 50th Battalion in reserve. Each battalion had a battery of machine guns, a mobile 6″ Mortar and two (one for support battalions) Stokes mortars attached. The Brigade also had a company of engineers. At the first objective (Red Line) 46th Battalion was to pass through 44th Battalion and continue to the second objective (Blue Line), Marly and the southern outskirts of Valenciennes. On the left 47th Battalion was to continue from the Red Line to the Blue Line.

The 44th Battalion's right company entered Aulnoy behind the barrage and swept on to the objective, in contact with 5th West Yorkshire (146th Brigade) on the right. Many prisoners were taken in Aulnoy. The left company cleared Mont Huoy thoroughly before moving on to the objective. The attached trench mortars were invaluable in suppressing the fire of various machine gun positions. The attached machine guns were set up to cover the right flank. The Battalion captured three field guns, twenty minenwerfer and eighty-three machine guns, in addition to about 800 prisoners. There were eighty-nine casualties, including seventeen killed. Later the Germans shelled the Mont with mustard gas and aircraft strafed parties on the roads. In cellars gas cylinders were discovered set for gradual leakage.

In support on the right, 46th Battalion had left its billets in Thiant at 1.00 a.m. and was in its assembly positions by 3.00 a.m. A Company (Major RW Gyles) was on the right and B Company (Lieutenant Phillips, later RJ Holmes) on the left, each with a frontage of two platoons. C and D Companies were in support respectively. The attached B Battery, 4th Canadian Machine Gun Battalion was to position four machine guns on Mont Huoy when 44th Battalion had taken the Red Line. Once 46th Battalion had seized the Blue Line, four machine guns were to be moved to the spur north of Aulnoy and east of the Aulnoy–Marly road. The remaining guns were to remain mounted in the vicinity of the church on the Aulnoy–Valenciennes road. The Battalion had a number of other attachments. An armoured car was to assist A Company on the right and a section each of cavalry and cyclists were at the disposal of the CO. The support companies were to mop up and deal with any opposition missed by the leading companies. At the Blue Line they were to take up positions about 275m behind the leading companies. Following consolidation, the support companies were to send patrols to exploit towards the Green Line.

In the initial attack 46th Battalion acted as moppers up for 44th Battalion, the latter being under strength and only able to concentrate on Aulnoy and Mont Huoy. On the right A Company followed the barrage, with 1 Platoon (Lieutenant Johnston) on the right, 2 Platoon (Lieutenant Cook) on the left and 3 Platoon (**Sergeant Hugh Cairns**) in support. Its right was on the Famars–Valenciennes road until reaching the cemetery near Aulnoy, when it was to swing right with the road on its left flank.

About 275m north of Famars, Cairns was advancing along the Valenciennes road when a machine gun opened fire from the upstairs window of a house. Cairns seized

The Famars – Valenciennes road just north of Famars looking north. It was in this area that Cairns first came under machine gun fire from the upstairs window of a house and rushed in to overcome the opposition.

a Lewis gun and rushed into the house. He dashed upstairs in the face of fire turned on him, killed the crew of five and captured the gun. After advancing about 450m behind 44th Battalion, the Company came under heavy machine gun fire from just behind Mont Huoy and the top of a building on the Famars–Valanciennes road. The latter was cleared by 1 Platoon, resulting in a large number of enemy dead and no prisoners. About 350m short of the sunken Aulnoy–Le Poirier Station road, the Company came under heavy machine gun fire from houses at the junction of the sunken road with the Famars–Valenciennes road. The 44th Battalion in front was struggling to clear the enemy resistance and 1 Platoon went forward to assist. Some prisoners and machine guns were taken and many more enemy were killed there.

About fifty metres beyond the sunken road, having crossed to the eastern side of the Valenciennes road, A Company came under direct machine gun fire from in front of the cemetery. Cairns rushed forward alone towards the strongly held machine gun post, firing the Lewis gun from the hip as he went. He silenced and captured two machine guns, killing twelve Germans and taking eighteen prisoners. By then 2 Platoon had merged with B Company on the left and there were insufficient men with A Company's commander to clear the area to the front when the barrage moved forward again. However, the halt of fifteen minutes on the Red Line allowed time to reorganise. A Company called forward two sections of C Company in support, one to reinforce the right flank and the other the left.

Looking west along the sunken road, with the cemetery on the right, towards the Famars–Valenciennes road. In this area Cairns silenced and captured two more machine guns. The area where the brickfields were in 1918 has been so closely built over that no meaningful photograph could be taken.

When the barrage lifted, A Company advanced in good order until in line with the junction of the Aulnoy–Valenciennes and Aulnoy–Marly roads. The Company was halted for a few minutes by machine gun fire. When the left Lewis gun section came into action, the right was able to continue. The Germans then retired along the road to the brickfields east of the Aulnoy–Marly road and came under very effective Lewis gun fire. Many Germans were routed out of the houses along the road and large numbers were sent back as prisoners.

A Company advanced again until reaching the area south of the brickfields, where it came under heavy fire from field guns and machine guns. The German party was well dug in and an inconclusive fire fight followed for about twenty minutes. Major Gyles ordered CSM FD Gibbons, Sergeant Cairns, who by then had been wounded in the shoulder, and four other men with two Lewis guns to outflank the enemy position. While fire was brought to bear on the enemy position, the small party moved on hands and knees to the right. They reached a point about seventy metres from the Germans and opened fire, causing such heavy casualties that the remainder surrendered. Three field guns, a trench mortar, seven machine guns and more than fifty prisoners were captured. The ground was also strewn with dead Germans. A Company then continued to the factory south of the railway, overcoming more opposition on the way. Cairns with eight other ranks and a Lewis gun were ordered to seize the railway/road junction at the station in Marly, which they did. The right flank was under heavy machine gun fire from the steelworks east of the Rhonelle, outside the Battalion's right boundary. Meanwhile, on the left, 1 Platoon, with twenty men of 44th Battalion, mopped up the factory and established posts on the railway. Cairns moved along the railway to connect with 1 Platoon. By 9.00 a.m. the Blue Line had been secured. A Company had forty-five casualties in this action.

In support on the right, C Company skirted the outskirts of Famars but it appeared that those in front had not gone through the village. Two sections were sent in and flushed out several Germans. In Aulnoy more opposition was dealt with and many enemy were killed or captured. Further into the village a field gun and a battery of light minenwerfers, with about fifty Germans, opened fire. C Company had some 44th Battalion stragglers and a party from D Company attached. They forced the enemy to retire, leaving behind their guns and many dead. The barrage by then had become ragged and there were a number of shorts.

At the Red Line, C Company sent a platoon out to the right to sweep the area north of Aulnoy, in support of A Company. The platoon completed the advance alongside A Company with its right on the Rhonelle. The rest of C Company advanced to the objective, overcoming several machine gun posts on the way. C Company captured a total of five field guns, four minenwerfers, four wagons, four machine guns and about 175 prisoners. The Company had eleven casualties, including five killed.

On the left of 46th Battalion, B Company passed to the west of Mont Huoy. Very little opposition was met until reaching the Aulnoy–Le Poirier Station road. Heavy machine gun fire and snipers were encountered and there was no sign of 44th Battalion in front. At the Red Line the Company reorganised and, when the barrage lifted, 5 Platoon worked forward over the open ground on the left, while the right mopped up the houses on the main road. A short distance after leaving the Red Line, the company commander was mortally wounded and there were many other casualties. The advance continued to the vicinity of the airfield alongside the Aulnoy–Valenciennes road. Just in front of the airfield contact was made with 1 Platoon, A Company. The advance of B Company continued across the main road to the objective on the Blue Line, without encountering much more opposition. By then Sergeant Irving was commanding the Company. The railway did not offer a suitable field of fire and a trench just to the south was occupied instead. Contact was established with A Company on the right and 47th Battalion on the left.

B Company lost all its officers in this action and was down to just thirty-three men. Only one magazine per Lewis gun remained. Lieutenants Holmes (14 Platoon) and Morfitt (15 Platoon) were sent from D Company and Holmes assumed command at 9.00 a.m. About midday an enemy party about forty strong was seen moving about in plain view where the Aulnoy–Valenciennes road crossed the railway. Small arms fire accounted for at least six but, in view of B Company's weakness, assistance was requested. At 3.30 p.m. a Stokes mortar arrived without ammunition. When this did arrive at 6.30 p.m. the crew could not be found. However, an artillery officer was able to arrange a barrage at 4.30 p.m. and there was little trouble from the enemy thereafter. At 6.30 p.m. two platoons of 50th Battalion arrived to reinforce the front on the right, allowing the rest of B Company to shift over to the left of its frontage. Of the eighty-eight all ranks that started this operation in B Company, fifty-seven were casualties by the end of the day.

D Company's 14 Platoon was to advance extended behind B Company, while 13 and 15 Platoons mopped up the houses along the main road. However, D Company soon found itself in the front line when it came up alongside B Company in the sunken road. Two platoons then worked along the Famars–Valenciennes road to outflank the enemy trench, 13 Platoon on the right and 15 Platoon on the left. When the platoons had advance about 200m, the enemy was seen to fall back on the left and the whole line was able to advance again. D Company captured a field gun, five mortars and about twenty machine guns in addition to about 300 prisoners. The Company had thirteen casualties.

The attack had been a resounding success. A, D and B Companies were on the Blue Line about 10.10 a.m., in contact with 47th Battalion on the left. Hundreds of the enemy had been killed or captured for comparatively light losses. The attached armoured car returned to report that it had reached the church in Valenciennes and that the city was full of Germans. The CO arranged for the armoured car to bring up a supply of Lewis gun magazines for B Company, while more were being carried up by tump liners.

Once the protective barrage in front of the Blue Line lifted, patrols were to push into Marly. However, such was the weight of enemy fire on the left from the south of Valenciennes, that the CO cancelled the left patrol. Major Gyles in A Company called forward the C Company patrol under Lieutenant JPG McLeod (recommended for the VC but awarded the DSO for this action), consisting of a sergeant and ten other ranks with a Lewis gun. The patrol moved off at 9.20 a.m., crossed the railway line and was met by Sergeant Cairns with information about a large German party in a factory just east of the main road. McLeod left seven men in houses as a covering party, while he, Cairns with a Lewis gun, and two men investigated the factory.

As they crossed the street, they came under fire. Cairns ran for the swinging gate that opened into the courtyard, firing the Lewis gun from the hip. Those enemy not killed fled into a back street. McLeod and one of the others then entered the courtyard. Rounding a corner they discovered about fifty Germans in a passage at the southern end of the courtyard. They ordered the Germans to surrender, which they did, but one retained his rifle. McLeod covered this man but a German officer drew his pistol and shot Cairns in the stomach. Cairns immediately opened fire killing or wounding around thirty. A German machine gun opened fire from a high brick wall and Cairns was hit in the wrist. He continued firing until another bullet almost severed his hand and blew away the Lewis gun trigger. About twenty Germans ran forward to overpower Cairns and he threw the useless weapon in the face of a German who was firing at him, knocking the man over. The rest of the

The final location in Cairns' VC action was on the road towards Valenciennes just north of the railway in Marly. This view is looking north to where the railway crossed this road in the vicinity of the large white van. The patrol under Lieutenant JPG McLeod advanced towards the camera position until reaching the factory on the east side (left in this view) of the road. The gateway on the left is believed to be the entrance to that factory.

patrol then joined in a skirmish with the surviving Germans. Cairns staggered out of the gateway and collapsed. He was carried back by one of the other men, who was killed by a burst from a machine gun. McLeod then dragged Cairns back to A Company's lines and reported what had happened to Major Gyles at 1.15 p.m.

Privates Marshall, 721012 J Fidler and 255806 P Lavery also displayed great gallantry in this action. Cairns died of wounds next day, the last of seventy-one Canadians to be awarded the Victoria Cross during the Great War. For the rest of the day the German machine guns, mortars and artillery were very active. On occasions the Canadian artillery was called upon to engage them.

On the left of 10th Canadian Brigade, 47th Battalion deployed A Company on the right and C Company on the left, supported by B and D Companies. D Company, 50th Battalion was to follow to mop up. The enemy counter-barrage was heavy and a large proportion of gas shell was used. However, there was no serious resistance until Le Poirier Station was passed, when well dug in positions were encountered. Many enemy were killed by the barrage but most posts still had to be cleared with the bayonet. The Red Line was reached on time at 6.50 a.m. Fifteen minutes later the advance resumed with B and D Companies passing through. Stubborn resistance was met all the way to the Blue Line, which was reached by 10.10 a.m. There was considerable machine gun and mortar fire from Valenciennes during consolidation. Numerous enemy targets were engaged by the Lewis gunners. At midday the enemy fire increased again. Parties of up to thirty Germans were seen moving around the streets about 275m ahead of the Blue Line. The artillery and 6″ Newton Mortars were brought to bear and stopped the enemy activities. A German barrage fell on the Blue Line at 4.30 p.m., but no attack developed and it was quiet by 5.05 p.m. The Battalion was relieved by 50th Battalion at 4.20 a.m. next morning, having taken about 600 prisoners and suffering 135 casualties, including sixteen killed and twenty-one gassed.

When 49th Division was forced back it exposed the right flank of 10th Canadian Brigade. The 44th Battalion was warned to be prepared to protect 46th Battalion's flank. In the afternoon, 50th Battalion was sent up to reinforce 46th Battalion and hold the Brigade's right flank. One company was attached to 46th Battalion, arriving at 4.15 p.m., with two platoons each being sent to A and B Companies. Those attached to A Company, consisting of two sergeants and twenty-three other ranks, arrived at 6.00 p.m. Two companies of 50th Battalion formed a defensive flank facing east on the spur north of Aulnoy, while the fourth company was near La Targette in support of 47th Battalion. Six batteries of 4th Canadian Machine Gun Battalion faced east but the fire from Marly was not suppressed. Contact was not made with 146th Brigade on the right until 7.25 p.m.

Meanwhile 12th Canadian Brigade and 3rd Canadian Division had established bridgeheads over the Escaut, crossing in collapsible boats and over cork float bridges. By midday most of 38th and 72nd Battalions (12th Canadian Brigade), on the left of 10th Canadian Brigade, had crossed over and were pushing into the city. They were held up at the railway and at the end of the day the Germans were still clinging to the east of Valenciennes and Marly. However, they had suffered enormous losses. Almost 1,800 prisoners were taken by the Canadians and more than 800 German dead were counted. Canadian losses were eighty killed and 300 wounded. The careful coordination of overwhelming artillery support had allowed the infantry to make significant advances.

During the night 10th Canadian Brigade was relieved by the 11th. The 46th Battalion was relieved by 54th Battalion at 10.00 p.m. and returned to Thiant for a hot meal. The Battalion had suffered 126 casualties (thirty-four killed, ninety wounded and two missing). About 800 prisoners had been taken, in addition to seven field guns, six mortars, two anti-tank guns and forty-five machine guns.

Overnight the Germans withdrew from Valenciennes and Marly. When the advance continued next morning, 12th Canadian Brigade was able to push through the city with little resistance. On the right 49th Division took the steel works in the afternoon.

Preparatory Operations for the Battle of the Sambre

2nd November 1918

484 Sgt James Clarke, 15th Battalion, The Lancashire Fusiliers (96th Brigade, 32nd Division), Happegarbes, France

By the end of October the right wing of the BEF had just about completed closing up to the west banks of the Sambre, Rhonelle and Schelde waterways, setting the scene for the final push of the war. In the next few days three offensives were unleashed against the already exhausted and battered Germans. The Group of Armies of Flanders on the left attacked on 31st October. Next day the Americans and French joined in on the right and, on 4th November, the British Fourth, Third and First Armies launched the main effort in the centre.

While preparations were being made for the central offensive (Battle of the Sambre) a number of small preparatory operations were carried out. Third and First Armies captured Valenciennes on 2nd November. In Fourth Army attempts were made to clear the Germans from points on the west bank of the Sambre. Aggressive patrolling cleared Ors, but enclaves at Catillon and le Donjon remained. However, the main difficulty existed on the left of IX Corps, which was still 1,800m from the canal northeast of Ors. The enemy held the spur at Happegarbes, which dominated the canal as far south as Catillon, and, during the main attack, would enable the Germans to fire into the flank of 32nd Division. The spur had to be captured beforehand.

On 30th October, 96th Brigade (32nd Division) relieved 16th Brigade (6th Division) in the line. On the right was 2nd Manchester, with 15th Lancashire Fusiliers on the left and 16th Lancashire Fusiliers in support. During the next two days vigorous patrolling and reconnaissances were carried out.

At 6.00 a.m. on 2nd November 15th Lancashire Fusiliers attacked on a frontage of three companies, supported by three Mark V tanks of 10th Tank Battalion. It took two hours to fight through to the objective, during which two tanks were lost. **Sergeant James Clarke** led his platoon in the attack until it was held up by heavy fire and suffered many casualties. Clarke dashed forward alone and got through a thick hedge that was held strongly by the enemy. Undeterred he systematically

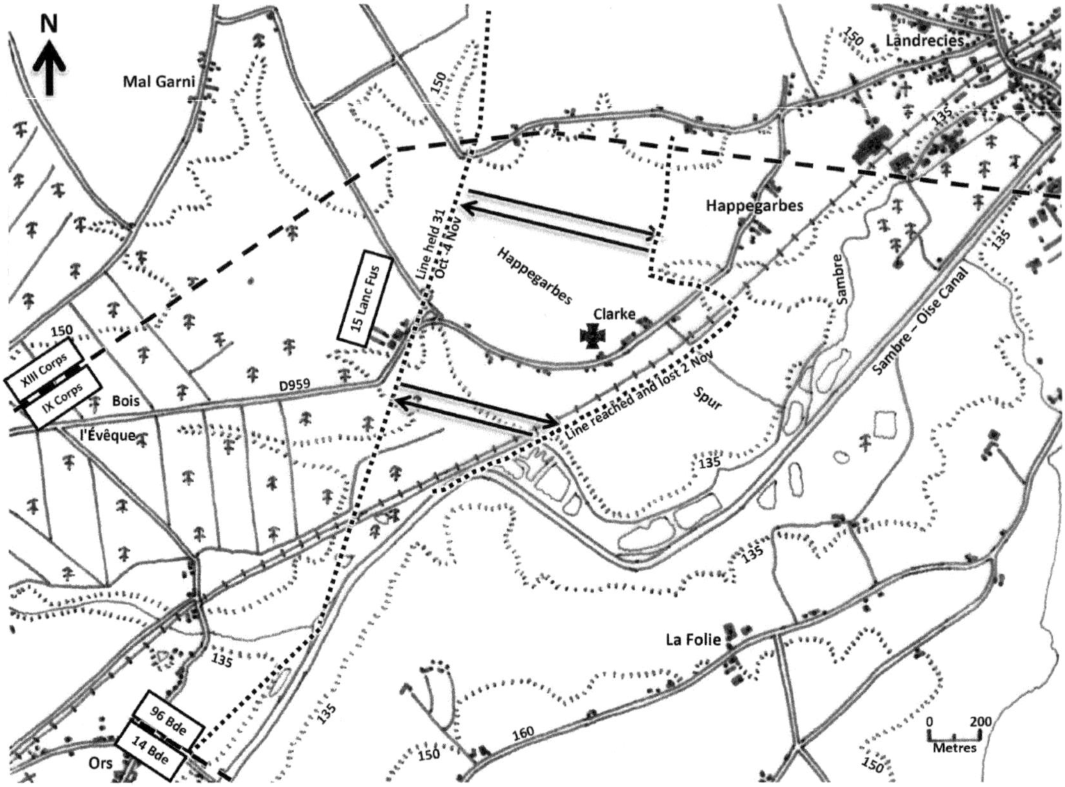

Few details of the attack on Happegarbes Spur are known, in particular the dispositions of the Battalion and precisely where James Clarke's VC actions took place. The position marked centrally on the spur is therefore representative rather than definitive. Drive east along the D959 through Bois-l'Évêque towards Landrecies. As the road emerges from the wood it swings left past some large farm buildings, beyond which is space to pull in on the roadside on the left. Follow the track to the northwest, which climbs gently, and turn back to look over the spur. Even with the height gained here it is not possible to pick out the railway and canal.

Looking southeast along the Happegarbes Spur from just behind the 15th Lancashire Fusiliers start line. The D959, railway and canal run across the picture in the low ground in the middle distance and are almost impossible to discern. Bois-l'Évêque is on the right. Happegarbes village is to the left of the power lines on the left of picture, beyond the light coloured field.

attacked four machine gun posts in succession, bayoneting the crews. He rallied the survivors of his platoon and led them forward again to take three more machine gun posts and many prisoners. Later another machine gun caused a further delay. Clarke gained the attention of a tank and guided it over exposed ground to where it could deal with the troublesome post.

After a long and difficult fight, the spur was seized, sixty-two prisoners were taken and a defensive line was established along the railway. A counterattack from the northeast was driven off at 9.00 a.m., but a stronger attack followed at 2.00 p.m., supported by a massive bombardment that included gas. The Germans infiltrated through gaps in the line and got behind the right and centre. The right flank was already in a dangerous salient and the whole unit had suffered many casualties. The CO led the reserve company forward to fill a gap in the centre, but it was clear that the Battalion could not hold the spur alone. Although reinforced by B and C Companies and a platoon of D Company, 16th Lancashire Fusiliers, the Battalion was back in its start positions at the end of the day.

At 6.15 a.m. on 3rd November 15th Lancashire Fusiliers and two companies of 16th Lancashire Fusiliers attacked again. The spur was taken within forty-five minutes and a counterattack was defeated. Clarke was again conspicuous and captured more prisoners. The Germans then penetrated behind the centre and right companies and the situation was critical. The troops rallied and the reserve company filled a gap to connect the two flanks together. The Germans were pushed back along the railway cutting towards Landrecies.

A second counterattack by five battalions was launched from the northeast at 1.00 p.m. Bitter fighting followed. All the Battalion's posts were knocked in by shelling, leaving the survivors exposed. Battalion Headquarters was almost surrounded and, although the position was held, heavy casualties were suffered. The Battalion was not strong enough to resist indefinitely and it pulled back to the start line. It was clear that the spur could be taken, but not held in isolation. The decision was therefore made to deal with it in the main offensive on 4th November, during which the Germans would be unable to launch such strong counterattacks.

The troops spent a very uncomfortable and wet night in the low ground west of the spur, prior to the offensive next morning, the details of which are related in

the next chapter. Zero hour was at 5.45 a.m. and 15th Lancashire Fusiliers, on the left of 96th Brigade, set off for the canal opposite La Folie and Le Sambreton. The Battalion was supported by two tanks and was covered by two 2nd King's Own Yorkshire Light Infantry companies, on the lower slopes of the spur. Enemy fire over the canal was terrific and Clarke dashed forward through the barrage with a Lewis gun team, which silenced machine gun posts on the far side in front of the right companies of the Battalion. The canal was reached and the west bank secured. The two companies on the left worked their way through Happegarbes village, clearing enemy posts as they went, before swinging north. By 7.00 a.m. all the ground west of the canal had been cleared. The Battalion passed two companies over two 25th Division (XIII Corps) footbridges southwest of Landrecies, in order to form the right of the bridgehead. The rest of the Battalion crossed the canal that night and advanced towards Le Sambeton. It was the Battalion's last action in the war.

Battle of the Sambre and Subsequent Operations

485 Maj George Findlay, 409th Field Company Royal Engineers (1st Division), Sambre-Oise Canal south of Catillon, France

486 Lt Col Dudley Johnson, South Wales Borderers att'd 2nd Battalion, The Royal Sussex Regiment (2nd Brigade, 1st Division), Sambre-Oise Canal south of Catillon, France

487 2Lt James Kirk, 10th att'd 2nd Battalion, The Manchester Regiment (96th Brigade, 32nd Division), Sambre-Oise Canal north of Ors, France

488 Maj Arnold Waters, 218th Field Company Royal Engineers (32nd Division), Sambre-Oise Canal north of Ors, France

489 Spr Adam Archibald, 218th Field Company Royal Engineers (32nd Division), Sambre-Oise Canal north of Ors, France

490 Lt Col James Marshall, Irish Guards att'd 16th Battalion, The Lancashire Fusiliers (96th Brigade, 32nd Division), Sambre-Oise Canal north of Ors, France

491 LCpl William Amey, 1/8th Battalion, The Royal Warwickshire Regiment (75th Brigade, 25th Division), Landrecies, France

4th November 1918

Germany suffered disaster upon disaster in October 1918 and, as November opened, stood alone. In Berlin there was revolution in the air, Ludendorff resigned and the fleet mutinied. Germany's allies had collapsed. Hungary separated from Austria and her troops mutinied. Bulgaria, Turkey and Austria all agreed armistices. A German collapse seemed inevitable and, although many troops continued to resist, the outcome was not in doubt. The danger was that the Germans would pull back to strong positions for the winter and bargain for a more advantageous peace deal. An immediate general offensive was therefore necessary to keep up the relentless pressure and not allow the Germans time to dig in. Two offensives were already underway in the north in Flanders and in the south, where the Americans and French attacked side by side. However, the key area was in the centre on the right wing of the BEF.

Haig ordered the Fourth, Third and First Armies to attack towards Mauberge and Mons on 4th November. The preliminary operations for this offensive were mentioned in the previous chapter. The attack frontage was fifty kilometres long from Oisy in the south to Valenciennes. South of Oisy the French attacked on a frontage of thirty kilometres.

Within the BEF it is the actions of the Fourth Army that are of most interest. The Army faced the difficult task of crossing the Sambre-Oise Canal on the right. The waterway was between ten and twelve metres wide at water level (considerably wider at the top of the banks) and two metres or more deep with a muddy bottom. However, at the locks the width was reduced to just over five metres. In places the overall width of the obstacle was increased by a series of reservoirs alongside the waterway. In other places there were substantial subsidiary streams on either side of the canal. The Germans flooded some of the low ground and, although it was only a few inches deep, it turned the whole area into a quagmire that was difficult to negotiate. South of Catillon the Germans had felled the trees on the west bank to clear their fields of fire and to create extra obstacles. On the left of the Army front was the Forest of Mormal with areas of thick undergrowth and deep drainage ditches. Elsewhere there were thick hedges and small villages that made ideal strongpoints. Everywhere the Germans enjoyed excellent observation over the obstacles.

The engineers devised a number of methods of getting over the canal. The 2nd Brigade produced lightweight single span bridges with wheels for the locks, which could be launched from the home bank without assistance from the far side. The 1st Brigade used captured German steel floats adapted into floating bridges that could be slid along the ground until launched. The 32nd Division used a similar design. Light footbridges were also made by lashing empty petrol tins or cork floats together into rafts that could be fastened in chains. As a last resort the assault troops had lifebelts and some light portable Berthon boats were held in reserve.

The IX Corps on the right was allocated an earlier zero hour (5.45 a.m.) than elsewhere, in order to gain maximum surprise in crossing the canal. The XIII Corps on the left started at 6.15 a.m., but both Corps had two objectives. The first, the Army objective (Red Line), was the minimum to be achieved. Beyond was a line of exploitation. It marked the limit of advance before a halt would be required to bring forward artillery, logistics and extend communications prior to another push forward. Assembly for the attack was achieved without difficulty and by the early hours there was a thick ground mist to obscure movement.

The IX Corps faced a number of complications. South of Lock 1 the width of the Canal was doubled by reservoirs on either side. Just about everywhere there were subsidiary streams, in places on both sides of the canal. In the centre of the Corps the west bank at Catillon was still held by the Germans. The 1st (right) and 32nd (left) Divisions were to make the attack either side of Catillon and seize separate bridgeheads. Having achieved the crossing, 1st Division was to press on to the Army objective (Red Line), maintaining a defensive right flank if the French to the south did not keep pace. HQ IX Corps laid down two preliminary objectives before the Red Line. The first, the Blue Dotted Line, was the initial bridgehead, where there would be a halt of ninety minutes to allow the field artillery to move forward. The second, the Blue Line, was an intermediate objective, where there would be a pause of fifteen minutes. The 32nd Division was to swing forward its right flank to an intermediate objective and later the left was to reach the Army objective, in contact with XIII Corps at the southwest corner of Landrecies.

The 2nd and 1st Brigades were detailed for the 1st Division attack, while 3rd Brigade made a number of feints and cleared Catillon on the west bank from the south. The crossing points were to be covered by a smoke screen east of the canal, which would add to the thick ground mist. In 2nd Brigade the 2nd King's

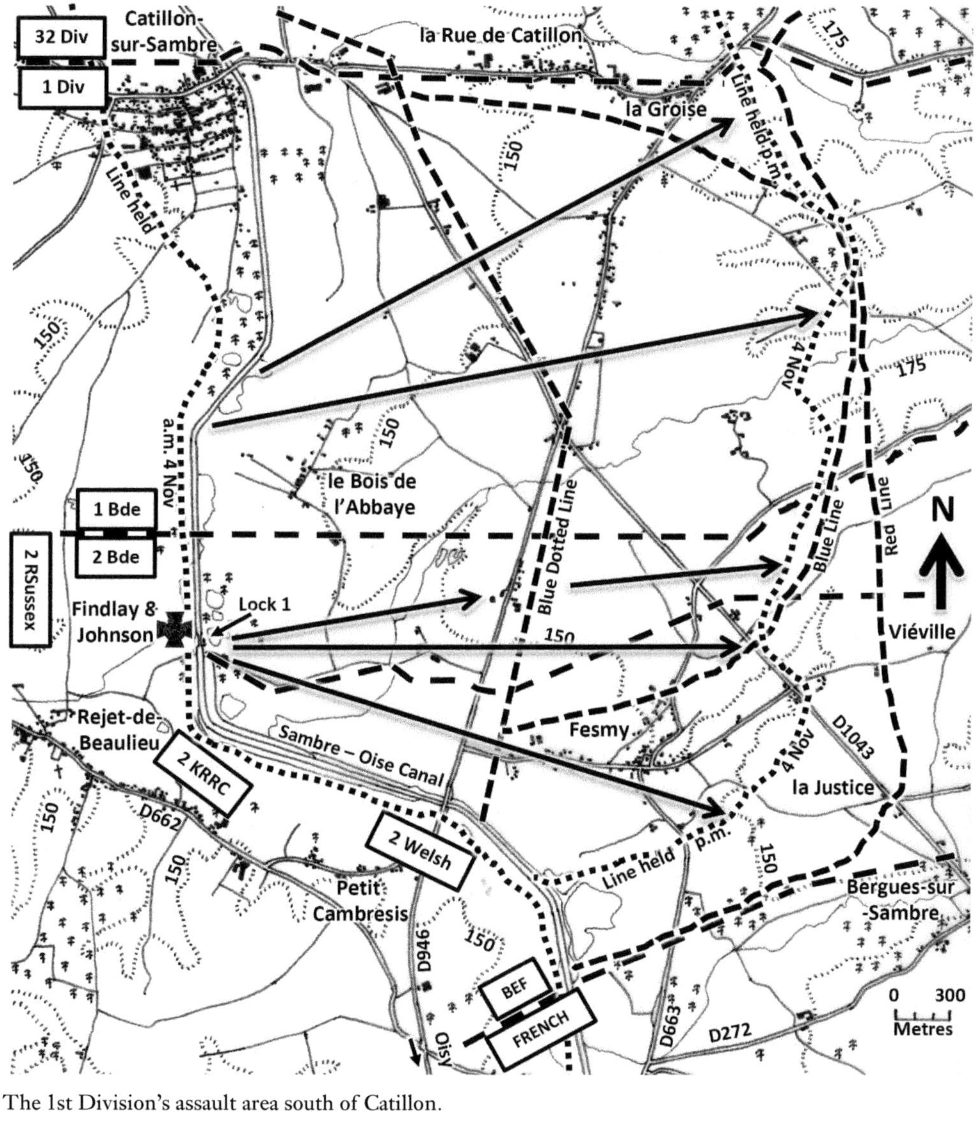

The 1st Division's assault area south of Catillon.

The remains of a German footbridge south of Lock 1 with the reservoirs either side of the canal.

Looking south from Lock 1 with the eastern reservoir on the left, which is wider than the canal on the right. On the other side of the canal, hidden by the trees, is the western reservoir. The totality of the three waterways adds up to a considerable obstacle.

Royal Rifle Corps was on the right and 2nd Royal Sussex was on the left, with 1st Northamptonshire in support to establish contact with the French at the crossroads at la Justice later. To the south of the reservoirs 2nd Welsh (3rd Brigade) held the line of the canal to the junction with the French. The 2nd Brigade's main crossing at Lock 1, north of the reservoirs and three kilometres south of Catillon, was to be made by 2nd Royal Sussex. This presented a number of difficulties, in addition to the obstacle of the waterway. The lock was on top of a five metres high steep bank and there were subsidiary streams at the base of both banks up to six metres wide. One company of 2nd King's Royal Rifle Corps was to attempt a subsidiary crossing at a footbridge south of the lock. If that had been destroyed, there were some Berthon boats with which to make the crossing.

A reconnaissance the day before the operation had been cancelled due to the close proximity of the enemy. There had been several other attempts to reconnoitre close to the crossing point in the days before. These had gleaned valuable information about the assembly areas and approaches but most of the information about the lock and the width of the waterway etc had come from air photos.

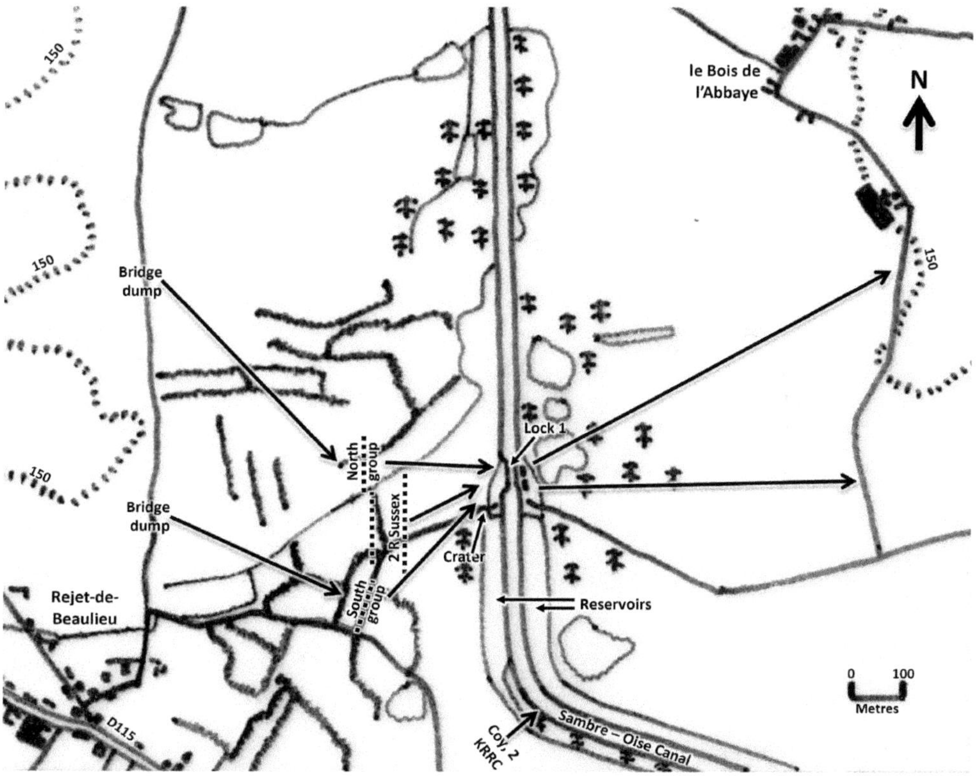

Significant streams (thin lines) and hedges (rough, thick lines) are shown west of the canal. Lock 1 is usually approached by road from the east. However, a route that follows the men who carried out the crossing operation starts in Rejet-de-Beaulieu. Approach the village along the D115 from the west from Mazinghien. Just after the church turn left and immediately right. Follow the road round a left bend and just after some houses turn into a lane on the right and park immediately on the right. Do not go too far as there is a deep ditch. Walk along the track eastwards around a few bends for just over 900m to reach Lock 1. On the way you pass through the assembly areas, cross the western subsidiary stream and see the western reservoir alongside the canal. The bank leading up to the lock is often covered in thick vegetation.

Despite the challenges the crossing plan was ambitious. The first two platoons of 2nd Royal Sussex were to cross at zero plus four minutes. Two complete companies were to be on the east side five minutes later. Initially they were to fan out along the north-south road 600m east of the canal. The support company was to form to the left and mop up the area up to the boundary with 1st Brigade. Once 2nd Royal Sussex had crossed, 2nd King's Royal Rifle Corps, less the company attempting the subsidiary crossing, was to follow over the lock. The final elements of the entire Brigade were due to cross at zero plus thirty-two minutes.

In addition to its Trench Mortar Battery, the Brigade was reinforced by a section of 10th Battalion Tanks Corps (two tanks), a supply tank of No.2 Tank Supply Company, a troop of the Royal Scots Greys, B Section of No.1 Special Company RE to produce the smoke screen, C Company of 1st Battalion MGC and 1 Section of 1st Australian Tunnelling Company. The latter was to construct a tank bridge later in the day, following which it was to search for mines and boobytraps east of the canal.

The infantry bridges for Lock 1 were brought by wagons to two dumps west of the canal, arriving at 6.00 p.m. on the 3rd. From there they were carried to the final assembly position during the night. By 1.30 p.m. they had been laid out in their proper order and gaps had been cut for the bridging parties through hedges and the enemy wire. The approach by 2nd Royal Sussex was covered by rain and mist and by 1.30 a.m. all were in position behind hedges 225–350m from the canal. Assembly was carried out so quietly that the Germans had no hint of the impending attack. Both leading companies, B on the right and C on the left, wore lifebelts and three men per section carried axes or billhooks. Two sections of machine guns were attached for the operation. The 409th Field Company RE accompanied the Battalion, manhandling thirty purpose-built bridges. Sixteen of these were footbridges for the subsidiary streams (eight per bank, for the west these were five metres long and for the east just over three and a half metres), eight bridges for the lock (including four with a reserve wave, each seven metres long) and six pack transport bridges (two for each subsidiary stream and two for the lock). Berthon boats were in reserve in case the bridging parties failed. The plan was for the infantry and sappers to advance in two groups and establish crossing points at the northern and southern ends of the lock, which was fifty metres long. The southern group had four west bank subsidiary bridges, two lock bridges and four supplementary lock bridges, plus six pack transport bridges. The northern group had four west bank subsidiary bridges, two lock bridges and all eight of the east bank subsidiary bridges.

At 5.44 a.m., a machine-gun barrage opened from the south and thirty seconds later from the north. One minute later the artillery barrage crashed down on the far bank, with one in eighteen shells being smoke. Four 18 Pounders were allocated to deal with the buildings on the far side of the lock by direct fire at zero hour. Eight Stokes Mortars fired a barrage 275m north and south of the lock until zero plus three minutes. Thereafter one mortar advanced with each of the two assault

The track leading to Lock 1 from the west. The lock buildings are mostly obscured by trees above the end of the lane. The northern group approached the lock over the field on the left. The southern group was on the other side of the hedgerow on the right.

battalions. The creeping barrage remained on the east bank for three minutes and then lifted ninety metres for another three minutes. It then rolled forward ninety metres every four minutes to the north-south road 600m east of the canal, where it halted for twenty minutes. Thereafter it moved forward ninety metres every six minutes to the Blue Dotted Line, where there was a ninety-minute pause before continuing to the Blue Line. If the French progressed satisfactorily on the right to La Justice, there would be a further advance by 1st Northamptonshire to Fesmy and the Red Line.

One of the guns fell ninety metres short on the right. As a consequence, the southern group had to slip to the left to avoid its fire after passing through the enemy wire. The sappers were up to ninety metres ahead of the infantry at zero hour but Captain Rhind was severely wounded, as were some of his men. A few seconds after the barrage lifted off the east bank at 5.49 a.m., the enemy barrage crashed down between forty-five and seventy-five metres west of the canal. The sapper and assault parties were hit by the heavy enemy barrage and machine gun fire from the lock houses and le Bois de l'Abbaye. The situation was in danger of collapsing into confusion. Although wounded, **Major George Findlay**, commanding 409th Field Company, steadied his men and got them moving forward again.

The western subsidiary stream with the buildings on the far side of Lock 1 on the right. The lock bank, now covered in thick vegetation, had been cleared by the Germans in 1918 and was covered by felled trees and stumps, making progress very difficult and arduous.

The sappers and the infantry in the northern group arrived at the subsidiary stream almost simultaneously, having suffered a few casualties on the way. A small stream had been encountered and Lieutenant Elmslie used two of the subsidiary west bridges to bridge it in order to allow the two lock bridges to continue. The first, under Corporal Dow, crossed and the second was just about to when an enemy shell knocked out Lieutenant Elmslie, his section sergeant and both bridge crews, except for two men. The two remaining subsidiary bridges, under Second Lieutenant White, followed by Corporal Dow's lock bridge, continued to move forward. One of the subsidiary bridge teams became casualties and, therefore, only one subsidiary bridge and one lock bridge reached the stream immediately west of the lock.

It was quickly realised that the southern part of the bank was blocked by roots, felled trees and barbed wire and it was not possible to cross the stream there. However, to the north the bank was relatively clear. The bridge carriers jumped into the waist deep water and two of the southern group subsidiary bridges were set up. The other two arrived shortly afterwards and were used in a V to form a single crossing. Once over the stream the infantry swarmed up the bank, over the barbed wire, and silenced resistance in a ruined house on the west side of the lock that had been causing so much trouble. Another infantry party made their way along the road and up the bank to the south.

From the top of the lock bank looking west. The northern group advanced over this field to reach the western subsidiary stream in the foreground.

Just after 5.55 a.m. the sole remaining west subsidiary bridge of the northern group arrived at the stream and was placed across it onto a tree. This enabled the first lock bridge of the southern group to be dragged over to bridge the stream. At about 6.05 a.m. the sole remaining northern lock bridge and the first of those of the southern group were carried across the stream and onto the lock side. A few minutes later one of the supplementary bridges was also placed over the stream.

While the leading infantry lined the canal bank to engage the garrison on the far side, one man crossed the canal over the remnants of the lock gate, but what became of him is not recorded. At 6.08 a.m. the first northern lock bridge had its wheels and launching lever fitted. In a hail of fire at 6.10 a.m. it was swung out over the lock and lowered onto the far side. Findlay supervised this delicate operation as one of the supporting steel guys had been shot away and it had to be lowered gently to avoid it being rendered unusable. Findlay was the first over to secure the far end. Two sapper NCOs followed and opened fire on the enemy covered by a Royal Sussex Lewis gunner who sprayed the enemy from the hip until he was hit and his No.2 took over.

Lieutenant Colonel Dudley Johnson, commanding 2nd Royal Sussex, came forward to see what was causing the delay. He found his men sheltering from the storm of fire which beat back every attempt to get over the bridge. Realising that delay would add to the casualties, he collected some men and tried again. Heavy

Lock 1 from the west. The assault came up the bank on the left and the bridges were positioned over the lock prior to assaulting the enemy positions in the lock buildings. There is a small memorial on the far side of the lock behind the white ladder.

enemy fire broke up the mixed infantry and sapper party. The rear waves were beginning to close-up, adding to the confusion and more casualties were suffered. Making another superhuman effort Johnson led his men over the canal and stormed the lock house. More troops dashed over and subdued the Germans in the other houses on the far side.

A few minutes later an east subsidiary bridge (Second Corporal Wardrop) and a west subsidiary bridge (Second Corporal White), no longer required for the western stream, arrived and crossed over the lock to be placed over the eastern stream. At 6.12 a.m. a southern lock bridge was placed over the lock, as were two supplementary bridges a minute later. At 6.15 a.m. two west subsidiary bridges were carried over the lock to bridge the eastern stream. Second Corporal Wardrop reported that the road bridge over the eastern stream was intact.

At 6.20 a.m. the remaining lock bridge of the northern group, which had been halted due to casualties amongst its crew, arrived and was launched over the lock. Five minutes later another supplementary bridge arrived and was also placed over the lock, as was a light German footbridge. Ten minutes later all seven bridges over the lock had been spaced out along its length. At 6.40 a.m. Lieutenant John Lawson Kelly RE was killed by a shell (Le Rejet-de-Beaulieu Communal Cemetery, France – B11). However, the sapper task had been completed successfully. Very quickly the whole of 2nd Royal Sussex crossed to the east of the canal, followed by 2nd King's Royal Rifle Corps. The sappers of 409th Field Company either assembled in the cellar of the lock building for a well-earned rest or searched the lock and neighbouring buildings for mines.

The King's Royal Rifle Corps company to the south encountered many difficulties. To reach the reservoir before the canal entailed crossing a two metres wide dyke and then scaling a two metres high bank. Manhandling the Berthon boats forward and assembling them proved to be impossible in the conditions. After struggling for quarter of an hour under heavy fire, the company commander decided to abandon the attempt, dumped the boats and led his men to the lock to rejoin the Battalion. There was a great deal of confusion as the battalions crossed, with platoons and companies mixed up in the fog and smoke. However, the men had been well briefed on where to go. The first objective was reached on time and contact was made with units on both flanks. There were some sharp exchanges early on, but the enemy resistance crumbled once the canal had been crossed and only a few machine guns had to be cleared.

By 8.30 a.m. the pack bridges were in place and animals were crossing. Findlay remained at the lock supervising until 10.00 a.m. when he went to have his wounds attended to. The tank bridge was constructed by 10.30 a.m. and a horse transport bridge by 4.30 p.m. A crater on the road leading to the west bank of the canal was also bridged. The lock was shelled periodically during the day. Findlay's Company suffered thirty-five casualties (twelve killed and twenty-three wounded, of whom seven remained at duty), which represented 100% of the officers and almost half of the other ranks engaged.

The 2nd Brigade was on the bridgehead objective (Blue Dotted Line) at 8.00 a.m., where there was a pause of ninety minutes, during which both leading battalions reorganised. The 1st Northamptonshire deployed one company behind the left of 2nd Royal Sussex and despatched another to take over from 2nd King's Royal Rifle Corps on the Petit-Cambresis–la Groise road (Blue Dotted Line) in preparation for the forthcoming attack on Fesmy.

At zero plus 229 minutes the advance resumed against little resistance, with the other 1st Northamptonshire companies forming behind the leading battalions. A cavalry patrol was sent to regain contact with the enemy along the Viéville – la Justice road. The Blue Line was reached by 12.10 p.m. At 12.30 p.m. 1st Northamptonshire was ordered to occupy Fesmy and entered the village successfully but was held up at the church. At 13.35 p.m. the cavalry patrol reported being fired upon from the crossroads and houses in Viéville and the artillery was turned on the village.

It was reported that the French were going to advance on their second objective at 4.00 p.m. Arrangements were made for 1st Northamptonshire to go forward with them supported by the artillery. This advance was successful. At the end of the day 1st Northamptonshire was holding a defensive right flank between Viéville crossroads and the canal, including Fesmy. A patrol reached la Justice and took six prisoners. However, the French did not intend moving that far until next morning and it was therefore decided not to move further forward until then. The other two battalions were on their objectives, each on a two-company frontage. The 2nd Brigade flank was also reinforced by 1/6th Welsh (Pioneers). La Justice was reached next morning and contact was established with the French. On the far right, south of the reservoirs, 2nd Welsh experienced little difficulty getting over the canal at the bridge at Petit Cambresis. The Battalion was in contact with the French, who ended the day on the western outskirts of Bergues-sur-Sambre.

The Brigade captured 419 prisoners, seven field guns and a large number of trench mortars and machine guns. It suffered 219 casualties, including twenty-five killed and fifteen missing. The 2nd Royal Sussex suffered 106 casualties (nine killed, ninety-three wounded and four missing) and took 200 prisoners, two field guns and fifty machineguns.

On the left, 1st Brigade had an easier passage at the bend of the Canal northwest of Bois l'Abbaye. Four floating bridges were over the canal within ten minutes of zero hour and the enemy barrage fell well behind the leading troops. Both assault battalions, 1st Cameron Highlanders on the right and 1st Loyal North Lancashire on the left, were over the canal at 6.10 a.m. Numerous small actions were fought but the bridgehead was established by 8.00 a.m. with large numbers of prisoners being taken. A pause followed and 1st Black Watch took over the lead from 1st Loyal North Lancashire.

The 3rd Brigade at Catillon caught many of the defenders coming out of the cellars after the barrage passed on. A tank and some infantry made a dash for the bridge and destroyed a machine gun covering it. Just after 8.00 a.m. six platoons of 1st Gloucestershire crossed the canal and established a bridgehead. Two companies of 1st South Wales Borderers reached Catillon from the west and assisted 1st Gloucestershire to overrun and mop up the town quickly, during which 573 prisoners were taken.

At 9.37 a.m. the enlargement of the bridgeheads commenced with the advance to the intermediate objective. Little resistance was met as the enemy was already pulling back. On the left of 1st Brigade there was no touch with 32nd Division and a company of 1st Loyal North Lancashire was tasked to form a flank until contact was made at 5.15 p.m. The line was almost everywhere on the Army objective by 5.00 p.m., although there were some hold-ups. The 1st Division had achieved a great victory. It had crossed the canal, advanced over 3,600m and captured 1,698 prisoners and twenty guns for under 500 casualties.

On the left of IX Corps, 32nd Division also faced an opposed crossing of the canal. Both assault brigades were allotted six mortars of No.1 Special Company RE to create a smoke screen. The artillery barrage was to lift from the eastern canal bank five minutes after zero hour and stand 275m beyond it (Yellow Line) for the next thirty minutes. During this time the bridges would be constructed and the first troops would cross. Thereafter the barrage was to move forward ninety metres every six minutes to the Blue Dotted Line. Artillery support from there to the Red Line was left to the brigade commanders. Seven artillery brigades were allocated to 32nd Division, one of which, 161st Brigade RFA, engaged special targets during the attack and was available to cross the canal as soon as the bridge at Ors was passable.

During the nights before the attack, constant and irregular artillery fire was directed against the eastern bank of the canal. The aim was to create uncertainty and nervousness, disrupt patrol activity and encourage machine gun teams to remain under cover. In addition to 32nd Division Machine Gun Battalion, three more units were attached – 6th Battalion MGC, 1st Company, Royal Horse Guards Machine Gun Battalion and 5th Cavalry Brigade Machine Gun Squadron. The former two units were to fire a barrage from the west bank of the canal. One company of 32nd Battalion MGC was attached to each assault brigade. The other two companies and 5th Cavalry Brigade Machine Gun Squadron were in reserve.

A troop of 20th Hussars was attached to the Divisional Signal Company. Each assault brigade also had a troop for liaison duties. A platoon of IX Corps Cyclist Battalion was attached to the Divisional Signal Company. A section of 1st Australian Tunnelling Company was distributed between both assault brigades to search for and destroy landmines and booby traps. As zero hour approached a thick mist formed in many parts of the valley. Routes from the forming up line, about 300m west of the canal, were marked with tapes and plank bridges were placed over streams and ditches.

On the right, 14th Brigade was to cross south of Ors, with 5/6th Royal Scots on the right, 1st Dorsetshire on the left and 15th Highland Light Infantry in reserve. The Brigade was commanded by Brigadier General Lewis Evans VC DSO, whose story is told in the fifth book in this series; *Victoria Crosses on the Western Front – Third Ypres 1917*. The Brigade was supported by 206th Field Company RE with two platoons of 16th Highland Light Infantry (Pioneers) attached. Three footbridges were to be constructed just south of Ors and another over the lock in the village. If the approaches were found to be usable by horses, a crossing for horse transport was also to be constructed over the lock. During the night before the attack, the

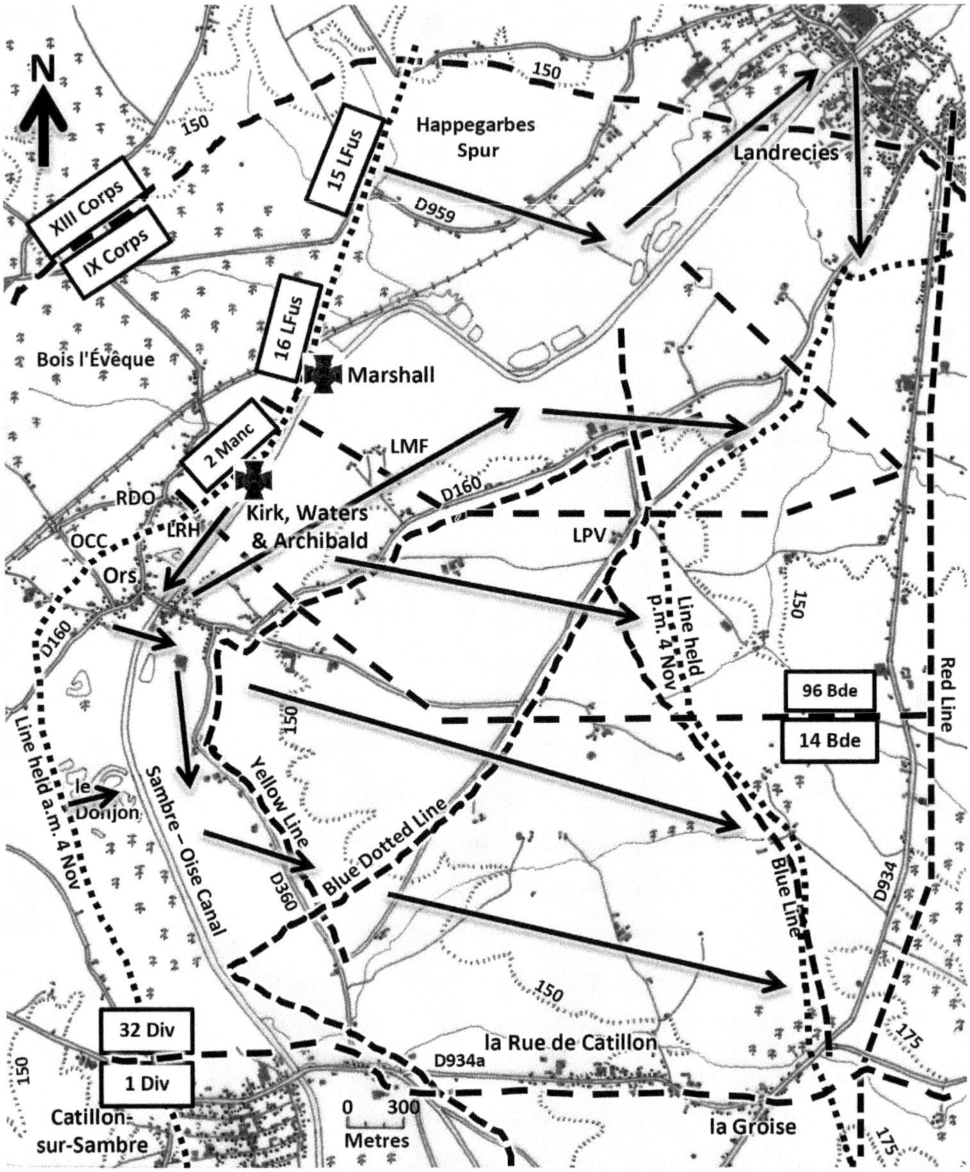

LMF = la Motte Farm, LPV = le PetitVersailles, LRH = la Rue d'Houis, OCC = Ors Communal Cemetery, RDO = Rue du Oui. Visit Ors Communal Cemetery on the D160a Rue de la Gare. The cemetery is on the right side just before the railway crossing. Return to Ors church and park in the little square there. The canal is just round to the right. Cross to the left side of the road and take the steps down to the canal bank. Walk northeast along the tow path for 900m to where the VC actions by Kirk, Waters and Archibald took place. Continue for another 700m to the site of Marshall's VC action. Alternatively to cut the walking distance, continue past the church and turn left (north) instead of right towards the canal. After 600m turn right along a dead end road for 300m to a small car park on the right. The canal is just over the bridge in front. Turn left along the tow path for 360m to the Kirk, Waters and Archibald VC site. Another option is to pass the church, turn left and follow this minor road northeast through la Rue d'Houis until you see the sign for Ors British Cemetery on the left. Park in front of the sign, cross the road and follow the grassy path 350m to the cemetery. Pass the cemetery on the right and swing left on the path over a footpath that crosses the subsidiary stream to the canal bank. Turn right for 200m to the Kirk, Waters and Archibald VC site and left for 500m for the Marshall VC site.

remaining villagers in Ors west of the canal were evacuated. This proved to be more difficult to achieve than envisaged as many of them were bedridden with influenza.

On the left, 96th Brigade, commanded by Brigadier General AC Girdwood DSO, was to cross north of Ors, just south of the elbow bend in the canal. All three battalions were in the line – 2nd Manchester on the right, 16th Lancashire Fusiliers in the centre and 15th Lancashire Fusiliers on the left, with two companies of 2nd King's Own Yorkshire Light Infantry (97th Brigade) in reserve. The remainder of 97th Brigade was held in reserve around St Souplet for operations the next day. The 96th Brigade was supported by 218th Field Company RE, with a company of 16th Highland Light Infantry (Pioneers) attached. They were to construct footbridges for the infantry to cross at zero plus five minutes. Thereafter the bridging equipment of 219th Field Company RE was at the disposal of 218th Field Company RE to erect a pontoon bridge at the end of the lane leading to the canal through la Rue d'Houis. In Ors, 219th Field Company RE, with two platoons of 16th Highland Light Infantry (Pioneers) attached, was to construct a tank bridge. Two mortars each were attached to 2nd Manchester and 16th Lancashire Fusiliers.

All the stores required for the bridges were brought forward and concealed under the canal bank well in advance of the attack commencing. When the barrage lifted in 14th Brigade's area, two platoons of 5/6th Royal Scots attacked le Donjon on the west bank but they were checked immediately. Elsewhere the infantry closed-up to the west bank. An attempt to float a bridge section downstream under cover of the mist to fill the gap in the Ors bridge failed. An attempt to cross 180m north of the bridge in a collapsible boat also failed when it capsized. The 1st Dorsetshire's first attempt to get over the road bridge at Ors was forced back by a hail of fire, including a field gun firing at point blank range. However, covered by the mist, a petrol tin bridge was established 180m south of the Ors road bridge and C, D and then A Companies, 1st Dorsetshire crossed over only twenty-five minutes after zero. The Germans were not aware of this crossing immediately and their artillery concentrated on other more likely crossing places. The 5th/6th Royal Scots took advantage of the Dorsetshire bridge to push two companies over the canal. Another petrol tin bridge was completed and by 8.15 a.m. a bridgehead had been formed. A horse transport bridge was open by 10.00 a.m. The enemy at le Donjon were then threatened from the rear and surrendered at 10.45 a.m. By the end of the day 1st Dorsetshire had taken 223 prisoners, thirty machine guns and three howitzers.

The 96th Brigade attacked with its three battalions in line, supported by 218th Field Company RE, with A Company, 16th Highland Light Infantry (Pioneers) attached to help move the heavy bridge sections and assist with their construction. **Major Arnold Waters**, commanding 218th Field Company RE, was tasked to produce four floating bridges, two for each assault battalion north of Ors. However, he had only forty-two men in three sections available. He protested that the job could not be done in the thirty minutes allocated. It was therefore decided to go with only one bridge per battalion.

The two bridges (one each for 2nd Manchester and 16th Lancashire Fusiliers) were carried forward through gaps cut in hedges and joined the infantry in their forming up positions just short of the canal bank late on 3rd November. On the right, 2nd Manchester had its right on the crossroads at Rue du Oui and the left on the railway line. Its C and D Companies were to lead. In the centre, 16th Lancashire Fusiliers formed up in an orchard close to the canal with C and D Companies leading the assault. The 15th Lancashire Fusiliers on the left was on the lower slopes of the Happegarbes Spur.

The artillery and machine gun barrages opened at 5.45 a.m. and five minutes later the assault parties moved forward. The sappers quickly bridged the subsidiary stream and began to manhandle the bridge sections up the steep west bank of the canal. The mist was not so thick here and the scene was lit by many flares.

At the southern bridge, 900m north of Ors, the 2nd Manchester assault parties were hit immediately they topped the embankment from directly across the canal and also from la Motte Farm, on the rising ground to the east. They were also heavily shelled. The 2nd Manchester's covering fire was not heavy enough to subdue the defenders hiding in hedges and tree lines almost on the canal bank. Most of the sapper bridging party were hit or suffered from gas poisoning, including Second Lieutenant Walter Oates and Lieutenant Thomas Chesman Barker who were killed (Ors British Cemetery – B35 & B34). Major Waters heard of the hold up and took control of bridging operations. The infantry continued to give as much supporting

This is where Kirk, Waters and Archibald tried to bridge the canal. Through a thinner section of trees on the right is la Motte Farm on the skyline.

fire as possible and **Second Lieutenant James Kirk** (2nd Manchester) paddled over on a bridge section and engaged the Germans with a Lewis gun from just ten metres. Ammunition was ferried over to him by an unknown and very brave soldier on another bridge section. Kirk did a splendid job of covering the bridging party until he was killed by a shot through the head. However, he enabled the bridge to be completed by Waters and **Sapper Adam Archibald**.

As the two worked on the bridge, pieces of it were shot off around them and sparks flew everywhere as bullets struck the binding wires. That they were not hit was nothing short of miraculous, as the enemy was only thirty metres away and the scene was lit by numerous flares. Just before the bridge was finished, Archibald collapsed from gas poisoning and Waters completed the job alone, a remarkable achievement given each bridge section weighed about 120 kilogrammes. When all was ready, Waters came back over and led two platoons of 2nd Manchester across. Shortly afterwards the bridge was smashed by shellfire. Attempts to repair it failed and the rest of the Battalion took shelter under the west bank. The war poet Lieutenant Wilfred Owen was killed close by while encouraging his men to provide covering fire and help with the bridging.

The sappers and pioneers succeeded in constructing the northern bridge, about 1,600m north of Ors, immediately south of the elbow bend in the canal. They were covered by the fire of 16th Lancashire Fusiliers. Heavy fire was received from the front and the left flank, where possession of the Happegarbes spur allowed the Germans to pour enfilade fire into the left rear of 96th Brigade. When the artillery lifted off the east bank, 16th Lancashire Fusiliers tried to cross. The bridges were ready in twenty-five minutes, with the sappers and pioneers suffering many casualties. A few men got over under Second Lieutenant Charles James Stapley but the anchors snapped on the east bank as Captain Harold Charles Pemberton crossed. He and Stapley managed to secure the bridge and Second Lieutenant Potts and three more men crossed before concentrated artillery fire broke up the bridge. Stapley and Pemberton were awarded the MC for this action, LG 2nd April 1919.

Lieutenant Colonel James Marshall, commanding the Battalion, was mindful that the barrage was about to move forward again. He organised a party of sapper and infantry volunteers to repair the bridge, but all were killed or wounded. Marshall was unharmed and formed another party to try again. He stood on the bank throughout, encouraging the men and assisting in the work until the bridge was ready. He then gathered the first assault company and charged across the bridge at its head. He was killed immediately and Captain TB Dunn MC assumed command. Shortly afterwards the bridge was damaged by fire and the survivors took cover behind the embankment.

Of the forty-two men of 218th Field Company committed to the crossing sites, there were thirty casualties, including twelve killed. Twenty-two men were decorated for gallantry in this action. In addition to Archibald's and Waters' VCs, there were three MCs, three DCMs, eleven MMs and three French medals.

This was where Marshall led his men over the canal. La Motte Farm can just be seen in the distance through a gap in the trees on the left.

On the left, 15th Lancashire Fusiliers secured the Happegarbes Spur and reached the west bank of the Canal at 7.00 a.m. By that time 96th Brigade had suffered 200 casualties at the two bridging sites but had achieved nothing. It was clear that another frontal assault stood no chance of success. At 8.30 a.m. GOC 32nd Division ordered 2nd Manchester and 16th Lancashire Fusiliers to move southwards under cover of the canal bank and cross over the 1st Dorsetshire bridge at Ors. Two companies of 2nd Manchester crossed and struck northwards to gain the Yellow Line by 11.30 a.m. Early in the afternoon the reserve battalion, 15th Highland Light Infantry, also crossed. There was almost no opposition at that time and, having secured the bridgehead, the battalions swept on to the Corps secondary objective, with only a short hold up at La Motte Farm. The 16th Lancashire Fusiliers crossed later, having recovered from the beating it had taken on the canal in the morning. This Battalion took over the line on the left and 97th Brigade crossed in support.

Having cleared the Happegarbes Spur on the far left, 15th Lancashire Fusiliers crossed the canal in 25th Division's area at Landrecies. It took its position in the line in contact with 25th Division on the left but not with 2nd Manchester on the right at le Petit Versailles. A transport bridge, completed at Ors by 219th Field Company RE, allowed artillery to cross the canal to come into action by 4.00 p.m. By the end of the day 32nd Division was on or beyond the Blue Line. The day's fighting cost 32nd Division 700 casualties. Only 238 prisoners were taken, plus twenty guns and numerous machine guns. However, although there had been hold-ups and setbacks, the Division was well established on the east bank by the end of the day and was ready for the next phase to be undertaken by 97th Brigade.

The XIII Corps, attacking half an hour after IX Corps, was led by 25th, 50th and 18th Divisions, with 66th Division in reserve. The Corps' task was a tall order,

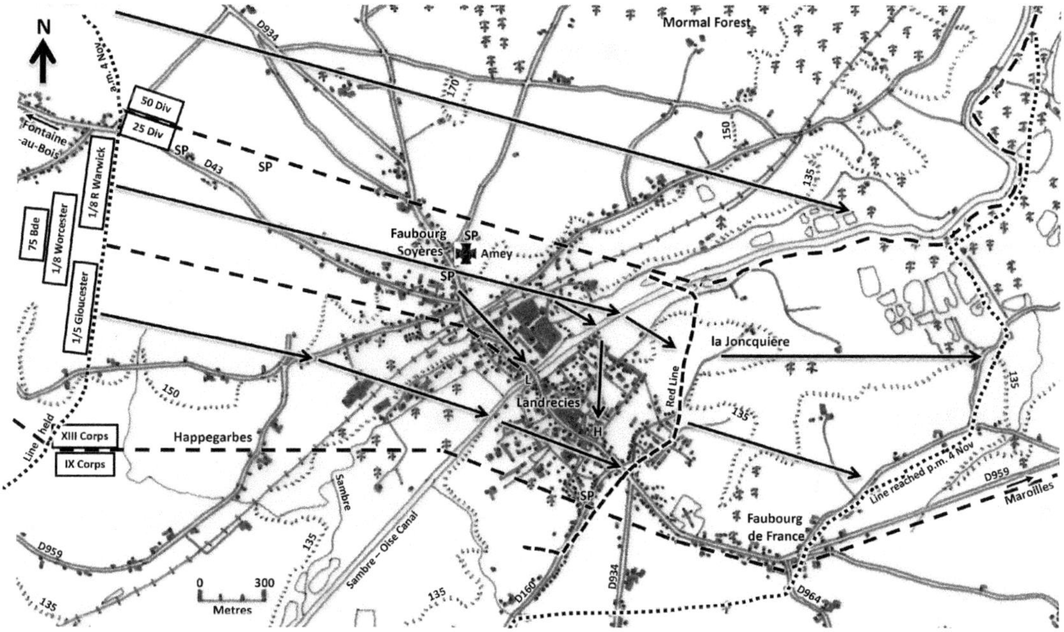

H = hospital, L = lock, SP = strongpoint mentioned in text. Approach Landrecies from the northwest along the D43, where there are opportunities to stop and consider the action fought by 1/8th Royal Warwickshire. It is not possible to be definitive about the locations of Amey's VC actions. The main strongpoints encountered by the Battalion are shown on the map. There are a number of buildings in the outskirts of Landrecies that could be described as châteaux and may be where Amey's final action took place.

entailing attacking through the southern part of the Mormal Forest, closing-up to Landrecies, capturing it, forcing a passage over the canal, establishing a bridgehead and capturing the intermediate objective (Green Line), including Maroilles. This entailed an advance of between seven and eight kilometres. In the second phase, 66th Division would pass through 25th Division and, in conjunction with 50th and 18th Divisions, secure the line of exploitation about nine kilometres further east.

On the right, 25th Division was to be led by 75th Brigade to the Red Line, including crossing the canal to establish a bridgehead to the south. Having achieved this, an outpost line was to be pushed forward. Then 74th Brigade was to pass through and capture the Green Line, while 7th Brigade remained in reserve. The other brigades in 25th Division doubted that a crossing could be made but 75th Brigade thought otherwise. The battalions were in competition with each other to get over the canal first. The 1/5th Gloucestershire and 1/8th Royal Warwickshire, on the right and left respectively, were to lead to the canal, each on a two-company frontage. Following them, 1/8th Worcestershire was responsible for forcing the passage of the canal and establishing the Red Line. It was also to establish the outpost line, once it was clear that at least one company of each following battalion had crossed the canal and occupied positions from where they could reinforce the Red Line.

If feasible the two leading battalions were to cross the canal immediately and not wait for 1/8th Worcestershire. In this case, the two battalions were to secure the south bank and provide covering parties to enable 1/8th Worcestershire to cross and continue to the Red Line.

The 105th Field Company RE and a company of 11th South Lancashire (Pioneers) were to carry ninety-five petrol tin rafts, each able to support one man. They were to be pulled back and forth across the canal with attached ropes, after the first man had paddled across. Twenty-five rafts were with the rear companies of 1/5th Gloucestershire. Fifteen of these were for crossing the Sambre stream southwest of Landrecies and ten for the canal. Thirty-five rafts were with the rear companies of 1/8th Royal Warwickshire for crossing northeast of Landrecies. Another twenty rafts were with the right forward company of 1/8th Worcestershire, in addition to those allocated to 1/5th Gloucestershire southwest of Landrecies. Two light bridges were to accompany 1/8th Worcestershire to span the lock at the road bridge in Landrecies, should it still be intact or only partially demolished. Two pontoon bridges were to be open seven hours after zero, one either side of Landrecies, each able to carry horse transport and field guns.

A number of men in each battalion practised on the River Selle, using the rafts and also swimming with lifebelts before the operation. It was stipulated that these men were not to wear puttees. Dry spare clothing and rum was to be provided to them as soon as possible after the crossing had been achieved. However, should a bridge be found fit for use (two were known about a kilometre southwest and northeast of the road bridge in Landrecies and others were discovered during the attack), the engineers accompanying the infantry were to remove any demolition charges. Word was to be sent immediately to Brigade HQ and the nearest RE officer in charge of bridging operations. The infantry was to push across at once and establish a bridgehead to protect the intact crossing. Other troops were to be diverted to it to speed the build-up on the far bank.

The 25th Division was allotted four tanks of 9th Battalion Tank Corps, two to each leading battalion. There were also four supply tanks. In addition to its divisional artillery, 25th Division was allocated 330th and 331st Brigades RFA (66th Division), 150th Army Brigade RFA (after the capture of the Red Line) and 27th Brigade RGA. A proportion of the Corps' heavy artillery was allocated to fire on selected targets in the Division's area. The creeping barrage was to move forward ninety metres every six minutes and stand 270m beyond the canal for sixty minutes, in order to allow time for the crossing to be made. A smoke screen was to be laid on the high ground east of the canal by the artillery, No.1 Special Company RE and 15th Wing RAF. When 66th Division passed through 25th Division, the artillery units would pass to the command of CRA 66th Division.

The 25th Machine Gun Battalion was reinforced by a company of 100th Machine Gun Battalion for the operation. Forty-eight machine guns were allocated to fire a supporting barrage and to cover the right flank during the advance. This was to include two sections firing on the bridge in Landrecies hopefully to prevent it from being demolished. Having fired the opening barrage, three sections were to accompany 75th Brigade to assist in consolidating the Red Line. Two sections of 6″ Newton Mortars were to follow the assault to fire on machine gun emplacements on the far side of the canal. A section of 75th Light Trench Mortar Battery was allocated to each battalion.

By 4.15 a.m. the assault units were in position. At 5.45 a.m. a noise barrage was opened by the machine guns and the German artillery opened fire on the right, causing ten casualties to 1/5th Gloucestershire. There was thick mist. The attack commenced at 6.15 a.m. when the creeping barrage fell 270m ahead of the start line. There was weak German artillery response, probably due to them believing that the attack was confined to 32nd Division's area to the south, as it had been in previous days.

By 8.15 a.m. two companies of 21st Manchester (7th Brigade), attached to 75th Brigade, had mopped up the ground on the right of 1/5th Gloucestershire between 25th and 32nd Divisions. Contact was established with 15th Lancashire Fusiliers to the south and many prisoners and machine guns were taken.

On the right 1/5th Gloucestershire encountered the enemy in strength. The advance was somewhat confused due to the thick mist, loss of officers, the number of untrained men and the close country. The forward companies became disorganised but B Company, in reserve, came up and carried the other companies forward. At 7.30 a.m. B Company reached a road junction west of Landrecies. It turned to the southeast, crossed the railway and the Sambre stream over an existing bridge, all under enemy artillery and mortar fire. The advance was then held up by machine gun fire from Landrecies.

D Company, which was to mop up later, moved towards Landrecies but suffered casualties from artillery, machine guns and road mines. It withdrew behind B Company. The enemy fire slackened as the British barrage advanced. D Company, 1/8th Worcestershire reinforced B Company, 1/5th Gloucestershire. A and B Companies, 1/8th Worcestershire kept further north to reinforce 1/5th Gloucestershire. With the assistance of a tank, these companies dealt with the machine guns on the main road at Faubourg Soyères, taking thirty-nine prisoners.

At 9.00 a.m., using the cover of hedges, B Company, 1/5th Gloucestershire and D Company, 1/8th Worcestershire reached the canal. Using two intact footbridges over a stretch of 450m of the canal, and covered by the barrage and Lewis guns, they crossed over under heavy machine gun fire from Landrecies. By 9.50 a.m. a line had been formed on the far side. Further north, on the Battalion boundary, A and B Companies, 1/8th Worcestershire reached the canal and covered the placing of bridges over the lock in Landrecies. The main road bridge had been blown earlier.

On the left of the Brigade, 1/8th Royal Warwickshire led with A Company on the right and B Company on the left. At 6.45 a.m. the Battalion came under heavy fire from enemy posts along the road leading to Faubourg Soyères. This was overcome

From the football ground southwest of the junction of the D43 with Rue du Cateau. The D43 is marked by the line of houses on the left. Landrecies is in the distance out of sight in the centre low ground. The start line for 1/8th Royal Warwickshire ran across the fields beyond the football pitch from left to right.

quickly with the help of a tank and the Lewis guns. The advance continued over a light railway (no longer there) and more resistance was encountered in Faubourg Soyères from machine guns and minenwerfers. This was also overcome with the assistance of a tank. However, some posts were overlooked in the mist north of the road and the support companies and C Company, 1/8th Worcestershire had to mop them up. The advance was delayed further by resistance in Faubourg Soyères. The support companies came forward to reinforce the leading elements. About 9.00 a.m. the enemy machine gun fire slackened and the Battalion pushed on and captured a strongpoint. It pressed on into Landrecies, still under machine gun fire. A company on the left, northeast of Landrecies found an intact bridge, while the right leading company was approaching the road bridge in Landrecies when it was blown up.

It is not clear where **Lance Corporal William Amey** earned his VC, except that most of the action took place before reaching Faubourg Soyères. The Brigade war diary mentions a number of strongpoints being overcome before reaching the canal. These were either on or north of the D43 Fontaine-au-Bois–Landrecies road. It is known that while leading his section forward he became detached from his company and joined another that was held up by heavy machine gun fire. Undaunted, he led his section to attack one of these posts under heavy fire and succeeded in dislodging it. The survivors ran for a neighbouring farm. Amey chased them and captured fifty prisoners and a number of machine guns. Later, he attacked another farm alone and killed two enemy, before driving the rest of the garrison into the cellar, where he held them until assistance arrived. After this a strongly held post, in a château at Faubourg Soyères, was holding up the advance. He rushed the château single-handedly, and with great determination, killed two defenders and held up the rest until he was reinforced. Another twenty prisoners were taken and the last resistance in this area was cleared.

Two platoons used a wooden plank bridge, constructed hurriedly by 182nd Tunnelling Company RE, to cross the canal at the lock in the town. The sappers had overcome a demolition party before it could blow the lock gates. The platoons took up positions in houses on the far side. The Battalion captured a battery of field guns, three minenwerfers, twenty machine guns, a battalion commander and staff and 230 other prisoners.

Landrecies could now be attacked from three directions. On the right, D Company, 1/8th Worcestershire advanced at 10.33 a.m., when the barrage moved forward. A strongpoint in a house on the southern boundary was captured with fifty-two

This château on Route de Faubourg Soyères (D934) north of Landrecies may be the one attacked by Amey.

Another possible château further north along Route de Faubourg Soyères (D934). This building is very close to where Lance Corporal George Wyatt, 3rd Coldstream Guards earned the VC on 25th August 1914, the story being related in the first book in this series, *Victoria Crosses on the Western Front, Mons to Hill 60, August 1914–April 1915.*

prisoners being taken. The objective on the Red Line was reached at 11.15 a.m. The 1/5th Gloucestershire companies crossing behind D Company, 1/8th Worcestershire faced south to form a protective flank. The 1/5th Gloucestershire mopping up company entered Landrecies and captured 219 prisoners, a field gun and twenty machine guns, bringing the Battalion's total prisoners for the day to 350.

On the left flank, two platoons of the left company of 1/8th Royal Warwickshire crossed the canal using an existing bridge. At the same time C Company, 1/8th Worcestershire reached the canal to the south of the bridge and came under machine gun and artillery fire. Under the cover of the Lewis guns and Newton 6″ Mortars, the rafts were launched and the crossing was made with light casualties. The Company pressed on and captured a hospital in Landrecies, taking forty-seven prisoners, before continuing to the Red Line objective.

In the centre, A and B Companies, 1/8th Worcestershire arrived at the canal too late to be supported by the barrage. They could not follow the two platoons of 1/8th Warwickshire over the plank bridge at the lock because of heavy machine gun fire. However, the enemy, aware that the town was being encircled from the flanks, slipped away. The two 1/8th Worcestershire companies crossed at the lock at 12.45 p.m. and captured two gun batteries and forty-six prisoners.

At 3.45 p.m. orders were issued for 1/5th Gloucestershire and 1/8th Worcestershire to form a defensive southern flank as 32nd Division (IX Corps) was behind. Due to considerable disorganisation amongst the various units, a general line of outposts was established. The Germans fell back, leaving 75th Brigade with 835 prisoners, twenty-seven field guns, thirty minenwerfer and seventy-seven machine guns. The Brigade suffered 268 casualties (thirty-six killed, 207 wounded and twenty-five missing), including 130 (fifteen killed, 110 wounded and five missing) in 1/8th Royal Warwickshire. The 74th Brigade moved up and extended the bridgehead in preparation for continuing the advance next day.

In the centre and left of XIII Corps, 50th and 18th Divisions, each on a two-brigade frontage, also reached the Army objective, although progress had been slow at times due to the mist and numerous hedgerows infested with machine gun posts. The assistance of tanks was invaluable. The 18th Division went on and reached a further Corps objective and 50th Division was not far behind.

Fourth Army had created a twenty-four kilometres long bridgehead, averaging five kilometres in depth and had taken 4,136 prisoners and eighty guns. The advance by Third, First and First French Armies had also been successful. German hopes of holding the line of the Sambre-Oise Canal, while preparations were made for a planned withdrawal to another line, were dashed. They had no alternative other than to fall back along the whole front. Provided the Allied pursuit was pressed home with vigour and there was no respite, the enemy would be compelled to accept the terms proposed to them in the armistice negotiations.

6th November 1918

492 Maj Brett Cloutman, 59th Field Company, Royal Engineers (5th Division), Pont-sur-Sambre, France

The successful crossing of the Sambre Canal by Fourth Army, and the advances made by Third and First Armies on 4th November, were a severe blow to the Germans. The extent of the success was not fully realised until later in the day, when it became clear that the Germans were in retreat along the whole line. However, they were well covered by rear guards and the retreat did not turn into a rout.

Third Army had renewed the offensive with four corps in line. In the right centre was IV Corps, led by 37th Division on the right and the New Zealand Division on the left, followed by 5th and 42nd Divisions respectively. During the assault on 4th November the garrison of Le Quesnoy surrendered and the final objective was reached. About 3,500 prisoners and 110 guns were taken by the two leading divisions.

Orders for the continuation of the advance on 5th November were issued, with 5th Division passing through 37th Division on the right to advance alongside the New Zealanders. The 5th Division's task was to capture the Pont-sur-Sambre – Bavai road and gain bridgeheads over the Sambre-Oise Canal. When 5th Division passed through, soon after dawn, it took under command 37th Division's attachments – five brigades of field artillery, 14th Tank Battalion, E Squadron, 3rd Hussars and A Company, IV Corps Cyclist Battalion. The advance was led by 95th Brigade on the right, with two battalions forward (1st East Surrey on the right and 1st Duke of Cornwall's Light Infantry on the left), and 15th Brigade on the left on a one-battalion frontage (1st Norfolk, followed by 1st Bedfordshire, with 1st Cheshire in reserve). The 15th Brigade RFA and D/123rd Battery RFA were affiliated to 95th Brigade and 27th Brigade RFA and D/124th Battery RFA to 15th Brigade. The infantry brigades each had a section of mobile trench mortars attached from the divisional artillery. One company of 5th Machine Gun Battalion was in close support and another was in reserve with 13th Brigade.

The advance commenced at 5.30 a.m. when 95th and 15th Brigades passed through 112th Brigade (37th Division). The artillery was slowed by poor road conditions and demolitions within the forest but there was little enemy resistance initially.

Having passed the Red Dotted Line at 7.30 a.m., 95th Brigade pushed on and met only slight resistance in reaching the Black Line at 9.30 a.m. The advance resumed at 10.15 a.m. and came under machine gun fire from the high ground, about 1,350m west of la Porquerie. Patrols located the enemy positions, which were driven out by a section of 52nd Battery RFA at 2.30 p.m. The Brigade then came under heavy enemy artillery fire and enfilade machine gun fire from the left, where 15th Brigade was held up. However, the Yellow Line was gained about 4.30 p.m. and patrols of 1st East Surrey on the right took seventeen prisoners at Hurtebise Farm.

The 15th Brigade reached the Red Dotted Line at 8.00 a.m., where 1st Bedfordshire passed through 1st Norfolk and continued towards the Black and

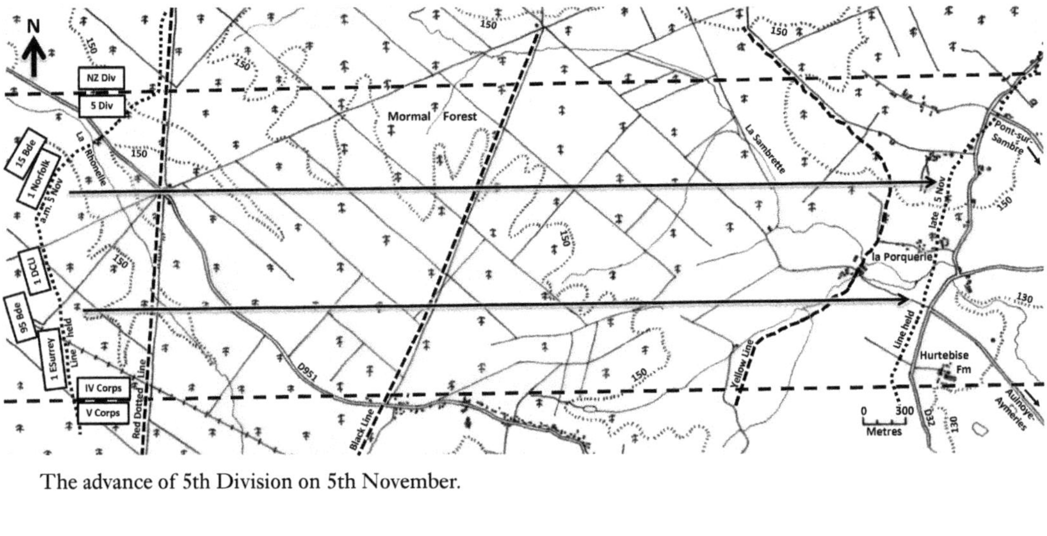

The advance of 5th Division on 5th November.

Yellow Lines. While 1st Norfolk fell back into reserve, 1st Cheshire was ordered forward to follow 1st Bedfordshire, which reached the Black Line in contact with 1st Duke of Cornwall's Light Infantry (95th Brigade) on the right. However, it was not in contact with the New Zealand Division on the left. Considerable opposition was then encountered. Two mobile trench mortars were brought forward which, with the artillery, bombarded the area west of la Porquerie and the attack was able to continue.

Patrols of 3rd Hussars informed the commander of 15th Brigade that the New Zealanders had passed the first objective. He decided to push 1st Cheshire through on the left of 1st Bedfordshire in order to turn the enemy flank. Despite an exceedingly arduous approach march along muddy and cratered roads, 1st Cheshire was in position by 2.45 p.m. The advance resumed and by 3.40 p.m. 1st Bedfordshire was on the Yellow Line and 1st Cheshire was pressing on. By 9.40 p.m. the third objective (Brown Line), the Pont-sur-Sambre–Bavai road, had been captured by 1st Cheshire, which remained in contact with 1st Duke of Cornwall's Light Infantry on the right but still had no contact on the left. This phase of the advance had met little opposition, except for heavy shellfire. Further advance was not possible in darkness until the situation on the left had been cleared up. Patrols were pushed towards the canal and bridging materials were brought forward over the atrocious roads. Any attempt to establish a bridgehead over the canal would have to wait until the next day.

Despite steady machine gun and artillery fire, 95th Brigade continued the advance during the night. The 1st Duke of Cornwall's Light Infantry set off at 3.30 a.m. on 6th November and entered Pont-sur-Sambre. The western edge of the village (Brown Line) was secured and sixteen prisoners and a machine gun were captured. At 6.30 a.m. 1st East Surrey reached the Brown Line along the Pont-sur-Sambre–Bavai road, in contact with 1st Duke of Cornwall's Light Infantry. Despite hold ups, by early on 6th November 5th Division had captured the whole of Mormal Forest and the line held was roughly along the Brown Line. Some 2,360 prisoners were taken.

The speed of advance slowed on 6th November due to heavy rain, which delayed the delivery of bridging material. The Germans also fought rearguard actions with great determination. Fourth Army set the La Capelle–Avesnes–Mauberge road as the objective. With more open operations being conducted, armoured cars and cavalry came into their own. The tanks were withdrawn into reserve in case they were needed to dislodge the enemy from prepared positions. The Germans cratered roads, blew bridges and did everything possible to delay the advance, but it ground on relentlessly and the objective was reached along the whole of the Army's front.

Despite the difficulties, Third Army's V Corps on the right crossed the Sambre-Oise Canal under heavy fire and pushed on towards its objective. In IV Corps, 42nd Division relieved the New Zealand Division and, at 6.30 a.m., continued the advance with 5th Division on its right. The objective for 5th Division was to

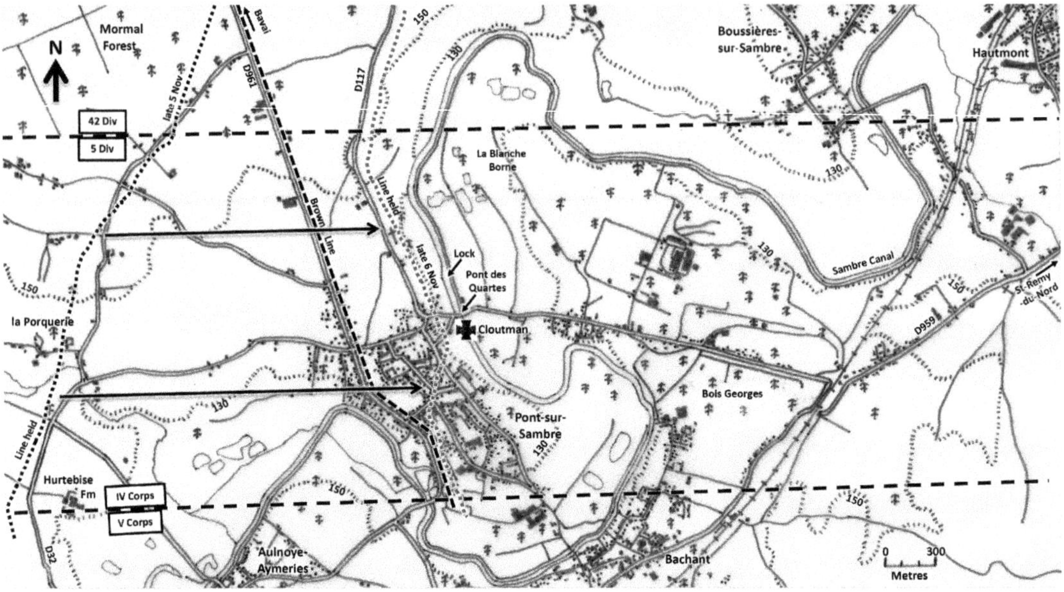

The continued advance of 5th Division late on 5th November and 6th November.

seize bridgeheads over the Sambre-Oise Canal, between Pont-sur-Sambre and Hautmont, before continuing to the final objective on the Avesnes – Mauberge road.

In 15th Brigade patrols of 1st Cheshire pushed forward to the canal, where they met heavy fire from the east bank and the high ground beyond. The situation in 95th Brigade was similar, with 1st East Surrey and 1st Duke of Cornwall's Light Infantry coming under heavy machine gun fire. By 10.50 a.m. 5th Division had closed up to the canal, the banks of which were reported clear of the enemy. However, all the bridges had been blown. The west side of the canal was found to be untenable due to the heavy rain and the line was pulled back 350m. An attempt to force a crossing was met with heavy machine gun fire. It was clear that the defenders on the opposite bank were prepared to resist attempts to cross the canal, which in that area was twenty-one metres wide and two metres deep, with a muddy bottom.

In the afternoon **Major Brett Cloutman**, commanding 59th Field Company RE, made a reconnaissance of the Pont des Quartes girder bridge northeast of Pont sur Sambre. Despite reports to the contrary, he found it was intact but noticed that it had been prepared for demolition. Having ensured that his men were in cover, he rolled over the towpath, slipped into the water and swam over the canal. He cut the demolition charge leads, although the bridge was swept by artillery fire and a machine gun in the factory north of the bridge. Having rendered the demolition charges useless, he swam back. Unfortunately, his bravery did not result in immediate success. A platoon of 1st Cheshire was ordered to the bridge to prevent the enemy from repairing the leads, while two mortars were to shell the approaches. However,

The modern Pont des Quartes bridge over the Sambre-Oise Canal at Pont-sur-Sambre. The lock entrance can be seen in the distance under the bridge.

these precautions came too late. The Germans blew the bridge at 5.15 p.m. and the platoon arrived fifteen minutes later. Cloutman also reconnoitred other crossing sites north of the Quartes bridge at la Blanche Borne and the damaged lock to the south of it.

Bridging operations continued overnight and plans were made to cross on 7th November at all three sites – la Blanche Borne, the lock and the Quartes bridge. Once the crossings had been secured, the advance was to continue to the Green and Red Lines. However, it proved impossible to build a bridge over the lock due to heavy machine gun fire. Two companies of 1st Cheshire were sent to cross the pontoon bridge being constructed by 59th Field Company RE west of la Blanche Borne. The 27th Brigade RFA covered the crossing point and laid down a light barrage on the east bank, while the sappers struggled forward with the bridging materials through the mud and cratered roads.

The two left Corps of Third Army had some success but in many places were short of the objective. South of the Condé Canal, First Army also made steady but unremarkable progress. Despite some corps and divisions not making as much ground as desired, it was still another successful day for the BEF, as it continued the remorseless grinding down of the enemy.

On 7th November 15th Brigade led the way in crossing the canal to seize the high ground to the east. Following behind, 95th Brigade was to pass through to the Green and Red Lines. By 6.00 a.m. the pontoon bridge was ready and two companies of 1st Cheshire crossed over, followed by 1st Norfolk. The two battalions reached the line of the railway east of Bois Georges, with the left flank thrown back where 42nd Division was behind.

At 9.00 a.m. 1st Devonshire (95th Brigade) began crossing the canal to pass through 15th Brigade in order to gain the Hautmont–Fontaine road (Green Line). However, heavy machine gun and mortar fire was received from the left flank at Boussières-sur-Sambre, in the deep bend of the Sambre, which was still occupied by the Germans. The advance was held up short of the railway west of St Rémy-mal-Bâti (now St Remy-du-Nord). However, the company on the right was less affected and met little resistance in reaching the Green Line and Fontaine beyond, where a 5.9″ Howitzer was captured. Touch was made with 21st Division on the right but the company was separated from the rest of the Battalion by a gap of 900m. As a result, it was pulled back to the Green Line. The line of the railway continued to be held by 15th Brigade until the whole of 95th Brigade passed through on the morning of 8th November.

Similar operations continued for the next three days. Early on the morning of 11th November Advanced GHQ sent out the longed for message, *Hostilities will cease at 11.00 hours today…..* Four years and three months of war were over. The most forward BEF troops were at Casteau, northeast of Mons, only a few hundred metres from where the first shots were fired by British troops in August 1914. In the intervening period the British Empire alone had suffered almost one million deaths, 560,000 of which were on the Western Front. Another two million were wounded, although most of these returned to duty.

The brunt of the final Hundred Days offensive was borne by the BEF. The French were exhausted and at the Armistice held only sixty-five kilometres of active front. The Americans had two million men in France and had the war continued into 1919 they would have assumed increasing importance. Very few men in the BEF in August 1918 had any experience of open warfare, but they adapted quickly and achieved a series of remarkable victories. Infantry, cavalry, artillery, tanks, engineers, communications, logistics and airpower combined in a devastatingly effective all arms battle. The lessons of this final campaign were not lost on the Germans, who used them to such effect in 1939 and 1940.

The pattern of the war had come full circle, starting with a period of open warfare before degenerating into years of stalemate in the trenches. The turning point was 1916, although it was not apparent at the time. In that year at Verdun and on the Somme the Germans suffered one million casualties, including a high proportion of pre-war professional NCOs and officers. By 1918 technological and tactical developments enabled the seemingly impenetrable trench defences to be overcome – tanks, gas, predicted artillery fire, trench mortars, grenades and rifle grenades, light machine guns and effective cooperation between air and ground forces. The infantry was also vastly superior to the battalions that went abroad in 1914 in terms of organisation, firepower and tactics.

The conflict witnessed staggering feats of bravery by soldiers of all nations. In all 634 VCs were awarded for the Great War. Of these 492 were earned on the ground on the Western Front. The story behind those VCs is effectively the story of the war on the Western Front.

Biographies

307817 LANCE CORPORAL WILLIAM AMEY
1/8th Battalion, The Royal Warwickshire Regiment

William Amey was born on 5th March 1881 at Mount Street, Aston, Birmingham, Warwickshire. His father, Charles Henry Amey (1833–27th January 1909), born at Heybridge, Essex, was a messenger in 1851, living with his parents. He married Elizabeth Callan/Callon (née Parry or West) (c.1821–62) on 19th April 1858 at Aston Juxta, Warwickshire. They were living at 1 Belvedere Place, St Francis Street, Aston in 1861. Elizabeth had married James Callan/Callon (c.1819–55), an engine driver born at Ashton-under-Lyne, Lancashire, in 1839, registered at Manchester, Lancashire. They were living at the Station, Wolverton, Buckinghamshire in 1841 and at Railway Cottages, Station, Fletton, Huntingdonshire in 1851. James and Elizabeth had five children – Maria Callan/Callon 1843, Elizabeth Callan/Callon 1848, Margaret Callan/Callon 1851, Mary Ann Callan/Callon 1852 and George Callan/Callon 1856. Charles Amey married Elizabeth née Clark (c.1841–1920) on 7th November 1864 at St Peter's & St Paul's Church, Aston, Birmingham, where she was born. Charles was a railway carriage fitter, living with his family at 3 Osborne Buildings, Mount Street, Aston in 1871 and 1881, at 47 Stuart Street, Aston in 1891 and at 58 Stella Street, Aston in 1901. They were still at Stella Street at the time of his death. Elizabeth was living there as a widow in 1911. William had seven siblings:

- Charles Henry Amey (1865–9th August 1911), born at Aston, was an iron moulder in 1881 and 1891, living with his parents. He married Emma Pate (1868–21st August 1923) in 1896. They were living at 296b Mount Street, Aston in 1901 and at 66 Mount Street by 1911. Charles died at the Homoeopathic Hospital, Birmingham. Emma was still living at 66 Mount Street at the time of her death there.

Mount Street Park, near where William was born.

- Kate Amey (4th July 1867–17th September 1950), married Henry 'Harry' James Swinburn (1871–1937) in 1897. They were living at 5 Brunswick Road, Birmingham in 1901. He was a labourer with the City Council in 1911, when they were living at 12 Trenville Avenue, Stoney Lane, Birmingham. There were no children. His death was registered at Bromsgrove, Worcestershire. Kate was living alone at Holly Cottage, Middle Road, Bromsgrove in 1939. She was living at 213 Erdington Road, Erdington, Birmingham at the time of her death there.
- Walter Amey (April 1869–1952) was a sawyer in 1891, living with his parents, a brass worker in 1901, living with his parents, and a general labourer in an engineering works in 1911, living with his mother. He was living at Third Road, Bromsgrove, Worcestershire in 1939 with George Parish, a single metalworker or fitter, born in July 1862. Walter never married.
- Annie Elizabeth Amey (2nd September 1872–6th April 1947), born at Nechells, Birmingham, was a metal burnisher in 1891, living with her parents, a silver burnisher in 1901, living with her parents, and 1911, living with her mother. She married Frank Parton Ellard (9th July 1874–28th May 1949), a buyer, in

Heybridge village is adjacent to the town of Maldon, Essex. There were Iron Age, Roman and Saxon settlements, as well as pre-historic sites in the area. The name Heybridge originates from a high bridge over the River Blackwater in the Middle Ages, which was replaced in 1870. Much of the flow along that part of the river had, by then, been diverted into the River Chelmer during construction of the Chelmer and Blackwater Navigation Canal. It was originally used to transport coal and wood inland to Chelmsford but went into decline when the Great Eastern Railway opened a line to Maldon in the 19th century. Today the canal is mainly used by pleasure boats and for fishing. The River Blackwater at Heybridge may be the site of the Battle of Maldon in 991, although this is contentious. Until the 1970s and 1980s, when new housing was built, much of the area was agricultural. The main industry until 1984 was the agricultural machinery manufacturer EH Bentall & Co, established in 1805. By 1914 Bentalls was employing up to 700 people. Francis Waring (1760–1833), vicar of Heybridge, had an extraordinary lifestyle. On Sundays he read church lessons at great speed, gave a sermon of one or two sentences and then ran down the aisle to leap onto his horse and gallop off to repeat the performance at two other churches. Although not poor, the vicarage was furnished with rough-hewn logs instead of chairs and his children ate from a trough. He and his wife slept in a wicker cradle suspended from the ceiling.

1928. He was a warehouseman in 1939, when they were living on Castle Street, Redditch, Worcestershire. They were living at 34 Woodville Road, King's Heath, Birmingham at the time of her death there. There were no children. Frank married Helena Wakefield née Brindley (13th June 1878–25th March 1967) in 1948. He was living at 259 Brook Lane, Kings Heath at the time of his death at The General Hospital, Birmingham. Helena was living at 1 Western Road, Winson Green, Birmingham at the time of her death there. Helena had married Charles Edwin Wakefield (21st April 1876–8th January 1944) in 1902. Charles was a printer's machinist in 1911, when they were living at 53 Kendal Road, Sparkbrook. By 1939 he was a printing machine minder and they were living at 259 Brook Lane, Kings Heath, Birmingham. They were still there at the time of his death at 1a Raddlebarn Road, Birmingham. Charles and Helena had two children – Lawrence Charles Wakefield (1905–77) and Edna Amey Wakefield (born 1907).

- Ellen 'Nellie' Amey (1875–17th September 1940), born at Aston, had no occupation and was living with her parents in 1891 and 1901. She was a servant in 1911, living with her mother. She never married and died at Rubery Hill Mental Hospital, Birmingham.
- Harry Amey (1879–1914) was a navvy in 1901, living with his parents, and a brass worker in 1911, living with his mother.
- Sidney Amey (1884–17th November 1934) was an errand boy in 1901, living with his parents, and an insurance clerk in 1911, living with his mother. He married Lydia Adelaide Ward (7th May 1889–18th January 1962) on 15th February 1913 at St Mary's, Aston Brook, Birmingham. They were both living at 53 Whitehouse Street at the time. She was a barmaid in 1911 living with her parents at 381 Nechells Park Road, Aston. Sidney served in the Worcestershire Regiment during the Great War. They were living at 70 Bridge Road, Saltey, Birmingham at the time of his death there. Lydia was a licensee manageress in 1939, living alone at 70 Bridge Road, Birmingham. They had a daughter:
    - Doris Amey (21st May 1914–5th August 2008) married Leslie George Martin (2nd February 1913–17th December 1993) in 1939. He was a district foreman with a patent roof glazier in 1939, when they were living at 78 Antrobus Road, Handsworth, Birmingham. They had a son – Brian ST Martin in 1946.

  Lydia married Frank Evans on 17th July 1943 at Birmingham. They were living at 56 Hyde Road, Birmingham at the time of his death at The General Hospital, Birmingham. She was living at 78 Antrobus Road, Handsworth at the time of her death there.

William's paternal grandfather, Thomas Amey (c.1801–66) married Hannah née Hardy (c.1807–80) on 29th March 1827 at Heybridge, Essex, where they were both born. He was a labourer in 1841, when they were living at Navigation Place,

Heybridge. He was a servant by 1851 and they were living at Seven Houses Building, Stratford, West Ham, Essex. By 1861 he was a general labourer and they were living at 11 George Street, Stepney, London. He was recorded as a shoemaker, bootmaker and cabinetmaker on his daughters' marriage certificates. Thomas' death was registered at Stepney. Hannah was living with her daughter, Harriet and family, at 43 Catherine Street, Tower Hamlets, London in 1871. Her death was registered as Hannah Amy at Lambeth, London. In addition to Charles they had seven other children:

The White Horse Inn, Great Baddow was Grade II listed in 1967. It was originally a 17th century timber-framed building and may have incorporated an earlier structure. The building was much altered in the 18th and 19th centuries and was renovated during the last century. The chimney stack is 17th century.

- Mary Amey (born c.1829), born at Heybridge.
- Elizabeth Amey (c.1832–September 1912) married William Green (born c.1831), but no record has been found. She was a widowed charwoman in 1871, living with her children at 3 Richards Street, Tower Hamlets. They had at least four children – Jane Green 1858, Henry Green 1860, Frederick Green 1864 and Walter Green 1867.
- Walter Amey (c.1835–22nd May 1913) was a servant in 1851, living with his parents. He married Adelaide Gotobed (27th May 1876–2nd August 1943), born at St Saviour, London, in 1896 registered at Romford, Essex. She was living with her parents at 75 Limehouse Causeway, Tower Hamlets, London in 1881 and at 13 Maypole Road, Ilford in 1891. By 1901 Walter was a licensed victualler and they were living at the White Horse Inn, Great Baddow, Essex. He subsequently died there but Adelaide continued to run the pub for some years after. They had a daughter:
  - Amy Adelaide Amey (1st October 1901–25th August 1989) married Harold Carlton Bonsor (7th May 1894–27th April 1952) in 1919, registered at Colchester. They had four children – Beryl B Bonsor 1922, Myrtle A Bonsor 1923, Valerie J Bonsor 1930 and Hewson A Bonsor 1936. Amy married Lancelot Telford Keel (28th November 1889–1974), birth registered at Newcastle upon Tyne, in 1958 registered at Bingham. Amy was living at 266 Botley Road, Burridge, Southampton when she died. Lancelot had married Evelyn M Lister (1891–1956) in 1915, registered at Newcastle upon Tyne, and they had two children – Kathleen J Keel 1919 and Henry E Keel 1925.

  Adelaide married Alexander Keiller Hamilton (23rd September 1891–1959), born at Torryburn, Fife, Scotland, on 1st October 1917 at St Mary the Virgin, Great

Baddow, Essex. Alexander enlisted in the Black Watch (1766) on 24th January 1910 and joined at Perth on 1st February. He was described as an engine driver, 5′ 4½″ tall, with fair hair, dark grey eyes, fair complexion and his religious denomination was Presbyterian. He was posted to 1st Battalion on 2nd March and attained 3rd Class Education on 13th April and 2nd Class on 30th November. On 18th January 1911 he was appointed lance corporal, paid from 18th July, and was promoted corporal on 28th December 1912. He qualified as Mounted Infantry (Longmoor) on 1st October 1912. Alexander reverted to private at his own request and transferred to the RFC on probation on 24th February 1913 (820) as airman 2. He qualified as a Skilled Technical Fitter at the Central Flying School on 14th August and his transfer to the RFC was approved next day. He was appointed airman 1 on 1st November with No.5 Squadron and embarked for France on 12th August 1914 with No.6 Squadron. Promoted corporal 23rd August, sergeant 20th November and flight sergeant on 1st March 1915. On 15th October he returned to Britain and reverted to sergeant on 21st January 1916 with No.27 Squadron. He re-embarked for France on 13th February, was appointed acting flight sergeant on 29 August and was promoted flight sergeant on 1st October. Awarded MM, LG 19th January 1917. On 1st February he was appointed acting warrant officer and sergeant major (T) and returned to Britain on 17th February to join 37 Squadron. Transferred to the RAF on 1st April 1918 as a Technical Supervisor and was promoted warrant officer on 2nd May. Alexander was posted to No.152 Squadron on 15th October and re-embarked for France on 18th October. On 1st January 1919 he was reclassified as sergeant major 1 and was posted to the Home Establishment on 13th February and Dispersal Centre Purfleet on 20th February. Alexander transferred to the RAF E Reserve on 20th March. He was mobilised by Royal Proclamation on 8th April 1921, joined E Reserve Henlow Reserve Pool on 11th April and reverted to E Reserve on 4th June as a sergeant fitter AE. He was discharged on 23rd January 1922. His address was Skinners, Great Baddow. He enlisted in the Class E Reserve for four years on 26th September 1938 as aircraftsman 2 at Andover, by when he was a public works general foreman, but did not volunteer for reserve training. His medical category was Grade II (GS). He was promoted sergeant next day and was brought into use on 15th October. Adelaide was living at Gable Cottage, Sandon, Essex in 1939. Living with her was Frederick Walker (born 30th August 1921), a single grocer's assistant. Adelaide subsequently died there. Alexander's death was registered at Wallasey.

- Harriet Amey (27th August 1837–1872) was a dressmaker in 1861, living with her parents. She married Henry Kneller (c.1836–February 1901), born at Bethnal Green, London, on 14th July 1861 at St Thomas, Stepney. He was a coal meter in 1871, when they were living at 43 Catherine Street, Tower Hamlets. Harriet's death was registered at Stepney. They had four children – Eliza Ann Kneller 1861, Harriett Elizabeth Kneller 1863, Helen H Kneller 1866 and Henry James Kneller

(1871–88). Henry senior married his sister-in-law, Elizabeth Green née Amey, on 4th July 1875 at St Thomas, Stepney. They were living at 18 Heath Street, Stepney at the time. They had a daughter – Emily Beatrice Kneller (1875–1961). Henry was a foreman at a coal wharf in 1891, when they were living at 14 Bridge Street, Stepney. By 1911 she was living with her son, Henry, who had changed his surname to Kneller, at 59 Bridge Street, Stepney. She subsequently died there.

- Henry Hardy Amey (31st July 1840–2nd December 1906), a boot and shoemaker born at Navigation Place, Heybridge, married Mary Ann Power (c.1841–91) on 14th July 1861 at Poplar, London. At the time of the census on 7th April 1861, Henry and Mary were living as man and wife at 2 Ann Street, Stepney, London. Henry was a bricklayer's labourer. He was a railway engine driver in 1871, when they were living at 8 Morville Street, Bow, London. Mary's death was registered at Shoreditch. Henry was a licensed victualler at the Weavers Arms, 36 Sun Street, Finsbury, London in 1891 and at the George the Fourth, 28 Redhill Street, Regent's Park, London in 1901. He subsequently died there.
- Maria Hester Amey (27th January 1843–1920) was a dressmaker in 1861, living with her parents. She married Charles James (c.1842–88), born at Spitalfields, London, on 23rd June 1861 at All Saints, Poplar, London. He was a coal meter in 1880, when they were living at 36 Maroon Street, Tower Hamlets and at 125 Brook Street, Tower Hamlets in 1881. His death was registered at Stepney. Maria was a charwoman in 1891, living with her family at 5 White Horse Street, Tower Hamlets and at 2 Green Street, Tower Hamlets in 1901. She was living with some of her children at 57 Adelaide Road, Leyton, Essex in 1911. Her death was registered at Edmonton, Middlesex. Maria and Charles had twelve children including – Charles William James 1861, Henry Hardy James 1863, Walter James 1869, Maria Hester James (1871–1914), Helen Hannah James 1873, George William James 1875, William James 1879, Elizabeth Jane James (1880–81), Frederick James 1884 and Florence James 1886.
- Helen 'Ellen' Hannah Amey (12th January 1848–1920), born at Stratford, Essex, was a dressmaker in 1861, living with her parents. She married George Willats (1844–1901), a brass finisher born at Stepney, London, on 16th June 1867 at All Saints, Poplar, London. They were living with her sister, Harriet and family, at 43 Catherine Street, Tower Hamlets, London in 1871. His death was registered at Whitechapel, London. She was a charwoman in 1911, living at 1 Dixon Street, Limehouse, London. Helen's death was registered at Pancras, London. They had nine children – George Hardy Willats (1868–99), Helen Hannah Willats (1869–85), Emily Willats (1871–1910), Louisa Willats (1875–1931), Henry Thomas Willats (1878–1941), Albert Willats (1880–1920), Thomas Willats (1883–1929), Frank Willats (1887–1964) and Clara Jane Willats (1890–1905).

His maternal grandfather, John Clark (c.1816–5th September 1862), born at Higham, Leicestershire, is believed to have married Ann Goodhew (c.1818–4th June 1876),

Lewisham in southeast London, about ten kilometres south of Charing Cross, was within Kent until 1889. It was a small village until the advent of the railways in the 19th century. The earliest written reference is a charter of 862. King Alfred was Lord of the Manor of Lewisham, which was given by his niece, Elthruda, to St Peter's Abbey, Ghent about 918. In the mid 17th century, the vicar of Lewisham, Abraham Colfe, built a grammar and primary schools and six almshouses. The Manor of Lewisham was purchased by George Legge, whose son, William, was a member of Queen Anne's privy council. On 5th September 1711 he was ennobled as Viscount Lewisham and Earl of Dartmouth. The original village centre was around the parish church of St Mary but moved northwards with the arrival of the railway to Dartford in 1849. In 1889 Lewisham became a Metropolitan Borough of the County of London. During the Great War the hospital became Lewisham Military Hospital. During the Second World War the hospital was hit by a V1, which destroyed two wards and killed a nurse. Another seventy people were injured. The town centre was also hit by a V1 in 1944, resulting in over 300 casualties, of which fifty-one were killed. In 1955 Sainsbury's opened a store in Lewisham, then Europe's largest self-service supermarket. On 4th December 1957 a crowded passenger express overran signals at danger in thick fog, crashed into a stationary train and brought down an overhead railway bridge onto the wreckage below. Ninety people died. Amongst those who were born or lived in Lewisham are:

- Ginger Baker (1939–2019) – drummer with the rock group *Cream*.
- Kate Bush CBE (born 1958) – singer, songwriter, record producer and dancer.
- General Sir John Crocker GCB KBE DSO MC (1896–1963) – GOC I Corps on D-Day and until the end of the war in Europe. He was later C-in-C Middle East Land Forces and Adjutant General.
- Lillie Langtry (1853–1929) – socialite, actress, producer and mistress of the future King Edward VII.
- Actors Jude Law (born 1972) and Gary Oldman (born 1958).
- Ian Wright (born 1963) – Crystal Palace, Arsenal and England footballer.
- John Simon Ritchie (1957–79) – Sid Vicious of the punk rock band, *Sex Pistols*.
- Henry Williamson (1895–1977) – author of *Tarka the Otter*.
- William George Wyman (born 1936) – bassist with the *Rolling Stones* 1962–93.

at Lewisham, Kent, where her birth was registered. He was an excavator in 1841, when they were living at Aston, Warwickshire. By 1851 he was a retail brewer and milkman, and they were living at Mount Street, Nechells, Birmingham. He was a publican in 1861 at the Jenny Lind, Church Road, Aston and subsequently died there. Ann was a laundress in 1871, living

The Jenny Lind public house closed in 1940.

with some of her children at 15 George Street, Aston. In addition to Elizabeth they had nine other children:

- Catherine Clark (born c.1839).
- Charles Clark (born 1844).
- Frederick Clark (born 1847).
- Ann Clark (born 1848).
- Sarah Ann Clark (born 1854), a twin with George.
- George William Clark (born 1854), a twin with Sarah, was a spoon filer living with his mother in 1871.
- Theodosia Clark (25th December 1859–1929) was a domestic servant in 1871, living with her mother. She married James Alder Pendrey (1850–17th October 1910), born at Uxbridge, Middlesex, in April 1878 at Aston. He was a general labourer, living with his family at 12 Laurel Cottages, George Road, Aston in 1881, at 1 Laurel Cottages in 1891 and at 1 Cranmore Street, Aston in 1901. They had nine children:
    - Clara Pendrey (24th April 1878–1953).
    - Sidney Pendrey (24th August 1879–2nd September 1934).
    - Ada Pendrey (6th January 1882–December 1970).
    - Jane 'Jennie' Pendrey (8th April 1884–1960).
    - Harry Pendrey (12th September 1886–4th July 1918) was a rubber worker when he enlisted in the Worcestershire Regiment on 5th November 1914 at Birmingham (19725, 29221 & 172249). He was described as 5′ 8½″ tall, weighing 133 lbs, with fresh complexion, grey eyes, brown hair and his religious denomination was Church of England. He was posted to 12th Battalion on 24th November and was promoted corporal on 28th November. On 18th June 1915 he married Beatrice Elizabeth Bryan (21st April 1890–1980) at St Catharine's Church, Nechells, Birmingham and they had a son, Albert James Pendrey (1916–97). Harry was appointed lance sergeant on 30th June 1915, transferred to 9th Battalion on 28th August and joined the Mediterranean Expeditionary Force next day. Harry was invalided from Mustapha Convalescent Camp, Egypt to Britain aboard HMHS *Egypt*, departing Alexandria, Egypt on 27th December. He was transferred to the strength of the Depot on 10th January 1916, while being treated at 2nd Birmingham War Hospital, Northfield until 25th March for valvular disease of the heart. He was demoted to corporal on 7th April and was posted to 5th Battalion on 9th April. Harry was tried by Regimental Court Martial on 26th June for conduct to the prejudice of good order and military discipline on active service. He was sentenced to take rank and precedence as a corporal with effect from 28th November 1915. He transferred to 13th Works Battalion, Devonshire Regiment (19125) on 19th July. On 28th April 1917 he transferred to 312th Labour Company, Labour Corps as acting

sergeant. He reverted to corporal on 11th August on posting to 380th Home Service Employment Company. A medical board at Fargo Military Hospital, Larkhill, Wiltshire on 8th April 1918 found him permanently unfit for service. On 29th April he was discharged no longer physically fit for war service due to a tubercule of the lungs. He was living with his family at 16 Freeman Road, Nechells.
    - James Pendrey (12th December 1888–10th May 1913).
    - Ernest Pendrey (16th September 1891–1960).
    - Walter Pendrey (18th August 1897–10th May 1918) served in 1/4th Wiltshire (17787) and was killed in action in Palestine (Ramleh War Cemetery, Israel and Palestine – N22).
    - Horace Pendrey (23rd October 1901–2nd May 1963).
- John Thomas Clark (born 1861).
- Lucy Clark (10th May 1863–1944) was a domestic servant in 1881 at 174 Acacia Terrace, Aston. She married John Edward Preece (27th December 1863–1942), a bricklayer, born at Hereford, on 5th February 1888 at St Clement's, Nechells. They were both living at 1 Laurel Cottages, Trevor Street, Nechells at the time. They were living with their family at 26 Court, 4 House, Clifton Road, Aston in 1891. They were living at 2 Back of 200 Clifton Road, Aston in 1939 with their spinster daughters, Edith, Annie and Dora. They had six children – Edith Preece (8th April 1888–1968), Elsie Preece (1890), John Edward Preece (3rd February 1891–1972), William Preece (15th September 1892–1967), Annie Lucy Preece (2nd June 1903–4th February 1965) and Dora Preece (13th January 1907–16th November 1984).

Very little is known about William's early life. He was a brass worker in 1901, living with his parents. By 1911 he was a chandelier maker for Verity's Ltd, electrical manufacturers at their Plume works in Aston, living with his mother.

William married Evelyn 'Eve' Matilda Haines née Gambles (4th March 1881–31st December 1970), born at Hackney, London, in 1938 registered at Edmonton, Middlesex. Eve had married Frederick Andrew Haines (21st May 1881–21st December 1937), a tobacconist's window dresser born at St Sepulchre, London, on 27th December 1909 at St Mark with St Bartholomew, Dalston, London. Frederick was living at 66 Havelock Road, Birmingham and Evelyn at 69 Graham Road, Dalston, London at the time. They were living at 5 William Cook Road, Ward End, Birmingham, Warwickshire in 1911. William and Eve met before the Great War and her marriage to Frederick broke down. Frederick moved in with another woman and William and Eve lived together at 13 Lansdowne Terrace, Leamington Spa in the 1920s. Frederick was living at 29 Arcot Road, Hall Green, Birmingham at the time of his death at The General Hospital, Birmingham. Only then did William and Eve marry. They were living at 13 Willes Street, Leamington Spa in 1939, by when she was a grocer's shop assistant. They had no children.

Eve's father, Herbert Edward Cartwright Gambles (24th April 1853–1917), born at Ashby de la Launde, Lincolnshire, was a farmer. He married Rosa Annie née Walker (1850–1933), born at Camberwell, London, on 12th October 1872 at St Matthew's Church, Upper Clapton, London. By 1879 he was a clerk and they were living at 109 Almack Road, London. He was unemployed in 1881, when he was living with his son, Herbert, and a visitor, Marion Giles, at 5 & 7 Gothic Villas, Tottenham, London. By 1891 he was a milk inspector, living with his family at Hackney, London. In 1901 he was a commercial clerk for a wool broker, living with his family at 57 Southey Road, Tottenham and at 117 Dunlace Road, Clapton, London in 1911. His death was registered at Hackney, London and hers at Edmonton, Middlesex. In addition to Evelyn they had six other children, all born at Clapton, London:

13 Willes Street, Leamington Spa, where William and Eve were living in 1939. There is a Heritage Blue Plaque to the left of the door (Memorials to Valour).

Ashby de la Launde in Lincolnshire is just west of Digby. In the Domesday Book it was recorded as Ashebi and consisted of two manors. The Lord of the Manor, William de Essheby, founded the Knights Templar preceptory, Temple Bruer, about 1150. Later the preceptory became the second wealthiest in Britain and helped to fund the Crusades from wool exports. In the 13th century, Cecilia, daughter of Jordan de Essheby, married Walter de la Laund. When Jordan died c.1260, Cecilia inherited the Ashby Manor, which thereafter was known as Ashby de la Launde. The de la Launde family lost the estate under King Henry VIII, who granted the manor to John Bellow and Robert Brocklesby in 1543. In 1580 it was sold to Edward King, who built Ashby Hall in 1595, using the original foundations of the Norman manor house. The Hall was home to Colonel Edward King (c.1606–81), MP for Great Grimsby, who served as a captain in the Parliamentary army and as Governor of Boston during the Commonwealth. Despite this and his nonconformist beliefs, he was probably the first MP to call for the restoration of King Charles II. In 1841 the estate passed to John William King, who was also parson of Ashby. He bred racehorses and in 1874 his filly *Apology* won the Triple Crown of the Thousand Guineas, Oaks and St Leger. When his activities came to the notice of the Bishop of Lincoln, he was forced to resign. The Hall was purchased in 1925 by George Canning, Baron Garvagh, having sold his Irish estates near Londonderry. He rebuilt and modernised parts of the Hall. Lord Garvagh moved to Keswick at the beginning of the Second World War and Ashby Hall became the officers' mess for RAF Digby. After the war the Hall stood empty until the estate was broken up in the late 1950s. The Hall became the Lake Rendezvous Club until 1960, when it was converted into Ashby Hall Country Club, later Ashby Country Club, which closed in 1992. The Hall then become the headquarters of a defence and security manufacturing company.

The first church of St Matthew in Upper Clapton was built in 1866 as a temporary iron structure,. The foundation stone of the permanent church was laid on 21st September 1867 and it was consecrated a year and a half later. In the 1950s the church was restored following damage in the war. The spire was demolished in 1962. In the early 1970s, the parish of St Matthew joined a group ministry with St Thomas', Stamford Hill and St Michael and All Angels, Stoke Newington Common. However, having been badly damaged by fire on 6th June 1976, St Matthew's church building was declared redundant the following January. The church hall was converted into the new church building and the parish became a plurality with St Thomas', Stamford Hill. The church bells were moved to Watton-at-Stone, Hertfordshire.

- Herbert Henry Charles Gambles (1873–1935) was a solicitor's clerk in 1891. He married Mary Annie Geear (1864–6th April 1936), birth registered at Llanelly, Carmarthenshire, in 1902 at Marylebone, London. His death was registered at Shoreditch, London. She was living at 10 Baring Street, Islington, London at the time of her death at 204 Hoxton Street, London.
- Claude Opfferman Gambles (12th July 1874–1942) was a civil engineer and clerk with the County Council in 1891. He married Gwendoline Kate Cull (1875–1922) in 1895 at Hackney, where she was born. They were living at 7 Devonshire Place, East Barnet, Hertfordshire in 1901. In 1911 he was single and a traveller in the dairy industry. Gwendoline was a resident at St Pancras Workhouse in 1920. Her death was registered at Pancras, London. Claude was a laundry traveller in 1939, living at 87 Gloucester Road, Tottenham, London. His sister, Rosa, and John Gambles (born 17th August 1909), assistant builders foreman, relationship unknown, were living with him. His death was registered at Edmonton.
- Marian Louise Gambles (1876–78).
- Aubrey Ernest Gambles (1879–80).
- William Douglas Gambles (29th April 1887–1957) was an assistant tobacconist in 1911. He married May Church (20th May 1890–1973) in 1916 at Edmonton. He was a laundry salesman in 1939, when they were living at 19 Fairbourne Road, Tottenham. His death was registered at Edmonton and hers at Enfield, Greater London. They had three children – Douglas A Gambles (1916–17), Joan C Gambles 1917 and Eric W Gambles 1919.
- Rosa May Gambles (12th May 1890–1967) was a typist in a wood flooring company in 1911. She was a telephone operator for a timber merchant in 1939, living with her brother, Claude. She died unmarried, registered at Haringey, London.

William enlisted in 1/8th Royal Warwickshire in Birmingham, possibly in May 1915, and was promoted lance corporal. It is not known when he went to France but

Dudley Road Hospital is in the Winson Green area of Birmingham. The hospital was built in 1889 as an extension of Birmingham Union Workhouse. It consisted of a single corridor about 400m long with nine Nightingale wards radiating from it. It was named the Birmingham Union Infirmary and later became successively Dudley Road Infirmary, Dudley Road Hospital and City Hospital. The Birmingham Treatment Centre opened on the City Hospital site in November 2005.

it was after 31st December 1915 because he was not entitled to the 1914–15 Star. The 1/8th Royal Warwickshire went to France on 22nd March 1915, so it is likely that William served in 2/8th Battalion, which formed in October 1914 at Birmingham. It moved to Northampton then Chelmsford and in March 1916 to Salisbury Plain, prior to deploying to France in May. It is not known if William deployed with it. He may have served with 2/8th Battalion until it disbanded in February 1918. However, the soldiers went to 2/7th Battalion and an entrenching battalion, rather than 1/8th Battalion, in which William subsequently served.

Awarded the VC for his actions at Landrècies, France on 4th November 1918, LG 31st January 1919. He was promoted corporal and was also awarded the MM but no details are known, LG 22nd July 1919. On 14th December he was granted leave, during which he was taken ill and underwent an operation at Dudley Road Hospital. The VC was presented by the King in the ballroom at Buckingham Palace on 22nd February 1919. William was demobilised in 1919.

William was a Turf Commission Agent in Leamington Spa, Warwickshire. He became a prominent member of the Leamington British Legion. He attended two VC Reunions – the VC Garden Party at Buckingham Palace on 26th June 1920 and the VC Dinner at the Royal Gallery of the House of Lords, London on 9th November 1929.

William died at Warneford Hospital, Leamington Spa, Warwickshire on 28th May 1940. The informant was Fred Chaulcey Maycock, who later married William's widow. A funeral with military honours was held on 1st June and he was buried in All Saints Cemetery, Leamington Spa, Warwickshire (Section 68, Grave 11). Arthur Hutt VC and Henry Tandey VC attended. The cemetery was cleared years later and his remains, together with those of Charles Goodfellow VC, were reinterred at Leamington Spa Cemetery, Tachbrook Road. The grave was refurbished by the Victoria Cross & George Cross Association, with support from RHQ Royal Regiment of Fusiliers and the Regimental Association in Warwickshire. A service of rededication was held on 21st August 2022, attended by regimental representatives, Viscount Montgomery, the Lord Lieutenant of Warwickshire, mayoral representatives and councillors from Warwick District Council, Royal

Warneford Hospital was Leamington Spa's main medical facility from 1834. It was named after the philanthropist, Samuel Wilson Warneford (1763–1855), who donated £3,000 of the £4,000 needed to build the hospital. It was initially funded by the patients, wealthy donors or collections from the general public. The maternity unit, the Cay Block, which opened in 1939, was financed by donations and collections organised by Mrs Annie Cay. Warneford closed in 1993, after services had been transferred to Warwick and Walsgrave Hospitals.

Leamington Spa, Warwick and Whitnash and members of the Royal Warwickshire Regiment, Royal Warwickshire Fusiliers and Royal Regiment of Fusiliers. He is commemorated in a number of other places:

- Accommodation Block, Infantry Training Centre Headquarters, Vimy Barracks, Catterick, Yorkshire.
- A Heritage Blue Plaque was dedicated at his former home at 13 Willes Road, Leamington Spa in October 2015.
- A Department for Communities and Local Government commemorative paving stone was unveiled by the Duke of Cambridge at Walk of Heroes, Hall of Memory, Centenary Square, Birmingham on 7th December 2015.

Eve married Fred Chaulcey Maycock (3rd May 1893–25th February 1963), born at Uxbridge,

William's grave in Leamington Spa Cemetery.

The Heritage Blue Plaque at his former home at 13 Willes Road, Leamington Spa.

The Department for Communities and Local Government commemorative paving stone at Walk of Heroes, Hall of Memory, Centenary Square, Birmingham.

Middlesex, on 14th May 1944 registered at Warwick. He was recorded as a nurse child in 1901, living with Elizabeth Coates (born c.1843) at Hockley Hole, Uxbridge. He was living at 25 Leicester Street, Leamington in 1940. Fred died at Warwick Hospital. Eve's death was registered at Haringey, London. Fred had married Lily Anstey (possibly 2nd December 1893–1940) in 1918 at Southwark, London. He was a foreman at HM Office Works in 1939, when they were living at 159 Leam Terrace, Leamington Spa. Lily was a patient at Warneford Hospital, Leamington Spa at the time of the 1939 Register and subsequently died there. Her age was recorded as fifty-three, indicating that she was born c.1887.

In addition to the VC and MM he was awarded the British War Medal 1914–20, Victory Medal 1914–19 and George VI Coronation Medal 1937. The medals were sold by William's widow for £650 at Sotheby's on 29th July 1963. They were purchased by Lieutenant Colonel Lewthwaite on behalf of the Friends of the Royal Warwickshire Regiment and were presented to the Regiment on 20th September. The VC is held by the Royal Warwickshire Regiment Museum, Pageant House, Jury Street, Warwick, Warwickshire.

213078 SAPPER ADAM ARCHIBALD
218th Field Company Royal Engineers

Adam Archibald was born on 14th January 1879 at 40 Balfour Street, Leith, Edinburgh, Midlothian, Scotland. His father, Rennie Archibald (1st January 1854–6th June 1931) was a plasterer, living at 18 Pilrig Street, Edinburgh, Midlothian in 1876. He married Christina née Anderson (22nd May 1849–13th July 1915), born at Aberdour, Fife, on 28th April 1876 at Easter Aberdour. They were living at 40 Balfour Street, Leith in 1881, at Broughton, Edinburgh in 1891 and at 24 Shaw's Street, Broughton in 1901. Christina died at 9 Shaw's Street, Edinburgh and Rennie at 4 Shaw's Terrace. Adam had four sisters:

- Sarah Blake Archibald (4th July 1876–15th May 1948), born at 40 Balfour Street, Leith, was a housemaid in 1891 at 6 Pilrig Street, Edinburgh, home of Mr and Mrs James Watson. She married John Croal (1st November 1874–1st February 1921), a printer/compositor born at 34 Carnegie Street, Edinburgh, on 29th June 1900 at 6 Nicholson Street, Edinburgh. John was living at

Balfour Street, Leith, where Adam Archibald was born. (*Rightmove*)

67 Cumberland Street, Edinburgh. They were living at 28 Beaverhall Terrace, Edinburgh in 1901. John died at 127 Broughton Road, Edinburgh. Sarah was living at 7 Shaw's Place, Edinburgh when she died at 22 James Street, Edinburgh. They had two children:

- John Croal (11th June 1901–22nd April 1970), born at 28 Beaverhall Terrace, Edinburgh, was an engineer's fitter. He married Jessie Walker Low (11th August 1901–1968), a spinner's assistant born at Canongate, Edinburgh, on 11th November 1921 at 2 Bellevue Crescent, Edinburgh. They had four children – John Croal (1921–83), Christina Anderson Croal (1925–27), George Croal (1931–2021) and James Croal (1937–2019).

Aberdour is on the north coast of the Firth of Forth in Fife. To the south is the island of Inchcolm, with Edinburgh beyond. The village was recorded as Abirdoure in 1179 and in 1126. Until the arrival of the railway in the 19th century, Aberdour was two villages, Wester and Easter Aberdour, on either side of the Dour Burn. The harbour was improved in the 18th century and a stone pier was constructed to load coal from nearby pits. In the 1850s the harbour became a popular destination for pleasure steamers from Leith and a deeper water pier was constructed at Hawkcraig. Hotels and other services followed and the railway came to Aberdour in 1890, following the building of the Forth Bridge. On the west side of Hawkcraig Point is a concrete jetty used in the development of radio-controlled torpedoes during the Great War. Aberdour Castle was begun as a hall house overlooking the Dour Burn in the 13th century. Over the next four centuries it was developed further. Some repairs were carried out following a fire in the late 17th century. However, in 1725 the family purchased Aberdour House, in Wester Aberdour, and the Castle fell into disrepair. St Fillan's Church, one of the best-preserved medieval parish churches in Scotland, dates mainly to the 12th century and was originally under the control of Inchcolm Abbey. A south arcade was added to the nave in the early 16th century. There is also the ruined 16th century church of St Drostan beside Dour Burn. When Lord Morton left the village for a large home in Edinburgh, he had the Aberdour Obelisk built. It is located between the Castle and the beach so that he could see his former hometown from the new house through binoculars. Inchcolm island was probably a monastic site well before the first documented mention in the 12th century. During the World Wars, the island was incorporated into the Firth of Forth defences. There are extensive remains of gun positions, barracks etc but the island is now more noted for its wildlife, particularly seabirds and seals. Aberdour was the birthplace of Lieutenant Colonel Geoffrey Charles Tasker Keyes VC MC (18th May 1917–18th November 1941). He was the son of Admiral of the Fleet Roger Keyes, 1st Baron Keyes (1872–1945), who planned and led the raids on Zeebrugge and Ostend in April 1918. He was also the first Director of Combined Operations during the Second World War.

- Christina 'Chrissie' Anderson Croal (21st November 1904–1957) was a baker's shop assistant living at 7 Shaw's Place, Edinburgh. She married James Carstairs Purves Foster (January 1901–1964), a chauffeur born at Leith, on 19th August 1932 at Masonic Hall, 19 Hill Street, Edinburgh. They had a son, John Croal Foster, in 1933.
- Janet Margaret Archibald, (17th August 1880–8th December 1954) married Robert Salmond Cumming Taylor (24th December 1877–21st June 1945), a printer/compositor born at Linktown, Abbotshall, Fife, on 27th December 1907 at 9 Shaw's Street, Edinburgh. Janet was recorded as Janet Menzies Archibald on her marriage and death certificates. Robert died at his home at 4 Shaw's Place, Edinburgh. Janet was still living there when she died at the Royal Infirmary Edinburgh. They had a son:
  - Robert Taylor (born 1908), lived at 49 Montague Street, Edinburgh.
- Christina Anderson Archibald (2nd October 1882–28th December 1945) was a baker's shop keeper in 1901 living with her parents. She married David Dunn McIntosh (21st October 1880–16th September 1948), a vanman born at 115 Kirkgate, Leith, on 11th October 1901. He was later an insurance agent. Christina died at her home at 4 Shaw's Terrace, Edinburgh and David at the Royal Infirmary Edinburgh. They had at least two children:
  - Rennie Archibald McIntosh (7th September 1905–3rd August 1988), born at South Leith, Edinburgh, was a plasterer, living at 3 Boswall Parkway, Edinburgh, at the time of his death at the Royal Victoria Hospital, Edinburgh. He never married.
  - Dorothea McIntosh (1921–2012) married Donald Thomas Parnham (7th February 1916–1990), a leatherworker born at Grantham, Lincolnshire, at St Andrew (Edinburgh) in 1947. She was living at 3 Boswall Parkway, Edinburgh with her brother at the time of his death. They had a son, David William Parnham, in 1953.

Carnwath village on the southern edge of the Pentland Hills in Lanarkshire is about fifty kilometres south of Edinburgh and Glasgow. It stands just north of the Roman road that connected the forts in Tweeddale with those on the Clyde. The castle dates to the mid 12th century but the only remains are the motte. At the centre of the village is Carnwath Cross, erected by 5th Lord Somerville in 1516 to celebrate the granting of burgh status in 1514. Carnwath collegiate church was established in 1386, although the only surviving part of the original church is St Mary's Aisle, built in 1424. A new parish church was built in 1869 beside the earlier buildings. Carnwath hosts the oldest foot race in Scotland and possibly Europe, the Red Hose Race. It dates back to 13th March 1508 and the local Laird provides a pair of red stockings as the prize.

Prestonpans is a former mining town, about thirteen kilometres east of Edinburgh, in East Lothian. The town is reputed to have been founded in the 11th century by Althamer, who was shipwrecked there. Monks arrived in the 12th century from Newbattle and Holyrood. By 1198 they were manufacturing salt in pans on the seashore and the settlement was renamed Prestonpans. Preston Tower was built by the Hamiltons in the mid-15th century. In 1596 one of the first post-Reformation churches was built in Prestonpans and ten years later the settlement became a parish in its own right. It was re-modelled in 1774. The memorial for the two World Wars, seen here on the right, also commemorates local people lost in the Spanish Civil War. Salt dominated industry in the early days of Prestonpans and, by the beginning of the 15th century, there were ten salt works. Other industries also flourished, including coal mining from 1210. There were many breweries, the first built in 1720, but all are now closed. Other sources of employment were a soap works and fishing, particularly herring and oysters. Nearby is the site of the 21st September 1745 Battle of Prestonpans (originally known as the Battle of Gladsmuir, then Tranent, before Prestonpans). It was the first significant encounter of the second Jacobite Rising. Charles Edward Stuart (Bonnie Prince Charlie or the Young Pretender) (1720–88), son of James Francis Edward Stuart (the Old Pretender) (1688–1766), led the Jacobite army and defeated the army loyal to King George II under Sir John Cope. Prestonpans was the birthplace of Same Shaw VC, who died in 1859. Also born there is Josh Taylor (born 1991), the first man from the United Kingdom to become undisputed world champion light welterweight boxer in the four-belt era.

- Elizabeth Archibald (born 13th December 1884), born at 38 Balfour Street, Leith, was a dressmaker in 1901 living with her parents.

Adam's paternal grandfather, also Adam Archibald (6th May 1819–21st January 1901), a gardener born at Prestonpans, East Lothian, married Janet née Menzies (c.1816–20th October 1899), born at Carnwath, Lanarkshire, at Colinton, Midlothian on 6th December 1839. They were living at Swanston Village, Colinton, Edinburgh in 1851, at 12 Simon Square by 1856 (he was a cab driver at the time) and by 1891 had moved to Broughton, Edinburgh. She died at 17 Shaw's Place, Edinburgh (where they were living by 1895) and he at Queensberry House, Edinburgh. In addition to Rennie they had six other children, all born at Colinton, Edinburgh:

- James Archibald (9th May 1841–1856) was a porter when he died of scarlet fever, registered at Newington and Grange, Edinburgh.
- Adam Archibald (4th May 1843–1903) married Grace Rush (1837–98), born at Lanteglos, Cornwall, on 7th September 1872 at St Mary's Church, Battersea, London. They were living at 11 Bolingbroke Road, Battersea at the time. Adam was an iron moulder in 1881 and 1891, when they were living at 25 Lucretia Road, Lambeth, London. Adam returned to Scotland after Grace died. His death was registered at St Giles, Edinburgh.

Swanston, a village on the southern edge of Edinburgh, is relatively isolated at the foot of the Pentland Hills and has been largely unaffected by development. It appears in 14th century charters granted in the reign of King David II and is listed as land owned by the Knights Templar. In the 16th century there were two large farms. Easter Swanston was owned by the Ross family and Wester Swanston originally by Sir John Cockburn and later the Foulis family. In 1670 the two farms were united under the Trotters. In 1758 Edinburgh Corporation was granted the right to extract water from springs in the area. The present village grew up in the 18th century for workers on Swanston Farm, which dates back to the 13th century. Thatched farm workers' cottages and a school were built around an informal green through which flows a small burn. Eight stone cottages on three sides of a communal green were added in the late 19th century. In the middle of the 20th century, the cottages still had earth floors and running water was not installed until 1934. Electricity reached the village in 1947. In 1956 Edinburgh's City Architect initiated a programme to renovate the cottages, which were then let to tenants. Most tenants purchased their properties under the Right to Buy scheme in the 1980s. Robert Louis Stevenson's (1850–94) family held a lease on Swanston Cottage 1867–80, which was used as a summer holiday home. He was attracted by the quiet country life and the feeling of remoteness, which may have had an influence on his later writing and his love of nature and wild places. Stevenson was a noted novelist, essayist, poet and travel writer, best known for *Treasure Island* and *Kidnapped*.

Queensberry House, built in the 17th century, is Category A listed. It stands on the south side of Canongate, Edinburgh and has been incorporated into the Scottish Parliament complex. About 1667 a Grand Lodging was constructed for Margaret Douglas of Balmakelly. The mansion house was built in 1681 for Charles Maitland, Lord Hatton and, in 1686, it was bought by the 1st Duke of Queensberry as his Edinburgh residence. His son, James, the 2nd Duke, inherited the house in 1695 and was one of the Scottish peers who signed the Treaty of Union in 1707. The public saw this as treasonous and self-serving and the house was attacked by the mob. While the Duke was involved in the negotiations surrounding the Treaty, he left his criminally insane son, James Douglas, Earl of Drumlanrig, unattended. James escaped from his room at the house and roasted and ate the kitchen boy. The building is said to be haunted by the boy's ghost. With the opening of the New Town, many of the wealthy moved out of the area. The house ceased to be the principal residence of the Dukes and became rented accommodation. It was sold to William Aitchison in 1801, who stripped the interior of its wooden panelling and fine fireplaces. From 1803 the building was a hospital, including during the cholera epidemic of the 1830s. In the 1850s it became a House of Refuge and Night Asylum for the homeless. In 1945 it became a home for the elderly homeless on a more long-term basis and was acquired by the Scottish Government in 1997. Queensberry House features in Ian Rankin's Inspector Rebus novel of 2000, *Set in Darkness*.

The Basra Memorial commemorates 40,682 members of Commonwealth forces (mostly Indian) who have no known grave and died on operations in Mesopotamia from autumn 1914 to the end of August 1921. It was designed by Edward Warren and was unveiled by Sir Gilbert Clayton on 27th March 1929. The panels record the names of all British personnel and Indian officers. However, Indian non-commissioned officers and other ranks are only commemorated by numbers and their names appear in a separate memorial register. The Memorial was originally eight kilometres north of Basra, on the main quay of the naval dockyard at Maqil, on the west bank of the Shatt-al-Arab. In 1997 it was moved by presidential decree thirty-two kilometres southwest, along the road to Nasiriyah, in the middle of what was a major battleground during the first Gulf War. The move was carried out by the Iraqi authorities and involved a considerable amount of manpower, cost and engineering to re-erect the Memorial in its entirety. It has suffered vandalism since, with some items missing, including the Cross of Sacrifice and the bronze plaques from the Wall of Remembrance that carry the names of the missing.

- William Archibald (22nd April 1846–16th May 1888) married Mary Ann Anderson (15th October 1849–14th December 1933) on 31st December 1869 at South Leith, Midlothian. They were living at 7 St Andrew Street, South Leith in 1871 and at 1 Richmond Place, Newington, Edinburgh in 1881. They had a son, Adam Archibald (1880–10th March 1957). Mary was a domestic servant in 1891, working for Robert Harrison at 56 Green Street, Calton, Glasgow, Lanarkshire. She had two sons with him – Robert Harrison 1890 and David Harrison (1892–7th January 1916), who was serving with 1st Seaforth Highlanders (642) when he died on active service (Basra Memorial, Iraq). Mary was a paper bag maker in 1901, living with her sons, Robert and David, at 10 Coulters Lane, Calton. She died of influenza and acute bronchitis at 271 Aitken Street, Glasgow.
- Margaret Archibald (5th June 1848–9th March 1909) married George Smith (c.1848–3rd September 1907), born at Keith, Banffshire, at Leith on 16th April 1875. He was a gardener (domestic servant) in 1881, when they were living at Strathclyde Street, Bridgeton, Glasgow and at Caldarvan East Lodge, Gartocharn, Alexandria, West Dunbartonshire in 1891 and 1901. They had five children – Janet 'Jenny' Smith 1875, James Smith 1878, Elizabeth Smith 1882, Adam Smith 1884 and George Smith 1887. She died at Alexandria, West Dunbartonshire.
- Elizabeth Archibald (28th June 1850–1926) married Robert Vallance (14th January 1848–1926) on 20th December 1872 at St George, Edinburgh. He was a gardener (domestic servant) in 1881, when they were living at Glenfullar Lodge, Dunbartonshire and at Ardgare Cottage, Dunbartonshire in 1891. By 1901 he was a dairyman, living with his family at Westerton Drive, Bridge of Allan, Stirlingshire. They both died at St Ninians, Stirlingshire. They had four

children – Margaret 'Maggie' Vallance 1873, Thomas Vallance (1874–97), Adam Vallance (1876–1932) and Janet 'Jessie' Vallance 1879. Her death was registered at St Ninians, Stirlingshire.
- Janet Archibald (born 1st January 1854), a twin with Rennie, born at Colinton, Midlothian.

His maternal grandfather, William Anderson (c.1806–17th July 1875), a carter, married Sarah née Blaik (c.1811–5th April 1884) on 29th September 1843 at Aberdour, Fife where they were both born. They were living on Main Street, Aberdour in 1861 and 1871 and she was still there in 1881. They both died at Easter Aberdour. In addition to Christina they had four other children, all born at Easter Aberdour:

- Robert Anderson (born 11th February 1844).
- James Anderson (17th April 1846–1887) was a message boy in 1861 and a mason in 1871, living with his parents.
- Janet Anderson (born 16th August 1851) was a dairy maid in 1871, living with her parents, and an outdoor worker in 1881, living with her mother. She had an illegitimate daughter, Janet 'Jessie' Young Anderson (born 2nd March 1875), who was living with her grandmother in 1881.
- Sarah Anderson (24th August 1856–1904) married John Thomson Alexander Fair (born 2nd March 1855), born at Kirkcaldy, in 1876 at Aberdour. He was a floor cloth printer in 1881 and 1891, when they were living at 17 Quality Street, Kirkcaldy. They were still there on 25th December 1895, when he was admitted to Fife and Kinross Asylum, suffering from depression. He was discharged on 7th March 1896. They were living at 20 Maryhall Street, Kirkcaldy in 1901. Her death was registered at Kirkcaldy and Abbotshall, Fife. They had five children:
    - James Fair (1876).
    - William Anderson Fair (1877–79).
    - Sarah Anderson Fair (1880).
    - John Anderson Fair (1883–84).
    - Helen 'Nellie' Alexander Fair (1885–1957).

Adam was educated at Leith Walk Public School, Edinburgh. He then trained at a technical school, gaining several trade certificates. Adam was a plasterer's apprentice at Leith and then worked as an outside foreman at Messrs Stuarts Granolithic Works, Duff Street, Edinburgh from July 1900.

Adam married Margaret Lauder Sinclair (10th July 1877–9th February 1958), born at 4 Arthur Street, Edinburgh, on 6th June 1902 at 6 Nicholson Street, Edinburgh. Adam was living at 24 Shaw's Street and Margaret at 33 James Street at the time. They lived at 53 Balfour Street, Leith, later moving to 39 Hillhouse Road, Blackhall, Edinburgh, where Margaret subsequently died. They had four children:

- Elizabeth Murray Archibald (29th June 1903–22nd February 1976), born at 41 Balfour Street, Leith, was a private secretary. She died unmarried at Western General Hospital, Edinburgh.
- Christina Anderson Archibald (27th December 1908–14th January 2000), born at 53 Balfour Street, Leith, was a bookshop manageress. She died unmarried at Brechin Infirmary, Angus, having lived at Bearhill Residential Home, 24 Castle Street, Brechin.
- Ada Margaret Rennie Archibald (7th May 1913–4th May 1989) was a telephonist. She died unmarried at Eastern General Hospital, Edinburgh.
- Rennie Archibald (15th February 1915–4th February 1988) was a joiner, living at 39 Hillhouse Road, Edinburgh, and

Leith Walk Primary School opened in 1876, replacing a previous institution in Pilrig. At the time the building was one of the largest and most expensive schools in Scotland, with a capacity for 1,057 pupils.

RAF Edzell in Aberdeenshire was first established during the Great War and closed in 1919. It was a civilian airfield in the 1930s but returned to military service in 1940. It was mainly an aircraft maintenance facility and by the end of the war held 800 aircraft in reserve. Various RAF units were based there:

- Relief Landing Ground for No.8 Service Flying Training School July 1940–March 1942 and No.2 Flying Instructors School January 1942–June 1945.
- No.44 Maintenance Unit August 1940–April 1949.
- No.1518 Beam Approach Training Flight June 1943–August 1944.
- Relief Landing Ground for No.8 Advanced Flying Training School May 1952–December 1953.
- No.5 Gliding School November 1952–September 1955 then No.662 Gliding School until May 1958.
- No.612 Squadron flying Vampires in the 1950s.

In the late 1950s the site was used for motor racing. One of the last sports car races was won by future double World Grand Prix Champion, Jim Clark (1936–68). It was leased to the United States Navy 1960–97 as part of the United States Navy Global High Frequency Direction Finding network, which tracked targets around the world. This included the AN/FRD-10 Circularly Disposed Antenna Array seen here, located in the quadrant formed between the two runways. By the end of the Cold War advances in technology had rendered the network obsolete, and the station closed in October 1997. RAF Edzell was also the home of the US 17th Space Surveillance Squadron from October 1993 until 1997, operating sensors in the Low-Altitude Space Surveillance System.

eventually became a clerk of works. He married Anne 'Annie' Belford Christie (28th February 1912–27th April 2006), a stationer's shop assistant, born at Gallowhill, Brechin, Angus, on 26th November 1942 at Queen Street Church, Edinburgh. Rennie died at 25 Castle Street, Brechin, Angus. Annie was living at Bearhill Nursing Home, 24 Castle Street, Brechin at the time of her death at Ninewells Hospital, Dundee. They had two children:

- ○ Annie Margaret Archibald (born 31st August 1946), born at Fyfe-Jamieson Maternity Home, Forfar, Angus, was a shoe shop assistant, living at 25 Castle Street, Brechin, Angus at the time of her marriage to Thomas Donald Aird (born c.1943), a US Navy Communications Technician 2nd Class, on 7th January 1967 at Dun House Hotel, Dundee, Angus. He was serving at the US Base, Edzell, Angus. She was living at Prince George, Virginia, USA in 1988.
- ○ Morag Archibald (30th October 1948) was a domestic maid, living at 25 Castle Street, Brechin, Angus at the time of her marriage to Charles Malcolm Barron (born 1947), a farm tractor man, on 8th July 1967 at Dun House Hotel, Dundee, Angus. They had two children – Malcolm Terence Barron (born 24th September 1967) and Caroline Ann Barron (born 25th July 1971).

Margaret's father, William Sinclair (23rd September 1833–4th February 1903), a mason, married Elizabeth née Murray (1st August 1835–15th April 1913), a domestic servant born at Olrig, Caithness, on 18th June 1858 at Castleton, Olrig. He was living at Durness Street, Thurso, Caithness at the time. By 1901 he was a postman. He died at 33 James Street, Edinburgh and she at 53 Balfour Street, Leith. In addition to Margaret they had six other children:

- Euphemia Sinclair (18th July 1858–1929), born at Bank Street, Thurso, married Robert Glover, a cooper at a brewery, on 5th December 1879 at 4 Arthur Street, Edinburgh. They had a daughter, Elizabeth Murray Glover (4th September 1880–1903), who never married.
- William Murray Sinclair (15th June 1862–1934), born at Newington, Edinburgh, married Janet Russell (31st October 1864–1943) at Leith in 1884. He was a stamper in the General Post Office in 1891, when they were living at 68 Drum Place, Leith South. By 1901 he was a head stamper, when they were living at 6 Wolseley Terrace, Canongate, Edinburgh and at 35 Meadowbank Crescent, Canongate in 1902. They had eight children:
    - ○ Janet Russell Sinclair (1884–1957) married James Williamson in 1908, registered at Canongate.
    - ○ William Murray Sinclair (born 1886).
    - ○ James Russell Sinclair (born 1887).
    - ○ Jane Liddle Sinclair (born 1890).
    - ○ John Sinclair (c.1894–1958).

    - Elizabeth Murray Sinclair (c.1896–1974) married William Brown Hamilton in 1923, registered at Canongate.
    - Alice Russell Sinclair (born 1899).
    - Arthur Russell Sinclair (1901–31st July 1943) married Margery Amy and they were living at Sandy Bay, Tasmania. He was serving in 2/3rd Machine Gun Battalion, Australian Imperial Force (TX2360) when he died on active service in Burma (Thanbyuzayat War Cemetery, Myanmar – A12 A 10).
- Christina Swanson Sinclair (23rd June 1864–1879), born at 169 The Pleasance, Edinburgh.
- Alexander Sinclair (5th December 1866–1882).
- John Sinclair (born 3rd April 1869), born at 4 Arthur Street, Edinburgh, was a postman in 1901, living with his parents at 33 James Street, Edinburgh.
- Elizabeth Murray Sinclair (24th February 1874–1949), born at 31 Richmond Street, Edinburgh, married Thomas Robertson in 1897, registered at St Andrew, Edinburgh.

On 8th December 1915 Adam enlisted at Edinburgh under the Derby Scheme and transferred to the Reserve next day (213078). He was described as just over 5′ 5½″ tall and his religious denomination was Presbyterian. He was mobilised on 9th November 1916 in the Royal Engineers and his trade was assessed as plasterer superior. Next day he reported to Depot Royal Engineers, Chatham, Kent and was posted to the RE Training Centre, Newark, Nottinghamshire on 26th March 1917. On 28th August he was posted to 5th Depot Company RE, Newark and transferred to the Durham Light Infantry (77054) on 16th September. Next day he proceeded to France from Folkestone, Kent and joined 1/7th Durham Light Infantry (Pioneers), 50th Division on 21st September.

On 28th October Adam was gassed and was evacuated to Britain on 6th November. He transferred to a command depot on 19th February 1918 and to the RE Depot, Chatham on 23rd May. Next day he joined 2nd Provisional Company at Chatham and transferred to 5th Reserve Battalion, Christchurch, Bournemouth, Hampshire on 29th June. On 5th August he transferred to Northern Command Discharge Centre, Ripon, Yorkshire for release to shipbuilding, but was rejected by the Admiralty as his trade was not suitable. Adam transferred to 645th West Lancashire Field Company RE, Colchester, Essex on 13th August and returned to France on 26th August from H Company, 5th Reserve Battalion RE. He joined the RE Base Depot and then 218th Field Company RE on 7th September. Adam was gassed again on 3rd November. **Awarded the VC for his actions on the Sambre-Oise Canal, north of Ors, France on 4th November 1918, LG 6th January 1919.**

Adam was admitted for treatment for gas injury and was discharged to 4th Convalescent Depot, Le Havre on 6th January 1919. However, he was still suffering from gas poisoning and was admitted to 6th General Hospital, Rouen on 10th January. He was evacuated to Britain on 29th January to join 5th Reserve

Battalion RE, Christchurch, Hampshire. By 14th February he was at Stoke-on-Trent War Hospital. He contracted rheumatism and myalgia and was discharged from the Army from 5th Reserve Battalion RE, no longer fit for war service, on 17th April 1919 and was awarded a 20% disability pension of £-/5/6 per week to be reviewed after a year.

The VC was presented by the King in the quadrangle of Buckingham Palace on 31st May 1919. He was one of the VC Honour Guard at the burial of the Unknown Warrior at Westminster Abbey on 11th November 1920. Adam returned to work at the Granolithic Ferro-Concrete Works. He later became the Works Manager and held this position until retiring on 28th February 1949.

Adam attended a number of VC Reunions – the VC Garden Party at Buckingham Palace on 26th June 1920, the VC Dinner at the Royal Gallery of the House of Lords, London on 9th November 1929, the Victory Day Celebration Dinner & Reception at The Dorchester, London on 8th June 1946 and the VC Centenary Celebrations at Hyde Park, London on 26th June 1956. He was a Freemason and a member of Elgin & Bruce Lodge No.1077 and St James' Operative Lodge No.97.

On 21st September 1944 he attended a civic luncheon hosted by the Lord Provost, Sir William Young Darling CBE MC, in Edinburgh at which John Alexander Cruickshank VC was the guest of honour. Among those present were fellow VCs Charles George Bonner, William Robertson and David Lowe Macintyre. Adam was present at the inspection of the British Legion in King's Park, Edinburgh by King George VI on 30th June 1946.

39 Hillhouse Road, Blackhall, Edinburgh. (*Rightmove*)

Warriston Crematorium is Edinburgh's oldest, based upon Easter Warriston House, which was built in 1808. A number of internal structural changes were required to adapt it and the work was completed in 1929. During the world wars 145 servicemen and women were cremated there and are commemorated on memorial panels at the end of the columbarium. Amongst those cremated there is Donald George Revie OBE (1927–89), the England international footballer and manager, best known for his successful management of Leeds United 1961–74. Other VCs cremated at Warriston are:

- Captain Charles George Bonner RN (1884–1951).
- Brigadier Arthur Edward Cumming (1896–1971).
- Lieutenant David Lowe MacIntyre (1895–1967).
- Captain Henry Peel Ritchie RN (1879–1958).
- Drum Major Walter Potter Ritchie (1892–1965).

Adam Archibald died at his home at 39 Hillhouse Road, Edinburgh on 11th March 1957. He was cremated at Warriston Crematorium, Edinburgh on 13th March and his ashes were scattered in the Garden of Remembrance there. He is recorded in the Book of Remembrance. Adam is commemorated in a number of other places:

- A Department for Communities and Local Government commemorative paving stone was dedicated on the corner of Shaw's Street and Spey Terrace, Broughton, Edinburgh on 2nd November 2018.
- Named on the For Valour Board at the Royal Engineers Museum, Brompton Barracks, Prince Arthur Road, Gillingham, Kent.

The For Valour Board at the Royal Engineers Museum. (*Memorials to Valour*)

In addition to the VC he was awarded the British War Medal 1914–20, Victory Medal 1914–19, George VI Coronation Medal 1937 and Elizabeth II Coronation Medal 1953. The medals were acquired by the Royal Engineers in 1998 and are held by the Royal Engineers Museum, Prince Arthur Road, Gillingham, Kent.

LIEUTENANT WILLIAM DAVIDSON BISSETT
6th Battalion, Princess Louise's (Argyll & Sutherland Highlanders)

William Bissett was born on 7th July 1893 at Bauchlands, St Martins, Perthshire, Scotland. He was registered as Bisset at birth, as were most births, marriages and deaths in his family. However, he signed his name as Bissett when he married and most official documents use this form. His father, John Bisset (8th January 1870–25th September 1922), born at Barnhill, Kinnoull, Perth, was a plumber in 1882. He married Helen 'Nellie' Milne née Davidson (born 14th September 1870), a domestic servant born at 16 St Andrew Street, Dundee, Forfarshire on 30th December 1892 at Bridgend Hall, Perth. He was living at Cornton Place, Crieff in 1901, when his wife and children were visiting her parents at 5 Ballantrae Place, Perth. John was living at Ewing Cottage, Comrie Road, Crieff when he died at 1 Burrell Street, Crieff. William had three siblings:

Crieff, a market town in Perth and Kinross between Perth and Crianlarich, is now a tourist hub with various attractions including whisky and glass. For centuries cattle were driven south to Crieff for sale to the growing population centres in Lowland Scotland and northern England. The Michaelmas cattle sale could see up to 30,000 animals. Rob Roy MacGregor and his followers passed through Crieff in October 1714, singing Jacobite songs and drinking toasts to the uncrowned King James VIII. In 1716 Highlanders returning from the Battle of Sheriffmuir burned most of the town to the ground. In 1731 James Drummond, Duke of Perth, laid out James Square and established a textile industry. In the 1745 uprising the Highlanders wanted to burn the town again, but it was saved by the Duke of Perth, a friend and supporter of Prince Charles. The following year the Jacobite army was quartered in the town and Prince Charles Edward Stuart held his final war council in the Drummond Arms Inn. During the 19th century, Crieff became a fashionable tourist destination for the wealthy. The railway arrived in 1856 and closed in 1964. The Crieff hydropathic establishment (now Crieff Hydro) opened in 1868. John Manson Craig VC (1896–1970) was educated at Crieff. Coincidentally two *Star Wars* actors, Ewan McGregor (born 1971) and Denis Lawson (born 1947), were both raised and educated in Crieff.

- John Milne Davidson Bisset (18th October 1897–1948) was also born at Bauchlands, St Martin's. He married Margaret Jane Watson (1883–1958) at Monifieth West in 1920. John was working at Elderslie Tramway Depot, Paisley, Renfrewshire in September 1922.
- Georgina Taylor Bisset (29th March 1901–30th December 1904) was born at 5 Ballantrae Place, Perth, and died at 1 Dollerie Terrace, Crieff. She was three days old and was recorded as Jane at the time of the 1901 Census.
- George Milne Davidson Bissett (born 12th June 1906) was born at 106 East High Street, Crieff, Perthshire.

William's paternal grandfather, James Bisset (c.1839–28th September 1872), a railway engine fitter born at Kinnoull, Perthshire, was living with his parents at Bellwood Lodge, Dundee Roadside, Perth in 1871. He married Elizabeth née McKillop (20th November 1844–7th August 1897), born at Tayview, Barnhill, Perthshire, on 22nd October 1869 at Perth. They were living at 17 James Street, Pilrig, Edinburgh, Midlothian in September 1872. He was a railway goods guard at the time of his death at the west end of the goods yard at Waverley Bridge Station, Edinburgh. She died at Balhepburn Fishing Station, Rhynd, Perthshire. In addition to John they had two other children born at Barnhill:

- Elizabeth Bisset (4th August 1871–1905).
- Janet Bisset (born 21st February 1873).

St Andrew Street, Dundee, where William's mother was born (Dundee Central Library). Dundee, on the Firth of Tay, is Scotland's fourth largest city. Historically within the county of Angus, it became a burgh in the late 12th century and a royal burgh in 1292. There were many turbulent times. The town was occupied by the English and recaptured by Robert the Bruce in 1312. It suffered during the Rough Wooing 1543–50 and was again occupied by the English in 1547. However, unable to defend the town the following year, it was burnt to the ground. In 1645 Dundee was besieged by the Royalists and was destroyed by Parliamentary forces in 1651. The town was held by the Jacobites in the 1715 rising and, on 6th January 1716, the Old Pretender (James VIII) made a public entry there. In December 1879 the town suffered one of the worst rail disasters in Britain when the Tay rail bridge collapsed during a storm, resulting in the loss of seventy-five lives. The economy in mediaeval times centred on raw wool and the production of finished textiles followed in the 15th century. The textile industry was revolutionised by the introduction of large mills and an expansion of the whaling industry followed a second Bounty Act in 1750. As a result of these changes the population increased rapidly in the late 18th and early 19th centuries. The linen export bounty was phased out between 1825 and 1832, resulting in demand for cheaper textiles. Jute, lubricated with whale oil, was processed in mechanised mills and sold for a quarter of the price of flax. The jute industry dominated Dundee in the second half of the 19th century, with up to sixty-two jute mills, employing 50,000 workers. Other industries expanded to support jute production, in particular whaling, maritime and shipbuilding. Up to 200 ships per year were built there, including Robert Falcon Scott's Antarctic research vessel, RRS *Discovery*, which is displayed at Discovery Point. Whaling ceased in 1912 and shipbuilding in 1981. In addition to jute, Dundee became known for smaller industries such as James Keiller's marmalade and the publishers, DC Thomson. The city was therefore said to be built on three Js - Jute, Jam and Journalism. In the early 20th century reduced demand for jute and competition from India caused the industry to fall into decline. Unemployment peaked in the inter-war period but, after the Second World War, there was a major recovery due to the introduction of light engineering and later microelectronics, biomedical and technological industries. A thirty-year regeneration project for Dundee Waterfront is expected to be completed in 2031. A new Victoria and Albert Museum opened in 2018, the first outside London. A notable resident was Adam Duncan, 1st Viscount Duncan of Camperdown, Baron of Lundie (1731–1804), born and educated at Dundee. He rose to Admiral in the Royal Navy and in October 1797 defeated the Dutch fleet off Camperdown, one of the most significant actions in naval history.

His maternal grandfather, William Davidson (11th November 1845–1906), born at St Martin's, Perthshire, was a journeyman joiner living at Gellatly Street, Dundee at the time of his marriage to Jane née Milne (20th September 1843–c.1916), a domestic servant born at Fordoun, Kincardineshire, on 3rd April 1868 at Auchenblae, Fordoun. They were living at 174 Seagate, St Andrew, Dundee in 1871, at 8 Ferry Road, Dundee in 1881, at Bauchlands Cottages, St Martin's, Perthshire in 1891 and at 5 Ballantrae Place, Perth in 1901. Jane was living at Dunfermline, Fife when she died at 53 High Street, Musselburgh. In addition to Helen they had three other children:

- George Milne Davidson (9th July 1868–5th July 1928) was born at Auchenblae, Fordoun. He married Maggie Scott Watson (1857–1936) at St Martin's,

Perthshire in 1890. Maggie and her daughter Eva were living with her father at St Martin's in 1891. George was an estate joiner in 1901, when they were living at Fotheringham Cottage, Inverarity, Angus. He was a clerk of works at Loretto School, living at 23 High Street, Musselburgh, at the time of his death at Huntly Lodge, Erkside. Maggie was later living at 60 Falcon Avenue, Edinburgh, Midlothian. They had at least four daughters – Eva Davidson (14th December 1890–1945), Jane Davidson (15th July 1895), Georgina Davidson (18th November 1897–1952) and Margaret Scott Davidson (13th October 1899–25th December 1978).

Seagate, Dundee, where William's maternal grandparents were living in 1871.

- John Davidson (born 30th June 1877), born at 8 Ferry Road, Dundee, Forfarshire, was a joiner in 1901 living with his parents.
- Jessie Davidson (born 25th July 1880) was a shop assistant in 1901 living with her parents.

William was educated at Taylor's Institution, Crieff. He was a member of the choir at St Columba's Episcopal Church, the town band and a minstrel troupe at the local Unionist Club in Crieff.

He enlisted in 6th (Renfrewshire) Battalion, Princess Louise's (Argyll and Sutherland Highlanders) (Territorial Force) on 29th April 1912 (1674), giving his occupation as engineer. It is believed that the future Captain A Henderson VC served in the same company. William was mobilised with 1/6th Battalion in August 1914 and went to France on 1st May 1915. He was promoted lance corporal on 25th July, corporal on 24th October and sergeant and Battalion Bombing Sergeant on 1st May 1916. He returned to England in September for officer training and was commissioned in 3rd (Reserve) Battalion on 19th December 1916. On 2nd May 1917 he returned to France and rejoined 1/6th Battalion on 22nd May. The Battalion

Taylor's Institution on Perth Road was founded for the education of the children of the poor of Crieff, with funds from a trust established in 1841 after the death of William Taylor of Cornton, a tallow-chandler. The school and master's residence were built in 1842–43. The average attendance was about 200. In 1859 the residue of Taylor's estate came into the hands of the trustees and the institution was enlarged by the addition of a Female Industrial School. The school building later became the British Legion Hall. In 1981 it was listed Category B by Historic Scotland.

An Episcopal church was consecrated in Lodge Street (formerly Lodge Brae), Crieff in 1848 in the name of St Michael and All Angels. Subscribers to the building included Queen Adelaide, William Gladstone, the Archbishops of Canterbury and Armagh and the Bishops of London and Gloucester. The building is now a tearoom. Disagreements with the Bishop of St Andrews led to the church being boarded up in 1862 and it fell into disrepair. The congregation raised money to build St Columba's Church to hold 200 people but, with a growing population, a larger church was soon needed. In 1877 the second St Columba's, seen here, was built. In the 1980s a survey revealed many faults, including problems with the tower. It was demolished and a modern building replaced it in 1986.

moved to Italy in December and remained there until April 1918. During this period it is possible that William was attached to the Machine Gun Corps, rejoining the Battalion when it returned from Italy. Promoted lieutenant on 19th June. **Awarded the VC for his actions east of Maing, France on 25th October 1918, LG 6th January 1919.**

Having been admitted to hospital he returned to duty on 16th November. He was also admitted to hospital on 18th January 1919 and served in 10th Battalion from April. The VC was presented by the King in the quadrangle at Buckingham Palace on 10th July. William was demobilised on 24th September 1919 and remained in

The French Croix de Guerre was first awarded in 1915 to individuals or units distinguishing themselves by acts of heroism. Some notable recipients include:

- Josephine Baker – American born French dancer, singer and actress for her work in the Resistance during the Second World War.
- Jacques Cousteau – pioneer diver and underwater filmmaker.
- General Dwight D Eisenhower – Supreme Allied Commander during Operation OVERLORD.
- Noor Inayat Khan GC and Violette Szabo GC – British SOE agents executed by the Nazis.
- Audie Murphy – American actor and the most decorated US soldier of WW2, including the Medal of Honor.
- General George S Patton – commander of US Third Army in the Second World War.
- Theodore Roosevelt – son of President Theodore Roosevelt, awarded the Medal of Honor for 6th June 1944 on Utah Beach.
- James Stewart – American actor for his role in the liberation of France as a USAAF Colonel.
- Major Richard D Winters – Easy Company, 506th Parachute Infantry Regiment, made famous by the TV series and book *Band of Brothers*.
- Sergeant Alvin C York – American First World War Medal of Honor winner and subject of a film in 1941 starring Gary Cooper.

6th Battalion. **Awarded the French Croix de Guerre, LG 15th December 1919.** He was granted a temporary commission as a lieutenant in 5th (Defence Force) Battalion, Manchester Regiment on 13th April 1921. On 1st July he transferred to the Defence Force General List and was appointed temporary staff captain. He relinquished the Defence Force commission on ceasing to be employed on 18th July and his Territorial Force/ Army commission on 30th September 1921, retaining the rank of lieutenant. On 14th June 1923 he applied for a recruiting officer's post but was ineligible because he had not been commissioned from the ranks and was not in receipt of an officer's pension.

Services started in a schoolroom at West End Green in 1846 and the church was founded formally in 1875. Construction of the current Emmanuel Church, on the corner of Lyncroft Gardens and Fortune Green Road, began in June 1897 and it was completed in June 1903. The building was Grade II listed by English Heritage in January 1999.

William was presented with an inscribed gold watch and War Bonds from Crieff at Porteous Hall. His parents were present at the ceremony, which was presided over by Provost Mungall. He was also presented with a silver cigar holder by the choir of St Columba's Church, Crieff and a silver cigarette case from his fellow officers.

William attended the funeral of AP Sullivan VC at the Guard's Chapel, Wellington Barracks, London on 13th April 1937. He was Chairman of the London Branch of the Argyll and Sutherland Highlanders Association in the 1940s and was also a member of the Royal British Legion at Overton-on-Dee, Flintshire. He attended two VC reunions – the Victory Day Celebration Dinner & Reception at The Dorchester, London on 8th June 1946 and the VC Centenary Celebrations at Hyde Park, London on 26th June 1956.

William Bissett married Hilda Heywood (6th February 1884–1971), born at Bury, Lancashire, on 9th July 1919 at Emmanuel Parish Church, West Hampstead, London. They both gave their address as 1 Lyncroft Gardens, Hounslow, London. In 1901 she was assisting her father in the family business. She was a visitor living with Harry Foster and Maud Francis Burt at 1 Patrick Road, Nottingham at the time of the 1911 Census. Hilda was a nursing sister with the Territorial Force Nursing Service and went to France on 20th February 1918. Her death was registered at Wrexham, Denbighshire. When she married her age was recorded as twenty-nine, indicating birth in 1890. When she died her date of birth was recorded as 6th February 1890. However, her birth was registered in 1884 and her age at successive censuses in 1891, 1901 and 1911 reflect this. They lived at various addresses:

Library Street, Wigan, where William and Hilda were living in 1921.

Queensbridge Hall, Overton-on-Dee (The Market).

Ins House, Thornygate, Barnard Castle, Co Durham – November 1920.
Poahatch, Startforth, Barnard Castle.
11 Library Street, Wigan, Lancashire – 1921.
Holly Cottage, Cousley Wood, Wadhurst, East Sussex – 1923.
38a Avenue Road, Hornsey, London – 1929.
17 Duke's Avenue, Muswell Hill, London – 1934.
Beechwood, Station Avenue, Walton-on-Thames – 1938.
Cae Gwegi, Capel Curig, Caernarfonshire.
Betws-Y-Coed, Caernarfonshire.
Queensbridge Hall, Overton-on-Dee, Flintshire – 1960s.

Hilda and William had one son:

- Donald Gardner Bissett (born 1922), born at Bridge of Weir, Renfrewshire, was educated at St Paul's School, London. He served in the East Surrey Regiment and rose to the rank of corporal. While on weekend leave with his parents at Walton-on-Thames, Surrey, he stole his father's medals, insignia, pay book and cheque book. He wore the VC, Croix de Guerre and major's rank crowns while cashing his father's cheques and defrauded him of £45. On 19th July 1946 he was jailed for nine months with hard labour at Belfast, Northern Ireland. Donald married Eunice Dangerfield (born 1930), born at Cardiff, Glamorgan, in 1952, registered at Pancras, London. They had a son, Alister Campbell Bissett (born 1953).

Hilda's father, Edward Wigley Heywood (1837–March 1927), born at Heywood, Lancashire, was living with his parents at Market Street in 1851 when he was employed in the family printing and stationary shop. He was a letterpress printer in 1861 living with his parents at Caxton Cottage, Fearn Street, Heywood, Lancashire.

He married Phoebe née Mason (c.1844–April 1928) on 19th September 1865 at Bury. They were living at 37 York Street, Heywood, Lancashire in 1871 and at 7 Market Place, Heywood in 1881, by when he was a pianoforte tuner and seller. They had moved to 12 Haymarket Street, Bury by 1891 and to 39 Manchester Road, Bury by 1901. He was a music professor in 1906. By 1911 they were living at 26 Newman Avenue, Springfield, Wigan. They both died at Wigan. In addition to Hilda they had nine other children, all born at Heywood:

- Eleanor Cecilia Heywood (1867–1944) was a music teacher and vocalist in 1891 and 1911, living with her parents. She never married and died at Stirling, Scotland.
- John Heywood (19th July 1870–11th April 1943) was a music teacher and vocalist in 1891, living with his parents. By 1901 he was a music teacher and musical instrument dealer still living with his parents. John was a music professor when he married Annie Gee (18th March 1874–19th December 1959), born at Hayfield, on 25th October 1906 at Hayfield Parish Church, Derbyshire. He was a pianoforte tuner and repairer in 1911, when they were living at 30 Linton Road, Bury. In 1939 they were living at 15 Swinley Road, Wigan, by when he was a musical instrument and radio dealer. John subsequently died there. Annie was living at 5 Melling Road, Southport, Lancashire at the time of her death at 11 Scarisbrick Street, Southport. They had three children:
    - Edith Heywood (1907–67) married Alfred Joseph Crossley (3rd October 1904–1991) at Wigan in 1927.
    - Marjorie Heywood (12th December 1908–1988) was an assistant ladies' hairdresser, living with her parents in 1939. She married Malcolm Earle Josiah Simpson (4th December 1914–1988) at Wigan in 1946. They had a son, John M Simpson, in 1947.
    - John Heywood (9th September 1913–1977).
- Edith Heywood (1872–73).
- Gilbert Heywood (1874–1st October 1953) was a music teacher and vocalist in 1891 living with his parents. He married Millicent Smith (1878–17th March 1926), born at Leytonstone, Essex, on 27th December 1902 at St Thomas Church, Bury. They were living at 20 Rock Street, Bury in 1911 by when he was a musical instrument dealer. Gilbert enlisted in the Army Service Corps on 18th April 1918 and was called up on 15th July at the Reception Depot, Bury (M/413252). He was living at 332 Hornby Street, Bury and was described as a managing director and piano tuner, 5′ 7″ tall, with fresh complexion, dark brown hair, brown eyes and his religious denomination was Church of England. He joined the ASC MT Depot at Sydenham on 18th July and transferred to Isleworth on 9th August. He passed the Learners Test as a lorry driver at Isleworth on 3rd October and was granted 4th Rate Corps Pay the next day. He served with No.3 Company, Norwood Depot, London from 9th October, transferred to the Dispersal Centre,

Kelsey Manor on 11th January 1919 and was demobilised to the Class Z Reserve from the Dispersal Unit, Wimbledon on 8th February. They were living at 3 Royal Avenue, Bury at the time of her death there. They had two daughters:

  - Doris Edith Heywood (23rd December 1904) married Herbert Butcher Webb (1891–1960) at Bury in 1940.
  - Norah Heywood (29th March 1910).

Gilbert married Gladys Hilda Hutchinson née Ramsden (31st October 1889–2nd December 1950), born at Bury, in 1928. She had married Harry Fleming Hutchinson (1882–2nd April 1921), a doctor born at Chorley. Lancashire, in 1917. He was a medical student in 1911, living with his parents at 2 Queen's Road, Chorley. They were living at 234 The Elms, Walmersley Road, Bury at the time of his death at 24 Rose Hill, Dorking, Surrey. Gilbert and Gladys were living at 951 Walmersley Road, Bury at the time of her death there. He was living at West Bank, Manchester Road, Bury at the time of his death.

- Frederick Heywood (1877–19th September 1907) was studying chemistry and was living with the Jenkins family at 24 Brighton Grove, Manchester at the time of the 1901 Census. He was a chemist's assistant when he married Irene Millicent 'Milly' Jenkin (12th June 1880–9th June 1956), born at Poplar, London, in 1904 at Chorlton, Lancashire. She was living with her parents at 5 Rippingham Road, Withington, Lancashire in 1891. They were living at 12 Campbell Road, Rusholme, Manchester at the time of his death at 95 Brackenbury Road, Preston. By 1911 Milly was a boarding housekeeper, living with her son at 85 Hamilton Road, Longsight, Manchester. She was living with Ellen Kennedy (born 18th May 1865), a retired teacher and spinster, at 97 High Street, Enfield, Middlesex in 1939. She was living at 54 Burlington Road, Blackpool, Lancashire at the time of her death at Victoria Hospital, Blackpool. They had a son:
  - Frederick Denis Heywood (28th July 1905–1974) is understood to have married Rhoda Hemingway at Manchester in 1931.
- Lilian Heywood (born 3rd February 1879) was a schoolteacher in 1911, boarding with her future sister-in-law's mother at Ivy Cottage, Rose Fold, Penwortham, Lancashire (see below under Wilfred Mason Heywood). She married Joseph Thomas Whiteside (14th January 1882–12th June 1959), born at Ormskirk, Lancashire, in 1911 at Preston, Lancashire. He was a professor of music in 1939, when they were living at 17 Oregon Square, Orpington, Kent. They were living at 23 East View Terrace, Black Bull Lane, Fulwood, Preston at the time of his death. They had a daughter:
  - Margaret Whiteside (born 1914) married Horace Olvanhill Winkfield (1st June 1911–1984), born at Kensington, London, in 1942 at Preston. They had three daughters – Rowena M Winkfield 1943, Christina A Winkfield 1944 and Marguerita D Winkfield 1948.
- Edward Geoffrey Russel Heywood (born and died 1881).

- Wilfred Mason Heywood (1887–1941) was an office boy at a calico bleach works in 1901. He married Vivienne Beck (6th January 1890–19th March 1977), a launderess born at Hartlepool, Co Durham, in 1911 at Preston, Lancashire. She was living with her parents at Ivy Cottage, Rose Fold, Penwortham, Preston. They lived at 116 Ribbleton Lane, Preston. Wilfred became a musician and member of a band. He travelled to New York, USA aboard RMS *Caronia* from Liverpool, departing on 20th April 1912 and to Boston, USA aboard SS *Arabic* departing Liverpool on 28th January 1913. He served as an acting corporal in 8th and 1/4th Battalions, South Lancashire Regiment during the Great War (29766). After the war he resumed his career as a musician. He travelled to Halifax, Nova Scotia aboard SS *Royal George*, departing Southampton on 27th November 1919 and arriving on 9th December. He travelled to New York aboard SS *Royal George*, departing Southampton on 30th March 1920 and returning to Liverpool aboard RMS *Caronia* on 5th July. They were living at 17 Molyneux Road, Waterloo, Liverpool in 1920. Vivienne was a nurse in 1939, living alone at 13 Oregon Square, Orpington, two doors away from her sister-in-law, Lilian Whiteside (see above). Wilfred was a resident at the County Mental Hospital, Lancaster and subsequently died there. Vivienne was living at 55 Arbour Street, Southport, Lancashire at the time of her death there. They had a daughter:
    - Dorothy Vivienne Heywood (17th September 1913–January 1987).
- Gladys Heywood (1889–1950).

Branston Depot in Staffordshire was originally the National Machine Gun Factory but by the time construction was completed in November 1918 the Great War was over and no machine guns were ever manufactured there. Crosse & Blackwell produced their famous Branston Pickle there 1920–25 and the Branston Artificial Silk Co produced Rayon there 1927–30. In the late 1930s the War Office again acquired the site as the Army's main clothing depot. It closed in 1961 when operations moved to Bicester. Parts of the site were used for storage for Royal Ordnance 1964–75. More recently parts of the site have been developed for housing.

On returning to civilian life William was in business in London. His final occupation was listed as an engineer at Queensbridge, Overton-on-Dee, Maelor, Flintshire. He was recalled to the Regular Army Reserve of Officers for service with the Royal Army Ordnance Corps as a lieutenant (108084) on 15th May 1939. On 28th September he was promoted war substantive captain and temporary major, serving as Deputy Chief Inspector Clothing Depot Branston, Staffordshire. On 24th May 1940 he transferred to the Pioneer Corps as a war substantive captain with seniority from 15th May 1939. He took command of 177th Company on 15th August 1940 and 206th

In 1833 Sir Watkin Williams Wyn founded the Dispensary and in 1838 the Infirmary was built in Regent Street, Wrexham. Many extensions and improvements followed and it was the town's hospital until 1918, when it was decided to build a new hospital as a memorial to those lost in the Great War. The foundation stone was dedicated on 2nd November 1923 with the Prince of Wales in attendance. The Wrexham and East Denbighshire War Memorial Hospital was opened in 1926. In 1934 Maelor General Hospital was opened by David Lloyd George MP. It was a combination of Croesnewydd Hospital, the Joint Fever Hospital and Plas Maelor. Maelor General Hospital, which had 276 beds, worked in conjunction with the War Memorial Hospital and in 1939 the Emergency Medical Services commandeered the buildings as a military hospital. In 1986 acute services at the War Memorial Hospital were integrated onto the Maelor campus with the completion of the first phase of development, which was opened by the Duchess of Kent and renamed Wrexham Maelor Hospital. In 1995 a new Acute Psychiatric facility opened.

Company on 8th June 1941 in Northern Ireland. Lieutenant John O'Neill VC MM was one of his subordinates. William's Company was involved in cable and airfield construction, agriculture, ordnance work and fire picquets. He commanded 295th Company from 2nd May 1942 at Ordnance Depot, Nesscliffe, Shropshire. The unit moved to Liverpool, Lancashire and the Wirral, Cheshire on fire-watching duties. He later commanded a unit in Devon and Hampshire, which was employed on road construction, and with the Royal Army Ordnance Corps. He relinquished command on 8th August 1944 and his

Pentrebychan Crematorium, Wrexham.

The Church of St Mary's the Virgin in Overton-on-Dee is famous for the ring of yew trees in the churchyard. There was probably a wattle and daub oratory on the site in the 7th century and by the 12th century the first stone church had been built. Towards the end of the 14th century a larger church was built and its tower remains. The nave was replaced in the 1450s and the bells were installed in the reign of James I. The church was damaged during the English Civil War. In 1710 the chancel was added on the eastern end of the nave. The north aisle and vestry on the south side of the tower were added in 1819 and by 1855 the north aisle had been widened and a south aisle built to match it. An extensive restoration was carried out 1868–70. In 1920 the north transept was made into Lady Chapel and the pulpit and choir stalls were moved to their present positions. In 1992 a new yew tree was planted by Queen Elizabeth II during her visit to Overton to mark the 700th anniversary of King Edward I's Royal Charter on 20th July 1292.

commission on 23rd September 1945, having exceeded the age limit of liability to recall, and was granted the honorary rank of major.

William died at Wrexham & East Denbighshire War Memorial Hospital, Wrexham on 12th May 1971. He was cremated at Pentrebychan Crematorium, Wrexham after a funeral service at St Mary's the Virgin, Overton-on-Dee on 17th May. His ashes are buried beneath a gravestone near the entrance of Aldershot Military Cemetery, Hampshire. Hilda was unable to attend the funeral as she was in hospital at Ellesmere, Shropshire. His son, Donald, was also absent, but his wife and son did attend. Department for Communities and Local Government commemorative paving stones were dedicated at Comrie War Memorial, Bridge Street, Comrie, Perthshire on 25th October 2018 and St Martin's War Memorial, Perth and Kinross on 28th October 2018.

The gravestone that marks where William's ashes are buried near the entrance of Aldershot Military Cemetery (Memorials to Valour).

In addition to the VC he was awarded the 1914–15 Star, British War Medal 1914–20, Victory Medal 1914–19, War Medal 1939–45, Defence Medal, George VI Coronation Medal 1937, Elizabeth II Coronation Medal 1953 and French Croix de Guerre 1918 with Bronze Palme. The VC is held by the Argyll and Sutherland Highlanders Regimental Museum, The Castle, Stirling.

The Argyll & Sutherland Highlanders Regimental Museum in the 15th century King's Old Building within Stirling Castle. The Castle, a Scheduled Ancient Monument, is one of the largest and most important in Scotland. It is surrounded on three sides by steep cliffs, creating a strong defensive position, guarding what was the farthest downstream crossing of the River Forth until the 1890s. Before the Union with England, Stirling Castle was one of the most used Scottish royal residences and several Scottish kings and queens were crowned there, including Mary Queen of Scots in 1542. The Castle has come under siege at least eight times, the last in 1746, when Bonnie Prince Charlie tried to take it.

472168 SERGEANT HUGH CAIRNS
46th Battalion (South Saskatchewan), Canadian Expeditionary Force

Hugh Cairns was born on 4th December 1896 at Ashington, Northumberland, England. His father, George Henry Cairns (1864–23rd September 1940), a coal miner born at Chatton, Northumberland, married Elizabeth Dores née Donkin (1869–22nd January 1948), born at Greenwell House, Lamesley, Co Durham, on 23rd May 1892 at Morpeth, Northumberland. She was a servant at the home of William and Elizabeth Atkinson, Pearson Cottage, Well Way, Morpeth in 1891. He was a deputy overman in 1901, when they were living at 59 Seventh Row, Ashington, Northumberland. By 1911 they had moved to 48 Third Row, Ashington. They emigrated to Canada aboard SS *Laurentic*, arriving at Québec on 13th May 1911, and settled at 713 29th Street, West Saskatoon, Saskatchewan. In 1913 they moved to 832 Avenue G, North Saskatoon and to 905 Avenue G North by April 1916. They both subsequently died at Saskatoon. Hugh had ten siblings, all born at Ashington:

- Henry 'Harry' Cairns (6th March 1893–26th November 1970) was a baker's apprentice in 1911 living with his parents. He married Elizabeth Davina Stobie (December 1895–1948), born at Edinburgh, Midlothian, Scotland. She was living with her parents at 69 Comiston Road, Edinburgh in 1901. They emigrated to Canada, departing Glasgow, Lanarkshire on 11th March 1911 aboard SS *Cassandra*, arriving at St John, New Brunswick on 20th March. They were living at Rusholme Road, Saskatoon at the time of the 1911 Census of Canada, by when Elizabeth was a laundry checker. Harry was a cook/baker living at 905 Avenue G North, Saskatoon when he enlisted in 8th Canadian Stationary Hospital (University of Saskatchewan) CEF at Saskatoon on 8th April 1916 (534199). He was described as 5′ 2″ tall, weighing 110 lbs, with dark complexion, brown eyes, dark brown hair and his religious denomination was Church of England. He embarked aboard RMS *Adriatic* at Halifax, Nova Scotia on 22nd May and disembarked at Liverpool, Lancashire on 30th May. He assigned $20 per month to his wife from his Army pay from May 1916. Harry was under instruction at the School of Cookery, Dibgate, Kent 8th-30th June and was attached to Shorncliffe Military Hospital, Kent 2nd November–20th January 1917. He rejoined 8th Canadian Stationary Hospital at Hastings on 22nd January and was attached to the Canadian Special Hospital, Witley, Surrey 9th October–10th November.

Ashington, on the River Wansbeck, is twenty-four kilometres north of Newcastle upon Tyne. Until the 1700s it was a hamlet of a farm and a few dwellings. There were some bell-pit and monastic mine workings, but volume coal mining developed when the Duke of Portland built housing to encourage Irish people to escape the famine and work in his mines in the 1840s. The Ashington Coal Co built parallel rows of colliery houses and miners came from as far afield as Cornwall. Ashington railway station opened in 1878 and in 1896 Ashington Urban District was created. The station closed in 1964. In 1934 some Ashington miners began producing paintings to sell at local markets. They achieved unexpected approval and were given gallery exhibitions as 'The Pitmen Painters'. In 2006 a museum housing their work was opened by the Princess Royal and a book and a play about them have been produced. Deep mining declined in the 1980s and 1990s and the last colliery closed in 2005, leading to large scale unemployment. Ashington has produced some outstanding footballers:

- John Edward Thompson 'Jackie' Milburn (1924–88) played mainly for Newcastle United and England. He was the cousin of Jack and Bobby Charlton's mother. Milburn made his debut in the FA Cup in the 1945–46 season. His two goals won the 1951 FA Cup Final and his forty-five seconds opening goal in the 1955 FA Cup Final was the fastest Cup Final goal until 1997. He was Newcastle United's highest goal scorer (200) until surpassed by Alan Shearer in 2006. A statue of him stands in Strawberry Place, just outside Newcastle United's ground at St James' Park.
- John 'Jack' Charlton OBE DL (1935–2020) spent his entire club career with Leeds United 1950–73, helping the club to the Second Division title (1963–64), First Division title (1968–69), FA Cup (1972), League Cup (1968), Charity Shield (1969) and Inter-Cities Fairs Cup (1968 & 1971). His 629 league and 762 total appearances are club records. He was part of the England team that won the 1966 World Cup. As manager, he led Middlesbrough to the Second Division title in 1973–74 and was Manager of the Year in his first season. He managed Sheffield Wednesday 1977–83 and gained promotion to the Second Division in 1979–80. He returned to Middlesbrough as caretaker-manager at the end of the 1983–84 season and managed Newcastle United 1984–85. As manager of the Republic of Ireland 1986–96, he took the team to the World Cup quarter finals in 1990.
- Sir Robert 'Bobby' Charlton CBE (1937–2023), younger brother of Jack, was one of the greatest football players of all time. He was a member of the 1966 World Cup winning team and also won the Ballon d'Or that year. He played almost all his club football for Manchester United and was cautioned only twice in his career. Bobby made his debut for Manchester United in 1956 and they became First Division champions the following year. He survived the Munich air disaster in February 1958 and was the club's last survivor of the crash. He helped United win the 1963 FA Cup, the Football League in 1965 and 1967 and captained the team when it won the European Cup in 1968, the first English club to win the competition. Bobby scored two goals in the final. After Manchester United he became manager of Preston North End in the 1973–74 season and was player-manager next season. He was a director of Wigan Athletic and a member of Manchester United's board of directors.

A medical board there on 23rd October found that he had defective teeth and deformed feet. Harry went to France with 8th Canadian Stationary Hospital on 5th December. He was awarded a Good Conduct Badge on 8th April 1918 and was granted fourteen days' leave in Britain 11th-26th December. On 16th April 1919 he returned to England from Rouen. He embarked aboard HMT *Regina* at Liverpool on 20th May and disembarked at Halifax, Nova Scotia on 28th May.

Hugh's father was born at Chatton, which has been inhabited since prehistoric times. There has been a church there since the 12th century. The current village is mainly 19th century.

He was discharged from Dispersal Station P, 12th Military District on 3rd June and was issued with War Service Badge Class A No.208626. Davina was living with her father at Caswell School, Saskatoon while her husband was serving in the Army. They were living at 618 Rusholme Road, Saskatoon in 1921. Elizabeth died in Saskatchewan and Harry at New Westminster, British Columbia. They had two children – George H Cairns (c.1915–October 1999), born at Saskatoon, and June Cairns (1920–92), who died at Vancouver, British Columbia.

- Albert 'Abbie' Cairns (28th January 1895–10th September 1918) was a coal mining cutter in 1911 living with his parents. He was a grocer when he enlisted in 65th Battalion CEF on 11th August 1915 at Saskatoon (472262), having served for one year with 105th Fusiliers. He was described as 5′ 5½″ tall, weighing 140 lbs, with fair complexion, blue eyes, fair hair and his religious denomination was Church of England. He was granted harvest leave 16th August–15th October and was treated at St Paul's Hospital, Saskatoon for measles 1st-7th March 1916. He sailed with his unit aboard RMS *Empress of Britain* from Halifax, Nova Scotia on 20th June and arrived in England on 28th June. Abbie transferred to 46th Battalion at Bramshott, Hampshire on 30th June. In his will dated 22nd July he left everything to his mother and assigned $20 per month to her from his Army pay. Abbie transferred to 10th Canadian Brigade Trench Mortar Battery on 23rd July but returned to 46th Battalion on 29th July. He went to France on 10th August, disembarking next day at Le Havre. He attended a Lewis gun course 3rd-9th September. Abbie was wounded on 4th April 1917. He was promoted lance corporal on 6th May and was sent to First Army Rest Camp on 23rd May, rejoining the Battalion on 6th June. He was granted ten days' leave in England 23rd August–5th September and was promoted corporal on 25th August. Abbie attended a Lewis gun course at 4th Canadian Division School 16th September–6th October. On 26th October he received a gunshot wound to the right arm at Ypres, Belgium, which fractured the upper third ulna, and he was admitted to No.37 Casualty Clearing Station next day. On 28th October he was transferred to 6th General Hospital, Rouen and next day was evacuated to England aboard HMHS *Warilda*, on the held strength of the Saskatchewan Regiment Depot, Bramshott. He was transferred to 3rd Southern General Hospital, Oxford on 1st November and to the Military Convalescence Hospital, Woodcote Park, Epsom on 4th December. On 21st January 1918 he was discharged from hospital and joined 15th Reserve Battalion, Bramshott. He returned to France on the strength

Lamesley is on the southern outskirts of Gateshead. The most prominent feature today is the contemporary sculpture, the *Angel of the North* by Anthony Gormley. It is reputed that Lewis Carroll wrote parts of *Alice's Adventures in Wonderland* in the Ravenworth Arms. The ruined Ravensworth Castle was the seat of the Liddells for three centuries from 1607, although the Castle dates back to 1315, with additions throughout the 14th century. There were a number of major alterations, including building mansions within the Castle. John Nash designed one version in the early 19th century. The Duke of Wellington visited in 1827. In the 1930s the family began mining for coal under the house and its demolition commenced. It was intended to use materials salvaged from the Castle to build a model village, but because of the Second World War only three houses were created. The majority of the Castle had been demolished by 1953.

Morpeth, a historic market town on the River Wansbeck, is close to Ashington and Bedlington. Settlement of the area commenced in Neolithic times and Roman artifacts have been found. The first written mention is in 1080, when the de Merlay family was granted the barony of Morpeth. Two castles were built in the late 11th and the 13th centuries. Only the inner gatehouse remains today. Newminster Abbey was founded in 1138 and was one of the first daughter houses of Fountains Abbey. A market charter was granted by King John in 1200 and, by the mid 18th century, it was one of the main markets in England. However, the advent of the railways caused the market to decline. The town was badly damaged in 1215 in an attempt to block King John during the First Baron's War. Margaret Tudor, sister of Henry VIII, Queen Consort of Scotland was laid up there through illness for some months in 1515–16. During the War of the Rough Wooing 1543–51, Morpeth was occupied by Italian mercenaries. During the Second World War, RAF Morpeth was an air-gunnery training school. Vice Admiral Cuthbert Collingwood (1748–1810) lived at Collingwood House in Oldgate. Emily Wilding Davison, a suffragette who died when she fell under the King's horse during the Epsom Derby in 1913, is buried in St Mary's churchyard.

of 46th Battalion on 7th April. He joined the Canadian Corps Reinforcement Camp on 9th April and 46th Battalion on 14th August. Abbie received a gunshot wound to the head during the Battle of Drocourt-Quéant on 2nd September. He was admitted to 3rd Canadian General Hospital, Boulogne on 4th September and 83rd (Dublin) General Hospital, Boulogne on 8th September, where he died (Terlincthun British Cemetery, Pas de Calais, France – III E 8).

- Norman Cairns (4th December 1896–17th November 1961), a twin with Hugh, was a grocer's apprentice in 1911 living with his parents. He was an accountant in 1916. He died at Vancouver, British Columbia.
- Lawrence Wilfred Cairns (1898–28th July 1966) was a bank teller in 1916. He married Marjorie Douglas Purdon (3rd September 1896–6th May 1976), born at Brandon, Manitoba, on 8th February 1923. He died at Saskatoon.

SS *Laurentic*, built in Belfast, Ireland and launched in 1908, was an early example of a ship propelled by reciprocating steam engines with a low-pressure steam turbine. She was one of two sister ships ordered in 1907 by the Dominion Line but completed for the White Star Line. *Laurentic* had a crew of 387 and berths for 1,660 passengers (230 first, 430 second and 1,000 third class). She left Liverpool on her maiden voyage on 29th April 1909. She was used on the Liverpool to Québec route and New York in winter. In July 1910 Detective Chief Inspector Walter Dew used *Laurentic*'s speed to reach Rimouski, Québec ahead of murder suspect Hawley Harvey Crippen, who was travelling aboard SS *Montrose*. Dew boarded *Montrose*, arrested Crippen and his lover, Ethel Le Neve, and brought them back to Britain aboard SS *Megantic*. On 13th September 1914 *Laurentic* was taken up as a troopship and on 3rd October left Gaspé Bay with thirty-one other ships bringing the Canadian Expeditionary Force to Britain. She reached Plymouth on 14th October. For more than two years she was an armed merchant cruiser. On 23rd January 1917 *Laurentic* departed Birkenhead, secretly carrying 3,211 gold bars to purchase munitions in Canada and the USA, valued at £5M (£515M in 2023). Two days later she called at Buncrana in Lough Swilly to disembark four ratings with symptoms of yellow fever. After leaving Buncrana in a blizzard, she struck a mine just north of the mouth of the Lough. laid by U-*80*. Seconds later she struck another mine. It was not possible to transmit a wireless distress signal but a distress rocket was fired. The vessel was listing twenty degrees, making it difficult to launch lifeboats. However, despite the conditions the crew did launch the lifeboats and rowed towards the shore. The temperature dropped to –13C and many men died of hypothermia before reaching land or being rescued by fishing boats. In total 354 men died and 121 survived. Most of the gold (forty-three tons) had been salvaged by 1924, but twenty-two bars remain unaccounted for.

- Ruby Blanche Evelyn Cairns (31st July 1900–7th May 1983) married John 'Jack' McAlpine Hamilton (25th March 1891–7th March 1969), born at Albany, Western Australia, c.1919 in Canada. Jack moved to Canada in June 1909 and was living at The Pas, Manitoba. When he enlisted in 65th Battalion CEF on 29th November 1915 at Saskatoon (472720) he was described as a teamster, 5′ 9½″ tall, with fair complexion, grey eyes, fair hair and his religious denomination was Church of England. His next of kin was his uncle, John McAlpine, of Kalgoorlie, Western Australia. He was appointed acting lance corporal on 28th February 1916, substantive on 5th April and corporal on 18th May. Jack sailed from Halifax, Nova Scotia aboard RMS *Empress of Britain* on 20th June, arriving in England on 28th June. He joined at Bordon Camp, Hampshire the following day and reverted to the ranks on transfer to 72nd Battalion there on 3rd July. He went to France on 12th August, disembarking at Le Havre next day. Jack was appointed paid acting corporal on 1st November. He attended a Junior Officers and NCO Course on 26th November and 23rd December. On 1st February 1917 he was promoted corporal and paid acting lance sergeant. On 1st March he received a severe gunshot/bomb wound to the left knee at Vimy Ridge and was admitted to 13th Canadian Field Ambulance and No.6 Casualty Clearing Station. Next day he was transferred to No.7 Canadian General Hospital Étaples. He later suffered from retinitis as a result of the blast. On 10th March he was evacuated to Britain and was admitted to 1st Northern General Hospital, Newcastle upon Tyne, Northumberland. Next day he was taken on the strength of the British Columbia Regiment Depot, Seaford, Sussex. The metal fragment was removed on 16th March. He continued his recovery at the Canadian Convalescent Hospital, Hillingdon House, Uxbridge, Middlesex 5th April–8th June. Next day he was taken on the strength of 3rd Canadian Command Depot, Seaford. He transferred to 1st Canadian Reserve Battalion, Seaford on 16th August and to the British Columbia Regiment Depot at Seaford on 25th September. On 12th October he was admitted to Cherry Hinton Military Hospital, Cambridge with syphilis and on 29th October transferred to Depot Company. On 1st August 1918 Jack was appointed paid acting sergeant whilst Orderly Sergeant, Regimental Depots, Seaford. He was admitted to 14th Canadian General Hospital, Ravenscroft, Eastbourne, Sussex on 6th March 1919 with a fifth metacarpal fracture of the right hand. He was transferred to Princess Patricia's Canadian Red Cross Hospital, Cooden Camp, Bexhill-on-Sea, Sussex on 8th March and to Woodcote Park Military Convalescent Hospital, Epsom, Surrey 16th-20th April. A medical at Epsom on 3rd June confirmed that he was still suffering from retinitis. He was taken on the strength of the Canadian Concentration Camp, Witley on 22nd June. He returned to Canada, departing Southampton, Hampshire on 2nd July and arriving at Halifax, Nova Scotia on 8th July. Jack was demobilised on 15th July and was discharged from 12th Military District Dispersal Station O on 25th July. Jack and Ruby travelled aboard RMS *Niagara* from Sydney, New South Wales, departing on 30th May 1929 and arriving at Vancouver, British Columbia on 21st June. He died at White Rock, Greater Vancouver, British Columbia and she at Coquitlam, Greater Vancouver. They had a son:

Albert Cairns' grave in Terlincthun British Cemetery.

- John 'Jack' Patrick Hamilton (10th August 1925–14th May 2008), born at The Pas, Manitoba, married Dorothy Tizzard (2nd September 1924–

19th January 1995), born at Ribstone, Alberta. She died at Costa Mesa, Orange Co, California, USA and he at Mount Vernon, Lawrence Co, Missouri, USA. They had a son and a daughter.

- Winifred 'Winnie' May Cairns (born 1903) married as Torbel.
- Edwin Donkin Cairns (1905–53) was a civil servant. He married Frances J Sears (1912–17th September 1999) c.1942. They were living at 488 Maclaren Street, Ottawa at the time. They were living at Somerset Street West, Ottawa in 1945 and at 59 Charon Street, Waterloo North, Ontario in 1949. They both subsequently died at Kitchener, Waterloo County, Ontario. Frances was a payroll control clerk in 1974, living with her mother at 37 Oxford Street, Kitchener.
- George Leslie Cairns (born 1907).
- Eva Rebecca Cairns (24th December 1908–28th December 1986) married William Ernest George Bell (19th July 1903–14th October 1989), born at Indian Head, Saskatchewan, on 18th January 1929 at Prince Albert, Saskatchewan. They both died at Saskatoon. They had six children:
    - Jacqueline 'Jacquie' Eva Bell (31st July 1929–28th October 2003), born at Rosetown, Saskatchewan, married Albert 'Al' Henry Gislain Bauche (14th March 1923–21st June 2013), born at Grande-Clarière, Manitoba, on 22nd July 1952 at Regina, Saskatchewan. They had four children. They both died at Saskatoon.
    - Ernest Dean Bell (15th August 1935–25th October 2009) was a buyer. He married Lois Beverly Compton (29th September 1939–8th November 2014), born at Rabbit Lake, Saskatchewan, on 5th September 1959 at North Battlefield, Saskatchewan. They lived at 36 Applewood Road, Sherwood Park, Alberta and both died at Edmonton, Alberta. They had six children.

Scremerston appears in written records as early as 1131. There is evidence of some habitation in the Neolithic, Bronze and Iron Ages. A Roman road passed 400m to the west and there was a small Romano-British settlement, later destroyed when the A1 road was re-routed. During the 18th and 19th centuries Scremerston was industrialised, due to the accessibility of coal, stone and clay. Jack Tar Pit was sunk in 1840 and was worked until 1878. Its largely intact engine house and pumping engine house are Grade II listed. Four other major mines were sunk in the village and there were a number of lime kilns along the coast. Scremerston Brick and Tile Works operated 1850–1943. During the Second World War there was a Chain Home Low radar station and a few buildings remain. Scremerston was also the operational base for an Auxiliary Unit, secreted in a cellar at Inlandpasture Farm. By the turn of the 20th century Scremerston's industry was in decline. The coal seams were exhausted and lime production was unable to compete against mechanised plants elsewhere. Many closures followed. The Great North Road (A1) passed through Scremerston and was the main coaching route between London, York and Edinburgh. However, coaches could not compete with the new railways and the last coach left Newcastle for Edinburgh in July 1847. Scremerston had a railway station from 1847 until 1951. The A1 passed through the village until 1983, when it was by-passed.

Bilton Banks was home to many miners from the late 19th to mid 20th centuries when the mines finally closed. The houses were then condemned and the last were demolished in the 1950s. Today there is nothing left. Coal mining in the area goes back to the monks of Hulne Priory in the 12th century. The mine most associated with Bilton Banks was Longdyke Pit, sunk in 1844/45. In 1841 Bilton Banks' population consisted of two families of agricultural workers. By 1891 there were 164 people living in the village.

  - Norman Larry Bell (27th January 1941–7th April 2018), born at Watrous, Saskatchewan, married Shirley Israel. He died at Luther Special Care Home, Saskatoon.
  - Phyllis Bell married as Graham.
  - Mavis Bell married as Orpen.
  - Hugh Bell.
- Thomas Cyril Cairns (1910–6th August 1959) married Myra Marie Dewson (born 31st July 1912), born at Colgate, Saskatchewan. He was living at 3079 Graveley Street, Vancouver at the time of his death there. They had two children:
  - Hugh Ross Cairns (12th May 1938–8th April 2010), born at Saskatoon, married Bonnie Gail Saywell (born c.1945) on 26th January 1974 at Norwalk, Fairfield Co, Connecticut, USA. He was an accounting assistant and she was a secretary/typist, both living at 149 West Rocks Road, Bridgeport, Connecticut at the time. Hugh died at Mississauga, Ontario.
  - Patricia Anne Cairns.

Hugh's paternal grandfather, Henry Cairns (c.1837–98), born in Scotland, was living with his parents at Inland Pasture Farm, Scremerston, Northumberland in 1851. He married Rebecca née Henderson (13th March 1832–1899), born at Wandon, Northumberland, on 17th February 1859 at Chatton, Northumberland. Rebecca had a son, Richard Henderson (born 1855), who was an agricultural labourer in 1871. Henry was an agricultural labourer in 1861, when they were living at Newlands Village, Warenton, Northumberland and at Hepburn, Northumberland in 1871. By 1881 he was an engineer (standing) and they were living at Bilton Banks, Lesbury, Northumberland. He was a coalminer by 1891, when they were living at Bothel Demesne, Ashington. Both their deaths were registered at Morpeth. In addition to George they had seven other children:

- John Cairns (born 1859), born at Chatton, Northumberland, was a coalminer in 1881, living with his parents. He married Catherine Ann Hindhaugh (1864–1933), born at Bedlington, Northumberland, in 1883. She was living with her father at Coach Road, Bedlington in 1871. In 1881 she was a domestic servant for the family of Thomas Straker, keeper of the Old Phoenix Inn, Morpeth. John and

Catherine were living at Haines Cottage, Spring Garden, Morpeth in 1891 and at 7 Hillgate, Morpeth in 1901. They had fourteen children:

- Ethel Cairns (1884–1954) married Thomas William Hall in 1908.
- Jane Cairns (1885).
- Kate Cairns (18th September 1886–1972) married William Rutherford (1895–1965) in 1912 and they had a daughter, Catherine M Rutherford, in 1916.
- Margaret Cairns (19th May 1888–1979) married Hugh Taylor Lockhart (1883–1960) in 1913 and they had two children – Hugh C Lockhart 1914 and Nancy Lockhart 1923.
- William Cairns (1889–1948) was a coal miner in 1911 living with his parents.
- Hannah Cairns (26 September 1891–1954) married Isaac Frazer (1876–1926) in 1915 and they had a son, James Frazer, that year. Hannah married William Theakston (28th January 1897–1984) in 1927.
- John Cairns (1893) was a coal miner in 1911 living with his parents.
- James Cairns (16th March 1895–1974) was a laundry assistant in 1911 living with his parents. He married Ann Toner (1902–74) in 1922. They had eleven children – Vera Cairns 1923, Catherine A Cairns 1924, James Cairns 1926, John Cairns 1928, Leslie Cairns 1930, Jean Cairns 1931, Frances G Cairns 1933, George E Cairns 1935, William A Cairns 1937, Patricia Cairns 1942 and Sheila Cairns 1948.
- Blanche Cairns (1897) married Robert Jobson in 1919 and they had two sons – John C Jobson 1921 and Robert Jobson 1923.
- George Cairns (1898–1965) married Eleanor Annie Aitchison (30th July 1899–1987) in 1920 and they had a daughter, Kate Cairns, that year.
- Bertram Cairns (born 1900).
- Stella Cairns (23rd December 1903–1981) married Robert Chater in 1924. Her death was registered at Derby.
- Harry Cairns (22nd November 1905–1984).
- Leslie Cairns (28th November 1907–1971).

- Margaret Ann Cairns (1860–1916), born at Newlands, Bamburgh, Northumberland, married John Mavin (1851–1927), a brickmaker born at Widdrington, Northumberland, in 1883, registered at Morpeth. They were living at Ivy Cottage, Benwell, Northumberland in 1891. By 1911 he was a foreman in a brickworks and they were living at Clairndene, North Terrace, Willington, Co Durham. Their deaths were registered at Tynemouth, Northumberland. They had six children, including three who died before the 1911 Census:
    - Robert H Mavin (born 1885).
    - Harold Seymour Mavin (born 1896) was a student and part time engine driver in 1911 living with his parents. He married Katherine Farrage in 1934, registered at Tynemouth.
    - Sidney Mavin (1903–51).

- Robert Cairns (1864–92), birth registered at Embleton, Northumberland, was a coalminer in 1881, living with his parents. His death was registered at Alnwick.
- William Miller Cairns (born 1866), born at Bamburgh, Northumberland, was baptised there on 1st April 1866. He was an errand boy in 1881, living with his parents, a banksman in 1891, still living with his parents, and was later a coalminer. William married Isabella Clark Storkey (6th May 1878–8th September 1941), birth registered at Tynemouth, in 1897, registered at Morpeth. They were living with her father in 1901 at 1 Tenth Row, Ashington. She was still with him and her stepmother at 20 Duke Street, Ashington in 1911 but William was not with her. Isabella was recorded as a widow in 1939, living at 22 Council Road, Ashington with her children, Alexander, Wilfred and Elsie. She subsequently died there. They had nine children:
    - John Donkin Cairns (19th September 1897–1981) married Elizabeth D Davison (22nd June 1902–1972) in 1920.
    - Aubrey Cairns (1899–1959) married Annie Maria Anderson nee Rossiter (3rd November 1901–1979) in 1940. They had a son, Colin Cairns, in 1949. Annie had married James Anderson in 1923.
    - Frederick Cairns (15th January 1902–1981) married Mary J Stone in 1926.
    - Rebecca Henderson Cairns (born 1903) married James Thomas Mackay (14th May 1907- 1977) in 1932. They had a daughter, Ann Mackay, in 1934.
    - Ivy Cairns (born 1908) married David Bramley in 1941. They had three children – David L Bramley 1943, Geoffrey Bramley 1948 and Alan Bramley 1952.
    - Harold Cairns (1910–59) married Emily Bland (6th February 1911–1970) in 1940. They had two sons – Eric Cairns 1943 and Nigel Cairns 1946.
    - Alexander Cairns (23rd June 1912–1992) was a journeyman butcher in 1939, living with his mother and siblings at 22 Council Road, Ashington. He married Patricia Wallace in 1940.
    - Wilfred C Cairns (born 2nd September 1914) was the manager of a newspaper office in 1939, living with his mother and siblings. He married Margaret J Wake (22nd December 1917–1986), born at Fareham, Hampshire, in 1940. They had two daughters – Joyce A Cairns 1943 and Diane Cairns 1945.
    - Elsie Cairns (1st February 1917) married John Hill in 1942, registered at Penrith. They had three children – Frederick Hill 1944, Carol IK Hill 1945 and Robin J Hill 1956.
- Jane Cairns (born 1867) married her brother-in-law, Thomas Donkin (January 1864–1933), born at Mitford, Northumberland, in 1890 at Morpeth. She was living with her parents in 1891. Thomas was a colliery banksman above ground in 1901, living with his children at 43 Tenth Row, Ashington. Jane was not with them and what became of her is not known. They had two children – Thomas Donkin (25th November 1892–1961) and Henry Donkin (9th January 1896–11th May 1915). Henry enlisted in the Royal Naval Volunteer Reserve on 9th November

Chatby Military and War Memorial Cemetery was used until April 1916, when a new cemetery was opened at Hadra. Some graves were brought into the cemetery after the war from other burial grounds and it was also used in the Second World War. There are now 2,259 Great War burials and 503 from the Second World War. The cemetery also contains graves of other nationalities and non-war and military graves, some dating from 1882. The Chatby Memorial at the eastern end commemorates almost 1,000 Commonwealth servicemen who died during the Great War at sea and have no known grave.

1914 (Z/1475), described as a miner, 5′ 11″ tall and his religious denomination was Church of England. He was serving as an able seaman in B Company, Nelson Battalion, Royal Naval Division from 24th February 1915. He was shot in the right hip and lumbar region at Gallipoli on 3rd May 1915 and was taken aboard HMHS *Gascon*. He was admitted to 17th General Hospital, Alexandria, where he died (Alexandria (Chatby) Military and War Memorial Cemetery, Egypt – C 156). Thomas senior was living with Mary Ann Donkin (born c.1877), born at Blaydon, Northumberland, as his wife in 1911 (no record of a marriage has been found) and his children at 43 Tenth Row, Ashington.

- Thomas Cairns (1869–1936) was a grocer's assistant in 1891, living with his parents, and an assistant butcher in 1911, living with his brother George and family.
- Rebecca Cairns (1876–1933), born at Lesbury, Northumberland, married Douglas Anderson (7th February 1881–22nd May 1956), a colliery foreman born at North Blyth, Northumberland, in 1901, when they were living at 3 Tenth Row, Ashington. By 1911 he was a police constable and they were living at 14 Warkworth Street, Newcastle upon Tyne. He was living at 17 Thoroton Street, Blyth with his children, Lionel and Audrey, in 1939. He was living at 7 Fontburn Terrace, North Shields at the time of his death. They had at least seven children:
    - Olga Minnie Anderson (born 1902).
    - Douglas Anderson (10th June 1904–1982) was a civil servant in 1956. He married Evelyn Murrell (born 1905) in 1922 at Hull, Yorkshire. They had at least four children – Marian J Anderson 1924, Marjorie E Anderson 1927, Evelyn J Anderson 1930, Jean M Anderson 1933 and possibly Marion Anderson 1936.
    - John Leslie Anderson (13th January 1906–1991).
    - Enid Ivy Anderson (1907–25).
    - Henry Cairns Anderson (15th January 1909–1987).
    - Lionel George Anderson (8th January 1911–1987).

Rothbury is an important road junction and crossing over the River Coquet. There are Neolithic and Bronze Age remains in the area but no evidence of Roman occupation, probably because the town was a considerable distance north of Hadrian's Wall. Fragments of a 9th century Anglo-Saxon cross are the only pre-Norman relics. In 1201 King John sealed the Rothbury Town Charter and visited four years later. King Edward I visited the town in 1291 and granted a charter for a market. The town became a centre for cattle and wool dealing. in 1334 King Edward III gave the town to Henry Percy, who had been given the castle and baronry of Warkworth six years earlier. Despite the border wars, Rothbury rose in prosperity during the 14th century but the 15th and 16th centuries were turbulent and bloody. Bands of Reivers burned the town on many occasions and the troubled times lasted until the unification of England and Scotland in 1603. The railway arrived in 1870 and closed in 1963. Amongst the town's noted alumni are:

- Imogen Stubbs (born 1961), actress, was born there.
- Alexander Armstrong (born 1970), actor, comedian and television presenter, was born in Rothbury, where his father was a doctor.
- William George Armstrong, 1st Baron Armstrong CB Kt FRS (1810–1900), the engineer and industrialist who founded Armstrong-Whitworth on Tyneside. He was also a scientist, inventor and philanthropist. He was knighted in 1859 after giving his gun patents to the government and, in 1887, was raised to the peerage as Baron Armstrong of Cragside. In collaboration with the architect, Richard Norman Shaw, he built Cragside, a country house just outside Rothbury, between 1862 and 1865. It was extended between 1869 and 1900 and was the first house in the world lit by hydroelectricity. The estate is now owned by the National Trust. The Prince of Wales (later King Edward VII) arrived at Rothbury by train in August 1884 to visit Lord Armstrong at Cragside.

Warkworth from across the Coquet. The castle in the background may have been first constructed by Prince Henry of Scotland in the middle of the 12th century but could also have been built by King Henry II of England. A timber castle was documented in 1157–64 when Henry II granted it to Roger fitz Richard. Roger's son, Robert, improved the castle and he hosted King John there in 1213. King Edward I also stayed in 1292. With the outbreak of the Anglo-Scottish Wars, King Edward II strengthened the garrison in 1319. Twice in 1327 the Scots besieged the castle successfully. During King Edward III's reign the castle passed to the Percy family and is still held by their descendants, the Dukes of Northumberland. It was designated a scheduled monument in 1915 and is now managed and maintained by English Heritage. One of the Percys, Sir Henry, known as Hotspur, may have been born at Warkworth (or Alnwick) in 1364. He led a number of rebellions against King Henry IV and was killed at the Battle of Shrewsbury in 1403.

The Church of St Lawrence in Warkworth is Grade I listed. The first record of the village dates from 737 when King Ceolwulf of Northumbria gave the church and village to the Abbot and monks of Lindisfarne. That wooden church was destroyed in the Danish raids in 875 and was rebuilt in stone during the 9th and 10th centuries. In 1120 King Henry I gave St Lawrence and three other churches to his chaplain, Richard de Aurea Valle. On his death all four churches became part of the newly formed Diocese of Carlisle and remained so until Newcastle became a separate diocese in 1882. Building of the existing church began in 1132 and is almost entirely Norman, which is unique in Northumberland. It was also a sanctuary for villagers in dangerous times. On 13th July 1174, the Earl of Fife entered Warkworth with a column of the Scottish King William the Lion's army and set fire to the town. Three hundred inhabitants who had taken refuge in the church were killed. About 1200 a tower was built at the western end of the church and the belfry and spire were added in the 14th century. In the 15th century the south aisle and entrance porch were added. On 9th October 1715 Warkworth was the first market town in England to proclaim the Old Pretender as King. His chaplain read morning prayers in the church. On 16th May 1761 John Wesley preached a sermon there. Extensive restorations were carried out in 1860 and in 1947 the floor was relaid. It was known from the 13th century, when the tower was built, that there was movement in the north wall. Buttresses were built to prevent lateral movement but the wall was built on shallow foundations. By 2006 the wall was almost half a metre out of line and the church was placed on English Heritage's Buildings at Risk Register. In March 2009 work started to secure and stabilise the wall and the church has since been removed from the Register.

- ◦ Audrey Alice Alma Anderson (22nd April 1913–1991) married Henry A Howard in 1940 and George Chalmers in 1965.
- ◦ Possibly Margaret V Anderson (born 1915).

His maternal grandfather, Thomas Donkin (c.1838–1900), an agricultural labourer born at Rothbury, Northumberland, married Isabella née Rogerson (1841–1908), born at Warkworth, Northumberland, on 1st December 1860 at St Lawrence Church, Warkworth. They were living at Greenwell House, Lamesley, Co Durham in 1871, at Coal Barn, Hepscott, Northumberland by 1881 and on a farm at Bothal Demesne, Northumberland by 1891. Isabella was living at 12 Eleventh Row, Ashington with her children, Isabella and Edward, in 1901. In addition to Elizabeth they had six other children:

- John William Donkin (1861–1919), born at Acklington/Warkworth, Northumberland (registered as Duncan) married Isabella Carr Black (1861–1938), born at Sheepwash, Northumberland, in 1889. He was a coalminer in 1901, when they were living at 2 Stable Row, Ashington and at 49 Scott Row, Ashington in 1911. They had three children:
  - ◦ Elizabeth Ann Donkin (born 1895) married Adam Lyall Fornear (born 1878) in 1912, registered at Tynemouth.

  - Isabella Rogerson Donkin (born 1896) married James Turnbull in 1916, registered at Morpeth.
  - John William Donkin (1900–52).
- Thomas Donkin (January 1864–1933), born at Mitford, Northumberland, was a colliery labourer in 1891 living with his parents. He married his sister-in-law, Jane Cairns (born 1867), in 1890 (see above).
- Mary Ann Donkin (1867–8th April 1903), born at Bothal, Northumberland, married Henry Familton (13th August 1870–13th September 1941) in 1893. He was a colliery deputy overman in 1911, living with his children at 13 Albert Terrace, Ashington. He was living at 201 Otley Road, Bradford, Yorkshire with his children, Henry and Elizabeth, in 1939 and subsequently died there. They had four children:
  - Elizabeth Familton (13th April 1893–10th November 1968) was a housekeeper living with her brother, Henry, in 1939. She never married and her death was registered at Wrexham.
  - John Familton (1895–11th September 1926) was a colliery screener above ground in 1911, living with his father. He married Ada Evelyn Woodland at Morpeth on 30th January 1915 and they had two children – Elizabeth Familton (1915–16) and John Familton 1917. John senior enlisted in the Royal Garrison Artillery (176858) at Ashington on 10th December 1915 and transferred to the Reserve next day. He was described as a lorryman and was 5′ 10¾″ tall. His wife was living at 240 Hawthorn Road and later at 25 Sycamore Street, Ashington. He was mobilised on 19th September 1917 to 4th Depot RGA and served in 67th Siege Battery RGA in France from 23rd January 1918. In April 1918 he was wounded by a gunshot to the right shoulder and was treated at 2nd Australian General Hospital, Wimereux from 6th April and Brook War Hospital, Woolwich from 8th April. John was discharged on 3rd February 1919 no longer physically fit for war service, assessed as 50% disabled, with a pension of 13/9d per week for twenty-six weeks and an allowance of 3/4d for the surviving child from 24th February.
  - Henry Familton (1897–10th February 1900).
  - Henry Familton (4th June 1901–1972) was a newspaper owner in 1939, living with his father and sister, Elizabeth, at 201 Otley Road, Bradford. He married Nellie Wood (13th November 1908–1985), born at Bradford, in 1946. Her death was registered at Bromley, Kent.
- Janet Donkin (1872–1914), born at Whickham, Co Durham, married Thomas Doyle (18th March 1872–1953), a coal hewer, in 1893. They were living at New Moor, Ashington in 1901 and 1911. Thomas was a surface colliery platelayer in 1939, living alone at 47 Eighth Row, Ashington. They had twelve children, all registered at Morpeth, including:
  - Isabella Doyle (1893–1961) married James Hart in 1912. They had nine children – Barbara Hart 1913, Thomas Hart 1914, George E Hart 1919,

  - Elizabeth D Hart 1920, John J Hart 1923, Doreen Hart 1923, William Hart 1925, Hannah A Hart 1930 and Joyce Hart 1934.
  - Margaret Ann Doyle (born 1895).
  - Janetta Doyle (born 1896) married Henry Fitzpatrick (1897–1958) in 1916. They had three children – Janet Fitzpatrick 1916, Thomas Fitzpatrick 1919 and Hilda Fitzpatrick 1924.
  - Norah Doyle (born 1897) was not with the family at the time of the 1911 Census.
  - Elizabeth Green Doyle (born 1900).
  - Thomas Donkin Doyle (born and died 1902).
  - Edward George Doyle (17th September 1903–1980) married Mary Bolam in 1928. They had two children – Elizabeth Doyle 1929 and Gordon Doyle 1937.
  - John Joseph Doyle (1905–07).
  - Jane Doyle (born 1908) married William Brown in 1932. They had a daughter, Kathleen M Brown, in 1940.
  - Hilda Doyle (1910) married Samuel R Milburn (1911–51) in 1933. They had three children – John Milburn 1933, Janet Milburn 1939 and Ann Milburn 1944.
  - Annie Doyle (born and died 1912).
- Isabella Donkin (born 19th April 1875), born at Bensham, Co Durham.
- Edward George Donkin (1877–1937) was a colliery horse keeper in 1901. He married Annie Rogers (27th December 1882–1975), born at Choppington, Northumberland, in 1905. She was an indoor pauper at Morpeth Union Workhouse in 1891. They were living at 25 Tenth Row, Ashington in 1911.

Hugh was educated at Bothal School, Ashington. He was a colliery labourer on screener in 1911 living with his parents. That year he emigrated to Canada with his family and worked as an apprentice plumber. His interests included football, long distance running and boxing. He

St Thomas Church was built on the corner of Avenue H and 20th Street in 1912. It was originally St Thomas Presbyterian Church, founded in 1908. In 1930 St Thomas Presbyterian and Wesley Methodist churches agreed to worship in the St Thomas building under joint ministry and formed St Thomas Wesley United Church in 1934. The Memorial Hall dedicated to those who served in both World Wars was added in 1956. The bell tower was demolished in 2008 after falling into disrepair. St Thomas was the first Saskatchewan United Church to openly welcome lesbians and gays.

RMS *Empress of Britain* (14,189 tons) was built by Fairfield Shipbuilding & Engineering Co at Govan on the Clyde in 1905–06. She was the first of three Canadian Pacific ships to be named *Empress of Britain* and was launched on 11th November 1905. There was accommodation for 310 first, 470 second and 730 third class passengers. She left Liverpool on 5th May 1906 on her maiden voyage to Québec and, except for during the Great War, operated on the transatlantic route between Canada and Europe until 1923. On her second voyage she made the trip from Moville, Ireland to Rimouski, Canada in the then record time of five days, twenty-one hours and seventeen minutes. Less than two weeks after RMS *Titanic* sank in the North Atlantic, *Empress of Britain* also struck an iceberg on 26th April 1912, but the damage was slight. On 27th July that year, *Empress of Britain* rammed and sank the British collier *Helvetia* in fog off Cape Magdelene in the estuary of the St Lawrence River. In 1914 she was requisitioned by the Admiralty and refitted as an armed merchant cruiser to join Admiral Archibald Peile Stoddart's squadron in the South Atlantic. In May 1915 she became a troop transport and carried more than 110,000 troops to Gallipoli, Egypt and India. She also carried Canadian and American forces across the North Atlantic. Passing through the Straits of Gibraltar on 12th December 1915 she collided with and sank a Greek steamer. Next night she collided with an empty French troopship, *Djuradjura*, which was cut in half and sank, with the loss of two French crewmen. *Empress of Britain* reverted to civilian use in late 1918 on the Liverpool–New York route but in March 1919 resumed the Liverpool–St John, New Brunswick service. Having returned a contingent of the CEF to Canada on 4th May, she returned to Fairfield's on the Clyde to be converted from coal to oil and modernisation of the passenger accommodation. On 9th January 1920 she returned to service on the Liverpool–Québec route. In October 1922 she changed to the Southampton–Cherbourg–Québec route. In 1924, the ship was renamed *Montroyal* and she was altered to carry 600 cabin and 800 third class passengers. On 19th April 1924, she resumed service on the Liverpool–Québec route. In 1926 the accommodation was again altered to carry cabin, tourist and third class passengers. In 1927 *Montroyal* transferred to the Antwerp–Southampton–Cherbourg–Québec route. She began her final voyage from Antwerp on 7th September 1929, having completed 190 North Atlantic round-trip crossings. On 17th June 1930 the ship was sold to Stavanger Shipbreaking Co and was scrapped. The lounge was incorporated into the Sola Strand Hotel, Sola, Norway as the Montroyal Ballroom and later the Montroyal Lounge, including the original fireplace, lead glass ceiling and windows.

played football for Christ Church, Saskatoon in the Canadian Champions Sunday School League in 1913 and for St Thomas' Church, the Saskatoon League Champions in 1915.

On 2nd August 1915 he enlisted in 65th Battalion CEF at Saskatoon, Saskatchewan. He was described as 5′ 6″ tall, weighing 138 lbs, with dark complexion, brown eyes, black hair and his religious denomination was Church of England. He was granted harvest leave 16th August–15th October. On 20th June 1916 Hugh sailed for England aboard RMS *Empress of Britain* with 65th Battalion, arriving at Liverpool, Lancashire on 28th June. He was taken on the strength of 46th Battalion (Saskatchewan Dragoons) at Bramshott, Hampshire on 30th June. The Battalion became known as the 'Suicide Battalion' due its heavy losses. He assigned $20 per month to his mother, from his Army pay from July, and in his military will

Bramshott Camp on Bramshott Common in Hampshire was used by the Canadian Army in both world wars.

left everything to her. On 23rd July he transferred to 10th Canadian Brigade Trench Mortar Battery but returned to 46th Battalion on 29th July. He went to France on 10th August and disembarked at Le Havre next day. Hugh attended a Lewis gun course 3rd-9th September. On 3rd June 1917 he was wounded by a shell in the back and was admitted to 12th Canadian Field Ambulance. Having returned to his unit on 9th June, he was granted ten days' leave in England 16th-31st July. He was awarded a good conduct stripe on 4th August and a pay increase.

Awarded the DCM for his actions at Vimy – he led a party forward at a critical moment and offered covering fire to the flank of an attacking battalion. He then recovered two guns which had been left behind, posted them, repelled three enemy attacks and successfully covered the withdrawal. He was wounded but held on until all his ammunition was expended before making his way back to the safety of his own lines, LG 25th August 1917. Hugh attended a Lewis gun course at 4th Canadian Division School 16th-29th September. He was promoted lance corporal on 11th November 1917 and attended an Anti-Aircraft Course at the Canadian Corps School 16th-18th March 1918. He was promoted corporal on 1st July and sergeant on 15th August. He was granted fourteen days' leave in England from 6th August. Hugh attended another Lewis gun course at the GHQ School 17th September–5th October.

The Distinguished Conduct Medal was instituted by Royal Warrant on 4th December 1854 for warrant officers and below for 'distinguished, gallant and good conduct in the field'. It ranked second only to the Victoria Cross and equated to the Distinguished Service Order for officers when awarded for gallantry. It was the first official decoration awarded by the British to recognise acts of individual gallantry in the Army. During the Great War there was concern that the number of medals being awarded would devalue it. As a result the Military Medal was instituted on 25th March 1916, as a lesser award for bravery. Nevertheless 24,591 DCMs were awarded during the Great War plus 472 Bars and nine second Bars. In 1942 other ranks of the Royal Navy and Royal Air Force also became eligible. In 1993 the DCM was discontinued after a major review of the honours system, which removed distinctions of rank in respect of awards for bravery. With the Conspicuous Gallantry Medal and the Distinguished Service Order when awarded for gallantry, these three decorations were replaced by the Conspicuous Gallantry Cross as the second highest award for gallantry for all ranks of all services.

Awarded the VC for his actions south of Valenciennes, France on 1st November 1918, LG 31st January 1919. He was the last Canadian to be awarded the VC for the Great War. Hugh died of the wounds he received during the VC action at No.1 Canadian Casualty Clearing Station, Auberchicourt, near Douai, at 3.45 a.m. the following day. He is buried in Auberchicourt British Cemetery (I A 8). As he died on operational duty, his next-of-kin is eligible to receive the Canadian Memorial Cross. The Victoria Cross was sent by the War Office to the Colonial Office for presentation to his father at North Saskatoon on 20th February 1919. Hugh is commemorated in a number of other places:

Hugh Cairns' grave in Auberchicourt British Cemetery (Memorials to Valour).

- Saskatoon, Saskatchewan
  - Sergeant Hugh Cairns VC Armoury, North Saskatchewan Regiment, 930 Idylwyld Drive, North Saskatoon, named in 1960.
  - Hugh Cairns VC Elementary School, now Hugh Cairns VC School, 2621 Cairns Avenue, opened in 1960.
  - Cairns Field Baseball Field.
  - An Imperial Order of the Daughters of the Empire chapter.
  - Hugh Cairns Street.
  - Statue of Hugh as a footballer in Kiwanis Park, North Saskatoon erected by the Saskatoon Football Association on 8th June 1921. The statue carries the names of seventy-five Saskatoon football players who did not return from the Great War.
  - A plaque dedicated in August 1995 at what was believed to be the Cairns home but is actually the wrong address. Hugh was identified in the 1913 and 1914 directories as the son of the Reverend Hugh Cairns (no relation) living at 418 10th Street East. The error was corrected in 1915 but was overlooked by planners eighty years later when erecting the memorial. The plaque has since been moved to 832 Avenue G, North Saskatoon, the family home before the Great War.
  - Hugh Cairns memorial, Christ Church Anglican Church.

The Saskatoon Football Association Memorial, modelled on Hugh Cairns.

832 Avenue G, North Saskatoon with the memorial plaque.

Bothal School war memorial at Ashington, Northumberland. Hugh's name is at the top of the left column. Albert's is four down in the next column to the right.

- Ontario
    - Victoria Cross obelisk to all Canadian VCs at Military Heritage Park, Barrie dedicated by Princess Royal on 22nd October 2013.
    - Named on one of eleven plaques honouring 175 men from overseas awarded the VC for the Great War. The plaques were unveiled by the Senior Minister of State at the Foreign & Commonwealth Office and Minister for Faith and Communities, Baroness Warsi, at a reception at Lancaster House, London on 26th June 2014 attended by The Duke of Kent and relatives of the VC recipients. The Canadian plaque was unveiled outside the British High Commission in Elgin Street, Ottawa on 10th November 2014 by Princess Royal in the presence of British High Commissioner Howard Drake, Canadian Minister of Veterans Affairs Julian Fantino and Canadian Chief of the Defence Staff General Thomas James Lawson.

The Victoria Cross obelisk in Military Heritage Park, Barrie, Ontario.

The Canadian VC memorial plaque (back right) outside the British High Commission in Ottawa (Memorials to Valour).

The 49 Cent postage stamps issued by Canada Post on 21st October 2004.

The York Cemetery VC Memorial.

The Books of Remembrance are housed in the Memorial Chamber of Canada's Parliament Buildings in Ottawa. The volumes record the names of more than 120,000 members of Canadian Forces and Canadian Merchant Navy who died on active service in wartime and other conflicts. The display case for the first book rests on an altar in the centre of the Chamber that was a British gift to Canada. Later books are displayed on altars against the walls of the Chamber. The pages of each book are turned every day, so that every name is displayed at least once each year. There are eight books:

- Great War is the largest, with 66,655 names.
- Second World War commemorates 44,893 Canadians.
- Newfoundland book commemorates over 2,300 Newfoundlanders who died in the world wars, before Newfoundland became part of Canada.
- War of 1812 – more than 1,600 dead in Canadian fencible or militia units.
- Nile Expedition 1884–85 (sixteen) and South Africa 1899–1902 (250).
- Korean War 1950–53 – 516.
- Seventh Book, dedicated on 11th November 2005 – members of the Canadian Forces who died on active duty since the Second World War, except Korea.
- Canadian Merchant Navy – more than 2,170 Canadian men and women who died during the world wars.

  - Plaque No.9 on the York Cemetery VC Memorial, West Don River Valley, Toronto, Canada dedicated on 25th June 2017.
  - Named in the Great War Book of Remembrance in the Memorial Chamber, Peace Tower, Parliament Buildings, Ottawa.
- Two 49 cents postage stamps in honour of the ninety-four Canadian VC winners were issued by Canada Post on 21st October 2004 on the 150th Anniversary of the first Canadian VC's action, Alexander Roberts Dunn VC.

Nos.3 & 5 Avenue du Sergent Cairns, Valenciennes, just before the dedication of the plaque, and detail of the memorial.

- A Department for Communities and Local Government commemorative paving stone was dedicated at Ashington Memorial Garden, Kenilworth Road, Ashington, Northumberland on 1st November 2018.
- Bothal School war memorial, Ashington, Northumberland dedicated in 1921, commemorates 128 former pupils, including Hugh and Albert Cairns.

Hugh Cairn's medals.

- The day before the dedication of the Vimy Memorial on 25th July 1936, a street in Valenciennes was renamed 'Avenue du Sergent Cairns' and a plaque was unveiled between Nos.3 and 5. A special medallion, inscribed with the arms of the town, was presented to his parents, who attended the ceremony.
- Named on The Ring of Remembrance (L'Anneau de la Mémoire or Ring of Memory) at Ablain-Saint-Nazaire, France, inaugurated on 11th November 2014. The Ring commemorates the 576,606 soldiers of forty nationalities who died in Nord-Pas-de-Calais in the Great War.
- His VC action featured in Issue 897 of the Victor Comic, entitled *A True Story of Men at War*, dated 29th April 1978.

Hugh was posthumously appointed Chevalier (Knight) of the French Légion d'honneur (Legion of Honour) in 1936, the first occasion that this award was given to a NCO of an allied country. In addition to the VC and DCM he was awarded the British War Medal 1914–20, Victory Medal 1914–19 and French Knight of the Legion of Honour. The medals eventually came to Hugh's nephew, William Milne who, with the approval of other family members, presented them to the Canadian War Museum in trust in November 1977, together with the medals to his brothers Albert, Henry and Lawrence. The VC is held by the Canadian War Museum, 1 Vimy Place, Ottawa, Ontario, Canada.

37721 SERGEANT JAMES CLARKE
15th Battalion, The Lancashire Fusiliers

James Clarke was born on 6th April 1894 at Greenfield Cottage, 8 High Street, Winsford, Cheshire. His father, John Clarke (12th May 1861–1955), born at Bunbury, Cheshire, was a labourer living with his mother at 3 Whitby's Lane, Over, Cheshire in 1881. He married Hannah Hodkinson (15th June 1870–1952), born at Tunstall, Staffordshire, in 1889 registered at Northwich, Cheshire. He was a salt boiler in 1891, when they were living at 4 Greenfield Cottages, Over. They had moved to 8 Greenfield Cottages by 1901 and they were still there in 1939. In addition to James, they had fourteen other children, five of whom had died by 1911, including:

- Joseph Clarke (6th July 1890–21st May 1973), born at Over, was a farm labourer in 1911 living with his parents. He married Georgina Stoneley Parkinson (12th June 1894–17th January 1963), born at Chester, in 1913. She was a lodger in 1901 at 526

High Street, Vale Royal, Cheshire, with the family of Thomas and Ann Hough. By 1911 she was a servant to the family of James and Catherine Thompson at 38 Earlston Road, Liscard, Cheshire. He was a general labourer in a chemical works in 1939, when they were living at 10 Greenfield Cottages, Over. They were still there at the time of her death at The Memorial Hospital, Crewe, Cheshire. He was living at 41 Pulford Road, Winsford, Cheshire at the time of his death there. They had seven children:

High Street, Winsford.

- John 'Jack' Clarke (17th January 1914–1986) married Phyllis Lea (7th January 1916–30th June 2008) in 1933. John was a waggoner and a cowman on a farm in 1939, when they were living at Chester Lane Lodge, Northwich. They are believed to have had four daughters, including Edna Ivy Clarke (born 4th January 1934).

Winsford, on the River Weaver, grew up around salt mining after the river was canalised in the 18th century. The Norman Earls of Chester had a hunting lodge at Darnhall. King Henry III annexed the title and the lands. In 1270 he gave the estate to the Cistercians, who built Darnhall Abbey in 1274. However, the land was not suitable and the locals were not cooperative, so the monks left and founded Vale Royal Abbey in 1281. King Edward I granted a charter to hold a market and annual fair at Over in November 1280. Winsford began to expand after 1721, when Parliament gave permission for improvements on the River Weaver that allowed sea-going vessels to reach Winsford from Liverpool. They brought china clay from Cornwall for the Potteries in northern Staffordshire. Locally produced salt was transported to the Potteries for use in salt-glazed stoneware. Finished ceramics were brought back to Winsford for export through Liverpool. That trade ended in the 1780s when the Trent and Mersey Canal opened, bypassing Winsford. The railway arrived in 1837. From the 1830s salt became important and the town expanded, with many buildings having timber frames because of the risk of salt subsidence. There was another major expansion in the late 1960s and 1970s to house overspill population from Liverpool. John Swanwick Bradbury, 1st Baron Bradbury GCB (1872–1950) was born in Crook Lane, Winsford. He was Private Secretary to the Chancellor of the Exchequer, Herbert Asquith (Prime Minister 1908–16) 1905–08, Principal Clerk in the Treasury and First Treasury Officer of Accounts 1908–11, Joint Permanent Secretary to the Treasury 1913–19 and the Principal British Delegate to the Reparations Commission in Paris 1919–25. During the Great War he was the Government's chief economic adviser. At the outbreak of the war, the Government needed to preserve its stock of bullion and asked the Bank of England to cease paying out gold for its notes. Instead the Treasury issued Ten Shilling and £1 notes, which were known as Bradbury pounds because the notes bore his signature.

Bunbury was listed in the Domesday Book of 1086, when the lord was Robert FitzHugh. On 23rd December 1642 some prominent gentlemen of Cheshire met in Bunbury to draw up the Bunbury Agreement, which was intended to keep Cheshire neutral during the English Civil War. It was a forlorn hope because of the strategic importance of Cheshire and the city port of Chester. In 1940 German aircraft returning from a raid on Liverpool jettisoned surplus bombs over the village, obliterating Church Row.

Northwich lies at the confluence of the rivers Weaver and Dane. The area around the town has been exploited for its salt since Roman times when the settlement was named Condate. Northwich appears in the Domesday Book. The salt beds beneath Northwich were re-discovered in the 1670s while searching for coal. During the 19th century it became uneconomical to mine the salt. Instead, hot water was pumped through the mines, the brine was pumped out and the salt extracted from it. However, this technique led to significant land subsidence. By 1732 the River Weaver had been improved to allow vessels up to 160 tons to travel up to Northwich. The Trent and Mersey Canal opened in 1775 and the Anderton Boat Lift opened in 1875 to connect the canal and river systems. The railway arrived in 1863. In 1874 soda ash manufacturing commenced using salt as a main raw material. Subsided land was used to dispose of the dangerous alkaline waste. Much of this unusable land has since been reclaimed and a programme to stabilise the abandoned salt mines was undertaken between 2004 and 2007. Bulk chemical industries also formed in the area, which became concentrated at the three Imperial Chemical Industries sites at Winnington, Wallerscote and Lostock.

- Joseph Clarke (5th March 1915–2009) was a baker in 1939, living with his parents. He married Lily Burgess (born 13th April 1916) in 1940. She was a domestic servant in 1939, living with her parents at 173 Delamere Street, Winsford. They are believed to have had a son, Alan Clarke, in 1951.
- Albert Clarke (22nd June 1918–4th March 1982) was a general labourer for Hutton's Contractors in 1939, living with his parents. He married Eileen 'Irene' Preston (born 1922) in 1940. She was living with her parents at 135 Gladstone Street, Winsford in 1939. They had two children – Joyce Clarke 1941 and Albert N Clarke 1944.
- Ivy Clarke (23rd March 1923–12th July 2009) married William Henry James (25th December 1917–12th May 1987), born at Cuddington, Cheshire, on 28th March 1942 at St John's Church, Over Winsford. He was working in motor haulage in 1939, when he was living with his parents at 58 Church Walk, High Street, Northwich. They both died at Tarporley, Cheshire. They had four children – Barry P James 1944, Christopher W James 1947, Marilyn B James 1948 and Michael J James 1950.

    - Leslie Clarke (13th August 1928–October 1993) married Edna Hornby (born 1931) in 1952. She was living with her parents at 65 Wall Street, Winsford in 1939. They had three children – Leslie Clarke 1954, Graham Clarke 1957 and Susan Clarke 1958.
    - Eric Clarke (2nd January 1932–1947).
    - Alec Clarke (born 1934).
- Alice Clarke (born 1892) was a farm servant in 1911 living with her parents.
- John Victor Clarke (28th May 1898–26th August 1972) married Olive Mary Kent (4th June 1903–29th September 1996) in 1930 at Nottingham. He was a blacksmith in 1939, when they were living at 75 Cromwell Road, Winnington, Northwich. They were living at 179 Cromwell Road at the time of his death there. They had a daughter, Margaret L Clarke (born 1933).
- Hannah Clarke (1900–02).
- Thomas Clarke (22nd March 1902–1966), born at Winsford, married Mary Ikin (20th June 1908–April 1974) in 1933. He was a permanent way labourer in 1939, when they were living at Moss House, Littler Lane, Winsford. They had three children – Brian Clarke (1934), Samuel Clarke (18th April 1935) and Mavis J Clarke (12th April 1938–1941).
- Naomi Clarke, (12th April 1904–12th December 1950) married Sidney Hatton (11th April 1905–11th January 1979) in 1924. He was a builder's bricksetter in 1939, when they were living at 532 High Street, Winsford. They had three children:
    - Freda May Hatton (25th January 1929–7th September 2001) married Alfred Fowles (1925–27th January 1966) on 20th September 1951. They had two children – Alfred M Fowles 1952 and Sandra M Fowles 1957.
    - Kenneth Hatton (15th February 1930–16th April 1988).
    - Joan Hatton (born 1937) married Roy Ashley (5th September 1936–April 1993) in 1962. He was living with his parents at 20 Chapel Street, Winsford in 1939. They had two children – Kathryn Ashley 1964 and Martin Ashley 1968.

Sidney married his sister-in-law, Florence Matilda Hatton late Evans née Randall (3rd March 1902–28th April 1977), birth registered at West Ham, in 1951 registered at Northwich. Florence had married Albert John Evans (5th August 1902–30th March 1973), at St Oswald's Church, Walthamstow, London on 24th September 1921. He was living with his parents at 85 Darwin Road, Ealing, London in 1911. He was a motor driver/window cleaner in 1939, when they were living at 24 Coppermill Lane, Walthamstow, London. Albert subsequently died there. They had three children – Leslie HJ Evans (1922–2007), Gordon A Evans (1925–94) and Brian R Evans (1929). The marriage ended in divorce. Florence then married Sidney's brother, John S Hatton (15th May 1902–23rd August 1951) in 1948, registered at Southend-on-Sea. They were living at 51 John Street, Winsford at the time of his death at Albert Infirmary, Winsford. John had married Florence Mills (4th March 1903–1945) in 1924. He was a joiner at a chemical works in 1939, when they were living at 51 John Street, Winsford. John and Florence Mills had two children – John Hatton 1926 and Florence M Hatton 1931.

- Sarah Clarke (19th October 1906–1958) married Joseph Oakes (28th July 1907–May 1937), born at Middlewich, on 4th July 1931 at St John the Evangelist Church, Over. Sarah married Albert Thompson (1st November 1901–1974) in 1938. He was a farm labourer in 1939, when they were living at 12 Greenfield Cottages, Winsford. Sarah had seven children from her two marriages and previously:
    - Roland Clarke (22nd July 1925–July 2001) was a farm labourer in 1939, living with his mother and stepfather. He married Joan Davies in 1951. They had two children – Alan Clarke 1955 and Shirley Clarke 1957.
    - Cyril Oakes (born 24th December 1931) married June Woodward (born 1937) in 1956. She was living with her parents at 2 Springvale, Rilshaw Lane, Winsford in 1939. They had two children – Alan J Oakes 1960 and Julie M Oakes 1963.
    - Rosina Ellen Oakes (16th July 1933–1956), died at Liverpool, Lancashire.
    - June Ellen Thompson (10th April 1939–January 2006) married Phillip J Donaldson (born 1937) in 1962. He was living with his parents at South View Cottage, Nantwich in 1939.
    - Alma S Thompson (born 1940) married Alan Lowndes (born 1933) in 1960. He was living with his parents at 17 Moss Bank, Winsford in 1939. They had three children – Denise A Lowndes 1963, Rachel Lowndes 1965 and Yvonne Jane Lowndes 1970.
    - David John Thompson (12th June 1944–20th April 1970) was living at 109 Dene Drive, Winsford at the time of his death.
    - Kathleen J Thompson (born 1948) married Carl Hodkinson (19th May 1948–April 1984) in 1967. They had two children – Wayne Anthony Hodkinson 1971 and Adele Karen Hodkinson 1973.
- Alfred Clarke (1st November 1907–1972) married Margaret Pickstock (30th March 1914–November 2005) in 1938. He was a cowman in 1939, when they were living at Chester Lane Brook, Northwich. They had seven children:
    - Elsie M Clarke (born 1939) married William H Lloyd in 1964. They had four children – William Lloyd 1965, Jane Lloyd 1966, Mary Lloyd 1973 and Peter Lloyd 1974.
    - Edith M Clarke (born 1940).
    - Alfred E Clarke (born 1942).
    - Mary H Clarke (born 1946) married Leonard Noden (born 1946) in 1966. They had at least one son, Mark Anthony Noden, in 1968.
    - Marion J Clarke (born 1948) married Robert F Tickle (born 1950), birth registered at Chester, in 1972. They had a daughter, Michelle Tickle 1974.

- James J Clarke (born 1950).
- Robert A Clarke (born 1953).

- Mary Clarke (20th October 1908–February 1994) married Bertram Hope (19th January 1903–1949) in 1934. He was living with his parents at 4 Worthing Street, Northwich in 1911. Bertram was a silica labourer in 1939, when they were living at 304 Station Road, Winsford. Mary married Patrick Duffy (July 1918–1988) in 1968. He was a farm labourer in 1939, living with his father at 42 Lewin Street, Middlewich. Mary had three children from her first marriage and previously:
    - Royston Clarke (born 10th October 1928).
    - Glenise Hope (6th June 1941–14th August 2005) married Alan J Dickenson in 1961. They had three children – Alan J Dickenson 1961, David G Dickenson 1964 and Paula Elaine Dickenson 1967.
    - Barbara Hope (born 1942) married Peter Foxley (1942–3rd November 2015) in 1964. They had at least two children – Jacqueline Foxley 1964 and Linda J Foxley 1965.
- Harry Clarke (12th May 1910–1966) was a gardener in 1939, living with his parents at 8 Greenfield Cottages, Over.

James's paternal grandfather, Joseph Clarke (c.1823–64), born at Tilston, Cheshire, married Eliza née Duckers (c.1835–1923), born at Audlem, Cheshire, on 16th February 1858 at St Boniface's Church, Bunbury, Cheshire. She was a servant for farmers James and Sarah Dobson at Wistaston in 1851. He was an agricultural labourer in 1861, when they were living at Bunbury. Eliza was a charwoman in 1871, living with her children at Blakeden Lane, Over and at 3 Whitby's Lane,

St Boniface's Church, on the highest point of the village of Bunbury on an older pagan site, is a Grade I listed building. There has been a church on the site since the 8th century, initially wooden but by 1135 there was a stone Norman church. It was rebuilt in 1320 and in 1385–86 Sir Hugh Calveley endowed it as a collegiate church and much of the existing structure dates from that time. A chantry chapel was added in 1527. After the chantries and collegiate churches were dissolved in 1547, the tithes passed to the Worshipful Company of Haberdashers. Nave galleries were added in the 18th century and major restoration work was carried out between 1863 and 1866. The church was damaged by German bombing in 1940 and the roof was replaced in 1950. Sir Hugh Calveley's (died 23rd April 1394) alabaster tomb and effigy is in the centre of the chancel. He took part in the Hundred Years' War, holding various military posts in Brittany and Normandy. There is some doubt as to whether he was buried there. In the north wall of the sanctuary is the tomb of Sir George Beeston, commander of *Dreadnought* in the fight against the Spanish Armada in 1588. The old churchyard contains the graves of five Great War soldiers and the churchyard extension four soldiers and a naval officer of the Second World War.

Over in 1881. In 1881 there was also a grandson, Thomas Clarke, aged five, living with her. Eliza was living at 3 Greenfield Cottages, Over in 1891 with her daughter, Eliza, and grandchildren, Tom Clarke (1876–1913) a farm labourer, Albert Clarke (1883–1953) and Lily Clarke (1889). Their parents are not known. Eliza married George Royle (1834–1914), a salt dealer born at Utkinton, Cheshire, in 1891. They were living at 3 Greenfield Cottages in 1891 with Eliza's grandsons, Tom and Albert Clarke. They were still living there in 1911, with Tom and Albert. In addition to John, James and Eliza had three other children:

- Ann Clarke (born 1857), birth registered as Clark, was a domestic servant with her sister, Elizabeth, for the Major family at Park Field House, Calveley, Cheshire in 1881.
- Charlotte Clarke (5th October 1859–1946), birth registered as Clark, married Reuben Egerton (1855–1930) in 1880. He was the son of Eliza Egerton (c.1836–1909), who married Samuel Hunt (c.1831–1906), a salt maker, in 1857. Reuben was recorded as Hunt in the 1861 Census, living with his mother and Samuel Hunt at Over Lane, Over. In 1871 Reuben was recorded as Edgerton, a farm servant working for John Bebbington, farmer of 122 acres at Over. Reuben was a salt boiler, living with his family at 530 Victoria Terrace, High Street, Over in 1881 and 1891. Charlotte was a fustian cutter in 1891. In the 1901 Census they appear inexplicably as Reuben and Charlotte Hunt, living at Oulton Low, Little Budworth, Cheshire. Reuben was a cowman on a farm in 1911, when they were living at Tetton, Middlewich, Cheshire. Charlotte was living at 516 High Street, Winsford in 1939 with her grandsons, Richard Egerton and Albert Capper. Charlotte had seven children from her marriage and previously, one of whom died before 1911, including:
    - Eliza Clarke (born 1879).
    - Sarah Egerton (born 1884).
    - Samuel Egerton (1888–1917) married Annie Peake in 1913. They had two children – Richard Egerton (born 6th July 1913) and Kathleen H Egerton (born 1914).
    - Ethel Egerton (15th January 1892–1970) married Alfred Hatton (1893–1966) in 1915. They had seven children – Florrie Hatton 1916, Alice Hatton 1918, Marjorie Hatton 1923, William Hatton 1924, Henry Hatton 1926, Sidney Hatton 1929 and Ruby Hatton 1931.
    - Catherine Egerton (20th December 1894–29th January 1974) married James Hatton (30th October 1896–1973) in 1922. They had five children – Marjorie Hatton 1923, William Hatton 1924, Henry Hatton 1926, Sidney Hatton 1929 and Ruby Hatton 1931.
    - Alice Egerton (1898–1928) married Richard Capper in 1920. They had four children – Albert Capper (15th July 1920), Phyllis M Capper 1923, Frank Capper 1924 and Denis Capper 1925.

- Elizabeth 'Eliza' Clarke (2nd June 1864–1952) was a domestic servant with her sister, Ann, working for the Major family at Park Field House, Calveley, Cheshire in 1881. She was a fustian cutter in 1891, living with her mother. Eliza married Philip Stoneley (1871–1937), a salt maker, in 1896. They were living at 4 Greenfield Cottages, Over in 1901 and 1911. She was still living there in 1939. Eliza had eight children from her marriage and previously, one of whom had died by 1911:
    - Lily Clarke (13th May 1889–1973) is believed to have married Thomas Hough in 1911.
    - Frederick Stoneley (9th June 1896–1976) was a domestic garden labourer in 1911 living with his parents. He is believed to have married Martha A Hickson (born 1897 or 1898) in 1931.
    - Annie Stoneley (21st April 1898–21st August 1980) married Walter Gunnery (1889–1922), registered at Chester in 1919. They had a daughter, Barbara A Gunnery, in 1920. Annie married William Walker in 1945.
    - Clarrie Stoneley (27th January 1901–March 1991) married John Fleet (1901–50) in 1922. He was a shunter in the salt industry in 1939, when they were living at 10 Winsford Hill, Winsford. They had three sons – Ronald Fleet 1922, Clifford Fleet 1926 and Kenneth Fleet 1928.
    - Philip Stoneley (3rd July 1903–1946) was a general labourer in 1939, living with his mother. He died at Albert Infirmary, Winsford.
    - Thomas Stoneley (13th July 1905–1955), a horse driver, married Mabel Ollier (12th January 1914–1982) in 1934. They were living at Greenfield Cottages, Winsford in 1939. They had two children – May Stoneley 1934 and Ian T Stoneley 1944. Mabel married Royston Walker (6th May 1907–1972) in 1958.
    - Leonard Stoneley (3rd November 1907–July 1943) married Doris Gardiner (26th November 1914–1981) in 1938. He was a permanent way labourer in 1939, when they were living at The Row, Sandiway, Northwich. They had two children – Barbara Stoneley 1938 and Kenneth Stoneley 1943. Doris married Harold L Hall in 1952.
    - Probably Edward Stoneley (1909–10).

His maternal grandfather, Matthew Hodkinson (1843–1918), born at Over, married Hannah née Prince (1846–90), also born at Over, in 1866. She was living with her parents at Rushton, Cheshire in 1851. She and her daughters, Betsy and Hannah, were living with her brother, Peter Prince, and family at Duke Street, Tunstall, Staffordshire in 1871. Matthew was a salt boiler in 1881, when they were living at 20 Dean Street, Over. He was living with his children at 498 High Street, Over in 1891 and with his daughter Hannah and family at 8 Greenfield Cottages, Over, Northwich, Cheshire in 1901. In addition to Hannah, Hannah senior had eight children from her marriage and previously:

The ancient borough of Over, which is mentioned in the Domesday Book, is now part of Winsford. Prehistoric tools have been found in the area. A Saxon stone cross was found between the World Wars when St Chad's Church was altered, although no church is mentioned in written records before the Normans. The Earls of Chester hunting lodge or summer palace at Darnhall was taken over by King Henry III, who spent some time there. At that time the brook was dammed to drive three water mills and create ponds to keep fish. King Edward I vowed to found an abbey in Cheshire when he was in danger of being shipwrecked. Cistercians chose to live in the wildest places, using their farming skills to clear forest and to bring unused land into use. A group of monks set up the new abbey but were allowed to move to a better site that became Vale Royal Abbey. During the Dissolution of the Monasteries in 1545, the Abbey and its lands were sold to Thomas Holcroft and almost immediately to Edmund Pershall, a London merchant. During the English Civil War in 1643, Royalists escaping from Nantwich sacked Over. The salt industry created massive pollution and, as the wind usually blew away from Over, it became popular for the homes of wealthier people.

- James Prince (1865–1933) was a salt labourer in 1881, living with his mother and stepfather as Hodkinson.
- Betsy (birth registered as Betsey) Hodkinson (1867–1933) married Arthur Billington (26th June 1866–1950) in 1890. He was a salt works labourer in 1891, when they were living at 34 Dean Street, Over. They had moved to 3 Dalk Cottages, Swanlow Lane, Winsford by 1901, by when he was a general labourer. In 1911 he was a general labourer for the Urban District Council. He was living alone at 53 Swanlow Lane in 1939. They had six children including:
    - Arthur Billington (1891–1967) was a jobbing gardener in 1911, living with his parents.
    - Annie Billington (22nd April 1893–1955) was a milliner in 1911, living with her parents. She married Laban Atherton (14th November 1899–1978) in 1923. He was a grocery shop assistant in 1939, when they were living at Delamere Street, Winsford. They had two sons – Kenneth Atherton 1924 and Sydney Atherton 1929.
    - Miriam Billington (1897–1914) was a domestic in 1911, living with her parents.
    - George Henry Billington (25th October 1898–1976) married Phyllis Hamlet in 1951.
    - Oswald Billington (29th July 1900–1978) married Ida Mary Holmes (16th November 1902–1992) at Sheffield in 1924. They had a son, Eric Billington, the following year.
- Catherine Hodkinson (15th December 1873–1960), born at Tunstall, Staffordshire and registered as Hodgkinson, was a domestic servant in 1891 at the home of Henry and Alice Cookson, farmers, at Fields Farm, Darnhall, Cheshire. She was

living with Thomas Ankers/Angus Simcock (1st October 1867–1909), a stone breaker road labourer born at Mobberley, Cheshire, at 84 Manchester Road, Lostock Gralam, Cheshire in 1901 as his wife but they never married. Thomas was born illegitimately and was adopted by William and Lucy Parkwood by 1871, when they were living at Sale. Thomas was reclaimed by his mother, Ann Simcock (1849–1927), after her marriage to Joseph Fowles in 1876. They were living at Bootle Lodge, Mobberley in 1881. Thomas's death was registered at Bucklow, Cheshire. Catherine was a charwoman in 1911, boarding with Peter Frederick Atkinson and family at 25 Thomas Street, Altrincham, Cheshire, along with her children, Thomas and Elsie. She was a nursery weeder living at 9 King Street, Altrincham when her son, George, was born in 1915. She was living at 3 Clifford Avenue, Altrincham in 1939, with the surname Simcock overscored with Hodkinson in the Register. Catherine's death was registered as Simcock at Bucklow. Thomas Simcock senior had married Margaret Letitia Jackson (13th January 1872–1899) in 1893, registered at Altrincham, where she was born. She was living with her parents at Peck Mill Farm, Little Warford, Marthall, Cheshire in 1891. Thomas and Margaret had two daughters – Maggie Simcock born 1894 at Mobberley and Ann Elizabeth Simcock born 1894 at Handforth, Cheshire. Catherine had three children:

  - Thomas Simcock (1901–74), born at Lostock Gralam.
  - Elsie Simcock (born 1907), birth registered at Stockport.
  - George James Hodkinson (16th June 1915–1965), born at 23 Paradise Street, Altrincham, was a charge hand in 1939, living with his mother. He married Eveline Southern (born 1912) in 1941, registered at Bucklow, where she was born. They had two children – Beryl Hodkinson 1941 and James Hodkinson 1945.

- Louisa Hodkinson (2nd September 1876–1952) was a laundress, lodging with two widowered general labourers, William Dunn (c.1867) and Thomas McLoughlin (c.1870), at 19 Old Market Place, Knutsford, Cheshire in 1911. She had seven of her children (Thomas to Alice) with her. Louisa married Michael Finn (5th November 1882–1952), a general labourer, in 1921, registered at Bucklow, Cheshire. They were living at 23 Market Place, Knutsford in 1939. Her death was registered at Leigh, Lancashire and his at Bucklow. Louisa had nine children:
  - Thomas Hodkinson (born 1895).
  - Mary Hodkinson (born 1896).
  - John Hodkinson (27th September 1898–1973) married Annie Steele in 1920. They are believed to have had three children – Samuel Hodkinson 1921, Hilda Hodkinson 1923 and Charles Hodkinson 1927.
  - Annie Louisa Hodkinson (born 1902), birth registered at Bucklow.
  - Catherine 'Katie' Hodkinson (4th March 1904–1986) married Richard Ball in 1936, registered at Bucklow.

  - Margaret Ellen 'Nellie' Hodkinson (24th June 1908–1970) married Walter Renshaw in 1943. They had a daughter, Margaret A Renshaw, in 1945.
  - Alice Hodkinson (born 1909) is believed to have married Roland Jones in 1930.
  - Winifred Hodkinson (born and died 1912).
  - Michael E Hodkinson (born 1914) married Gladys Moss in 1936. They had two sons – Anthony T Hodkinson 1939 and Stewart Hodkinson 1947.
- Alice Hodkinson (6th December 1878–1960) married Samuel Hunt (1866–1930) in 1893. He was living with his parents at Victoria Terrace, Over in 1871. Sam was a general labourer in 1901, when they were living at 500 High Street, Winsford. By 1911 he was a salt worker and they were living at 512 Victoria Terrace, Winsford. Alice was still living there with some of her children in 1939. They had twelve children:
  - Mary Hannah Hunt (1893–1939) was a domestic servant in 1911, living with her parents. She married John Ellis in 1915, registered at Leigh, Lancashire. They had four children there – Lilian M Ellis 1920, Joyce Ellis 1925, Bessie Ellis 1928 and Jennie Ellis 1932. Mary's death was registered at Wigan, Lancashire.
  - John Hunt (7th September 1895–1963).
  - James Hunt (24th August 1897–1946) was an agricultural labourer in 1939, living with his mother.
  - Catherine Hunt (1899–1965) married Hector Davies (1900–58) in 1921. They had at least three children – Eva Davies 1921, Hector Davies 1925 and William Davies 1928.
  - Tom Hunt (born 1902) married Elsie M Carrick (4th May 1908–1982) in 1939. They had three children – Sam Hunt 1940, Barbara A Hunt 1942 and Maureen G Hunt 1945.
  - Matthew Hunt (10th March 1904–1970) was a chemical labourer in 1939, living with his mother.
  - Samuel Hunt (4th February 1908–1969).
  - George Hunt (14th December 1908–1965) was a public contractor's labourer in 1939, living with his mother.
  - Alice Hunt (1910–25).
  - Nellie Hunt (1912–20).
  - Alfred Hunt (11th November 1916–January 1974) was a farm horseman in 1939, living with his mother. His death was registered at Liverpool. He may have married Frances M Brown in 1943.
  - Ernest Hunt (20th August 1921–1979) was a private service gardener in 1939, living with his mother. He is believed to have married Phyllis M Capper (born 1923) in 1940. They had at least four children – Alice Hunt 1942, Susan Hunt 1946, Vivienne Hunt 1949 and Maralyn (sic) Hunt 1952.

- Fanny Hodkinson (29th March 1881–1971) appears as Mary in the 1881 Census. She married William Williams (20th December 1839–14th August 1909), a shipwright, on 26th February 1907 at Whitegate Church, Cheshire. They were living at 16 School Road, Meadow Bank, Winsford at the time of his death there. Fanny was a servant for Sarah Hitchinson at 21 Main Road, Moulton, Cheshire in 1911. Her daughter was living with her. Fanny was a housekeeper at the County Mental Hospital, Chester in 1939. They had a daughter:
    - Violet Williams (20th September 1907–1984) married Albert Whitney (born 1904) in 1925. They had two daughters – Sheila Whitney 1926 and Joyce Whitney 1933.

  William Williams had married Mary Ann Buckley (8th January 1843–23rd August 1899), born at Liverpool, Lancashire, on 21st January 1861 at Wharton Church, Northwich. William and Mary had eleven children – William Williams (1862–1905), George Hulme Williams (1864–1921), Thomas Williams (1866–1935), Walter Buckley Williams (1868–1871), Priscilla Williams (1870–1906), Maud Williams (1872), John Williams (1874), Joseph Williams (1876), Sarah Annie Williams (1879–1952), Mary E Williams (1881) and Frederick Hulme Williams (1885). Frederick Hulme Williams enlisted in the Army Service Corps (3529) at London on 5th September 1914 and joined at Aldershot next day. He had served a six-year apprenticeship with the Salt Union Ltd in Cheshire. He was described as a motor driver, 5′ 8½″ tall, weighing 149 lbs, with fresh complexion, brown eyes, brown hair and his religious denomination was Church of England. His next of kin was his wife, Minnie Elizabeth Williams née Cross (20th May 1882–April 1972), living at 8 Woodfield Terrace, Thornwood, Epping, Essex. They married on 23rd January 1912 at Ascot, Berkshire and had two children – Marjory Eileen Williams born 17th May 1912 and Jack Noel Williams born 25th December 1913. Frederick went to France on 21st September and served with 71st Company MT ASC. He suffered severe rheumatic fever and was ill for twenty-nine weeks. As a result, he was discharged on 26th March 1915 no longer physically fit for war service. He was granted a pension of 1/6d per day for twelve months, later reduced to 9d per day. In October 1916 he enquired if he could receive the Silver War Badge as he was being asked constantly why he was not serving. Minnie was a widow in 1939, living with her daughter, Marjory Prowse, wife of William Prowse (1901–76), at Grove Cottage, Ross, Herefordshire.
- Thomas Hodkinson (11th March 1883–1951) was an agricultural labourer in 1901 at Old Grove, Minshull Vernon, Cheshire. He married Catherine/ Katherine Leigh (23rd March 1870–1942), born at Brooklands, Cheshire, in 1907 registered at Bucklow. She was a servant for Rebecca Jones at 40 St Bees Street, Moss Side, Hulme, Lancashire in 1901. Thomas was an assistant gardener in 1939, when they were living at 15 Kara Street, Seedley, Salford, Lancashire. They had two children:

- ◦ James Leigh Hodkinson (26th May 1908–1967) married Emily Bird (born 11th January 1914), a capstan lathe hand, in 1934. James was a textile dyer in 1939, when they were living with Job and Thurza E Bird at 22 Ashcroft Avenue, Salford. They had a daughter, Jean Hodkinson, in 1945. The marriage is believed to have ended in divorce. Emily married John Brokenshire (1901–56) in 1955, registered at Barton, Lancashire. James married May Dean née Hogan (29th April 1907–1992) in 1955. May had married Thomas R Dean in 1933.

St John's School, Over Winsford has been the local school for Over since the 1860s. The original building dates back to 1840.

- ◦ Mary Hannah Hodkinson (24th July 1909–November 1988) was a cotton doubler, living with her parents in 1939. She never married.

Rochdale lies at the foot of the Pennines on the River Roch. A Saxon castle, of which nothing remains, was one of twelve constructed against the Danes in the 10th and 11th centuries. Rochdale appears in the Domesday Book in 1086 as *Recedham*. Weekly markets were held from 1250 and, by 1251, the town was important enough to be granted a Royal Charter. The town expanded due to the wool trade, particularly in the 19th century when it became a mill town for textile manufacturing during the Industrial Revolution. The Rochdale Canal was built to move cotton, wool, coal, limestone, timber and salt. It became a major artery for commerce between Lancashire and Yorkshire by linking the Bridgewater Canal in Manchester with the Aire and Calder Navigation at Sowerby Bridge. The railway arrived in 1841. The town's economic success led to its rise to borough status. However, during the 20th century textiles production declined and eventually halted. Rochdale is the birthplace of the modern Cooperative Movement in 1844. The Grade I listed Town Hall of 1871 is one of the finest examples of Victorian Gothic revival architecture. John Byron bought the manor in 1638 and it was in the family until sold by the poet, Lord Byron, in 1823. The first seven series of the BBC school drama *Waterloo Road* were filmed in Rochdale 2006–12. The Rochdale Crisis Intervention Team co-ordinator, Sara Rowbotham, made more than 180 attempts to alert police and social services to the Rochdale child sex abuse ring from 2003. She was ignored until 2014 because witnesses were considered to be unreliable. Amongst the town's notable people are:

- Sir Cyril Richard Smith MBE MStJ DL (1928–2010), a Labour and Liberal politician, who was MP for Rochdale 1972–92. His reputation was marred by his involvement in covering-up a health risk posed by an asbestos factory, in which he owned 1,300 shares. After his death the Crown Prosecution Service admitted that Smith should have been charged with the sexual abuse of young boys. There had been 144 complaints against Smith but attempts to prosecute him had been blocked. A number of public authorities were implicated in covering up his alleged crimes.
- Dame Gracie Fields DBE OStJ (1898–1979), the actress, singer, comedian and star of cinema and music hall, was the highest paid film star in the world in 1937.
- Sajid Javid (born 1969) was the Conservative Home Secretary 2018–19, Chancellor of the Exchequer 2019–20 and Secretary of State for Health and Social Security 2021–22.

William Tatham & Sons was established at Rochdale in 1866. It manufactured machinery for the textile industry and in its heyday employed 300 people. The company closed after 136 years with the loss of ninety jobs.

- Lottie Hodkinson (6th August 1885–1966) was living with George Yarwood (born 1874), a horse driver whose birth was registered at Ashton, Lancashire, as his wife at 14 York Place, Northwich in 1911, with William and Annie Evans. In the Census that year they claimed to have been married for six years but were not married until 1913. They had one child who had died by 1911. Lottie married Arnold Cecil Crosby (18th February 1887–1961), born at Allostock, Cheshire, in 1918, registered at Bucklow. He was a labourer in a brickyard in 1901, living with his mother at London Yard, Allostock. He was a thrashing machine attendant in 1939, when he and Lottie were living at 24 Wincham Lane, Northwich. His death was registered at Northwich and hers at Wirral, Cheshire.

James was educated at St John's School, Over Winsford, Cheshire. He was employed as a farm labourer before moving to Rochdale, Lancashire in 1913, where he was a carter with Butterworth Bros, Carters of Milnrow and later for William Tatham & Sons in Rochdale.

James married Betty Sophia Wood (6th July 1891–1972), a cotton mill cardroom hand born at Milnrow, Lancashire, on 7th August 1915 at St James, Milnrow. They were both living at 2 Whitworth Street, Rochdale at the time. They were living at 29 Clyde Street, Rochdale in February 1919 and had moved to 174 Milnrow Road, Rochdale by 1933. They were living at 20 Back Clyde Street, Rochdale in 1939, by when he was a pensioner and she was a cardroom drawer. Her death was registered at Littleborough, Lancashire. They had five children:

- James Clarke (born 1916), born at Rochdale.
- Vera Clarke (23rd October–22nd November 1919), born at 35 Swanlowe Lane, Winsford, Cheshire and died at 29 Clyde Street, Rochdale.
- Edith Clarke (born and died 1921), born at Rochdale.
- Hilda Clarke (28th August 1922–2nd July 1995) was a ring room gaiter up in 1939, living with her parents. She married Leslie Walter Dobson (2nd October 1920–2nd September 2007) on 23rd March 1948. He was a bleaching hand in 1939, living with his parents at 996 Edenfield Road, Rochdale. Leslie served in the Royal Air Force. Hilda inherited her father's VC medal group. Hilda and

Milnrow, on the River Beal at the foot of the South Pennines, now forms a continuous urban area with Rochdale. Occupation of the area goes back to the Mesolithic period and there are Bronze Age, Iron Age, Saxon and Norman remains. The Byron family was endowed land in Milnrow during Norman times. In 1253, King Henry III granted rights to the Knights Hospitaller to try suspected thieves, regulate the production and sale of food and erect a gallows for public executions. The area was primarily used for marginal hill farming during the Middle Ages. Shallow coal mining was recorded in 1610. The population increased with the wool trade in the 17th century. In the 19th century, the Industrial Revolution replaced domestic woollen industries and converted the area into a mill town. Cotton spinning was the main industry with mass-produced textiles from Milnrow being exported globally with the arrival of the railway in 1863. Throughout the 20th century coal mining and cotton spinning declined.

Leslie were living at 96 Norden Road, Bamford, Rochdale in 1984. She died at Bamford, Rochdale and he at Morecambe, Lancashire. They had two children, births registered at Littleborough, Lancashire:

- ◦ Renee Dobson (born 1947) married John P Dobson in 1971 registered at Colchester, Essex. They had triplets – Antoinette Mary, Julie Ruth and Lee Paul Mason in 1974.
- ◦ Jeanette Dobson (born 1949) married Paul AC Ferrigia in 1980 at Rochdale.

- Elsie Clarke (7th September 1927–May 1995) married John Whitworth (9th February 1923–January 1997) in 1949, registered at Littleborough. He was a ring doffer in 1939, living at 29 Wellington Street, Milnrow. The marriage ended in divorce. John is believed to have married Helen G Janssen in 1956 and they had a son, John R Whitworth, in 1957. Elsie is understood to have lived with Albert Edward Hughes from 1952. They were living at 20 Back Clyde Street, Rochdale in 1957. Elsie married Frank Kemp on 25th March 1964. She was living at 36 Deane Street, Blackpool, Lancashire when she attended the dedication of her father's headstone in November 1994. Her death was registered at Blackpool and Fylde. Elsie had five children from her various relationships – Patricia Whitworth (31st October 1947), Denis Whitworth (1953), David Whitworth (1955), Susan A Whitworth (23rd July 1957) and Gary Kemp (1967).

A chapel of worship had been built by the River Beal in 1496 and was enlarged in 1537 but it often flooded and a new site was sought. The medieval church was rebuilt in 1798 and 1815. The current Church of St James was built close to the original in 1868–69.

Betty's father, Joshua Wrigley Wood (9th February 1855–7th December 1918),

1 Nall Street, Milnrow, where Betty was living with her father and sisters in 1901.

born at Saddleworth, Yorkshire, was living with his parents at Ginnell, Butterworth, Lancashire in 1861. By 1871 the family had moved to Milnrow, Butterworth, by when he was a warehouseman. Joshua married Elizabeth Ann née Mellowdew (c.1859–98), born at Blatchinworth-with-Calderbrook, Lancashire, registered as Melladew, in 1878 at Rochdale. He was a colliery banksman in 1881, when they were living at Hollingsworth Fold, Butterworth. He was a fellmonger in 1891, when he was living with part of his family at 3 Lily Street, Butterworth. By 1901 he was living at 1 Nall Street, Milnrow with his daughters, Beatrice, Nellie and Betty. Joshua was living with his widowed sister, Betty Fielding in 1911. In addition to Betty, Elizabeth and Joshua had eight other children:

- Eliza Wood (1878–1945) was raised by her grandparents. She was a cardroom back tenter in 1911.
- Charles Joshua Wood (1879–20th August 1918) was a cotton doffer in 1891, living with his parents. He was serving as a private in 1st Border (4261 & 202604) when he died of wounds (Longuenesse (St Omer) Souvenir Cemetery, France – V D 78).
- Hannah Wood (12th April 1882–1963) was a cardroom engine head tenter in 1891, living with her parents. By 1901 she was a cotton ring piecer, living with her aunt, Betty Sophia Fielding, at 26 Bridge Street, Rochdale. She had a son, Fred Wood (17th April 1902–1973). Hannah married Francis 'Frank' Stonewall Jackson (5th October 1880–1961), born at Manchester, Lancashire, at Rochdale in 1907. He was a tool machinist in 1911, when they were living at 1 Whatmough Square, Milnrow. He was a salesman in 1939, when they were living at 18 New York Street, Rochdale.
- Beatrice Wood (14th January 1885–1955) was a cotton ring piecer in 1901, living with her father. She married William Henry Irvine (1882–1906) in 1906 (sic). William's brother, Fred Butterworth Irvine (1885–10th July 1918) was serving as an air mechanic 2nd class in the Royal Air Force (61949) when he died (Rochdale Cemetery – Plot O, Grave 14155). Beatrice was living alone at 29 Clyde Street, Rochdale in 1939.

Charles Joshua Wood's grave in Longuenesse (St Omer) Souvenir Cemetery. The inscription is very difficult to read.

- Nellie Wood (11th January 1889–1st January 1967) was a cotton ring piecer living with her parents in 1891 and with her father in 1901 and 1911. She never married. She had a daughter, Beatrice Wood (1913–66), who married Fred Taylor Sutcliffe (18th December 1909–1974) in 1937. They had two sons – Douglas Sutcliffe 1947 and William Sutcliffe 1948.
- Godfrey Wood (22nd March 1896 – later in 1896).
- Albert Wood (22nd June 1897–1940), a twin with Fred, was living with his aunt, Betty Sophia Fielding, at 26 Bridge Street, Rochdale in 1901 and 1911, by when he was a reacher in a weaving firm. He was a labourer when he married Margaret Buckley (10th April 1900–1991) on 29th August 1921 at St James's Church, Blatchinworth-with-Calderbrook, Lancashire. They were both living at 5 Mount Pleasant, Calderbrook Road, Littleborough. She was living with her parents at 7 Ward Street, Manchester in 1901 and at 5 Mount Pleasant, Calderbrook Road, Littleborough in 1911. They are believed to have had a daughter, May Wood, in 1921. Albert was a general labourer in 1939, living with Ellen Raymond (born 2nd March 1897), a spinster, at 77 Newhey Road, Milnrow. Margaret was a cotton spinner in 1939, living with John Greenwood, a married general labourer (14th December 1896–1972) at 1A Salley Street, Littleborough. Margaret married Anthony Nell (16th August 1877–2nd October 1959), a colliery hewer born in Finland, in 1945. Anthony had married Clara Hodgson (13th April 1874–31st August 1943), born at Barnsley, Yorkshire, on 25th December 1900 at St Paul's Church, Monk Bretton, Barnsley. They were living at 15 Wakefield Road, Old Mill, Monk Bretton in 1911 and at 40 Eldon Street North, Barnsley in 1939. Anthony and Clara had a daughter, Elsie Annie H Nell (24th January 1904–23rd March 1991) who married Edward Hunter in 1929 and they had six children – Brian Hunter 1929, Terence Hunter 1931, Gordon Hunter 1933, Betty Hunter 1934, Leslie Hunter 1936 and Jean M Hunter 1937. Margaret married thirdly Ernest Preece (28th June 1911–September 1994), a cotton mill labourer, in 1960. He was living at 395 Queensway, Rochdale.
- Fred Wood (22nd June 1897–1898) was a twin with Albert.

James Clarke with his barrel organ.

James enlisted in 6th Lancashire Fusiliers on 10th October 1915 and transferred to 15th Battalion after training in 1916. He was promoted sergeant and was appointed acting company sergeant major but, because of a shortage of NCOs, he also continued with his platoon. **Awarded the VC for his actions at Happegarbes, France 2nd-4th November 1918, LG 6th January 1919.** The VC was presented by the King in the ballroom at Buckingham Palace on 13th February 1919. Rochdale honoured him with a public reception on 1st February and Winsford

The Volunteer Drill Hall was opened on 26th June 1901 by Lieutenant General The Earl of Dundonald KCVO KCB, just after the return of Winsford men from the Boer War. He took part in the Nile Expedition and commanded the Camel Corps for the relief of Khartoum. He was the first to enter Ladysmith after the town had been under siege from 2nd November 1899 to 28th February 1900. In 1914 the drill hall was used by a detachment of E Company, 7th Battalion, The Cheshire Regiment TF. It contained a shooting gallery, main hall for drill, offices, kitchen and an armoury. Adjoining the building was a house for the sergeant instructor and a large yard for outdoor drilling. By 1935 the hall had been converted into the Palace Cinema. It became a bingo hall in the 1970s. The hall burned down in February 2021.

The Grade II listed Marlborough Street Magistrates Court on Great Marlborough Street, London was a court of law from the early 19th century. It saw many trials, including those of Oscar Wilde, Christine Keeler, Mick Jagger and Keith Richards of the Rolling Stones and John Lennon. It closed in 1998 and is now The Courthouse Hotel London. Charles Dickens worked there in 1835 as a reporter for the *Morning Chronicle*. Louis Napoleon (the future Napoleon III) appeared as a witness in a fraud case in 1847. The current building was designed in 1912–13.

Belle Vue Stadium in Manchester was the venue for the first race around an oval track in Britain on 24th July 1926. It has also been used for speedway, stock car and banger racing. The track was owned and operated by the Greyhound Racing Association. It was bought by The Crown Oil Pension Fund in 2014. The name of the stadium came from the nearby Belle Vue Zoological Gardens built in 1836. By June 1927, the stadium was attracting almost 70,000 visitors a week. Its closure was accelerated by the Covid-19 pandemic. At Belle Vue there was also a funfair and scenic railway that enjoyed a boom in the 1950s and 1960s, when up to 150,000 people would flock to the park on public holidays. The King's Hall opened in 1910 and became a popular music venue hosting some of the world's biggest names such as Jimi Hendrix, The Who, Rolling Stones, Eric Clapton and the Bay City Rollers. The King's Hall also hosted circuses until 1981. The zoo closed in 1977 and the amusement park in 1980. The Stadium was subsequently demolished to make way for housing.

on 14th February. The Winsford procession commenced at St John's School before moving to the Drill Hall for the civic reception. He was presented with an illuminated address, £10 in cash and £50 in war savings certificates. His wife received a gold necklace and a pendant. James was discharged on 13th May 1919.

James and Betty about to depart for the Victory Day Celebrations in London in June 1946.

He worked as a stoker in Wilmslow for eight years until 1927. He was then in and out of jobs through ill health following a serious mastoid infection. At one time he was a temporary road worker in Manchester. In desperation he worked as a busker with a barrel organ in Manchester after being unemployed for ten months. He went to London and wore his VC while playing his barrel organ with Arthur Collins in Marlborough Street and Coventry Street. In March 1933 he was charged with obstruction. At Marlborough Street Magistrates Court he asked for the charges against Collins to be dropped as he took full responsibility. In his defence he stated that he was a VC recipient and had a wife and three children to support. He had been out of work trying to make an honest living but had been unable to send anything home lately. He owed £3 on the organ and had just 2½d in his pocket. He had not eaten that day and concluded by saying that he was supposed to be one of Lloyd George's heroes. The magistrate discharged both men under the Probation Act. James was later employed as an attendant at Belle Vue Greyhound Racing Track, Manchester.

James attended three VC reunions – the VC Garden Party at Buckingham Palace on 26th June 1920, the VC Dinner at the Royal Gallery of the House of Lords, London on 9th November 1929 and the Victory Day Celebration Dinner & Reception at The Dorchester, London on 8th June 1946.

Birch Hill Hospital has its origins in the Dearnley Union Workhouse, which opened in November 1877. An infirmary was added in 1902 and during the Great War parts of the hospital were used for service personnel. It became the Dearnley Public Assistance Institution in 1930 and joined the National Health Service as Birch Hill Hospital in 1948. Services transferred to Rochdale Infirmary and Birch Hill closed in January 2013. The site was sold for residential development with the clock tower being retained. Other parts of the hospital were retained including a psychiatric hospital on a smaller site.

James Clarke died of pneumonia at Birch Hill Hospital, Rochdale on 16th June 1947. His funeral, with full military honours, was followed by burial in an unmarked grave in Rochdale Cemetery (Plot O, Grave 14155). The Lancashire Fusiliers Regimental Association arranged for a wooden cross to be erected over the grave in 1992. A proper headstone was erected in 1993 and it was dedicated on 11th November 1994, with his daughter, Elsie Kemp, and other family members in attendance. The VC & GC Association was represented by Lieutenant Commander Ian E Fraser VC DSC RD. James is commemorated in a number of other places:

James Clarke's grave in Rochdale Cemetery (Memorials to Valour).

- RSM James Clarke VC Walk, Memorial Gardens, Rochdale named on 21st June 2015.
- Winsford, Cheshire
    - James Clarke Road.
    - A rose garden outside Winsford Lifestyle Centre, The Drumber, with a granite bench bearing his name.
    - Named on the War Memorial on a panel to those 'Died from wounds received 1914 to 1918'.
    - A Department for Communities and Local Government commemorative paving stone was dedicated in the rose garden outside Winsford Lifestyle Centre on 2nd November 2018.
- His VC action featured in Issue 782 of the Victor Comic entitled 'A True Story of Men at War' dated 14th February 1976.

The granite bench and commemorative paving stone in the rose garden outside Winsford Lifestyle Centre (Memorials to Valour).

In addition to the VC he was awarded the British War Medal 1914–20, Victory Medal 1914–19 and George VI Coronation Medal 1937. The medals were owned by his daughter, Hilda, who sold them at auction at Christie's for £8,800 on 24th July 1984. The group was sold to Lord Michael Ashcroft at Spink's on 12th March 1996 for £22,800. The VC is held by the Michael Ashcroft

Winsford War Memorial and details of the panel to those 'Died from wounds received 1914 to 1918' (Graham Flatt and Memorials to Valour).

Trust, the holding institution for the Lord Ashcroft Victoria Cross Collection, and is displayed in the Imperial War Museum's Lord Ashcroft Gallery.

MAJOR BRETT MACKAY CLOUTMAN
59th Field Company, Royal Engineers

Brett Cloutman was born on 7th November 1891 at Marsden House, Colney Hatch Lane, Muswell Hill, London. His father, Alfred Benjamin 'AB' Cloutman (1861–9th August 1933), was a furniture salesman born at Calverton, Buckinghamshire. He married Charlotte (also seen as Clarissa) Jane née Reeve (1862–96), a machinist whose birth was registered at Wells, Somerset, in 1887 at St George, Hanover Square, London. She was living with her parents in 1881. In 1891 they were living at Brooklyn, Harrow, Middlesex. Alfred became Governing Director of Maple & Co. Charlotte's death was registered at Marylebone, London. Alfred married Alice Mary Marnham (23rd January 1858–6th May 1938), born at Blackheath, Kent, on 17th March 1898 at the Baptist Chapel, St Leonard's-on-Sea, Sussex. Alfred was described as a house furnisher in 1901, when they were living at The Gables, Green End, Southridge, Grosvenor Terrace, Hemel Hempstead, Hertfordshire. They were living at Hillcrest, Waverly Road, Crouch End, North London in 1911 and at Old Hall, 17 South Grove, Highgate, London at another time. Alfred was a Baptist layman in later life. In 1929 he donated anonymously a site at the corner of Elmfield Avenue and Tottenham Lane to the Ferme Park Baptist Church, which became a YMCA with Alfred appointed

The earliest records of Muswell Hill date from the 12th century. The Bishop of London granted land to the east of Colney Hatch Lane, on which a newly formed order of nuns built a chapel, named Our Lady of Muswell. By the 18th century Muswell Hill was a scattered village of detached villas. Towards the end of the 19th century it was developed into the London village that it is today. Nearby Alexandra Palace opened in 1873, served by a railway from Highgate, with a station at Muswell Hill. More development took place in the early 20th century. The first public television broadcasts were made from Alexandra Palace before the Second World War. In 1964, three Muswell Hill residents, brothers Ray and Dave Davies and Pete Quaiffe, formed *The Kinks*, one of the most important and influential rock groups of that time. Former KGB agent, Alexander Litvinenko, lived in Muswell Hill from 2000 until his assassination in 2006.

Calverton, is situated south of Stony Stratford, six and half kilometres west of Milton Keynes. The parish consists of Lower Weald and the hamlets of Upper and Middle Weald. In the Domesday Book of 1086 Calverton was recorded as Calvretone. All Saints parish church was rebuilt between 1818 and 1824. Calverton Manor (Grade 2* listed) was sold in 1616 to Sir Thomas Bennet, Lord Mayor of London in 1603, and was extended in 1659. The Manor is reputedly haunted by Lady Grace Bennett, who was murdered there in 1694.

Old Hall, South Grove, Highgate began as a detached house with extensions added later. It is now divided into flats. Francis Bacon, 1st Viscount St Alban (1561–1626), died there. He served as Attorney General and Lord Chancellor under James I. It is contended that he wrote some of Shakespeare's plays. He became the first Queen's Counsel in 1597, when Elizabeth I appointed him her legal advisor.

President. The fact that he was the benefactor was only announced at his funeral. He was living at 19 South Grove, Highgate, London at the time of his death there, leaving effects valued at £51,015/8/5 (£4.25M in 2023). Alice was living at 4 Holly Lodge Gardens, West Hill, Highgate at the time of her death there, leaving effects valued at £54,371/14/2 (£4.5M in 2023). Brett had two brothers from his father's first marriage:

The first Baptist Church in Crouch End formed in 1807 and met in Broadway Hall, which was once part of the outbuildings of Old Crouch Hall, until 1837. From 1879 a second Baptist congregation met in Broadway Hall, until increasing population led to the erection of Ferme Park Baptist Church in 1889 with seating for 630. Congregations continued to grow, and a new chapel was built adjacent to the old between 1897 and 1900, with a capacity of 1,250. The old chapel was converted into halls and a flat. The Baptist Chapel merged with the United Reformed Church in 1973 and opened on the same site as the Union Church in 1980.

- William Alfred Cloutman (1888–1946), born at Harrow, Middlesex, was a merchant who worked in Chile. He married Lina (born c.1887) at Valparaiso, Chile. They arrived at Liverpool from Valparaiso aboard SS *Ortega* on 28th June 1922, giving their address as Old Hall, Highgate Village. He died at Santiago, Chile.
- Wolfred Reeve Cloutman (9th July 1890–21st August 1915), born at Wealdstone, Harrow, was a mining student, living with his father in 1911. He was educated at London University (BSc (Eng), where he was a member of the OTC, and the Royal School of Mines (1st Class Diploma). He applied for a commission on 28th January 1915 and was described as just over 5′ 9½″ tall and weighing 145 lbs. He was commissioned in the Royal Engineers on 19th February 1915 and went to France on 25th February. Mentioned in Despatches, LG 22nd June 1915. He was promoted lieutenant on 9th July and joined 178th Tunnelling Company RE at Méaulte, France on 13th August. The Company had just taken over the notorious Tambour mining section in front of Fricourt from the French. A survey was being conducted underground when a camouflet was fired on 21st August. The unit war diary states that a Royal Engineers sergeant and an infantryman were asphyxiated, and Lieutenant Jameson and three other ranks were gassed. Wolfred rescued an injured sergeant in the mine and carried the man fourteen metres up a ladder. Immediately after handing him over, Wolfred was overcome by fumes and fell to his death. For his devotion to duty, he was again Mentioned in Despatches, LG 1st January 1916. He is buried in Norfolk Cemetery, Becordel-Becourt, near Albert, France – I A 14. In the grave next to him is buried 88958 2nd Corporal Edwin Hart, also 178th Tunnelling Company, who died on 22nd August 1915, aged thirty-two.

Brett's paternal grandfather, William Curtis Cloutman (17th February 1825–8th April 1899), married Elizabeth Alice née Brett (7th August 1828–16th May 1900) on 26th April 1847 at Camberwell, London, where she was born. He was a master carpenter, employing five men, in 1851, when they were living at 39 St George's or Commercial Road, Camberwell, London. By 1861 he was a builder's foreman and

Barbara Kent with Harold Lloyd in the 1930 film, *Feet First*. She was less than five feet tall. In 1925 she won the Miss Hollywood Beauty Pageant and was contracted by Universal Studios. She starred with Greta Garbo in the 1926 film *Flesh and the Devil*. In 1927 she appeared to be swimming naked in the film *No Man's Law* but was actually wearing a flesh-coloured bathing suit, something that was considered very daring at the time. She starred opposite Harold Lloyd in the 1929 comedy *Welcome Danger* and in 1930 in *Feet First*. Barbara married Harry Edington in 1932 and Jack Monroe in 1954. She led an active life, flying light aircraft until her 85th birthday and was still playing golf in her nineties.

they were living at Calverton End, Calverton, Buckinghamshire. By 1871 he was a surveyor of land and buildings, living with his family at 4 County Place, Bedminster, Somerset. They had moved to Carleton Villa, Stapleton, Gloucestershire by 1881. William died at his home at 137 Wells Road, Totterdown, Gloucestershire and Elizabeth at Bristol, Gloucestershire. In addition to Alfred they had nine other children:

- Louisa Elizabeth Cloutman (18th October 1848–26th March 1950), born at Peckham, London, was a housekeeper at 33 Portman Street, Chorlton, Lancashire in 1911. She was incapacitated in 1939, living at 145/7 Bishop Road, Bristol. She died at The Eventide Nursing Home, Chesterfield Road, Bristol.
- Curtis William Cloutman (1850–24th December 1927) was a stationer in 1871. He married Emily Jane Jullion (13th November 1855–23rd February 1957), birth registered at Poplar, London, in 1876 at Bristol, Gloucestershire. They were living at The Laurels, 2 Bellevue Road, Bedminster, near Bristol in 1891 and were still there in 1911. They were living at The Laurels, 3 Wells Road, Totterdown, Bristol at the time of their deaths. They had six children including:
    - Ivy Cloutman (1877–3rd January 1941) married Charles Frederic George Newcombe (1876–December 1938) in Bristol in 1903. They had a daughter,

Valentine George Crittall JP, 1st Baron Braintree, (1884–1961). He was elected Labour MP for Maldon, Essex in the 1923 general election, with a majority of only forty-nine. He served as Parliamentary Private Secretary to Lord Thomson, Minister of Air but lost his seat in the 1924 general election. In 1926 he founded the garden village of Silver End, near Braintree, Essex to accommodate people who worked in the Crittall family's growing factories. He was knighted in 1930, was elevated to the peerage in 1948 and was a director of the Bank of England 1948–55. Crittall married three times - Olive Lillian MacDermott in 1915, Lydia Mabel Revy in 1933 and Phyllis Dorothy Cloutman in 1955. He had no male children, and the barony died with him.

Joan Marjorie Newcombe in July 1905. She was living at 8 Alma Road, Clifton, Bristol when she died.

- Jullion Curtis Cloutman (4th February 1880–25th October 1955) was a stationer in 1901, living with his parents. He married Lily Louise Kent and they had a daughter, Barbara Cloutman (later Kent) (16th December 1907–13th October 2011), born at Gadsby, Alberta, Canada, who became a Canadian actress of the silent and early talking film eras in the 1920s and 1930s. Jullion died at Los Angeles, California, USA.
- Phyllis Dorothy Cloutman (15th October 1889–8th October 1972) married George Henry Nelson Parker (1881–1938) in 1912 at Bristol. He was later manager of an insurance company. They had five children – Curtis PN Parker 1913, Barbara MN Parker 1915, Jullion CN Parker 1917 and twins Greville CN and John CN Parker 1922. Phyllis married Valentine George Crittall, 1st and last Baron Braintree, in 1955. She was living at Queen's Meadow, Bocking, Braintree, Essex when she died.
- Enid Audrey Cloutman (16th April 1893–23rd December 1971) married Henry James Drew-Smythe MC TD MS FRCS NMSA FRCOG (1891–1983) at Bristol in 1914. Henry served in both world wars in the RAMC, rising to colonel. They were living at 17 Withyholt Park, Charlton Kings, Cheltenham, Gloucestershire at the time of her death there. Henry was living at 2 Charlton Close, Charlton Kings at the time of his death there. They had two sons:
  - Richard 'Dickie' David Somerset Drew-Smythe (1920–87) received an emergency commission in the Indian Army on 12th December 1942 and served with 1st King George V's Own Gurkha Rifles and 43rd Armoured Division in India and Burma. Dickie farmed in Wiltshire, became Master of Foxhounds of the North Hereford Hunt and an Inspector with The British Horse Society. He married Jean Dionis Anstruther (1927–61) in 1949 at Holy Trinity Church, Brompton, Kensington, London, and they had two children – Ian David Drew Smythe 1950 and Janet D Drew-Smythe 1954. He married Mary Georgiana Glyn (formerly Mrs John William Talbot Lewes) (1935–93) in 1965 at Weymouth, Dorset. They divorced in 1982.
  - John 'Johnny' Roderick Smythe (1923–90) was commissioned in the Indian Army on 7th December 1942 and was Mentioned in Despatches for his service with 7th Rajput Regiment in Burma, LG 19th July 1945. He married Pamela Margaret Swiney (1920–98) in 1947 at Bristol. She was a doctor's secretary in 1939, living with her parents at 28 Queens Court, Bristol. They divorced and Pamela never remarried. They had two children – Jonathan J Drew-Smythe 1949 and Barnaby M Drew-Smythe 1958. Johnny married his cousin, Jill Margaret Cloutman (1920–2010) in 1964 (see below under Brett's second daughter).

    - Norman Frayne Cloutman (27th November 1894–September 1941) was commissioned in 3/6th Gloucestershire on 5th November 1914 and was promoted lieutenant on 20th March 1916. He later served in 2/6th Battalion and last appears in the Army List in April 1917. He married Esme Gerrish (1891–1960) at Bristol in March 1922. Norman was a divorced retired insurance official, living at Edson's Farm, Long Ashton, near Bristol in 1939. He died at Taunton, Somerset.
- Alice Isabel Cloutman (1852–1912) was living with her younger sister, Lavinia and family, in 1911. She died unmarried at Bristol.
- Walter James Cloutman (1853–30th January 1929) was a clerk in a surveyor's office in 1871, living with his parents. Later he was a commercial traveller. He married Marion Evans (1852–1915) in 1877 at Bristol, where she was born. He was living with his brother Alfred at the time of the 1891 Census. They were living at Glen Cottage, Wells Road, Knowle, Bristol in 1901 and at 21 Lancashire Road, Bishopston, Bristol in 1911. Her death was registered at Worcester. He was living at Brentwood, 103 Malvern Road, Worcester at the time of his death there. They had five children:
    - Walter Evans Cloutman (30th September 1884–12th April 1954), a vicar, was a boarder at Plymouth, Devon in 1911. He married Dora Harris Balkwill (1888–1978) in July 1913 registered at Kingsbridge, Devon, where she was born. She was living with her parents at Dodbrooke, Devon in 1891 and 1901. They had two children – Margaret M Cloutman 1917 and Geoffrey W Cloutman 1920. They were living in Cheltenham, Gloucestershire in 1936. Walter died at Epping, Essex and Dora at Welwyn Garden City, Hertfordshire.
    - Gertrude Ellen Marion Cloutman (6th March 1886–1972) married Leslie Gordon Kinnersley (1885–29th October 1960), a dental surgeon, in Bristol in 1914. They had two daughters – Ruth Marion Kinnersely 1919 and Elizabeth Kinnersley 1921.
    - Harold Evans Cloutman (1891–11th June 1932) enlisted in 1st South Midland Brigade Royal Field Artillery on 2nd September 1914 and was discharged on medical grounds on 14th November (1552). He was deemed to have been enlisted on 2nd March 1916 and was called up in the Royal Artillery (239381 & 553784) at Bristol on 19th May 1917. He joined next day at No.3 Depot RFA, Hilsea, described as 5′ 8″ tall and weighing 138 lbs. He was found fit for C1 at Aldershot on 19th June and C2 on 21st September and was posted to 6C Reserve Brigade. Harold transferred to the Labour Corps (555984) on 28th April 1918 and served in 677th (Home Service) Employment Company. He transferred to 18th (Home Service) Battalion, Essex Regiment (58095) on 13th July and was found fit for B service abroad on 16th August but not General Service. He was transferred permanently and compulsorily to the RASC MT (M/417075) as a learner heavy driver

on 4th December and joined at Sydenham. He refused several vaccinations on 5th December but despite this he was found fit for overseas service. He was treated in hospital 14th December–21st January 1919 for influenza and dermatitis. On 22nd March 1919 he was transferred to the Class Z Reserve from No.1 Dispersal Unit, Wimbledon.

- Marion Doris Winifred Cloutman (1894–1935).
- Leslie Evans Cloutman (4th June 1896–28th January 1966), a clerk, enlisted in 1st South Midland (Gloucester) Brigade RFA (1858 & 825633) as a driver at Bristol on 13th November 1914. He was living at 67 Cotham Brow, Bristol and was 5′ 4″ tall. He was posted to 240th Brigade RFA, 48th Division, embarked at Southampton on 29th March 1915 and disembarked at Le Havre next day. Leslie was admitted to 1/2nd South Midland Field Ambulance with dyspepsia on 1st July, transferred to the Divisional Rest Station on 5th July and rejoined his unit on 7th July. He was in hospital 29th-31st March 1916 and was granted seven days leave on 28th April. On 10th November at Montecourt he was mounting a horse when it bolted and threw him against a gate post, resulting in him landing with full force on his knee. He was admitted to 1/1st West Riding Field Ambulance with synovia left knee on 19th November and joined 50th Base Depot, Le Havre on 23rd December. Leslie was posted to 18th Division Ammunition Column on 7th February 1917 and to A Battery, 83rd Brigade RFA, 18th Division on 1st May. He was granted leave 12th-26th September. On 7th October he was admitted to 3rd Anzac Field Ambulance and No.10 Casualty Clearing Station, Remy Siding, Lijssenthoek, Belgium with a synovitis injury right knee and was later transferred to 2nd General Hospital, Le Havre. He was discharged to the Base Depot on 29th October. On 11th November he was admitted to 40th Stationary Hospital, Harfleur, not yet diagnosed. He was transferred to 4th Convalescence Depot, Harfleur on 22nd January 1918 and was posted to C/306th Battery RFA on 29th January. He was admitted to No.53 Casualty Clearing Station, Roye, France on 23rd March, not yet diagnosed, and was transferred to 47th General Hospital, Le Tréport next day with myalgia. On 8th April he was discharged from 3rd Convalescence Depot to the Base Depot and joined First Army Royal Artillery Reinforcement Camp on 16th April. Leslie was granted leave 12th-26th September. On 27th September he was admitted to Worcester Military Hospital and was transferred to the Special Section, Chiseldon, Military Hospital next day with gonorrhoea. He was discharged to rejoin his unit on 9th December and joined First Army Royal Artillery Reinforcement Camp on 19th December. Leslie embarked for Britain aboard SS *Charles* to proceed to No.1 Dispersal Unit, Fovant, Wiltshire on 17th January 1919. He was disembodied on 15th February, giving his address as 103 Malvern Road, Worcester. He was discharged on demobilisation on 31st March 1920. Leslie married Marjorie

Woodruff (15th February 1900–14th March 15th April 1968), born at 10 Salisbury Terrace, Cassell Road, Fishponds, Bristol, at St Mary's, Fishponds on 10th September 1921. He was living at Fremantle Square, Kingsdown and she at Downend Road, Fishponds. They had a son, Basil WE Cloutman (1924–83). They were living at 166 Dorchester Road, Weymouth, Dorset in 1939, when he was a commercial traveller. He was living at 24 Southwoods, Yeovil, Somerset and Marjorie at Crestwood, Southwoods at the time of their deaths.

- Charles Arthur Cloutman (1855–65), born at Bloomsbury, Middlesex and died at Bedminster, Somerset.
- Lydia Slatter Cloutman (1857–30th September 1937), born at Calverton, Buckinghamshire, married Stuart Moore Rochead (8th September 1846–31st August 1926), a widower born at Glasgow, Lanarkshire, on 18th July 1893 at Russell Town Congregational Church, Cobden Street, Russell Town, Gloucestershire. He was a turkey red dyer in 1901, when they were living with the children from his first marriage at Stretford, Lancashire. By 1911 they were boarding at 130 St Andrews Road, St Anne's on the Sea, Fylde, Lancashire. He was living at 16 Athol Road, Alexandra Park, Manchester at the time of his death there. Lydia was living at 43 Townsend Drive, St Albans, Hertfordshire at the time of her death at St Albans and Mid-Hertfordshire Hospital. They had two daughters:
    - Lydia Gladys Rochead (1894–95).
    - Alice May 'Midge' Rochead (April 1896–1979), an elocution teacher born at Barton upon Irwell, Lancashire, married William Stainer Valentine (18th September 1895–9th March 1964), born at Earlestown, Lancashire, at Warrington, Cheshire in June 1922. They had one daughter, Jean M Valentine, in 1926. William was educated at Ashton Grammar School, Ashton-under-Lyne, Lancashire and Edinburgh University, where he studied medicine 1913–15. He was a cadet sergeant in the University Senior Division, Officers' Training Corps from February 1914 and was commissioned on the Unattached List, Territorial Force for service with the infantry unit of Edinburgh University Officers' Training Corps on 15th December. He was commissioned in 4th Queen's Own Cameron Highlanders on 14th April 1915, with seniority from 15th December 1914. William served in France July 1915–August 1916 and August–November 1917. Regular Commission 15th September 1915. Promoted temporary lieutenant on 1st October 1915 and was attached to the Machine Gun Corps in March 1916. He was wounded on the Somme in August and promoted lieutenant on 15th September. He transferred to the Indian Army to serve with 3/9th Gurkha Rifles from 8th February 1918. William transferred to 4/39th Garhwal Rifles on 5th November and was invalided home in January 1919. He transferred to 5th Prince of Wales's Volunteers (South Lancashire

Regiment) on 18th May 1920, with seniority from 9th September 1916. Promoted temporary lieutenant 10th April 1921 and captain 1st July 1921. He last appears in the Army List in September 1922. They were living at Greenways, Old Harpenden Road, St Albans, Hertfordshire in 1938. William was appointed captain and administrative officer Royal Artillery Territorial Army 2nd May–2nd September 1939 (90602) and was promoted war substantive major on 27th September 1943. He was appointed SO2 Education, British Advisory Staff, Polish Resettlement Corps, Northern Command on 15th July 1946. He transferred to the General List on promotion to major on 1st December 1946, with seniority from 27th April 1943 and continued in the same appointment. William relinquished his commission on completion of service on 1st December 1949 with the honorary rank of lieutenant colonel. Awarded the Territorial Efficiency Decoration, LG 21st April 1950. William died at Nobles Hospital, Douglas, Isle of Man. Alice also died at Douglas.

Stuart had married Sophia Hay Telfer (1849–8th December 1891), born at West Derby, Lancashire, in 1880 at Rochdale, Lancashire. Her death was registered at Barton upon Irwell, Lancashire. Stuart and Sophia had five children – Katharine Sophia Rochead (30th October 1881–24th July 1974), Mary Stuart Rochead (10th November 1882–1941), Constance Muriel Rochead (9th April 1884–10th December 1943) and twins, Stuart Percival Rochead (2nd December 1885–1949) and Marguerite Evelyn Rochead (2nd December 1885–18th July 1908).

- Albert Edward Cloutman (1864–27th October 1951), born at Bedminster, Somerset, was a clerk salesman to a cold merchant in 1881, living with his parents. He married Blanche Furlowe (1867–15th September 1961), birth registered at Pontypool, Monmouthshire, on 17th September 1891 at Holy Trinity and St Philip's, Bristol. She was living with her parents at George Street, Trevethin, Monmouthshire in 1871. Albert was a builder's merchant in 1901, when they were living at 3 Drummond Villas, Fishponds Road, Stapleton, near Bristol. They sailed for Wellington, New Zealand on 9th January 1908 and were living at Todd's Road, Ashurst, North Island in 1916 before moving to Drury, near Auckland. They had four children:
    - Albert Reginald Cloutman (26th June 1892–28th December 1975), a farmer, enlisted in 35th Reinforcements (25810) on 30th May 1916, described as 5′ 7½″ tall, weighing 131 lbs, with medium complexion, blue eyes, brown hair and his religious denomination was Church of England. Posted to E Company, 17th Reinforcements. Transferred to Featherston Details on 26th August, Trentham Details on 28th August, E Company, 17th Reinforcements on 30th August and HQ Staff on 10th September. A medical board at Trentham on 17th April 1917 reviewed an old fracture of the lower left leg and found him fit for active service. He transferred to the NZASC as a driver on 22nd April, to Trentham Details and Featherston

Details on 25th August, 34th Reinforcements NZASC on 28th August, 36th Reinforcements NZASC on 3rd October, 34th Reinforcements NZASC on 13th October, 36th Reinforcements NZASC on 16th January 1918 and 35th Reinforcements NZASC on 26th January. Active service commenced on 23rd February. He embarked at Wellington aboard HMNZT 101 *Tofua* on 2nd March and disembarked at Suez, Egypt on 8th April. He embarked at Suez on 30th April, disembarked at Southampton on 15th May and joined at Durrington Camp, Larkhill, Salisbury Plain. Albert was attached to HQ NZEF on 21st May, marched into Sling Camp, Bulford on 6th July and joined the NZ Infantry Reserve Brigade from Larkhill on 12th July. On 14th October he was admitted to Tidworth Military Hospital with influenza, transferred to the New Zealand Convalescent Hospital, Hornchurch on 30th October and was discharged on leave on 26th November, to report to Codford, Wiltshire on 11th December. On 25th January 1919 he embarked at London aboard SS *Port Melbourne* and was admitted to the ship's hospital 1st-10th February. He arrived in New Zealand on 7th March and was discharged on 21st April 1919 no longer physically fit for war service due to bronchitis contracted on active service. He was only awarded the British War Medal. He married his sister-in-law, Frances Jessie Aurora Rolfe (4th November 1902–5th March 1988), in 1925.

- Charles Wilfred Cloutman (14th October 1896–1st November 1942), was a farm hand employed by W Doole of Pukekohu. He enlisted in the NZ Rifle

The building of Sling Camp commenced in 1903, but it expanded rapidly once war broke out. By 1916 it had been taken over by New Zealand forces and comprised four main sections - Auckland, Wellington, Otago, and Canterbury Lines. Its main purpose was to train reinforcements and recovering casualties. At the end of the war, there were 4,600 New Zealand troops there and it became a repatriation centre. The men were eager to return home, but no troopships were available due to overuse during the war and strikes. Eventually the men rioted in frustration. In the aftermath they were put to work carving an enormous Kiwi into the chalk hillside in February and March 1919. Although Sling Camp was removed in the 1920s, the Bulford Kiwi remains to this day. It covers 6,100 m2 and is 130m long. In the post-war years the Kiwi Polish Co maintained it and during the Second World War it was covered over to prevent it being used by enemy aircraft as a navigation marker. In 1948 local Boy Scouts removed the covering and added fresh chalk. Military units then took over the maintenance including the author's own unit, 249th Signal Squadron (AMF(L)), in the 1980s and 90s.

Brigade, H Company, 14th Reinforcements (14762) on 15th March 1916 and joined at Trentham. He declared previous service in the Cadets and was described as 5′ 10″ tall, weighing 161 lbs, with fair complexion, blue eyes and fair hair and his religious denomination was Methodist. He was on foreign service from 26th June, embarking at Wellington aboard HMNZT 57 *Tahiti*. He disembarked at Devonport on 22nd August and joined 3rd NZ Rifle Brigade Training Battalion. On 4th September he was admitted to No.1 NZ General Hospital, Brockenhurst and joined the NZ Command Depot, Codford on 28th October. He was confined to barracks for three days and forfeited two days' pay for being absent off pass from 11.00 p.m. on 13th November until 7.45 a.m. on 14th November. On 5th March 1917 Charles transferred to the NZASC and joined at Sling Camp, Bulford on 9th March. He joined No.4 Company NZASC on 23rd April as a driver, transferred to 4th NZ Field Ambulance on 25th May and went to France to join the unit on 29th May. He was attached to the NZ Wing, 2nd Anzac Reinforcement Camp on 11th October and rejoined 4th NZ Field Ambulance on 12th November. Charles joined XXII Corps Reinforcement Camp on 8th February 1918, was attached to Reinforcement Company, NZ Division Wing, XXII Corps Reinforcement Camp on 10th March and marched out to 2nd Entrenching Battalion, Étaples on 10th May, joining on 19th May. He was attached to the NZ Training Company on 8th June and proceeded to England on leave 31st August–17th September. He was promoted corporal on 28th December. On 14th March 1919 Charles embarked at London aboard SS *Ionic* for return to New Zealand. He was discharged on 16th June 1919. Charles married Edna Mabel Hannah Hall (1902–3rd August 1981) in 1925 and they had at least two children – Nola Clare Cloutman 1927 and John Edward Cloutman 1938.

- Olive Marjorie Cloutman (1898–15th July 1988) married Arthur Vere George Rolfe (6th February 1891–2nd March 1971) in 1920. They had at least three children – Ivan Wilfred Rolfe 1922, Leslie George Rolfe 1923 and Enid Irene Rolfe 1926. Arthur was a farmer, living at Swanson, Auckland, when he enlisted in 6th Company, Auckland Infantry Battalion. He attested at Trentham on 19th December 1914 (12/1783) but his service reckons from 14th December. His next of kin was his mother, Mrs Amelia Rolfe. Arthur declared previous service in D Squadron, Waikino and was described as 5′ 10½″ tall, weighing 168 lbs, with dark complexion, brown eyes, dark brown hair and his religious denomination was Church of England. He was promoted corporal on 30th December and sergeant on 18th January 1915. On 13th February he embarked aboard HMNZT 18 *Tahiti* with 3rd Reinforcements and disembarked at Suez on 26th March. He landed at Gallipoli on 5th May and was promoted sergeant on 8th May (nothing in his service record suggests that he was demoted after the promotion in

The Lady Hardinge Hospital for Wounded Indian Soldiers was established in the Balmer Lawns and Forest Park Hotels at Brockenhurst in 1914. Temporary structures in the grounds providing additional accommodation. The location was ideally situated close to railway links and the port of Southampton. The facilities were soon found to be insufficient and in 1915 a 500-bed facility of tented and hutted accommodation was constructed at Tile Barn, known as Tin Town. Almost 3,000 Indian soldiers were treated at Brockenhurst before the Indian Corps moved to Egypt in November 1915. Three Indian servicemen are buried in the CWGC cemetery at St Nicholas' Church, Brockenhurst. No.1 New Zealand General Hospital, one of three New Zealand general hospitals in Britain operated by the RNZAMC, was established at Brockenhurst in June 1916, after moving from Abasseyeh, Egypt. Over 21,000 patients, mainly New Zealanders, were treated there before the hospital closed at the end of January 1919. Ninety-three New Zealand servicemen died while being treated at Brockenhurst and are buried in the CWGC cemetery.

Codford Camp, Wiltshire was used by ANZAC forces as a training and transit depot. The AIF badge was carved into the chalk on the hillside above the camp (53 x 45m) in 1916. The soldiers of 13th Training Battalion, who had to maintain the badge, named it 'Misery Hill'. The nearby CWGC cemetery contains the graves of sixty-six New Zealanders and thirty-one Australians. The local community still feels a strong bond with the ANZAC troops and hold a remembrance ceremony on Anzac Day every year. A similar bond exists at nearby Sutton Veny (Australian War Memorial).

January). On 7th August he received a gunshot wound to the left side back and was also suffering from dysentery when taken aboard HMHS *Delta*. He was admitted to the NZ General Hospital, Cairo on 11th August, embarked aboard HMNZT 101 *Tofua* at Suez on 23rd September and disembarked in New Zealand on 26th October. Arthur was discharged medically unfit on 23rd February 1916. He re-enlisted on 7th July 1917 (15889) and joined 29th Specialist Company on 27th July. He was promoted QMS at Featherston on 3rd August. He embarked aboard HMNZT 91 *Mokoia* at Wellington for foreign service with 29th Reinforcements on 13th August. He disembarked at Glasgow on 2nd October, marched into Sling Camp, Bulford, Wiltshire to join 4th (Reserve) Battalion, Wellington Regiment (C Company) next day and reverted to temporary sergeant. He transferred to 4th Reserve Battalion, Auckland Regiment on 6th October and was taken on strength on 8th October. Having failed to qualify in an NCO's class of instruction on 27th October, he remained a temporary sergeant 28th October, and was attached to Details Company Camp and rejoined his unit from No.7 Camp on 14th December. Having achieved a very good pass in the last NCO class of instruction, he was confirmed as sergeant on 16th January 1918 and joined 4th Reserve Battalion, Auckland Regiment on 12th February. Arthur went to France on 20th March from 3rd Reserve Battalion, Auckland Regiment and joined 1st Auckland on 1st April. He was admitted to 6th General Hospital, Rouen (not yet diagnosed) on 4th May and later that day to 1st Stationary Hospital with venereal disease. He was transferred to 51st Stationary Hospital, Rouen on 13th May with syphilis and stomatitis. He was discharged from the venereal hospital but remained at 51st Stationary Hospital as a non-venereal patient. He was discharged to the NZ Infantry and General Base Depot on 30th June and transferred to 1st NZ Entrenching Battalion on 10th July. He was admitted to 6th General Hospital with a left inguinal hernia on 6th September and was evacuated to England on 15th September for admission to 2nd NZ General Hospital, Walton-on-Thames with debility. He rejoined the Auckland Regiment on 16th October. On 18th January 1919 Arthur embarked aboard HMT *Zealandic* in England and returned to New Zealand on 26th February. He was discharged on 27th August no longer fit for war service on account of illness contracted on active service. His address in August 1921 was Stafford Road, Northcote, Auckland.

    - Arthur Cecil Cloutman (14th October 1906–5th May 1982) married Eileen Isabel Margaret Norris (born 1910) in 1931 and Doris 'Dot' Ellen Huzziff (1st February 1910–30th June 1992) in 1938.

- Lavinia Bates Cloutman (10th February 1867–4th February 1960), born at Bristol, married James Bowland (28th June 1857–1st October 1943), a commercial traveller in stationery born at Bowdon St Mary's, Cheshire, in 1890 registered at Barton Regis. They were living at 12 Berkeley Road, Bishopston, Bristol in 1911 and at the time of his death at Snowdon Buildings, Fishponds, Bristol. Lavinia was living at 75 Belmont Road, St Andrews, Bristol at the time of her death at Ivywell, Church Lane, Backwell, Somerset. They had five children:

- ◦ Unnamed male (born and died 1892).
- ◦ Conrad Cloutman Bowland (24th August 1894–26th October 1918) enlisted in 26th Royal Fusiliers (19786) at Bristol on 7th December 1915 and joined at High Beech. He was described as a bank clerk, 5′ 6¼″ tall and his religious denomination was Congregationalist. In his will dated 24th April 1916 he left everything to his father. Conrad went to France on 4th May. He applied for a commission on 9th January 1917 while serving in 10 Platoon, C Company. He was treated for dental caries at 41st Division Rest Station 19th-21st February. He returned to Britain on 28 June on the strength of the Royal Fusiliers Depot and joined No.20 Officer Cadet Battalion, Crookham on 11th August. Conrad was discharged to a commission in 6th Gloucestershire on 27th November. He died of wounds at No.45 Casualty Clearing Station, Awoingt (Awoingt British Cemetery, Nord, France – I D 29).

Conrad Cloutman Bowland's grave in Awoingt British Cemetery.

- ◦ John Denis Bowland (1896–21st May 1965) emigrated to Australia. He married Constance Edith Macdonald in New Zealand in 1925 and died at Napier, Hawkes Bay, New Zealand.
- ◦ Doreen Mary Bowland (27th May 1899–June 1980) married Sidney Ewart Ralph (17th December 1897–6th February 1981), born at Clifton, at Bishopston, Bristol on 17th July 1925 and they had two daughters – Patricia Kathleen Ralph (1927–95) and Christine Norah Ralph 1930. Sidney was an office manager when he retired in 1962. Doreen died at Weston-super-Mare and Sidney at Backwell, Bristol.
- ◦ James Ritchie Bowland (16th June 1902–19th May 1974) married Marjorie E Williams (23rd March 1906–1987) at Bristol in 1929. James was a company deputy manager. He died at Bath, Somerset.

- Amelia Jessie Cloutman (1868–90), born at Bedminster, died unmarried at Barton Regis, Gloucestershire.

His maternal grandfather, William Frederick Reeve (16th November 1823–1891), born at Craven Street, Shoreditch, London, married Maria Matilda née Strickland (c.1832–91), born at St Luke's, London, on 19th December 1847 at St Mary, Islington, London. He was a foreman engineer in 1851, when they were living at

Craven Street in Westminster, originally Spur Alley, was rebuilt about 1730 when the land was owned by the Craven family. It has been home to a number of historical figures:

- Aaron Burr (1756–1836), 3rd Vice President of the United States, lived abroad in the years 1808–12, mostly in England on Craven Street.
- Benjamin Franklin (1706–90), the writer, publisher, scientist, inventor, statesman and diplomat, lived at No.36 for sixteen years before the American Revolution. The house is Grade I listed and is now a museum, Benjamin Franklin House.
- The German poet Heinrich Heine (1797–1856) lived at No.32 in 1827.
- Haematology pioneer, William Hewson (1739–74), also lived at No.36 for two years from 1772, at the same time as Benjamin Franklin. In 1998 the remains of six children and four adults discovered under the house may relate to medical experiments carried out there.
- Herman Melville (1819–91), author of *Moby-Dick*, lived at No.25 in 1849.

The Church of St Mary the Virgin, Islington is Grade II listed. The churchyard was enlarged in 1793, closed for burials in 1853 and was laid out as a public garden in 1885. The first recorded church building in the 12th century was replaced in the 15th century. In July 1738 George Stonehouse, Vicar of St Mary's, invited Charles Wesley to take charge as Curate, but did not possess a licence to do so from the Bishop of London. Wesley's preaching was unpopular with some of the congregation and within a year he was expelled and embarked on field-preaching. The church was in a ruinous condition and had to be rebuilt, the new building being consecrated on 26th May 1754. In 1759 Philip Quaque, son of King Birempong Cudjo, was baptised at St Mary's and became the first black African to be ordained in the Church of England. He returned to Ghana as a missionary. Daniel Wilson (1778–1858) was the Vicar 1824–32, then became Bishop of Calcutta. In 1831 he was one of the founders of the Lord's Day Observance Society. The Islington Clerical Conference, founded by Daniel Wilson, ran from 1827 until 1983 and was held at St Mary's. Samuel Ajayi Crowther from Sierra Leone studied at the church's school and attend services from 1826. He was ordained by the Bishop of London, served in West Africa and later became the first African bishop in Nigeria. A portico of Portland stone was built at the west door in 1904, designed by Sir Reginald Blomfield, a prolific architect of his age and designer of many war memorials, including the Menin Gate Memorial at Ypres, the RAF Memorial in London and the Cross of Sacrifice in most CWGC cemeteries. Donald Coggan, later Archbishop of Canterbury, was Curate 1934–37.

On 9th September 1940, during the Blitz, a bomb destroyed most of the church, leaving only the tower and spire intact. The rebuilt church was dedicated in 1956. David Sheppard, later Bishop of Liverpool, played cricket for England while an assistant curate 1955–57. In 1967 brothers Majeeb, Najeeb and Waheeb Chowdhry and friend Emmanuel Din started the first Asian Christian Church in the UK at St Mary's.

Islington. By 1861 he was a millwright and engineer and they were living at Horse Catch, Wookey, Somerset. They had returned to Islington by 1871 and were living there at 88 Bride Street and were still there in 1881. Both their deaths were registered at Islington. In addition to Charlotte they had eight other children:

- William Frederick Reeve (9th December 1850–7th March 1938), born at Islington, married Ida Ada Mary Glynn (6th July 1862–23rd December 1942), born at Whitechapel, London, in 1880 at Romford, Essex. He was a wharf manager in 1901, when they were living at 101 Erlanger Road, Deptford, London. They were living at 52 Palace View, Bromley at the time of his death at Bromley and District Hospital. She was living at 9 Greencourt Road, Orpington, Kent in 1939 and at 16 Towncourt Crescent, Petts Wood, Orpington at the time of her death at The County Hospital, Farnborough, Kent. They had four children:
  - Ruby Frederica Mary Reeve (30th December 1880–6th May 1972) married John Edward Rogers (10th January 1875–2nd July 1949), born at Whittington, Salop, on 5th August 1903 at St Catherine's, Hatcham, London. He was later a director. They were living at Croydon in 1911 and in Buckinghamshire in 1939. Ruby died at Eastbourne, Sussex.
  - Stewart William Reeve (born and died 1882).
  - Keith Glynn Reeve (5th September 1886–June 1965) married Daisy Lawrence (2nd November 1897–December 1973) in October 1931 at Winchester, where she was born. Both their deaths were registered at Brentwood.
  - Pearl Reeve (29th December 1893–March 1982), born at Greenwich, married Lloyd Harry Richards (9th January 1894–September 1970), an insurance official born at Deptford, London, at St Catherine's, Hatcham, London on 9th July 1921. He was living with his parents at Hornsey, Middlesex in 1901. They had one child – Pamela Richards in 1924. His death was registered at Bromley and hers at Croydon.
- Henry Charles Reeve (1853–64) died at Wookey, Somerset.
- Maria Matilda Reeve (1856–63) died at Wookey.
- Alfred John Reeve (1859–14th April 1940) was a watchmaker in 1881, living with his parents. He married Helen Candland (1855–2nd September 1949), birth registered at St Pancras, London, in 1882 at Islington. They were living at 29 Lucerne Road, Islington in 1901 and at 135 Newington Green Road, Islington in 1911. They were living at 73 Mildmay Park, London in 1915 and at 63 Clissold Crescent, Stoke Newington, London at the time of his death there. She was living at 6 St Mary's Road, Ealing, London at the time of her death at 35 Ravensbourne Gardens, Ealing. They had four children:
  - Alfred John Reeve (1883–84).
  - William Frederick Reeve (21st September 1884–1949) was a clerk at a wharf in 1911, living with his parents. He was still living with them at 73 Mildmay

Park, London when he enlisted in the Royal Field Artillery (83858) at Holloway, London on 21st January 1915. He was described as 5′ 5½″ tall and weighed 120 lbs. He joined at No.6 Depot RFA, Glasgow next day. Posted to 18th Reserve Battery, 3B Reserve Bde RFA, Topsham Barracks, Exeter as a driver on 8th March and to 20th Reserve Battery, 4A Reserve Brigade RFA, Woolwich on 1st May. Appointed acting bombardier on 27th August and was promoted on 9th November. Posted to the Mesopotamian Expeditionary Force, embarking at Devonport on 23rd December and disembarked on 10th March 1917. Joined 222nd Brigade Ammunition Column RFA at Makina on 18th March. He was granted one month's leave in India, embarking aboard HT *Aronda* on 28th April 1918. Embarked at Bombay aboard HT *Sicilia* on 21st June 1918 and disembarked at Basrah on 27th June. Rejoined his unit on 11th July. He left the unit at Sheikh Habil for demobilisation on 27th January 1919. Embarked aboard SS *Chakdina* on 22nd February and was struck off the strength of the Mesopotamian Expeditionary Force. Demobilised on 21st March. Discharged on 31st March 1920. William married Grace Irene Madley (28th April 1888–December 1966), birth registered at Holborn, London, on 22nd May 1915 at St Paul's Church, Canonbury, London, when they were living at 73 Mildmay Park. They were living at 30 Shelver's Way, Banstead, Surrey in 1939. They had two children – Grace Margaret Reeve (1916–2001) and Stanley William Reeve (1924–2006). William's death was registered at Lambeth, London and Grace's at Hounslow, London.

- Ernest Alfred Reeve (1886–1932) married Lily Anderson (1889–1919), born at Newington, London, on 23rd January 1909 at St Paul's Church, Canonbury. She was living with her parents at 260 Red Post Lane, East Ham in 1901. He was a telegraph clearing house clerk in 1911, when they were living at 25 Carysfort Road, Clissold Park, Stoke Newington, London. They had two children – Clifford Alfred Reeve (1909–2008) and Constance Grace Alma Reeve (1911–70). Lily's death was registered at Rochford, Essex and Ernest's at Hackney.
- Claude Harold Reeve (1890–23rd August 1918), a dental mechanic, married Eva Winifred Nash (24th March 1889), born at Cranbrook, Kent, on 21st November 1909 at St Paul's Church, Canonbury, London. They were both living at 9 St Paul's Place, Islington at the time. They later lived at 171 Fulham Road, Chelsea. Eva was living with her parents at The Hill, Cranbrook in 1891 and at Spring Cottages, Cranbrook in 1901. He enlisted in 3/28th Battalion, London Regiment (Artists' Rifles) (3504 & 760505) at Dukes Road, Euston Road, London on 19th March 1915, when he was living at 24 Green Lanes, Stoke Newington. He had served in 5th Middlesex but was discharged when the Territorial Force formed. He transferred to 1/28th London on 30th July, went to France from Southampton on 11th August

The Mailly-Maillet to Serre and Puisieux road entered no man's land 1,300m southwest of Serre. On 1st July 1916, 31st and 4th Divisions attacked north and south of the road unsuccessfully. On 13th November 3rd and 31st Divisions attacked again without success. Early in 1917, the Germans fell back to the Hindenburg Line and the battlefields of the Somme and Ancre were cleared by V Corps. A number of new cemeteries were made, three of which are named from the Serre Road. Serre Road Cemetery No.2 was begun in May 1917 and by the end of the war contained c.475 graves. After the war it was enlarged by burials brought in from the surrounding area and graves from sixteen smaller cemeteries. The cemetery, designed by Sir Edwin Lutyens, was completed in 1934. It contains 7,127 Commonwealth burials of the Great War, of which 4,944 are unidentified.

and joined the unit on 16th August. Claude was admitted to hospital 8th–9th March 1918. He died on active service on 23rd August 1918 (Serre Road Cemetery No.2, Serre, France – X G 12). Eva lived at various addresses, including 63 Park Lane, Stoke Newington until September 1918 and then at 75 Mildmay Park, Islington. She was granted a pension of £1/9/7 per week for her and her three children from 10th March 1919. She married Francis Frederick Bennett (1883–1969) at Islington in 1919 and they had two children – Trevor F Bennett 1919 and Joan Winifred Bennett 1921. Claude and Eva had three children:

- Claude William John Reeve (1910–73).
- Denis Harold Reeve (1913–22).
- Wallace Arthur Reeve (1914–69).

Eva married Francis Frederick Bennett (1883–1969), in 1919 at Islington, London and they had two children – Trevor F Bennett 1919 and Joan Winifred Bennett 1921.

- Thomas Alfred Reeve (1861–September 1918), birth registered at Wells, was a watchmaker in 1881, living with his parents. He married Louisa Annie Baker (1868–5th August 1937), born at Holborn, London, in 1891 at Islington. He was a licensed victualler by 1901, when they were living at 20 Shambles, Worcester. They were living at 3 Derby Road, Worcester in 1911. His death was registered at Upton upon Severn, Worcestershire and hers at Croydon, Surrey. They had four children:
    - Doris Maude Reeve (2nd September 1889–25th February 1980) was a hotel servant at Colwall, Herefordshire in 1911, with her future husband. She married Leonhard Grubinski (1885–19th April 1917), born in Germany, at Westminster in September 1912. They had a son, Leonhard Grubinski (born

and died 1915). Leonhard senior died in Berlin. Doris married Richard J Curtis (born c.1885) in October 1928, registered at Kingston upon Thames. She died at Ramsgate, Thanet, Kent.

- Ernest Victor Reeve (October 1891–January 1902).
- Ivy Ruby Louisa Reeve (3rd October 1894–23rd January 1991), was a boot shop assistant in 1911, living with her parents. She married Walter Leonard Smith (July 1891–15th March 1949) in September 1917 at Upton upon Severn, Worcestershire, where he was born. They had a daughter, Mary Irene Smith (6th January 1920–2002). Walter died at Brighton, Sussex. Ivy married George William Porter (6th May 1891–14th January 1966), a French polisher born at Newington, London, in Surrey in 1949. They already had a son, Jim Porter (11th August 1931–2009). George enlisted in the King's Royal Rifle Corps (A/1114) at London on 19th August 1914 and joined at Winchester on 23rd August. He was described as almost 5′ 6″ tall, weighing 122 lbs, with fresh complexion, hazel eyes, dark brown hair and his religious denomination was Church of England. He was posted to 7th Battalion on 25th August and embarked for France on 19th May 1915. On 29th September he was wounded by a gunshot to the back and was admitted to 9th Stationary Hospital next day. He was transferred to Britain on 1st October on the strength of the Depot. He joined 5th Battalion on 26th November and transferred to the strength of 9th Battalion on 2nd February 1916. He embarked for France on 4th February and joined 9th Battalion on 14th February. Granted Class I pay on 19th August and leave in November 1917. He was taken prisoner between 21st and 27th March 1918 and was held at Cassell. He returned to the Depot on 9th January 1919 and transferred to the Class Z Army Reserve on 9th April. His address was 29 Woodside Road, Norwood, London. He was discharged on demobilisation on 31st March 1920. George and Ivy both died at Croydon.
- Mabel Helen Reeve (31st August 1899–1st June 1949), born at Worcester, married Sydney/Sidney Jesse Goddard (November 1890–April 1965), a railway clerk born at Twickenham, Middlesex, at Upton upon Severn in 1921. They are believed to have had three children – Eric Sidney James Goddard (1925–2008) and twins Mavis Doris Goddard (1930–81) and Ruby Mabel Goddard (1930–75). Both their deaths were registered at Brighton.

- Maria Matilda Reeve (1865–1913), birth registered at Whitechapel, London, married Frederick Augustus Rodway (1854–1915), born at Chelsea, London, in 1898 at St Olave, London. He was a general shop dealer in 1901, when they were living at 8 Clifton Street, Shoreditch. By 1911 he was a carter and she was a cook, living at 66 Sayer Street, Newington St Mary, London. Both their deaths were registered at St Olave. They had three children, two of whom were deceased by 1911:

In 1541 John Incent applied to Henry VIII to purchase land. By 1544, Berkhamsted School's first building, Old Hall, had been completed. A period of legal and religious turmoil followed but the school survived and thrived. Amongst its famous alumni are:

- Sir Algernon Methuen (1856–1924), founder of Methuen publishers.
- Clementine Churchill (1885–1977), wife of Winston Churchill.
- Graham Greene (1904–91), author, and his brother, Sir Hugh Greene (1910–87), Director-General of the BBC 1960–69.
- Sir Robin Knox-Johnston (born 1939), yachtsman.

The School has two other VC recipients – Arthur Mayo and George Pearkes.

Stanley House School, Margate.

  - Horace Frederick Rodway (10th August 1899–2nd May 1982), born at Bermondsey, was deemed to have enlisted on 9th September 1917. He was called up to 45th Training Reserve Battalion (26365) at the Central London Recruiting Depot, Whitehall on 6th October and was graded medically B1. He was described as a clerk, 5′ 3½″ tall, weighing 106 lbs and his religious denomination was Church of England. He was living at 4 Mountgrove Road, Stoke Newington with his next of kin, his uncle and aunt, Beverley and Charlotte Jane Wakeling. Horace was posted to L Company, 45th Training Reserve Battalion at Perham Down, Wiltshire on 2nd December and transferred to 2/8th (Cyclist) Battalion, Essex Regiment (46323) at Hollesley Bay, Suffolk on 16th December. He was medically graded B1 on 4th April 1918 and B2 on 18th October at Woodbridge. He was demobilised from No.2 Dispersal Unit, Crystal Palace on 22nd January 1919, giving his address as 79 Park Lane, Clissold Park. Horace married Winifred Clara Instance (26th December 1903–January 1990), born at Islington, in 1940 at Berkhamsted. She was living with her parents at 66A Aberdeen Park, Islington, London in 1939. He was living at 254 Elmsleigh Drive, Leigh-on-Sea, Essex at the time of his death there. Her death was registered at Southend-on-Sea.
- Henry Charles Reeve (born 1866), birth registered at Islington, was an engineering apprentice in 1881.
- Frederick Charles Reeve (born 1871).

Bishop's Stortford College was founded in 1868 by prominent Nonconformists in East Anglia as a public school for Evangelical Nonconformists to provide their boys with effective and Christian education, within the means of the middle class. Bishop's Stortford Collegiate School, founded in 1850, was acquired, renamed The Nonconformist Grammar School and was inaugurated on 23rd September 1868 with forty pupils. It was renamed Bishop's Stortford College in 1901, to avoid confusion with the town's rival Grammar School, and the number of pupils increased steadily in the early 20th century. In 1902 an existing school was taken over to form a new preparatory department. In 1945 Bishop's Stortford became a fully independent public school. In 1977 the first girls were admitted and in 1995 the college became fully coeducational.

Brett was educated at:

- Berkhamsted Preparatory School, Hertfordshire.
- Stanley House School, Margate, Kent.
- Bishop's Stortford College, Hertfordshire 1907–08, where he was a member of the choir, played the clarinet in the orchestra and was an accomplished swimmer. He received a prize for Modern Languages from the Chairman of the Governors on Prize Day 1908. When Brett's VC was announced, the Headmaster decreed that Monday 3rd February 1919 be taken as a holiday.
- London University 1909–12 reading Modern Languages. He was fluent in French, German, Italian and Spanish and graduated BA with Honours 1913. Brett was a member of the London University Officers' Training Corps (Royal Engineers) 1909–13.

He was employed as a junior assistant by Maple & Co, Tottenham Court Road, London, the furnishing company, of which his father was the Governor.

On 2nd September 1914 Brett enlisted in 12th London (The Rangers), having initially been refused a commission due to poor eyesight. He was commissioned in the Kent (Fortress) Works, 6th Company, Royal Engineers at Southborough, Kent on 3rd March 1915. He was appointed acting captain on 2nd July and was promoted lieutenant on 1st June 1916. He went to France on 15th June 1917 and was involved in operations at Vimy and in the Ypres Salient. He served on the Piave in Italy between December 1917 and the spring of 1918. Returning to France, he took part in the advance of the Third Army from the Somme to the Sambre. Promoted acting major on 31st August 1918 and assumed command of 59th Field Company RE (now 59th Independent Commando Squadron RE). **Awarded the MC for his actions at Banteaux, France on 30th September 1918, when he made a personal reconnaissance under heavy machine gun fire to ascertain the possibilities of bridging the Canal de L'Escaut, LG 1st February 1919. Awarded the VC for**

Maple & Co, the furniture manufacturer, was founded by John Maple (1815–1900) in 1841 and became one of the prime makers and suppliers of furniture to the aristocracy and royalty worldwide. The company's main establishment was in Tottenham Court Road, London, with trading locations abroad in such places as Paris and Buenos Aires. John Maple completed his apprenticeship with James Constable in Surrey. He partnered with former co-worker James Cook and in 1841 they opened Cook & Maple at 145 Tottenham Court Road. The partnership was dissolved in 1851, leaving Maple sole proprietor of the company. Maples began a close association with the royal family, beginning with Queen Victoria, and the company furnished numerous royal palaces and cottages. After the Second World War sales went into decline. In 1980, the furniture maker Waring & Gillow joined with Maple & Co, to become Maple, Waring & Gillow. It became part of Allied Maples Group Ltd, which was acquired by supermarket chain Asda in 1988. It went into administration in 1997 and was taken over by Allders. Notable commissions undertaken by Maple & Co include:

- The Grand Hotel, Trafalgar Square, London.
- York Cottage, Sandringham, Norfolk.
- Furniture for royal yachts and a number of ocean liners.
- The Viceregal Lodge, residence of the Viceroy of India in Simla (1892).

his actions at Quartes Bridge, Pont-sur-Sambre, France on 6th November 1918, LG 31st January 1919. The VC was presented by the King in the Ballroom at Buckingham Palace on 13th February 1919.

Brett relinquished acting major on 16th April 1919. He was presented with a writing table by the directors and staff of Maples. He last appears in the Army List on active service in September 1919 but remained in the Territorial Reserve of Officers. He was promoted major in the Kent Fortress Engineers, Territorial Force on 20th September 1919 and last appears in the Army List in April 1921.

Brett Cloutman married Louisa Margaret 'Peggy' Emily Hunter (13th January 1893–20th December 1976), birth registered at Brentford, Essex, on 17th February 1916 at Gunnersbury Congregational Church, Chiswick. The ceremony was conducted by Brett's cousin, the Reverend Walter Evans Cloutman. Peggy was a china assistant in 1911, living with her parents. She and Brett were living at Marsden House, 36 Colney Hatch Lane, Muswell Hill, London in 1919 and at Fallowhurst, Bow Lane, Finchley, London in 1939, when he was also an air raid warden and she was a member of the Women's Voluntary Service. They later moved to 2 Old Hall, Highgate Village, North London. Peggy succeeded her husband as President of the Hornsey YMCA in August 1971. She was still living at 2 Old Hall at the time of her death. Peggy and Brett had two daughters:

- Mary Reeve Cloutman (25th February 1917–1st April 1989), born at Chiswick, London, was a shorthand typist and member of the Women's Voluntary Service

in 1939, living with her parents. She married Gordon Ellis Eberhardt (4th April 1916–22nd December 1991), born at Edmonton, Middlesex, in 1940 at Hendon, Middlesex. The family changed their surname to Everard by Deed Poll about 1943. Gordon was a director of a company of merchants and manufacturers of automatic machinery in 1939, living with his grandmother, Gertrude Eberhardt (1858–1952), father, Stanley Leopold Henry Eberhardt (1893–1983) and his sister, Joy (born 1917) at Glenwathen, Ballards Lane, Finchley. Joy was a teacher, Licentiate of the Royal Academy of Music, and a Nursing Auxiliary at Finchley Memorial Hospital. Mary and Gordon were living at Pinkneys, Bush End, Takeley, Bishop's Stortford, Hertfordshire at the time of her death at Uttlesford, Essex. Gordon was still living at Pinkneys at the time of his death, registered at Brentwood, Essex. They had two children:
    - Jennifer M Everard (born 1944), born at Hampstead, London, married Trevor D Ingram (born 1944), birth registered at Amersham, Buckinghamshire, in 1970 at London City. They had at least two children – Mark Christopher Ingram 1971 and Sarah Ann Ingram 1975.
    - Christopher J Everard (born 1946), born at Edmonton.
- Jill Margaret Cloutman (25th August 1920–13th November 2010), born at Edmonton, was living with her parents in 1939 and was a member of the Women's Voluntary Service. She married her cousin, John 'Johnny' Roderick Drew-Smythe (29th September 1923–16th September 1990), born at Bristol, Gloucestershire, on 14th October 1964. They later moved to Ireland. He was living at Nepcroft Steep Lane, Findon, West Sussex at the time of his death. She was living at 14 Admirals Walk, Funtington, Chichester, West Sussex at the time of her death. They had two children – Christopher Drew-Smythe and Jennifer Drew-Smythe.

Louisa's father, Walter Hunter (12th November 1858–1926), born at Dover, Kent, married Emily Bessy née Barber (1856–1918), born at Richmond, Surrey, in 1888 at Lambeth, London. He was a draper's assistant in 1891, when they were living at 8 Heathfield Gardens, Chiswick, Middlesex. By 1901 he was a shoe buyer and in 1911 a commercial traveller in footwear, living at 25 Fairfax Road, Chiswick, Middlesex in both census returns. Their deaths were registered at Brentford, Middlesex. In addition to Margaret, they had two other children:

- Alfred Walter Hunter (8th December 1889–9th November 1972), born at Chiswick, London, was a warehouseman for a florist in 1911, living with his parents. He served in 5th Battalion, London Regiment (London Rifle Brigade) for four years until February 1912. He enlisted in 2/1st London (City of London) Field Ambulance RAMC (138) on 7th August 1914. He was described as a warehouseman working for Cook, Son & Co, St Paul's Churchyard, 25 Fairfax Road, Chiswick, London. Promoted corporal 3rd October and acting sergeant 6th March 1915. On 21st August 1915 he applied for a commission and was commissioned in 2/6th Works Company, Kent Fortress Engineers on 1st September 1915. At that time he was described as a hotel and steamship contractor, 5′ 11″ tall and living at 40 Reading Road, Ipswich. He served with 249th Field Company RE in the Royal Naval Division (63rd) and was awarded the MC – he extricating two men buried in a front line dugout broken in by shell fire. After thirty-six hours' unceasing work, during which he and his party were exposed to shell and machine gun fire, the two men were got out. It was due to the energy and disregard of danger which he showed that these two men were rescued alive (LG 16th September 1918). Promoted lieutenant 1st June 1916, acting captain 13th February 1919 and acting major on 16th February. Alfred was demobilised from No.1 Dispersal Unit, Purfleet on 26th June 1919, giving his address as 14 Valkyrie Road, Westcliff on Sea, Essex. He married Dora Cecile Leffler (1st July 1892–18th January 1979), born at Blackpool, Lancashire, on 4th March 1916 at Holy Trinity, Barnes, Surrey. He was managing director of a private cloth manufacturing company in 1939, when they were living at Four Oaks, Station Road, Beaconsfield, Buckinghamshire. Alfred was living at Flat 3, Kinellan Court, Penn Road, Beaconsfield at the time of his death, registered at Windsor, Berkshire. Dora was living at 28 Dingle Lane, Solihull, Warwickshire at the time of her death there. They had a daughter:

  - Audrey M Hunter (born 1st July 1922) was a shorthand typist in 1939, living with her parents. She married Eric B Biggs (born 1920) in 1947 at Amersham. They had two sons – John H Biggs 1950 and David A Biggs 1953.

- Agnes Mary Hunter (21st July 1894–17th February 1982), birth registered at Brentford, was a milliner's assistant in 1911, living with her parents. She married Samuel Alexander Gordon (8th September 1888–1st May 1958), born at Ferns, Wexford, Ireland, at Brentford Register Office on 10th April 1915. They were living at 25 Fairfax Road, Bedford Park, London in 1915, at 13 Prebend Gardens, Chiswick, London and 34 Stamford Brook Road, Hammersmith, London in 1917 and at 5 Vaughan Avenue, Stamford Brook, Chiswick, London in 1918. Samuel enlisted in 22nd Royal Fusiliers (657) at Kensington Town Hall on 22nd September 1914 and joined at White City. He was described as a stationery salesman, 5′ 7¼″ tall, weighing 126 lbs, with fresh complexion, blue eyes, brown hair and his religious denomination was Church of England. He was promoted lance corporal and went to France on 16th November 1915. On 12th December 1916 he applied for a commission while serving in D Company and returned to Britain on 29th December. Samuel joined No.14 Officer Cadet Battalion, Berkhamsted on 1st February 1917 and was commissioned in 3rd Battalion, East Kent Regiment on 29th June. He served with the 1st Battalion in France. He embarked at Calais and disembarked at Dover on 8th August to be admitted to 24 Park Street Hospital, London with debility and anaemia. Medical boards on

22nd August, 22nd September and 22nd October found him unfit for General Service for two to three months, Home Service for six weeks to two months and light duty for one month. Medical boards on 1st December, 25th February 1918 and 27th March found him unfit for A for three to four months and C1 for six weeks. The board on 27th March found him fit for C2 but he was granted leave to 17th April. Medical boards on 26th August, 28th October and 28th November found him unfit for A, B and C1 for two to six months but fit for C2 and he was to return to the Air Board. Samuel transferred to the RAF in December, with effect from 10th June 1918 and seniority from 1st April 1918. A medical board on 11th February found him unfit for A & B for three months and C1 for two months. They were living at 5 Vaughan Avenue, Chiswick in 1921. He was an airport manager for a public company in 1939, when they were living at The Cape, Balcombe Road, Horley, Surrey. They were living at 125 Wick Hall, Furze Hill, Hove, Sussex at the time of his death at Hurstwood Park Hospital, Haywards Heath, Sussex. She was living at 2 Sackville Road, Hove at the time of her death. They had two children:

- Jack Arthur Gordon born at Woolwich on 11th July 1915.
- Doreen Lindsay Gordon (8th September 1920–May 1998), a shorthand typist born at Hammersmith, arrived at Liverpool from Colombo, Ceylon on 19th January 1946 and was living at The Cape, Balcombe Road, Reigate, Surrey. She married Dacus Patrick Reginald Stokes (27th June 1922–May 1997) in Surrey in July 1947. Dacus was commissioned in the Royal Air Force (1576951 & 178791) as a pilot officer in the RAF Reserve of Officers, General Duties Branch on 20th June 1944. Promoted flying officer 20th December 1944 and flight lieutenant 20th June 1946. Appointed to a Class Civilian Component Commission as a flying officer on 11th July 1952 and was promoted flight lieutenant on 1st October 1952. Dacus relinquished his commission on 1st August 1954. They were living at 85 Station Road, Reigate in 1948. They had two children – Roger D Stokes 1949 and Gillian Stokes 1951. The marriage ended in divorce. Dacus married Della M Jordan in July 1955 at Aldershot, Hampshire. That marriage also ended in divorce. Della married Derek JKA Butcher in 1967. Dacus married Agnes M Fleming in 1965. Dacus' death was registered at Worthing, West Sussex. Doreen did not marry again. Her death was registered at Brighton, East Sussex.

After the war Brett returned to Maples, working in London and Buenos Aires, Argentina, where he was President of Maples in the region. On 2nd April 1924 he was admitted to Gray's Inn to study law and finished in the top echelons. He was called to the Bar in Trinity Term 1926. Before the ceremony he wrote to the Treasurer of the Inn requesting that his decorations were not mentioned as he did wish to be treated differently from anyone else. Brett subsequently practised Common Law

The Honourable Society of Gray's Inn is one of four Inns of Court, professional associations for barristers and judges in London. To be called to the bar and practise as a barrister in England and Wales, an individual must belong to one of the inns. Gray's Inn is at the intersection of High Holborn and Gray's Inn Road. Its gardens, the Walks, have existed since at least 1597. None of the Inns of Court claim to be older than the others but law clerks and their apprentices have been on the site since at least 1370. It grew during the 15th and 16th centuries and was home to many important barristers and politicians, including Francis Bacon (1561–1626). Queen Elizabeth I was a patron and Gray's Inn became the largest of the Inns by number, with over 200 members. The English Civil War disrupted legal education, calls to the bar and new admissions. As a result, Gray's Inn never fully recovered. Fortunes continued to decline and, although now more prosperous, Gray's Inn is today the smallest of the Inns of Court. During the Second World War the Inn was badly damaged in 1941 and rebuilding took until 1960. Today many buildings are offices for barristers and solicitors and there are about sixty apartments. The Inn also contains the Inns of Court School of Law, a joint venture between all four Inns for the vocational training of barristers and solicitors.

at 1 Garden Court, Temple, London. On 28th October 1929 at West Ham Police Court, he defended Job HC Drain VC, who was accused of blocking a tramway at Plaistow with his bus. Drain claimed that he could not pull over due to his way being blocked by cyclists. The case was dismissed, with Drain being awarded two guineas costs.

Garden Court, Temple, London.

One of Brett's high-profile clients was the American vaudeville star, Sophie Tucker, who was prosecuted by HM Customs in April 1932. He joined the Western Circuit and also appeared frequently in the North London Sessions. On 28th April 1930 he was opposing barrister to EP Bennett VC at Southwark Crown Court. On 13th April 1937 he attended the funeral of AP Sullivan VC at the Guard's Chapel, Wellington Barracks, Birdcage Walk, London.

Brett was recalled on 11th March 1940 as a lieutenant in the Royal Engineers (Emergency Commission)

Job Drain was awarded the VC for his actions at Le Cateau on 26th August 1914 and was also mentioned in Field Marshal Sir John French's despatch dated 8th October 1914. Following demobilisation in 1919 Job was employed at various times as a Whitehall messenger, fishporter at Billingsgate, London Passenger Transport Board bus driver from 1924 and by the London Electricity Board. His story is told in the first book in this series, *Victoria Crosses on the Western Front, Mons to Hill 60, August 1914–April 1915*.

Eugene Bennett was awarded the VC for his actions near Le Transloy, France on 5th November 1916. After the Great War he returned to the Bank of England until 1921, then studied law and was called to the Bar (Middle Temple) in October 1923. He held various other appointments:

- Deputy-Umpire under the Unemployment Insurance Act 1920 on 16th June 1930.
- Prosecuting Counsel to the Post Office, South East Circuit 1931–35.
- Metropolitan Stipendary Magistrate at West London Magistrates Court 1935–46 and at Marlborough Street Court 1946–61.
- Governor of Regent Street Polytechnic.

His story is told in the third book in this series, *Victoria Crosses on the Western Front, The Somme 1916, July–November 1916.*

and was posted to Aldershot, Hampshire (122929). He was confronted by a group of sapper officers who had returned from Dunkirk, suffering physically and emotionally. However, he was able to restore their morale and they were able to return to active service. Brett was appointed Second-in-Command of 26th Field Company RE, which reformed at Dumfries after most of the unit was taken prisoner at St Valery in June 1940. He was promoted acting captain and temporary major on 4th February 1941 and war substantive major and temporary lieutenant colonel on 26th February 1943. He served in Syria and commanded the Royal Engineers Training & Reinforcement Depot in Egypt. He was appointed Chief Royal Engineer, Levant Engineer Battalion in Italy, with the unit consisting of Syrians, Lebanese and Cypriots. **Mentioned in a War Office Despatch, LG 6th January 1944.** Appointed honorary lieutenant colonel in April 1946 and participated in the London Victory Parade that June. He last appears in the Army List in October 1946.

Brett Cloutman's second legal publication.

In 1945 he was appointed to the executive committee of the Finchley Labour Party and stood unsuccessfully for the Finchley West Ward in the same year. He was later Chairman of Finchley Labour Party but stood down in 1948 when he was appointed to the Supreme Court. He was appointed King's Counsel on 12th April 1946 and became a divorce commissioner in the same year. He was also Senior Chairman of the War Pensions (Special Review) Tribunal 1947, Official

Referee of the Supreme Court of Judicature 1948–63 and Senior Official Referee of the Supreme Court of Judicature 1954–63. **Created Knight Bachelor in the Queen's Birthday Honours List for services while Senior Official Referee of the Supreme Court of Judicature, LG 13th June, 16th July and 23rd July 1957.** He wrote jointly with Francis William Luck – *The Law Relating to Authors and Publishers* 1927 and *The Law for Printers and Publishers* 1929.

Brett held a number of other appointments:

- President of the Hornsey (North London) YMCA from 1951. The club had been re-established by his father in 1929.
- President of the Metropolitan Union of YMCAs 1951, a position held by his father until 1933. On 7th November 1971 (his 80th birthday) he was to have been given the Golden Order of the Red Triangle (the YMCA's highest honour) by National President Sir Rupert Neville.
- Chairman of the Brotherhood of Ferme Park Baptist Church.
- Governor of Eltham College 1965–66.
- High office within the Royal British Legion.
- Master of the Worshipful Company of Glass Sellers of London 1939–40 and 1965–66 and was presented with the Jewel of a Past Master on his retirement from the post.
- He helped develop Hornsey Carnival in 1959 into a format that is still used today.

Brett attended a number of VC Reunions:

- The VC Garden Party at Buckingham Palace on 26th June 1920.
- The VC Dinner at the Royal Gallery of the House of Lords, London on 9th November 1929.
- The Victory Day Celebration Dinner & Reception at The Dorchester, London on 8th June 1946.
- The VC Centenary Celebrations at Hyde Park, London on 26th June 1956.
- The 1st, 2nd, 3rd, 4th and 5th VC & GC Association Reunions at the Café Royal, London on 24th July 1958, 7th July 1960, 18th July 1962, 16th July 1964 and 14th July 1966.
- The 7th VC & GC Association Reunion at the Connaught Rooms, Covent Garden, London on 18th June 1970.

The Worshipful Company of Glass Sellers ranks 71st in precedence among the City of London livery companies. The company received its royal charter from Charles II in 1664, to regulate glass selling and pot-making within the City and ensure quality and fair trade. Today the company stimulates interest in glass and carries out charitable works, with the emphasis on education.

Golders Green Crematorium.

Wolfred Cloutman's grave on the right, in which Brett Cloutman's ashes were placed after his death in 1971. On the left is the grave of 2nd Corporal Edwin Hart, also a member of 178th Tunnelling Company RE.

He returned to his home at 2 Old Hall, Highgate Village, London following a meeting with the Secretary of the YMCA on 15th August 1971, sat in an armchair, fell asleep and passed away quietly. He was given a YMCA funeral and was cremated at the West Chapel, Golders Green Crematorium, Hoop Lane, North London on 18th August. His ashes were interred in his brother's grave at Norfolk Cemetery, Albert, France (1 A 14). Brett is commemorated in a number of other places:

- Sir Brett Cloutman Wing of the YMCA building at Hornsey, London was dedicated by the Bishop of London on 22nd March 1974.
- A Department for Communities and Local Government commemorative paving stone was dedicated at Hornsey Central Neighbourhood Health Centre, 151 Park Road, London on 6th November 2018.
- The Cloutman Award – he set up a trust in 1969 to finance an engraved tankard for the most promising lance corporal in 59th Field Squadron RE (later

The VC memorial plaque at Golders Green Crematorium.

On 8th July 1943, the 1939–43 Star (later the 1939–45 Star) and the Africa Star became the first two campaign stars instituted for the Second World War. The first Africa Star ribbons were issued later that year. It was awarded for a minimum of one day's service in an operational area of North Africa between 10th June 1940 and 12th May 1943. By March 1944 1,500,000 personnel had received Africa Star ribbons. There were three clasps – North Africa 1942–43, 8th Army and 1st Army. Only the first earned could be worn on the ribbon. Australians who served in Syria 8th June–11th July 1941 qualified for the Africa Star but service in West Africa did not.

59th Independent Commando Squadron RE) to be presented on 6th November, the anniversary of his VC action.

- Cloutman Block, Gibraltar Barracks, Minley, Hampshire.
- Named on the For Valour board at the Royal Engineers Museum, Prince Arthur Road, Gillingham, Kent.
- Named on a memorial plaque to the fourteen VCs cremated at Golders Green Crematorium, Hoop Lane, London dedicated on 7th April 2013.
- Framed biography, photograph and copy VC and MC in the University of London Officers' Training Corps Dining Room, Handel Street, London.

In addition to the VC and MC he was awarded the British War Medal 1914–20, Victory Medal 1914–19, 1939–45 Star, Africa Star, Italy Star, Defence Medal, War Medal 1939–45 with Mentioned-in-Despatches Oakleaf, George VI Coronation Medal 1937 and Elizabeth II Coronation Medal 1953. His medals, and those of his brother Wolfred, were bequeathed as a deed of gift to the Corps of Royal Engineers in November 1970. The VC is held by the Royal Engineers Museum, Prince Arthur Road, Gillingham, Kent.

14107 SERGEANT HORACE AUGUSTUS CURTIS
2nd Battalion, The Royal Dublin Fusiliers

Horace Curtis was born on 7th March 1891 at Cellars, St Anthony-in-Roseland, St Just-in-Roseland, Cornwall. He was baptised on 1st May 1891 at the Wesleyan Methodist Church, St Mawes. His father, Thomas Curtis (1858–3rd November 1894), born at Newlyn, was a miner in 1882. He married Catherine 'Kate' Meluish née Ball (16th October 1859–30th September 1940), born at St Goran, Cornwall, on 18th November 1882 at the Register Office, St Columb, Cornwall. She was living with her grandparents, Eleazar and Charlotte Ball, at Penhallow, St Newlyn East, Cornwall in 1881. Thomas was a

St Goran (or Gorran) is a coastal parish ten kilometres south-southwest of St Austell. The largest settlement is Gorran Haven seen here. Saint Guron or Goronus is said to have gone there from Bodmin. The church dates from Norman times but the current structure is 15th century, as is the Chapel of St Just at Gorran Haven.

Penhallow farmhouse, which dates from the 18th or early 19th centuries, is Grade II Listed (Savills).

gamekeeper by 1891, when they were living at 5 Cellars House, St Anthony-in-Roseland. Kate was a pauper in 1901 living with her children at Fiddler's Green, St Newlyn East and was still there in 1939. Horace had four siblings:

- Hilda Maria Curtis (16th April 1883–8th June 1967), born at Fiddlers Green, St Newlyn East, married Sydney Vincent (8th January 1882–4th May 1937), born at Prospect Place, Falmouth, Cornwall, on 28th November 1903 at Wesleyan Methodist Chapel, Union Place, Truro, Cornwall. He was a packer for the Great Western Railway in 1911, when they were living at Vincents, Fiddlers Green, St Newlyn East. He died at Goonhavern, Cornwall and she was still living at Fiddlers Green at the time of her death there. They had eleven children:

Station Road, St Newlyn East, which leads to Penhallow farmhouse. St Newlyn East village is five kilometres south of Newquay and is known locally as Newlyn East. The parish is named after the patron saint of the church, St Newlina. The church was founded in Norman times but most of the present building is 14th and 15th centuries. The listed 15th century Cargoll Farm Barn belonged to the manor of Cargoll, which is recorded in the Domesday Book in 1086. On 9th July 1846 there was a disaster at nearby East Wheal Rose mine when an unusually heavy thunderstorm flooded the workings and thirty-nine miners drowned. The St Newlyn East Pit, an abandoned quarry that was used for Cornish wrestling, was later used to preach sermons. After the mining disaster the Pit was tiered and dedicated to those who died in the disaster.

- Eldred Thomas Henry Vincent (1903–22nd April 1932), born at St Columb and died at St Newlyn East.
- Elsie Doreen Melluish Vincent (22nd February 1905–October 1978) married Arthur Sydney Kiddell (15th October 1906–10th March 1991), born at Aston, Warwickshire, in 1928 at Birmingham, Warwickshire. Arthur was a gas fitter in 1939, when they were living at 30 Ulleries Road, Solihull, Warwickshire. Elsie's death was registered at Truro. Arthur was living at 21 Winchcombe Road, Solihull, Warwickshire at the time of his death. They had three children – Sydney Arthur Kiddell (3rd August 1929–1990), Eldred W Kiddell (1931) and Enis HM Kiddell (1934).
- Horace Wilfred Sydney Vincent (7th September 1907–11th April 1991), born at St Newlyn East, had no roof to his mouth and had difficulty talking. He was a permanent way labourer with Great Western Railway in 1939, living with his mother. He was also a beekeeper. Horace was living at Fiddlers Green at the time of his death at St Newlyn East.
- Marion Avis Vincent (15th July 1908–January 1996) married Lewis Harris (5th September 1910–6th January 1979) in 1936 at St Columb, where he was born. He was a general haulage contractor in 1939, when they were living at 6 Trevena Terrace, Newquay. He died there and she at St Austell. They had two children – Rosina L Harris (1938) and Marie L Harris (1943).
- Enis 'Enie' Pauline Vincent (2nd June 1910–23rd February 1976) suffered from arthritis. She never married and lived in the family home at Fiddlers Green, where she subsequently died. She had a daughter, Myra Pauline Vincent (31st March 1928–21st June 2009).
- Hilda Beryl Georgina Vincent (13th May 1912–19th May 1963), born at Fiddlers Green, was a general domestic servant and companion help to Annie Maria Complin (1853–1946) at 8 Adelaide Terrace, Truro in 1939. She never married and died at Tehidy Chest Hospital, Camborne, Cornwall.
- Clifford Augustus Vincent, a twin with Esme (22nd July 1920–30th July 1992), born at St Newlyn East, was a motor mechanic in 1939, living with his mother. He married Rosamond Joyce Hooper (1921–23rd December 2012), born at St Columb, in 1942 at Truro. He died at St Newlyn East and she at Truro. They had two children – Elizabeth SI Vincent (1943) and Greta Diane Vincent (1950–2006).
- Esme Cliffodia Vincent, a twin with Clifford (22nd July 1920–18th November 1992) was living with her mother in 1939. She married Albert Victor Gatland (25th July 1912–22nd July 1997), born at Brentford, Middlesex, in 1946 at Truro. He was educated at Soham Grammar School, Churchgate Street, Beechurst, Cambridgeshire 1923–24 and served as a sergeant in the Army during the Second World War. He was a baker in 1954. They were living at 1 Moorfield Road, Bromley, Kent in 1964 and at Curtis Cottage, Fiddlers

Green at the time of her death there. He died at St Newlyn East. They had a son, David P Gatland (1948).

- Rona Averil Vincent (28th August 1921–21st February 1997), born at St Columb, was incapacitated in 1939 and was living with her mother. She never married and died at St Newlyn East.
- Dudley Cecil Vincent, a twin with Everett, (12th December 1923–8th October 1989), born at St Newlyn East, was an errand boy in a chemist's shop in 1939. He married Dorothy May Carter (18th September 1925–1982), born at St Columb, on 12th November 1947 at St Austell. She was living with her parents at 23 St Piran's Road, Newquay in 1939. Her death was registered at Truro. He was living at 10 Halt Road, St Newlyn East at the time of his death there.
- Everett Barrington Vincent, a twin with Dudley, (12th December 1923–16th August 2007) married Mary Eileen Hooper (27th August 1927–8th February 2010) in 1945 at Truro, where she was born. She was living with her parents at Sunnyside, Cubert, Truro in 1939. They both died at Truro. They had a daughter, Susan EM Vincent (1949).

- Eldred Barrington Curtis (22nd August 1884–9th July 1958), born at Penzance, Cornwall, was a groom in 1901 and a clay labourer in 1911. He was living with his mother at Fiddlers Green, St Newlyn East, Cornwall in 1939, by when he was a Cornwall County Council labourer. He never married.
- Wilfred Thomas Curtis (25th April 1886–19th December 1971), born at St Newlyn East, Newquay, Cornwall, was a teamster in 1901. He married Louie Odgers (16th September 1882–12th May 1961) on 24th July 1909 at St Columb, where she was born. By 1911 he was a clay labourer and they were living at Well Lane, St Dennis, Cornwall. Wilfred attested for the Army on 6th June 1916, transferred to the Reserve next day, was mobilised on 2nd August and assigned to the Army Service Corps at Aldershot, Hampshire (173071). His religious denomination was Wesleyan. He sailed for Boulogne, France from Folkestone, Kent aboard SS *Invicta* on 31st August with 53 Section, Heavy Artillery MT, 154th Siege Battery RGA. He moved to different units frequently – 402 Motor Transport Company 4th September, 335 Company attached to XIII Corps Royal Artillery 4th October, 363 MT Company 12th January 1917, 611 MT Company 23rd March, 594 MT Company 31st May, 717 MT Company 4th September, 594 MT Company 23rd December, 717 MT Company 9th January 1918, 403 MT Company 30th January, 406 MT Company 12th May, 884 MT Company 2nd November and 604 MT Company 21st November. He was granted leave 13th-27th December 1917 and received the Good Conduct Badge on 4th August 1918. Wilfred returned to Britain on 30th December 1918 and was admitted to 4th Southern General Hospital, Devonport, Devon next day. He transferred to the Class Z Reserve on demobilisation from the Dispersal Unit, Woolwich, London on 27th April 1919. Wilfred and Louie were living at 2 Wellington Road,

St Austell in 1939. Her death was registered at Bodmin, Cornwall. Wilfred was living at Four Winds, Mitchell, near Newquay, Cornwall at the time of his death there. They had three children, all registered at St Austell:

- Maisie Pearl Curtis (19th February 1910–9th May 1979) married Leonard Royce Maurice Bullen (5th August 1910–27th November 1997), born at St Stephens, Cornwall, in 1932 at St Austell. His family was living at Grampound Road, Little Treviscoe, St Stephens in 1911. Leonard was an engine driver and fitter in a clay works in 1939, when they were living at Little Treviscoe, St Stephen-in-Brannel, St Austell. They were living at Four Winds, Mitchell, Newquay at the time of her death there. He died at Truro. They had two sons – Eric R Bullen (1938) and Peter Roy Bullen (1952–92).
- Narissa May Curtis (25th September 1911–July 1994) married George Francis Stedman (26th August 1911–May 1994), born at Helston, Cornwall, in 1934 at St Austell. He was a clay worker in 1939, when they were living at Carpalla Foxhole, St Austell. His death was registered at Truro and hers at St Austell.
- Stephen Rex Curtis (9th November 1913–December 2000) was a contractor's labourer in 1939, living with his parents. He married Barbara Rae Billing (26th November 1920–3rd January 1994), born at St Blazey Gate, Cornwall, in 1940 at St Austell. She died at Truro and he at St Austell. They had a son, Michael T Curtis (1943), and possibly a daughter, Christine G Curtis (1953).

- Henry 'Harry' Trudgen Curtis (28th February 1894–6th March 1969) was a butcher's assistant in 1911. He married Lilian Maud Stribley (1892–1937) in 1916 at St Columb, where she was born. Her death was registered at St Austell. Harry was a supervisor at an electric motor plant in 1939, living with his daughter at 64 Currian Road, Nanpean, Cornwall. They had a daughter:
  - Sybil Maud Curtis (22nd May 1918–1983), born at Biggleswade, Bedfordshire, married Eric James Hawkey (20th December 1916–23rd April 1950) in 1943 at St Austell. He was a stone quarry labourer in St Austell & District Hospital, Edgcumbe Road, St Austell at the time of the 1939 Register. They lived with her father at 64 Currian Road, Nanpean and Eric subsequently died there.

  Henry married Phyllis K Crook (31st December 1919–6th June 2008) in 1944 at Poole, Dorset, where she was born. Phyllis was a Post Office assistant and telephone operator at North Street Post Office, Pewsey, Wiltshire, in 1939. Henry's death was registered at Chippenham, Wiltshire. Phyllis married Albert Edward Green (31st May 1913–1984), birth registered at Wirral, Cheshire, in 1975 registered at Delyn, Clywd. Phyllis died at Mold, Flintshire. Albert had married Winifred Nora Colclough (1917–2001) in 1936 registered at Wirral. Albert was a shearer in a steel sheet mill in 1939, when they were living at 2 Girton Road, Ellesmere

St Columb Major, ten kilometres east of Newquay, is referred to locally as St Columb. It is named after the 6th century Saint Columba of Cornwall, also known as Columb. Major distinguishes it from the nearby St Columb Minor. Twice yearly, on Shrove Tuesday and the Saturday eleven days later, the town hosts the medieval game of hurling. It was common throughout Cornwall but is now only played at St Columb and St Ives. Two teams of unlimited numbers (townsmen and countrymen of St Columb parish) endeavour to carry a silver ball to goals three kilometres apart or across the parish boundary. As the parish covers about forty-five square kilometres, it is the largest sports ground in the world. There are Bronze and Iron Age monuments in the area, including Castle an Dinas and the Nine Maidens, the largest row of standing stones in Cornwall. In 1333 King Edward III granted a market in St Columb Major to Sir John Arundell as a reward for supplying troops to fight the Scots. After the 1549 Prayer Book Rebellion, William Mayow was hanged outside a tavern in St Columb for leading an uprising in Cornwall. During the English Civil War in 1645 there was a skirmish near St Columb between the Prince's regiment and a Parliamentary detachment, in which the latter was victorious. In 1676 most of the church of St Columb was blown up by three youths. There were three royal visits during the 20th century, including by Queen Elizabeth II and Prince Philip in August 1977 during the Silver Jubilee tour of Cornwall. On 27th May 1983 the Prince and Princess of Wales visited to commemorate the 650th anniversary of the signing of the town charter by King Edward III. In 1860 plans were drawn up for the church, which is dedicated to St Columba, to become the cathedral of the diocese of Cornwall, but it was built at Truro instead. St Columb features in the 1961 novel *Castle Dor* by Daphne du Maurier. It also features in *Kangaroo* by DH Lawrence, published in 1923. St Columb was the birthplace of Richard Bullock (1847–1921), a legendary figure of the Wild West era in America, where his quick-shooting working on the Deadwood stage earned him the name 'Deadwood Dick'.

Port, Cheshire. It is assumed that the marriage ended in divorce. Phyllis' father, Reginald Augustus Crook (1882–1953), served in the Army Service Corps during the Great War (T/370845). He enlisted at Poole, Dorset on 10th December 1915 and was mobilised at Dorchester, Dorset on 2nd May 1918, described as a baker, 5′ 4″ tall, weighing 122 lbs, with black hair, sallow complexion and brown eyes. He served with 666th Company ASC, Reserve Depot, Blackheath, London, until being transferred to the Class B Army Reserve on 20th July 1918, having been wrongly called up. He was discharged surplus to military requirements on 14th December.

The early 18th century Grade II listed Plume of Feathers Inn at Mitchell, where Horace's paternal grandparents were living in 1861.

Horace's paternal grandfather, Thomas Curtis (c.1814–78), born at Newlyn, Cornwall, married Margaretta née May (c.1821–87), also born at Newlyn, in 1840 at St Columb. He was a lead miner, living with his family at the Plume of Feathers Inn, Mitchell, St

Newlyn East in 1861. Margaretta was living with her son in 1881. In addition to Thomas they had another son:

- William Curtis (1850–21st May 1918), born at Newlyn, was a butcher and farmer. He married Mary Jewell (c.1850–77) in 1874 at St Columb and they had a son, William Curtis (1875). William senior married Jane Benny (23rd September 1862–13th September 1943) in 1888 at St Columb, where she was born. She was living with her parents at 48 Churchtown, St Newlyn East in 1871. William and Jane were living at Downey Lane, Newlyn in 1891. William died at St Newlyn East. Jane was living next door to the VC and his wife at Shop, St Newlyn East in 1939. Jane was living at The Cross, St Newlyn East at the time of her death at Penhallow, Perranzabuloe, Cornwall. They had two children:
    - Celia Rhoda Curtis (6th January 1889–11th March 1976) married William J Jewell registered as Rhoda C Curtis at Truro in 1910.
    - Nicholas Benny Curtis (22nd March 1891–1974).

His maternal grandfather, John Drew Ball (17th November 1833–1899), a millwright born at St Issey, Cornwall, married Maria née Thomas (c.1840–67) on 16th July 1859 at St Goran, where she was born. Her death was registered at Truro. John and his children were living with his father at Penhallow Moor, Newlyn in 1871. John married Helen Jane Appledore (registered as Appledon) (c.1838–1902), born at St Stephen's, Saltash, Cornwall, in 1878 at Truro. They were living with her father at Lanner Mill, St Allen, Cornwall in 1881 and by 1891 had moved to Penhallow, St Newlyn East. Both their deaths were registered at St Columb. In addition to Catherine, John had four other children from his two marriages:

- James Thomas Ball (1861–63) born at Truro.
- Charlotte Louisa Ball (15th December 1863–22nd May 1949), born at St Columb, was a dressmaker, living with Thomas and Kate Curtis at 5 Cellars House, St Anthony-in-Roseland at the time of the 1891 Census. She married Robert Trenerry (1864–1903), born at Truro, on 13th February 1893 at St Enoder, St Columb. His death was registered at St Columb. Charlotte was a charwoman in 1911, living with three of her children at Chapel Town, near Summercourt, Cornwall. She was incapacitated in 1939, living with her daughter, Bertha, and husband at Tresallyn, Wadebridge, Cornwall. She died at Trecerus, Padstow, Cornwall. They had five children:
    - Bertha Mary Trenerry (2nd March 1893–1987) married John Kestell (24th May 1892–1970) in 1920 at St Columb, where he was born. They had a son, Dennis J Kestell, in 1923.
    - Ella Maud Trenerry (26th January 1895–1984) married Frederick Harris in 1930 at Crediton, Devon. They had a son, Frederick F Harris in 1931.

- Hugh William Trenerry (15th April 1896–1980) served as a corporal in the Army Service Corps (T2/015927) and Duke of Cornwall's Light Infantry (32015) and went to France on 22nd July 1915. He later transferred to the Class Z Reserve. Hugh married Florence EE Strongman (1898–1969) at St Columb in 1927.
- Walter Vincent Trenerry (1897–2nd May 1916) served as a private in 1/4th Hampshire (4692) and died on active service (Amara War Cemetery, Iraq – XXI G 19).
- Samuel Thomas Trenerry (5th March 1900–August 1988) enlisted in the Royal Navy on 14th March 1918 (J86331), described as 5′ 6¼″ tall, with dark brown hair, blue eyes and fresh complexion. He served aboard HMS *Vivid I* and HMS *Roxburgh* from 18th August as an ordinary seaman. He was discharged on 11th February 1919. Samuel married Elizabeth A Webber (24th March 1899–1982) at St Columb in 1921. They had two sons – Kenneth John Trenerry (1st November 1921–1986) and Eric T Trenerry (1925).

• Barrington 'Barney' Britton Ball (17th September 1864–3rd September 1923), born at Gervarnick, St Allen, Cornwall. His first name was registered at Truro as Barantine. He and four other grandchildren were living with his paternal grandparents at Penhallow Farm, Newlyn East in 1871. He was still there at the time of the 1881 Census, with his two sisters, by when he was an agricultural labourer. Barney married Emma Jane Halls (17th April 1863–16th January 1921), born at St Newlyn East, in 1887 at St Columb. They travelled to New York, USA from Liverpool, Lancashire aboard SS *Alaska*, arriving on 6th June 1887, and returned from New York aboard SS *City of Berlin*, arriving at Liverpool on

SS *Alaska*, built by John Elder & Co of Glasgow, carried 350 first class passengers and 1,000 in steerage. She held the Blue Riband as the fastest liner on the Atlantic in 1882 and in 1883 became the first liner to make the crossing to New York in under a week. However, in doing so she burned 250 tons of coal per day. One of her passengers was Hugh Simpson Rodham, grandfather of Hillary Clinton. *Alaska* completed 100 voyages before sailings were suspended in 1894. In 1897 she was chartered as a troop transport and in 1899 was sold for scrap. However, she was resold to the Barrow shipyard as an accommodation hulk until broken up in 1902.

21st May 1892. He was a farmer and bus proprietor in 1901, when they were living at Penhallow, East Newlyn. He abandoned Emma before 1911, when she was living at Grampound Road, St Stephen's, with her three youngest children. She died at Coomb, St Stephen, Cornwall. They had four children:

- George Drew Ball (27th July 1889–3rd February 1961) born in Iowa, USA. He was living at Clearwater, Florida in 1937.
- Cliffodia Halls Ball (25th April 1891–3rd August 1965) married Francis Herbert James Lanyon (21st January 1892–1952), a general merchant, at St Austell in 1913. They had a daughter, Frances EC Roberts (23rd August 1914–1981), who never married.
- Stanley Llewellyn Ball (1896–16th August 1962) married Susan Dorothy Martin (6th March 1897–1987) at Liskeard in 1926.
- Myrtle Jane Ball (1899–1948) married Robert Wesley Richards (29th August 1899–1977) at St Austell in 1923. They had three children – Terence H Richards 1930, Jean Richards 1933 and Dennis J Richards 1935.

Barney had a relationship with Susan 'Susie' Ann Argall née Hubber (17th January 1875–9th June 1969), born at St Columb. They cohabited in the USA and may have married but no record has been found. She was living with her parents at Trencreek Village, St Columb Minor in 1881. In 1891 she was living with her mother at Pilgrim Hill, Newlyn East. Barney died at Tarpon Springs, Pinellas, Florida, USA. Susie was living at Precinct 25, Tarpon Springs in 1930 and 1935. In 1937 she was living at the residence of George D Ball (Barney's son from his first marriage) at Clearwater, Florida and at Precinct 71, Tarpon Springs in 1945. She was living at 33589 Tarpon Springs when she died and was buried with Barney. Susie and Barney had two children, both born at Tarpon Springs:

- Arthur Cecil Ball (7th October 1913–5th March 1999) served as a lieutenant colonel in the US Army during the Second World War and Korean War and was awarded the Bronze Star with Oak Leaf Cluster.
- Adeline B Ball (13th June 1915–15th May 1999).

Susie had married Philip Martin Argall (4th September 1871–4th January 1922), a carpenter, on 11th May 1895 at St Newlyn Parish Church. Philip is believed to

The Bronze Star Medal is awarded to members of the US armed forces for heroic achievement, heroic service, meritorious achievement or meritorious service in a combat zone. When the medal is awarded for acts of valour a 'V' device is worn on the ribbon and this constitutes the fourth highest US military decoration for valour. The medal can be awarded to foreign military personnel serving with or alongside US forces. Civilians may also be eligible for the award. For example, reporter Joe Galloway received it during the Vietnam War for rescuing a badly wounded soldier under fire in 1965. Another civilian recipient was Ernest Hemingway. The oak leaf cluster is worn to denote additional awards.

have deserted her after the birth of their son, Philip, and she later abandoned her two surviving children, Francis and Norah, sometime between 1907 and 1911, in a doorway opposite Truro Cathedral. Her brother-in-law, John Charles Grey (1869–1941), a bus driver, who was married to Philip Argall's sister, Ellen Batten Argall (1873–1922), collected them and they were living with their grandmother, Clarissa Argall (c.1837–1912), and her unmarried daughter, Mildred (1877–1946), a dressmaker, at St Newlyn East in 1911. Susie went to the USA and may have joined her father there. Philip died at Johannesburg, South Africa. Philip and Susan had six children:

- Frances Olive Argall (25th October 1895–21st February 1896).
- Francis Stanley Argall (14th November 1896–30th September 1977) married Winifred K Matthews (1897–1918) at Redruth in 1918. She died later that year.
- An unnamed son (29th-30th April 1900).
- Nora Beatrice Argall (7th October 1901–31st January 1990) married William J Prout (25th October 1894–1975) in 1923. They had three children – Esme Lorna Prout (1924–99) and twins Martyn G and Philip J Prout 1931. Philip died at birth.
- George Martin Argall (21st July 1903–26th August 1905).
- Philip Edwin Argall (23rd February–20th March 1907).

- Annie Peters Ball (30th September 1878–1957), born at Truro, married John Trebilcock (1874–1923), a farm labourer, in 1903 at St Columb, where he was born. John was living with his parents at Newlyn East in 1901. John and Annie were living at Grampound Road, Cubert, Truro in 1911. His death was registered at St Columb. Annie was living with her widowed son-in-law, David Bryce Currah, and two others at Churchtown, Cubert in 1939. Her death was registered at Truro. They had two daughters:
  - Helen Jane Trebilcock (1904–39) married David Bryce Currah (25th December 1908–1996), a highways timekeeper, in 1930. They had two sons – Derek DJ Currah 1931 and Alan D Currah 1933. David married Lilian M Carhart (born 1918) in 1963.
  - Elsie Trebilcock (1906–67) married Richard J Crewes at St Columb in 1933. They had two children – Richard B Crewes 1934 and Hazel J Crewes 1942. Elsie's death was registered at Bodmin.

Nothing is known about Horace's education. He worked as a Cornish clay labourer. He enlisted in the Duke of Cornwall's Light Infantry (15833) on 12th September 1914 at St Austell. He was described as 5′ 8½″ tall, weighing 136 lbs, with fresh complexion, grey eyes, dark hair and his religious denomination was Wesleyan. His next of kin was his mother at Fiddlers Green, Newlyn East. He joined at Bodmin later the same day and transferred to 7th Royal Dublin Fusiliers (14107) on 18th September. The Battalion embarked at Devonport aboard HMT

RMS *Alaunia* (13,405 tons), a Cunard Line ship built at Greenock in 1913, was sister ship to RMS *Andania* and *Aurania*. She is seen here at Alexandria. When war broke out she was requisitioned as a troopship and was widely employed in the role bringing Canadian troops to Europe, supporting the Gallipoli campaign and carrying troops to Bombay before returning to the North Atlantic route in 1916. On 19th October 1916, outbound for New York from London, she struck a mine in the English Channel laid by UC-16 and sank off Hastings, Sussex with the loss of two crewmen. Cunard named another vessel RMS *Alaunia*, which was in service 1925–57.

Lieutenant General (later Field Marshal) George Francis Milne GCB GCMG DSO (1866–1948). He was commissioned into the Royal Artillery in September 1885 and served in India, Aldershot and Malta before taking part in the Suakin Expedition in 1896. While at the Staff College, Camberley he became friends with William Robertson, the future CIGS. Milne took part in the Nile Expedition in 1898 and at Omdurman scored a direct hit on the Mahdi's tomb. During the Second Boer War he was Deputy Assistant Adjutant General and was promoted major. For his service in South Africa he was Mentioned in Despatches and was awarded the DSO. Various appointments and promotions followed including with HQ North Midland Division and HQ 6th Division at Cork, Ireland. In 1912 he was appointed CB and became Brigadier General Royal Artillery, 4th Division at Woolwich in October 1913. He went with 4th Division to France on the outbreak of the Great War and joined HQ III Corps in January 1915 as a major general. In July 1915 he was appointed GOC 27th Division in Salonika and in January 1916 GOC XVI Corps there. On 9th May he was appointed C-in-C Salonika. Milne was promoted substantive lieutenant general on 1st January 1917. He undertook a number of costly offensives in support of his French and Serbian allies, with limited resources and troops constantly suffering from malaria. He was appointed GCB on 1st January 1918. In September 1918 Milne became responsible for the military administration of a vast area around the Black Sea at a time of disorder resulting from the Russian Revolution and Turkish War of Independence. Withdrawal of British forces was completed early in June 1920 and from Persia in spring 1921. Milne was appointed KCMG on 1st January 1919 and was advanced to GCMG on 3rd June 1919. In March 1920 he occupied Constantinople when the administration was collapsing. On 26th April 1920 he was promoted general and was appointed Lieutenant of the Tower of London on 15th December. He was appointed GOC Eastern Command in June 1923 and ADC to the King on 31st July. On 19th February 1926 he became Chief of the Imperial General Staff and promoted the mechanisation of British land forces, although only limited progress was made during his term. He was advanced to GCB in January 1927 and was promoted field marshal on 30th January 1928. He retired in 1933 and was raised to the peerage as Baron Milne of Salonika and Rubislaw, Aberdeenshire. Milne held numerous other appointments including - Colonel Commandant Royal Artillery from 21st November 1918, Master Gunner St James' Park from 1929, Constable of the Tower of London from 1933 and Colonel Commandant Pioneer Corps from 1940. During the Second World War he served as an ARP Warden in Westminster.

Alaunia on 9th July 1915 for service with the Mediterranean Expeditionary Force and arrived at Alexandria, Egypt via Malta. The Battalion departed Alexandria on 22nd July and arrived at Mudros two days later. On 7th August it landed at Suvla Bay, Gallipoli, although Horace's Medal Index Card gives his qualification date for the 1914–15 Star as 9th August. In early October the Battalion moved to Salonika via Mudros. Horace was appointed unpaid lance corporal on 7th February 1916. He was wounded by a gunshot to the head and also suffered from malaria, but the dates are not recorded in his service record. He was appointed paid acting corporal on 14th August and paid acting sergeant on 8th September. He was promoted corporal on 23rd September and sergeant on 17th November. **Mentioned in the Despatch of GOC Salonika Army, Lieutenant General George Francis Milne on 29th March 1917, LG 21st July 1917.**

The Battalion moved to join the Egyptian Expeditionary Force for service in Palestine on 2nd September 1917 and left 10th Division on 27th April 1918. The Battalion departed Egypt by ship on 23rd May, arriving at Marseille, France on 1st June. It was reduced to cadre on 6th June and the surplus manpower, including Horace, was transferred to 2nd Royal Dublin Fusiliers. Horace was posted to the Depot in England on 20th June and was granted leave from Bermondsey Military Hospital, Ladywell Road, Lewisham, London 24th July–3rd August. He was transferred to the 3rd Battalion and declared unfit for posting to a theatre other than France or Italy due to malaria. On 13th September he joined the British Expeditionary Force Base in France and joined 2nd Royal Dublin Fusiliers on 21st September. **Awarded the VC for his actions east of Le Cateau, France on 18th October 1918, LG 6th January 1919.**

Horace later served in the same platoon as Sergeant Robert Downie VC in 2nd Royal Dublin Fusiliers. Horace had a discharge medical at Le Quesnoy on 26th January 1919 and no disability was found due to his military service. He returned to Britain on 31st January and the VC was presented by the King in the ballroom of Buckingham Palace on 8th March. Horace was demobilised to the Class

In 1897 work began on a new workhouse for St Olave's (Bermondsey) Union Board of Guardians. It was to be an infirmary to accommodate the elderly poor and infirm. The Ladywell Workhouse was opened in 1900 by the Prince and Princess of Wales. It had 812 beds and was designed to provide the maximum light and space. In 1904 St Olave's Union joined with St Margaret's to become the Bermondsey Union and the workhouse became the Bermondsey Institution. During the Great War the Institution became the Bermondsey Military Hospital, with 796 beds. In 1929 Boards of Guardians were abolished and the Institution came under London County Council as the Ladywell Institution. It did not join the NHS and continued as a residential home for the elderly managed by London County Council. It closed about 1975, since when most of the buildings have been demolished and the land redeveloped for housing. The remaining buildings have been converted for residential use.

Z Reserve on 28th March. The Lord Lieutenant of Cornwall presented him with £150 from his fellow workers in the china clay industry on 30th October. Horace was discharged on 31st March 1920.

Horace returned to the china clay industry at Newlyn and later worked in the building trade. In later years he was a ganger for a firm of builders and civil engineers. He re-enlisted in 5th Duke of Cornwall's Light Infantry (Territorial Force) (5431368) at St Columb on 20th May 1920 and was promoted sergeant the same day. He was described as 5′ 7″ tall, weighing 150 lbs, with dark complexion, blue eyes, black hair and his religious denomination was Wesleyan. He attended annual camps 7th-14th August 1920, 23rd July–6th August 1921 and 29th July–5th August 1922. On 27th August 1920 he was promoted WO2 and appointed company sergeant major. He transferred to 4/5th Duke of Cornwall's Light Infantry on 20th December 1921 and was discharged on 19th May 1923.

Robert Downie was awarded the VC for his actions on 23rd October 1916 near Lesboeufs, France during the Battle of the Somme. His story is told in the third book in this series, *Victoria Crosses on the Western Front – Somme 1916: 1st July–13th November 1916.*

Horace married Rhoda Grose Phillips (10th September 1898–1974), born at St Newlyn East, in 1922 at St Columb. They made their home at Glenburn, St Newlyn East. Living with them in 1939 were Leopold George Butler (1874–1940), a retired railwayman, and his wife, Emma Jane Oxnam (1874–1951), who was Rhoda's aunt on her mother's side. Rhoda and Horace had a daughter:

- Kathleen Hilary Curtis (22nd January 1924–18th March 2013), born at St Newlyn East, married John Henry Charles Watts (19th February 1912–25th May 1969), born at Colchester, Essex, in 1945 at Truro. He was a public works lorry driver in 1939, living at 98 London Road, Colchester. They were living at Glenburn, St Newlyn East at the time of his death there. Kathleen died at Newquay. They had a daughter:
    - Margaret A Watts (born 1948) married David W Payne (born 1946) in 1970. They had two daughters – Victoria Ann Payne 1971 and Joanne Kate Payne 1974. The marriage ended in divorce. Margaret married Arthur T Sampson (born 1942) in 1981. David married Helen S Harvey (born 1953) in 1985.

Horace Curtis back at work in the clay industry after the Great War.

Camborne Redruth Community Hospital, where Horace died. The hospital began as the Redruth Mines Infirmary in 1863. An accident ward was added in 1871 and the West Cornwall Women's Hospital was built on an adjacent site in 1899. The two hospitals amalgamated in 1901 and became the West Cornwall Miners and Women's Hospital in 1915 and the Camborne-Redruth Miners and General Hospital in 1940. It joined the NHS as Camborne-Redruth Hospital in 1948. A major redevelopment in 2002 resulted in the old hospital being converted into flats. New medical facilities became the Camborne Redruth Community Hospital.

Rhoda's father, John Henry Phillips (c.1868–1935), born in Scotland, married Agnes Ann née Oxnam (17th April 1870–1948), born at St Newlyn East, in 1895 at St Columb. John was a navvy on the railway in 1901, when they were living at St Newlyn East. By 1911 he was an iron ore miner and they were living at Grampound Road, St Newlyn East. Agnes was living with her daughter, Rhoda, and son-in-law, Horace, in 1939. In addition to Rhoda they had another daughter:

- Frances Kathleen Phillips (31st July 1896–4th February 1966) married Francis Hubert Carhart (27th May 1895–1972) on 19th February 1939. They were living at 5 Halt Road, Truro in 1939, by when he was a Cornwall County Council labourer. Frances was living at 14 Halt Road, St Newlyn East at the time of her death at Camborne-Redruth Hospital, Barncoose Terrace, Redruth.

During the Second World War Horace trained as an Air Precautions Warden before serving as a lieutenant (1st February 1941) in 11th Cornwall (Newquay) Battalion, Home Guard. He commanded the St Newlyn East platoon and last appears in the Home Guard List in March 1942. He attended two VC Reunions – the VC Dinner at the Royal Gallery of the House of Lords, London on 9th November 1929 and the Victory Day Celebration Dinner & Reception at The Dorchester, London on 8th June 1946.

A Wesleyan Chapel was built in Newlyn East in 1832 (the building on the right). In 1884 a new chapel, Newlyn East Wesleyan Chapel, for 600 people was constructed and can be seen on the left. The 1832 chapel became the Wesleyan Hall and was converted to a Sunday school. In 1932 the Wesleyan, Primitive Methodist and United Methodist Churches amalgamated to become the Methodist Church of Great Britain and the Chapel became the Newlyn East Methodist Church. It closed in 1982 and was sold for development. The 1832 building became a chapel again.

Curtis V.C. Close in St Newlyn East (Memorials to Valour).

The commemorative paving stone at St Newlyn East War Memorial (Memorials to Valour).

The last few years of Horace's life were troubled by illness and he was virtually paralysed towards the end. He died at Camborne-Redruth Hospital, Barncoose Terrace, Redruth, Cornwall on 1st July 1968. His funeral was held at St Newlyn East Methodist Church and he was cremated at Penmount Crematorium, Truro on 4th July 1968. His ashes were scattered in the Garden of Remembrance (Lawn E) and his name is recorded in the Book of Remembrance. Horace is commemorated in a number of other places:

- Curtis V.C. Close, St Newlyn East, Newquay.
- A Department for Communities and Local Government commemorative paving stone was dedicated at St Newlyn East War Memorial, The Butts, Carrick, Cornwall on 11th November 2018.

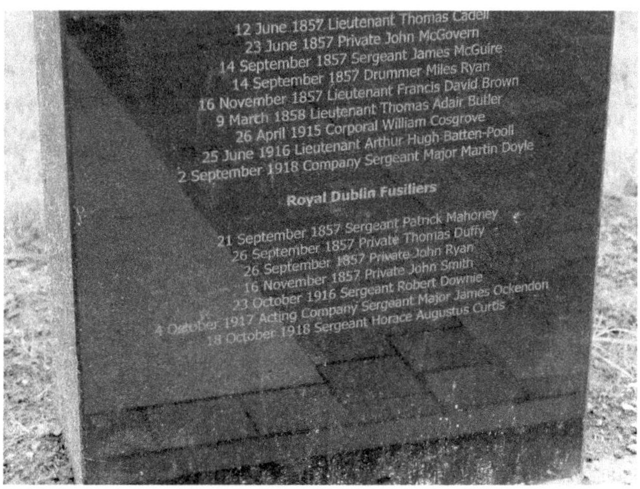

The Irish Infantry Regiments VC Memorial at the National Memorial Arboretum. Horace Curtis' name is at the bottom.

The 1914–15 Star was instituted in December 1918 for personnel who served in any theatre between 5th August 1914 and 31st December 1915. Those awarded the 1914 Star, Africa General Service Medal or Khedive's Sudan Medal 1910, were ineligible to receive it. The 1914–15 Star was awarded with the British War and Victory Medals, the trio known as Pip, Squeak and Wilfred after comic strip characters. A total of 2,366,000 medals were awarded to members of the British, Dominion and Empire forces.

- Named on the Irish Infantry Regiments VC Memorial at the Irish Infantry Grove, National Memorial Arboretum, Alrewas, Staffordshire.

In addition to the VC he was awarded the 1914–15 Star, British War Medal 1914–20, Victory Medal 1914–19, George VI Coronation Medal 1937 and Elizabeth II Coronation Medal 1953. The VC was sold at a Christie's auction of 27th November 1990 for £7,800 and at a Glendining's auction of 25th March 1992 for £10,000 to Lord Ashcroft. The VC is held by The Michael Ashcroft Trust, the holding institution for the Lord Ashcroft Victoria Cross Collection and is displayed in the Imperial War Museum's Lord Ashcroft Gallery.

205353 SERGEANT JOHN BRUNTON DAYKINS
2/4th Battalion, The York & Lancaster Regiment

John Daykins was born on 26th March 1883 at Ormiston Farm, Hawick, Roxburghshire, Borders, Scotland. His father, also John Daykins (c.1855–23rd June 1924), born at Hawick, was a farm steward in 1881 living at Ormiston Cottage, Cavers, Roxburghshire. He married Betsy 'Bessie' née Brunton (12th November 1854–26th March 1936), a spinner born at Teviothead, Roxburghshire, on 17th November 1882 at 1 Bridge Street, Hawick. The family lived at Sunnyside and then Kaimend Farm, Hawick. John senior and his brother-in-law, Samuel Brunton, took over the tenancy of Howden Farm on the estate of the Marquess of Lothian, near Jedburgh, Roxburghshire in 1885. John had three siblings:

- Samuel Brunton Daykins (2nd March 1884–23rd January 1940), born at Ormiston Farm, was a farmer at Howden Farm, Jedburgh. He married Isabella Elliot Bell (26th May 1888–17th May 1934), a housekeeper born at 77 High Street,

Hawick, on 22nd November 1922 at Primside, Morebattle, Roxburghshire. They were living at Ancrum Mains, Ancrum in 1930. She died in a nursing home at 39 Palmerston Place, Edinburgh, usual residence Wester Ulston, Jedburgh. He died at Howden, Jedburgh.

- James Brunton Daykins (22nd September 1885–18th January 1914), born at Hawick, was a law clerk in 1901 and later a bank clerk. He travelled to Montréal, Québec, Canada aboard RMS *Empress of Britain* on 9th June 1906 and lived at Galt, Ontario. He returned to Britain aboard RMS *Victorian* from Montréal, arriving at Liverpool, Lancashire on 20th October 1911. He died at Howden.
- Elizabeth 'Lizzie' Rodgerson Daykins (22nd February 1887–27th September 1974), born at Howden, married John Swanston (23rd April 1868–30th October 1927) born at Duns Mill, Berwickshire, at Howden on 24th February 1911. There were no children. He was a farm manager at the home farm at Burnbrae on the Neathorn Estate. He became the estate agent for Harold Gray at Babraham, Cambridgeshire in 1910 and ran his own farm there, whilst living at Magog House. Lizzie returned to Scotland and died at Queen's House, Kelso, Roxburghshire.

Ormiston House close to the Farm, near Hawick.

Bridge Street, Hawick. Hawick, in the Scottish Borders at the confluence of Slitrig Water and the River Teviot, was historically in Roxburghshire. It lies sixteen kilometres southwest of Jedburgh and is one of the furthest towns from the sea in Scotland. Settlement in the area goes back many centuries and there are the remains of a 12th century motte-and-bailey castle. Hawick was formally declared a town after the Battle of Hornshole in 1514 between an English raiding party and Hawick locals. On 11th October 1537 the town was declared a free burgh since time immemorial. St Mary's and Old Parish Church was constructed in 1764 on the site of a 13th century church and was reconstructed after a fire in the late 19th century. The town grew during the Industrial Revolution, mainly due to textile knitting and weaving. The first knitting machines arrived in 1771. The town manufactured different textiles, hosiery and knitwear, including cashmere, and adapted as fashions changed. In the 1930s over 1,200 people were employed in producing knitwear but by the late 20th century the textile industries had shrunk to just a few small businesses. Amongst the famous people associated with the town are:

- William Pollock McLaren CBE (1923–2010) the rugby union player and commentator, teacher and journalist, known as 'the voice of rugby'.
- James Paris Lee (1831–1904) the British, Canadian and later American arms designer, best known for inventing the bolt action and magazine for the Lee-Metford and Lee-Enfield rifles.
- Sir Charles 'Chay' Blyth CBE BEM (born 14th May 1940) the yachtsman and rower, who was the first person to sail single-handed non-stop westwards around the world in 1971.

John's paternal grandfather, John Daykins (c.1812–21st September 1879), a woollen stocking framework knitter born at Jedburgh, Roxburghshire, married Ann née Clark or Clegg (c.1815–26th April 1880), born at Lanark, Lanarkshire. They were living at Appletreehall, Roxburghshire in 1861. He was found dead at Hilliesland Loch, near Hawick, usual residence Ormiston, Kirkton, Roxburghshire. She died at Ormiston. They are not believed to have had any other children.

Howden Farm. (*Martin Dawes*)

His maternal grandfather, John Brunton (born c.1809), an agricultural labourer born at Stitchill, Roxburghshire, married Elizabeth 'Betsy' née Rodgerson (c.1813–28th June 1895), born at Hutton Currie, Dumfriesshire. They were living at Falnashmill, Teviothead, Roxburghshire in 1851, when he was a surfaceman. In 1861 they were living at Dodlands, Cavers, Roxburghshire and were still there

Jedburgh, the county town of Roxburghshire, lies on Jed Water, a tributary of the River Teviot, sixteen kilometres from the English border. A church was founded in the 9th century and King David I made it an Augustinian Priory between 1118 and 1138. The Abbey, founded in 1147, was left a ruin in the border wars with England in the 16th century but it still dominates the town. King Malcolm IV died at Jedburgh in 1165. King David I built a castle, which in 1174 was one of five ceded to England. The castle was occasionally a Scottish royal residence until it was demolished in 1409. In 1258 negotiations took place in Jedburgh between Alexander III of Scotland and Henry III of England over the succession to the Scottish throne. In 1307, James Douglas, fighting for King Robert Bruce, took Jedburgh from the English. However, its proximity to England resulted in many raids and skirmishes by both Scottish and English forces. Despite this, trade flourished and there were horse, cattle, corn and butchers' markets. In 1566 Mary Queen of Scots stayed at a house in the town. It is now a museum. In 1745, the Jacobite army led by Prince Charles Edward Stuart passed through the town and the Prince stayed there. Amongst the famous people associated with Jedburgh are:

- Mary Somerville (1780–1872), the scientist and writer, who studied mathematics and astronomy. In 1835 she and Caroline Herschel were the first female honorary members of the Royal Astronomical Society. Somerville College, Oxford is named after her and she appeared on the 2017 Royal Bank of Scotland £10 note.
- James Thomson (1700–48) the poet and playwright, who wrote the lyrics of *Rule Britannia*.
- Greig Laidlaw (born 12th October 1985), who was educated at Jedburgh Grammar School, holds the record for the most caps as captain (39) of the Scottish rugby union team and has scored over 700 points for Scotland in his career, one of the highest points scorers in rugby union history. He has also represented the British & Irish Lions.

in 1881. He died before 1891. She died at Howden, Jedburgh. In addition to Betsy they had three other children:

- John Brunton (born 6th August 1839), born at Teviothead, was an agricultural labourer in 1851.
- Samuel Rodgerson Brunton (5th March 1841–18th March 1930) was a journeyman joiner in 1881 and was living with his sister and brother-in-law at Howden in 1901. He died at Howden.
- James Brunton (born 27th August 1842).

The village of Appletreehall is about three kilometres northeast of Hawick.

John was educated at Jedburgh Grammar School May 1889–1896 and also at Kelso School. He worked on his father's tenant farm at Howden. He enlisted in A Squadron, 1st Lothian & Border Horse Yeomanry on 7th September 1914 (1718) described as 5′ 9½″ tall, weighing 139/150 lbs, with ruddy complexion, blue eyes, dark hair and his religious denomination was Presbyterian. He reduced his age to twenty-seven years and six months. John had enormous feet and the Army had trouble finding boots to fit him. He joined at Haddington, East Lothian on the same day that he enlisted and after eight months transferred to Sutton Veny, Salisbury Plain, Wiltshire. He went to France on 20th September 1915, arriving at Le Havre next day, when the Squadron became 26th Division's Cavalry Squadron. He sprained his knee at Parc Borély, Marseille on 5th December while taking two horses to water. Two days later he embarked there for the Mediterranean Expeditionary Force in Salonika, arriving on 17th December. He contracted malaria in September 1916. A Squadron transferred to 8th Mounted Brigade in November.

Stitchill is three kilometres north of Kelso and eight kilometres from the English border. It is mentioned as a manor in 1308, when it was considered forfeited to King Edward I of England. Nearby is Flodden Field, site of the battle in September 1513. The village is in the historic territory of the Pringles, a notorious family of Border Reivers. Robert Pringle of Baitingbush purchased the lands of Stichill in 1628, and his grandson, also Robert Pringle, was created 1st Pringle Baronet of Stichill.

Jedburgh Grammar School was founded in the 15th century by William Turnbull, Bishop of Glasgow. The school was originally at Jedburgh Abbey. The modern school was created as a result of the Education (Scotland) Act 1872, which required children to receive an education. The school was extended at the turn of the century when secondary education was introduced. The original buildings were started in 1882 and have listed status. Amongst its notable alumni is Lieutenant Francis Anthony Blair Fasson GC RN (17th July 1913–30th October 1942), who served aboard the battleship HMS *Rodney* and the light cruiser HMS *Curacoa* before being attached to the RAF 1935–36. He returned to the Navy and served aboard the minesweeping sloop HMS *Salamander*, the escort HMS *Shoreham* and the destroyer HMS *Windsor*. He was first lieutenant of the destroyer HMS *Hostile* in April 1940 during the First Battle of Narvik, for which he was mentioned in despatches. After a spell ashore at the naval headquarters at Alexandria, Egypt, he joined the destroyer HMS *Petard* in March 1942 as first lieutenant. On 30th October 1942 *Petard*, in conjunction with destroyers HMS *Pakenham*, *Hero*, *Dulverton* and *Hurworth*, and an RAF Sunderland, attacked and badly damaged the German U-*559* in the Mediterranean. The crew was forced to abandon the submarine with seven dead. Fasson, with AB Colin Grazier and NAAFI canteen assistant Tommy Brown, jumped onto the deck of the sinking submarine and went below. Working in complete darkness and aware that the submarine could sink without warning, Fasson and Grazier located documents which Brown carried up to a whaler. They continued searching until the submarine suddenly sank, drowning Fasson and Grazier, who were awarded the George Cross. Brown survived and received the George Medal. The codebooks were immensely valuable to the codebreakers at Bletchley Park, allowing the German naval Shark Enigma code to be read.

John embarked aboard HMT *Royal George* on 27th November, arriving on 7th December for home leave until 6th January 1917. He was on the held strength of 3/1st Lothian & Border Horse Yeomanry, Aldershot, Hampshire. At the end of his leave on 3rd January, John was ordered to join No.1 Officer Cadet Battalion, Membland Hall, Newton Ferrers, Devon in a War Office letter dated 26th December 1916. However, he reverted to 3/1st Lothian & Border Horse Yeomanry on 30th January after being found unfit for further service following a medical examination. He was posted to 2nd Reserve Regiment of Cavalry, Aldershot on 11th February, which was absorbed by 4th Reserve Regiment of Cavalry the following day. Following a medical he was transferred to 2/2nd County of London Yeomanry (Westminster Dragoons) on 13th March (20645). He embarked at Southampton the same day and arrived at Rouen, France on 14th March. John joined 2nd Advanced Remount Squadron, Abbeville and on 28th April he was admitted to hospital with a recurrence of malaria, returning to duty on 13th May. On 16th August he embarked for Britain from Rouen. On 20th August he transferred to the Tank Corps Recruit Depot (300686), when the personnel of 2/2nd County of London Yeomanry (Westminster Dragoons) transferred to the infantry or the Tank Corps. However, on 26th August he transferred to 3rd York & Lancaster (205353) and returned to France on 31st October, on the strength of 13th York & Lancaster. Having joined

SS *Heliopoli* (11,146 tons), built for the Egyptian Mail Steam Ship Co of London by Fairfield Shipbuilding & Engineering Co, was launched on 28th May 1907. She carried up to 1,154 passengers as well as cargo. In 1909 she was laid up in Marseille, France when she was taken back by the builders. The following year she was purchased by Canadian Northern Steamships of Toronto and renamed *Royal George*. Following a refit she commenced Avonmouth-Montréal-Québec sailings. On 6th November 1912 she was stranded near Québec and, having been refloated, sailed for Halifax for repairs. On 3rd October 1914 she sailed from Gaspe Bay for Plymouth with part of the Canadian Expeditionary Force and was then taken over as a British troopship. She was involved in the Gallipoli campaign in 1915. The fleet was purchased by Cunard Steam Ship Co in 1916, but *Royal George* continued as a troopship for the remainder of the war. Passenger voyages resumed on 10th February 1919 with the first of five Liverpool-Halifax-New York sailings. Her first Southampton-Halifax-New York voyage commenced on 15th August. Her last voyage commenced on 10th June 1920, after which she was an emigrant depot ship at Cherbourg, before being laid up in the River Fal. She was broken up at Wilhemshaven in August 1922.

Membland is an historic estate about thirteen kilometres southeast of Plymouth, first mentioned in the 14th century. The Hillersdon family was seated at Membland by the 16th century. Richard Hillersdon (c.1639–1703), was MP for Plympton Erle in 1679. His only son died and Membland passed to his son-in-law, Arthur Champernowne, who died childless. The next occupant was Arthur Stert (died 1755), MP for Plymouth 1727–54, who rebuilt the house with detached wings. He was predeceased by his only son. Membland was purchased in 1757 by John Bulteel (1733–1801). He inherited his paternal estate of Flete and, having no further use for Membland, sold it to Peter Perring (1743–96) of London, who had made a fortune in the East Indies. He died childless and Membland passed to his nephew, Sir John Perring, 1st Baronet (1765–1831), senior partner of Perrings Bank and Lord Mayor of London in 1803. The bank failed in 1825 and he sold his estates. Robert Robertson (1777–1859) purchased Membland in 1827. In 1836 he was High Sheriff of Devon. About 1860 Membland was purchased by John Delaware, MP for Devonport. The estate was purchased about 1877 by Edward Baring, 1st Baron Revelstoke (1828–97), senior partner of Barings Bank. He rebuilt Membland Hall and visitors included the Prince of Wales (later Edward VII). After the collapse of Barings Bank the property was sold in 1899 to a property developer. A year later it was bought by shipbuilder William Cresswell Gray. In 1904 he purchased another estate in Yorkshire, which he preferred but could not find a buyer for Membland, although he did sell off much of the land, reducing the estate to 227 acres by 1924. After its use in the Great War as an officer cadet training facility the house became derelict. After Gray's death it was purchased by Stanley Thomas Pitts, who demolished the building and sold the salvaged materials in 1927–28. Several estate buildings survive, including the gatekeeper's lodge, stables, gasworks, forge and laundry. A smaller dwelling was built on the site of the house in the 1960s.

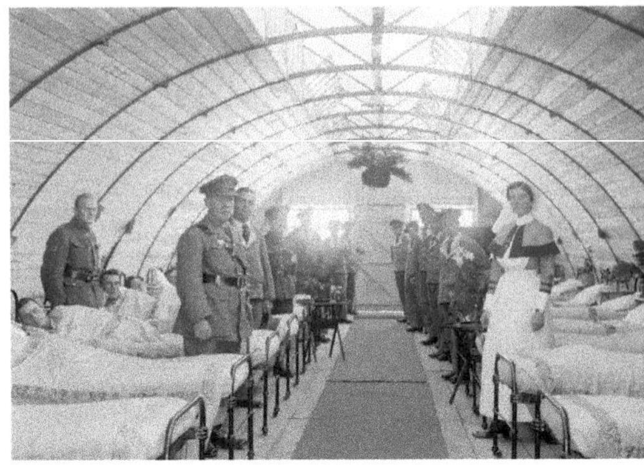

Staff and patients of 1st Canadian General Hospital awaiting a royal visit. The hospital formed at Valcartier on 14th September 1914 with most of the personnel coming from No.5 Field Ambulance (Active Militia), Montréal. It left Québec on 30th September aboard SS *Scandinavian*, arriving at Devonport on 14th October. The hospital arrived at West Down North Camp on Salisbury Plain on 20th October, with a strength of thirty officers and 168 other ranks. It was operational before the end of the week. The King and Queen visited on 4th November. No.1 Canadian General Hospital transferred to Bulford Manor on 10th November. On 18th November the hospital had its first fatality, 37123 Private John J Laroe CASC (Bulford Church Cemetery – I 4 4). An outbreak of meningitis followed in December and January, resulting in many deaths. The Hospital moved a few miles north to Netheravon on 1st January 1915. Whilst on Salisbury Plain, No.1 Canadian General Hospital treated 3,993 patients, of whom 1,249 were venereal cases. There were sixty-nine deaths, one-third due to cerebro-spinal fever. On 13th May 1915 the hospital embarked for France, arriving at Boulogne next day, before moving to Étaples. The hospital was in tents but, as winter approached, it was clear that the canvas made for the tropics was not up to the weather on the French coast. Gradually all the hospitals in the area had their tents replaced by huts. The first fifty patients arrived on 31st May. By the end of 1915, 10,621 patients had been treated, of whom 139 died (1.3%). Captain Francis Alexander Scrimger VC was posted to No.1 Canadian Field Hospital on 30th December. His story is told in the second book in this series, *Victoria Crosses on the Western Front, Second Ypres to the Eve of the Somme – April 1915–June 1916*. On 3rd August 1916, the King made a surprise visit. The busiest day for the hospital so far came on 19th April 1917, when 2,205 patients were being treated. On 10th January 1918, No.1 Canadian General Hospital was chosen to specialise in compound femur fractures. On 14th April a record 2,218 patients were in the hospital. A bombing raid on 19th May killed three Canadian nursing sisters, the first Canadian nurses killed in action. On 21st November, ten days after the Armistice, there were still 1,108 patients in the hospital. The last 163 patients were discharged on 29th January 1919. On 12th February all personnel, except for a small rear party, proceeded to the Canadian Embarkation Camp, Le Havre. The rear party arrived on 28th February and on 16th March all the staff embarked aboard SS *Lorina*. They arrived at Weymouth next day for onward travel by train to London and Shorncliffe, Kent. The entire unit was granted eight days leave, followed by medical boards and documentation for the return to Canada. On 11th April three officers and 176 other ranks embarked aboard SS *Adriatic* at Liverpool. No.1 Canadian General Hospital was demobilised in Montréal in April 1919 and was disbanded on 15th November 1920.

SS *Cambria* was built for the London & North Western Railway for the Holyhead to Dublin service. She was requisitioned by the Admiralty in 1914 as an armed boarding steamer until being converted to a hospital ship in 1915. She worked the Dover to France route until May 1917, when she was transferred to the Holyhead–Dublin route. She returned to the Channel in December 1917 as a troop carrier before again moving to the Holyhead–Dublin route in February 1918. She was renamed TSS *Arvonia* in 1919 and in August 1922 was requisitioned as a troopship by the Irish Free State. She was scrapped in 1925.

The VAD Military Hospital at Barry Road, Northampton was lodged in a school and baths. (*Alan Murray-Rust*)

The Auxiliary Hospital at Guilsborough occupied Guilsborough Hall, which was demolished c.1955.

34th Infantry Base Depot, Étaples the following day, he was posted to 2/4th York & Lancaster (62nd Division) on 4th November.

John was promoted corporal on 29th December. He was admitted to 2/3rd West Riding Field Ambulance on 23rd March 1918 with pyrexia of unknown origin. He passed through No.30 Casualty Clearing Station and was admitted to 1st Canadian General Hospital, Étaples the following day. He returned to Britain on 28th March aboard HMHS *Cambria* on the strength of the Depot. He was treated at the VAD Military Hospital, Barry Road, Northampton 28th March–2nd April and then the Auxiliary Hospital, Guilsborough, Northampton until 14th May. On 26th May he joined the 4th Reserve Battalion and was posted to the Royal Engineers Pioneer Depot, Reading, Berkshire on 15th June. He embarked at Folkestone for France on 24th July and joined the 7th Battalion (Pioneers) on 5th September. John returned to 2/4th Battalion on 8th September and was appointed paid acting sergeant on 3rd October. **Awarded the VC for his actions at Solesmes, France on 20th October 1918, LG 6th January 1919.**

The Military Medal, seen here with a Bar, was awarded to other ranks of the British Army (later extended to other services) and Commonwealth countries for bravery on land. It was established on 25th March 1916 as the other ranks equivalent of the Military Cross, which was awarded to commissioned officers and warrant officers. It was the third level gallantry award, ranking below the Distinguished Conduct Medal. Over 115,000 MMs were awarded during the Great War, as well as 5,700 bars and 180 second bars. Private Ernest Corey, a stretcher-bearer with 55th Australian Infantry Battalion, was awarded three bars. Over 15,000 MMs were awarded during the Second World War. It was discontinued in 1993, since when the Military Cross has been awarded to all ranks within the British honours system. Most Commonwealth nations established their own honours systems after the Second World War and award their own gallantry decorations.

John Daykins being received at Jedburgh Town Hall on 31st May 1919.

The rank of sergeant was confirmed on 20th October. **Awarded the MM for his actions with B Company, the right forward assault company, in the attack on Fresnoy on 4th November 1918, LG 20th August 1919.** He opted to have the MM delivered by post and not to have a formal presentation. John continued to serve with the British Army of Occupation at Köln (Cologne), Germany until returning to Britain on 7th April 1919. No disabilities were found on his final medical at York on 9th April. John was disembodied on demobilisation on 7th May 1919. Next day the VC was presented by the King in the quadrangle at Buckingham Palace.

John Daykins' family grave in Castlewood Cemetery, Jedburgh. (*Memorials to Valour*)

On 31st May, John was transported by horse and carriage through Jedburgh until soldiers carried him shoulder-high to the Town Hall. He signed the Burgess Roll and received the 'Burgess Ticket', equivalent to being granted the freedom of the town, in a silver-mounted cask made of oak from the one thousand years old Jed Forest Capon Tree. He also received a silver tea and coffee set from the people of Jedburgh. The machine guns that he captured

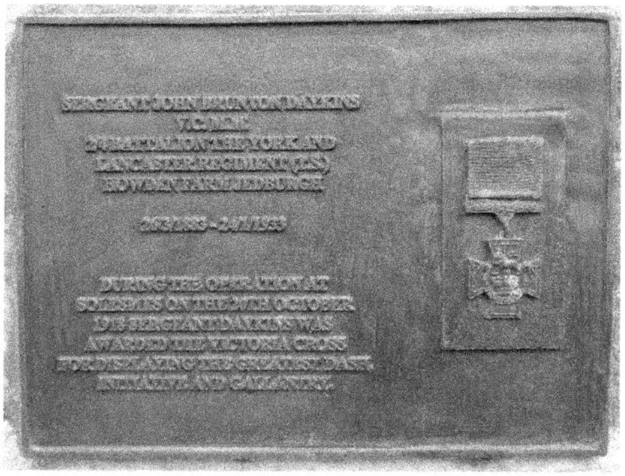

Memorial plaque outside the British Legion, Jedburgh (Memorials to Valour).

The Department for Communities and Local Government commemorative paving stone at Jedburgh War Memorial (Memorials to Valour).

The Victory Medal (or Inter-Allied Victory Medal) was first proposed by French Marshal Ferdinand Foch as a common award for all the nations allied against the Central Powers. Regardless of nationality, each medal is 36mm in diameter, the ribbon is a double rainbow and the obverse shows winged victory (except Japan and Siam, where winged victory has no relevance). For British Empire forces the medal was issued to all who received the 1914 Star or 1914–15 Star and to almost all who received the British War Medal. The British alone struck 6,335,000 Victory Medals. These three medals were known as Pip, Squeak and Wilfred after a popular newspaper comic strip. To qualify for the Victory Medal recipients had to be mobilised for war service and have entered a theatre of war between 5th August 1914 and 11th November 1918, plus Russia 1919–20 and mine clearance in the North Sea until 30th November 1919. Those Mentioned in Despatches wore an oakleaf on the Victory Medal ribbon, as shown here.

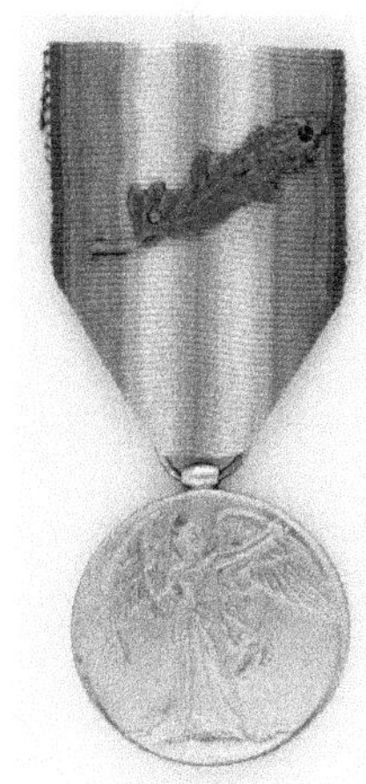

at Solesmes were mounted in Jedburgh until they were scrapped in 1940 for the war effort. John took over the tenancy of his father's farm after his death in 1924 and lived there with his mother and sister. He never married. John attended two VC reunions – the VC Garden Party at Buckingham Palace on 26th June 1920 and the VC Dinner at the Royal Gallery of the House of Lords, London on 9th November 1929.

On the evening of 24th January 1933 John heard a disturbance outside his house and took his gun to investigate. A stray cat had been giving trouble in the area. When he failed to return, his sister went out and found him with a bullet wound to the head. John died in Jedburgh on the way to Edinburgh Royal Infirmary. He is buried in the family plot in Castlewood Cemetery, Jedburgh (Grave 1431). He left effects valued at £5,013/19/6, probate granted to his brother, Samuel. John is commemorated in a number of other places:

- Daykins Drive, Hawick named in 1981.
- Plaque outside the British Legion, Jedburgh unveiled in September 2000.

Clifton House was built in 1783 as a residence for the Walker family. It was sold in 1891 to Rotherham Corporation as a municipal park, which was opened by the future King Edward VIII. The Museum, which opened in 1893, incorporates the York & Lancaster Regiment Museum. Clifton Park Museum and Park are both Grade II listed.

- A Department for Communities and Local Government commemorative paving stone was dedicated at Jedburgh War Memorial, Abbey Bridge Road, Jedburgh on 20th October 2018.

In addition to the VC and MM he was awarded the 1914–15 Star, British War Medal 1914–20 and Victory Medal 1914–19. The VC was given on long loan by his sister, Elizabeth Swanston, to the Regiment in May 1957. The VC is held by the York & Lancaster Regimental Museum, Clifton Park Museum, Clifton Lane, Rotherham, South Yorkshire.

MAJOR GEORGE DE CARDONNEL ELMSALL FINDLAY
409th (1/1st Lowland) Field Company, Royal Engineers (Territorial Force)

George Findlay was born on 20th August 1889 at Leabank House, Cardross, Dunbartonshire, Scotland. His father, Robert Elmsall Findlay DL JP (25th April 1855–19th November 1928), born at Manila, Philippines, was educated at Harrow and Balliol College, Oxford (BA 1877, MA 1878). He served in the Queen's Own Royal Glasgow Yeomanry from 1st July 1881 until 1892, retiring as a major. He served again in the Lanarkshire Yeomanry as a lieutenant from 11th April 1900 and was promoted captain on 25th January 1902. He last appears in the Army List in April 1908 but was appointed immediately afterwards as a Co-opted Member of the Dumbarton Territorial Force Association. He held this position in the Army List until June 1922. Robert served again as a major in the Queen's Own Royal Glasgow Yeomanry from 25th July 1915 and last appears in the Army List in August 1918. Robert was a director of Findlay, Richardson & Co, a Glasgow firm of East India Merchants trading with Manila and Japan. He was also a director of the Scottish Amicable Life Assurance Society

Leabank House, where George was born.

George's father, Robert Elmsall Findlay.

and a director of the Union Bank of Scotland. He was a member of Kilmaronock School Board, Chairman of the Parish Council and a member of the County Council. He took a leading role in the affairs of Dunbartonshire Constitutional Association and of the Primrose League. Robert married Jane Cecilia Louise née Scott (2nd October 1858–16th July 1949), born at 34 Lynedoch Street, Glasgow, Lanarkshire, on 10th August 1882 at St Mary's Church, Birnam, Perthshire. He was living at Boturich Castle, Balloch, Dunbartonshire and she at 1 Woodside Place, Glasgow at the time. They lived at Leebank, Cardross and Boturich Castle. Robert died at Henry Brock Vale of Leven Cottage Hospital, Alexandria, Dunbartonshire and Jane at Drumfork House, Helensburgh, Dunbartonshire. George had four siblings:

The population of Birnam increased with the arrival of the Highland Railway and resulted in the need for a new place of worship. Land for the new church was donated by Sir William Stewart, Laird of Murthly, and the building was completed in 1858, dedicated to St Mary the Virgin by Charles Wordsworth, Bishop of St Andrews, nephew of the famous poet. A tower was added in 1870, a new parsonage in 1872, an organ in 1874 and a choir vestry later that decade. A side aisle had to be added in 1883 to accommodate the number of worshippers. Two windows are the work of William Morris & Co.

1 Woodside Place, Glasgow became a Category A listed building in December 1970. It was built in 1838. Woodside Place is in the prestigious Park Area of Glasgow's West End.

Drumfork House is believed to be the oldest house in Helensburgh, possibly built as early as 1720, although it is also reputed to have been built for John Stevenson, a Glasgow merchant, in 1748. After George's death there in 1967, the house was empty until 1986, when it was restored as a guest house.

- Charles Bannatyne Findlay (19th October 1883–9th June 1965), born at Old Kirkpatrick, Dunbartonshire, was educated at Harrow. He was commissioned in the Royal Artillery on 24th June 1903 and was promoted lieutenant on 24th June 1906. He married Violet Alice Gunter (1892–14th November 1919), born at Chelsea, London, on 30th July 1914 at St Saviour's Church, Chelsea. She was the daughter of Major General James Gunter, 1st Dragoon Guards (1833–1908) and Laura Elizabeth Alice Inglis (1860–1942), of Aldwark Manor, Yorkshire. Violet's address was 29 Lennox Gardens, London at the time of the marriage. Charles went to France on 27th October 1914 and was promoted captain on 30th October 1914. He returned to Britain on 24th July 1915 and redeployed to France on 3rd September. He transferred to Salonika on 21st November and remained there for the rest of the war. Appointed acting major 16th June 1916, Deputy Assistant Adjutant General Salonika 31st October 1917 and GSO2 to GOC RA Salonika 26th December. Appointed acting lieutenant colonel on 1st July 1918 to command 130th Brigade RFA until 20th July 1919. Appointed brevet lieutenant colonel on 3rd June 1919 and promoted lieutenant colonel on 22nd June 1922. He was Mentioned in Despatches on 25th September 1916 and was awarded the MC (LG 1st January 1917) and the Greek Military Cross 2nd Class (LG 7th October 1919). Violet died of Spanish flu at Adara, Ladytown, Newbridge, Co Kildare, Ireland soon after the birth of her son, Robert. Charles married Mary Helen Paterson (1896–12th August 1986), birth registered at Chester le Street, Co Durham, on 22nd January 1921, registered at Samford, Suffolk. She was the daughter of the Reverend Thomas Frederick Paterson (1856–1928) and Alice Clara Fleming (1862–1958), of East Bergholt, Suffolk. Charles was promoted colonel on 3rd June 1923. He inherited Boturich Castle on his father's death on 19th November 1928 and sold it the same year to his cousin, Brigadier (Ret'd) Thomas Dunlop Findlay (1895–1950). Charles was appointed temporary brigadier as Commander Royal Artillery, Aldershot Command on 17th January 1936. Appointed ADC to King George V 12th December 1936–1st October 1939. He was CRA 2nd Division in France 1939–40 (CBE, LG 11th July 1940) and was acting GOC 2nd Division 12th-15th August 1940. Appointed Inspector General RA (Field Branch), War Office on 1st September 1940. Major General DG Johnson VC CB DSO MC was Inspector of Infantry at the same time. Transferred to the Reserve of Officers mid-1943. Charles was a member of the Displaced Persons Allied Commission

The Legion of Merit is awarded for exceptionally meritorious conduct in the performance of outstanding services and achievements. The Legion of Merit is seventh in the order of precedence of US military awards. There are four degrees – Chief Commander, Commander, Officer (shown here) and Legionnaire.

1943–47 and the International Refugee Organisation in Italy 1947–48. Awarded the American Officer of the Order of Legion of Merit (LG 18th July 1947). They were living at The Oaks, Letty Green, near Hertford at the time of his death there. Mary died at Orpington Hospital, Bromley, London. Charles had six children from his two marriages:

- Jean Frances Findlay (16th June 1915–16th November 2003), birth registered at Chelsea, married her second cousin, Dr Neil Ripley Ker (28th May 1908–23rd August 1982), born at Brompton, London, in 1938 at Chelsea. His parents were living at 46 Pont Street, Chelsea, London in 1908, at Friningham Lodge, Detling, near Maidstone, Kent in 1911 and later at Dougalston, Milngavie, Dunbartonshire, Scotland. Neil was educated at Eton and Magdalen College, Oxford and became a scholar of Anglo-Saxon literature. He was a lecturer at Oxford University in 1939, when they were living at 8 Sollershalt Flats, Oxford. He was also a member of Oxford City First Aid Party and she was a member of the Red Cross detachment. Neil registered as a conscientious objector at the outbreak of the Second World War and was assigned work as a porter at Radcliffe Infirmary, Oxford. He published *Medieval Libraries of Great Britain* 1941, *Catalogue of Manuscripts Containing Anglo-Saxon* 1957 and another 123 publications. He became a Fellow of the British Academy in 1957 and was created CBE for services to palaeography (LG 30th December 1978). They were living at Brambles, Hinksey Hill, Abingdon, Berkshire in 1945. Neil died following a fall while hiking in Scotland. The Neil Ker Memorial Fund was established by his family and friends to promote the study of western medieval manuscripts. Jean died at Aberfeldy, Perthshire. They had four children – Robert Frances (sic) Ker 1940, Christina Mary Ker 1942, Helen Elizabeth Ker 1944 and Janet Margaret Ker 1952.
- Robert Bannatyne Findlay (6th November 1919–24th January 1921) was born in Ireland and his death was registered at Dartford, Kent.
- Mary Buchanan Findlay (5th February 1922–21st October 2010), birth registered at Bromley, worked as a State Registered Nurse. She never married and her death was registered at Dunkeld, Perth and Kinross.

One of the many publications by Neil Ker.

The US Distinguished Flying Cross was established on 2nd July 1926 to recognise single acts of heroism or extraordinary achievement while participating in aerial flight. The first recipient to actually be presented with the DFC was Charles Lindbergh, following his trans-Atlantic flight in 1927. Amelia Earhart became the first woman to receive the DFC on 29th July 1932 for her solo flight across the Atlantic.
Amongst the many other distinguished recipients are:

- Colonel Buzz Aldrin USAF – Lunar Module pilot for Apollo 11 and the second man to walk on the Moon.
- Lieutenant George HW Bush USNR, later President of the USA.
- Orville and Wilbur Wright – aviation pioneers.
- Squadron Leader Robert Stanford-Tuck – RAF flying ace.
- Brigadier General James Stewart USAFR – B-24 pilot, Group Operations Officer and Academy Award-winning actor.
- Major Clark Gable USAAF – bomber observer-gunner and star of *Gone with the Wind*.

The US Air Medal was created in 1942 for single acts of heroism or meritorious achievement while participating in aerial flight. The original award criteria were a naval vessel or three enemy aircraft in flight destroyed, or twenty-five operational flights during which exposure to enemy fire was expected or one hundred operational flights during which exposure to enemy fire was not expected. These criteria were altered by commanding generals of Air Forces to fit the conditions of their theatre of operations. Notable recipients include the first men to land on the Moon in 1969 – Neil Armstrong and Buzz Aldrin.

- Nan Margaret Findlay (born 19th August 1926), birth registered at Ipswich, Suffolk, married Squadron Leader John 'Jock' Ramsay Maitland (11th October 1924–16th March 2012), born at Forfar, Angus, on 29th October 1952. He was the son of Lieutenant Colonel Sir George Ramsay Maitland 7th Bt DSO DL (1882–1960) and Jean Hamilton Findlay MBE (1890–1982). John was educated at Rugby School. His military career started in the Fleet Air Arm but he had to transfer to the RAF to complete flying training because the Navy decided his eyesight was not adequate. He served in Palestine and Cyprus flying Spitfires with No.32 Squadron. He then flew Meteors with No.247 Squadron in Britain, before volunteering for an exchange posting with the USAF. In January 1953 he was attached to 25th Fighter Interception Squadron in Korea, flying Sabres from Suwon. On 24th June he shot down a MiG. A few weeks later he damaged another, which was seen going down, but was unconfirmed. When the Korean War ended in July 1953, he had flown seventy-seven operational missions. He was awarded the American DFC and the Air Medal. Back in Britain he was a day fighter instructor before commanding No.249 Squadron

The annual Biggin Hill Air Fair or Biggin Hill International Air Show, at the former RAF fighter station, was one of the largest civilian airshows in the world and the largest privately organised in Europe. Jock Maitland purchased a lease to run Biggin Hill as an airport in 1958 and ran the first show in 1963. It continued until 2010 and has been succeeded by a smaller air show, The Festival of Flight, since 2014.

in Jordan and Cyprus flying Venoms. He was involved in ground attack sorties during the Suez operations in 1956. The following year he flew operations in Oman before resigning his commission. He then developed Biggin Hill as a commercial airport, founded a flying club and a small airline, an executive charter business and the Biggin Hill Air Fair. In 1975 he established Air Displays International and over thirty years organised almost one hundred air shows, in addition to the annual Biggin Hill event. He retired in 2006. Nan and Jock divorced in 1966. They had three children – David Ramsay Maitland 1954, James Maitland 1957 and Jean Findlay Maitland 1959. John married Kathleen Mary Desmond (25th July 1931–18th December 1984), born at Dinard, Ille-et-Vilaine, Brittany, France, on 7th February 1968. She died at Otford, Kent. John and Kathleen had a son, Keith John Maitland, in 1969.

  - John de Cardonnel Elmsall Findlay (29th June 1928–2001) was educated at Wellington College. He was commissioned in the Royal Artillery on 15th July 1948 (393130) and was promoted lieutenant on 15th July 1950. He transferred to the Regular Army Reserve of Officers, Class III on 5th June 1954 and was promoted captain in the Territorial Army on 9th December 1959. John married Rosemary Katherine Boyd (1931–2019), born at Ayr, Scotland, on 22nd November 1958 registered at Winchester, Hampshire. He was appointed JP and DL for Ayrshire and died at Girvan. Her death was registered at Perth, Perthshire. They had three children all registered at Colmonell, Ayrshire – Charles Boyd Findlay 1960, James de Cardonnel Findlay 1961 and Alice R Findlay 1964.
  - Barbara AH Findlay (born 20th January 1933), birth registered at Aldershot, Hampshire.

- Jane Cecilia 'Cis' Hope Findlay (9th November 1885–17th November 1965), born at Boturich Castle, married Captain Claude Gray-Buchanan (17th February 1878–4th November 1914), born at Timaru, New Zealand, on 2nd July 1914 at St Augustine's Church, Dumbarton. He was the eldest son of Lieutenant Colonel

Michael Rowland Gray-Buchanan (1846–1933) and Frederica Stuart (1855–1936) of Ettrickdale, Port Bannatyne, Bute. Claude was educated at Summerfield, Harrow and the Royal Military College Sandhurst, passing out first in 1898. He was commissioned on 20th July 1898 and was attached to 1st Hampshire as a probationer for the Indian Army. He served at Landi Kotal (Khyber Pass) and on the North West Frontier of India October 1898–October 1899. Appointed to the Indian Army on 13th October 1899. He was promoted lieutenant and appointed to 35th Sikhs on 30th October 1900. Claude was in action during the Waziri Campaign 1901 and was promoted captain and appointed double company officer in 35th Sikhs on 20th July 1907. He attended the Staff College, Quetta, passing out in December 1913. At the outbreak of the Great War, he was appointed to HQ RFC, BEF. On 2nd November 1914 he was attached to 2nd/8th Gurkha Rifles. He was initially reported missing on 4th November but was later accepted to have been killed in action near Festubert, France (Neuve-Chapelle Memorial, France – Panel 30). Jane was living at Bayfield House, Nigg, Ross-shire at the time. She was living at Craigie Cottage, Monteith, Stirlingshire and Cameron House, Cluny, Aberfeldy, Perthshire at the time of her death.

- Robert Scott Findlay (17th April 1887–22nd May 1915), born at Glasgow, Lanarkshire, was educated at Harrow School (Cadet Corps and 27th Middlesex Rifle Volunteers) and Oxford University (UOTC 1905–09 and 1st Volunteer Battalion, Oxford Light Infantry). He applied for a commission in 9th Argyll & Sutherland Highlanders on 11th January 1910 but the Battalion was manned to its establishment of junior officers. He was allowed to join as a supernumerary in

Claude Gray-Buchanan's name on the Neuve-Chapelle Memorial. The Neuve-Chapelle Memorial commemorates 4,742 members of the then Indian Army and labourers (including Nepal and Pakistan) with no known grave, who died in the Great War. The Memorial was designed by Sir Herbert Baker, with sculpture by Charles Wheeler. Half of the inside of the circular enclosure consists of panels with names of the dead. The Memorial was unveiled by the Earl of Birkenhead, Secretary of State for India on 7th October 1927. He had served in France 1914–15 as a staff officer with the Indian Corps and co-wrote *The Indian Corps in France* in 1917. French Marshal Ferdinand Foch gave a speech in French and contingents of Indian troops represented the units that fought in France. Later additions commemorate other Indian Army dead of both World Wars. Two VCs are commemorated – Gabar Singh Negi and William Arthur McCrae Bruce. The Memorial bears the scars of fighting in the area during the Second World War. The Memorial was visited in April 2015 by Indian Prime Minister Narendra Modi.

The Quintinshill rail disaster on 22nd May 1915 was the worst in British history. The Quintinshill signal box controlled two passing loops on either side of the double-track main line from Glasgow to Carlisle. At the time of the accident both passing loops were occupied by goods trains and a northbound passenger train was stood on the southbound main line. A southbound troop train, carrying 1/7th Royal Scots from Larbert to Liverpool on the way to Gallipoli, collided with the stationary passenger train and a minute later the wreckage was struck by a northbound express from London Euston to Glasgow Central. Gas from the lighting system of the troop train ignited and the fire engulfed all five trains. Only half the soldiers on the troop train survived. The precise number of those killed is unclear as some bodies were consumed completely by the fire. The official death toll was 227 (215 soldiers, nine passengers and three railway employees). However, the Army later reduced its losses to 214. There were also four victims thought to be children who are not included in the total. Their remains were never claimed or identified. The soldiers were buried in a mass grave in Rosebank Cemetery, Edinburgh. An official inquiry concluded that the collision was caused through neglect of the rules by two signalmen. They were convicted of culpable homicide in Scotland. After being released in 1916, they were re-employed by the railway, although not as signalmen. (*Dumfries & Galloway Libraries*)

July on the understanding that he would not be paid or claim any allowances until a vacancy occurred. He was serving as a captain with 9th Argyll & Sutherland Highlanders when he was killed in the worst disaster in British railway history at Quintinshill, near Gretna, Scotland, whilst on home leave from France (Boturich Castle Private Cemetery, Dunbartonshire). There were 226 deaths in the disaster, plus another 246 injured.

- James Buchanan Findlay (7th January 1895–1983), born at Kilmaronock, Dunbartonshire, trained at the Royal Naval Colleges Dartmouth and Osborne from 15th September 1907. He was appointed midshipman on 15th May 1912 on the battleship HMS *St Vincent*. Appointed acting sub lieutenant on 15th September 1914 and was loaned to the Government of Australia for service aboard the battlecruiser HMAS *Australia* on 24th May 1913, while on the strength of HMS *Victory*. He was assigned to HMS *Pembroke* whilst awaiting an appointment on 1st February 1915 and joined HMS *St George* for HMS *Kale* on 12th February. James was promoted sub lieutenant on 15th March 1915 and joined HMS *Blake* for HMS *Lyra* on 2nd June. He joined HMS *Diligence* for the destroyer HMS *Mischief* in December. He was treated aboard Hospital Ship No.6, 2nd-7th October 1916. Appointed acting lieutenant on 15th December 1916, later substantive from 15th September. He joined HMS *Blake* for HMS *Magic* on 9th January 1917 and HMS *Versatile* in January 1918. James was on half pay from 15th April 1919 and transferred to the Emergency List on 15th October. He was granted permission to proceed to Manila on 11th November. James married Mary Sancroft Findlay-Hamilton (1897–1993), born at Carmunnock, Glasgow, on 17th March 1923 at Holy Trinity Episcopal Church, Kilmarnock. He was promoted lieutenant commander gunnery on the Emergency List on 15th September 1924. James was reinstated on 13th October 1938 and joined HMS *Osprey* additional for an anti-submarine course on 10th September 1939 and HMS *Dryad* additional for a course on 25th September. He joined HMS *Lord Stanhope* additional for duty with No.20 Group Anti-Submarine Trawlers on 9th October. On 8th December he was appointed commander of the Group. He joined HMS *President* additional for duty at the Admiralty with the Directorate of Anti-Submarine Warfare on 18th December and the Anti-Submarine Warfare Division of Operations Division on 1st July 1943. He was treated at St Mary's Hospital, Paddington, London for an abscess 27th June–3rd July 1944. James was dispersed on 1st August 1945 and released on 26th September, reverting to the Emergency List next day. Promoted commander on the Emergency List on 8th May 1946. He was appointed CBE (Civil Division) for political services in Ayrshire (LG 13th June 1957). He held a number of civil appointments – DL Ayrshire 1945, President of the Kilmarnock Division Unionist Association from 1947, director Bank of Scotland and other companies. Mary and James both died at Kilmarnock, Ayrshire. They had four children:

The Royal Company of Archers, The King's/Queen's Bodyguard for Scotland is a ceremonial unit that has served the Sovereign since 1822. It is also known as The Royal Company. Having been established by the Monarch, the Company has many unique prizes, influential supporters and ceremonial roles. Its associated charity, The Royal Company of Archers Charitable Trust, helps disadvantaged individuals with health and wellbeing in Scotland.

- Anne Georgina Findlay (17th July 1924–2005) married Lieutenant Commander David Crawford Marshall VRD RNVR (1915–2004), born at Hillhead, Glasgow, Scotland, on 3rd June 1949. He was commissioned as a probationary sub lieutenant in the Clyde Division RNVR on 22nd June 1938. He was promoted sub lieutenant 22nd June 1939 and lieutenant 8th October 1940. He was Mentioned in Despatches (LG 11th December 1945) and last appears in the Navy List in July 1946. David was an export manager when he sailed from Britain on 30th April 1946 for the USA aboard HMS *Reaper*. She was a lend-lease aircraft carrier and on arrival at Norfolk, Virginia on 13th May was decommissioned and returned to the US Government. David became a member of The Queen's Bodyguard for Scotland, Royal Company of Archers. He was a farmer at Broughton, Biggar, Scottish Borders when he was awarded the MBE (LG 14th June 1986). Anne and David had five children – Susan Ferrier Findlay MA 1950, Philippa Mary Marshall 1952, Lucinda Katherine Marshall 1955, John Julian Marshall 1957, and Georgina Margaret Vanessa Marshall 1959. Both their deaths were registered at Peebles, Scottish Borders.

- John Robert Findlay (29th April 1927–17th October 2016), educated at Harrow, was a cadet (14485340) when granted an Emergency Commission in the Queen's Own Cameron Highlanders on 27th April 1946 (365125). He was promoted war substantive lieutenant on 27th October 1946 and was granted a Regular Commission as a lieutenant on 8th May 1948, with seniority from 29th April. John was appointed ADC to Lieutenant General Sir Colin M Barber KBE CB DSO, General Officer Commanding-in-Chief, Scottish Command, on 27th February 1952 as an acting Captain. He transferred to the Regular Army Reserve of Officers Class III on 1st May 1955. He was a member of The Queen's Bodyguard for Scotland, Royal Company of Archers in 1961. He married Eira Govett (born 1936), born at Westminster, London, on 6th August 1955 registered at Winchester, Hampshire. She was living with her parents at the Manor House, Newton Stacey, Hampshire in 1939. They had three children – James Anthony Findlay 1957, Michael Andrew Findlay 1960 and Alastair John Findlay 1963. The marriage ended in divorce. John married Tessa Milne Moore (23rd January 1940–29th September 2014), born at Hartley Wintney, Hampshire, on 13th June 1984 at Kensington, London. They both died at Kilmarnock, Ayrshire. Tessa had married Noel Robert Cunningham-Reid (26th December 1930–26th September 2017), birth registered at St George, Hanover Square, London, in 1960 at Westminster. Noel and Tessa had three children – Mark J Cunningham-Reid 1962, Jane M Cunningham-Reid 1964 and Charles Ashley Cunningham-Reid 1968. Noel married Wendy Seeley on 30th August 1997, registered at Hay-on-Wye, Powys. Noel was the son of Alec Stratford Cunningham-Reid (23rd April 1895–26th March 1977) who was commissioned in the Royal Engineers on 25th November 1914. He was posted to Farnborough on 9th September 1915 and joined 11th Reserve Air Squadron there on 15th November. On 15th December he transferred to the General List for duty as a flying officer RFC. He was posted to 19th Reserve Squadron on 22nd March 1916. On 14th April he was involved in a flying accident at Hounslow, suffering minor injuries and traumatic neurasthenia, which was compounded by the loss of his only brother, Second Lieutenant Duncan Flower Cunningham-Reid, who was killed on 19th December 1915 serving with 12th Squadron RFC in Belgium. On 26th May Commander 18th Wing RFC recommended that Alec return to regimental duty as the medical authorities did not consider he would ever return to flying. At various times he suffered irregular sleeping, loss of concentration, loss of nerve for flying, stammering speech, depression, debility, over anxiety, easily fatigued, headaches and recurrent insomnia. A medical board at Caxton Hall, London on 31st May found him unfit for General Service for six months, Home Service for four months and light duties for three months and granted him sick leave until 31st August. On 14th July Commander 18th Wing RFC informed GOC 6th Brigade RFC, Adastral House, Victoria Embankment, London that Cunningham-Reid was unfit for flying or related staff duties. On 8th August GOC Training Brigade RFC did not consider Cunningham-Reid would make a suitable flying officer and did not wish to retain his services. A medical board at Caxton Hall on 12th August found him unfit for General Service for four months, Home Service for six weeks and light duties for three weeks. Leave was granted until 1st September, then he was attached to 39th Squadron RFC, Woodford Green. A medical board at Caxton Hall on 7th September found him unfit for General Service for six weeks, Home Service for one month but fit for light duties. He reported to Chief Engineer, Aldershot Command on 25th September for duty at the Training Depot for Field Units RE. A medical board at Aldershot on 11th October found him unfit for General Service for five months, Home Service for four months and light duties for three months. He was granted leave until 11th January 1917. Medical boards at Caxton Hall on 9th January, 7th February and 4th April found him unfit for General and Home Service for periods of two to six months and light duties between three weeks and three months. A medical board at Caxton Hall on 5th June found him unfit for General Service for six months and Home Service for three months but fit for light duties in clerical work or as an aide. He was assigned to recruiting duties in the London Recruiting Region from 4th July. A medical board at Caxton Hall on 30th October found him fit for General Service but he was not required by the RFC. However, something changed as he was ordered to report to the Air Ministry, Hotel Cecil, Strand, London on 29th December and was appointed flying officer RFC on 1st January 1918. He joined 85th Squadron on 17th January, 56th Training Squadron on 22nd January, 40th Training Squadron, Croydon on 24th January and No.1 School of Air Gunnery on 28th March. Alec was posted to 85th Squadron on 12th May but was admitted to hospital on 8th July. Despite this he was awarded the DFC – when engaging a column of infantry at a very low altitude, this officer saw a hostile balloon on the ground. This he attacked and burnt. On the two following days he shot down two aeroplanes, and a few days later destroyed a third, LG 3rd August 1918. He was fit for General Service ground duties from 7th August and joined 2nd Fighter School on 22nd August. He joined the BEF on 25th September and was appointed SO3 on 2nd October. Alec was credited with seven air victories and transferred to the Unemployed List on 18th February 1919. He was a Conservative MP at various times between 1922 and 1945 for St Marylebone and Warrington. He married Ruth Mary Clarisse Ashley, 'England's wealthiest girl' at the time, in 1927 (divorced 1940) and Angela Williams in 1944 (divorced 1949).

- Charles George Findlay (19th April 1929–10th October 2017), educated at Harrow, married Anne Marguerite Barnard (born 1934), birth registered at East Ashford, on 14th December 1963. She was the daughter of Major Andrew Norman Barnard (1905–23rd April 1940) and May Valentine L Wagemans (1907–80), of 29 Elvaston Place, Kensington, London in 1939. Andrew served in the Royal Irish Fusiliers (38675) and was promoted captain on 9th May 1936. He was appointed Military Assistant Secretary to the Committee of Imperial Defence on 20th April 1939 and was promoted acting major on 18th October. He died in service and is buried in Wye (Sts Gregory and Martin) Churchyard, Kent. Charles served as a Kent County Councillor from 1997. They had two children – Andrew Hamilton Findlay 1965 and Mary Sancroft Findlay 1969.
- Neil James Findlay (29th May 1930–9th September 2008), educated at Harrow, married Barbara Jean Houison-Craufurd (5th May 1934–7th July 2004), birth registered at Brixworth, Northamptonshire, on 16th October 1955 at Westminster. They lived at Aytoun House, Aytounhill, Newburgh, Cupar, Fife. They had two children – Jeremy Findlay 1958 and Amanda Findlay 1964. Neil married Audrey Carol Haldane née Jones at Cupar in 2008. She was known as Carol and had married Major John Morton Haldane (14th April 1929–1st March 2001), born at Bridge of Allan, Stirlingshire, at the Royal Hospital Chelsea Chapel on 24th July 1971. John was commissioned in The Scots Greys on 14th July 1949 (403478). He was promoted lieutenant on 14th July 1951, temporary captain 14th April 1954–2nd May 1956 and captain 3rd May 1956. He transferred to the Reserve of Officers on 5th March 1959 and joined the Ayrshire Yeomanry (TA) as a captain with seniority from 3rd May 1956. He resigned his commission on 26th August 1965 but appears in the Army List until March 1966. John was chairman of HABAR, 17 Abercromby Place, Edinburgh, Midlothian, when the Company was wound up voluntarily on 9th March 1961. His death was registered at Kilbirnie, Beith and Dalry, Ayrshire. They had two daughters – Nicola Diana Haldane 1973 and Katharine Joanna Haldane 1974.

George's paternal grandfather, Charles Bannatyne Findlay (1st June 1821–9th August 1877), born at Easterhill, Lanarkshire, was in business in Manila, Philippines. He married Georgiana de Cardonnel née Elmsall (c. 1829–9th January 1892), baptised at Adwick le Street, Yorkshire, on 12th August 1829. She was the daughter of Colonel Joseph Edward Greaves Elmsall (died 1851), 1st Royal Dragoons, and Hannah Mary de Cardonnel (died 1854) of Woodlands, Yorkshire. Charles purchased Boturich Castle, Dunbartonshire in 1872 from his brother, Colonel John Findlay. He died at Kissingen, Bavaria and she at Boturich, Dunbartonshire. In addition to Robert they had four other children:

Boturich Castle is believed to have been built by Isabelle, the last Duchess of Albany and Countess of Lennox, who died c.1460. The current Castle was built c.1830 on part of the ruin of the old castle, the walls of which can be traced to a height of six metres in places.

- Mary Georgiana de Cardonnel Findlay (14th October 1853–2nd July 1856).
- Mansfeldt de Cardonnel Findlay (7th April 1861–31st December 1932), born at Edinburgh, Midlothian, was educated at Harrow and joined the Diplomatic Service as an attaché in 1885. He was Minister Resident at Dresden and Coburg, Germany 1907–09, Envoy Extraordinary and Minister Plenipotentiary at Sofia, Bulgaria 1909–11, Christiania, Norway and Stockholm, Sweden during the Great War and later at Constantinople in Turkey, Vienna in Austria, Buenos Aires in Argentina and Belgrade in Serbia. He was appointed CMG (LG 9th November 1904), CB (LG 23rd June 1908), KCMG (LG 2nd June 1916), Norwegian Grand Cross of the Order of St Olaf (LG 15th February 1924) and GBE (LG 3rd June 1924). Mansfeldt married Cora Sybil Alexander (22nd May 1872–25th February 1959), birth registered at Stoke Damerel, Devon, on 27th April 1895, registered at St George, Hanover Square, London. They were living at Moreton House, Moreton, near Dorchester, Dorset at the time of his death there. She died at the Manor House, Bradford Peverell, Dorchester. They had four children:
    - Joyce Evelyn Findlay (22nd April 1898–28th April 1987).
    - Noel Charles Mansfeldt Findlay (18th November 1899–9th April 1976) married May C Legge in 1929, registered at Canterbury, Kent. Noel served in the Royal Navy as a midshipman 8th September 1915, acting lieutenant aboard HMS *Mischief* December 1915 and sub lieutenant 15th May 1918. He had retired by January 1919. They had three children – Jane E Findlay 1930, Jonathan M Findlay 1933 and Martin C Findlay 1935. His death was registered at Ashford, Kent.
    - Bridget Sybil Findlay (15th December 1903–30th January 1985) married Roger HC Fetherstonhaugh-Frampton (5th February 1899–22nd March 1985) in 1927, registered at Wareham, Dorset. They had four daughters – Mary B Fetherstonhaugh-Frampton 1928, Sybil G Fetherstonhaugh-Frampton 1930, Philippa E Fetherstonhaugh-Frampton 1934 and Teresa J Fetherstonhaugh-Frampton 1937. Roger joined the Royal Navy in January 1912 and served aboard HMS *Amphitrite* 2nd August 1914–22nd June 1915. Appointed midshipman on 21st December 1914 and served aboard HMS

Barham from 22nd July 1915, including at the Battle of Jutland. He failed examinations for torpedo, gunnery and engineering in May 1917 but passed them in July. Appointed acting sub lieutenant on 15th July and joined HMS *Victory* for HMS *Vernon* on 29th October. He joined Woolwich for HMS *Vectis* on 7th November. Promoted sub lieutenant on 15th January 1918 and joined HMS *President* for a course at Cambridge University 15th January–27th August 1919. He joined HMS *Columbine* additional for HMS *Wolsey* on 27 August and was promoted lieutenant on 15th January 1920. He joined HMS *Victory* additional for unemployment, time not to exceed six months, on 26th April and joined HMS *Iron Duke* on 2nd June. Roger departed Liverpool aboard SS *Patricia* for Constantinople via Egypt on 26th June. He joined HMS *Victory* on 9th March 1921 and was placed on the Retired List at his own request on 4th November 1922. Promoted lieutenant commander on the Retired List on 15th January 1928. He was employed as a fishery officer and, from August 1931, was Assistant King's Harbour Master, Pembroke Dock. Appointed Admiralty Requisitioning Officer, Milford Haven on 1st March 1934 and Assistant King's Harbour Master, Pembroke Dock again on 7th August 1937. Roger was appointed to HMS *Eaglet*, Flagship of CinC Western Approaches, Liverpool on 3rd July 1940 but reverted to the Retired List on 16th August. He joined HMS *Drake* additional on 1st October and HMS *Eaglet III* as the First Lieutenant on 4th October. He joined HMS *Mersey* on 25th December. Roger commanded HMS *Glen Strathallan*, a trawler requisitioned as an anti-submarine vessel, from 14th May 1941. He received the displeasure of their Lordships when she grounded in the Menai Straits on 3rd January 1943. He was to blame because he navigated the straits when unsure if there was sufficient depth of water, placed undue reliance on a RNVR officer who had no qualifications to advise him and failed to use a hand lead in accordance with regulations. He joined HMS *Excellent II* additional on 24th February 1943 for special service and joined HMS *Drake* on 18th October, when he was found fit but was not to be sent to the Mediterranean or a hot climate for six months. He joined HMS *Odyssey* additional on 15th November for special service with Naval Assault Group Channel and Force S from 22nd January 1944. He served aboard LSIs HMS *Glenearn* and *Empire Arquebus*. The Ministry of Agriculture & Fisheries requested he be released as soon as possible on 26th June 1944 but this does not appear to have happened. Appointed acting commander on 21st July 1945. He was dispersed on 1st August 1945 and released on 26th September, having been promoted commander on 5th September 1945. Bridget and Roger both died at Moreton House, Moreton, Dorchester.

- John Cecil Alexander de Cardonnel Findlay (13th November 1909–1972).

The Battle of Atbara took place during the Second Sudan War on 8th April 1898. A combined British and Egyptian army under Herbert Kitchener advanced down the Nile into Sudan against the Sudanese Mahdists under Khalifa Abdallahi ibn Muhammed. He ordered Emir Mahmud Ahmad and his 10,000 strong army of western Sudan to advance northward towards the junction of the Nile and Atbara River to engage the Anglo-Egyptian army. Kitchener realised that Mahmud was unwilling to attack, so he quietly advanced towards the Mahdist fortified camp just outside Nakheila. The Anglo-Egyptian attack, by three brigades, began at 6.20 a.m. with a brief artillery bombardment of the Mahdist camp. After forty-five minutes the battle was over. A few thousand warriors retreated to the south, but the majority of the 15,000 Mahdists were killed or captured, including Mahmud. The battle was the turning point in the conquest of Sudan. In the picture the Seaforth and Cameron Highlanders bury their dead after the battle.

- Charles Findlay (28th July 1864–8th April 1898) was commissioned in the Gordon Highlanders on 6th February 1884. He was promoted lieutenant in the Cameron Highlanders on 12th March 1884 and captain on 7th December 1891. He took part in the Nile Campaign 1884–85 and was with the Sudan Frontier Field Force in 1889 and the Sudan Campaign in 1898. He married Lilian Vaughan Barron (1st December 1878–16th August 1949), born at St Helier, Jersey, Channel Islands, on 29th September 1897 at the Cathedral, Gibraltar. She was the daughter of Colonel Harry Barron RA (1847–1921) and Clara Emily Kelly (1857–1936). Charles was killed in action serving with the 1st Battalion at Atbara, Sudan. He left effects valued at £36,848/0/1 (£5.7M in 2023). They had a son:
    - Victor Alexander Charles Findlay (10th September 1898–17th August 1946) was commissioned in the Royal Artillery on 19th February 1916 and was promoted lieutenant on 19th August 1917. He served in the Egyptian Expeditionary Force 12th December 1917–31st October 1918 and last appears in the Army List in April 1921. Victor married Joan Gilbert Casson (15th October 1898–1979), born in Bengal, India, on 21st June 1920 at Simla, India. He died while big game hunting and is buried at Shinyanga, Tanzania. Their son, Charles de Cardonnel Findlay (1921–28th August 1942), born at Marylebone, London, was killed when the aircraft he was ferrying from America to Britain crashed off the coast of Donegal, Ireland. Another son, Anthony G Findlay, was born in 1923 at Dolgelly, Merionethshire, Wales. Victor and Joan divorced and she married Lieutenant Colonel Adam Duncan Chetwynd RA, 9th Viscount Chetwynd of Bearhaven (14th November 1904–12th June 1965) on 28th April 1928 and had three children – Philippa Mary Agnes Joan Chetwynd 1930, Julian Isabella Chetwynd 1932 and Adam

Richard John Casson Chetwynd 1935. Joan served in G Branch, WAAF from 4th January 1939 and was promoted squadron officer (squadron leader) on 1st January 1943. She last appears in the Air Force List in July 1945. Adam was commissioned in the Royal Artillery TA on 17th May 1939 and was mobilised on 24th August. He was promoted war substantive captain and temporary major 14th July 1941 and major 15th April 1946. He last appears in the Army List in June 1952. They divorced in 1951 and he married Dorothea Marianne Duncan-Johnstone on 17th January 1952. They had two daughters – Catherine Sophia Marianne Chetwynd 1956 and Frances Diana Dorothea Chetwynd 1959.

Lilian married Captain Francis Edward de Carteret Chevallier RA (31st July 1873–4th June 1942), born at Aspall, Suffolk, on 2nd October 1901 at St Nicholas, Cole Abbey, London. He was a gentleman cadet at the Royal Military Academy Woolwich and was commissioned in the Royal Artillery on 15th August 1893. Promoted lieutenant 15th August 1896, captain 1st April 1900 and supernumerary major. He was appointed Adjutant School of Gunnery 2nd January 1901–31st December 1903 and Adjutant 1st November 1904–8th August 1907. Francis was restored to the establishment on 18th May 1914 and served in the RGA during the Great War. He deployed on operations to Kamerun (Cameroons) and Nigeria 4th January 1915–18th February 1916. Appointed temporary lieutenant colonel 16th November 1916–3rd March 1918 and was promoted lieutenant colonel on 4th March 1918. He retired on retired pay due to ill-health on 6th January 1921. Lilian filed for divorce on 2nd May 1905 and the final decree was issued on 30th April 1906. She married Angus John McNeill (31st May 1874–22nd June 1950), born at Stanley, Yorkshire, on 8th July 1907, registered at Kensington, London. He was commissioned in the Seaforth Highlanders on 29th May 1895. He was 6′ ½″ tall and was promoted lieutenant on 22nd August 1897. He took part in the Occupation of Crete 1897 and the Soudan Campaign 1898, including the Battles of Atbara and Khartoum (MID). Angus took part in the South African War from 1899 as ADC to GOC 3rd Division and later in command of Montmorency's Scouts (MID twice). Promoted captain 19th March 1901 and brevet major 29th May 1901. He retired from the Seaforth Highlanders on 20th July 1910, when his address was Fawley Manor, Wantage, Berkshire. He was appointed major in Lovet's Scouts Yeomanry on 21st July 1910, later backdated to 29th May 1901. He embarked at Devonport on 7th September 1915, disembarked at Mudros on 26th September and rejoined the Regiment at Suvla, Gallipoli on 8th October. Appointed temporary lieutenant colonel on 10th November 1915 to command 1/2nd Lovat Scouts. He disembarked at Alexandria from HT *Scotian* on 28th December. Attached to HQ Kharga Detachment on 19th June. MID, LG 13th July 1916 for distinguished and gallant conduct during the period of General Sir Charles Munro's command of the Mediterranean Expeditionary Force. Angus was promoted lieutenant colonel on 19th September 1916, later backdated to 1st June 1916. Mentioned in General Sir Archibald Murray's Despatch (C-in-C Egyptian Expeditionary Force), LG 25th September 1916. Angus commanded 230th Brigade, MEF as a temporary brigadier general from 8th February 1917, assuming the appointment on 21st February. Awarded the Serbian Order of Karageorge 4th Class (with Swords), LG 19th February 1917. Mentioned in General Sir Archibald Murray's Despatch of 1st March 1917, LG 6th July 1917. He disembarked at Alexandria from Sollum on 9th March. He was admitted to a field ambulance and No.75 Casualty Clearing Station on 14th December. Transferred to 44th Stationary Hospital, Kantara with malaria on 16th December. Relinquished command due to illness on 21st December. Transferred to Naerich Hospital, Cairo on 27th December. A medical board there on 7th January 1918 found he had malignant malaria. He was classed B1 for two months and was discharged from hospital on 30th January. He was granted leave in Britain to 25th March, embarking aboard HT *Kashgar* at Alexandria on 17th February, arriving at Folkestone on 25th February. His address was 25 Palace Gate, London. He embarked at Taranto, Italy on 29th March and disembarked at Alexandria on 3rd April. Awarded DSO, LG 3rd June 1918. Mentioned in General Sir Archibald Murray's Despatch of 3rd April 1918, LG 11th June 1918. Angus commanded 163rd Brigade, 54th Division in Palestine and Syria from 27th April 1918. He embarked at Beirut aboard HT *Ellenga*, disembarking at Kantara on 28th November. He commanded 161st Brigade from 16th March 1919. On 10th April he was ordered to Combined Base Depot, Kantara to await passage to Britain. Embarked aboard SS *Goentoer* at Alexandria on 10th June for Taranto and disembarked at Folkestone on 16th June. Also awarded CB, CBE and TD (LG 20th July 1926). He transferred to the Reserve as lieutenant colonel and honorary brigadier general on 30th July 1919. Angus was promoted colonel on 2nd March 1920 to command the Norfolk and Suffolk Infantry Brigade, relinquishing honorary brigadier general. His retired pay was suspended while he served in the Defence Force 8th April–23rd July 1921. Angus relinquished command of the Norfolk and Suffolk Infantry Brigade on 18th February 1922. On the same date he was appointed Commandant Palestine Gendarmerie for four years, ending on 30th April 1926, based at Sarafand Camp, Lydda, Palestine. He ceased to belong to the Regular Army Reserve of Officers on 31st May 1924, having reached the age limit. They moved to Jerusalem after the Great War and lived in the Mashashibi Quarter, running a stud farm for the Department of Agriculture, Palestine. She died at her home in Palestine and he at Nicosia, Cyprus. They had a son:

- John Malcolm McNeill (22nd February 1909–1996), who was commissioned in the Royal Artillery on 31st January 1929. He received numerous promotions – lieutenant 31st January 1932, captain 1st August 1938, acting major (41179) 7th January–6th April 1941, temporary major 7th April 1941–12th March 1943, acting lieutenant colonel 13th December 1942–12th March 1943, war substantive major 13th March 1943, temporary lieutenant colonel 13th March 1943–6th July 1945, acting colonel 7th January–6th July 1945, war substantive lieutenant colonel 7th July 1945–5th December 1948, temporary colonel 7th July–4th November 1945, major 31st January 1946, temporary lieutenant colonel 5th September 1949–31st March 1951, lieutenant colonel 1st April 1951, colonel 1st February 1953, temporary brigadier 28th October 1955–7th February 1957, brigadier 8th February 1957, local major general 27th–29th June 1960, temporary major general 30th June–2nd August 1960 and major general 3rd August 1960. Amongst his appointments were – Instructor 1st December 1936–11th May 1940 (Class GG to 31st July 1938), GSO1 AF 4th February 1943–20th February 1944, GSO1 HQ 21st Army Group 21st February–9th December 1944, Colonel General Staff (Air) South East Asia Command 7th January–4th November 1945, GSO1 School of Air Support 5th November 1945–30th January 1948, Secretary Joint Planning Staff Ministry of Defence 1st February 1953–31st January 1954, Deputy Secretary Chiefs of Staff Committee Ministry of Defence 1st February 1954–13th August 1955, Commander Royal Artillery Infantry Division British Army of the Rhine 28th October 1955–15th April 1958, Commander Royal Artillery HQ Division 16th April–30th December 1958, ADC to the Queen 12th September 1958–2nd August 1960, Commandant School of Artillery Southern Command 26th January 1959–26th June 1960, Commandant (Major General) British Army Staff and Military Member British Joint Staff Mission Washington DC 30th June 1960–5th February 1963. He was awarded the MBE (LG 18th February 1943), Mentioned in Despatches (LG 23rd March 1945), CBE (LG 1st January 1959) and CB (LG 1st January 1963). John retired on 6th May 1963. He was appointed Colonel Commandant, Royal Regiment of Artillery on 21st July 1964.

Francis married Elizabeth Louise Fleming (25th July 1872–3rd December 1944), born at Kintyre, Argyllshire, in 1916, registered at Kingston upon Thames, Surrey. They were living at Glebe House, Aspall, Suffolk in 1939. He died at Aspall Rectory and Elizabeth was living at North Park, Campbeltown, Argyllshire at the time of her death there.

- Francis Richard Sandford Findlay (3rd August 1866–15th February 1877), born at Edinburgh and died at Cookham, Berkshire.

His maternal grandfather, James Scott (21st May 1810–24th April 1884), born at Glasgow, Lanarkshire, was educated at Glasgow Grammar School and Polmont School, Stirlingshire. He joined the calico printers of James Black and Co in 1826 and became a partner in 1830. He developed an interest in the railways 1835–45 and retired from his business in 1847. James married Jane Martha née Galbraith (7th May 1830–10th February 1917) on 13th September 1848 at Glasgow, where she was born. He was a member of Glasgow Town Council 1846–55 and was City Treasurer and

Woodside Crescent, Glasgow.

deputy-chairman of the Clyde Trust during that time. The formation of Kelvingrove Park was largely his work. He founded the firm J & JW Scott & Co in 1852, with one of his younger brothers, and rejoined his old firm of James Black & Co in 1856, to establish what became Scotland's largest cotton spinning firm. James was instrumental in establishing the great mineral and goods depots adjacent to the Queen's Dock, Glasgow. They were living at 1 & 2 Woodside Place, Glasgow in 1861. In 1871 he turned his attention to the Scottish oil industry and established works at the mineral fields at Clippens, Renfrewshire. He acquired extensive shale fields at Pentland and merged the business into Clippens Oil Co Ltd in 1882, with him as chairman. James served as DL Renfrewshire and JP for Lanark, Renfrew and Dunbarton. He was also appointed HM Income Tax Commissioner. James and Jane both died at Woodside Crescent, Glasgow. In addition to Jane they had nine other children:

- Margaret 'Maggie' Bogle Scott (14th July 1850–22nd March 1864), born at 16 Woodside Crescent, Glasgow.
- Thomas Inglis Scott (24th September 1851–1898) was an oil merchant. He married Abigail Johnston Robertson Reid (5th May 1854–6th May 1914), born at Greenock, Renfrewshire, on 2nd June 1880 at Rutherglen, Lanarkshire. They lived at Gallowflat House, Rutherglen before moving to Clippens House, Johnstone, Renfrewshire. He died at Rutherglen and she at Kilmacolm, Renfrewshire.
- Andrew Corbet Scott (16th May 1853–1st June 1923), born at Kelly, Renfrewshire, was a merchant in 1884. He married Amy Evelyn Alston Stewart (24th November 1856–8th July 1908), born at Moulin, Perthshire, on 3rd February 1886 at the Episcopal Chapel, Pitlochry, Perthshire. She was the daughter of Captain Benjamin Hallowell-Boxer RN. She died at Bonhill, West Dunbartonshire and he was living at The House, Urrard, Killiecrankie, Perthshire at the time of his death there, leaving effects valued at £56,567/19/7 (£3.8M in 2023).
- Helen Bethia Scott (16th July 1855–1950), born at Inverkip, Renfrewshire, married Thomas Ripley Ker (c.1854–18th July 1947), born at Blantyre, Lanarkshire, on 20th June 1877 at St Mary's Tower, Birnham, Perthshire. He was educated at Brasenose College, Oxford, graduating on 5th June 1873. They were living at Bardowie House, Baldernock, Stirlingshire in 1881 and at Mansion House, Dougalston in 1901. He was appointed DL and JP for Dunbartonshire. Thomas was living at Eastertoun, Milngavie when he died at Glasgow. Helen also died at Eastertoun. They had three children:

◦ Robert McNeil Ker (18th February 1878–15th October 1953), born at Dunmullin, Strathblane, Scotland, was educated at Rugby School. He married Margaret Lilian Blagden at Donhead St Mary Church, Wiltshire on 13th October 1903. He was commissioned in 3rd Argyll & Sutherland Highlanders on 8th February 1900 and undertook embodied service with the Militia at home February–December 1900 and 20th September–2nd November 1901. He served in South Africa January–October 1902, including as a staff officer May–August. He was selected for an appointment in the Royal Garrison Regiment from 28th January 1903 and served in Malta April 1903–28th April 1904. Appointed Adjutant 1st Battalion, Royal Garrison Regiment October 1903 and served in South Africa from 29th April 1904. Promoted lieutenant on 30th May 1904 and retired from 1st Battalion, Royal Garrison Regiment on 20th September 1905. Robert was embodied as a captain on 4th September 1914 with 3rd Argyll & Sutherland Highlanders. He was appointed to 10th Argyll & Sutherland Highlanders at Aldershot on 14th September and Adjutant 12th Argyll & Sutherland Highlanders at Codford on 23rd September. He was the Machine Gun Officer, HQ 77th Brigade from June 1916. On 2nd September he reported sick at Salonica with dyspepsia and was sent to Malta, embarking on 9th September. A medical board at Tigne Military Hospital, Malta on 20th September found him unfit for three months and granted leave until 3rd December. He embarked aboard HMHS *Goorkha* on 23rd September and disembarked at Southampton on 2nd October. A medical board at 1st Western General Hospital, Fazakerley, Liverpool on 4th October found him unfit for two months. A medical board at 3rd Scottish General Hospital, Stobhill, Glasgow on 5th December found him unfit for General & Home Service for two months and light duty for one month. Leave was extended to 4th January 1917. A medical board at 3rd Scottish General Hospital on 16th January found him unfit for General Service for two months, Home Service for one month but fit for light duty. He joined the Machine Gun Training Centre, Grantham on 18th January and was posted to No.1 Cadet Battalion, Bisley on 14th February. A medical board at the Military Hospital, Inkerman Barracks, Woking on 7th March found him unfit for General Service for two months, Home Service for one month but fit for light duty. Medical boards at Woking on 7th April, 12th June and 11th July found him unfit for General Service but fit for Home Service. A medical board there on 10th August found him fit for General Service. Appointed temporary major on 9th November. A medical board on 19th April 1918 found him unfit for A for three months but fit for C1. He had contracted gastralgia in Switzerland in 1914 prior to service. A medical board on 19th July found him unfit for A & B for two months but fit for C1. A medical board on 20th September found him fit for A and ordered him to report to the Machine Gun Training

Centre, Grantham. He was demobilised on 7th January 1919 and was granted the rank of major in the Reserve of Officers. His address was the Army & Navy Club, Pall Mall, London and Dougalston, Milngavie, Scotland. Robert transferred from Class 1 Regular Army Reserve of Officers to Class 2 on attaining the age limit on 18th February 1923. He ceased to belong to the Reserve of Officers having reached the age limit on 18th February 1928.

  - Ronald Scott Ker (1879–7th November 1915) married Elma Katherine Guthrie Smith (1878–1949), born at Strathblane, in 1906 at Killearn. He died at Bournemouth, Hampshire and she at Bridge of Weir.
  - Helen Ripley Ker (25th July 1887–1975) born at Baldernock and died at Inverness.

- James Black Scott (27th January 1857–28th July 1913), born at 17 Woodside Place, Glasgow, was a merchant in 1884. He was living at Clippens House, Linwood, Renfrewshire in 1901. James married Janet 'Jenny' Brown (born 11th August 1871), born at Dreghorn, North Ayrshire, on 26th February 1907 at 122 Holland Street, Anderston, Glasgow. He was a farmer at the time of his death at West Fulton Farm, Renfrewshire.
- Agnes Norah Scott (30th April 1860–27th February 1878), born at Inverkip, Renfrewshire and died at Anderston, Glasgow.
- Archibald Galbraith Scott (18th February 1862–27th May 1900), born at Anderston, was a merchant in 1884. He was commissioned in the Royal Artillery as a lieutenant on 22nd February 1882. Archibald was Initiated into Freemasonry at Western District United Service Lodge on 19th March 1890. Promoted captain 26th April 1890. He served in Malta and joined the Lodge of St John & St Paul there on 2nd May 1892. He was seconded as Adjutant of Militia Artillery 15th November 1893–7th September 1894 and was placed on half-pay due to ill-health on 3rd August 1895. He died at Clippens House, near Johnstone, Renfrewshire.
- Mina Hope Scott (30th March 1864–30th December 1949), also seen as Maria Christian Hope Scott, was boarding at Manor House School, Wandsworth in 1881. She married Henry William Johnston (1853–13th August 1924) in 1883 at Kelvin. She was living with her brother, James, and mother at the time of the 1901 Census. They were living at Dunros, Strathtay, Perthshire at the time of their deaths.
- Charles Inglis Scott (11th April 1866–14th October 1941), born at Inverkip, was commissioned as a lieutenant in 3rd Dragoon Guards from the Militia on 8th December 1886. Appointed Adjutant 3rd Dragoon Guards 6th July 1891–5th July 1895 and promoted captain 24th May 1893. Transferred as Paymaster to the Army Pay Department on 30th October 1897. Promoted major and Staff Paymaster 14th December 1904 and 1st Class Assistant Accountant Army Accounts Department 1st May 1905–31st December 1909. Promoted lieutenant colonel 14th December 1909, temporary colonel and Chief Paymaster

St Ninian's Preparatory School was founded in 1879 by Arthur John Caswall Dowding, father of Air Chief Marshal Hugh Dowding (1882–1970), who was born and educated at the school. Dowding commanded RAF Fighter Command during the Battle of Britain. The school was attended by two other VC's – David Younger and Donald Mackintosh. Mackintosh's story is told in the fourth book in this series, *Victoria Crosses on the Western Front, 1917 to the Eve of Third Ypres, January–July 1917*. In 1987 the RAF Association and RAF Benevolent Fund bought the school, which was renamed Dowding House. It provides sheltered housing for former RAF personnel and dependants.

Harrow School, founded in 1572, is one of the original ten public schools regulated by the 1868 Public Schools Act. Amongst its alumni are seven British Prime Ministers, including Robert Peel, Henry Palmerston, Stanley Baldwin and Winston Churchill, members of various royal families, Jawaharlal Nehru first Prime Minister of India and twenty VC and one GC winners. Other notables include Lord Byron, Wimbledon champions Spencer Gore and Frank Hadow, FA Cup founder Charles W Alcock, actor Benedict Cumberbatch, singer/songwriter James Blunt, rugby international Billy Vunipola and racing pundit John McCirick.

1st September 1914–31st December 1916 and brevet colonel 1st January 1917. He was awarded the CMG in the King's Birthday Honours 1918. Charles retired on retired pay on 31st August 1918. He married Mary Harriet Sophia Inglis (1862–20th March 1924) on 15th January 1903, registered at Wetherby, Yorkshire, where her birth was registered. She was living with her parents and siblings at Eastcote Road, Ruislip, Middlesex in 1891 and with her sister, Laura Elizabeth Alice Gunter (1860–1942), and family at Boston Hall, Boston, Lincolnshire in 1901. She died at Killiecrankie, Perthshire and he was living at Urrard and Druimuan, Killiecrankie at the time of his death.

George was educated at St Ninian's Preparatory School, Moffat, Dumfriesshire, where he was captain of the Football XI and Rugby XV, and Harrow School, Middlesex 1903–08. At Harrow he won the Spencer Cup for the best schoolboy shot at Bisley in 1907 and was captain of the winning Eight at Bisley in 1908.

The Harrow Eight after winning the Ashburton Shield, below the score board, at Bisley in 1908.

George entered the Royal Military Academy, Woolwich in 1908 and won the revolver shooting competitions in 1909. He

The Royal Military Academy Woolwich trained officers of the Royal Artillery and Royal Engineers, and later officers of the Royal Corps of Signals and other technical corps. Woolwich was known as The Shop because its first building was a converted workshop of Woolwich Arsenal. After a false start in 1720, the Academy was created by Royal Warrant in 1741 to produce *good officers of Artillery and perfect Engineers.* Gentlemen cadets were initially aged from ten to thirty and were accommodated in lodgings in Woolwich. However, the cadets gained a reputation for riotousness and in 1751 a Cadets' Barracks was built and they had to adjust to stricter military discipline. The Cadets' Barracks was demolished in the 1980s for road widening. The idea of moving the Royal Military Academy out of the Warren was mooted in 1783, as it outgrew the available accommodation. A new complex of buildings facing the Royal Artillery Barracks at the southern edge of Woolwich Common was built between 1796 and 1805. The following year 128 cadets moved to the new Academy. In 1810 cadets of the East India Company moved to a new college at Addiscombe. After the Crimean War the minimum age for cadets was raised to fifteen and more specialist training was added. The Academy was enlarged in the 1860s. In 1873 the central block had to be entirely rebuilt following a devastating fire. In 1936 it was decided to merge Woolwich and Sandhurst but the Second World War intervened. The last Commandant of Woolwich was Major General Philip Neame VC, whose story is told in the first book in this series, *Victoria Crosses on the Western Front, Mons to Hill 60, August 1914 – April 1915.* In 1947 the Royal Military Academy Sandhurst opened to provide officer training for all arms and services. The old Academy at Woolwich was used to house troops of various types and the central block was taken over by the Royal Artillery Institution for a museum, archives and offices. The chapel became the Garrison Church, replacing the bombed-out St George's Church. The site closed in 2003. Two stained glass windows from the chapel were moved to the Garrison Church of St Alban the Martyr at Larkhill, Wiltshire. The Woolwich buildings, some of which are Grade II listed, were converted and extended into 334 houses/apartments.

was commissioned in the Royal Engineers on 30th January 1910, serving initially with 5th Field Troop. He was promoted lieutenant on 28th February 1912 and was appointed Assistant Adjutant for Musketry at Chatham. He broke both legs in a riding accident and was granted sick leave for ten months. As he was still recovering when the Great War broke out, he trained recruits before proceeding on operational service to France with 24th Field Company RE on 5th March 1915. Appointed temporary captain on 28th September 1915 and was promoted captain on 30th January 1916. He carried out works on the lines of communication until May 1916 and was a staff officer to Chief Royal Engineer V Corps 7th April–23rd June 1917.

George was appointed acting major 27th June 1917–23rd September 1919 and commanded 409th (1/1st Lowland) Field Company RE June 1917–September 1919. **Awarded the MC for his actions on 10th November 1917 at Passchendaele, Belgium when he worked for hours in heavily shelled areas and deep mud to establish communications and undertook successful night reconnaissances over difficult ground. He went forward to carry out a reconnaissance and tape extensions to a new track and No.6 Track forward of Source Farm. The positions in this area were very obscure and he had to inform the**

The Military Cross was created on 28th December 1914 for officers of the rank of captain and below and warrant officers. In August 1916 bars were awarded for further acts of gallantry. In 1931 the MC was extended to majors and to members of the RAF for ground actions. In the 1993 honours review the Military Medal for other ranks was discontinued and the MC became the third level decoration for all ranks of the British Armed Forces for acts of gallantry on land.

infantry holding the farm of their positions, LG 18th January and 25th April 1918. Awarded a Bar to the MC for his actions 17th-19th October 1918 in the area of Vaux Andigny and Vallée Mulatre. He carried out personal reconnaissances prior to and during the fighting under heavy shell and machine gun fire to effectively ensure the maintenance of lateral communications across a river, a task entrusted to his company, LG 11th January 1919.

Awarded the VC for his actions at the Sambre-Oise Canal, France on 4th November 1918, LG 15th May 1919. He was initially awarded the DSO (LG 2nd April 1919) but this was subsequently upgraded to the VC and the DSO was cancelled in LG 8th August 1919. **Mentioned in Field Marshal Sir Douglas Haig's Despatches on 9th April 1917 and 16th March 1919, LG 15th May 1917 and 7th July 1919.** George represented the Western Division RE at the Paris Victory Parade on 14th July 1919. The VC and MC & Bar were presented by the King at Buckingham Palace on 27th November 1919.

George Findlay married Dorothy Bertha Gordon (10th October 1900–1981), born at Aikenhead House, Cathcart, Renfrewshire, on 8th September 1921. There were no children. The marriage was annulled c.1933. Dorothy was boarding at 14 Kendrick Mews, Kensington, London in 1939, when she was a volunteer with the Auxiliary Ambulance Service. Dorothy married William John L Williams (25th December 1907–8th January 1984), birth registered at Camberwell, at Kensington in 1942. He was living with his parents at 52 Grove Hill Road, Denmark Hill, Camberwell in 1911. He was a company director in 1939, boarding at 37–49 Brick Street, Westminster, London. That address was the rear of the Park Lane Hotel on Piccadilly (now the Sheraton Grand). He was living at Tailors, Snow Hill, Crawley Down, Sussex at the time of his death. Both their deaths were registered at Tunbridge Wells.

Dorothy's father, Henry Erskine Gordon JP DL (11th September 1849–12th April 1929), birth registered at Kensington, was an Advocate of the Scottish Bar. He was living with his uncle, Henry L Harvey, a landed proprietor, at 113 St George's Square, Hanover Square, London in 1881. Henry married Bertha Agnes née Finlay (6th December 1869–25th May 1947), born at 70 Queen Street, Edinburgh, Midlothian, on 1st October 1895 at Windlesham, Surrey. She was the daughter

Aikenhead House in King's Park was built in 1806 for the West Indies merchant and prominent Glasgow Tory, John Gordon. The wings were added in 1823. It was on the site of a house built for James Hamilton, 1st Earl of Abercorn, who died in 1633. In 1930 the estate was acquired by Glasgow Corporation and was opened as King's Park. In 1986 the house was converted into fourteen flats.

of Major John Finlay, 78th Highlanders (1834–1911), and Mary Marcella Taylor (1843–1930), of Castle Toward, Argyllshire. Henry was serving as a major (from 13th January 1897) and honorary lieutenant colonel in the Lanarkshire Imperial Yeomanry in 1901, when they were living at Aikenhead House, Meikle Aikenhead Farm, Cathcart, Renfrewshire. Henry subsequently died there, by when Cathcart was part of Glasgow. Bertha died at Nairn. In addition to Dorothy they had four other children, all born at Aikenhead House, Cathcart:

- Joan Victoria Christian Erskine Gordon (30th August 1897–10th April 1924). She never married and died at Cairo, Egypt.
- Nancy Althea Gordon (26th November 1898–25th April 1985) never married and was living at Hertfordshire Seaside Convalescent Home, 123 West Hill Road, St Leonards-on-Sea, East Sussex at the time of her death there.
- Violet Erskine Gordon (1st April 1903–13th September 1985) married John Digby Welch (5th April 1903–12th December 1963), born at Maymyo, Burma, in 1932 at Nairn. He was at boarding school in 1911 at Glenholm, Burgess Hill, Sussex and was living at Oak Hall, Burgess when he travelled to Port Said, Egypt aboard SS *Nellore*, departing London on 14th July 1922. John was commissioned in the King's Own Scottish Borderers on 1st February 1923. He was promoted lieutenant on 1st February 1925 and was appointed Adjutant on 17th June 1931. He transferred to the South Wales Borderers and was promoted captain on 21st January 1934. He was appointed Brigade Major, 14th Infantry Brigade on 17th January 1939 (24781). Promoted major on 1st February 1940, war substantive lieutenant colonel on 7th January 1944 and lieutenant colonel on 18th March 1947. He retired with the honorary rank of brigadier on 23rd August 1948. John ceased to belong to the Reserve of Officers having exceeded the age limit on 9th August 1958. They were living at The Walled Garden, Hurley, Berkshire at the time of his death at King Edward VII Hospital, Clewer, Berkshire. She was living at Cockham House, Fontbridge Lane, Burwash, Etchingham, East Sussex at the time of her death. They are believed to have had two sons – Anthony DG Welch (1934) and John Peter Erskine Welch (28th July 1936–28th July 2009).
- Barbara Isobel Gordon (21st May 1906–7th July 1987) was aboard SS *Laconia* on a world cruise starting at Liverpool, Lancashire on 23rd May 1926. She was living

at Flat 3, Eccleston Square, London at the time. She married John Hamilton Piesse (27th April 1906–1st January 1972), a solicitor born at Chertsey, Surrey, on 9th April 1931 at St Mark's Church, North Audley Street, London. He was living at 13 North Audley Street, London and she at Invernairne House, Nairn, Scotland at the time. The marriage ended in divorce. He was living at 29 Ashley Drive, Walton-on-Thames in 1939, when he was a member of the Auxiliary Fire Service. Barbara was living at Leydene, Rosers Cross, Waldron, Heathfield, East Sussex at the time of her death there. They had three children – Caroline M Piesse 1934 and twins Donald G and Richard G Piesse 1936. John married Avice Margaret Dixon (30th April 1920–3rd June 2004) in 1949 at Chelsea, London. They were living at Flat 9 Somerville House, Manor Fields, London in 1962 and at the time of his death there.

George was appointed Adjutant 52nd (Lowland) Divisional Engineers (TA) 26th March 1920–28th March 1924. He commanded 59th Field Company RE in 1924 and was later appointed Deputy Chief Royal Engineer (Works) in Liverpool. He took up works appointments at Dehra Dun, North-West Frontier Province, India and Karachi (now Pakistan). George returned to regimental duty as Assistant Commandant, Queen Victoria's Own Madras Sappers & Miners at Bangalore, India. He later commanded the training battalion there. Promoted major on 23rd February 1926 and lieutenant colonel on 1st December 1933. He returned to England in 1934 on sick leave and was appointed Chief Royal Engineer, Highland Area, Perth that October. In March 1936 he was fined £5 for driving without a licence in Richmond Park, London and complained bitterly to the court over the amount. He was placed on Half Pay on 1st December 1937 and retired due to ill health on 1st August 1939. Appointed lieutenant colonel and honorary colonel with seniority from 1st November 1933 in the Regular Army Reserve of Officers, Royal Engineers Class II.

George was recalled in September 1939 and appointed temporary colonel on 3rd March 1940. He was appointed Chief Royal Engineer, Northern Ireland District on 14th July but retired due to ill health as honorary colonel on 27th January 1941. He served in 2nd Dunbarton Battalion, Home Guard as a major from 25th March 1942 and later transferred to Z Battery, 136th (101st Dunbartonshire HG) Anti-Aircraft, part of the Clyde Heavy Anti-Aircraft Group. George served in Italy with the Allied Military Government 1943–46.

George was elected to Dunbartonshire County Council as member for Cardross and Craigendoran in 1941. He also became a member of Helensburgh District Council until 1964. He was a prominent member of the local British Legion and was president for several years before being appointed the branch life president. He was a member of the county's War Pensions Committee and was appointed DL Dunbartonshire on 27th May 1957, LG 4th June 1957.

St Bride's Episcopal Church in the Hyndland area of the West End of Glasgow. It began as a temporary church in the new suburbs of Glasgow in the late 19th century. In 1891 a group of local businessmen proposed a new church in Beaconsfield Road, Kelvinside, on land provided by the owner of the Kelvinside estate, JB Fleming. A small wooden chapel was acquired from the grounds of Douglas Castle, seat of the Earls of Home. The chapel, which accommodated 114 people, was dedicated to St Bride of Kildare, patron saint of the Douglas family. In 1899 a site on the Hyndland estate at Hanover Terrace (now Kingsborough Gardens) and Hyndland Road was selected and the chapel was moved there. However, a permanent building was required and plans were drawn up. Through the generous aid of a wealthy benefactress, Sarah Mackie, husband of James Logan Mackie of Mackie and Co., creator of White Horse whisky, progress was swift. The foundation stone of the chancel was laid on 9th May 1903 and was completed on 30th April 1904. The foundation stone of the nave was laid on 5th May 1906 and it was dedicated on 25th May 1907. Sarah Mackie died soon afterwards and work on the building ceased. The nave had to be torn down due to shoddy workmanship and the future was uncertain. However, the philanthropic Reid Brothers provided funds for the building in memory of their sister, Elizabeth, who died in 1912. The new church was consecrated on 1st February 1915. It is now Category B listed.

George married Nellie Constance 'Connie' Clark (18th February 1901–24th March 1991), born at 18 Mount Road, Montrose, on 3rd June 1959 at St Bride's Episcopal Church, Kelvinside, Glasgow, Lanarkshire. She was appointed a telephonist on 10th December 1920 (Edinburgh Gazette 7th January 1921). She was President of Cardross Old People's Welfare Committee and Commandant of the Cardross Red Cross Detachment. Connie died at Bristol, Gloucestershire.

Connie's father, John Clark (1866–8th November 1924), born at Montrose, was a sorting clerk and telegraphist, when he married Helen Thow Barclay (28th April 1866–6th January 1949), a dressmaker, at St Mary's Church, Montrose on 20th April 1892. John was living at 4 Mill Lane and Helen at 3 Murray Street, Montrose. They were living at 1 Mill Lane, Montrose in 1892 and at 18 Mount Road, Montrose in 1901. He was the Postmaster at Bo'ness, West Lothian in 1917, living at Helen Villa, Braehead, and the Postmaster at Uddingston, South Lanarkshire in 1918, when they were living at Clydeview, Main Street. John was retired when he died at 53 King Street, Montrose, while living at 63 Polworth Gardens, Hyndland, Glasgow. Helen was living at Connella, Cardross, Dunbartonshire when she died. They had three other children, all born at Montrose:

- James Barclay Clark (1894–3rd December 1947) was serving in A Company, 1/6th Highland Light Infantry (332338), Egyptian Expeditionary Force in 1917. He never married and died at Cardross.
- Andrew Scott Duncan Clark (16th December 1895–22nd April 1917), known as Duncan, was educated at Montrose Academy before being apprenticed to McClure, Naismith, Brodie & Co at St Vincent Street, Glasgow. He also studied

During the Great War, Kantara was an important point in the defence of Suez against the Turks. The town developed into a major base and hospital centre. The cemetery was begun in February 1916 to serve the various hospitals. After the Armistice, the cemetery more than doubled in size when graves were brought in from other cemeteries and desert battlefields. Kantara was a hospital centre again during the Second World War. The cemetery now contains 1,562 Commonwealth burials of the Great War and 110 of the Second World War. There are also 341 graves of other nationalities, many of them Polish. Near the entrance is the Kantara Memorial, commemorating sixteen New Zealand servicemen of the Great War who died in action at Rumani and Rafa and have no known grave. In 1961 the nearby Kantara Indian Cemetery became inaccessible. The 283 Great War servicemen buried there are now commemorated on the Kantara Indian Cemetery Memorial on the wall of Kantara War Memorial Cemetery behind the Stone of Remembrance.

law at the University of Glasgow and was a member of the UOTC. Having taken his exams in October 1915, he was commissioned in 9th (Reserve) Battalion, Royal Scots Fusiliers on 19th November. Duncan disembarked at Port Said, Egypt on 31st May 1916. He was attached to 1/4th Battalion on 26th July 1917 and joined B Company on 3rd August. He took part in the attacks of 52nd (Lowland) Division during the Second Battle of Gaza on 17th April. He was seriously wounded by gunshots to the hip and stomach on 19th April and was evacuated to 24th Stationary Hospital at Kantara on the east bank of the Suez Canal. He died of wounds there and is buried in Kantara War Memorial Cemetery, Egypt (C 58). He is commemorated on the Montrose War Memorial and on his father's gravestone in Rosehill Cemetery. In his will, dated 2nd July 1916, he left everything to his parents.

- Roland Clark (1897–5th September 1923) served as a sapper in the Royal Engineers during the Great War (WR/265856). However, in his brother's service record he is recorded as 242448 in 12th Light Railway Operating Company RE, BEF. He was discharged due to being disabled on 15th January 1919. He died at Milton, Lanarkshire.

George Findlay in later life.

George attended a number of VC Reunions – the VC Garden Party at Buckingham Palace on 26th June 1920, the VC Centenary Celebrations at Hyde Park, London on 26th June 1956 and the 1st and 3rd VC & GC Association Reunions at the Café Royal, London on 24th July 1958 and 18th July 1962. He was a keen sportsman, particularly game shooting, rifle shooting and horse riding. He was also an excellent pianist.

Kilmaronock Parish Church. There has been a Christian community there since the time of St Kessog in the 6th century. In 1324 King Robert the Bruce transferred the patronage from the Earls of Lennox to the Abbey of Cambuskenneth at Stirling. The present building dates from 1813. Kilmaronock Church closed in May 2017 and services are now held at Gartocharn Church. The building is Grade B listed.

George and Connie's grave in Kilmaranock Churchyard.

The VC Memorial at Glasgow Central Station.

The Italy Star was instituted in May 1945 for British Commonwealth forces who served in the Italian campaign 1943–45. On 8th July 1943, the 1939–43 Star (later 1939–45 Star) and the Africa Star became the first two campaign stars instituted by the United Kingdom. By May 1945 there were eight stars and nine clasps. The Arctic Star and Bomber Command Clasp were added in February 2013. No-one could be awarded more than six campaign stars with five of the ten clasps. Only one clasp can be worn on any campaign star. No clasps were awarded with the Italy Star. The eligibility criteria for the Italy Star were different for service at sea, on land and in the air.

The King George V Silver Jubilee Medal commemorated the 25th anniversary of the coronation. 85,235 medals were issued, with a proportion to each Commonwealth country. The medals were awarded at the discretion of the local government, but in general went to members of the Royal Family and household, ministers, government and local government officials and members of the armed forces.

George died at Drumfork House, Helensburgh, Dunbartonshire on 26th June 1967 and was given a private funeral at his own request at Kilmaranock. He is buried in the family plot at Kilmaranock Churchyard, Gartocharn, near Loch Lomond. In his will he left £63,183 (£1.4M in 2023). George is commemorated in a number of other places:

- A British Legion bench in Hermitage Park Garden of Remembrance, Helensburgh.
- Harrow School Speech Room along with the other School VCs.
- Royal Military Academy Woolwich VC Honour Board, Woolwich, London, now in the RMA Sandhurst Library.
- For Valour board at the Royal Engineers Museum, Gillingham, Kent.

The Royal Engineers Museum, Library & Archive at Gillingham, Kent tells the story of the Corps of Royal Engineers and British military engineering in general. The Library was founded in 1812. The Museum and Library received Designated status in 1998, being recognised as having an outstanding collection of national and international significance, one of only three military museums in the country with this status. The Museum and Library have over 500,000 objects relating to the history of the Corps of Royal Engineers and the development of military engineering. These include:

- Waterloo map, with markings made by Wellington himself.
- Revolver used by Lieutenant Chard VC against the Zulus at Rorke's Drift in 1879.
- Russian glass grenades from the Crimea.
- A large collection of items belonging to Charles Gordon found on his travels in China and the Sudan.
- Twenty-five of the fifty-two VCs awarded to REs and three GCs.

- A Department for Communities and Local Government commemorative paving stone was dedicated at Drumfork House, Drumfork Road, Helensburgh, Strathclyde on 4th November 2018.
- Memorial dedicated at Glasgow Central Station on 8th May 2022 honouring fifty-five VCs from Glasgow and the West of Scotland.

In addition to the VC and MC & Bar he was awarded the 1914–15 Star, British War Medal 1914–20, Victory Medal 1914–19 with MID Oakleaf, 1939–45 Star, Italy Star, War Medal 1939–45, George V Silver Jubilee Medal 1935, George VI Coronation Medal 1937 and Elizabeth II Coronation Medal 1953. The VC is held by the Royal Engineers Museum, Prince Arthur Road, Gillingham, Kent.

LIEUTENANT COLONEL HENRY 'HARRY' GREENWOOD
9th Battalion, The King's Own (Yorkshire Light Infantry)

Harry Greenwood was born on 25th November 1881 at Windsor Infantry (later Victoria) Barracks, Sheet Street, Windsor, Berkshire. He was baptised at the Garrison Chapel, Cork, Ireland on 28th March 1882. He was known as Harry or Stalky in the family due to his fondness for the Rudyard Kipling character in *Stalky and Co*. Harry's father, Charles Greenwood (5th November 1853–8th April 1927), a plumber born at St Mary, Nottingham, was living with his sister, Maria and family, at 170 Sherwood Street, Sherwood, Nottingham in 1871. Charles enlisted in the Grenadier Guards on 1st September 1875 (5016) at Nottingham for twelve years. He joined the 2nd Battalion in June 1876. He was promoted lance corporal February 1878, corporal June 1878 and lance sergeant May 1879. He gained the 2nd Class Certificate of Education in June 1876 and was promoted sergeant in November 1879. Charles passed the Instructor of Musketry course in October 1880. Charles married Margaret née Abernethy (4th June 1855–30th August 1926), born at Loughkeen, near Birr, Co Tipperary, Ireland, on 2nd October 1880 at Holy Trinity Church, Marylebone, London. He was living at 4 Bolsover Street and she at 11 St Andrews Place at the time. Margaret arrived in London in 1870 and was employed as a maid. Charles served in Cork, Ireland from February 1882 and in Egypt for four months that year on operations against the mutinous Egyptian Army (Khedive's Star and Egypt Medal). He returned to Britain for service in London at Wellington Barracks, Chelsea Barracks, the Tower of London and Windsor, before returning to Dublin. He extended his service to complete twenty-one years on 8th September 1884. Charles returned to Victoria Barracks, Windsor in October

Windsor Infantry Barracks were built in 1853 and were enlarged in 1911. The barracks were demolished in 1988 and new barracks were built 1989–93.

An 1821 Act of Parliament provided up to £1M for building additional churches 'to promote the established religion of the country and improve the morals of all orders of society' and as a thankful offering for the deliverance of the country from invasion by Napoleon. Holy Trinity was built in 1828, one of the so called 'Waterloo churches'. The architect was Sir John Soane, who designed the Bank of England. Use of the church declined and from 1936 it was a warehouse for Penguin Books, although part of the church remained available for services. In 1937 the Anglican missionary organisation, the Society for Promoting Christian Knowledge, took over the building until it relocated in 2006. In 1952 the Bishop of London proposed reuniting Holy Trinity parish with that St Marylebone, from which it had been formed. The church is currently a wedding department store and function venue. Noted members of the congregation at various times were William Gladstone, Viscountess Nelson (widow of Lord Nelson), the Duke of Wellington, Florence Nightingale and Lord 'Bobs' Roberts VC.

1888 and was posted to Bermuda for twelve months, sailing on 22nd July 1890. Bermuda was not a popular posting at the time as it was disease-ridden. It is not known if his family accompanied him, but it is known that Harry remained with neighbours in England. Charles returned to Britain in early July 1891. He was discharged in September 1896 and settled in Tottenham, London. He returned to plumbing before becoming a Yeoman of the King's Bodyguard at St James' Palace in December 1903. He kept watch during Edward VII's lying in state at Westminster Hall in May 1910.

The family lived at 35 Westerfield Road, Tottenham from 1898 and had moved to 235 Park Lane, Tottenham by 1901. In 1904 they moved to rented accommodation at 2 West Road, Tottenham and purchased the property when Margaret received an inheritance. In 1908 they moved briefly to a smallholding, selling eggs at Medstead, near Alton, Hampshire. The venture was not a success and they returned to their property at West Road, Tottenham in 1909.

Charles re-enlisted on 30th January 1915 in 3rd Battalion, Cheshire Regiment at Birkenhead (12417). Next day he was promoted successively to corporal, sergeant and colour sergeant. He served with 50th Training Reserve Battalion (which had been 14th (Reserve) Battalion, Cheshire Regiment), at Prees Heath from 1st September 1916 (TR3/8180). He was attached to 8th Battalion, Cheshire Volunteer Regiment, Northwich from 18th April 1917 as acting regimental sergeant major. On 9th July he joined 225th Graduated Battalion, which had been 50th Training Reserve Battalion and on 1st November became 51st Graduated Battalion, Manchester Regiment at Great Yarmouth. Charles was posted to the Cheshire Regiment Depot on 26th January 1918 and was demobilised to the Class Z Army Reserve on 9th March 1919 from No.1 Dispersal Unit, Crystal Palace. He returned to his former appointment as a Yeoman of the King's Bodyguard.

Margaret died in a nursing home at 19 Derby Road, Ponders End, London and bequeathed her entire estate, gross value £737/0/2, to her daughter, Kitty. Charles was still living at 2 West Street at the time of his death at North Middlesex Hospital, Edmonton, leaving effects valued at £273/4/2 (£19,800 in 2023) to his son, John. Harry had eight siblings:

Charles and Margaret Greenwood.

- Maria Annette Greenwood (12th January 1883–23rd March 1955), born at Wellington Barracks, Westminster, married Ernest William Baker (11th February 1884–14th May 1918), a meat salesman born at Islington, London, on 6th May 1907 at St Mary's Church, Tottenham, London. He was living at 100 Norfolk Road, Seven Kings, Ilford, London and she at 4 Lansdowne House, Lansdowne Road, London. Ernest was a cashier in 1911, when they were living at Gloucester House, Bolingbroke Road, Fulham, London. Ernest went to Australia alone before the outbreak of the Great War. He enlisted in D Company, 1st Tropical Battalion, Australian Naval and Military Expeditionary Force on 16th August 1914 at Sydney, New South Wales (1038). He was described as a labourer, 5′ 5½″ tall, weighing 155 lbs, with fair complexion, blue eyes, light brown hair and his religious denomination was Church of England. His next of kin was his wife living with her parents at 2 West Road, Tottenham, London, England. Ernest embarked at Sydney aboard HMAT A35 *Berrima* on 19th August. He was discharged time expired on 4th March 1915 but re-enlisted at Liverpool, NSW on 17th April (1032), described as a cook. His wife was living at the same address and later at 6 Dundas Terrace, Dryden Street, Nottingham, England and 13 Harley Street, Castle Boulevard, Nottingham. Ernest landed at Gallipoli on 16th August and was promoted corporal on 21st August and temporary RQMS on 27th September. He disembarked at Alexandria, Egypt from Mudros on 9th January 1916 and embarked for France aboard HMT *Ingoma* on 18th March, disembarking at Marseille on 25th March. He was bitten by a dog and admitted to 7th Australian Field Ambulance 11th-12th October. On 17th July 1917 he was appointed Chief Instructor of Cooking at 1st Anzac Corps School and was attached to Second Army Cookery School 8th-18th September. He was granted leave in England

2nd-17th November. On 27th March 1918 he joined the Reinforcement Camp, Caestre, France and transferred to 20th Battalion AIF next day. Ernest was hit by shell fragments on 14th May and was admitted to 5th Australian Field Ambulance, where he died (Querrieu British Cemetery, France – C5). Pensions were granted to his wife and three children in July 1918. Maria and Ernest had three children:

Harry's brother-in-law, Ernest William Baker, and his grave in Querrieu British Cemetery, France.

- Edmund 'Ted' Charles Baker (5th July 1908–12th December 1995), born at West Kensington, London, was a farmer, living with his mother at 6 Dundas Terrace, Nottingham when he emigrated to Montréal, Québec, Canada aboard RMS *Duchess of Atholl*, departing Liverpool, Lancashire on 9th May 1930. He married Robina 'Ruby' Swanson (17th December 1909–22nd March 2010), born at Burghead, Elgin, Moray, Scotland. He returned to Britain aboard SS *Montcalm*, departing Montréal and Québec and arriving at Southampton, Hampshire on 11th October 1936. Ted and Ruby travelled to England to attend his mother's funeral, returning to Montréal aboard RMS *Empress of France*, arriving on 29th June 1955, by when he was an electrical engineer. He died at Devon, Alberta and she at Montréal. They had three daughters – Patricia Annette Baker (1934–2017), Kathleen Baker and Alexandra Baker.
- Ernest John Baker (19th September 1911–1990), born at Romford, Essex, was educated at Trent Bridge and Nottingham High Schools before working in the chemical department of Boots the Chemist. He emigrated to Canada as a mechanic and lived at Montréal, Québec. He returned to England with his brother, Ted, arriving at Southampton, Hampshire on 11th October 1936. He was living at his mother's address while in Britain. Ernest married Marjorie Ethel Ware (20th June 1915–1993) in 1937 at Nottingham, where she was born. Her father, 56082 Lance Corporal Ernest Edward Ware (1882–8th October 1918) served in 13th Royal Welsh Fusiliers and died on active service in France (Moulin-de-Pierre British Cemetery, France – A15). He and his wife, Maria, were living at 16 End Avenue, Sneinton, Nottingham in 1915. Ernest and Marjorie lived at 19 Sneinton Hermitage, Nottingham. He served as a staff sergeant in the Royal Artillery during the Second World War (784486) and

was awarded the MM for service in Italy (LG 3rd August 1944). Ernest's death was registered at Lancaster, Lancashire and Marjorie's at Kendal, Cumbria. They had two children – Peter Dane Baker (1939–2019) and Penelope D Baker (1941).

- Kathleen Mary Baker (3rd June 1916–13th July 2012), born at Nottingham, was serving in 16th Nottinghamshire, Auxiliary Territorial Service in 1939 (W9030). She married Frank Hillyard (3rd June 1914–16th November 1989) in 1945. His father, 6991 Lance Corporal James Albert Hillyard (c.1882–25th September 1916) 9th Sherwood Foresters died on active service (Norfolk Cemetery, Becordel-Becourt, France – II A 36). Frank was a chef at HMS *Royal Arthur*, a shore training establishment at Skegness, Lincolnshire at the time of the 1939 Register. He died at Basford, Nottinghamshire. Kathleen was living at 53 Coronation Road, Nottingham in 2010 and subsequently died there. They had three children, including Victor CF Hillyard 1951.

Maria married Arthur Gorst Anderson (2nd February 1880–22nd February 1959), born at Northwich, Cheshire, in 1925 at Nottingham. He was living with his parents at Heath Lane, Northwich in 1891. Arthur was a process foreman in a chemical works in 1939, when they were living at Beech House, 35 Beech Avenue, Mapperley, Arnold, Nottinghamshire. He was also a refuge warden at the time of the 1939 Register. Maria died at Beech House and Arthur was still living there at the time of his death at the Royal Infirmary, Lancaster. Arthur had married Annie Massey (1880–1924) in 1907 at Runcorn, Cheshire and they had a daughter, Edith Anderson (1908–2000).

- Margaret 'Maggie' Greenwood (14th August 1884–17th November 1918), born at Aldershot, Hampshire, was a shorthand typist in 1911, working with her sister, Kate, and brother, Harry, for Robert Williams' mining company. She replaced Harry as Williams' private secretary in 1914 but suffered a nervous breakdown and resigned from the company. She emigrated to Wellington, New Zealand, where she married Lawrence Abel Whitaker (15th March 1883–1945), a clerk born at Wooburn, near Wycombe, Buckinghamshire, in 1915. He had served in the Kings Royal Rifles Corps (London Regiment) TF for thirteen years, including five as a sergeant, for two years of which he was in charge of motor cyclist scouts. Lawrence was a musketry instructor and won a gold medal for shooting at Bisley. In 1911 he was a clerk for a mechanical engineer, living with his mother at Elmwood, Wellington Road, Bush Hill Park, Enfield, Middlesex. He emigrated to New Zealand in 1913 and settled at Wellington, working for the Imperial Government Supplies Department. They lived at Disley Street, Kelburn, Wellington. Lawrence was commissioned in the Wellington Garrison Artillery Division TF on 7th July 1916 and was assigned to 5th Company, New Zealand Garrison Artillery. He was described as 5′ 7¼″ tall, weighing 145 lbs, with fresh complexion, blue eyes, fair hair and his religious denomination was

Church of England. He volunteered for the New Zealand Expeditionary Force at Wellington Town Hall on 26th March 1917 but was unfit due to flat feet and deafness. On 29th January 1918 he passed an examination for promotion to lieutenant at Fort Ballance, Wellington. On 30th July 1919 he applied to resign his commission and this was granted on 7th August. Margaret died at Wellington. He was living at 1 Crescent Road, Wellington in 1919. Lawrence married Dorothy Sparrow (c.1891–1961) in 1920. He was a carrier in 1925, when they were living at Brandon Street, Seatoun, Wellington and at Ventnor Street, Wellington in 1935. Lawrence died at Wellington. Dorothy was still living at Ventnor Street in 1954. They had at least one child, Mary Doreen Whitaker in 1921.

- Charles Greenwood (3rd July 1886–27th May 1968), born at Chelsea, London, emigrated to Canada in 1907, joined the Toronto Police Force and later became an inspector. He married Rachel 'Rae/Lottie' Matilda Lester (6th August 1889–21st November 1973), born at Hackney, London, England, on 5th June 1911 at Toronto. He was living at 278 Berkeley Street and she at 358 William Avenue at the time. Charles is reputed to have served in the Canadian Army in Canada during the Great War, but no service record has been found. The family lived at various addresses in Toronto – 358 Milton Avenue in 1912, 1 Badgerow Avenue in 1914, 21 Cassells Avenue in 1921 and at 347 Huron Street in 1946. They had four children, all born at Toronto:
    - Charles Albert Greenwood (20th April 1912–21st September 1979), married Veronica Doreen Murray (13th January 1921–5th August 2006). He served as a captain in the Royal Canadian Armoured Corps during the Second World War and returned to Canada via No.3 Canadian Repatriation Depot, Cove, near Aldershot, Hampshire, England, on 20th February 1946. The family was living at his parents' home at 347 Huron Street, Toronto at the time. They had a son.
    - Margaret Rachel 'Rae' Greenwood (8th October 1914–3rd July 1971) married Lieutenant Rolf Kristiansen (11th October 1918–13th January 1983), born at Kristiansand, Vest-Agder, Norway. They sailed from Bergen, Norway on 6th March 1946 aboard SS *Norefjord*, arriving at New York, USA on 17th June. They lived at Toronto, Canada. She died at Women's College Hospital, 76 Greville Street, Toronto and he at Beeton, Simcoe Co, Ontario. They had two children – Wayne Kristiansen and Wendy Kristiansen.
    - Violet Victoria Greenwood (24th May 1916–12th December 1928).
    - Lloyd Henry Greenwood (c.1920–30th March 2016) served in the Royal Canadian Air Force during the Second World War. He married Myril and they were living at 57 Hammersmith Avenue, Danforth, Ontario in 1945. Lloyd was a salesman in 1949, when they were living at 15 Hubbard Boulevard, Danforth. By 1968 he was a manager and they were living at Stouffville, Simcoe, Ontario. They were still there in 1972, by when he was

a store owner. They had two children – Lloyd Mark Greenwood and Lee Greenwood.

- Arthur Abernethy Greenwood (18th June 1888–22nd March 1965) enlisted in the Royal Artillery in 1906 and served on the North-West Frontier in 1908. He was with 79th Battery RFA at Dinapore, India in 1911. Arthur married Mary Justine Anderson (born 28th August 1892) on 24th July 1911 at St Joseph's Cathedral, Allahabad, India. They had a son – Illtudis Abernethy Greenwood (August 1912–5th September 1912). The marriage was annulled c. 1913. Mary married Isaiah Hale (1885–30th October 1934), born at West Bromwich, Staffordshire, on 18th November 1919 at Allahabad. Mary and Isaiah had a son, William Trevor Hale (19th September 1922–4th December 1994), born at Bangalore, India. Isaiah died at Asansol, Bengal, India. Arthur was commissioned (Special Reserve) on 28th August 1915 and served in East Africa. He transferred to the Royal Horse Artillery in France in 1915 and was wounded in 1916. Promoted Lieutenant 1st July 1917. Home service followed until 1918, when he transferred to the Royal Air Force but he last appears in the Army List in July 1920. Arthur married Kate 'Katie' Miriam Lidbetter (24th August 1893–1942), born at Islington, London, on 22nd July 1918 at Islington Register Office. She was living with her parents at 59 Carleton Road, Tufnell Park, Islington in 1911. Arthur was in charge of commercial sales at Frigidaire Ltd, Edgware Road, London 18th April 1925–15th April 1929. At the outbreak of the Second World War he was recalled as a captain to train recruits in a reserve regiment. He attended the Gunnery Staff Course and was promoted major. He served with the Army Welfare Service from 1943 and served in India until 1945. Arthur married Doris Evelyn Buck (15th July 1920–October 1994) in 1955, registered at Kensington, London. They were living at 65 Harrington Gardens, Kensington at the time of his death at St Mary Abbots Hospital, Kensington. Arthur had three children from two of his marriages:
    - Grahame Charles 'Charlie' Arthur Greenwood (18th February 1919–12th August 2008), born at Andover, Hampshire, was educated at Haileybury before working for a firm of stock jobbers in the City and for Unilever. Charles, as he was known, joined the Honourable Artillery Company in 1936 and was granted an Emergency Commission in the Royal Artillery (91364) on 27th May 1939. He was mobilised from the Supplementary Reserve of Officers on 24th August and served with 22nd Field Regiment in France. He was evacuated from Dunkirk aboard the paddle-steamer *Medway Queen*. Promoted war substantive lieutenant 1st January 1941, lieutenant 18th August 1941, acting captain 29th May 1942, temporary captain 29th August 1942, acting major 24th July 1944 and war substantive captain and temporary major 24th October 1944. He saw action in Algeria in 1943. He was awarded the MC for his actions at Monte Cassino, Italy, on the night of 11th May 1944 he was forward observation officer with the

leading company of 1/6th East Surrey in an attack. He got his party onto the objective, but they were in a highly precarious situation. For the next thirty-six hours, under constant sniping, shelling and attack from mortars, by quick calls for fire, he saved the infantry in what was an almost untenable position. When their last officer was wounded, he took charge and continued to consolidate the defences (LG 26th October 1944). Charles later served in Greece with 30th Field Regiment. Appointed acting lieutenant colonel 26th September–9th November 1945. He was promoted lieutenant on a Regular Commission on 12th December 1945 and captain on 1st July 1946. Post war he served in Germany, Korea, Hong Kong, Aden and Singapore. Appointed GSO2 HQ Eastern Command 31st January 1949–30th January 1951. In Korea he survived an appendix operation, haemorrhagic fever, a Jeep accident and some heavy fighting. Promoted major 18th February 1953. Appointed GSO2 Singapore Base District 31st August 1953–27th July 1955. Awarded the MBE for services in Singapore during the unrest leading up to independence (LG 26th October 1955). Appointed GSO2 Joint Planning Staff 6th July 1959–10th February 1962. Appointed temporary lieutenant colonel 26th March 1962 and promoted lieutenant colonel 4th July 1962. He was awarded the OBE for services as CO 34th Light Anti-Aircraft Regiment RA in the East (LG 1964). Appointed GSO1 Ministry of Defence 28th August 1964–5th March 1967. Colonel 6th August 1966. Appointed Chief Instructor Tactics Wing, School of Artillery, Manorbier 11th March 1967–6th May 1970. Appointed Colonel GS, HQ Wales 22nd May 1970. Appointed Deputy Commander and Brigade Colonel to GOC Wales at Brecon 1972. Awarded the Emergency Reserve Decoration. After retirement from the Army (last appears in the Army List in 1973), he was appointed Deputy Secretary of the Territorial Army & Volunteer Reserve Association for Wales and Monmouthshire. Secretary 1975. He was made a Serving Brother (Member) of the Most Venerable Order of the Hospital of St John of Jerusalem (LG 11th December 1975) and was appointed DL for South Glamorgan (LG 22nd January 1980). He completed a Masters in Education, University of Wales in July 1988. He was created a Knight of the Most Venerable Order of the Hospital of St John of Jerusalem (LG 20th March 1990). Charles married Margarita 'Margi' Isabel Bailward (3rd April 1920–23rd October 2013), born in Trinidad and Tobago, West Indies, on 19th August 1950 at Windsor, Berkshire. They both died at Cardiff, Glamorgan. They had four daughters including – Angela Greenwood 1951, Phillippa A Greenwood 1952 and Prudence J Greenwood 1958.

- Henry David John Greenwood (5th October 1920–9th March 2013), born at Islington, was educated at Haileybury College, where he was a member of the Cadet Contingent, Officer Training Corps. He enlisted in the Honourable Artillery Company (Infantry Battalion) and was commissioned in the

Royal Artillery on 27th May 1939 (91365). He transferred to the Reserve of Officers as a captain (seniority from 27th May 1949) and relinquished his commission on 7th September 1950. Henry married Kathleen 'Kay' Mary Andrew (7th March 1918–25th February 2012), born at Oldham, Lancashire, on 19th August 1944. They both died at Harrogate, Yorkshire. They had two children – Sarah FM Greenwood 1946 and Michael AJ Greenwood 1948.
    - Elizabeth A Greenwood (born 1955).
- David Abernethy Greenwood (13th March 1890–11th October 1952), born at Wellington Barracks, London, enlisted in the Royal Berkshire Regiment in 1906. He was serving with the 2nd Battalion at Meerut, India in 1911 and was subsequently claimed by his elder brother, Arthur, and transferred to the Royal Artillery. David married Mary Rachel Greenwood (not related) (10th May 1895–12th August 1977), born in India, on 10th September 1913 at St Patrick's Church, Agra, India. He served in France and Mesopotamia during the Great War and retired as a battery sergeant major. He was awarded the MSM for valuable services in India in connection with the War (LG 3rd September 1920). He joined the Indian Prison Service on 14th November 1919 and was appointed superintendent of the central jail at Vizagapatam on 1st November 1920. He was also employed at Coimbatore, Madras and Bellary, where he was appointed Officiating Superintendent at Alipuram Jail in December 1924. He received the Kaisar-i-Hind Medal (2nd Class) for his service in January 1924. David and Mary separated. They had a son:
    - Charles David Abernethy Greenwood (12th July 1914–7th August 1975), born at Jhansi, Uttar Pradesh, India, received an emergency commission on 5th July 1941. He trained at Belgaum, Karnataka before joining 2nd Battalion, 9th Gurkha Rifles. Promoted war substantive lieutenant 1st October 1942. He was captured by the Japanese in Singapore and held in Changi Jail, with a period in forced labour camps near Kanchanaburi, Thailand during 1942 and

The Kaisar-i-Hind Medal for Public Service in India was awarded by the Empress/Emperor between 1900 and 1947, to 'any person without distinction of race, occupation, position, or sex … who shall have distinguished himself (or herself) by important and useful service in the advancement of the public interest in British Raj'. The medal was instituted by Queen Victoria on 10th April 1900 and the name translates as Emperor of India. The medal had three grades. The Gold Medal was awarded directly by the monarch on the recommendation of the Secretary of State for India. Silver and Bronze (seen here) Medals were awarded by the Viceroy. The most famous recipient is Mohandas Karamchand (Mahatma) Gandhi (1869–1948). His award, by Lord Hardinge, was for his contribution to ambulance services in South Africa. He returned the Medal in 1920.

1943. He was released in September 1945 and lived in India. Appointed war substantive captain and relinquished his commission on account of disability on 23rd January 1948, retaining the rank of captain. Charles married Margaret 'Peggy/Peg' Elizabeth Harris (25th October 1913–16th February 2012), born at Woking, Surrey, on 22nd April 1946 at Loyola College Chapel, Madras. She was living with her parents at Ardnardeen, Danes Hill, Hockering Estate, Woking, Surrey in 1939, when she was a civil nursing reservist. They were living at Cheyne Cottage, Doles Lane, Wokingham, Berkshire at the time of his death there. They had at least one son – Sean David Aberneathy Greenwood (1947–99).

David married Gladys Hildred Dee (8th October 1913–January 1976) on 9th June 1933 at Coimbatore, India. They had two children, including Heather A Greenwood. During the Second World War David was commissioned and served as Adjutant, Southern Provinces Mounted Rifles, Madras as a captain. David and Gladys divorced on 30th July 1945 in the High Court, Madras. David died at Nottingham. Gladys married Arthur Wilfrid Taylor Allan (28th October 1903–c.1959) in 1954 at Kensington, London. Arthur was granted an Emergency Commission in the Indian Army on 27th May 1942. Promoted war substantive lieutenant on 16th September, acting captain to 15th September and temporary captain to 14th December 1944. He later worked for the United Nations Health Organisation. Arthur died at Delhi, India and Gladys at Paddington, London.

Mary married Henry Crawshaw (2nd August 1902–23rd February 1991), a foreman painter born at Manchester, Lancashire, on 16th October 1936 at Karachi, India (now Pakistan). Henry was working for the Carriage & Wagon Department, East India Company at Bombay in 1927. They returned to England on holiday in 1938 aboard SS *California*, sailing from Bombay and arriving at Liverpool, Lancashire on 19th April, giving his address as 60 Tillery Street, Miles Platting, Manchester, Lancashire. They returned to England aboard SS *Asturias*, arriving at Southampton, Hampshire in April 1947 and lived at 62 Kennett House, Smedley Road, Manchester. Mary died at 5 Kingsdown Road, Wythenshawe, Manchester and Henry at Old Vicarage Nursing Home, Frampton-on-Severn, Gloucestershire. Henry and Mary had two daughters born in India – Joan Mary Crawshaw (2nd November 1927–November 1995) and Eva Geraldine Crawshaw (4th May 1929–c.2002).

- Kate 'Kitty' Greenwood (20th November 1892–27th April 1951), born at Caterham, Surrey, joined her brother, Harry, working for Robert Williams' mining company in 1909. She was a shorthand typist in 1911 and replaced her sister, Margaret, as Williams' private secretary in 1915, remaining with him until his death. Kitty accompanied Harry to Buckingham Palace when he was invested with the DSO on 10th July 1918. When Sir Robert, who was created a baronet in 1928, died on 25th April 1938, he left Kitty a generous legacy of £10,000 (£811,000 in 2023) plus 300 shares in Zambesia Exploring Co and 1,000 shares in

Tanganyika Concessions Ltd. She was able to retire and move to Scotland. Kitty never married and was living at Brokinstone Kellas, near Elgin, Morayshire at the time of her death at 19 Great King Street, Edinburgh, Midlothian.

- Mary Ann 'Mollie' Greenwood (1st December 1894–16th March 1914) was a shorthand typist in 1911. She died at 2 West Road, Tottenham, London.
- John Greenwood (14th September 1897–15th June 1973), born at Tottenham, London, was a member of 1st Cadet Battalion, King's Royal Rifles, Finsbury Square, London from 13th August 1914 and was promoted lance corporal. He was living at Moorlands, Sewardstonebury, Chingford when he applied for a commission on 14th September 1915, initially in the RFA with 36th Division as an older brother was serving there as a subaltern. He passed a medical next day. John went to France in May/June 1916. He was serving with 19th Liverpool on 2nd November 1917, when he came out of a HQ at Wytschaete, Belgium and was hit by a shell splinter in the upper left arm, fracturing it and passing through near the shoulder. He embarked at Le Havre on 11th November and disembarked at Southampton next day. His address was 92 Queens Gate, South Kensington, London. A wound pension was paid from the date of wounding. He was treated at 4th London General Hospital, Denmark Hill, London and on 21st February 1918 a fragment of bone was removed and some pus was drained. A medical board in London on 13th March found him unfit for A & B for an uncertain period and C1 for three months. A medical board on 3rd June, by when he was at the Officers Convalescent Hospital Barrington, Paignton, South Devon, found he was unfit for A & B for an uncertain period and C1 for two months. Medical boards on 2nd August, 13th September and 12th November found he was unfit for A & B for six months and C1 for between six weeks and two months. A medical board on 21st February 1919 found he was unfit for the same periods and he was returned to the Officers Convalescent Hospital Barrington, Paignton, for six weeks more treatment. A medical board on 7th April found he was unfit for A & B for three months but fit for C1 and was granted three weeks leave. A medical board at Cambridge Military Hospital, Aldershot on 3rd May found he was unable to raise the arm above the horizontal, the joint was deformed and there was marked loss of shoulder muscles. He was assessed as being 25% disabled permanently but, despite this, was found fit for General Service. John was released from service from the Dispersal Unit, Crystal Palace on 7th May. A medical board at Cheltenham Terrace, London on 2nd September found much the same as the board in May. A medical board on 6th August 1920 extended the wound pension to 5th August 1921. He was living at Allbright Leigh, Buckhurst Hill, Essex at the time. He relinquished his commission on 1st September 1921, retaining the rank of lieutenant. He worked in India post war as a merchant but was too badly injured to serve in the Second World War. John married Kathleen Isabel Sheridan (16th July 1899–2nd November 1973), born at Mendoza, Argentina, on 19th July 1924 at Paignton Parish Church, Devon. They lived at Holmwood, Horsell Vale, Woking, Surrey, where they both subsequently died. They had a daughter:

  - Patricia 'Pat' Kathleen Greenwood (25th September 1928–2nd November 2006), born at Paignton, Devon, married Stanley Leonard Roberts (2nd July 1928–23rd July 2010), born at Edmonton, Middlesex, in Surrey in 1955. He was living with his parents at 10 Sandhurst Avenue, Surbiton, Surrey in 1939. Pat and Stanley were living at 6 The Avenue, Chobham, Surrey at the time of her death. They had two sons and a daughter.

Apple Row, Nottingham.

Harry's paternal grandfather, Henry Greenwood (c.1815–16th August 1862), married Mary Ann née Lumley (c.1817–7th April 1879), on 9th March 1835 at St Mary, Nottingham, where they were both born. He was a fishmonger in 1841, when they were living at Apple Row, Nottingham. By 1851 they had moved to 113 Parliament Street. By 1861 he was a greengrocer and fish salesman. He was still living at Parliament Street when he died. In addition to Charles they had ten other children, all born at Nottingham:

- Eleanor 'Ellen' Greenwood (c.1836–17th June 1880) was a lace drawer in 1851 living with her parents. She married Edwin Wallace (1835–83), a brush maker, on 1st November 1856 at Nottingham. They were living with her parents at Parliament Street in 1861 and at 11 Charlotte Street, Nottingham in 1871. At the time of the 1871 Census he was absent from the family home and she was a fish dealer. They had three children:
  - Henry 'Harry' Wallace (1857–1920) was living at 11 Charlotte Street, his mother's address, when she died in 1880. He married Catherine Cain (c.1857–1904) in 1885.
  - Kate Wallace (1860–19th March 1937) died unmarried.
  - Nellie Maria Wallace (1863–1903) married Roland Edmund Brookhouse (1861–1939) in 1883. He was born at Leeds, Yorkshire and died at Hendon, Middlesex. Nellie died at Chelmsford, Essex.
- Ann Greenwood (born 1838) was a domestic servant for the Williamson family in 1861 at Garner's Hill, Nottingham. She is believed to have married Edward Kirk on 3rd October 1865 at St Peter's Church, Nottingham.
- Henry Greenwood (28th April 1840–1850).
- Maria Greenwood (born 1843) was a lace hand in 1861, living with her parents. She married Charles Henry Savage (born 1842), born at Hoxton, London, in 1863. He was a greengrocer in 1871, when they were living at 179 Sherwood Street, Sherwood, Nottingham. Maria's brothers, Charles and Arthur, were living with them at the time of the 1871 Census. By 1881 he was a fishmonger and they were living at 192 Sherwood Street. They emigrated to Pennsylvania, USA between 1881 and 1900. They had six children:

- Annie Maria Savage (27th April 1864–1st October 1949) married Frederick Murray. She died at 4100 Locust Street, Philadelphia, Pennsylvania.
- Charles Henry 'Harry' Savage (born 1866).
- Arthur Percy Savage (born 1867).
- Frederick Augustus Savage (born 1870).
- Ethel Florence Savage (born December 1880).
- Harold Edwin Savage (born December 1885).

- George Greenwood (24th November 1844–27th February 1889) was assisting his father in the family business in 1861. He returned home drunk on the evening of 12th September 1864 and began arguing with his mother over money. He grabbed a knife and threatened her until one of his married sisters intervened. He rushed at her but fell over and the knife pierced his thigh. He was apprehended by Police Constables Foster and Howell and taken to the General Hospital in Nottingham. George was sentenced to one month's imprisonment in default of paying £5. He was a fishmonger in 1881, living at 9 Cole Court, Sherwood, Nottinghamshire. Living with him was Mary A Anderson (born 1848), a spinster housekeeper, and her daughter, Lily (born 1876). George died at Nottingham Workhouse.
- Eliza Greenwood (born 1847).
- Sarah Greenwood (October 1849–17th November 1850).
- Arthur Greenwood (1855–1914) was a lace maker. He married Lizzie Fannie Hardwick (1860–31st August 1909) in 1881. She was living with her parents at 17 Berkeley Street, Nottingham in 1861. Arthur was a grocer in 1891, when they were living at 184 & 186 Long Hedge Lane, Sneinton, Nottingham. They were living at 19 Waterloo Promenade, Nottingham at the time of her death there. Arthur was living at the Nottingham Workhouse and Infirmary, Ragthorpe, Nottinghamshire in 1911.
- Kate Greenwood (27th November 1856–28th September 1893) married Arthur Wellington Loverseed (December 1853–4th September 1894), born at Sneinton, Nottingham, on 18th October 1875. He was a contractor in Nottingham in 1879 and they were living at 16 Pelham Crescent, The Park, Nottingham in 1891. They both subsequently died there. They had six children:
  - John Henry L Loverseed (14th September 1875–1946) married Catherine K Houghton in 1916.
  - Ida Katherine 'Kate' Loverseed (1877–1959) married William Bonser Thurman (1875–1954) in 1901. She died in Grantham, Lincolnshire. They had at least one child, Ronald J Thurman in 1911.
  - Ethel Laura Loverseed (1878–1957) married Frank Herbert Tomlinson (1881–1953) in 1907 registered at Melton Mowbray. They had at least one child, Lucy M Tomlinson in 1912. His death was registered at Nottingham and hers at Cheltenham.
  - Arthur William Loverseed (25th December 1879–1954) married Mary K Booth (26th May 1886–1976) in 1914. Both their deaths were registered at

Wandsworth. They had three children – Mary S Loverseed 1916, Maire K Loverseed 1917 and Arthur J Loverseed 1919.

  - Aubrey Wellington Loverseed (1884–30th April 1958) married Kathleen Lawrence (23rd July 1900–1985) in 1933. He was living at 68 Harlaxton Drive, Derby Road, Nottingham when he died at the General Hospital, Nottingham.
  - Ernest Harry Loverseed (1885–1931) married Winifred Rosina A Case (24th January 1894 -1976) in 1918 registered at Brentford. They had four children – Richard B Loverseed 1920, Daphne B Loverseed 1923, Daphne B Loverseed 1927 and Jeffrey E Loverseed 1928.
- Mary Ann Greenwood (born 1859) was living with her sister, Maria and family, at the time of the 1881 Census. She married Harry Brown (c.1854–1934) on 17th April 1881 at St Andrew's Church, Nottingham. He was a lacemaker, living at Mansfield Road, Nottingham and she was living at Welbeck Street, Nottingham at the time. They were living at 73 Raglan Street, Nottingham in 1891 and 1901. He was still living there as a widower in 1911. They had two sons:
  - Harry Brown (born 1882) was a packer in an apron factory in 1901 living with his parents.
  - Charles Brown (born 1884) was a lithographic printer in 1901 living with parents. He married Ada (born c.1888) and they had a daughter, Muriel Brown c.1909.

His maternal grandfather, David Fawcett Abernethy (10th October 1827–25th September 1903), born at Tipperary, Ireland, was a farmer. The Abernethy family originated in Moray, Scotland and emigrated to Ireland with Prince William of Orange, fighting at the Battle of the Boyne. The name is often seen as Aberneathy. He married Charlotte née Mathers (1829–21st December 1904), born at Dublin, Ireland, on 29th July 1852 at St George's Church, Dublin. He was living at 20 Nelson Street and she at 2 Willow Place, Booterstown, Dublin. They moved to Liverpool, Lancashire before 1875. In 1881 he was a milk dealer and they were living at 1 St Georges

St George's Church, Dublin was designed by Francis Johnston, who is best known for the General Post Office building on O'Connell Street in Dublin. With St Andrew's Church in Chennai, India, it is considered one of the finest stylistic daughter churches to London's St Martin-in-the-Fields. The new St George's Church was deemed to be in Drumcondra when it was built in 1802 as a new parish (established 1793) church for the Church of Ireland. By the 1950s the parish was the largest in Ireland. The building was sold in 1991. The bells, which are mentioned in James Joyce's *Ulysees*, were moved to Taney Parish Church, Dundrum and the ornate pulpit was carved up to decorate a pub in Parliament Street. The former church became a theatre, then a night-club and later office facilities.

Road, Great Crosby, Lancashire. They returned to Dublin and were living at 37 Upper Wellington Street in 1901. He died there and she at Pembroke Cottages, Merrion, Co Dublin. In addition to Margaret they had nine other children:

- John Abernethy (10th October 1854–21st December 1912), born in King's (now Offaly) Co, Ireland, served in the Royal Irish Constabulary. He married Adelaide Emily Fitzgerald (1858–3rd December 1923) in September on 11th August 1879 at St John's Church, Limerick, Ireland. They were living at 17 Pembroke Estate Cottages, Dublin in 1911 by when he was a pensioner. They both subsequently died in Dublin, he at Sir Patrick Dun's Hospital and she at 17 Pembroke Estate. They had six children:
    - Walter Thomas Abernethy (born 16th August 1880).
    - Rowland Abernethy (5th December 1881–28th February 1948) served in the Coldstream Guards in 1897 (986) and was discharged by purchase. He was a clerk when he enlisted in the Army Service Corps on 10th September 1900 at Dublin (S/16722), described as 5′ 3½″ tall, weighing 115 lbs, with fresh complexion, blue eyes, fair hair and his religious denomination was Church of England. He gained the Second Class Certificate of Army Education upon entry and was posted to Aldershot, Hampshire on 20th September. Posted to the Curragh, Ireland on 11th December and gained First Class Army Education on 29th October 1901. He returned to Aldershot on 3rd December and deployed to South Africa with B Supply Company ASC on 11th December (Queen's South Africa Medal with clasps South Africa 1902 and Cape Colony). Rowland was assigned to the Deputy Assistant Adjutant General's office at Kimberley on 12th January 1902 and to OC ASC HQ Office there on 20th November. He was a ration clerk 17th-27th May 1903 and then worked in supply accounts at Middelburg from 28th May and at Bloemfontein from 5th March 1906. Promoted lance corporal on 28th October 1903 and was granted Class 1 pay of 6d per day on 1st April 1904. He extended his service to complete eight years on 20th April and was promoted second corporal on 12th July. On 10th September 1905 he was granted Class 1 pay of 7d per day. He returned to Dublin on general duties on 22nd January 1907 and was promoted corporal on 30th January. He extended his service to complete twelve years on 30th July 1908 and was promoted lance sergeant on 23rd March 1909. He qualified for Nos.1, 2 & 3 Drill Certificates on 17th May 1909 and for No.4 Drill Certificate on 9th June. Promoted sergeant on 6th November 1909. Rowland was assigned to the Recruiting Staff Office, Dublin on 6th February 1910 and was at West Down Camp, Salisbury Plain, Wiltshire from 6th August working on supply accounts on manoeuvres until 18th October. When he returned to Dublin he was assigned to the Garrison Office on 20th December. He was a sergeant in the Supply Office at Curragh on 12th April 1911 and was appointed Chief

Clerk there on 26th November. He extended his service to complete twenty-one years on 27th January 1912. He sailed for Egypt on 22nd March and was assigned to the Embarkation Office, Alexandria on 4th April. He returned to Britain on 20th February 1914 and was discharged with a pension on 15th September 1914, no longer physically fit for war service due to being insane. However, a squadron quartermaster sergeant (S4/039070 & 403931) of the same name went to France on 9th May 1915 and was later an acting warrant officer. This man was discharged in 1916. Rowland was living at 17 Pembroke Estate, Merrion when he died at Grangegorman Mental Hospital, Dublin.

- ◦ Michael Abernethy (born 21st October 1882), a twin with John.
- ◦ John Abernethy (21st October 1882–12th December 1883), a twin with Michael.
- ◦ Oliver Abernethy (1883–1935).
- ◦ Adelaide Christina Abernethy (25th December 1883–12th March 1928) married Patrick Fitzpatrick, a soldier of Portobello Barracks, Dublin, at Booterstown Church, Blackrock, Rathdown, Dublin, on 7th January 1908.

- Emily Abernethy (c.1856–18th August 1919) emigrated to Australia aboard SS *Duke of Westminster*, departing Plymouth, Devon and arriving at Cooktown, Queensland on 21st August 1883. She married Joseph Robert Hamm (c.1855–27th July 1921), born in the Channel Islands, on 19th July 1884 in Queensland. They moved to Sydney, New South Wales and they both subsequently died there.
- Walter Abernethy (12th July 1861–20th March 1918), born at Carrig Locheen, Co Tipperary, joined the Royal Navy on 20th August 1880 (112796) and served aboard HMS *Valiant*, the First Reserve guard ship for Southern Ireland, as a gun room servant. He was described as 5′ 7″ tall, with light brown hair, blue eyes and fair complexion. He was discharged at his own request on 1st March 1881. He married Sarah Ellen 'Nellie' Ward (3rd October 1869–28th July 1951), born at Sculcoates, Yorkshire, on 5th December 1888 at St Anne's Church, Belfast, Ireland. She was living with her parents at Devonshire Buildings, Barrow-in-Furness, Lancashire in 1881. He appeared as Walter Fitzgerald in the 1891, 1901 and 1911 Censuses of England. He was a gatekeeper in a shipyard in 1891, when they were living at 11 Steamer Street, Barrow-in-Furness. By 1901 they had moved to 9 Abercorn Street and were still there in 1911, by when he was a commissionaire in a shipbuilder's yard. His death at Barrow-in-Furness was registered as Walter Abernethy Fitzgerald. Sarah was living at 11 Island Road, Barrow-in-Furness in 1939, recorded as Sarah E Abernethy-Fitzgerald, as was her death in 1951. They had thirteen children:
  - ◦ Annie Charlotte Abernethy (1889–1966) married Thomas Harvey in 1909.
  - ◦ James Abernethy (14th January 1891–1953) was a shipwright in 1911 living with his parents. His surname was registered as Abernethey at birth. James married Margaret Elsie Bailey (1900–18) in 1917. They had one child, Leslie

E Abernethy in 1918. James married Catherine B Kearney (1896–1966) in 1921. They had three children – Sheila P Abernethy 1921, Margaret M Abernethy 1923 and Rosena E Abernethy 1931.
    - Ethel Abernethy (25th February 1892–1963).
    - Margaret 'Maggie' Helena Abernethy (1893–6th June 1968), registered as Abernethey at birth.
    - Walter Abernethy (1895–1960) was a sheet iron worker in 1911 living with his parents. His surname was registered as Abernethey at birth. He married Minnie Varle (1901–67) in 1919. They had three children – Walter Abernethy 1919, James E Abernethy 1922 and Elizabeth Abernethy 1930. Walter married Winnifred M Scott (7th June 1923–1987) in 1947.
    - Roland/Rowland Abernethy (3rd July 1897–26th September 1970) married Mary J Bayle (18th December 1897–1976) in 1919. They had four children – Thomas R Abernethy 1919, Josephine Abernethy 1921, Vera W Abernethy 1925 and Gerard R Abernethy 1929. Roland was living at 14 Andover Street, Barrow-in-Furness when he died.
    - Annie Elizabeth Abernethy (27th October 1898–1975) married John Newsham (1887–1955) at Liverpool in 1927. They had a son, John G Newsham in 1930.
    - John 'Jack' Abernethy (9th May 1901–1971).
    - Mary Ellen 'Nellie' Abernethy (1903–28th April 1958) married Peter A McArdle (12th December 1897–1973) in 1927. They had a son, Peter A McArdle in 1937.
    - David Abernethy (19th July 1908–26th October 1981) was a bread salesman living with his mother in 1939. He married Louisa D Treanor (11th April 1914–1991) in 1940. They had three children – Dympna M Abernethy 1941, David JD Abernethy 1942 and Daniel K Abernethy 1946.
    - Walter Abernethy (born and died 1910).
    - Thomas Gerard Abernethy (29th May 1911–1974) married Phyllis M Marr (8th March 1916–1992), born at Ipswich, in 1935. They had three children – Maureen G Abernethy 1936, Gerard Abernethy 1938 and Phyllis S Abernethy 1944.
    - Winifred M Abernethy (April 1914–11th September 1958) married William L Campbell (October 1909–1983) in 1936. They had a daughter, Winifred J Campbell in 1939.
- Rowland Abernethy (born 30th October 1862).
- Charlotte Helena Abernethy (c.1866–20th May 1906) moved to Liverpool, Lancashire and married William Hugh Dalrymple (1865–28th August 1930), a cabinet maker, at St Saviour's Church there on 1st August 1887. They were both living at 1 Parliament Place, Liverpool at the time. They were living at 37 Tagus Street, Toxteth Park, Lancashire in 1891 and 1901. They had three children:

- Charles Dalrymple (7th March 1888–1962) married Lavinia Maud Morgan (born 1892) in 1914, registered at West Derby. They had a daughter, Helena Dalrymple in 1916.
- William Dalrymple (17th February 1890–18th November 1963) married Florence Davies (c.1887–1960) in 1911, registered at West Derby. They had at least three children – Florence Dalrymple 1918, Rowland Dalrymple 1920 and Muriel Dalrymple 1924.
- Walter Dalrymple (18th August 1892–1966) married Mary Robinson (27th August 1897–1984) in 1916, registered at West Derby. They had a daughter, Mary Dalrymple in 1917. They both died in Surrey.

William married Hannah Griffiths née Woods (1867–12th June 1932) in 1908, registered at Toxteth Park. They were living at 71 Claremont Avenue, Wavertree, Liverpool at the time of his death there. Hannah had married Samuel Griffiths (born c.1856) in 1888 at West Derby. He was a cabinet maker in 1891, when they were living at 10 Leda Street, West Derby. Living with them were twin daughters, Mary Jane and Sarah Rachel Griffiths (born 1880), probably from Samuel's previous marriage. They were still at 10 Leda Street in 1901. They had a son, Albert Herbert Milburn Griffiths (2nd February 1890–12th September 1949), who was a commercial clerk.

- Lily Florence Abernethy (c.1868–24th July 1880) was born at Dublin. She was tending her father's cattle on 24th July 1880 at Crosby but did not return home. Her body was discovered that evening under a pile of timber at Cambridge Road, Litherland. A servant girl, who saw the cattle near the timber but not Lily, reported that the timber fell suddenly.
- Jessie Edith Abernethy (20th April 1871–March 1905), born at Donnybrook, Dublin, married Thomas Wise (born 15th December 1869), born at Blarney, Co Cork, on 15th October 1895 at Cork, Ireland. She died at Balrothery, Ireland.
- James Abernethy.
- David Abernethy.

Harry was educated privately because his parents moved frequently. He was employed as an apprentice compositor with *The Times* newspaper at Printing House Square, London. Later he was employed by Robert Williams' (1860–1938) (Sir Robert in 1928) mining company as his private secretary from

The Times newspaper was produced at Printing House Square from 1785 to 1974. The offices were on the site of Blackfriars Priory's refectory where Shakespeare, who lived next door, staged his plays in the winter, when the Globe theatre was closed (News UK).

May 1902 until 1914. Williams was an associate of Cecil Rhodes and formed the Zambesia Exploring Co and Tanganyika Concessions Ltd. Harry met him while serving in the South African Constabulary. He accompanied Williams on frequent trips to South Africa.

Harry married Helena Emily Anderson (14th March 1878–22nd October 1969), born at Ashburton Crescent, Gosforth, Northumberland, on 9th January 1909 at St Clement Danes Church, Strand, London. She was a lady's help at Astwick Farm, Evenley, Northamptonshire in 1901, working for Thomas and Isabel Trevor. They met when she was a nurse and he was in hospital having his appendix removed. They lived at various addresses:

Aspley, Lime Grove, Kingston upon Thames, Surrey 1911.
Cantley, Connaught Avenue, Chingford, Essex c.1914.

St Clement Danes Anglican Church, on the Strand in Westminster, is situated on an island in the road outside the Royal Courts of Justice. The first church on the site was reputedly founded by the Danes in the 9th century, but there are other theories to how the church became so named. King Harold I, also known as Harold Harefoot, King of the English 1035–40, is recorded as being buried in the church but there is no memorial. The original church was rebuilt by King William I and again later in the Middle Ages. It was expanded in 1608 and 1618. After the 1666 Great Fire of London, repairs were attempted to the steeple, but these were impractical, and the whole tower was rebuilt and completed in 1669. Soon afterwards it was decided that the rest of the church, which was also in a poor state, should be completely rebuilt. The rebuilding, to Sir Christopher Wren's design, was completed in 1682. The interior was created by Edward Pierce, with whom Wren worked on many churches. The existing tower was reclad and a steeple was added in 1719. William Webb Ellis, often credited with inventing Rugby football in 1823, was once a rector of the church and there is a memorial tablet. The building was burned out on 10th May 1941 during the Blitz and was not restored until the late 1950s following an appeal for funds. It was re-consecrated on 19th October 1958 as the Central Church of the Royal Air Force. Outside the Church are statues of Sir Arthur 'Bomber' Harris and Hugh Dowding. The statue of Harris was controversial due to the bombing of Dresden. Despite protests, including from Germany, the Bomber Harris Trust went ahead with it in 1992. It was unveiled by Queen Elizabeth, the Queen Mother. Inside the Church there are numerous memorials, including one to the Polish Air Forces. The floor is inscribed with the badges of over 800 RAF commands, groups, stations, squadrons and other formations. Books of Remembrance list the names of all RAF personnel who have died in service and American airmen based in the United Kingdom who died during the Second World War. Near the altar are plaques listing RAF, RFC, RNAS and Commonwealth personnel who have been awarded the VC and GC. There are also memorials to several people whose ashes are buried in St Clement Danes, including Sir Archibald McIndoe (1900–60), the pioneering plastic surgeon who worked for the RAF during the Second World War, and Marshal of the RAF Lord Tedder (1890–1967). In the gallery hang the Queen's Colours and Standards of active RAF squadrons, together with standards of several disbanded squadrons and the Royal Banner of the Royal Observer Corps. It is claimed that the church features in the nursery rhyme *Oranges and Lemons*, but it may also refer to St Clement Eastcheap. However, the bells of St Clement Danes do play the tune every day at 9.00 a.m., midday, 3.00 p.m. and 6.00 p.m.

Moorlands, Sewardstonebury, Waltham Abbey, near Chingford, Essex c.1915.
7 Courtland Road, Paignton, Devon – temporarily to avoid Zeppelin raids c.1917.
Albrightleigh, High Road, Buckhurst Hill, Essex c.1919.

7 Courtland Road, Paignton, Devon, on the right, where Harry's family lived in 1917.

They had four children:

- Mollie 'Molly' Helena Margaret Greenwood (10th April 1914–8th July 1933), born at Chingford, Essex, married Carlos Ferreira Martins, of Portuguese origin, and settled in Angola. She died of blackwater fever during childbirth and is buried at Mossamedes (now Moçâmedes), Namibe Province, Angola.
- Harry Charles Gillespie Greenwood (20th -24th July 1915), born at Moorlands, Sewardstonebury, Waltham Abbey, near Chingford, died four days later from complications and jaundice exhaustion.
- Alice Stella Evelyn 'Evie' Greenwood (7th July 1917–1st July 1998), born at 7 Courtland Road, Paignton, Devon, was educated at Wimbledon High School and in Switzerland with her sister, Cynthia, in 1934. She was living with her parents at West Winds, South Cliff Avenue, Bexhill-on-Sea, Sussex in 1939. She served as an ambulance driver in the Auxiliary Territorial Service during the Second World War in Northern Ireland. Evie married Lieutenant Malcolm Brooks Onwood (3rd December 1919–29th July 2013), born at Wanstead, Essex, on 21st August 1946 at the Brompton Oratory, Brompton Road, London. Malcolm enlisted in the Army and was promoted lance sergeant. He was commissioned in the 19th Hyderabad Regiment, Indian Army (Emergency Commission) on 9th July 1942 and promoted war substantive lieutenant on 9th January 1943. On 16th July 1945 he transferred to 2nd Duke of Wellington's (355748) retaining his seniority. He relinquished his commission on 8th December 1946 and was granted the honorary rank of captain. They emigrated to the USA and were living at 45 Eton Court, Ramsey, Connecticut when US citizenship was granted on 4th September 1958. Evie died at Cohasset, Norfolk Co, Massachusetts. They had a daughter, Michelle Onwood, who married Peter Laney and they had two children – Andrew and Stephen Laney.
- Violet Cynthia Marion Greenwood (1st April 1919–16th March 2006), born at Albrightleigh, High Road, Buckhurst Hill, Essex, was educated at Wimbledon High School and in Switzerland with her sister Evelyn. She was living with her parents in 1939. She served as an ambulance driver in the First Aid Nursing Yeomanry and the Auxiliary Territorial Service during the Second World War at Liverpool, Lancashire and London. Violet married Richard List (28th December

1916–19th July 1992), born at Croydon, Surrey, on 1st May 1948 at Wimbledon Parish Church, Surrey. He worked for Westminster Bank. He was commissioned in the Royal Corps of Signals (TA) on 10th May 1939 and was mobilised on 24th August. Promoted war substantive lieutenant 1st January 1941 and appointed temporary captain 19th August 1941. He was serving with Tripoli District Signals, Libya in October 1943. Promoted captain 29th July 1945, major 20th February 1952 and was awarded the TD. They emigrated to Canada and the USA and lived in New York and Edmunds, Snohomish Co, Washington State. He died at Edmunds and she at Sacramento, California. They had three children:

- Anne List (born 15th March 1949), born at Nelson Hospital, Merton, Surrey, married as Clarke on 12th October 1974 at Pelham, New York. They divorced on 25th February 1983 at Sacramento, California. They had two daughters – Monica Clarke and Nicole Clarke (1979–2019). Anne married Robert on 20th April 1996 at Sacramento.
- Helen List (12th April 1951–15th October 2011), born in Surrey, was a linguist with masters' degrees from McGill University and the University of British Columbia. She married Douglas 'Doug' Gordon Hawes (10th February 1948–23rd November 2014), an engineer and architect born at Montréal, Québec, Canada, c.1972 at Pelham, Westchester Co, New York. They had two daughters – Catherine McGill and Emily McGill. The marriage ended in divorce c.1975 at Montréal. Doug remarried. Helen married Jeffrey 'Jeff' Ireland McGill (1st November 1949–10th August 2018), born at the Royal Victoria Hospital, Montréal, in June 1982 at Vancouver, British Columbia, Canada. He was a salesman in 1968 at London, Ontario. He graduated from Bishop's University, Sherbrook, Québec (BSc Physics 1970) and Concordia University, Montréal (MSc Mathematics 1973). Jeff carried out operations research on the Canadian Northern Railroad. He began teaching at the British Columbia Institute of Technology in 1979 and later at the University of British Columbia (PhD Management Science 1990). He taught at the University of Denver, Colorado, USA in 1992 and at Smith School of Business, Queens University, Kingston, Ontario in 1993. Helen and Jeff divorced. Helen died at the Royal Jubilee Hospital, Victoria, British Columbia and Jeff at Kingston, Frontenac, Ontario.
- Christopher List (29th April 1953–6th June 2020) married Carly in April 1974 at Pelham, Westchester Co, New York. He died at Port Angeles, Clallam Co, Washington, USA.

Helena's father, Daniel Gillespie Anderson (1845–26th May 1911), born at Inverkeilor, Forfarshire, Scotland, married Helena Amy née Cracknell ((1850–89), born at Gainsborough, Lincolnshire, on 11th August 1868 at Christ Church, Newcastle upon Tyne. They were living at Ashburton Crescent, Gosforth, Northumberland in 1878. He was an India rubber agent in 1881, by when they

Gainsborough, a market town on the River Trent in Lincolnshire, is England's furthest inland port, ninety kilometres from the North Sea. It was one of the capital cities of Anglo-Saxon Mercia and is mentioned in the Anglo-Saxon Chronicle. For five weeks in 1013 Gainsborough was the capital of England and Denmark under Swyn Forkbeard and his son Cnut (Canute). Cnut's alleged attempt to turn back the tide may have been the tidal bore on the Trent. The 1086 Domesday Book records that Gainsborough was a community of tenants of Geoffrey de Guerche. A weekly market was granted by King John in 1204. Gainsborough Old Hall was built between 1460 and 1480 and is one of the best-preserved manor houses in Britain. King Richard III stayed there in 1483 and King Henry VIII in 1541. Gainsborough supported the King in the English Civil War and there were battles there and at Winceby. Parliamentary forces captured Gainsborough on 20th July 1643, but it was immediately besieged by the Royalists and forced to surrender after three days. It was captured again by Parliament on 18th December 1643, but its force had to withdraw in March 1644, having razed the town's defences. The first church recorded at Gainsborough was in 1180. The medieval Church of All Saints was demolished in 1736, less the west tower, and replaced by a new parish church completed in 1748. As the town's population increased in the 19th century, a second church, Holy Trinity, opened in 1843 (closed 1971), followed by St John the Divine Church in 1882 (closed 2002) and St George's Church in the 1950s. It has been claimed that some of the Mayflower Pilgrims worshipped in secret at the Old Hall before sailing for Holland to find religious freedom in 1609 but there is no evidence for this. However, a congregation that met in the town developed into the Baptists. The John Robinson Memorial Church was dedicated in 1897, named in honour of John Robinson (1576–1625), pastor of the Pilgrim Fathers. John Wesley preached in Gainsborough several times between 1759 and 1790 and the town's first Methodist chapel opened in 1788. It is believed that Gainsborough is the fictional town of St Ogg's in George Eliot's *The Mill on the Floss*. Amongst the famous people associated with the town are two actors who were born there:

- Dame Agnes Sybil Thorndike, Lady Casson CH DBE (1882–1976) toured internationally in Shakespearean productions, often appearing with her husband, Lewis Casson. George Bernard Shaw wrote *Saint Joan* specially for her.
- John Alderton (born 1940) is best known for his roles in *Upstairs, Downstairs* and *Please Sir!* He often starred alongside his wife, Pauline Collins.

were living at Rectory Terrace, South Gosforth, Northumberland. Helena's death was registered at Castle Ward, Northumberland. Daniel married Elizabeth Carrick (born 1861), born at Greenwich, Kent, in 1892 at Sunderland, Durham. They were living at Ashburton Crescent, Gosforth, Northumberland in 1896. By 1901 Daniel was manager of an India rubber works at Whitley, Northumberland and they were living there at 5 Windsor Court. He was living at 17 Brandling Park, Newcastle upon Tyne at the time of his death at Victoria Nursing Home, 2 Victoria Square, Newcastle upon Tyne. In addition to Helena Emily Anderson, Daniel had eight other children from his two marriages:

- Daniel William Frederic Anderson (born 1869), registered at Newcastle upon Tyne.

- Amy Alice Anderson (1871–1929) married William Edward Goddard (25th August 1867–15th July 1943), born at Wallsend, Northumberland, on 4th June 1889. He was an India rubber agent in 1891, when they were living at 9 Ashburton Road, Coxlodge, South Gosforth, Northumberland. By 1901 they had moved to 20 North Terrace, Newcastle upon Tyne, next door to his widowed father. By 1911 he was an agent for a leather and India rubber manufacturer and they had moved to 14 North Terrace. They were living at 54 Jesmond Road, Newcastle upon Tyne in 1929. William was living at 44 Regent Road, Gosforth, Northumberland in 1939. He was living at Rose Farm, New Ridley Road, Stocksfield, Northumberland at the time of his death at the Emergency Hospital, Ponteland, Northumberland. They had three children, two of whom died very young. The surviving child, Amy Hope Goddard (1892–1966), married George Anderson in 1911. They had four children – John G Anderson 1911, Doreen HK Anderson 1917, Mary P Anderson 1920 and Sheila Anderson 1922.
- Gillespie George Anderson (born 1873) married Alice Amy Downing (20th July 1879–1970), born at Newburn, Northumberland, in 1910. He was a photographer in 1911, when they were living at 37 Chaddock Street, Preston, Lancashire. Gillespie enlisted on 3rd October 1915 and served in the South Wales Borderers and South Lancashire Regiment. He transferred to the Royal Flying Corps as an airman 3 on 15th December 1917 and the Royal Air Force (115155) on 1st April 1918 as a photographer. He was described as 5′ 6¾″ tall, with light brown hair, grey eyes, fresh complexion and his religious denomination was Church of England. His RAF records show his civilian occupation as draughtsman and his birth as 1878 or 9th March 1882. He was posted to Egypt on 5th November 1918. Gillespie transferred to the RAF G Reserve on 19th March 1919. He was deemed to have been discharged on 30th April 1920, when his address was 36 Acomb Street, Moss Side, Manchester. However, in the meantime he re-enlisted (336512) on 29th August 1919 as airman 2 at the Recruit Centre, Henlow for four years regular service followed by eight years on the reserve. His wife was living at 20 Normanton Terrace, Newcastle upon Tyne and later at 134 Atkinson Road, Benwell. He reclassified as leading aircraftsman photographer on 30th August and joined the Depot at Henlow on 3rd September. He was posted to India on 27th September and joined No.99 Squadron, which was flying patrols over the North West Frontier. He was posted to No.114 Squadron at Quetta on 18th January 1920 and the unit was renumbered No.25 Squadron in April. Appointed acting corporal unpaid 17th February–7th September 1920. He was posted to the RAF School India on 9th September and to No.1 Squadron on 31st March 1921, which moved to Iraq in May. However, Gillespie was posted to the RAF School India and was detached to Bangalore on 20th April. On 31st July 1921 he was admitted to Hospital at Barian. Promoted corporal on 1st July 1922 and moved to Bombay for the Home Establishment on 29th October. He was granted leave 6th December 1922–3rd January 1923 and joined the School of

Photography, Farnborough on 10th February. He was granted annual leave 17th March–13th April and was awarded the Good Conduct Badge on 18th June, effective from 29th August 1919. He was posted to the Depot on 31st July, was granted leave from 1st August and transferred to the RAF Reserve on 28th August 1923. Gillespie was discharged from the Reserve on 28th August 1931, when his address was 28 Gainsborough Grove, Newcastle upon Tyne.

- Alfred Gustav Anderson (1875–1937). His death was registered at Greenwich, Kent.
- Ethel Jane Anderson (1877–1st February 1896), born at Gosforth, Northumberland, and died unmarried at Roermond, Limburg, Netherlands.
- Lewis Anderson (born 1880) was an accountant and clerk working for a removal and carting contractor and horse dealer in 1911, boarding with the family of John and Edith Mackie at 205 South Eldon Street, South Shields, Co Durham.
- John Douglas Anderson (4th December 1895–1970) was boarding at Felstead School, Dunmow, Essex in 1911. He joined the Royal Navy as a midshipman on 17th May 1917 and served on HMS *Excellent* and *Dido*. He was granted a Watchkeeping Certificate on 3rd October 1918 and was appointed temporary acting sub lieutenant on 23rd March 1919. He was demobilised on 18th April 1919. John married Rosemary Daphne Truscott (14th October 1907–November 1999), birth registered at Atcham, Shropshire, in 1931 at Oxford. He was an assistant rivers purification inspector with Thames Conservatory in 1939, when they were living at Oak Cottage, Oak Street, Cirencester, Gloucestershire. At the time of the 1939 Register he was an Air Raid Precautions fire services section officer and she was also a member of the ARP and British Red Cross. His death was registered at Cirencester, Gloucestershire and hers at Hastings and Rother, East Sussex.
- Mary Dorothea Anderson (born 1896) married Fenwick Bowman in 1926. She is believed to have died in 1955 at Cape Province, South Africa.

Harry was a member of 1st Cadet Battalion, King's Royal Rifle Corps based at 2 Finsbury Square (42 Sun Street from 1904), London from 21st July 1897 (1401) and was promoted sergeant in 1899. His father was sergeant major and all his brothers also joined the Cadet Battalion as they became old enough. Harry enlisted in the City of London Imperial Volunteers on 1st January 1900 (851). He departed from Southampton, Hampshire later in the month and arrived in South Africa in mid-February. He served in the Second Boer War with the CIV until October 1900 and took part in the Battle of Diamond Hill 11th-12th June. When the unit was ordered home in October, Harry remained in South Africa and transferred to the South African Light Horse. Winston Churchill had served previously in the unit. In June 1901 Harry transferred to the South African Constabulary, a mounted unit raised by Major General Robert Baden-Powell. However, he was an inexperienced horseman and as a result of being thrown from his horse, was invalided home in

October 1901. He rejoined the Cadet Battalion as a colour sergeant and was later an instructor of musketry. Harry served in cadet units and the London Rifle Brigade until 1909.

Harry, on the left, with three of his brothers – Arthur second left, David third left and John on the right.

Harry was commissioned as a temporary captain on 4th April 1915 and joined 9th King's Own Yorkshire Light Infantry. The Battalion was inspected by King George V as it marched through Windsor, whilst being billeted at Maidenhead, Berkshire. The Battalion moved frequently and was based successively at Pontefract, Berkhamsted, Tring, Maidenhead, Tring again and Witley. Harry was granted compassionate leave following the death of his infant son on 24th July 1915. He proceeded with the Battalion on operational service from Folkestone to Boulogne, France on 11th September aboard SS *St Seviol*. **Awarded the MC for his actions near Hill 70, Loos on 26th September 1915, LG 14th January 1916. Mentioned in Field Marshal Sir John French's Despatch dated 30th November 1915, LG 1st January 1916.**

Harry was appointed temporary major on 27th October. He was on parade with the Battalion when it was inspected by the King next day. During the inspection the King's horse threw him and he broke his pelvis. Harry commanded the Battalion 18th-31st January 1916, while the CO was on leave. He contracted epididymitis and was admitted to a field hospital on 20th April, before being evacuated to Britain aboard HMHS *St Patrick* from Rouen on 24th April, arriving at Southampton, Hampshire the following day. A medical board on 2nd May sent him on six weeks sick leave. He was posted to 11th (Reserve) Battalion (8th Training Reserve Battalion from 1st September), Rugeley, Cannock Chase, Staffordshire on 5th July

HMHS *St Patrick* (2,531 tons) was built by John Brown & Co in Scotland in 1906 for the Fishguard & Rosslare Railways and Harbours Co as a ferry between Fishguard and Rosslare. With her sister ships, *St David* and *St Andrew*, she was one of the first five ships to be requisitioned during the Great War and was converted to a hospital ship with a capacity of 146 berths and twenty-eight cots. She remained in service until January 1919. In April 1929 she was destroyed by fire while moored at Fishguard and was sold for scrap the following year. Her engines were transferred to the *St Andrew*.

The Great War camps on Cannock Chase accommodated up to 40,000 men and more than 500,000 soldiers trained there.

on light duties. Harry rejoined 9th King's Own Yorkshire Light Infantry at Blaireville, France on 17th April 1917. The Battalion was in action on 1st October at Polygon Wood, east of Ypres, Belgium and Harry was appointed acting lieutenant colonel 19th-31st October while temporarily in command. Promoted major on 19th October with seniority from 27th October 1915. He was temporarily in command again on 31st December while the CO was on a course.

Awarded the DSO for his actions on 23rd March 1918 on the Longavesnes–Péronne road while second-in-command. Two heavy enemy attacks made under cover of mist were repulsed during which a hostile machine gun crew got to within fifty yards of the British line. Being short of machine gunners due to casualties, Greenwood dashed out with a lance corporal from 1st East Yorkshires and 38787 Private Harold Wright of his own Battalion and forced an enemy officer and two soldiers hiding in a hollow to carry back the machine gun. They were under intense fire throughout. The machine gun (there were two according to the regimental history but one in the citation) was then put to use on the enemy with great effect, LG 26th July 1918. Private Wright was awarded the MM. The DSO was presented by the King at Buckingham Palace on 10th July.

Harry was appointed acting CO 26th April–17th May, when the CO was wounded. As acting CO he presented the MM ribbon to fourteen men of the Battalion, including Private Harold Wright, on 3rd May at Lederzeele. The Battalion moved south to the Champagne and Aisne regions in early May. Harry was appointed acting CO 28th May–8th June when the CO was wounded again. Harry also commanded the Brigade temporarily while the commander was on leave 5th-8th June. On 28th July he assumed command of the Battalion as an acting lieutenant colonel. **Awarded a Bar to the DSO for his actions near Battery Valley, Le Sars**

The Distinguished Service Order, seen here with a Bar, was instituted by Queen Victoria on 6th September 1886 and is usually awarded to majors (or equivalent) or above. In the past it was occasionally awarded to valorous junior officers. There were 8,981 awards in the Great War. The order recognised meritorious or distinguished service in war. Prior to 1943 the order could only be given to someone mentioned in despatches. Since 1993 the order has been restricted solely to distinguished service and not for gallantry. Although the DSO is now open to all ranks, it has yet to be awarded to a non-commissioned rank.

Harry Greenwood leaving Buckingham Palace after being presented with the DSO by the King on 10th July 1918. On the left are his sister Kitty and daughter Molly and, on the right, his wife, Helena (Cynthia List).

on 23rd/24th August 1918. Although ill he refused to leave the Battalion. During the action he was wounded by friendly fire when several shells from heavy batteries fell among his men as they approached the Grandcourt–Thiepval road, after clearing some dugouts in Battery Valley. He was thrown off his feet against a post, resulting in internal injuries. Notwithstanding this, he led the first wave of the attack and on reaching the second objective on the Grandcourt–Thiepval road he reorganised his and another battalion, beat off two counterattacks and held the ground until relieved. Next day when the advance was held up by very heavy machine-gun fire, he made a daring reconnaissance and succeeded in getting around a flank. He remained at his post for four more days before handing over the Battalion to Major Walsh on 29th August. Only then did he go to a dressing station, LG 2nd December 1918.

Harry returned to the Battalion on 15th October. **Awarded the VC for his actions at Ovillers, France on 23rd/24th October 1918, LG 26th December 1918. Mentioned in Field Marshal Sir Douglas Haig's Despatch dated 8th November 1918, LG 28th December 1918.** He was appointed temporary commander of 64th Brigade, while Brigadier General CV Edwards DSO was on leave 14th December 1918–4th January 1919. Harry was demobilised from the Officers' Dispersal Unit, London on 12th March 1919. The VC and DSO Bar were presented by the King in the quadrangle at Buckingham Palace on 8th May.

Harry was made a life member of West Essex Golf Club, Chingford, Essex on 2nd May 1919. He attended the VC Garden Party at Buckingham Palace on 26th June 1920 and was one of the Honour Guard at the burial of the Unknown Warrior at Westminster Abbey on 11th November 1920.

Harry returned to his old employment with Robert Williams' mining company and went to Africa as commercial manager of the Benguela Railway in Portuguese West Africa (now Angola) in the early 1920s. In about 1924 he became resident director at Lobito Bay, Angola of the Williams Group companies, including the Benguela Railway Co, Benguela Estates Ltd, Angola Estates Ltd and Zambesia Exploring Co. He remained there for about ten years and then returned to work at head office in Gresham Street, London. In the 1939 Register he was described as a company director and publicity manager.

The Benguela Railway (Caminho de Ferro de Benguela) runs through Angola from west to east, terminating at Lobito on the Atlantic. It is the largest and most important railway in the country, connecting with the Democratic Republic of the Congo and the Cape to Cairo Railway. The line roughly follows old trade routes. The Portuguese government initiated construction in 1899 in order to gain access to the central Angolan plateau and the mineral wealth of the Congo. A concession, running for ninety-nine years, was granted to Sir Robert Williams on 28th November 1902. His Benguela Railway Co took over construction on 1st March 1903. By 1914, 500 kilometres had been completed but construction halted during the Great War and did not recommence until 1920. The border with the Belgian Congo was reached in 1929. The Benguela Railway was the shortest way to transport mineral riches from the Congo to Europe. Its operational peak was in 1973 when it transported 3.3 million tons of cargo, generated $30M in freight revenue and had 14,000 employees. Steam locomotives outnumbered diesels as late as 1987. Angola gained independence from Portugal in 1975. In the Angolan Civil War the railway was heavily damaged and fell into disuse. By 1992, only 340 kilometres of the railway remained operational. When the concession expired in 2001, and ownership of the railway passed to the Angolan government, only thirty-four kilometres remained in service. The railway was reconstructed between 2006 and 2014 by the China Railway Construction Co, which employed 100,000 Angolans.

Helena and her daughters arrived at Southampton on 25th March 1930 from Lobito, Angola via Las Palmas aboard SS *Adolf Woermann*, giving their address as 92 Queens Gate, Kensington. The family was living at Dulwich Village, London c.1931, at 77 Holme Park Road, Wimbledon Park, overlooking Wimbledon Golf Course, from 1935 and at West Winds, South Cliff Avenue, Bexhill-on-Sea, Sussex by 1939.

Harry served in the Army Officers Emergency Reserve from 15th February 1940. He received a Regular Army Emergency Commission as a lieutenant in the Pioneer Corps on 4th July (141511). On 5th October he was appointed war substantive major and temporary lieutenant colonel to command No.12 Pioneer Corps Training Centre, Dingle Vale School, Liverpool. The school received a direct hit during an air raid on 7th May 1941 and the Centre moved to Pheasey Farm Estate, Great Barr, Birmingham, Warwickshire. It moved again in June 1942 to Oldham, Lancashire, where it remained until July 1943. It then moved to Prestatyn, North Wales to the LMS holiday camp. Eventually all Pioneer Depots were merged under Harry's command as No.12 Pioneer Corps Holding and Training Unit of 7,000 men. During his command the

Dingle Vale School, where No.12 Pioneer Corps Training Centre was based in 1941, was rebuilt after being damaged in an air raid. The School was later attended by Beatles drummer, Ringo Starr, and is now Shorefields Technology College.

The seafront camp, built as a joint venture between Thomas Cook and the LMS railway, opened on 24th June 1939. Designed as an upmarket family holiday centre it featured modernistic architecture, especially the Hamlyn Tower. There were 900 chalets, accommodating up to 2,000 guests, a ballroom, gymnasium, massive dining hall, lounges, swimming pool and lido and numerous sports facilities. On 3rd September 1939, only a few months after opening, a Royal Signals subaltern arrived to break the news that the site was being requisitioned as No.2 Signal Training Centre. By the late 1960s there was a downturn in business as customers sought more freedom from regimented entertainment and mealtimes. Some chalets were converted to self-catering and static caravans were installed. The situation worsened in 1971, when Pontins opened a new self-catering camp a mile away. The camp was sold to Pontins in 1975 and was renamed Tower Beach. Brand new chalet blocks were built, more old chalets were converted, the caravan park was expanded and an area was created for touring caravans and tents. An indoor pool was built and the outdoor pool was filled in. However, the camp closed in 1984 and was derelict for seventeen years, during which it was used for police riot training and TV/movie filming. It was demolished in 2001 and the land is a housing estate known as Tower Gardens.

unit trained 124,000 recruits, including friendly aliens, conscientious objectors and other non-combatants.

Greenwood offered to take a unit over to France in June 1944 but was refused due to his age. **Appointed Officer of the Order of the British Empire (Military Division) for his work in reorganising the Pioneer Corps, LG 8th June 1944.** Promoted acting colonel on 6th July 1945 and appointed temporary colonel 6th January–3rd October 1946. He relinquished command of No.12 Pioneer Corps Holding and Training Unit on 3rd June 1946. On 7th June he suffered severe abdominal pain and was rushed to Nelson Memorial Hospital, Merton, Surrey, where an intestinal obstruction was operated on the same day. This was followed by a second operation on 6th July for carcinoma of the sigmoid colon (bowel cancer) and a tumour was removed. Harry was discharged from hospital on 30th July. He relinquished his commission and was granted the rank of honorary colonel on 16th May 1947.

Harry Greenwood during the Second World War. (*Cynthia List*)

Harry was invited to attend the Victory Day Celebration Dinner in June 1946 but was unable due to being in hospital. He died at his home at 77 Home Park

The Most Excellent Order of the British Empire was established on 4th June 1917 by King George V to honour those who served in non-combat roles during the Great War. The Order comprises five classes, both civil and military. The two most senior classes make the recipient a knight/dame. The five classes are:

Knight/Dame Grand Cross (GBE).
Knight/Dame Commander (K/DBE).
Commander (CBE).
Officer (OBE).
Member (MBE).

The British sovereign is the supreme head of the order and appoints all other officers on the advice of the UK and some Commonwealth governments. The second most senior officer is the Grand Master and Prince Philip was the last incumbent until his death in 2021. The order is limited to 300 Knights/Dames Grand Cross, 845 Knights/Dames Commander and 8,960 Commanders. There are no limits to the number of the fourth and fifth classes, but no more than 858 Officers and 1,464 Members may be appointed each year. Foreign appointees, as honorary members, do not contribute to the numbers. Although intended to recognise meritorious service, the order was also awarded for gallantry. From 1958, these awards were designated Commander, Officer or Member of the Order of the British Empire for Gallantry. This was replaced in 1974 by the Queen's Gallantry Medal.

Road, Wimbledon Park, London on 5th May 1948 after a long illness. He is buried in Putney Vale Cemetery, London (Block N, Grave 71 – C). His will, dated 11th November 1947, appointed as executors the Standard Trust Bank of South Africa Ltd. His estate was bequeathed to his wife, gross £20,722/2/3, net £18,734/3/7. Probate was granted on 23rd August 1948. Harry is commemorated in a number of other places:

- Greenwood Road, Putney Vale Cemetery, named in 1997 by Wandsworth Borough Council. Six other roads and paths in the Cemetery are named after other VCs buried, cremated or commemorated there:

77 Home Park Road, Wimbledon Park, where Harry died.

Harry Greenwood's grave in Putney Vale Cemetery. (*Memorials to Valour*)

Alexander Way – Ernest Alexander VC CB CMG
Boulter's Path – William Boulter VC
Hayward Avenue – Reginald Hayward VC MC & Bar
Paton's Path – George Paton VC MC
Richard's Way – Alfred Richards VC
Schofield Road – Harry Schofield VC.

Greenwood Road in Putney Vale Cemetery. (*Memorials to Valour*)

- A Heritage Blue Plaque was unveiled at Victoria Barracks, Windsor where Harry was born, by the Mayor of the Royal Borough of Windsor and Maidenhead, Councillor Mrs Ady Sheldon, on 8th April 1997. Colonel Pat Porteous VC attended.

The Blue Plaque at Victoria Barracks, Windsor. (*Memorials to Valour*)

- A Remembrance Garden in Kidwells Park, Maidenhead opened in June 2015. A display board unveiled on 25th August 2015 by the Mayor of Windsor & Maidenhead, Councillor Eileen Quick, gives information about the part played by the town during the Great War and details of VC recipients connected with the Royal Borough – Oliver Brooks, Charles Doughty-Wylie, William Thomas Forshaw, Harry Greenwood, Francis Grenfell, Thomas Tannatt Pryce and Ferdinand West.
- A VC Memorial Garden at Bachelor's Acre, Windsor was opened by the Deputy Mayor of the Royal Borough of Windsor & Maidenhead, Councillor John Lenton, on 25th November 2016. Seven VCs with connections to the Royal Borough are named, including Harry Greenwood, whose life story is on Panel 2. There is also information about the other six VCs – Oliver Brooks, Charles Doughty-Wylie, William Thomas Forshaw, Francis Grenfell, Thomas Tannatt Pryce and Ferdinand West.
- A Department for Communities and Local Government commemorative paving stone was dedicated at Bachelors Acre Memorial Garden, Windsor on 23rd October 2018.
- Memorial outside Wandsworth Town Hall, London to commemorate recipients of the George Cross and Victoria Cross who were born, lived, studied, worked or died in the borough of Wandsworth. Those GCs named are James Scully and Cyril Martin,

The VC and GC memorial outside Wandsworth Town Hall. (*Memorials to Valour*)

and the VCs are Ernest Alexander, George Cairns, Michael Campion, James Collis, Matthew Dixon, George Dorrell, Edward Foster, Harry Greenwood, Reginald Haine, Frederick Johnson, Herbert Jones, Arthur Lascelles, Brian Lawrence, Jack Mantle, John Norwood, Alfred Richards, Harry Schofield and John Sinnott.

The Castle of Good Hope, Cape Town.

- Named on a bronze memorial plaque in a set of eleven country-related plaques honouring the 175 men from overseas who were awarded the VC during the Great War. The plaques were unveiled by Senior Minister of State in the Foreign & Commonwealth Office and Minister for Faith and Communities, Baroness Warsi at a reception at Lancaster House, London on 26th June 2014. The reception was attended by the Duke of Kent and relatives of the VCs. The South African plaque is mounted at the Castle of Good Hope, Cape Town.

After her husband's death, Helena went to live in Canada with her daughter, Cynthia. She died at 404 Jerusalem Road, Cohasset, Norfolk Co, Massachusetts, USA.

In addition to the VC, DSO & Bar, OBE and MC he was awarded the Queen's South Africa Medal 1899–1902 with four clasps (Cape Colony, Orange Free State, Johannesburg & Diamond Hill), King's South Africa Medal 1901–02 with two clasps (South Africa 1901 & South Africa 1902),

The Queen's South Africa Medal was instituted in 1900 for military personnel, civilian officials and war correspondents, who served during the Second Boer War from 11th October 1899 to 31st May 1902. Approximately 178,000 were awarded. There are twenty-six clasps.

The Defence Medal was instituted in May 1945 for non-operational military and certain types of civilian war service (Home Guard, Civil Defence, Royal Observer Corps, Fire Service and other approved civilian services) from 3rd September 1939 to 8th May 1945 and for the Pacific Theatre until 2nd September 1945. In the United Kingdom military personnel in headquarters, training units and airfields were eligible for the award. Qualifying service varied. In the United Kingdom the requirement was three years or three months in a Mine and Bomb Disposal Unit. In a non-operational area, not subjected to air attack and not closely threatened, the requirement was one year's service overseas outside the individual's country of residence. In a non-operational area subjected to air attack or closely threatened, the requirement was six months.

1914–15 Star, British War Medal 1914–20, Victory Medal 1914–19 with Mentioned-in-Despatches Oakleaf, Defence Medal, War Medal 1939–45, George V Silver Jubilee Medal 1935 and George VI Coronation Medal 1937. He wore the ribbon of the King George V Jubilee Medal 1935 while serving in the Pioneer Corps, but it has not been proven that he was entitled to wear it. His service in the Pioneer Corps entitled him to the Defence Medal and the War Medal 1939–45 but he appears not to have claimed them. The medals passed to his wife and then his daughter, Cynthia, and were held in safe custody in a US bank. Cynthia eventually decided that they should go to his old Regiment and were handed over at a ceremony in Doncaster, Yorkshire on 17th July 2002. His granddaughter, Mrs. Anne Meagher, travelled from Washington State, USA for the ceremony. The VC is held by the King's Own Yorkshire Light Infantry Regimental Museum, Museum & Art Gallery, Chequer Road, Doncaster, South Yorkshire.

The King's Own Yorkshire Light Infantry Regimental Museum in Doncaster.

LIEUTENANT FREDERICK WILLIAM HEDGES
The Bedfordshire Regiment, attached 6th Battalion, The Northamptonshire Regiment

Frederick Hedges was born on 6th June (also seen as 22nd November) 1896 at the Women's & Children's Hospital, Umballa (now Ambala), India. He was known as Fred, Freddie and Bill. His father, Henry George Hedges (c.November 1857–1931), born at sea in the Bay of Bengal, India, was a draper's assistant. He enlisted at Hounslow as a boy bandsman in 12th Royal Lancers on 20th February 1872 (1307), aged fourteen years and three months. He was described as 4′ 9″ tall, with fresh complexion, grey eyes and brown hair. He was treated for a sprain 9th October–13th November 1872, congestion of the liver 12th-18th February 1873 and rheumatism 5th-11th February 1874. He was appointed trumpeter on 23rd March 1874 and gained the Second Class Certificate of Army Education on 8th September. Henry was treated for boils 20th-26th August 1876. He was awarded Good Conduct Pay of 1d per day on 20th November and embarked for India on 28th December, arriving on 1st February 1877. He was treated for

Umballa (now Ambala) in Haryana, India is close to the border with Punjab state, about 200 kms north of New Dehli. Ambala is divided into two areas – Ambala Cantonment, known as Ambala Cantt, and Ambala City. Ambala Cantt is mentioned in the novel *Kim* by Rudyard Kipling. In a battle in 1709 the Sikhs captured Ambala from the Mughals. The Army Cantonment was established in 1843 after the British were forced to leave Karnal Cantonment following the malaria epidemic of 1841–42. Ambala was given district status in 1847. In November 1949 the assassin of Mahatma Gandhi, Nathuram Godse, was hanged at Ambala Central Jail. The Indian Army and Air Force have a large presence there. The air base is one of the oldest and largest that were inherited from the British at independence. Spitfires and Harvards based there took part in the Indo-Pakistan War 1947–48. The airbase was attacked in 1965 by the Pakistan Air Force. Harold Adrian Russell 'Kim' Philby (1912–88), the British double agent and member of the Cambridge Five, was born in Ambala. He was nicknamed Kim after the boy spy in Kipling's novel.

febricula 23rd May–23rd July and 31st July–27th August 1877. On 13th September he was promoted lance corporal. He was treated for fever 7th-19th September 1878, gonorrhoea 21st July–3rd August 1879, febricula 5th-9th October 1879, hepatitis 11th-29th February 1880 and gonorrhoea 4th-14th July. He was awarded Good Conduct Pay of 2d per day on 20th November. Promoted corporal 2nd July 1882, lance sergeant 28th July 1883 and sergeant 13th February 1885. He was awarded Good Conduct Pay of 3d per day on 20th November and was treated for rheumatism 19th-25th January 1886. Henry departed India for Britain aboard HMS *Malabar* on 29th October 1887 and was based at Colchester on 25th November. He gained

HMS *Euphrates*, an iron-hulled troopship was built by Laird Brothers of Birkenhead and launched on the Mersey on 24th November 1866, the fourth and last Royal Navy ship of that name. A single screw gave a speed of fourteen knots and she was also barque-rigged. Her top speed was reduced to eleven knots in 1873 when a more efficient, but less powerful, engine was installed. She carried three 4 Pounder guns. The hull was painted white to help reflect heat. *Euphrates* could transport up to 1,200 passengers and operated between Portsmouth and Bombay. A return trip via the Suez Canal took about seventy days. She was involved in a number of accidents:

- 28th February 1870 – collision with the British merchant ship *Bates Family* at Bombay.
- 19th December 1883 – ran aground off Gibraltar and was refloated next day.
- 6th February 1892 – collision with the German steamer *Gutenfels* in the Suez Canal.

Euphrates was sold to I Cohen in Portsmouth on 23rd November 1894 and was resold to Henry Castle & Son for breaking the following August.

St John's Church, St John's Hill, Cleveland Town, Bangalore Cantonment, where Frederick's parents married in 1882. The church traces its origin to a small chapel and school in Haines Road. The Reverend R Posnett, Assistant Chaplain, East India Company, played a significant role in establishing the church and school. At the time the Bangalore Cantonment was populated mainly by pensioned officers and employees of the East Indian Company, Europeans and their native wives and Eurasian children. These children were not allowed to enrol in the European schools and Posnett recognised the need to provide a church and school for these residents. A single room on Haines Road served as a school during the day, a library during the afternoon and a church on Sundays. This building was built with funds raised by officers of the East India Company. Services were attended by up to 115 people and the school educated almost seventy pupils, mainly girls. However, a larger building was needed and Posnett raised the funds by appealing to different congregations in India and abroad. A plot of land beside the Roman Catholic chapel (later St Francis Xavier's Cathedral) was purchased in October 1853. The church, schools and library were designed with matching Gothic architecture. The schools, one each for boys and girls, and library were inaugurated on 28th May 1854. By 1914 St John's School had 135 children. Today it is St John's High School. St John's Church was consecrated on 12th April 1858 by the Bishop of Madras. The tower was raised at the end of 1858 and the building was extended in 1895–96. In front of the church is a memorial to members of the congregation who lost their lives in the Great war. Officers of the Madras Regiment offer their tributes at the memorial every 11th November.

First Class Education on 8th October 1888 and was appointed bandmaster on 1st November 1890, transferring to 18th Hussars the same day. He served in India from 28th January 1891, travelling there aboard HMS *Euphrates*. He was treated for influenza 3rd-26th February 1892, a sore throat 29th December–12th January 1893 and rheumatism 20th-26th August 1895. Henry returned to Britain aboard SS *Nubia* on 14th October 1897 and was discharged on 16th November from Gosport, Hampshire after giving three months' notice.

Henry married Harriet Eliza née Loader (7th June 1865–1st November 1950), born at Bangalore (now Bengaluru), India, on 28th November 1882 at St John's, Bangalore. Her first language was Tamil. They were living at 16 Lydford Terrace, Linkfield Road, Isleworth, Middlesex in 1899 and at 14 Linkfield Road in 1900, by when he was an insurance agent for the Wesleyan & General Assurance Society. They had moved to Girgeh, 24 Lansdowne Road, Heston, Hounslow, Middlesex by 1901, when he was an assurance superintendent. They were still there in 1911. She was living with her son, Bertie, at 233 High Street, Hounslow, Middlesex in 1939 and subsequently died there. Frederick had eight siblings:

- Emily Olive Edith Hedges (15th October 1883–31st May 1958), born at Bangalore, India, married Arthur William Leetch (11th March 1887–26th February 1973), born in India, on 18th March 1916 at Gunnersbury Register Office, Brentford, Middlesex. His address at the time was the Liberal Club, Wellingborough and he was the son of William Leetch, a former lieutenant and quartermaster. He is believed to have served as plain Arthur Leetch as a sergeant in 20th King's Royal Rifle Corps (C/9668), enlisting on 29th November 1915 and went to France on 28th March 1916. Medical board forms in his service record indicate that he had served previously, enlisting c.April 1903. He was commissioned in 11th Middlesex on 15th April 1917 but fell ill and left his unit on 4th May, suffering from subacute rheumatism originating on service in Nigeria in 1913. He embarked at Boulogne aboard HMHS *St Denis* and disembarked at Dover on 12th May. Medical boards at Bath War Hospital on 6th June and 6th July found him unfit for General Service for two months and Home Service for one month but fit for light duties. He was granted leave to 27th July. A medical board at Chatham on 23rd August found him unfit for General Service permanently, Garrison and Home Service for five months but fit for light duties without marching. He was serving with 2nd Training Battalion, RAMC Depot, Blackpool by November 1917 and was relieved of duty there and sent to 2nd Western General Hospital, Manchester on 13th December. A medical board there on 22nd December found him unfit for any service for an uncertain period. A medical board at Eastbourne on 28th February 1918 found him unfit for General Service for six months, Home Service for four months but fit for light duties C2. From 20th March 1918 he served with the Labour Corps Office, Nottingham on probation. Promoted lieutenant on 15th October. Medical boards on 30th July 1918, 24th October and 30th January 1919 found he was unfit for Category A permanently, Category B & C for three months but fit for Category CII and he continued at the Labour Corps Office. A medical board at Nottingham on 5th May found him fit for Category A. he last appears in the Army List in September 1920. In 1939 Arthur was an unemployed clerk living with Emily at 14 River Court, Surbiton, Surrey. They both died at 130 Lower Richmond Road, Putney, Surrey. When he died, Arthur was described as a retired works superintendent.

- Harriet Ethel Hedges (22nd December 1884–5th March 1965) was a schoolteacher when she married Arthur Charles Patrick Handover (17th March 1885–23rd July 1941), also a schoolteacher born at 10 Elcom Street, Paddington, London, on 26th December 1909 at Holy Trinity, Hounslow, Middlesex. They were both living at Lansdowne Road, Hounslow. In 1911 he was an elementary schoolteacher teaching maths at Isleworth County School, Middlesex. Arthur enlisted in the Norfolk Regiment on 29th July 1916 (38125) and served as an acting sergeant. He was discharged on 9th September 1918 no longer physically fit for war service. They were living at 54 Clare Road, Hounslow, Middlesex at the time. They were living at 14 Alexandra Gardens, Hounslow, Middlesex in 1939 by when he was a secondary schoolmaster. He died at West Middlesex Hospital, Isleworth, Middlesex. She was living at St Cross, Cedar Road, Hook Heath, Woking, Surrey from January 1957 until the time of her death at Whitehanger Nursing Home, Haslemere, Surrey. The had two children:

  - Roy Arthur Handover (22nd April 1913–26th February 1986), born at 54 Clare Road, Hounslow, was an insurance clerk in 1939, living with his parents. He married Kathleen Frances Watkins (16th May 1914–6th February 1980), born at 30 Reighton Road, Upper Clapton, London, on 10th February 1940 at Edmonton, Middlesex. Roy was a chartered secretary in 1965. They lived at St Cross, Cedar Road, Hook Heath, Woking, Surrey until 1969. Kathleen died at West Brow, Telham Lane, Battle, East Sussex. He was living at 1 Norman Close, Marley Lane, Battle at the time of his death at Conquest Hospital, Hastings and East Rother, Sussex. They had three children – John Handover (1942–2004), Clare Handover 1947 and Frances Handover 1957.
  - Brian Ronald Handover (27th March 1921–1927) born and died at Brentford.
- Constance Amy Hedges (11th August 1886–12th July 1973) was a cashier in a provisions department in 1911, living with her parents. She married John Charles Charrington (c.1890–7th October 1917), a provisions dealer born at St Arvans, Monmouthshire, on 24th March 1913 at Heston Parish Church, Middlesex. He was living at 22 Corporation Road, Newport, Monmouthshire and she at Church Road, Heston at the time. John was a grocery shop assistant living with his father at Gatlas House, Caerleon, Monmouthshire in 1911. He served during the Great War as a driver in the Royal Engineers (161384) with the Cable Section and was killed in action in Mesopotamia (Basra Memorial, Iraq). Constance was living at 4a Oliver Grove, Croydon, Surrey in 1939 and was subletting part of the property to William McGregor Smith, a travelling coal salesman (5th November 1878–9th June 1957). She never remarried and was living at 8 Bedford Park, Croydon at the time of her death at Queen's Hospital, Croydon.
- Ernest Henry Hedges (8th January 1888–11th June 1951), born at 31 Elthiron Road, Fulham, London, was a printer/compositor in 1911, living with his

The Basra Memorial, where John Charles Charrington is commemorated, is located near Zubayr, Iraq. It commemorates 40,605 Commonwealth forces, mainly Indians, who died during the Mesopotamia Campaign 1914–21 and whose graves are not known. Originally located eight kilometres north of Basra, on the main quay of the naval dockyard at Maqil on the Shatt-al-Arab River, it was moved by presidential decree southwest in 1997 to a battleground from the more recent Gulf War of 1990–91. The memorial has suffered deliberate sabotage, with some items being removed including the Cross of Remembrance and the bronze plaques from the Wall of Remembrance. Of the total of those commemorated there, 33,256 are Indian, 7,336 British, eleven Australians, a Canadian and a New Zealander. There are five VCs. Sadly 30,000 Indian other ranks are not named, just their number by regiment. (*CWGC*)

parents. He married Marie Gough (2nd October 1892–1st February 1981), born at Kettering, Northamptonshire, on 14th August 1915 at St Leonard's Church, Heston, Middlesex. She was living at 120 Standard Road, Heston at the time. He was a printer's manager in 1939, when they were living at 24 Charnwood Avenue, Merton, Surrey. They were living at 47 Broughton Avenue, Aylesbury, Buckinghamshire at the time of his death at Tindal General Hospital, Aylesbury. She was still living at 47 Broughton Avenue at the time of her death there.

- Walter Henry Hedges (26th February 1890–22nd August 1947), born at Whitton, Middlesex, was serving as a corporal in the Army in 1917. He married Flora 'Florrie' Georgina Sanders (13th December 1887–27th October 1979), a clerk born at Hounslow, on 3rd August 1917 at Holy Trinity, Hounslow, Middlesex. She was living at The Cottage, Staines Road, Hounslow, Middlesex at the time. He was a clerk in the Civil Service Finance Department in 1939, when they were living at 21 Hibernia Gardens, Hounslow. They were still living there at the time of his death at the Hospital of St John and St Elizabeth, St John's Wood, London. Flora was still living at 21 Hibernia Gardens at the time of her death there. They had a son:
    - Derek Henry Hedges (21st March 1920–1986), born at Brentford, was an engineer's clerk in 1939, living with his parents. He married Florence Louise Clark (27th June 1921–1989) in 1942 at Lewisham, London. She was a clerk in 1939, living with her parents at 48 Layard Road, Bermondsey, London. His death was registered at Lewisham and hers at Bromley, Kent.
- Elsie Maud Hedges (29th April 1892–11th April 1983), born at Bangalore, was baptised on 22nd June 1892 at Umballa, India. She was a parlourmaid for the Bell family at The Old House, Westham, Slough, Buckinghamshire in 1911. She married George Kennedy (10th May 1881–28th February 1931), a chauffeur born at Waringstown, Lurgan, Co Down, Ireland, on 9th April 1912 at St Leonard's Church, Heston, Middlesex. He was living at Church Road, Heston. His death was registered at St George, Hanover Square, London. She was manageress of an off-licence in 1939, living with her mother and brother, Bertie, at 233 High Street, Hounslow, London. Elsie was living at Carlton Dene, 45 Kilburn Park Road, London at the time of her death. Elsie and George had two children:
    - Kathleen Kennedy (3rd October 1915–11th December 2001), birth registered at St George, Hanover Square, married Kenneth John Hume (27th December 1911–20th February 1984), born at Leytonstone, London, in 1937 at Lambeth, London. They met as children in 1925. Kenneth gained a BSc and worked at the National Physical Laboratory at Teddington, London. They were living at 49 Mallard Way, Wembley, Middlesex in 1939, by when he was a chief gauge inspector. He joined de Havilland Aircraft Co Ltd as a metrology superintendent working on the development of the jet engine. This was a reserved occupation during the Second World War, so

The de Havilland Aircraft Co Ltd was established in late 1920 by Geoffrey de Havilland initially at Edgware but later at Hatfield, Hertfordshire. The company was renowned for its innovation and produced many famous aircraft, including the Gipsy Moth in which Amy Johnson flew to Australia in 1930, the wooden WW2 multirole Mosquito and the pioneering passenger airliner the Comet. The company became part of Hawker Siddeley in 1960 and lost its separate identity in 1963. Hawker Siddeley merged into what eventually became BAE Systems. However, the de Havilland name lives on in De Havilland Canada.

he joined the company's Home Guard unit. Later he took up teaching and lecturing and had a number of appointments:

Head of the National College of Horology.

Apprentice training officer, Dowty Group, Cheltenham, Gloucestershire.

Professor of Engineering Metrology, Loughborough College (later University).

UNESCO 1962 to set up the equivalent of the National Physical Laboratory at Durgapur, India.

They lived in India during his time with UNESCO. Kenneth published several books on metrology, including *A History of Engineering Metrology* 1980, which became recognised as the leading authority in its field and was translated into several languages. Kenneth and Kathleen both died at Cheltenham, Gloucestershire. They had two daughters – Jean Margaret Hume 1940 and Bridget Mary Hume 1946.

- ○ Eileen Kennedy (1st March 1921–13th February 1929).

- George Henry Hedges (29th September 1898–10th August 1962), born at Isleworth, Middlesex, married Gladys Annie Sutton (23rd December 1901–6th February 1994), born at Richmond, Surrey, in 1924 at Brentford. She was living with her parents at 95 Kew Road, Richmond in 1911. George and Gladys were living at 26 Cranbrook Road, Hounslow, Middlesex in 1939, by when he was a newspapers and printing works manager. She was living at 31 Rothbury Gardens, Isleworth, Middlesex at the time of her death there. He was still living at 26 Cranbrook Road at the time of his death at West Middlesex Hospital, Isleworth. They had two daughters:

Kenneth Hume's book.

- ◦ Renee Meriel Gladys Hedges (8th November 1925–31st October 2013), born at Isleworth, married Eric John Bunyan (12th July 1921–15th December 2014), born at Margate, Kent, on 12th August 1944 at St Michael and St Martin Church, Hounslow. They had three children – Marie Cecilia Bunyan 1946, Christopher John Bunyan 1950 and Peter Montague Bunyan 1952. The marriage ended in divorce. Eric is understood to have married Ethel Rose Bagley (26th September 1921–April 1989), born at Camberwell, London, at Brentwood on 11th October 1968. Ethel was a shop assistant in 1939, living with her parents at 233 St Helier Avenue, Merton and Morden, Surrey. Ethel died at Slough, Berkshire and Eric at Wells, Somerset. Renee married David Burke in 1960 at Pancras, London. They had a daughter, Kathleen Renee Burke in 1967. Renee married John H Sams (1st February 1915–February 1993), born at Tower Hamlets, London, in 1974 at Poplar and Bethnal Green, London. Renee was a journalist in London for twenty-five years. She died in Hertfordshire.
- ◦ Joan Pamela Hedges (8th October 1927–2009), born at Brentford, married Lloyd Montague Parsick Joaquim (30th May 1916–26th May 1988), a mining engineer born at Kingston upon Thames, Surrey, in 1948 in Middlesex. They emigrated to New Zealand and by 1958 he was a commercial assistant. They travelled aboard SS *Canton* from Hong Kong to Singapore, departing on 18th June 1958. Their address was 26 Cranbrook Road, Hounslow. The marriage ended in divorce. She was a hairdresser in 1969 at Access Road, Kerikeri, Northland. By then Lloyd had retired and was living at Coopers Beach, Mangonui, Kaitaia. He was living at 55 Main Road, Coopers Beach at the time of his death. Joan married Thomas George McGuinness (5th March 1925–11th December 2003), born at Timaru, Canterbury, New Zealand. He was living at Torkar Road, Clarks Beach, Papakura, Auckland in 1978 and she at Clarkes Beach, RO4, Pukekohe. They were both nurses in 1981, when he was living at Torkar Road and she at 4/6 Ray Small Drive, Papakura.

- Bertie Lionel Hedges (18th April 1900–19th February 1959) was the manager of an off-licence in 1939, living with his mother at 233 High Street, Hounslow, London. Also living there was Elsie Maud Kennedy, his widowed sister, manageress of an off licence. Bertie remained with his mother until her death. He was living at 15 Windsor Avenue, London at the time of his death at Nelson Hospital.

Frederick's paternal grandfather, William Hedges (1827–13th August 1901), born at Hampton, Middlesex, was a great friend of John William Loader (Frederick's maternal grandfather) and they served in the Army in India and during the Crimean War together. William is believed to have married Anne née Watters Tarant (c.1829–1910) on 18th December 1849 at the Registrar's Office, Cork, Ireland, where she was born. He was a mess waiter with 12th Lancers at the Barracks, Cork at the time. He was a domestic servant/coachman in 1861, when they were living at Hampton, Middlesex. He was a groom and gardener in 1871, when they were living at Twickenham, Middlesex. In 1881 they were living at the hamlet of Whitton. By 1891 they had moved to 1 Hope and Anchor Cottages, Twickenham and they were still there in 1901. William died at Richmond upon Thames, Middlesex and Anne at Brentford, Middlesex. In addition to Henry they had six other children:

- William Henry Hedges (c.1852–25th June 1857) died of cholera at Kirkee, Bombay, India.

Frederick, standing on the left, with his father and four brothers.

Cork is the second largest city in Ireland. Originally a monastic settlement founded in the 6th century, Cork was expanded by the Vikings about 915. Its charter was granted by Prince John, Lord of Ireland, in 1185. In medieval times the town was fully walled. In 1349 almost half the population died in the Black Death. It is often referred to as 'the rebel city' because of its support for the Yorkists during the Wars of the Roses. Perkin Warbeck landed there to recruit support for a plot to overthrow Henry VII of England. In the Irish War of Independence, the centre of the city was burnt down by Black and Tans and there was fierce fighting between Irish guerrillas and British forces. During the Irish Civil War, Cork was held by anti-Treaty forces until it was retaken by the pro-Treaty National Army. Locals sometimes call the city 'the real capital' because of its opposition to the Anglo-Irish Treaty in the Irish Civil War.

- George Vigilant Hedges (c.1854–25th June 1857) died of cholera at Kirkee, the same day as his brother William.
- Frederick William Hedges (born 1862), born at Kingston upon Thames, Surrey and baptised on 4th May 1862 at St Mary's, Hampton, was a florist in 1881, living with his parents. By 1891 he was a head gardener living at The Gardens, Richmond Road, Isleworth, Middlesex.
- Ernest William Hedges (1863–2nd September 1920), born at Staines, served as a sergeant in 4th Dragoon Guards in India. He married Kate Bateup (1858–6th September 1893), born at Ticehurst, Sussex, on 11th September 1886 at Hartley Wintney, Hampshire. He was serving as a sergeant in 1st Middlesex at North Camp, Aldershot, Hampshire in 1888. Kate died of enteric fever at Mhow, Bengal, India. They had two sons:
    - Ernest Henry Hedges (19th December 1887–5th April 1958), born at Aldershot, Hampshire, married his cousin, Agnes Ketchell on 18th December 1915 (see below under maternal grandparents). They had four children – Philip J Hedges 1917, John A Hedges 1921, Peter E Hedges 1923 and Anne E Hedges 1924.
    - Herbert William Charles Hedges (24th January 1890–22nd March 1954), born at Kamptee, India and died at Park Prewett Hospital, Sherborne Street, Basingstoke, Hampshire.

  Ernest married Caroline Smith Price (1857–3rd August 1937), born at Deal, Kent, on 25th December 1895 at Colaba, Bombay, India. He was a general dealer in 1911, when they were living at 9 Stanley Terrace, Malling Road, Snodland, Kent. Ernest enlisted in the Buffs (Special Reserve) on 2nd October 1914 at Hythe, Kent (679). He was promoted sergeant major the same day and appointed drill instructor in 9th Battalion. He was described as 5′ 8¼″ tall, weighing 161 lbs, with blue eyes, dark brown hair and his religious denomination was Church of England. He claimed he had been born at sea and had served previously in the Indian Army, retiring voluntarily with the Long Service & Good Conduct Medal but no campaign medals. He was discharged on the grounds of not likely to become an efficient soldier on medical grounds on 24th March 1915 at Canterbury, Kent. They were living at 22 St Leonards Road, Hythe, Kent at the time and at 31 Albert Road, Hythe, Kent at the time of his death there. Caroline was living at Wembley, Herschell Road, Walmer, Kent at the time of her death there.
- Emily Maria Hedges (1865–1923) was a domestic servant in 1881, living with her parents. She married James Ketchell (1865–1936), born at Whitton, Middlesex, on 10th September 1887 at St Philip and St James' Church, Whitton, Middlesex. He was a florist in 1901, when they were living at 2 Hope and Anchor Cottages, Twickenham, next door to her parents. By 1911 he was a nurseries packer and they were living at 6 Stanhope Terrace, Hounslow Road, Whitton, Twickenham and at

12 Hounslow Road, Whitton in 1916. Both their deaths were registered at Brentford. They had six children:

- Ernest George Ketchell (1888–1967) was living with his grandparents in 1901 and was a nursery labourer in 1911 living with his parents. He married Harriet K Mitcham (12th June 1895–1972) in 1920 and they had twins, Esther K and Rose E Ketchell in 1921.
- George Albert Ketchell (born and died 1891).
- Agnes Ketchell (4th November 1892–18th October 1975) was a dressmaker in 1911, living with her parents. She married her cousin, Ernest Henry Hedges, on 18th December 1915 (see above under paternal grandparents).

William Ketchell's grave in the Guards' Cemetery, Lesboeufs.

- William Ketchell (1895–15th September 1916), was a butcher in 1911, living with his parents. He enlisted in the Rifle Brigade (S/10116) at Hounslow on 26th April 1915 and joined at Winchester next day. He was described as a grocer's assistant, 5′ 7½″ tall and weighing 119 lbs. On 1st May he was posted to 6th Battalion at Sheerness and to 9th Battalion on 23rd February 1916. William went to France on 24th February, joined 14th Infantry Base Depot next day and 9th Battalion on 6th March. He was reported wounded and missing on 15th September 1916 and on 2nd August 1917 was accepted to have died (Guards' Cemetery, Lesboeufs, France – VI H 10).

Harry Ketchell's grave in London Cemetery & Extension, Longueval. He and his brother, William, were killed six days apart and lie in cemeteries five kilometres from each other.

- Harry Ketchell (1897–9th September 1916), was a nurseryman errand boy in 1911, living with his parents. He enlisted in the East Surrey Regiment on 27th October 1915 and joined at Kingston upon Thames, described as a nurseryman and 5′ 7″ tall. He was posted to 3rd Battalion on 1st November and transferred to the Machine Gun Corps (43941) on 21st July 1916. He went to France on 6th August and joined 164th Company, Machine Gun Corps on 9th August. Harry was killed in action on 9th September 1916 (London Cemetery & Extension, Longueval, France – 10 B 44).
- Arthur Ketchell (14th January 1903–1981) married Mabel Slaughter (1903–67) at Brentford in 1930. They had three children – Marjorie Ketchell 1931, Alan Ketchell 1934 and James Ketchell 1937.

Bangalore (now Bengaluru) is the capital and largest city of Karnataka. In the last century it has grown enormously from 400,000 in 1941 to over 8,000,000 today. Located on the Deccan Plateau over 900m above sea level, Bangalore has a pleasant climate throughout the year. Stone Age artefacts date human settlement to as early as 4000 BC. There are Iron Age burials on the outskirts of Bangalore and Roman coins indicate that the region was involved in trade with Rome and other civilisations in 27 BC. The modern era began in 1537 when a mud fort was established. Ownership of the area changed hands many times. The Mughals captured Bangalore in 1687 and sold it to the Kingdom of Mysore. Bangalore fort was captured by the British under Lord Cornwallis in 1791, during the Third Anglo-Mysore War, and it became a centre of resistance against Tipu Sultan. The British East India Company captured it after victory in the Fourth Anglo-Mysore War in 1799 and returned administrative control to the Maharaja of Mysore, whose Princely State of Mysore existed as a nominally sovereign entity under the Raj. The Residency of Mysore State shifted to Bangalore in 1804. It was abolished in 1843, revived in 1881 and closed in 1947. In 1809 the British shifted their cantonment to Bangalore. It expanded throughout the 19th century and was known as the Civil and Military Station of Bangalore. A telegraph connection arrived in 1853 and a railway to Madras (now Chennai) in 1864. In 1898 an outbreak of plague claimed 3,500 lives. In 1912, the Bangalore Torpedo was devised in Bangalore by Captain McClintock of the Madras Sappers and Miners. Following the independence of India in 1947, Bangalore became the capital of Mysore and the new Indian state of Karnataka was formed in 1956. The city has been a major aerospace and technology centre since the 1960s.

- William Hedges (born 1868), born at Kingston upon Thames and baptised on 8th November 1868 at St James, Hampton Hill, Richmond upon Thames.

His maternal grandfather, John William Loader (24th January 1817–5th August 1892) was born, according to various sources, at Newington St Mary, Surrey, or Sydenham, Kent or Pitt Street, Lambeth, Surrey. He enlisted in 13th Light Dragoons on 8th November 1836 (496) and went to India. He transferred to 15th Hussars on 1st March 1840. John married Hannah née Waters (2nd October 1824–6th August 1904), born at Bangalore, India, on 15th February 1840 at St Thomas Garrison Church, Madras, India. He received Good Conduct Pay of 1d per day on

St Thomas Garrison Church (also known as St Thomas English Garrison Church) was built by the British government at the request of army officers in the area in 1827 and was opened officially in 1830. Most of the materials for the construction were imported from Britain and the design has similarities with St Clement Danes in London. The church is located in the foothills of St Thomas Mount, where St Thomas, one of the twelve apostles, lived during his final years. The original tall spire was trimmed to accommodate passing flights from the nearby airport.

The Crimea Medal was approved on 15th December 1854 for issue to officers and men of British land and naval units that fought in the Crimean War 1854–56 against Russia. The Medal is notable for its unusually ornate suspender and clasps. Most were issued unnamed but could be returned for naming free of charge. Five clasps were authorised, four for land battles:

- *Alma* – 20th September 1854.
- *Balaklava* – 25th October 1854.
- *Inkerman* –5th November 1854.
- *Sebastopol* – the siege 11th September 1854 – 9th September 1855. Anyone receiving the Balaklava or Inkerman clasps was also issued this clasp.
- *Azoff* – naval expedition in the Sea of Azoff 25th May – 22nd September 1855. Only awarded to RN personnel.

The medal was also issued to Turkish, and a limited number of French, forces who served in the Crimea.

28th January 1845, forfeited on 3rd June 1846 and regained on 3rd June 1847. He received Good Conduct Pay of 2d and 3d on 3rd June 1849 and 8th November 1851 respectively. On 1st February 1854 he transferred to 12th Lancers and received Good Conduct Pay of 4d and 5d on 8th November 1856 and 1st March 1860 respectively. He was in action at Sebastopol during the Crimean War before returning to India and transferred to 1st Dragoon Guards on 1st March 1860. John was discharged unfit for further service (chronic rheumatism and debility due to extended service in a tropical climate) at Saidepot, India on 28th January 1862 and settled at Bangalore, India. He was described as a labourer, 5′ 7¾″ tall, with fair complexion, grey eyes and brown hair. He was awarded the Crimean Medal with Sebastopol clasp, Turkish Crimean Medal and Good Conduct Medal. He died in Karnataka, India and she at Bangalore. In addition to Harriet they had thirteen other children:

- Mary Jane Loader (28th November 1840–1918), born at Bangalore, married Joseph Anderson (1829–6th April 1866) on 7th June 1856 at Madras (now Chennai), India. Mary married William Edward Sheppard (1839–30th March 1900), born at Devizes, Wiltshire, on 14th November 1866 at Trinity Church, Bangalore. They returned to England before April 1880 and were living at 104 Khyber Road, Battersea, London in 1881, when he was a domestic groom of chambers. They had moved to 26 Salcott Road, Battersea by 1883 and to 31 Elthiron Road, Fulham, London by 1891. Her death was registered at Chelsea, London. Mary had eight children from her two marriages – Henry 'Harry' Anderson (1st August 1857–14th June 1914), Charles Anderson (born 21st March 1859), Edwin Anderson (27th February 1862–23rd May 1899), Maria Agnes Anderson (born 2nd August 1864), William Edward Sheppard (21st November 1868–6th February 1942), Frederick Sheppard (3rd March 1870–1950), Albert

Frank Sheppard (3rd July 1873–November 1882) and Herbert Albert Sheppard (10th April 1880–29th October 1959).

- William John Loader (3rd April 1843–23rd April 1914) married Alice Gardner (born c.1855). They had six children:
  - Mildred Verona Loader (28th October 1889–1982).
  - William Ewart Loader (born 20th September 1891).
  - Olga 'Olive' Frances Loader (19th June 1893–1923) married Valentine Norman Bogle (1893–25th December 1918), born in India on 25th May 1918 at Rangoon, Burma. He was a mechanic sergeant major (050633) serving with 1024th No.2 Burma MT Company RASC, attached to Supply and Transport, when he died on active service (Tehran War Cemetery, Iran – V C 15). Olga married Sergeant Herbert Dudley Whiskens (born 1898), Rangoon Police Force, on 14th January 1920 at Epworth, Bengal.
  - Alice Merlyn Loader (11th January 1896–1978).
  - Victor Gerald Loader (26th May 1899–7th December 1949).
  - William George Loader (11th June 1904–1904).
- Elizabeth Loader (24th May 1845–13th April 1861), born at Bangalore, married John Cleave (c.1836–21st April 1862), a farrier in 1st Dragoon Guards, at Trinity Church, Bangalore on 9th April 1861. She died just four days later of spasmodic cholera. He contracted dysentaria acuta and died at Bangalore.
- Alfred Henry Loader (15th June 1847–11th August 1919) was an engine driver on the Madras Railway. He married Elizabeth Hannah Conyers (15th September 1848–22nd April 1898), born at Bangalore, on 4th August 1869 at St John's, Bangalore. She died of fever at Madras. He married Alice Virginia Gay (18th February 1865–7th September 1918), born at Pondicherry, India, on 21st November 1901 at All Soul's Church, Coimbatore, India. He was a locomotive foreman at the time. They both died at Bangalore. Alfred had ten children with his first wife – Alfred Henry Loader (3rd January 1871–25th March 1906), Florence Louisa Loader (7th April 1872–7th January 1927), Frederick

Tehran War Cemetery is on the southern edge of the British Embassy's Gholhak compound on Dowlat Street (Kolah Dooz) in north Tehran. Within the Cemetery is the Tehran Memorial, which commemorates British, Indian and New Zealand casualties from both World Wars in Iran (formerly Persia), who have no known grave. It also commemorates some who died in regions of Russia whose graves are unknown or unmaintainable.
The Cemetery was completed in 1963 and contains 412 burials of the Great War, thirteen unidentified, and 152 burials of the Second World War. There are also fourteen non-world war and twenty-five foreign national burials.

The Madras Railway Co played a pioneering role in developing railways in southern India. It formed in 1845 and its first track, from Royapuram, Madras to Arcot, opened in 1856. It was to connect Madras on the east coast with the west coast, also link with Bangalore and the Nilgiri Hills and the line from Bombay. The link with the west coast was established in 1862 and Bangalore Cantt in 1864. In 1871 an extension to Raichur linked with an extension of Great Indian Peninsula Railway to establish the Madras-Bombay link. In 1877 the Company owned 150 locomotives, 391 coaches and 3,223 goods wagons. The southern part of the East Coast State railway was taken over by Madras Railway in 1901. It merged in 1908 with Southern Mahratta Railway to form Madras and Southern Mahratta Railway.

Lewis Loader (16th October 1873–25th July 1905), Alice Maud Loader (born 1st March 1876), Winifred Harriet Loader (5th May 1879–23rd May 1902), George Melville Loader (23rd May 1880–6th April 1949), Albert Percival Loader (born 4th April 1884), Clifford Hope Loader (9th August 1885–24th October 1912), Janet Mary Loader (born 24th October 1886) and Frank Loader.

- Caroline Loader (7th March 1849–17th February 1914) married Private Terence McAnally/ McNally (c.1838–20th March 1869), 1st King's Dragoon Guards, on 20th July 1864 at St John's, Bangalore. He transferred to 16th Lancers and died following a rupture of the gut at Bangalore. They had two daughters – Catherine 'Kate' Eliza McAnally (5th July 1865–1936) and Mary Ann McAnally (25th December 1867–15th July 1869). Caroline married William George Maddocks (11th January 1847–10th March 1917), born at 44 Stockwell Street, Old Kent Road, London, in India in 1871. They returned to Britain between 1891 and 1894 and were living at 29 Mersey Road, Bishop's Stortford in 1896. He was an Army pensioner and caretaker in 1901, when they were living at New Town Road, Bishop's Stortford, Hertfordshire, moving to 29 Nursery Road, Bishop's Stortford by 1911. They both subsequently died there. They had ten children:
    - Alice Mary Maddocks (1st November 1871–25th November 1922).
    - William George Maddocks (9th December 1873–18th October 1956).
    - Florence Rebecca Maddocks (23rd April 1876–30th November 1962).
    - Arthur Brenchley Maddocks (2nd August 1878–4th April 1953), born at Bangalore, India, enlisted in 16th Lancers (4303 & L13036) at Bishop's Stortford on 3rd November 1896. He was described as a light porter and a draper warehouseman, just over 5′ 8½″ tall and weighing 138 lbs. He was in hospital at Canterbury 14th November–7th December and received a wound there on 4th January 1897 and was in hospital until 9th January. He was in hospital again at Canterbury 25th May–2nd June and 5th-11th June with neuralgia. Arthur embarked aboard SS *Nubia* on 16th September, disembarked in India on 10th December and was posted to Ambala on

20th December. He was in hospital there 2nd-31st October with tonsillitis. He was granted Good Conduct Pay of 1d per day on 3rd November 1898. He was treated for gonorrhoea at the Cavalry Camp, Dehli 12th-13th January 1899, hospital in Dehli 14th-17th January and at Ambala 17th-21st January. Arthur served in South Africa from 7th January 1900 (Queen's South Africa Medal and King's South Africa Medal with clasps) and was severely wounded at Tafelkop in the right side, left hip and foot on 20th December 1901. He was brought to favourable notice by C-in-C South Africa, LG 25th April 1902. Arthur was appointed unpaid lance corporal on 13th July 1902 and was promoted on 30th August. He extended his service to complete eight years on 5th October and was granted Good Conduct Pay of 2d per day on 3rd November. Promoted corporal on 1st April 1903 and attained 3rd Class Army Education on 16th September. He extended his service to complete twelve years on 5th October and returned to Britain on 5th November. He was granted Class 1 Service Pay of 7d per day on 1st April 1904 and attained 2nd Class Army Education on 14th October. He passed the examination for promotion to sergeant on 13th March 1905. Forfeited the Good Conduct Badge on 2nd April 1907 and was in arrest on 11th May. He was tried by Regimental Court Martial at Aldershot on 15th May for 'conduct to the prejudice' and reduced to the ranks. On 9th January 1908 he was reduced to Class II Service Pay of 5d per day for inefficiency. However, he was allowed to extend his service to complete twenty-one years on 18th October. Arthur transferred to Eastern Cavalry Depot on 20th March 1912 and was attached to the Army Veterinary Corps, Woolwich on 6th December 1915. He was posted to 1st Reserve Cavalry Regiment at Waterford, Ireland on 27th May 1918 and Curragh Camp from 23rd July. He continued in service from 2nd November with Depot Army Veterinary Corps, Woolwich and was allowed to draw his pension whilst still serving from 4th November. Arthur volunteered for one year retention at Woolwich on 6th August 1919. He was discharged at Canterbury on 24th April 1920, giving his address as 65 High Street, Walthamstow, London. A pension of 1/1½d per day for life was revised to 2/9d from 25th April 1920, when he was assessed as being 50% disabled – deafness (caused by a bomb in 1917) and gunshot wounds to lung and foot. Arthur married Lilian Maud M Lawrence (8th October 1890–1971), birth registered at Pancras, London, at Southwark in 1921. They had two daughters – Elsie L Maddocks 1922 and May F Maddocks 1924. His death was registered at Southwark and hers at Lambeth.

- Charles Edward Maddocks (27th May 1881–1966) married Juliet MacDonald (c.1884–1927) at Newmarket, Suffolk in 1911. They had two daughters – Norah A Maddocks 1912 and Mary M Maddocks 1916. He married Honor Fenn (4th August 1891–1974) there in 1931. Both their deaths were subsequently registered there.

  - Winifred Caroline Elizabeth Maddocks (8th September 1883–1954) married Ralph S Carter (1887–1941) in 1913 registered at Bishop's Stortford, Hertfordshire. They had two children – Ivan C Maddocks 1913, who changed his name to Carter in 1934, and Leslie R Carter 1920.
  - Walter Edward Maddocks (29th May 1886–1967) married Jessie Carter at Edmonton in 1910. His death was registered at Enfield.
  - Norah Maddocks (10th April 1888–26th September 1951).
  - Charlotte Madeleine Maddocks (born 1891).
  - Frederick Henry Maddocks (12th December 1894–March 1966) married Bridget Martin (c.1895–1939) at Kensington in 1916. They are believed to have had seven children – Norah E Maddocks 1917, Frederick H Maddocks 1919, Margaret PF Maddocks 1921, Phyllis M Maddocks 1924, Victor E Maddocks 1926, Ronald G Maddocks 1928 and Mary T Maddocks 1932. Frederick's death was registered at Lambeth.
- Hannah Loader (22nd May 1851–27th June 1853).
- Amelia Loader (20th May 1853–1st April 1919) married Sergeant James Frederick Lees (c.1825–10th January 1877) on 20th May 1869 at Bangalore. He died of cholera at Arcot, Madras. James had married Evelina Jane Royle (1833–13th January 1869) on 10th September 1850 at Trinity Church, Bellary, Madras. She died at Bangalore. Evelina and James had five children – twins Alice Amelia Jane and Jane Alice Lees (born 14th June 1860), James Royle Lees (born 19th September 1861), Harcourt Cecil Rundle Lees (10th September 1865–29th March 1938) and Jane Evelina Maude Lees (25th December 1868–13th July 1869). Amelia married Joseph Henry Corkery (born c.1857) on 29th April 1878 at Bangalore. He was an overseer at the Department of Public Works. She died at Darbhanga, Bengal.
- John Edward Loader (23rd March 1855–11th April 1913), an engine driver for Madras Railway, married Theresa Parkinson (c.1862–20th October 1880) on 4th July 1877 at St Mark's Church, North Black Town, Madras. Theresa died of cholera at Tharrawaddy, Burma. John married Mary Louise Maartenz (15th January 1864–25th December 1909), born at Kumbakonam, Tamil Nadu, India, on 26th June 1883 at St John's, Bangalore. Mary died of consumption at Mandalay, Burma. John and Mary had three daughters – Eunice Elsie Loader (12th July 1885–1946), Gladys Leonora Loader (16th November 1886–27th January 1905) and Clarice Frederica Loader (1st February 1889–1969). John married Narsama 'Susan' Wadathy (born c.1883), born in India, on 18th January 1910 at Immanuel Baptist Church, Rangoon (now Yangon), Burma (now Myanmar). He died at Rangoon.
- Alice Loader (born 31st January 1858), born at Secunderabad, India, married Joseph John Clarke (born c.1854), born at Innerleithen, Peeblesshire, Scotland, on 23rd August 1876 at Bangalore. They had four children – Thomas Andrew

Clarke 1877, Albert Edward Clarke (1880–1913), Malcolm Kenneth Clarke 1883 and Daisy Mary Ann Clarke (3rd March 1884–25th April 1971).
- Frederick Loader (born 27th February 1861) married Mary.
- Albert Loader (22nd January 1863–10th September 1915) married Mabel Evelyn McMahon (c.1866–21st May 1942) on 2nd February 1887 at Holy Trinity Church, Bangalore. He died at Kharagpur and she at Bungalow 518 there. They had four children – Sybil Beryl Loader (17th October 1889–1953), Maurice Albert Lancelot Loader (born 5th August 1892), Mervyn Leslie McMahon Loader (6th March 1894–1967) and Gladys Clare Loader (30th April 1898–26th January 1965).
- Walter Edward Loader (20th July 1867–30th January 1937) married Mya Zin 'Alice' Fisher, also seen as Alicia Maud Baecher (10th April 1877–26th January 1961), born at Myingyan, Burma, on 6th November 1901 at Maymyo, Burma. He died at Rangoon, Burma and she at Taunggyi, Burma. They had six children – Walter Gerald Loader (16th February 1897–28th June 1980), Percival Frederic Loader (12th June 1899–16th December 1986), Constance Beatrice Loader (17th November 1901–2000), Bertram Harold loader (11th June 1904–7th March 1926), Lionel Herbert Loader (21st May 1906–6th May 1990) and George Gilbert Loader (16th July 1908–15th March 1928).
- James Herbert Loader (4th October 1869–6th March 1872).

Frederick was educated at Grove Road Primary School, Hounslow, Middlesex 1901–07 and Isleworth County School, Middlesex 1907–14. He was employed as a clerk. Frederick enlisted in 1/9th (County of London) Battalion (Queen Victoria's Rifles), The London Regiment on 6th August 1914 at 56 Davies Street, London (2182). He was just over 5′ 8″ tall. He proceeded with the Battalion to France on 4th November 1914. He was injured in some way, possibly frostbite, in the trenches at Wulverghem, Belgium in the period 19th-24th January 1915 and was evacuated to England on 27th January for treatment at 3rd Northern General Hospital, Sheffield, Yorkshire 28th January–16th March. He applied for a commission while serving at Tadworth Camp, Epsom, Surrey on 10th April and joined B Company, 3/9th Battalion on 15th April. He was passed fit at a medical board at Tidworth, Hampshire on 8th June and applied for a commission the same day. Frederick was discharged on 5th July and was commissioned in 9th (Reserve) Battalion, Bedfordshire Regiment next day. On 10th July he reported to the School

Grove Road Primary School, Hounslow.

Isleworth County School (now Isleworth & Syon School) originated as a charity school in 1715 using a bequest from William Cave, Vicar of Isleworth. It was known as the Blue School after the school uniform. Due to expansion it became a boys' school and the girls moved to a separate building in North Street in 1870. An upper school was added in 1883 and in 1896 it moved to St John's Road. As a model school it was used to train teachers. Early in the 20th century it came under the Blue Schools Foundation. In 1903 it became a state school, when Middlesex County Council assumed control, and was renamed Isleworth County School a few years later. In 1930–31 it moved to Ridgeway Road, where it has been ever since. Under the 1944 Education Act it became Isleworth Grammar School and during the 1950s and 60s gained a high academic reputation. Hounslow Council adopted the comprehensive system and the Grammar School merged with Syon School for Boys in 1979 to form the current Isleworth & Syon School. The School now admits girls in the sixth form and is part of a consortium with other secondary schools in the borough.

The Davies Street Drill Hall was designed by Charles Herbert Shoppee as the headquarters of 1st Middlesex (Victoria and St George's) Volunteer Rifle Corps and was completed in December 1890. The unit amalgamated with 19th Middlesex (St Giles and St George's, Bloomsbury) Volunteer Rifle Corps to form 9th (County of London) Battalion, London Regiment (Queen Victoria's) in 1908. The Battalion was mobilised in August 1914 before deploying to France. When the London Regiment was broken up in 1937, the battalions were allocated to other units and Davies Street became the home of Queen Victoria's Rifles, King's Royal Rifle Corps. On 30th November 1940 the building was badly damaged by a bomb and was rebuilt between 1950 and 1952. Since then the units based at the Drill Hall have been renamed a number of times.

of Instruction, St Mary's House, Sea Road, Felixstowe, Suffolk. The 3rd Reserve Battalion was there throughout the war.

Frederick served in France again 5th November–29th January 1916, although it is not known where. He returned again on 2nd September and served with 6th Bedfordshire, taking part in the Battle of the Ancre in November and the Battle of Arras in April 1917. On the night of 10/11th April he received a shrapnel splinter to the right hand at Le Bergère crossroads, near Monchy-le-Preux and was evacuated to Rouen. He was transferred to England aboard HMHS *St George* on 19th April, disembarking at Southampton, Hampshire for treatment at 5th Southern General Hospital, Portsmouth, Hampshire and later at Osborne House, Isle of Wight. A medical board at Portsmouth on 12th June found him unfit for General Service for two months, Home Service for six weeks and light duties for one month. Promoted lieutenant on 1st July. Medical boards at Portsmouth on 14th July, 15th August and 7th September found him unfit for General Service for between two and three months, Home Service between six weeks and two months and light duties between one month and six weeks. A medical board at Osborne, Isle

The 3rd Northern General Hospital TF had a staff of fifty-seven officers and 1,360 other ranks. It remained in Sheffield until 1920. The base hospital was in a teacher training college on Collegiate Crescent, fitted out with operating theatres and wards. Today it is the Collegiate Campus of Sheffield Hallam University. Wards in existing hospitals were turned over for military use:

- Fir Vale Infirmary (now Northern General Hospital) – 500 beds.
- Ecclesall Infirmary (later Nether Edge Hospital) – 150 beds.
- Royal Hospital, West Street – 140 beds.
- Royal Infirmary, Infirmary Road – 133 beds.
- Winter Street Hospital (St George's) – 120.
- Wadsley Lunatic Asylum, Middlewood (Wharncliffe Hospital) – 2,000 beds.

Most of the wounded arrived at Midland Station at night from the southern ports. They were taken to one of the hospitals in open-topped buses for the walking wounded and ambulances for the more badly injured. Staffing for these centres came from the Royal Army Medical Corps, based at the drill hall on Glossop Road, existing doctors and nurses from various hospitals, general practitioners, university staff and volunteer nurses from the Red Cross etc. The base hospital controlled convalescent homes as far away as Derby, with local centres at Greystones School (150 beds), Bramall Lane cricket pavilion (150 beds), Lydgate Lane School (130 beds) and Carterknowle School (115 beds). At times the city's hospitals were almost overwhelmed by the influx. Some hospitals were funded by public donations and came under financial pressure, necessitating appeals to the government for assistance. The local population also had difficulty being admitted for routine treatment. At the former lunatic asylum, more than 1,600 inmates were transferred into the wider society. Staff there were given two weeks medical training at the Royal Infirmary to prepare them for dealing with the wounded. However, it was only natural that Wharncliffe specialised in treating shell shock and other psychiatric conditions.

of Wight on 20th September found him unfit for General Service for one month but fit for light duties after three weeks leave ending on 11th October. He joined 3rd (Reserve) Battalion at Felixstowe, Suffolk on 12th October. A medical board on 20th October found him unfit for General Service for one month but fit for Home Service. A medical board at Felixstowe on 22nd November found him unfit for A for one month but fit for C1. On 21st December he was passed fit for General Service at a medical board at Felixstowe. He may have qualified as a machine gun officer about this time.

Frederick returned to France on 25th September 1918 and was attached to 6th Northamptonshire. **Awarded the VC for his actions on 24th October 1918 at Renuart Farm, northeast of Bousies, France, LG 31st January 1919.** On 4th November he received a three and

HMHS *St George* was built for the Great Western Railway to operate on the Rosslare to Fishguard route until 1913. She was sold to Canadian Pacific and was requisitioned as a hospital ship until 1919. *St George* was later purchased by the Great Eastern Railway for the Harwich to Hook of Holland route and was scrapped in 1929.

The 5th Southern General Hospital opened in August/September 1914 at Priory School, Fawcett Road, Southsea and Milton Hospital in Milton Road (later Priorsdean Hospital). The site in Fawcett Road, seen here, was purchased by Portsmouth School Board in 1890. Construction of the school was completed in May 1892. Later extensions covered the site of an old priory and Priory Farm. In 1907 Francis Avenue School for girls moved to a building next to the boys' school. Post war the school became overcrowded and an extension to the girls' school was completed in 1934. As Portsmouth was a prominent bombing target during the Second World War, the girls' school moved to Salisbury. On 10th January 1941 a German bomb destroyed the boys' school and the extension of the girls' school. The boys moved to St Ronan's Road School. The bombed out remains of the old school were demolished in the late 1950s and replaced with a gymnasium for the girls' school. In 1946 the girls' school became Portsmouth Southern Grammar School for Girls. The Southern Grammar School for Boys was on Eastern Road and was later part of Portsmouth College. In 1974 the boys school returned to the site, merging with the girls' school to form Priory Comprehensive School. The school became a specialist sports college, with the opening of the Priory Tennis Centre in 2006, and an academy, part of the Bohunt Education Trust, in 2014.

Osborne House, a former royal residence in East Cowes, was built between 1845 and 1851 for Queen Victoria and Prince Albert as a summer home and retreat. Albert designed the house himself. The builder was Thomas Cubitt, whose company built the main facade of Buckingham Palace in 1847. Queen Victoria died at Osborne House on 22nd January 1901. Her son, Edward VII, never liked Osborne and presented it to the nation on his coronation day, although Princesses Beatrice and Louise were granted houses on the estate. The royal pavilion was retained as a private museum to Victoria. Part of the estate around the stables was used as a Royal Navy officer training college 1903–21, known as Royal Naval College, Osborne. Students included Queen Victoria's great-grandsons, the future Kings Edward VIII and George VI. Another alumnus was Jack Llewelyn Davies, one of the five Llewelyn Davies boys who inspired JM Barrie's *Peter Pan*. During the Great War the secondary wings of the house were a convalescent home for officers. Robert Graves and AA Milne were two of the patients. It became the King Edward VII Retirement Home for Officers, accommodating military and civil service convalescents, including retired officers, until the late 1990s. In 1954, Elizabeth II gave permission for the private apartments on the first floor of the royal pavilion to be opened to the public. In 1986, English Heritage took over the management of the House and in 1989 the second floor was also opened to the public. The House is Grade I listed and the landscaped park and gardens are Grade II* listed.

a half inches long gunshot wound to the right side of the scalp and a gunshot through his right shoulder. He was evacuated to England from Le Havre on 7th November, arriving at Southampton, Hampshire the following day and was treated at a hospital in Bournemouth. A medical board at Millbank on 15th November found him unfit for A & B for two months and C for three weeks. A medical board on 6th December found him unfit for A & B for two months and C for one month and he was sent to a convalescent hospital. A medical board on 16th January 1919 found him unfit for A & B for two months and C for one month and he was granted leave until 15th February. Medical boards at Hounslow on 21st February and 26th March 1919 found him unfit for any service for one month and leave was extended to 25th April. A medical board on 2nd May passed him fit for light duties and he rejoined his unit. The VC was presented by the King in the quadrangle at Buckingham Palace on 15th May.

Frederick was appointed Commandant No.8 Group Prisoner of War Camp, Fulwell, Guildford, Surrey on 19th June. As the camp held fewer than 200 prisoners, he was not entitled for acting captain rank. On 27th September he suffered a compound fracture of the right leg in a motorcycle accident while on duty. Blame was attributed to the driver of a touring car that was being driven at excessive speed by Henry Spurrier, managing director of Leyland Motors Ltd. A medical board on 9th February 1920 found him unfit for any service for two months and recommended two months leave. He was demobilised following a medical board on 9th April 1920 at the Military Hospital, Edmonton. The fracture had united soundly and his leg movements were good but there was some dermatitis of the skin. His disability was assessed as 40% and he was judged not fit for general or overseas service for six months. Frederick was demobilised from the Officers' Dispersal Unit, London, relinquishing his commission and retaining the rank of lieutenant on 14th April 1920. He worked for some time as an insurance manager at Sunbury-on-Thames, Surrey.

Frederick Hedges married Mollie Lorna Kenworthy (23rd June 1898–15th August 1983), born at Brentford, Middlesex, on 26th July 1919 at Holy Trinity, Hounslow, Middlesex. He was living at 23 Lansdowne Road, Hounslow and she at 117 St Stephen's Road, Isleworth, Middlesex. They lived at 136 The Avenue, Sunbury-on-Thames, Teddington, Middlesex.

Holy Trinity on the High Street, Hounslow was built about 1864 and was destroyed by fire in 1943. A replacement was constructed in 1961.

On 17th December 1922 he attended the unveiling of a memorial to the eighty-one old boys of Isleworth County School who died in the Great War. As secretary of the memorial committee, he was instrumental in creating the memorial, an oak screen in the Assembly

Hall. Frederick attended two VC reunions – the VC Garden Party at Buckingham Palace on 26th June 1920 and the VC Dinner at the Royal Gallery of the House of Lords, London on 9th November 1929. Frederick and Mollie were active members of the British Legion. He assisted former soldiers with claims for disability allowances and was elected Chairman of the Teddington Branch in 1939. He attempted to re-enlist at the outbreak of the Second World War but was rejected and served in Civil Defence instead. In 1939 he was an insurance inspector and Organiser/Chief Air Raid Precautions Warden and Mollie was an ambulance driver. They had one son:

Frederick and Mollie with their families on their wedding day.

The Hedges' home at 136 The Avenue, Sunbury-on-Thames. (*The Move*)

- John Grosvenor Hedges (5th February 1924–14th November 1941) joined 31st Middlesex Home Guard and was a member of the Upper Thames Shore Patrol. He attended a birthday party at a friend's house in Thames Ditton on 13th November 1941 and arrived at Sunbury Lock for duty at about 2.00 a.m. He was rowed across the river from the Middlesex bank but just before landing on the opposite bank the boat started leaking. Both men stood up and the dinghy capsized. The other man swam to the landing stage, removed his greatcoat and dived in to assist John but was unable to locate him. He returned to the shore and raised the alarm. The police dragged the river unsuccessfully. John's body was recovered on 13th December, still fully clothed in his uniform but without his helmet and rifle. An inquest on 18th December decided that the cause of death at Sunbury Court Island was asphyxia due to drowning. A verdict of accidental death was recorded. John was not a good swimmer and was unable to stay afloat with the weight of his equipment. The ferryman was not experienced. He discovered that the usual boat had a damaged rowlock that night and had taken a nearby dinghy. John's body was cremated at Mortlake Crematorium on 19th December.

Mollie's father, Herbert Charles Kenworthy (7th July 1872–1945), born at Teddington, Middlesex, married Catherine Laura née Cummins (17th March 1869–24th March 1950), born at Queenstown (now Cobh), Co Cork, Ireland, at Twickenham Parish Church, Middlesex on 4th September 1897. Herbert was a candle mould caster in 1901, when they were living at 1 Edgar Villas (later known as 119 St Stephen's Road), St Stephen's Road, Isleworth. They were living at 117 St Stephen's Road by July 1919, when he was an engineer, and they were still there in 1939. Herbert's death was registered at Edmonton, Middlesex. Catherine was living at 60 Duchy Road, Harrogate, Yorkshire at the time of her death.

The Sunbury ferry site in earlier times.

Frederick and Mollie moved to Leeds, Yorkshire in 1942, where he was Branch Manager in the Company office and a member of Leeds & Harrogate Rotary Club. He suffered from neurosis and depression after the death of his only son and started drinking heavily. He became intoxicated during his farewell function at Teddington. As a result he was charged with being drunk-in-charge of a motor vehicle. He offered a plea in mitigation regarding his head injury and the case was dismissed.

They moved to 60 Duchy Road, Harrogate, Yorkshire in the autumn of 1949. Frederick was later Area Manager for Cornhill Insurance Co. He was charged with a drink-driving offence on 18th December 1951, fined £50 and banned from driving for two years. His company paid for private treatment in a local clinic. He signed a pledge to abstain and, after attending a few counselling sessions at the clinic and some medication, was discharged late in January 1952. His employers wanted him to return to the London area to take up a new appointment but Frederick resisted on the grounds that his recovery was progressing well and he was settled in Leeds. He returned to work on 3rd March 1952.

Frederick retired as the Leeds Area Manager at the end of March 1954 because of ill health and was confined to his bed until May 1954. However, he seemed to be in high spirits on 27th May and was allowed to get up. He remained outwardly

Stonefall Crematorium, Harrogate.

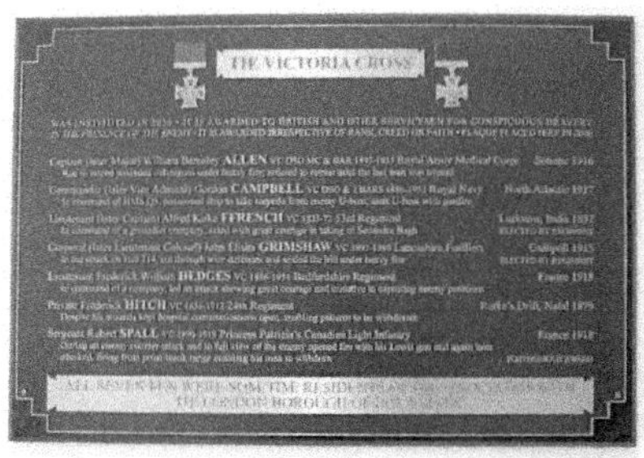

The Victoria Cross Memorial at the Civic Centre, Hounslow. (*Memorials to Valour*)

The 1914 Star was authorised for the Army in 1917 and for the Royal Navy in 1918. It was awarded to officers and men who served in France and Belgium between 5th August and midnight on 22nd-23rd November 1914, the formal end of the First Battle of Ypres. The recipient's number, rank, name and unit are stamped on the reverse. In October 1919 a clasp was authorised, '5th Aug–22nd Nov. 1914', for those who had been under fire or within range of enemy artillery during the period. A total of 365,622 medals were awarded. Approximately 145,000 clasps were awarded but the precise number is unknown as it had to be claimed personally and many of those eligible died before 1919 or simply failed to apply. Some Royal Navy personnel qualified by landing at Antwerp. A few women also qualified, serving as nurses or auxiliaries. However, the majority of recipients were members of the pre-war regular British Army and its reservists, the Old Contemptibles, and the medal became known as the 'Mons Star'. A small number were awarded to Canadians, mainly members of 2nd Canadian Stationary Hospital, which served with the BEF from 6th November 1914. The 1914 Star was always awarded with the British War Medal and Victory Medal. Anyone awarded the 1914 Star did not qualify for the 1914–15 Star.

The Queen Elizabeth II Coronation Medal 1953 was awarded immediately after the coronation on 2nd June 1953 as a personal souvenir from the Queen to members of the Royal Family, selected officers of state, members of the Royal Household, government and local government officials, mayors, public servants, members of the armed forces and police in Britain, the colonies and Dominions. It was also awarded to members of the Mount Everest expedition, two of whom reached the summit for the first time four days before the coronation. A total of 129,051 medals were awarded.

in good spirits and at 10.30 a.m. on 29th May his wife felt she could leave him for a short while. She returned about forty-five minutes later to find him hanging from the landing newel post. She immediately phoned for an ambulance and the driver cut the body down. An inquest on 31st May decided that Frederick had taken his own life while the balance of his mind was disturbed. He was cremated at Stonefall Crematorium, Wetherby Road, Harrogate on 2nd June. His ashes were collected by D Henderson and taken by the family, who are believed to have scattered them discretely over the flower beds of the local public gardens in which he had enjoyed walking. He is commemorated in a number of places:

The Bedfordshire & Hertfordshire Regimental Museum is part of Luton Wardown Park Museum.

- Roll of Honour at Isleworth County School (now Isleworth and Syon School), Middlesex.
- Communities and Local Government commemorative paving stones for the 145 VCs born in Australia, Belgium, Canada, China, Denmark, Egypt, France,

Germany, India, Iraq, Japan, Nepal, Netherlands, New Zealand, Newfoundland, Pakistan, South Africa, Sri Lanka, Ukraine and United States of America were unveiled at the National Memorial Arboretum, Alrewas, Staffordshire by Prime Minister David Cameron MP and Sergeant Johnson Beharry VC on 5th March 2015.

- Named on the Victoria Cross Memorial, Civic Centre, Hounslow, West London.

Mollie died at Langley Court Rest Home, 9 Langley Avenue, Surbiton, Surrey.

In addition to the VC he was awarded the 1914 Star with 'Mons' clasp, British War Medal 1914–20, Victory Medal 1914–19, George VI Coronation Medal 1937 and Elizabeth II Coronation Medal 1953. The group was loaned to Leeds City Museum after his death, before being presented to his Regiment by his widow. They were displayed in the Officers' Mess at the Regimental Depot but were later moved to the Bedfordshire & Hertfordshire Regimental Museum, Luton Wardown Park Museum, Wardown Park, Luton, Bedfordshire.

LIEUTENANT COLONEL DUDLEY GRAHAM JOHNSON
The South Wales Borderers, attached 2nd Battalion, The Royal Sussex Regiment

Dudley Johnson was born on 13th February 1884 at Rockcliffe, Eyford, Upper Slaughter, near Bourton-on-the-Water, Gloucestershire. His father, William Johnson (16th June 1840–9th September 1899), born at Furths, Northamptonshire, served in 6th Inniskilling Dragoons as a captain. He married Rosina 'Rose' Marguerite née Arnott (16th August 1852–25th December 1926), born at Glasgow, Lanarkshire, on 30th October 1872 at the Cathedral, Cork, Co Cork, Ireland. They lived at Rockcliffe House, Eyford Estate, Upper Slaughter, Gloucestershire and at Fern Bank, Oddington, Moreton-in-Marsh, Gloucestershire. William was a farmer in 1881, employing nine men, two boys and six women. Following the death of his eldest son in 1896, William suffered from insomnia and melancholia. The family employed two attendants to accompany him at Fern Bank. By the spring of 1899 his health appeared to have improved. Thereafter the family kept just one attendant, who heard a noise about 5.00 a.m. on 9th September but assumed that it came from outside the house. However, at 7.30 a.m. he went to William's bedroom and discovered him dead from a self-inflicted gunshot wound to the head. The inquest recorded a verdict of suicide

Upper Slaughter, near Bourton-on-the-Water in the Cotswold area of Gloucestershire, is just off the old Roman road, the Fosse Way. It is one of a handful of Doubly Thankful Villages that lost no men in either of the World Wars. Upper Slaughter was settled up to 2,000 years ago and Roman burial mounds have been found nearby. The manor is recorded in the Domesday Book of 1086. It was owned by Roger de Lacy before the Slaughter family acquired it in the late 12th century. The current building dates back to Tudor times but the crypt is probably 14th century. The remains of a Norman castle are on the northern edge of the village. In 1906 cottages around the square were reconstructed by architect Sir Edwin Lutyens, chief architect of New Dehli, India, the Cenotaph and Thiepval Memorial in France. On the night of 4th February 1944 a German bomber dropped 2,000 incendiary bombs on Upper Slaughter. Some buildings were damaged but there were no fatalities or injuries. St Peter's Church dates back to the 12th century.

during a fit of temporary insanity. Rose also subsequently died at Fern Bank. Dudley had eight siblings:

- William Bertie Stuart Johnson (1874–96), born at Newbridge, Co Kildare, Ireland, was educated at Bradfield College, Berkshire May 1888–July 1892. He was commissioned in 3rd Battalion, The Duke of Edinburgh's (Wiltshire Regiment) in 1894 and was promoted lieutenant on 24th April 1895. He was on a family holiday in Belgium in 1896 when he spotted a swimmer in trouble and went to the rescue but was drowned.

Bourton-on-the-Water is within the Cotswolds Area of Outstanding Natural Beauty and much of the village centre is a conservation area, with 114 Grade II or Grade II* listed buildings. The River Windrush runs alongside the village main street. Neolithic remains from 4,000 BC have been found nearby. Salmonsbury Camp was inhabitated from the Neolithic through to the Roman periods. A Roman road, Icknield or Ryknild Street, ran from the Fosse Way at Bourton to South Yorkshire. Roman artifacts have also been discovered in the village. A Saxon timber church was built in about 708 AD on the site of a Roman temple. By the 11th century there was a stone church. Some of the current St Lawrence church on the same site was built in the 14th century, but most of it is from the 17th and 18th centuries, with modifications in the late 19th century. The village was served by a passenger railway between 1862 and 1962. Tourism become a significant factor from the 1920s onwards. There are now about 300,000 visitors each year, whereas the village has only 3,500 residents. Parts of the James Bond film *Die Another Day* (2002) were filmed in Bourton and the nearby former RAF Little Rissington. The actor Wilfrid Hyde-White (1903–91), born at Bourton-on-the-Water, achieved international recognition for his role as Colonel Pickering in the film version of *My Fair Lady* (1964). He lived in the USA but his body was returned for burial in the family grave at Bourton.

The procession through Oddington on 26th February 1921 when the village war memorial was dedicated. Oddington was acquired by St Peter's Abbey, Gloucester in 681 and transferred to the see of York in 1061. In 1552 the barony of Churchdown, including Oddington, was granted to Sir Thomas Chamberlayne, who served the Tudors as an ambassador. The estate was in the Chamberlayne family until 1787. It was then owned by various people until the estate was broken up and sold. Oddington House became a school and the manor house a farmhouse and later the parsonage. There are two parts to the village, Upper and Lower Oddington. The number of tenants of the manor remained constant from the 9th to the middle of the 16th centuries. In the Middle Ages Oddington was a staging post with at least seven inns. King Henry III often stayed there when travelling between Woodstock and Evesham, Tewkesbury or Gloucester. The parish church of St Nicholas, dating from the 12th to the 15th centuries, stands a little apart from the two villages. It was restored in 1913, when medieval mural paintings, including a large *Last Judgement* were revealed under whitewash. In 1852 a new Holy Ascension Church was built midway between the two villages and St Nicholas was then only used for funerals. There is no electricity and services are only held in the summer and at Christmas. A nonconformist chapel was established about 1884 and a Methodist chapel was built in 1903. Since 1937 the latter has been a house. By 1835 there were five-day schools and a new national school was built in 1844. By 1871 it was the only school in the parish. It closed in 1977.

- Leslie George Arnott Johnson (1875–21st June 1929), born at Dublin, Ireland, was educated at Bradfield College September 1888–December 1890 and became a land agent. He married Hilda Eckstein (c.1890–26th June 1963), born at Cape Town, South Africa, on 2nd June 1910 at St George, Hanover Square, London. He was living at Laragh House, Bandon, Co Cork, Ireland and she at 25 Charles Street, Berkeley Square, London at the time. Hilda was the sister of Lilian, who married Leslie's brother, Raymond. They lived at 10 Airlie Gardens, Middlesex and Fern Bank, Oddington, Moreton-in-Marsh, Gloucestershire. Leslie died at Fern Bank and Hilda at Landsdowne House, Taplow, Berkshire. They had six children:
    - Daphne Rosemary Hilda Johnson (c.1911–29th September 1974), born at Bandon, Co Cork, Ireland, married Thomas Bloor, but no other details are known. She later married Douglas Alfred Withers Ross (born 1904), an engineer, and they were living at 5/7 Elgin Avenue, Armadale, Victoria, Australia in 1972. Daphne died at Cape Woolamai, Phillip Island, Victoria. Douglas had married Ellen Ransbottom (born 1893), birth registered at West Derby, Lancashire, in 1929 registered at Willesden, London. She was living with her parents at 14 Skelton Road, Forest Gate, London in 1911. Douglas and Ellen were living at 5 Green Gables, Appel Street, Griffith, Queensland in 1937, at 32 Docker Street, Elsternwick, Victoria in 1942 and at New Street, Ringwood, Victoria in 1949 and 1954. Douglas married Sylvia Jean (surname unknown) and they were living at Torquay Terrace, Torquay, Queensland in 1977 and at Hervey Bay Retirement Village, Torquay in 1980.

- Viola Diana Leslie Johnson (25th May 1912–November 1998), born at Laragh House, Bandon, Co Cork, married Lieutenant Henry Melville de Berdt Romilly (8th August 1914–August 1997), born at Ranikhet, India, on 31st August 1939 at Chelsea, London. Viola was living with her mother-in-law at The Briars, Romney Marsh, Kent in 1939. Henry's father, Francis Henry Romilly (1st October 1878–25th September 1915) was commissioned in the Welsh Regiment on 4th January 1899 and took part in the Second Boer War in South Africa 1899–1902 and in Northern Nigeria 1903. He was promoted lieutenant in March 1908 and was promoted captain and transferred to the Leicestershire Regiment on 9th February 1910. He was wounded in February 1915 serving with the 2nd Battalion but remained at duty. Awarded the DSO for his actions at Neuve Chapelle on 10th March when he led a small party in capturing about one hundred yards of enemy trenches, LG 8th May 1915. Francis was killed in action and is buried in Rue-du-Bacquerot No.1 Military Cemetery, Laventie, France (II D 13). Henry was commissioned in the Leicestershire Regiment on 31st January 1935 and was in action on the North West Frontier 1937–39. He received numerous promotions – lieutenant 31st January 1938 (64595), acting captain 20th July–22nd September and 24th September–19th October 1940, temporary captain 20th October 1940–3rd June 1941 and 19th October 1941–22nd March 1942, acting major 23rd December 1941–22nd March 1942, war substantive captain 23rd March 1942, temporary major 23rd March 1942–9th January 1944, captain 31st January 1943, local lieutenant colonel 10th September–9th October 1943 while specially employed, acting colonel 10th October 1943–9th April 1944, war substantive major 10th January 1944, war substantive lieutenant colonel 10th April 1944–12th August 1948, temporary colonel 10th April 1944–30th June 1946 and major 31st January 1948. Henry retired, with the honorary rank of colonel, on 1st June 1958 and ceased to be a member of the Reserve, on reaching the age limit, on 16th June 1965. The marriage ended in divorce. They had three children including Barry Henry de Berdt Romilly (1940–2007) and Sara Diana de Berdt Romilly (1942). Henry married Maria Vilma Pogonyi (27th September 1926–3rd March 2006), born at Rákospalota, Budapest, Hungary, in 1952 at Trieste, Italy. He died at Hastings and Rother, East Sussex and she at Worthing, West Sussex. They had a son, George H de Berdt Romilly (born 1955), and a daughter. Viola married Reuben Astley-Jones (7th June 1899–1978), born at Worthen, Shropshire, in 1953 at Bodmin, Cornwall. His father, Richard Jones (born 1867) enlisted in the Army Pay Corps at Shrewsbury on 23rd March 1915, giving his age as forty-four years and 120 days. His next of kin, his wife Mary, was living at 15a Market Square, Wellington, Shropshire. He was just over 5′ 8½″ tall and his religious denomination was Calvinist Methodist. He was discharged, services no longer required, on 9th October 1915. Reuben died at North

Walsham, Norfolk and Viola at Windsor and Maidenhead, Berkshire. Reuben had married Nancy Podmore (3rd March 1908–17th January 1993), born at Wellington, Shropshire, in 1935 registered at Forden, Montgomeryshire. Reuben was a chief finance and local government officer in 1939, when they were living at Tarn Hows, Barnfield Crescent, Wellington. The marriage ended in divorce. Reuben and Nancy had a son, Philip W Astley-Jones in 1946. Nancy married John McGinnis (1916–1991) in 1959 at Shrewsbury. She died at Radbrook Green Nursing Home, Shrewsbury, Shropshire.

- Pamela Geraldine Leslie Johnson (12th September 1913–16th March 1981) married Malcolm Fayerweather Gordon CBE DSc (Queen's University Belfast) (21st May 1913–17th June 2005), born at Hilden House, Lisburn, Co Antrim, Ireland, on 6th November 1938 at Eton, Buckinghamshire. He was chairman of the Linen Research Association, Belfast, Northern Ireland in 1967. Pamela died at Newtownards, Co Down, Northern Ireland. They had five children, including Michael Leslie Gordon (1939–2009) and Gail Patricia Gordon (1941–2016). Malcolm married Margaret 'Peggy' Phipps Comersall (1926–2008). He died at Killinchy, Newtownards.
- William Leslie Arnott Johnson (27th October 1915–8th April 1991) married Margaret Boyd Jardine (3rd June 1914–20th August 1991), born at London, England, on 22nd December 1962 in Rhodesia. He was living at 17 Compton Avenue, Tilehurst, Reading, Berkshire when he died in South Africa. She died at Johannesburg, South Africa. Margaret had married William 'Roy' Alfred Jardine (11th March 1911–1961), born at Kimberley, South Africa, on 24th August 1937 in South Africa. William died in Zimbabwe. They had two sons.
- Valerie Leslie Johnson (16th November 1916–January 1985) never married and died at Maidstone, Kent.
- Mervyn John Leslie Arnott Johnson (1918–11th May 1944) married Mary Joy Knobel (born c.1910) on 14th January 1942 in South Africa, where she was born. They were living at Landsdowne House, Bath Road, Taplow, Buckinghamshire in 1944. Mervyn received a Regular Army Emergency Commission in the South Wales Borderers (145131) on 17th August 1940 and was promoted war substantive lieutenant on 7th February 1942. He was serving as a major in Burma, attached to 15th Punjab Regiment, when he was killed in action (Kohima War Cemetery – 6 D 1).

• Raymond Bazley Johnson (30th January 1877–27th November 1948), born at London, was educated at Bradfield College September 1890–July 1893. He was commissioned from the Militia in 6th (Inniskilling) Dragoons on 4th May 1898 and promoted lieutenant on 5th July 1899. He was later a captain in 6th Inniskilling Dragoons. Raymond embarked for South Africa with B Squadron, 6th Inniskilling Dragoons aboard SS *Jamaican* at Queenstown, Ireland on 29th October 1899. He took part in operations in:

Orange Free State March–May 1900, including actions at Vet River and Zand River. He travelled from Driefontein with six men at night, accompanied by the Australian poet and correspondent, Andrew Barton 'Banjo' Paterson, carrying General French's Despatches to Lord Roberts at Germiston. They eluded several parties of the enemy and completed their mission.

Transvaal May–June 1900, including actions near Johannesburg, Pretoria and Diamond Hill (11th-12th June).

Transvaal east of Pretoria July–20th November 1900, including actions at Reit Vlei and Belfast (26th–27th August).

Cape Colony south of Orange River, including actions at Colesberg (1st June–12th February).

Transvaal and Orange River Colony 30th November 1900 to 31st May 1902.

Raymond was mentioned in Lord Kitchener's Despatches of 4th September 1901 (LG 10th September 1901) and 8th October 1901 (LG 3rd December 1901), for gallant and dashing conduct on the Vaal River on 23rd September, in killing two Boers, wounding one and capturing fifteen before they could get to cover. Promoted captain 15th March 1902. Appointed Adjutant 6th Dragoons 1st April–31st May 1902. In June 1902 he was sent to England with a small contingent to represent the Regiment at King Edward VII's Coronation. Awarded the DSO (LG 26th June 1902), which he received from the King on 24th October 1902. Raymond last appears in the Army List in March 1906 and was living with his mother in 1911. Raymond married Lilian Eckstein (c.1891–30th August 1937), born in South Africa, on 15th February 1912 at St Gregory's, Welford Park, Newbury, Berkshire. Lilian was the sister of Hilda, who married Raymond's brother Leslie. They were living at Hill Side, Little Compton, Warwickshire in 1914. He served in the Great War as a temporary lieutenant commander RNVR, with HMS *Pembroke II* additional for duty with the Royal Naval Air Service 3rd December 1914–15th October 1915, when he resigned. He then served in 4th Reserve Regiment of Cavalry as a captain from 9th March 1916 and was Commandant School of Instruction 1916–17. He was attached to Quartering Branch RAF from 4th Cavalry Reserve Regiment on 5th June 1918 and joined HQ South Western Area next day for administrative duties. However, he does not appear in the Air Force List. Promoted captain 7th November 1918 and dispersed on 12th March 1919. He last appears in the Army List in May 1920. They were living at The Old Forge, Great Rissington, Bourton-on-the-Water, Gloucestershire at the time of her death at Holme Lacy Hospital, Herefordshire. Raymond was living at the Ellenborough Hotel, Oriel Road, Cheltenham in 1939. He was living at The Cavalry Club, London at the time of his death at the Mayfair Hotel, Berkeley Square, London. Lilian and Raymond had three children:

- Diana Vivien Raymond Johnson (18th January 1914–9th September 2015), born at Little Compton, Gloucestershire, married Harold Banning Richardson in 1937 at Westminster. They had a daughter, Rhea Richardson (born 17th April 1941). Harold is believed to have married Maria B Berkelaar at Hitchin in 1968. Diana married Brandon Barringer (11th June 1899–23rd September 1991), born at Cape May, Cape May Co, New Jersey, USA, in 1967. He graduated from Haverford School, Pennsylvania in 1916 and Princeton University. New Jersey in 1921 (Phi Beta Kappa). He served in the Students Army Training Corps at Princeton University (4.347.200). He was employed by First Pennsylvania Banking & Trust Co 1921–49. He held numerous appointments – member of the finance committee of the Wellington Fund 1929–59, director of Lehigh Valley Railroad 1938–42, treasurer and director of Curtis Publishing Co 1948–62, director of New York & Pa County Inc 1950–62, director of Bantam Books Inc 1957–61, trustee of Thomas Jefferson University and the Academy of Natural Sciences, an overseer of the Franklin Institute and a governor of the Nature Conservancy. He was living at 1530 Locust Street, Philadelphia, Pennsylvania when he enlisted in the US Army Air Force on 27th April 1942 (0–903589), reaching the rank of colonel and being appointed Deputy Chief of Statistical Control Division USAAF. He was discharged from Andrews Field, Washington DC on 26th March 1946. Awarded the Legion of Merit. He died at Beaumont, Bryn Mawr Retirement Community Inc, Delaware Co, Pennsylvania. Diana died at Wayne, Delaware Co. Brandon had married Sonia Elizabeth Louise Converse (27th December 1909–23rd November 1964), born at Philadelphia, Pennsylvania, in 1945. They were living at Hilldale and Ashwood Roads, Villanova, Delaware Co, Pennsylvania in 1946. Sonia died at Philadelphia. She and Brandon had three daughters – Carla Sonia Barringer (married as Rabinowitz), Elizabeth Brandon Barringer (married as Fentress) and Felicity Barringer (married as Taubman).

  - Lilah Mervyn Raymond Johnson (23rd March 1915–26th September 1942), born at Newbury, Berkshire, was a student living at 37 St Leonard's Terrace, Chelsea in 1939. She was a VAD at the time of the 1939 Register. She never married and was living at The Grenville Hotel, Bude, Cornwall at the time of her death at The Holloway Sanatorium, Virginia Water, Surrey.
  - Michael Hugh Raymond Johnson (born 29th January 1917), born at Farnham-Royal, Eton, Buckinghamshire, moved to California, USA before 1942 and worked for Robert Walsh, at the California Yacht Club, Wilmington Marina, Los Angeles. He ran and lived aboard the fishing boat *Windward*. He was described as 5′ 11″ tall with grey eyes, brown hair, freckled complexion and weighed 200 lbs. Michael married Helen Dallas (born 9th September 1912), born at Los Angeles, on 14th April 1942 at Alexandria, Virginia, USA.

- Cecil John Douglas Johnson (12th September 1878–5th November 1966), born at Eyford, Gloucestershire, was a farmer, living with his mother at Fern Bank, Oddington in 1911. He suffered an accident while at school at Bruges, Belgium, resulting in respiratory issues that prevented military service. Cecil was a

Freemason, member of Bowyer Lodge, Chipping Norton, Initiated in June 1905 and Master in 1912. He married Gladys Barton (17th June 1881–1974), born at Yardley, Birmingham, Warwickshire, on 27th April 1921 at St Matthew's Church, Westminster. They were living at Plough Cottage, Oddington, Gloucestershire in 1939, when he was an ARP Warden. Cecil subsequently died there. Gladys's death was registered at Cheltenham, Gloucestershire. They had four children, all registered at Stow-on-the-Wold, Gloucestershire:

- Ruth Mary Johnson (22nd February 1922–15th September 1988) married Jozef/Josef Nowakowski (5th March 1915–30th November 1973), born in Poland, in 1956 at Abingdon, Berkshire. They were living at 59 Russell Road, Nottingham at the time of his death there. She was living at 9 Chawley Lane, Cumnor Hill, Oxford at the time of her death there. They had three children – David JJ Nowakowski 1956, Johnathan M Nowakowski 1958 and Elizabeth MJ Nowakowski 1962.
- John Cecil Johnson (20th March 1923–19th February 2010) was commissioned as a pilot officer (on probation) in the RAFVR on 7th August 1942 (127958). Promoted war substantive flying officer 7th February 1943 and was awarded the DFC (LG 15th October 1943). He served with No.104 Squadron and was promoted war substantive flight lieutenant 7th August 1944 and later acting squadron leader. Awarded a Bar to the DFC (LG 20th April 1945). Posted to Training Branch on 15th May 1950 and resigned his commission, on 24th November 1950. John became a Clerk in Holy Orders. He died at Telford, Shropshire.
- Angela Margaret Johnson (born 1924) married Frank Alfred Glover (5th November 1897–23rd January 1979), born at Chedworth, Gloucestershire, at Cheltenham in July 1968. Frank was living with his widowed grandmother and widowed father at Clifden Cottage, Chedworth in 1911. He enlisted in the Royal Flying Corps on 4th January 1916 (17160) and carried out basic training at Hendon airfield, qualifying as a rigger air mechanic 2nd class. He transferred to the Royal Air Force on 1st April 1918 as air mechanic 3rd class, rigger (aero) and was assigned to No.2 Aircraft Acceptance Park, Hendon and later No.1 Communications Squadron, Hendon. He was discharged on 30th April 1920 and returned to Clifden Cottage. Frank was living at 20 Vineries Close, Leckhampton, Cheltenham at the time of his death there. Frank had married Isabel/Isabella Watt Allan (30th January 1904–13th August 1950), born at Banff, Banffshire, Scotland, in 1927 at Hamilton, Lanarkshire. They were living at 19 Painswick Road, Cheltenham in 1939, by when he was a foreman joiner. Isabel subsequently died there. Frank and Isabel had two children – Philip William Glover (1931–2018) and Isabel M Glover (1935–2019).
- Christopher Dudley Johnson (16th April 1926–3rd July 2018) became a Clerk in Holy Orders. He married Anne 'Anna' B Smythe (born 1924) in

1960 at Winchester, Hampshire, where she was born. She was living with her parents at 52 St Cross Road, Winchester in 1939. Christopher died at Winchester. They had three children – Rosemary D Johnson 1961, Kathryn L Johnson 1963 and Nicholas S Johnson 1964.

- Rose Marguerite Mary Johnson (28th April 1881–16th March 1932), born at Rockcliffe, Eyford, Gloucestershire, never married and lived with her mother at Fern Bank, Oddington, Moreton-in-Marsh, Gloucestershire. She was living there at the time of her death at Highways, Oddington.
- Victor Neville Johnson (14th August 1882–2nd October 1972) was educated at Bradfield College May 1898–December 1899. He served in the Militia and was embodied with 3rd Wiltshire Regiment for two years and 208 days. Promoted lieutenant 2nd May 1900 and received a regular commission in the Royal Garrison Artillery on 12th August 1902. Promoted lieutenant on 21st March 1903 and transferred to the Gloucestershire Regiment on 8th July 1905. He was promoted captain on 15th July 1911 and was based at Verdala Barracks, Malta with the 2nd Battalion at the time of the 1911 Census. Victor married Claire Eleanor Alicia Nevinson (1892–14th November 1970), born at Chelsea, London, on 30th January 1913 at St Luke, Chelsea. She was living at 14 Sydney Street, Chelsea at the time. He was living at Kinnersley, Severn Stoke, Upton-on-Severn, Worcestershire in 1939. Victor was appointed adjutant with the TF 18th April 1912–5th October 1915. Victor served in France March 1915–5th August 1918. Appointed Brigade Major 6th October 1915–9th February 1917 and was promoted brevet major on 3rd June 1916 and major 18th January 1917. Appointed GSO2 in France 10th February 1917–5th August 1918. Appointed GSO1 War Office as a temporary lieutenant colonel 1st September 1918–31st March 1919. Appointed GSO1 North Russia 9th April–17th October 1919, where he was wounded. Victor was Mentioned in Despatches (LG 1st January 1916, 15th June 1916, 4th January 1917, 11th December 1917 and 3rd February 1920). Awarded the DSO (LG 1st January 1918) and the French Legion d'Honneur 5th Class (LG 5th November 1920). Promoted brevet lieutenant colonel on 3rd June 1919. Appointed Brigade Major, Western Command 11th March 1920–31st March 1922. He was employed with the Royal West African Frontier Force 9th November 1927–13th October 1929. Promoted lieutenant colonel on 2nd July 1931 and was appointed OIC Infantry Records & Pay Office, Warwick on 28th March 1935. Promoted colonel on 28th March 1935 and retired on 28th March 1939. Eleanor was living at Hill House Farm, Rushock, Worcestershire at the time of her death there. Victor died at Kirkleacham, 15 Lansdowne Croft, Malvern, Worcestershire. They had a daughter:
  - Priscilla Neville Johnson (25th May 1918–30th November 2006), born at Stow-on-the-Wold, was a farm assistant at Goldburn, Okehampton, Devon in 1939. She married Lieutenant Denys William Clegg Solven RA (22nd November 1917–10th December 1997), birth registered at Aston,

Warwickshire, in 1941 at Upton upon Severn, Worcestershire. He was a cadet sergeant, Bromsgrove School Contingent, Junior Division, Officer Training Corps and was commissioned in 67th (South Midland) Field Brigade RA TA on 24th July 1938. He was mobilised on 24th August 1939 (76480) and was promoted lieutenant 8th January 1941 and captain 1st July 1946. Awarded the Territorial Efficiency Decoration (LG 20th June 1950). Promoted major on 8th July 1952 and retired on 19th November 1958. They both died at Hereford. They had two children – Pauline C Solven 1943 and Guy DN Solven 1946.

- Mervyn Taylor Johnson (13th March 1886–14th September 1914) was educated at Bradfield College March 1899–March 1904. He was commissioned in 3rd Wiltshire (Militia) on 26th November 1904 and transferred to 2nd South Wales Borderers on 24th April 1907. Promoted lieutenant on 15th May 1909. He was based with his brother, Dudley, at Artillery Barracks, Pretoria, South Africa in 1911. Mervyn served at Tientsin, China 1911–14. He was fatally wounded serving in 1st Battalion at the Battle of Aisne and was originally buried by the Reverend Joseph DS Parry-Evans (1876–1936) 'outside the farm at the crossroads in Vendresse'. After the war his remains were exhumed and reburied in Vendresse British Cemetery, Aisne, France (I C 18).
- John Charles Eric Arnott Johnson (25th September 1897–18th December 1983), born at Oddington, Gloucestershire, was a cadet at the Royal Naval College, Osborne, Isle of Wight, Hampshire in 1911. He served as a midshipman aboard HMS *Carnarvon* and was promoted sub lieutenant on 15th May 1917 and acting lieutenant. Promoted lieutenant 15th February 1919 and retired at his own request on 27th September 1920. He was commissioned in the Royal Air Force on 14th July 1923 as a flying officer (honorary flight lieutenant), Flying & Observation Officer in General Duties Branch (18004). He was under instruction at No.2 Flying Training School, Duxford, Cambridgeshire in 1924 and was posted to No.24 (Communications) Squadron, Kenley, Surrey. He was under

Vendresse British Cemetery, where Mervyn Taylor Johnson is buried. The area was the scene of severe fighting involving British troops in 1914 and 1918. The cemetery was created after the Armistice by concentrating graves from at least thirteen other cemeteries and the battlefields. Over 700 Great War casualties are commemorated on this site. Over half are unidentified and there are special memorials to three soldiers, known or believed to be buried there in unnamed graves. Special memorials also record fifty soldiers buried in other cemeteries whose graves were destroyed by shell fire. There are thirty-seven graves identified collectively but not individually marked by headstones superscribed, *Buried near this spot*.

instruction at the Electronics & Wireless School, Flowerdown, Winchester from 1st December 1924 and was posted to No.208 (Army Cooperation) Squadron, Moascar, Ismailia, Egypt on 18th November 1925. Promoted flight lieutenant on 1st January 1928. He was held on depot strength from 29th July 1930 whilst sick and non-effective. Posted to No.99 (Bomber) Squadron, Upper Heyford, Oxfordshire on 7th November 1930 and No.33 (Bomber) Squadron, Bicester, Oxfordshire on 6th September 1931. John attended the Staff College, Andover, Hampshire from 23rd January 1933 and was appointed Station Adjutant, HQ Worthy Down, Winchester, Hampshire on 9th January 1934. He was appointed ADC Camp to the Viceroy of India on 1st January 1935 and was promoted squadron leader on 1st April 1936. John took command of No.62 (Bomber) Squadron, Cranfield, Bletchley, Buckinghamshire on 25th June 1937 and was promoted wing commander on 1st March 1939. He retired on 24th March 1943. He married Pamela Muriel Ismay (8th September 1913–29th November 1988), born at Chelsea, London, on 7th September 1940 at Westminster. They were living at Fir Cottage, Winkfield Road, Ascot, Berkshire at the time of their deaths. They had three children:

- Bruce Johnson (born 1945), born at Isle of Wight, Hampshire.
- David Johnson (born 1946), born at Windsor, Berkshire.
- Phylleen Johnson (born 1955) married Bradley Paul Roynon (born 1950), born at Wandsworth, London, in 1979 at Bracknell, Berkshire. Bradley was a National Health Service management adviser with London Teaching Hospitals. He was appointed Director of the Chief Executive's Office, London Borough of Richmond. He was CEO East Hampshire District Council 1988–97, CEO Southampton City Council 2001–07 and CEO Carmarthenshire County Council 2007–10. He was appointed to the Board of Solent Healthcare. The marriage ended in divorce. Bradley married Janet Lennox in 1988 at Richmond upon Thames. Phylleen married Anthony Cunningham (born c.1955) in May 1994 in Surrey.

Dudley's paternal grandfather, William Johnson (April 1806–20th April 1877), born at Thurmaston, Leicestershire, married Mary née Sansom (1811–October 1882),

Old Stratford, Northamptonshire lies immediately north of where the Roman road, Watling Street, crossed the River Great Ouse. The Buckingham Arm of the Grand Union Canal, which passed through the village, has been disused since 1964.

also born at Thurmaston, Leicestershire, in 1838 at Leicester. He was a cattle dealer and grazier in 1851, when they were living at Old Stratford, Northamptonshire. By 1861 he was a farmer at The Green, Passenham, Northamptonshire. He was living at Deanshanger House, Passenham at the time of his death there. Mary was a farmer of 315 acres employing three men and a boy at Calverton Lodge, Calverton, Northamptonshire in 1881. Her death was registered at Potterspury, Northamptonshire. In addition to William they had three other children:

- Sarah Johnson (6th November 1838–1906), born at Furtho, Northamptonshire, was living with her sister, Mary, at 16 Linton Terrace, Lampton Road, Heston, Hounslow, Middlesex in 1901. She never married and subsequently died there.
- John Johnson (born 1845).
- Mary Louisa Johnson (17th November 1849–20th November 1908), born at Cosgrove, Northamptonshire, was living with her sister, Sarah, at 16 Linton Terrace, Lampton Road, Heston, Hounslow in 1901. She never married and subsequently died there.

His maternal grandfather, John Arnott (26th July 1814–28th March 1898), born at Auchtermuchty, Fife, Scotland, went to Cork, Ireland in 1837 and worked in the retail business. He established his own business in Belfast, followed by a chain of drapery stores in both Ireland and Britain. He was proprietor of the *Irish Times* newspaper, which remained in the family until the 1960s. He was a noted philanthropist and promoter of Irish industries. Amongst his many appointments, he was Lord Mayor of Cork on three occasions, MP for Kinsale, Cork 1859–63 and JP for the City & County of Cork. John married Margaret 'Mary' Jane née McKinlay (c.1816–

Auchtermuchty, Fife was, until 1975, a royal burgh established under King James V in 1517. Human habitation in the area dates back 2,000 years. The Romans had a camp in the southeast of the town. Linen was the main industry until the early 18th century, when the firm of John White established the first foundry in the town. Stratheden Whisky Distillery opened in 1829 but closed in 1926 when Prohibition was imposed in the USA and reduced demand. The old part of the town has many buildings from the 17th and 18th centuries. The church is a simple Georgian box chapel, with gravestones dating back to the 17th century. The town was the location of Tannochbrae in the 1990s TV series *Dr Finlay*. Amongst the town's famous alumni are:

- *The Proclaimers*, Charlie and Craig Reid, born on 5th March 1962 at Leith, grew up in Edinburgh, Cornwall and Auchermuchty, where they attended Bell Baxter High School. The duo is best known for *Letter from America* 1987 and *I'm Gonna Be (500 Miles)* 1988.
- Sir James Shand MBE (1908–2000), the accordion musician, was born in East Wemyss, Fife. The family moved to Auchermuchty and there is a statue of him there.

29th July 1866) on 20th January 1852 at 11 Landsdowne Crescent. Glasgow, Lanarkshire. She died at Cork, Ireland. John married Emily Jane Fitzgerald (1854–22nd October 1938) at St Mary's Church, Youghal, Co Cork on 7th November 1872 and they lived at Woodlands and South Mall, Cork. He was created baronet on 12th February 1896. John died at Woodlands leaving effects valued at £160,371/12/- (£24.8M in 2023). Emily changed her name to Emily Jane Arnott-Fitzgerald by Royal Licence on 20th September 1902. She was living at Dunardagh, Blackrock, Co Dublin at the time of her death at Strand House, Youghal. In addition to Rose, John had eleven other children from his two marriages:

South Mall, one of the main streets in Cork, Ireland, was built over what was once a channel of the River Lee. The street is a centre for banking, financial services, legal offices and solicitors.

- John (later Sir John) Alexander Arnott (1st November 1853–26th July 1940), born at Cork, served in 4th Battalion, The Cheshire Regiment. Promoted captain 19th January 1884, major 5th June 1893 and retired as a lieutenant colonel on 1 December 1897. As a lieutenant colonel he was appointed a Governor of the Royal Hibernian Military School, Phoenix Park, Dublin. He married Caroline Sydney Williams (1859–28th December 1933), born at Bath, Somerset, on 27th September 1881. He was a ship owner in 1890. Caroline was invested Lady of Grace, Order of St John of Jerusalem. She was a JP and was created DBE in 1918. John was JP and DL, Co Cork. They were living at 12 Merrion Square, Dublin in 1918 and later at Shearwater, Ceanchor Road, Baily, Howth, Co Dublin. Caroline died at the Private Hospital, Regent Street, Leicester. John died at Shearwater, leaving effects valued at £93,774/6/11 (£7.3M in 2023). They had seven children, born at Barton Regis, Gloucestershire:
    - Margaret Christian Salome Arnott (1883–14th March 1952).
    - John 'Punch' Arnott (25th July 1885–30th March 1918) was commissioned on probation in 15th (The King's) Hussars on 25th July 1906 and was at Muttra, India in April 1908. His seniority as second lieutenant dated from 25th July 1908 and he was promoted lieutenant on 9th October 1911. Appointed Adjutant 24th November 1912. He was seconded as ADC to GOC 1st Cavalry Division 5th August 1914–13th April 1915 and embarked for France on 14th August, landing next day. MID 20th November. John was promoted captain on 25th February 1915 and rejoined the Regiment as Adjutant on 14th April 1915. MID 30th November, LG 1st January 1916. MC, LG 14th January 1916. He was admitted to 7th Stationary Hospital, Boulogne with laryngitis 12th March–5th April. Appointed Staff Captain

HQ 2nd Cavalry Brigade on 1st November and rejoined the Regiment on 25th December. John was killed in action and is buried Fouilloy Communal Cemetery, Somme, France (A6).

John Arnott's grave in Fouilloy Communal Cemetery.

- Lina Victoria Arnott, a twin with Mary, (1887–25th October 1974) married Baron Francis C de Freyne (1887–1935) in 1916 at Kensington.
- Mary Christian Arnott, a twin with Lina, (1887–26th May 1936).
- Lauriston John Arnott (27th November 1890–2nd July 1958) was educated at Wellington College September 1904–August 1907 and at West Wratting Park, Cambridge from September 1907. He was commissioned in 1st Cameronians on 5th October 1910 and was promoted lieutenant on 26th February 1913. Due to misconduct with excessive drinking at Stobs Camp his leave was stopped for one year from 24th June 1913. He was drunk and misbehaved at Alhambra Music Hall, Glasgow on 19th March 1914, while based at Maryhill Barracks there, and was to be tried by general court martial. However, he was allowed to resign in April 1914 after his father requested this option to GOC Lowland Division. He enlisted in 3rd Royal Irish Rifles (1312) at Dublin on 3rd November 1914, described as a rancher, 5′ 11″ tall, weighing 147 lbs, with grey eyes, black hair and his religious denomination was Church of Ireland. He was appointed unpaid lance corporal on 6th November and acting sergeant on 9th November. Lauriston went to France on 5th or 11th November and returned to Britain on 14th or 30th December or 3rd January 1915. He was commissioned as a lieutenant in 3rd Royal Irish Rifles on 24th March 1915 and went to France on 15th June to join 2nd Royal Irish Rifles. He was very severely wounded by a gunshot in the right elbow and forearm on 23rd June and was evacuated from Dieppe to Dover on 29th July for admission to King Edward VII Hospital for Officers, London. The wound resulted in limited movement of the arm and some wasting. A medical board at Caxton Hall, London on 23rd August found him unfit for General Service for four months and Home Service for three months. He was granted leave until 22nd November. Lauriston was promoted captain on 18th September. A medical board at King George V Hospital, Dublin on 29th November found him unfit for General Service for four months, Home Service for three months and light duties for two months. His leave was extended until 28th January 1916. A medical board at Aylesbury on 8th February 1916

found him unfit for service for four months and leave was extended until 7th June. Medical boards at Caxton Hall on 7th June and 12th September found him unfit for General Service for between six and three months, Home Service between four and two months and light duties between three and two months. Leave was extended until 11th November. A medical board at King George V Hospital on 20th November found him unfit for General Service for three months, Home Service for two months and light duties for one month. Leave was extended until 19th December. Medical boards at King George V Hospital on 19th December and 27th January, 27th February and 30th March 1917 found him unfit for General and Home Service for the same periods but fit for light duty office work. By 2nd April he was working under HQ Irish Command. A medical board on 26th June found him unfit for General Service for three months but fit for Home Service. A medical board at Lower Castle Yard, Dublin on 24th July found him unfit for General Service for six months and Home Service for three months but fit for light duty. A medical board there on 28th September found him unfit for General Service permanently and Home Service for two months but fit for light duty. A medical board at Lower Castle Yard on 4th or 11th December found him fit for A and he returned to France in January 1918. Lauriston was admitted to No.8 British Red Cross Hospital, Boulogne about 25th May because of the old wound. A medical board at Harfleur, Le Havre on 28th May found him fit for B3. A medical board on 16th September found him unfit for General Service. He was admitted to No.10 Casualty Clearing Station, Remy Siding, Lijssenthoek, Belgium with insomnia and weakness, probably following influenza. He was transferred to No.5 British Red Cross Hospital, Wimereux, France and was evacuated to Britain for treatment at 1st Western General Hospital, Fazakerley, Liverpool. A medical board there on 13th December found him unfit for A & B and C for one month and he was sent for convalescence to Monkstown House Auxiliary Hospital, Co Dublin. A medical board at Dublin on 12th March 1919 found him unfit for service permanently and he was assessed as 30% disabled. Lauriston relinquished his commission on account of ill-health on 11th May.

- Robert John Arnott (19th August 1896–25th July 1966).
- Thomas John Arnott (12th April 1899–16th July 1979), educated at Eton College, Windsor, married Lettice Mary Crompton-Roberts (23rd April 1903–1986), born at Chelsea, at St George, Hanover Square, London on 29th September 1927. He served in the 15th Hussars and was mentioned in despatches and awarded the US Silver Star. Thomas died at Swindon, Wiltshire. They had four children – Peter John Arnott (25th January 1929–October 2001), Mariegold [sic] Winifred Arnott (14th November 1931–2nd April 1987), Guy Arnott (9th November 1932–21st August 2010) and Caroline Arnott (born 28th April 1934).

Major General Sir Eric Stanley Girdwood KBE CB CMG (14th October 1876 – 24th May 1963) was educated at Belfast Royal Academy and was commissioned in the Cameronians (Scottish Rifles) on 20th May 1899. He served in the Second Boer War 1899–1902 with the 2nd Battalion, including in the Ladysmith Relief Force, at the battles of Colenso (December 1899), Vaal Krantz (February 1900) and Tugela Heights (February 1900) and in Natal March–June 1900. He was Brigade Major of the Scottish Rifles Brigade in 1911. During the Great War he served at Gallipoli and commanded 156th Brigade in Egypt and Palestine in 1916. He was later GOC 74th Division in Palestine and France. He was appointed Commander 9th Brigade 1919, Commander Military Forces in Iraq 1924, GOC Bombay District, India 1926, Commandant Royal Military College, Sandhurst 1927 and GOC Northern Ireland District 1931. He retired in 1935. In 1955 he became President of the Legion of Frontiersmen. At Sandhurst one of the officer cadets was the future actor, David Niven. He and Dick Hobson were Commandant's Orderlies for six months. Part of their uniform was a white cross-belt with a silver message box on the back. The boxes should have been empty but Niven loaded his with Woodbine cigarettes, Swan Vestas matches, toilet paper and a pack of ten condoms. When other cadets enquired, he told them they were the Commandant's personal supplies. On long Sunday morning inspections by the Commandant, the cadets were amused that the inspection was preceded by this unusual cargo. However, one morning the Commandant decided to inspect his orderlies. Both were immaculately turned out until General Girdwood walked round the back and opened Niven's message box. Dick Hobson had great difficulty controlling his laughter and Niven thought that his military career was at an end. After an eternity searching the box, Girdwood stood before Niven and said, *I had heard about that…thank you very much…you are very considerate…*' Immediately after church parade Niven cleared out the message box.

- David Taylor Arnott (28th April 1855–22nd July 1915), born at Newcastle upon Tyne, Northumberland, was a journalist. He married Ethel Marion Napier late Jessop née Bell (24th September 1863–21st November 1893), born at Downham, Norfolk, in 1890 at Marylebone, London. He was a newspaper editor by 1892. They were living at 37 Boundary Road, St Johns' Wood, London at the time of her death there. Ethel had married George Henry Jessop (c.1857–90) in 1884 at Taunton, Somerset. His death was registered at Axbridge, Somerset. David married Blanche Emma Girdwood (1st January 1872–7th January 1962), born at Belfast, Co Antrim, Ireland, on 11th December 1895 at Paddington, London. She was the sister of Major General Sir Eric Stanley Girdwood KBE CB CMG (1876–1963). They were living at Rose Bank, Binstead, Isle of Wight, Hampshire at the time of his death there. Blanche was living at 10 Porchester Terrace, London at the time of her death. David had three children from his two marriages:
  - Maria Ethel Arnott (24th March 1891–11th March 1961).
  - John Frederic Arnott (2nd June 1892–24th October 1969) was educated at Bradfield College, Berkshire until July 1910 (OTC). He was a rancher in Canada when he enlisted in 2nd Canadian Mounted Rifles (107064) at Victoria, British Columbia on 31st December 1914. He was described as 5′ 11½″ tall, with ruddy complexion, blue eyes, light brown hair and his

religious denomination was Church of England. The unit sailed for Britain on 12th June 1915. From July he assigned $10 per month from his military salary to Miss Arnott, c/o Miss Fox, Cowichan Bay, Vancouver Island, BC. He applied for a commission in the Wiltshire Regiment Special Reserve on 26th August, while serving with C Squadron, 2nd Canadian Mounted Rifles, 1st Canadian Mounted Rifles Brigade at Shorncliffe, Kent. He was commissioned in 3rd Wiltshire Regiment on 25th September. John suffered from periostitis of the left tibia. A medical board at Weymouth on 28th April 1916 found he was unfit for General Service for two months and Home Service for one month. A medical board there on 6th June found he was fit for General Service. Awarded the MC, LG 20th October 1916. He was attached to 1/1st Buckinghamshire, 145th Brigade, 48th Division at St Gratien when he fell ill with influenza and jaundice on 1st February 1917. He was treated at 1st New Zealand Stationary Hospital, Amiens until 25th February when he was transferred to 8th General Hospital, Rouen. On 7th March he embarked aboard HMHS *St David* at Rouen, disembarked at Southampton next day and was sent to the Royal Victoria Hospital, Netley, Hampshire. A medical board there on 17th March found he was unfit for General Service for one month and Home Service for three weeks but fit for light duties at home. He was granted leave until 7th April. He joined 3rd (Reserve) Battalion at Littlemoor Camp, Preston, Weymouth on 30th April. A medical board at Nothe Hospital, Weymouth on 5th May found he was unfit for General Service for one month and Home Service for three weeks but fit for light duties. He was attached to 92nd Training Reserve Battalion, Chiseldon Camp, Wiltshire. A medical board at the Military Hospital, Chiseldon Camp on 6th June found he was fit for General Service. Promoted lieutenant on 1st July and appointed acting captain 2nd May 1918–11th July 1919. John was taken prisoner at Guyencourt on 27th May 1918. That day 1st Wiltshire was in 25th Division in Corps Reserve. The enemy attacked at dawn, but it was not until 2.00 p.m. that 1st Wiltshire was engaged. At 3.00 p.m. John's company was driven back and formed up again around Battalion HQ in conjunction with A Company. Casualties were heavy and shortly afterwards they were ordered to withdraw to hold a wood about 275m away. During the withdrawal the CO was wounded, and he went to help, assisted by Lieutenant Reid, the Battalion Lewis Gun Officer. They were then cut off and forced to surrender. He was repatriated on 15th December and arrived in England on 20th December. By January 1919 he was serving with the 1st Battalion at Royal Barracks, Dublin. On 10th July the War Office investigation into the circumstances of his capture found he was not to blame. John relinquished his commission on 27th February 1920. However, he was granted a special appointment (Class GG) as Intelligence Officer, Curragh Internment Camp, Ireland on 30th April 1921. This was changed to another special

appointment (Class HH) as Censor Officer, Curragh Internment Camp on 15th August. He relinquished the special appointment on 19th January 1922. He was disembodied and relinquished his commission retaining the rank of captain on 11th February. His address was 81 King's Road, Chelsea, London. John was living at the Soo Hotel, Weyburn, Saskatchewan, Canada in January 1940. He died at Prince Albert, Saskatchewan.
  - David Terence Edmond Arnott (27th September 1899–27th May 1933).
- Mangerton William Arnott (14th August 1856–16th December 1901), of Drumdiah, Killeagh, Co Cork, was JP (Cork) and High Sheriff 1896. He married Eliza Mary Arnott [sic] (12th November 1864–17th July 1898), born at Partick, Lanarkshire, on 10th November 1886 at Edinburgh, Midlothian, Scotland. She died at Marylebone, London and he at Cork. They had a daughter – Eliza Mary Arnott (1887–1st February 1956).
- Margaret Jane Arnott (10th April 1859–5th August 1936), born at Cork, married Lieutenant Francis Augustus St Maur Sheil (15th February 1855–17th September 1887), born at Kinnitty, Kings Co (now Co Offaly), Ireland, at St Luke's Parish Church, Cork on 28th September 1880. He served in the North Cork Rifles as a sub lieutenant and transferred to 9th King's Royal Rifle Corps. He resigned his commission on 23rd June 1883 and died at Charlton House, Southsea, Hampshire. She lived at 6 Worcester Road, Pembroke Vale, Clifton, Gloucestershire. Margaret married Major Harry Wetherell Rowden, Wiltshire Regiment (14th September 1853–18th November 1921), born at Oxford, on 6th August 1892 at St John's Wood, London. Harry was commissioned as a lieutenant in 3rd West Yorkshire, Militia on 6th April 1872 and transferred as a lieutenant to 99th Duke of Edinburgh's (Lanarkshire) Regiment of Foot on 2nd December 1874. He served during the Zulu War in South Africa in 1879. On 1st July 1881 under the Childers Reforms the 99th amalgamated with 62nd (Wiltshire) Regiment of Foot to form the Duke of Edinburgh's (Wiltshire Regiment). Harry served with the 2nd Battalion at Nowshera, Bengal, India and was promoted captain on 25th October 1881. On 1st September 1890 he was appointed Adjutant 3rd Battalion, Wiltshire Regiment, Militia and was promoted major on 8th August 1894. He retired on 14th September 1901. They were living at 37 Banbury Road, Oxford in 1911. Harry was living at 26 Polstead Road, Oxford at the time of his death there. Margaret was living at Cranford, Sidmouth, Devon at the time of her death. She had four children from her two marriages:
  - John Francis Arthur St Maur Sheil (16th June 1881–2nd August 1938), birth registered at Barton Regis, was commissioned in 3rd Cheshire on 2nd February 1900. He last appears in the Army List in September 1904. John married Ethel Lloyd (1880–19th December 1958), born at Carlton Villas, Marsland Road, Sale, Cheshire, at Kendal, Westmorland in 1907. Ethel was living with her mother and her two children at the time of the

1911 Census at Woodhouse, Milnthorpe, Westmoreland. He was living at Ashfield Park, Ross, Herefordshire when he applied for a commission on 30th September 1914, which was granted with effect from 14th September. He was serving at Donard Camp, Co Down, Ireland at the time and claimed five years previous service in the Cheshire Regiment, including two and a half years in South Africa. John was appointed captain and Adjutant, 10th Royal Irish Rifles on 26th September and transferred to 17th (Reserve) Battalion on 16th February 1915. He was appointed temporary major in 17th (Reserve) Battalion, Royal Irish Rifles on 8th May 1918 with seniority from 20th May 1915. A medical board on 2nd December 1918 found him unfit for A & B permanently but fit for C1. He was recommended for one week's leave then to report to HQ Southern Command. Medical boards on 24th February, 6th June and 14th July 1919 found him unfit for A & B permanently and C1 for between one and two months. After the last board he was recommended for two month's leave. John was admitted to hospital at Exeter suffering from asthma whilst on leave on 26th August. A medical board at Exeter on 26th September found him permanently unfit for service. He relinquished his commission on account of ill-health contracted on active service on 29th October 1919. He was living at Stratford-sub-Castle, Salisbury, Wiltshire at the time of his death at the Nursing Home, Crane Street, Salisbury. She was living at Privetts Convalescent Home, Totland Bay, Isle of Wight, Hampshire at the time of her death at St Georges Nursing Home, Milford-on-Sea, Hampshire. They had three children:

- Frances Elizabeth St Maur Sheil (25th October 1908–1996), birth registered at Ross-on-Wye, Herefordshire, married Hamilton A Shotter (27th December 1905–1986) registered in 1935 at Bournemouth, Hampshire and 1936 at Salisbury, Wiltshire [sic].
- Francis Patrick St Maur Sheil (17th June 1910–8th October 1944), born at Ludlow, was educated at Highfield School, Liphook, Hampshire and Abbey House, Sherborne School, Dorset 1924–28, where he played in the 2nd XV rugby and cricket XI (corporal OTC). Francis was trained at the Royal Military Academy, Sandhurst and, when he was commissioned in the South Wales Borderers on 30th January 1930, Dudley Johnson VC gave him his old swagger stick. Francis married Pauline Adele Kunhardt (14th April 1912–1972), registered at Portsmouth in 1932. They had three children – John WM Sheil 1938, Shaun Sheil and Elizabeth Ann Sheil 1942. Francis was promoted lieutenant on 30th January 1933 and was seconded to the Nigeria Regiment for service under the Colonial Office from 9th August. Promoted captain on 1st August 1938 (44997). He was awarded the DSO for attacking a machine gun position near Cassino and killing two of the enemy with rifle and bayonet. Francis was a lieutenant colonel commanding 1st Duke of Wellington's

(West Riding Regiment) at Monte Cece, Palazzuolo Sul Senio, northeast of Florence, Italy, when he was killed in action (Florence War Cemetery – IX G 7).

- John Augustus St Maur Sheil (18th March 1918–1998) married Alice MPA Badham (born 1918), born at Southampton, Hampshire, at Westminster in 1940. They divorced. Alice married Carlo Fornara at Paddington, London in 1944 and they had a son, Christopher C Fornara the following year. John married Doreen AV Bradley (born 1921) in the Cotswolds in 1946. They had a son, Michael P St Maur Sheil, in 1946, registered at Oxford.

The top of the swagger stick given by Dudley Johnson to Francis Patrick St Maur Sheil when he was commissioned in the South Wales Borderers. (*Mike St Maur Sheil*)

- Eileen Mabel St Maur Sheil (17th May 1882–19th December 1931), born at Woodlands, Banwell, Somerset, married John William Frederick Arthur Crawfurd (15th November 1878–22nd June 1939), a brewer born at St John, Dulwich, London, in 1905 at Dublin. They were living at 14 Pembroke Road, Donnybrook, Dublin in 1907 and at 9 Herbert Street, Dublin in 1916. They were living at Park Cottage, Sandyford, Co Dublin at the time of her death there. He died at Dublin. They had four children:
  - Phyllis Nancye Crawfurd (2nd August 1907–6th April 1991), born at 14 Pembroke Road, Donnybrook, Dublin, married Gontran I Goulden (5th April 1912–1986), born at Canterbury, at Westminster, London in 1937. They had a daughter, Elizabeth NA Goulden, registered at Pwllheli, Caernarvonshire in 1942. His death was registered at Fulham and hers at Leicester.
  - Geoffrey Desmond Crawfurd (5th March 1910–1969), born at 9 Herbert Street, Dublin. He was a Catholic Priest, Chaplain to St Bernard's Convent in 1939, living at 1 Langley Road, Slough living with housekeeper, Teresa Rudd, born 17th September 1890.

Florence War Cemetery, on the banks of the River Arno, contains 1,632 Commonwealth burials of the Second World War. Following the fall of Rome in June 1944, the Germans retreated through a series of defensive positions. Florence, in the centre of the Arno Line, was taken by the Allies on 13th August 1944. The subsequent attack on the Gothic Line was launched from there. The cemetery was begun in November 1944, initially for burials from hospitals in and around Florence. However, the majority of the burials are from fighting in the area from July to September 1944. After the war, eighty-three graves were also moved there from nearby Arrow Route Cemetery.

    - Joan Eileen Crawfurd (born 11th July 1916), a twin with Hillary.
    - Hillary John Crawfurd (11th 1916–16th October 1966), a twin with Joan. His death was registered at Bristol, Gloucestershire.
  - Sybil Violet St Maur Sheil (October 1885–7th October 1917), born at Banwell, married John Carson Parker (1878–23rd October 1945) on 29th June 1912 at St Giles, Oxford. He was living at Ainsdale-on-Sea, Southport, Lancashire and she at Burcott, 37 Banbury Road, Oxford at the time. John was a tea planter in Ceylon and also a lieutenant in the Ceylon Mounted Rifles. They were living at Tyspane Estate, Kotmale, Ceylon at the time of her death there. John was a captain in the Ceylon Mounted Rifles when he married Dorothy Maud Sweet (7th October 1891–21st October 1934), born at Winterbourne Kingston, Dorset, on 15th January 1920 at Symondsbury Parish Church, Dorset. She was an Associate of the Royal Red Cross. They were living at Shawlands Estate, Lunugala, Ceylon at the time of her death at the Joseph Fraser Nursing Home, Fraser Road, Colombo, Ceylon. John was living at Stretton, Meyrick Road, Babbacombe, Torquay, Devon at the time of his death at Asheldene Nursing Home, Asheldon Road, Torquay. John had two children from his two marriages:
    - Sybil Evelyn Carson Parker (31st March 1913–7th April 1995).
    - Peter John Carson Parker (29th April 1928–31st October 2007).
  - Marguerite Violet Wetherell Rowden (17th October 1893–12th July 1985) never married and died at Oxford.
- Loftus Percival Arnott (7th November 1873–2nd December 1956) was commissioned in 3rd Leinster Special Reserve on 5th February 1896 and was promoted lieutenant on 26th May 1897 and captain on 6th December 1899. He resigned as an honorary major on 24th April 1912. Loftus served again as a captain in 3rd Royal Dublin Fusiliers from 10th September 1914 and was promoted major on 26th August 1915. A medical board on 4th October 1916 found him unfit for General Service for six months but fit for Home Service. A medical board on 4th December found him unfit for General Service for two months but fit for Home Service. A medical board on 3rd February 1917 found him unfit for General Service permanently but fit for Home Service. He was serving at No.1 Dispersal Centre, Ripon in February 1919. A medical board on 12th March found him unfit for A permanently and B for three months but fit for C. He relinquished his commission on account of ill-health on 18th March 1919 retaining the rank of major. Loftus was living c/o Sir CR McGregor Bt & Co at 39 Panton Street, Haymarket, London in 1919 and later at 53 Sydney Parade Avenue, Ballsbridge, Dublin and 5 College Street, Dublin. He died at 53 Sydney Parade Avenue, leaving effects valued at £106,922/10/- (£3.3M in 2023).
- Emmeline Louisa Arnott (27th October 1874–10th August 1966) married Captain Godfrey Herbert Bloomfield (5th March 1865–21st November 1946), born at Waterford, Ireland, at St Luke's Parish Church, Cork on 16th September 1896.

His parents were Fitz-Maurice Gustavus Bloomfield JP (11th February 1824–5th January 1894), of New Park, Co Waterford, and Henrietta Sophia Commerell (14th November 1824–19th February 1906), sister of Admiral Sir John Edmund Commerell VC. Godfrey was commissioned as a captain in 7th Rifle Brigade (The Prince of Consort's Own) on 6th October 1889 and resigned his commission on 29th June 1896. They were living at New Park, 89 Lower Baggott Street, Kilculliheen, Co Waterford in 1901. He was a magistrate and breeder of horses and hunted with the Waterford Hounds. He was living at Lisnafillon House, Gracehill, Co Antrim at the time of his death there. She was living at Ardvarna, Strandtown, Belfast, Northern Ireland in 1946. They had five children:

- ◦ Fitzmaurice John Commerell Bloomfield (born 4th September 1897), born at Newpark, Ferrybank, Waterford.
- ◦ Gustavus William Herbert Bloomfield (2nd March 1899–21st July 1979) was educated at Bilton Grange, Rugby and Winchester College (sergeant OTC). He applied for a commission in the Irish Guards Special Reserve on 19th March 1917 but enlisted in 3rd Royal Munster Fusiliers (3/7445) at the Central London Recruiting Depot, Whitehall on 7th December. He was described as a student, 5′ 8¼″ tall, weighing 139 lbs, with fresh complexion, hazel eyes and auburn hair. He was posted to the Household Brigade Officer Cadet Battalion, The Hall, Bushey, Hertfordshire on 28th December. He transferred to No.1 Cavalry Cadet School, Netheravon on 28th February 1918, when he became a candidate for 2nd Life Guards, but rejoined the Household Brigade Officer Cadet Battalion on 22nd April, when he became a candidate for the Guards Machine Gun Regiment. Gustavus was commissioned on 31st July 1918 in the Guards Machine Gun Regiment and was released from service on 23rd March 1919. He married Zeyle EHG Gardner in 1926 registered at St George, Hanover Square, London.
- ◦ Kathleen Lily Ives Bloomfield (22nd March 1901–21st November 1934) married Eric H de Bunsen (1889–1942) in 1929 registered at St George, Hanover Square, London. Her death was registered at Marylebone and his at Westminster.
- ◦ Dorothy Sophia Caldwell Bloomfield (25th July 1903–18th May 1991).
- ◦ Judith Irene Bloomfield (3rd September 1919–7th May 1997), born at 89 Lower Baggot Street, Dublin, married Albert BBJ Goor at Westminster in 1948. He married Margaret McCarthy at Kensington in 1978.

- Jessie Alexandra Fitzgerald Arnott (9th October 1875–16th January 1971) married Lieutenant General Sir William Pulteney Pulteney GCVO KCB KCMG DSO (1861–1941) on 17th October 1917 at The Annunciation, St Marylebone, London. He was the son of the Reverend Richard Thomas Pulteney Pulteney (1812–74), Rector of Ashley, Market Harborough, Northamptonshire and Emma Dalison. They were living at 3 Fitzhardinge Street, Portman Square, London

Lieutenant General Sir William Pulteney Pulteney GCVO KCB KCMG DSO (18th May 1861–14th May 1941) was educated at Eton and commissioned in the Scots Guards from the Militia on 23rd April 1881. He was promoted lieutenant on 1st July 1881 and served in the Egyptian War 1882 at Mahuta and the Battle of Tel-el-Kebir. He was appointed Adjutant 24th February 1891–14th February 1895 and was promoted captain on 4th May 1892. He was employed under the Foreign Office in Uganda 15th February 1895–22nd September 1897, including the Unyoro Expedition 1895 and Nandi Expedition (MID) 1895–96. Awarded the DSO for operations against slave-trading Arabs in Uganda Protectorate, LG 3rd November 1896. The DSO was presented by the Queen at Windsor Castle on 9th July 1897. Promoted major 1st May 1897 and appointed Vice-Consul, Congo Free State 31st December 1898–17th June 1899. During the Second Boer War 1899–1902 he was in action during the advance on Kimberley, Belmont, Enslin, Modder River and Magersfontein, in Orange Free State February–May 1900, including actions at Poplar Grove, Driefontein, Vet River (5th–6th May), Zand River, Transvaal (May–June 1900), including actions near Johannesburg, Pretoria and Diamond Hill (11th–12th June),Transvaal east and west of Pretoria (July–29th November 1900), Orange River Colony (May–29th November 1900), Transvaal (December 1900–April 1902) and Cape Colony (December 1900). Promoted brevet lieutenant colonel 11th November 1899 and commanded 1st Scots Guards 9th April 1900–17th January 1901. He commanded a column 17th January 1901–April 1902. Mentioned in Despatches, LG 26th January 1900, 10th September 1901 and 29th July 1902. Promoted lieutenant colonel on 1st April 1904 and was awarded the CB in 1905. Promoted brevet colonel 29th November 1900 and colonel 1st January 1908, when he was on half pay until 7th February 1908. Appointed Brigadier General, 16th Brigade, Irish Command 7th February 1908–31st March 1909. Promoted major general 1st January 1909 and appointed GOC 6th Division, Irish Command 16th July 1910–15th July 1914. Appointed temporary lieutenant general 5th August 1914 to command III Corps, which he did until 19th February 1918. Promoted lieutenant general on 4th May 1915. Commanded XXIII (Reserve) Corps in Britain 20th February 1918–15th April 1919. KCB 1915, KCMG 1917, KCVO 1918 and GCVO. Sir William was specially employed with the British Military Mission to Japan 18th May–8th September 1918, retired on 8th January 1919 and was Black Rod in Parliament 1920–41.

at the time of his death at Pines Hill, Stanstead, Essex. Jessie died at Ivy Hall Nursing Home, Crowborough, Sussex.

- Lily Eleanor Arnott (11th February 1878–12th December 1967) married Arthur Edward Rogers AMICE (18th July 1871–1st January 1950), born at Sevenoaks, Kent, on 12th August 1902. He was the son of Lieutenant Colonel John Thornton Rogers DSO (1834–1900) and Margaret Bagwell (1842–1904). They were living at Patrickswell, Inishlounaght, Co Tipperary, Ireland in 1911 and Angle House, Wildernesse Avenue, Seal, Kent in 1939. They both subsequently died there. They had two children – Frances Eleanor Rogers (25th August 1903–16th January 1927) and Arthur John Patrick Rogers (28th October 1913–18th May 1934).
- Florence Geraldine Arnott (5th August 1879–26th July 1958) married Henry Herbert Ronald White (9th February 1879–12th March 1939), born at Teignmouth, Devon, on 24th June 1906 at All Saints' Church, Knightsbridge, London. He was living at Lough Eske Castle, Co Donegal, Ireland and she at Woodlands, Cork at the time. He was the son of Major General Henry George

White DL (1836–1906) and Frances Cromwell late Pelly formerly Ferguson (1846). He was educated at Rugby School, Warwickshire and the Royal Military College, Sandhurst, Surrey. Henry was commissioned in the King's Royal Rifle Corps on 27th July 1898 and was promoted lieutenant on 4th December 1899. He served in the Second Boer War with the Mounted Infantry 1901–15th January 1903 (Queen's South Africa Medal with clasps Transvaal and Orange Free State). He served on operations in Somaliland 16th January 1903–8th February 1904 and was promoted captain and appointed Adjutant, 1st Mounted Corps from 5th October 1903. Henry was severely wounded at Jidballi on 10th January 1904 (Africa General Service Medal with clasp Jidballi). A medical board in Somaliland on 19th January found him unfit for six months and recommended no duties on the homeward voyage, on which he was to be accompanied by his servant. He embarked aboard SS *Marmora* at Berbera on 8th February for Marseille, France and arrived in Britain on 21st February. He was on leave until 8th August but a medical board at 68 Victoria Street, London on 3rd March found him unfit for three months. He was posted to the strength of the 2nd Battalion on 17th May. A medical board at 68 Victoria Street, London on 25th July found him unfit for three months and his leave was extended to 25th October. A medical board at 68 Victoria Street on 10th October found him unfit for two months and his leave was extended to 10th December. A medical board at 68 Victoria Street on 28th November found him fit. He embarked for Bermuda on 15th December and served there until 24th October 1905. On 1st May 1906 he was appointed Adjutant 5th Battalion, 60th Rifles and resigned his commission on 2nd June 1908. Henry was appointed High Sheriff, Co Donegal in 1912. He served again as a captain from 3rd March 1915, backdated to 18th September 1914, and was in East Africa May 1915–March 1917. He was promoted major in 25th Royal Fusiliers on 8th September 1915 and served as Adjutant and Second-in-Command. He was in hospital with malaria 30th September– 24th October 1915. On 24th July 1916 he was admitted to 26th Field Ambulance and transferred to 52nd General Hospital on 27th July. Mentioned in the GOC's Despatch of 22nd November 1916, LG 6th March 1917 and was awarded the DSO (LG 13th February 1917) and later the OBE. Henry embarked for South Africa on 27th February 1917 and was a brigade major in Cape Town in 1918. He served in the Nyasaland Field Force as a lieutenant colonel 16th July–29th November 1918. He was demobilised from the Officers Dispersal Unit, London on 17th August 1919 and relinquished his commission, retaining the rank of major, on 5th January 1921. He was appointed to the Regular Army Reserve of Officers, Class 2 on 26th February 1921 as a major with seniority from 23rd July 1917. Henry was removed from the Regular Army Reserve of Officers on 9th February 1929, having reached the age limit for liability to recall. In November 1938 he wrote to the War Office from the Army & Navy Club, Pall Mall, London asking if there was anything he could do in the event of war or before. In reply he was warned that, in view of his age, he was unlikely to be utilised and he may therefore wish to offer his services elsewhere such as Air Raid Precautions duties. They were living at 10 Bury Street, St James, London at the time of his death at 6500 Yucca Street, Los Angeles, USA. She was living at Cronkbane, 20 Somerset Road, Douglas, Isle of Man at the time of her death. They had two sons:

  - Henry George Ronald White (born 17th April 1907) married Mildred Hawksby (born 1922) in 1945 at Bulmer, Northumberland. They had two sons – George W White 1947 and Christopher White 1955.
  - John Maxwell White (12th July 1909–6th August 1988) was commissioned in The King's Royal Rifle Corps 29th August 1929 (44206) and was promoted lieutenant on 29th August 1932 and captain on 3rd March 1938. He was appointed Adjutant 15th July 1940–14th January 1941, GSO3 War Office 15th January–5th March 1941 and GSO3 (O) Western Command 1st April 1941–21st December 1942. Appointed acting major 21st April–20 July 1941 and temporary major 21st July 1941–26th May 1942, 22nd December 1942–21st April 1944 and 23rd May–22nd August 1944. Appointed Instructor RAC Tactical School 22nd December 1942–30th December 1943. SO1 (CA) Civil Affairs Staff 21st Army Group 23rd May 1944–2nd June 1945. Acting lieutenant colonel 23rd May–22nd August 1944, war substantive major 23rd August 1944, temporary lieutenant colonel 23rd August 1944–23rd March 1949 and 30th November 1950–5th July 1951. Appointed Assistant Director Civil Affairs/MG BAOR 3rd June–23rd September 1945, ADCA 24th September–21st November 1945, ADCA/MG (Admin) 22nd November 1945–14th January 1946 and Commander Det CC for G 15th January–30th October 1946. Promoted major 1st July 1946. Appointed Senior Regional Officer (SO1) 31st October–20th November 1946 and Senior Cont Officer (SO1) 21st November 1946–22nd November 1948. OBE, LG 1st January 1948. Promoted lieutenant colonel 6th July 1951 and temporary colonel 2nd October 1953–1st December 1956. Appointed Deputy Director Public Relations, GHQ Middle East Land Forces 2nd October 1953–10th October 1956. Employment List (1) 21st October 1953, supernumerary 6th July 1954 and retired as honorary colonel on 12th July 1957.

- Cecil John Maxwell Arnott (4th August 1882–31st August 1954) was commissioned in 3rd Leinster on 9th January 1900. The Battalion was embodied 18th January 1900–26th May 1902. He was promoted lieutenant on 5th October 1901 and at some time in his service he was attached to a regular unit. He last appears in the Army List in July 1903. He was living at The Cottage, Clonsilla, Dublin at the time of his death.
- Mary Louisa Mabel Arnott (5th May 1886–10th August 1966), born at Woodlands, Cork, was known as Mabel. She married Captain Sir Francis Hugh Brooke (10th November 1882–4th November 1954), born at Kildrought House,

Celbridge, Co Kildare, on 5th May 1915 at St George, Hanover Square, London as Mary Louisa Mabel Fitzgerald-Arnott. He was commissioned in 3rd Duke of Edinburgh's (Wiltshire Regiment) on 16th January 1901 and transferred to the King's Royal Rifle Corps on 11th March 1903. Transferred to the South Irish Horse, Special Reserve of Officers as a lieutenant on 8th March 1912. He was a captain in the Cavalry Special Reserve from 17th July 1915 and was attached to the Royal Irish Regiment, Service Battalions from 27th August 1917. He last appears in the Army List in May 1921. They were living at Pickering Forest, Celbridge, Co Kildare at the time of his death. They had two children:

- George Francis Cecil Brooke (30th March 1916–27th December 1982).
- Emily Alma Brooke (3rd November 1918–July 1985).

Dudley was educated at Bradfield College, near Reading, Berkshire May 1898–April 1901. He was boarding at Army College House under Andrew Low at the time of the 1901 Census. He was commissioned in the Militia, 3rd The Duke of Edinburgh's (Wiltshire Regiment) on 4th March 1901, described as 6′ 4″ tall and fluent in French. He was promoted lieutenant on 31st October 1901 and served on St Helena guarding Boer prisoners in 1901. Dudley returned to Britain in May 1902 and passed the qualifying examinations for transfer to a Regular Army commission in March 1903. He was commissioned in 2nd South Wales Borderers on 4th July 1903. He served in South Africa January–June 1904 and was promoted lieutenant on 2nd March 1907. He served in South Africa again from December 1910 and was based with the Battalion at Artillery Barracks, Pretoria at the time of the 1911 Census. Appointed Adjutant 5th February 1909–4th February 1912 and served in North China from November 1911.

Dudley married Marjorie Ailsie Grisewood (1886–13th October 1950), born at Daylesford, near Stow-on-the-Wold, Worcestershire (Gloucestershire from 1931), on 5th June 1912 at Daylesford Parish Church (St Peter's). They lived at Abbey House, Colchester, Essex and Orchard House, Church Crookham, Hampshire. Marjorie died at Orchard House. They had three children:

Bradfield College, formally St Andrew's College, is a public school in the village of Bradfield, Berkshire. The school is now part of the Rugby Group, which also includes Rugby, Harrow, Shrewsbury, Wellington College and Charterhouse. Bradfield was founded in 1850 and has been fully co-educational since 2005. Bradfield is renowned for its Greek plays and outdoor amphitheatre. The first was performed in the original language in 1881 to save the school from bankruptcy. The Greek play is normally performed on a three-year rota. The amphitheatre was built in a disused chalk pit and opened in 1890.

From 1900 to 1902 St Helena housed many Boer prisoners. They were treated with respect and dignity consistent with the rules of war at the time. One of the shipments is seen here being marched to Deadwood Camp. The first shipment of 514 arrived on 10th April 1900, including General Cronjé and his wife, and another on 26th April. By February 1902 there were about 5,500 on the island. Some prisoners wished to become British subjects, but this caused friction with others who were bitterly against the British. A separate camp was created to house the pro-British prisoners. There was also tension between Freestaters and Transvaalers resulting in the authorities opening Broad Bottom Camp in early 1901 for the burghers of the Orange Free State. Several of the most intractable prisoners were confined in High Knoll Fort.

Daylesford is a privately owned village on the north bank of the River Evenlode in the Cotswolds Hills Area of Outstanding Natural Beauty. The village was a detached part of Worcestershire until 1931 when it was transferred to Gloucestershire. In medieval times the manor was held by the Hastings family. Warren Hastings (1732–1818), Governor-General of India, acquired Daylesford House in 1788. A church was founded in the 10th century. Hastings rebuilt the Norman Church of St Peter in 1816 and was buried there two years later. The church was rebuilt again in 1859–63 and is now Grade I Listed.

- Peter John Dudley Johnson (August 1914–1995), birth registered at Stow-on-the-Wold, was commissioned in the Royal Artillery on 30th August 1934. He was promoted lieutenant on 30th August 1937 and appointed ADC 1st August 1939–10th January 1940. Appointed acting captain 11th January 1940, temporary captain 11th April 1940–11th January 1941 and 2nd June–1st September 1941, war substantive captain 2nd September 1941, acting major 2nd June 1941 and temporary major 2nd September 1941. MID, LG 24th June 1943. Promoted captain 30th August 1943, war substantive major 30th December 1943 and appointed temporary lieutenant colonel 30th December 1943. OBE (LG 28th June 1945). After the war he commanded No.8 Information Control Unit, British Control Commission, controlling German newspapers, radio and films in Hamburg and Schleswig-Holstein. On 11th October 1946 he pleaded guilty at a court martial in Hamburg, having assisted Fräulein Ingelore Heldern, his German secretary, to travel to Britain. She was half Jewish and her father was a naturalised British subject living in Australia. She was sentenced to twelve months' imprisonment by the German civil government for unauthorised

Abbey House, a large Regency house, was owned by the Ministry of Defence for many years and was the Garrison Commander's residence. It has since been completely restored.

possession of leave passes. However, this was suspended when Peter petitioned the court, accepting responsibility. In a plea of mitigation to the court martial, Mr JH Collier, defence counsel, described the journey as 'a light-hearted frolic as a result of a love affair, when passion was running at its highest...' and the trip was an 'unfortunate and foolish escapade with drastic consequences'. Peter had an excellent record and testimonials were read from Lieutenant General Sir Ronald Scobie and four major generals. Despite this, on 25th November he was sentenced to be dismissed from His Majesty's service but appears to have carried on serving. Promoted major on 30th August 1948 and last appears in the Army List in April 1952, having qualified on an Intermediate Staff Course during the Second World War. Peter married three times:

- Marion Georgina Wikeley (23rd March 1912–27th May 1980) in June 1938 at Singapore. She was the daughter of Lieutenant Colonel James Masson Wikeley, late 17th Cavalry, Indian Army (1867–1952), of Ravensdale, Bellraugh, Isle of Man. They divorced and she never remarried. She was living at 9 Redcliffe Place, London at the time of her death in a London hospital.
- Fräulein Ingelore Martha Heldern (born c.1926), born in Germany, in 1947 at Trowbridge, Wiltshire. They travelled from Montréal, Canada aboard SS *Empress of France*, arriving at Liverpool, Lancashire on 10th August 1951. They were living at Orchard House, Church Crookham, Hampshire at the time. They divorced after having had two sons – Patrick PG Johnson c.1947 and David Anthony Johnson 1951.
- Sylvia Joyce Knights née Allen (c.1919–22nd September 1987). born at Calcutta, India, in 1956 at Chelsea, London. They were living at 14 Chelsea Court, 95 Elmpark Gardens, London at the time of her death. He reportedly died at Hounslow, London. They had a daughter, Joanna Johnson (born 27th November 1962). Sylvia had married Patrick James Knights (17th March 1911–31st July 1970), also born at Calcutta, in 1940 at

Hendon, Middlesex. Patrick was a sales ledger accounts clerk in 1939, when he was living with his widowed mother and brother, Frederick G Knights, an estate clerk with London County Council at 15 The Crescent, Wembley, Middlesex. They are believed to have had four children – David Knights 1944, Colin Patrick Knights 1946 and twins Nigel and Patricia Knights (born 4th January 1952). The marriage ended in divorce. He was working as an accountant in Brazil in 1958 when his address in England was 92 East Towers, Pinner, Middlesex. He was living at Woodhay, The Crescent, Hampton-in-Arden, Warwickshire at the time of his death there.

- Patience Mary Johnson (6th April 1917–26th November 1998) was living at Glenelm, Darras Road, Castle Ward, Northumberland in 1939. She married Lionel Douglas Arthur De Hochepied Larpent (26th October 1910–28th March 1977), born at Farnham, Surrey, in 1939 at Colchester, Essex. Lionel was distantly related to Daniel Burges VC. He was commissioned in the Northumberland Fusiliers (Royal from 1935) on 29th January 1931 and was promoted lieutenant 29th January 1934 and captain 29th January 1939. He was appointed Adjutant 2nd September 1939–26th May 1940, acting major 17th September 1941 and temporary major 17th December 1941–7th August 1942, 18th August–15th October 1942 and 8th February 1943–30th June 1946. Lionel served in India and Burma 1942–46, including during the 2nd Chindit operation in Burma (MID, LG 26th April 1945). Promoted major 1st July 1946, local lieutenant colonel 9th June–30th August 1947 and temporary lieutenant colonel 7th March 1948–15th August 1949. He retired from the Army in 1952 and served as Retired Officer Grade 3, MS Branch, HQ British Army of the Rhine 1955–69. They were living at Keepers Cottage, Hall Road, Copford, Colchester, Essex at the time of his death there. Patience's death was registered at Colchester. They had three children:
    - Stephen Douglas John De Hochepied Larpent (6th March 1940–6th May 1986), birth registered at Newcastle upon Tyne, Northumberland, was educated at Bradfield College, near Reading, Berkshire and Britannia Royal Naval College, Dartmouth, Devon. He was appointed midshipman in the Royal Navy on 1st September 1959. Promoted acting sub lieutenant 1st May 1961, lieutenant 1st July 1963 and later commander with Allied Forces, Southern Europe. Stephen married Elisabeth Helen Tyner (born 1938), birth registered at Warwick, in 1966 in Surrey. He died at Piddletrenthide, Dorset. They had two sons – Benjamin Jeremy H De Hochepied Larpent 1973 and Jolyon De Hochepied Larpent 1978.
    - Marianne M De Hochepied Larpent (born 31st January 1943), born at Aldershot, Hampshire, married Captain Valentine Freeman West (born 31st July 1932), born at Easthampstead, Berkshire, on 12th December 1964 at the Royal Military Academy, Sandhurst, Berkshire. He was commissioned in the King's Royal Rifle Corps on 6th February 1953 (427026). He was

promoted lieutenant 6th February 1955, temporary captain 1st August 1956–18th June 1957, 22nd September–6th November 1957 and 26th March 1958–5th February 1959, captain 6th February 1959, temporary major 11th December 1964–5th February 1966 and major 6th February 1966. The Regiment became 2nd Green Jackets in 1958 and the Royal Green Jackets on amalgamation in 1966. He retired on 13th April 1970. They had three children – Timothy James West 1966, Christopher Robert West 1968 and Alexandra Lucy West 1973.

- Andrew Lionel Dudley De Hochepied Larpent (born 10th February 1951), born at Aldershot, was educated at Bradfield College, near Reading, the Royal Military Academy Sandhurst and Reading University (BSc Hons). He was commissioned in the Royal Regiment of Fusiliers on 30th July 1971 (491441). Promoted lieutenant 30th January 1973, captain 30th July 1977 and major 30th September 1983. He was appointed SO3 Protocol and Visits, Berlin 1982–83 and attended the Army Staff College, Camberley (psc) in 1984. Appointed SO2 Operations/Organisation & Deployment, HQ 3rd Armoured Division 10th December 1986–19th February 1989. Appointed SO1 Directing Staff, Staff College 20th February 1989–12th January 1990 and was promoted lieutenant colonel on 30th June 1989. CO 3rd Battalion, The Royal Regiment of Fusiliers 13th January 1990–26th July 1992, including on Operation Granby in Iraq during the 1991 Gulf War (OBE, LG 13th June 1992). Appointed SO1 Directorate of Infantry 27th July 1992 and retired on 1st November 1994 to the Reserve of Officers Class 1. On 1st April 1997 he joined the TA as a lieutenant colonel, with seniority from 30th June 1989, and served until 30th June 2002. He was then employed as CEO Cancer and Leukaemia in Childhood 1997–2001, CEO Somerset Care Group 2001–11, CEO Southern Cross Care (South Australia & Northern Territory) 2011–16 and was founder and Chairman of the Commonwealth Association for the Ageing. Andrew married Anne Marion Knights (born 1949), born at Ealing, Middlesex, on 22nd June 1974 at Ickenham, Middlesex. They had three children – John Douglas De Hochepied Larpent 1977, David Andrew De Hochepied Larpent 1979 and Katherine Anne De Hochepied Larpent 1984.

- Primrose Lucy Johnson (23rd October 1922–30th March 1975), born at Elham, near Hythe, Kent, married Frank Ian Cordeux Wetherell (16th June 1910–19th July 1997), born at Ipswich, Suffolk, in 1953 at Aldershot, Hampshire. He was living with his parents at The Old House, Carr Street, Ipswich in 1911. Frank attended the Royal Military College, Sandhurst and was commissioned in the Royal Tank Corps on 30th January 1930 (45008). Promoted lieutenant on 30th January 1933 and served on the North West Frontier of India (Mohmand) 1935 (India General Service Medal 1908–35 with Mohmand 1933 [sic] clasp. Promoted captain on 1st August 1938 and was appointed Chief Instructor,

Officer Producing Unit on 17th January 1939 (45008). Promoted major 1st July 1946 and lieutenant colonel 1st April 1952. He was appointed GSO1 in the Directorate of Staff Duties, War Office on 13th August 1954 and was placed on the Supernumerary List on full pay on 1st April 1955. He ceased to belong to the Reserve of Officers, having attained the age limit, on 16th June 1965. They were living at Melfort Cottage, Chandlers Lane, Yateley, Hampshire at the time of her death there. He also died at Yateley. They had a daughter:

 - Philippa 'Pippa' Ann Cordeux Wetherell (born 16th March 1961) married David Felton at Sydney, New South Wales, Australia. They had a son. The marriage ended in divorce.

Marjorie's father, the Reverend Arthur George Grisewood (16th April 1855–26th November 1918), born at Wandsworth, London, was Rector of St Peter's Daylesford, near Stow-on-the-Wold, Worcestershire. He married Lilian née Lockwood (7th July 1861–11th March 1952), born in India and christened on 19th October 1861 at Barrackpore, West Bengal, in 1885 at Chipping Norton, Oxfordshire. He died at St Luke's Hostel, Fitzroy Square, London. She was living at Westwood, Aldershot Road, Church Crookham, Hampshire at the time of her death there. In addition to Marjorie they had two other children, born at Daylesford Rectory:

- Frederick 'Freddie' Henry Grisewood (11th April 1888–15th November 1972 was educated at Radley College, Abingdon, Berkshire and Magdalen College, Oxford (Greek & Latin 1908). He played one first-class cricket match for Worcestershire against Oxford University at The University Parks in June 1908, winning by 332 runs. He studied singing in London, Paris, and Munich and later gave singing lessons to, among others, John Cyril Maude, brother-in-law of Major William La Touche Congreve VC. Freddie was commissioned in 1/4th Oxfordshire and Buckinghamshire Light Infantry on 12th September 1914 and was promoted lieutenant on 19th October 1915. He relinquished his commission on 29th April 1917 due to ill-health contracted on active service and was granted the honorary rank of lieutenant. The Silver War Badge was applied for on 8th October. It took him six years to recover from his disabilities. Freddie broadcast several times as a singer before joining the BBC as an announcer in 1929, including on *Children's Hour* and *Scrapbook*. He moved from announcing to outside broadcasting in 1937 on *The World Goes By*. He was the commentator for the Coronation of King George VI and Queen Elizabeth on 12th May 1937, the BBC's first large live outside television broadcast. The equipment failed just as the Royal carriage appeared. However, a hefty kick by the engineer in charge brought it back to life. He also commentated on the first televised broadcast of a tennis match at Wimbledon on 21st June 1937 and hosted the first UK game show, *Spelling Bee*, broadcast from Alexandra Palace on 31st May 1938. During the Second World

War he was a full-time announcer on the overseas service and was the regular speaker on *The Kitchen Front*, a programme by the Ministry of Food, and on *The Brains Trust*. However, Freddie is best-known for being the host of *Any Questions?* from its first broadcast from Winchester in October 1948 until 1967. The programme continues to this day. Awarded the OBE, LG 1st January 1959. He published *My Story of the BBC* in 1959. Freddie married Gladys 'Betty' Elizabeth Roffey (4th August 1889–11th March 1976), born at Little Laver, Essex, at Writtle in 1915. The marriage ended in divorce. Gladys did not remarry and was living at 213 Ongar Road, Writtle, Chelmsford, Essex at the time of her death there. They had a daughter, Anne Grisewood (17th April 1921–2008), who married Brian Joseph Gordon Kaye (23rd December 1920–14th February 1984) on 26th September 1947 at Westminster. They had a son, Angus FG Kaye, in 1962. Freddie was living at Redbourne Hotel, New Cavendish Street, St Marylebone, London in 1939. He married Aileen Croft Scriven (13th February 1903–19th April 1986), birth registered at Leeds, Yorkshire, on 8th March 1941 at Petersfield, Hampshire. She was living with her parents at Lidgett Lane, Harrogate, Yorkshire in 1911. Aileen was the sister of Margaret Croft Scriven (1912–2001), who was ranked fifth tennis player in the world in 1933 and 1934. She had particular success in the French Championships, winning the singles in 1933 and 1934, mixed doubles in 1933 and doubles in 1935. She was a Wimbledon quarter finalist on four occasions. Freddie and Aileen died at Hewshotts, Bramshott, Liphook, Hampshire.

- Arthur Archdale Grisewood (19th September 1892–24th June 1934) was educated at Radley College, Oxfordshire and was a cadet in the OTC when he was commissioned in 1/4th Oxfordshire & Buckinghamshire Light Infantry on 1st November 1913. Promoted lieutenant 9th January 1915. He suffered from albuminuria and Bright's Disease about five years before enlisting and was on sick leave 16th January–15th March. A medical board at Oxford on 16th April found him unfit for General and Home Service for one month and leave was granted to 14th May. A medical board at Caxton Hall, London on 28th May found him unfit for General Service permanently and Home Service for two months. Although active service was out of the question, the medical authorities believed that service in Egypt in a non-arduous post would be advantageous. This was not taken up by the military authorities. A medical board at Warley Military Hospital, Brentwood, Essex on 28th July found him unfit for General Service permanently and Home Service for two months but fit for light duties. He reported for duty with 3/4th Battalion on 19th July, was found unfit, sent to 2nd Southern General Hospital, Bristol on 29th July

Freddie Grisewood.

and was sent home the same day. A medical board at Oxford on 27th September found him permanently unit for service and he relinquished his commission on account of ill-health on 26th October 1915. Arthur travelled to Australia aboard SS *Omrah*, departing from London on 3rd November 1916. He was an overseer at Maxland, Mungindi, Maranoa, Queensland in 1919. He was living at 94 Lonsdale Road, Oxford at the time of his death at Acland Nursing Home, Oxford.

Dudley was promoted captain on 11th March 1914. He served at Tsingtao, China 23rd September–7th November 1914, and was present at its capture. **Awarded the DSO for his ability and gallantry on the night of 5th/6th November 1914, including rescuing several wounded men while exposed to heavy machine gun fire, LG 16th March 1915. He was mentioned in Brigadier-General NW Barnardiston's despatch dated 9th October 1914, LG 30th May 1916.** Dudley returned to Britain via Hong Kong aboard HMT *Delta*, arriving in Plymouth, Devon on 12th January 1915. The Battalion was stationed at Rugby, Warwickshire until embarking at Avonmouth on 17th March aboard SS *Canada*, bound for Alexandria, Egypt. The Battalion sailed aboard RMS *Alaunia* on 11th April for Mudros. It transferred to HMS *Cornwallis* and landed at S Beach, Gallipoli on 25th April. He was wounded in the shoulder and embarked for Britain on 20th June.

Human settlement at Tsingtao, now Qingdao, dates back 6,000 years. In 1891, the Qing Empire made Tsingtao a base against naval attacks. German naval officials reported on this activity in May 1897 and subsequently German troops occupied the fortification. The waning Qing Empire was forced to concede the area to Germany the following year. The growing Imperial German Navy based its Far East Squadron there. The enclave was conquered by Japanese and British forces in 1914. The city reverted to Chinese rule in December 1922, but Japan maintained economic dominance of Shandong Province as a whole. Japan re-occupied Qingdao in 1938 during the Second Sino-Japanese War. Nationalist Chinese forces returned after the Japanese surrender in September 1945. On 2nd June 1949, the city was taken by Chairman Mao Zedong. In recent years Shandong has developed considerably economically, much of this has been concentrated in Qingdao. Internationally, Qingdao is best known for the Tsingtao Brewery, founded by a German-British joint venture in 1903 that produces Tsingtao, the best-known Chinese export beer.

SS *Delta* (8,024 tons) was built by Workman Clark at Belfast for the Peninsular & Oriental Steam Navigation Co and was launched in 1905. During the Great War she was a troop transport, a hospital ship on the Tsingtau operations and at Gallipoli and in 1918 a supply liner under the Requisition Scheme. As a hospital ship she was staffed by six medical officers, twelve nurses and forty-five other staff. The ship had 287 cots and 210 berths. In 1919 she repatriated Australian troops before being refitted and returning to the Far East service. In 1929 *Delta* was sold for scrap in Japan.

Dudley was appointed Second-in-Command, 11th South Wales Borderers at Hazeley Down, Winchester, Hampshire. On 3rd December he was appointed GSO3, Third Army, Central Force, Home Defences and GSO3 Northern Army, Home Forces on 19th December. He was appointed Brigade Major, 14th Reserve Infantry Brigade, Home Forces 25th May–22nd October 1916. He went to France on 31st October and was Deputy Assistant Adjutant & Quarter Master General, HQ 19th Division November–December. He was appointed temporary major whilst Deputy Assistant Adjutant General, HQ 1st Division 5th January–26th December 1917. **Awarded the MC, LG 1st January 1918.**

On 4th December 1917 Dudley was promoted major. He was appointed acting lieutenant colonel to command 1st South Wales Borderers from 5th January 1918, while the CO was recovering from wounds. He reverted to major and Second-in-Command on 17th February 1918 when the CO returned. Appointed acting lieutenant colonel whilst in command of 2nd Royal Sussex Regiment from 5th April. He was wounded on 26th May and was evacuated to Britain on 2nd June. The wound required daily attention for the rest of his life. He returned to France on 3rd September. **Awarded a Bar to the DSO for his actions at Pontruet on 18th September when he led his Battalion over difficult terrain. He then reorganised his men after the objective was reached and subsequently carried out a night attack on 24th September advancing 900m against strong opposition, LG 11th January 1919.**

RMS *Alaunia* (13,405 tons) was built by Scotts Shipbuilding & Engineering Co at Greenock for Cunard and was launched on 9th June 1913. She had only 2nd and 3rd class accommodation. Her maiden voyage commenced on 27th December. When the Great War broke out, she was requisitioned as a troopship, HMS *Alaunia*, the first Cunard ship to transport Canadian troops. She was involved in the Gallipoli campaign and carried troops to Bombay later the same year. In 1916 she again carried troops from Canada. On 19th October 1916, sailing from London to New York, she struck a mine laid by UC-16 in the English Channel off Eastbourne. Attempts to tow her to shore or beach her failed and she sank. Two crewmen were lost.

HMS *Cornwallis*, a pre-Dreadnought battleship, was laid down in July 1899 and completed in February 1904. She was able to steam at nineteen knots, making it, and the rest of the *Duncan* class, the fastest battleships in the world. Her main battery was of four 12″ guns. *Cornwallis* was assigned to the Mediterranean Fleet and in 1905 to the Channel Fleet. Two years later she moved to the Atlantic Fleet until 1909, then returned to the Mediterranean Fleet. In 1912 she was assigned to the Home Fleet, first to the 4th Battle Squadron and then the 6th. Having covered the crossing of the BEF to France in August 1914, it transferred to the 3rd Battle Squadron to reinforce the Grand Fleet. *Cornwallis* fired the first shots of the Gallipoli campaign on 19th February 1915 during a bombardment of Ottoman coastal defences. She supported the landings at Cape Helles on 25th April and shelled Ottoman troops over the following month, as Allied soldiers sought to push further inland. She served with the Suez Canal Patrol and briefly on the East Indies Station until March 1916, when she returned to the Mediterranean. She was torpedoed and sunk by U-32 on patrol off Malta on 9th January 1917.

The Army Staff College at Camberley originated from Colonel Le Marchant's staff college founded in 1799. In 1802, it became the Senior Department of the new Royal Military College, then at High Wycombe and later at Sandhurst. In 1858, the Senior Department became the Staff College and in 1870 separated from the Royal Military College. The purpose-built accommodation seen here was constructed 1859–63. From 1903, Colonial forces officers were admitted and in 1905 a few Royal Navy and Royal Marines officers were also introduced each year. Except for during the world wars, it operated until 1997, when it merged into the Joint Services Command and Staff College, together with its Royal Navy and Royal Air Force equivalents. Its Commandant in 1936–37 was a fellow VC, the then Major-General Viscount Gort.

Dudley was temporary Commander of 2nd Brigade 26th September–5th October, then resumed command of 2nd Royal Sussex Regiment. **Awarded the VC for his actions at the Sambre-Oise Canal, France on 4th November 1918, LG 6th January 1919. He was mentioned in Field Marshal Sir Douglas Haig's despatch dated 16th March 1919, LG 8th July 1919.** Dudley embarked for Britain on 11th November. Appointed temporary lieutenant colonel while commanding 2nd Royal Sussex 1st January–29th April 1919. He was in Germany as part of the Army of Occupation. The VC, Bar to the DSO and MC were presented by the King in the quadrangle at Buckingham Palace on 14th June.

Appointed temporary lieutenant colonel and Chief Instructor (Class AA), Lewis and Hotchkiss Gun Wing, Small Arms School, Hythe, Kent on 22nd July. Appointed Chief Instructor (Class AA) Small Arms School, Hythe 22nd September 1919–21st September 1923. He was a member of the VC Guard at the Interment of the

Unknown Warrior on 11th November 1920. Promoted brevet lieutenant colonel on 29th December 1923. Attended Staff College, Camberley 1923–24 and the Senior Officers' School, Belgaum, India in 1925. Promoted lieutenant colonel on transfer to the North Staffordshire Regiment (The Prince of Wales's) on 12th April 1928. Appointed Chief Instructor (Class AA), Netheravon Wing, Small Arms School, Wiltshire on 2nd December 1926. Appointed CO 2nd North Staffordshire Regiment on 12th April 1928. Half-pay on 12th April 1932 on relinquishing command of 2nd Battalion. Promoted colonel the same day, with seniority from 29th December 1927, and attended the Royal Naval Staff College, Greenwich 1932–33. Resumed full pay on 1st July 1933.

Dudley was appointed temporary brigadier whilst Commander 12th (Secunderabad) Infantry Brigade 1st July 1933–20th January 1936. Appointed Commandant, Small Arms School, Netheravon, Wiltshire and Officer i/c Records, Small Arms School Corps (remaining a temporary brigadier) on 13th February. He was appointed ADC to King George VI 10th September 1936–6th January 1939. He was promoted major general to command 4th Division on 7th January 1938, with seniority from 25th December 1937. **Appointed an Ordinary Member of the Order of the Bath (Military Division), LG 8th June 1939.**

At the outbreak of the Second World War, 4th Division, in common with other British formations, was not ready for operations. It took two weeks to gather manpower, equipment and supplies before the Division began to move to France as part of the BEF, under command of II Corps (Lieutenant General Alan Brooke). The Division was in reserve behind Lens and in late November moved into the line northeast of Lille. Throughout the winter, the Division trained and prepared defences. When the Germans invaded in May 1940, the BEF moved into Belgium. Major General TR Eastwood DSO MC arrived to take command of 4th Division, but Dudley pleaded to remain in command once combat operations had commenced. Eastwood was appointed Vice Chief of the General Staff, HQ BEF. The 4th Division was northeast of Brussels by 14th May. At midnight on 17th May, with 4th Division

The Most Honourable Order of the Bath was founded by King George I in 1725. It is the fourth senior of the British Orders of Chivalry. The name derives from the medieval ceremony for appointing a knight, which involved bathing as a symbol of purification. The Order consists of the Sovereign, the Great Master and three Classes of members:

- Knight or Dame Grand Cross (GCB).
- Knight or Dame Commander (K/DCB).
- Companion (CB).

Members belong to either the Civil or the Military Division. Recipients of the Order are now usually senior military officers or civil servants. Commonwealth citizens who are not subjects of the British monarch and foreign nationals may be Honorary Members.

Lieutenant General Alan Brooke (later Field Marshal Alan Brooke, 1st Viscount Alanbrooke), Commander of II Corps, in France with his divisional commanders, Major General Bernard Montgomery (later Field Marshal Bernard Law Montgomery, 1st Viscount Montgomery of Alamein) (3rd Division) on the left and Major General Dudley Johnson (4th Division), on the right.

in contact with advanced German units, General Gort ordered all British forces to withdraw across the River Dendre. By 19th May, the Division was holding the front west of the Escaut. Next day German probes developed into a full-scale assault. The 4th Division repelled all attacks, but further north, in 44th Division's sector, a German force got across the river and to the south the Germans had reached Arras. Although 4th Division drove back every attack, it was a matter of time before the

HMS *Worcester*, the eighth of her name, was laid down by J Samuel White at Cowes, Isle of Wight on 20th December 1918 and completed on 20th September 1922. *Worcester* saw service in the Atlantic and Mediterranean Fleets before transferring to the Reserve Fleet and being placed in reserve at Portsmouth in the early 1930s. She was recommissioned in 1939 with the 16th Destroyer Flotilla at Portsmouth for convoy escort and patrol duties in the English Channel and Southwestern Approaches. In May 1940 she came under C-in-C Dover to support the evacuation of forces from France, making six trips to Dunkirk and rescuing 4,350 troops. She suffered damage in an air attack on 27th May. In July 1940 she returned to 16th Destroyer Flotilla at Harwich before transferring to Western Approaches Command for convoy defence. In January 1941, *Worcester* again transferred to 16th Destroyer Flotilla at Harwich. On 6th March 1941, she and HMS *Whitshed* were escorting Convoy FS29 southwards along the east coast of Britain, when they came under German air attack. Next day the destroyers chased a German S/E-boat, which was a decoy for the 1st S-Boote Flotilla to attack the convoy. *Worcester* and *Whitshed* were too far away to intervene, and two merchant ships were sunk. During the Channel Dash in February 1942 *Worcester* made an unsuccessful torpedo attack and was hit by 11″ shells from the German battlecruisers and 8″ shells from *Prinz Eugen*, suffering twenty-six dead and forty-five wounded. *Worcester* was under repair and conversion until August 1942 and was assigned to the Home Fleet at Scapa Flow to support Arctic convoys. In January 1943, *Worcester* again returned to 16th Destroyer Flotilla and resumed operations in the North Sea. On 24th October 1943, she deployed off Norfolk with other craft to intercept S/E-boats gathering to attack on two convoys. The German 4th Torpedo Boat Flotilla was prevented from attacking the convoys and lost four S/E-boats. On 23rd December 1943 *Worcester* detonated a mine in the North Sea and was towed to Great Yarmouth. She was beyond economical repair and became an accommodation ship in London as HMS *Yeoman*. She was sold for scrap in September 1946 and was broken up at Grays, Essex.

Division was outflanked. Late on 22nd May the Division withdrew to the positions it held during the winter. Over the next few days 4th Division delayed the German advance while being gradually pushed northwest towards Dunkirk. On the night of 31st May/1st June, less than 400 men from 4th Division reached boats off the beaches. Dudley telephoned Dover and the War Office to plead for more ships to be sent. As a result, the bulk of the Division was embarked. The last 500 embarked aboard the destroyer HMS *Worcester* from the Mole, including Dudley and his staff. A new HQ was established at Crewkerne, Somerset. At the age of fifty-five Dudley was considered too old to continue in an active command appointment. On 25th June he handed over 4th Division to Major General Eastwood and was appointed GOC Aldershot Command. He was mentioned in the War Office despatch dated 20th December 1940, LG 20th December 1940, and General Lord Gort's despatch dated 25th April 1940, LG 17th October 1941.

Dudley was appointed Honorary Colonel, 4th Battalion, Monmouthshire Regiment 26th February 1941–27th September 1949. He was supernumerary to establishment 13th-20th March 1941 on full-pay. He was appointed Inspector of Infantry 21st March 1941–30th April 1942 and Adviser (Training) to the Home Guard at GHQ Home Forces 11th May 1942–20th December 1943. He retired on 27th January 1944. Appointed Colonel South Wales Borderers 30th June 1944–31st December 1949.

Dudley took up a number of civil employments and appointments:

- Borough Councillor, Fleet Urban District Council, Hampshire and Chairman 1948–50. He had a special interest in housing and the welfare of the elderly.
- President of Hampshire British Legion 1952–63, thereafter Life Vice President.
- President of the Secunderabad Club, Hyderabad, India 8th March 1934–29th March 1936.
- President, League of Friends of Winchfield Hospital, Odiham Road, Winchfield, Hook, Hampshire.
- Life President Fleet Town Football Club.
- Church Warden Christ Church, Church Crookham, Hampshire 1948–68.

The Secunderabad Club is one of the five oldest clubs in India. It had four name changes before Secunderabad Club was settled upon. The club was established on 26th April 1878 by British Army garrisons in the area under an agreement with the 3rd Nizam, Sikandar Jah. The club came to its current location in March 1903. Until 1947 there were only British Presidents but a few high-ranking members of the Indian nobility were offered membership. In the early hours of 15th January 2022, a devastating fire completely gutted the main building.

He attended a number of VC Reunions – the VC Garden Party at Buckingham Palace on 26th June 1920, the VC Dinner at the Royal Gallery of the House of Lords, London on 9th November 1929, the VC Centenary

The Church Crookham village war memorial was unveiled on 10th October 1920 at the crossroads of Gables Road and Galley Hill Road.

Celebrations at Hyde Park, London on 26th June 1956 and the 1st, 2nd, 3rd, 4th, 5th, 7th, 8th and 9th VC & GC Association Reunions at the Café Royal, London (the 7th was at the Connaught Rooms, Covent Garden) on 24th July 1958, 7th July 1960, 18th July 1962, 16th July 1964, 14th July 1966, 18th June 1970, 14th July 1972 and 23rd May 1974.

Dudley unveiled the War Memorial in his home village of Oddington, Gloucestershire on 26th February 1921. He also unveiled the VC memorial display at the South Wales Borderers Museum in 1973. He regularly attended the Remembrance Day commemorations at Church Crookham War Memorial and read out the names of those listed on the memorial.

Dudley died at his home at 2 Heathfield Court, Fleet, Hampshire on 21st December 1975. He is buried in Christ Church churchyard, Church Crookham, Hampshire with his wife. His coffin was borne by warrant officers and sergeants of the Royal Regiment of Wales. A memorial service was held at Brecon Cathedral in February 1976. He is commemorated in a number of other places:

- Church Crookham, Hampshire

Heathfield Court, Fleet.

Dudley Johnson's grave in Christ Church churchyard, Church Crookham.

Memorial plaque in Havard Chapel, Brecon Cathedral. (*Memorials to Valour*)

  - Johnson Way and the adjacent sheltered housing development, Dudley Court.
  - Memorial at Christ Church.
- Bourton-on-the-Water, Gloucestershire
  - Dudley Johnson Close.
  - A Department for Communities and Local Government commemorative paving stone and plaque were dedicated at Bourton-on-the-Water War Memorial on 10th November 2018.
- Brecon, Powys
  - Plaque at Havard Chapel, Brecon Cathedral unveiled on 31st January 1976.
  - Victoria Cross Roll, The Royal Welsh Museum, The Barracks.
- The Royal British Legion General Johnson Homes near Guildford, Surrey and the General Johnson Flatlets at Stanmore and Winchester.
- Johnson Mews, Roussillon Park, Broyle Road, Chichester, West Sussex.
- Memorial paving stone unveiled outside Freemason's Hall, Covent Garden, London on 25th April 2017 by the Duke of Kent KG.

On 8th July 1943, the 1939–43 Star (later 1939–45 Star) and the Africa Star became the first two campaign stars instituted by the United Kingdom. By May 1945 there were eight stars and nine clasps. The Arctic Star and Bomber Command Clasp were added in February 2013. No-one could be awarded more than six campaign stars with five of the ten clasps. Only one clasp can be worn on any campaign star. The 1939–1945 Star was awarded for operational service between 3rd September 1939 and 2nd September 1945. It is the only campaign star that covers the full duration of the Second World War. The Battle of Britain Clasp was instituted in 1945 for award to air crew members on fighter aircraft who took part in the Battle from 10th July to 31st October 1940. A total of 2,936 airmen qualified for the clasp. The Bomber Command Clasp was instituted on 26th February 2013 for aircrew on aircraft participating in at least one operational sortie in a Bomber Command operational unit between 3rd September 1939 and 8th May 1945. The broad criteria for award of the 1939–45 Star were 180 days service between these dates. Naval personnel qualified after 180 days afloat between certain specified dates in areas of operations laid out in the regulations. Army personnel had to complete 180 days service in an operational command. However, airborne troops qualified if they had participated in any airborne operations and had completed sixty days service in an operational unit. Aircrew qualified after sixty days service in an operational unit, including at least one operational sortie. Ground crew and other air force personnel qualified by completing 180 days service in an area of operational army command. Merchant Navy personnel qualified upon completion of 180 days service with at least one voyage through an operational area. The award of a gallantry medal or MID qualified the recipient for the 1939–1945 Star, regardless of service duration. Service terminated prematurely by death or disability due to service also qualified the recipient for the Star. In some special circumstances just one day's service was required–Battle of France 10th May–19th June 1940, St Nazaire Raid 22nd-28th March 1942, Dieppe Raid 19th August 1942, Anglo-Iraq War 10th April–25th May 1941, Japanese conquest of Burma 22nd February–15th May 1942 and Battle of Madagascar 5th May–5th November 1942. These were actions for which a specific campaign medal was not awarded.

- Citation and replica VC at the Army Reserve Centre, 23 Guildford Road, Farnham, Surrey.
- Framed photograph with VC citation in Holy Ascension Church, Oddington, Gloucestershire.
- Victoria Cross Memorial Plaque, Bradfield College, Berkshire.
- Named on Past Presidents Board, Secunderabad Club, Hyderabad, India.
- Memorial at Lock 1, Sambre-Oise Canal, France.

The entrance to the Royal Welsh Regimental Museum at Brecon.

In addition to the VC, DSO & Bar and MC he was awarded the Queen's Mediterranean Medal 1899–1902, 1914–15 Star, British War Medal 1914–20, Victory Medal 1914–19 with Mentioned-in-Despatches Oakleaf, 1939–45 Star, Defence Medal, War Medal 1939–45 with Mentioned-in-Despatches Oakleaf, George V Silver Jubilee Medal 1935, George VI Coronation Medal 1937 and Elizabeth II Coronation Medal 1953. The VC is held by the Regimental Museum of The Royal Welsh (Brecon), The Barracks, Brecon, Powys, Wales.

The Queen's Mediterranean Medal was awarded to Militia troops who replaced regular units in Gibraltar, Malta and Egypt, to allow them to serve in the Second Boer War. Dudley served on St Helena guarding Boer prisoners in 1901. Troops who guarded Boer prisoners there were awarded the Queen's South Africa medal without clasps. The inclusion of the Queen's Mediterranean Medal in his medal group cannot be explained but it appears that he was awarded the wrong medal.

SECOND LIEUTENANT JAMES KIRK
10th, attached 2nd Battalion, The Manchester Regiment

James Kirk was born on 27th January 1897 at Willow Bank, Ladybridge Road, Adswood, Cheadle Hulme, Cheshire. His father, also James Kirk (9th November 1869–1940s), was born at Little Lever, Lancashire. He married Rachel née Simpson (1870–4th May 1933), born at Newton Heath, Lancashire, in 1895, registered at Prestwich, Lancashire. She was a linen weaver in 1891. He was a dyer's traveller in 1901, when they were living at Wilmslow Road, Stockport, Cheshire. They had moved to 530 Edge Lane, Droylsden, Manchester by 1901. James was living with his son,

Reginald, at 15 Rostherne Avenue, Fallowfield, Manchester in 1939. James junior had three siblings, all born at Cheadle Hulme:

Ladybridge Road, Cheadle Hulme.

- Jessie Kirk (5th February 1896–1953) was a corset maker in 1911 living with her parents. She married Charles James Fox (25th October 1893–18th September 1953), born at Droylsden, Lancashire, in 1921 at Ashton-under-Lyne, Lancashire. He was a commercial clerk in the paper trade in 1939, when they were living at 171 Wilbraham Road, Manchester. Jessie died there and Charles at 20 Nell Street, Manchester. They had three children:

Newton Heath is less than five kilometres from Manchester city centre. Historically part of Lancashire, it was formerly a farming area but changed to engineering during the Industrial Revolution, particularly in mining and textiles. French Huguenots settled in the 16th century, bringing cotton and linen weaving and bleaching skills. The arrival of textile mills changed a cottage industry into full mechanisation. In 1825 Newton Silk Mill was built and Monsall Silk Dye Works soon afterwards. The Rochdale Canal allowed raw materials and finished products to be moved in bulk. Other industries followed, including soap, match manufacturing, rope works and glass making. During the 19th century the population increased almost twenty-fold. Newton Heath was home for a number of famous companies – Mather & Platt produced pumps, electrical machinery and fire sprinkler systems, Avro Aircraft was based there until relocating to Chadderton and Woodford and Heenan & Froude, which designed and manufactured the steelwork for Blackpool Tower. In 1943 the artist LS Lowry painted *Going to Work* of workers walking to Mather & Platt's stainless-steel foundry. The picture is now owned by the Imperial War Museum. The railways arrived in the 1840s. Locomotive repair sheds were opened in 1877 and become a major local employer. Newton Heath Station closed in January 1966 but the area is now served by Metrolink. Newton Chapel, later the Parish Church of All Saints Newton Heath, built in 1556 of wattle and daub, was the first of eight Chapels of Ease under Manchester Collegiate Church. The Chapel stood on the highest ground on the site of the Roman Road from Chester to Manchester, at its junction with the roads to Moston and Droylsden. Newton Chapel was rebuilt in 1598 and 1738. On 2nd May 1808 the building collapsed. The present church was constructed in 1814 and was extended in 1879. There was a major unsympathetic re-reordering in the late 1960s, described by Historic England as a 'heritage crime'. The building is currently on the At Risk Register of Listed Buildings. Manchester United FC was formed from Newton Heath Lancashire & Yorkshire Railway FC. The Club was established in 1878 and played in green and gold jerseys. By 1892 it had been admitted to the football league and the following year moved to Bank Street, Clayton. The name was changed to Manchester United FC in 1902.
Amongst Newton Heath's famous people are:

- Mike Atherton OBE (born 1968) Lancashire and England cricket captain.
- Judy Finnigan (born 1948) television talkshow host and journalist.
- George Stringer VC (1889–1957).

    - Bernard Fox (31st December 1922–14th December 2006), was a municipal clerk in 1939, living with his parents. He married Audrey Jones (14th November 1926–4th October 2019) in 1953 at Manchester, where she was born. Her parents were living at 392 Oldham Road, Manchester in 1939, when Audrey was an evacuee living with Selina J Sherwin (1870–1944) at Rose Cottage, Ashbourne, Derbyshire. Audrey and Bernard had three children including Robert Fox 1954 and Gail M Fox 1959. They both died at Macclesfield, Cheshire.
    - Sheila E Fox (1924–2015) was a domestic servant, living with her parents at 171 Wilbraham Road, Manchester, when she travelled to Halifax, Nova Scotia aboard RMS *Aquitania*, departing Southampton, Hampshire on 19th April 1949. She married Freddrick 'Fred' Hurbert [sic] Westwick (29th May 1926–6th March 1990), a rancher born at Springhouse, British Columbia, Canada. They lived at Box 4629, Bunting Lake Road, 150 Mile House, BC. He died at Cariboo Memorial Hospital, Williams Lake, BC. They had a son, James 'Jim' Westwick (15th December 1953–9th November 2018).
    - Charles Fox (born 1925) married Josephine 'Josie' Ore (21st September 1932–8th April 1999) on 20th February 1953, registered at Burnley, Lancashire. She was living with her parents at 74 Lockyer Avenue, Burnley in 1939.
- Reginald Kirk (20th October 1900–1961), born at Willow Bank, was a packer, cotton and piece goods in 1939, living with his father at 15 Rostherne Avenue, Fallowfield, Manchester.
- Donald Kirk (1906–11).

James' paternal grandfather, Squire Kirk (25th April 1834–1881), born at Prestwich Cum Oldham, Lancashire, married Margaret née Sharples (1839–9th August 1897), born at Horwich, Lancashire, in 1860 registered at Bolton, Lancashire. She was living with her parents at Lever Lane, Little Lever, Bolton in 1851. Squire was a carter in January 1870, when they were living at 25 Adelphi Street, Salford, Lancashire. By the time of the 1871 Census they had moved to 12 Turner Street, Salford. By 1881 he was a former coal miner and they were living at Douglas Green, Pendleton, Salford. In addition to James they had four other children, all born at Little Lever:

- Moses Kirk (1862–28th December 1864).
- Ann Kirk (born 1864) was working in a bleach works in 1881, living with her parents. She married Thomas Jackson (born c.1862), born at Wrea Green, Lancashire in 1882 registered at Prestwich. He was a dyers mangler in 1891, when they were living at 24 Mill Lane, Newton Heath, Lancashire. They were

Prestwich, in the Metropolitan Borough of Bury, Greater Manchester, is about five kilometres north of Manchester city centre and was historically part of Lancashire. The oldest part is known as Prestwich Village and there is a large Jewish community, the second largest in the United Kingdom. Prestwich Manor was held by Robert de Prestwich in 1193. In 1371 Robert de Holland claimed the manor as the right of his wife and the following year seized it by force, retaining it until 1389. The Langley family regained the manor after 1403 and it subsequently passed to the Coke family, who held it until 1777, when Thomas William Coke, Coke of Norfolk, a leader of the Agricultural Revolution, sold the land in order to increase his Norfolk estates. The manor was later sold to Salford Corporation and Prestwich Council. In the late 18th century the area was mainly rural with scattered farms and small settlements. The population was about 670. Hand loom weaving and silk weaving began soon afterwards. The arrival of the railway encouraged affluent merchants from Manchester to build villas in the town. By 1912 the population had increased to 12,800. By 1961 the population had reached 31,000 and Prestwich was a suburb of Manchester. Prestwich Hospital, an asylum, was established in 1851 and by 1900 was the largest in Europe. Bury Old Road was turnpiked in 1754 and Bury New Road, the main thoroughfare, was constructed by a turnpike trust in 1826. The railway arrived in 1879 and in 1916 the line was converted to electric operation. It continued until August 1991 and reopened as the Manchester Metrolink in April 1992. Electric trams arrived around 1900. Amongst the famous people from the town are:

- Howard Jacobson (born 1942), author and Man Booker Prize winner.
- William Sturgeon (1783–1850), physicist and inventor, who created the first practical electric motor and electromagnetic solenoid.
- Victoria Wood (1954–2016), writer, comedian and actress.

still there in 1911. They had four children – George Jackson 1885, Margaret 'Maggie' Jackson 1887, Elizabeth 'Lizzie' Jackson 1890 and May Jackson 1892.

- Elizabeth Mary Kirk (26th May 1867–19th August 1944) married William Rowland Stanfield (1864–1907), born at Uppingham, Rutland, in 1888 registered at Prestwich. Elizabeth was running a sweet shop in 1939, assisted by her daughter, Emily, at 300 Edge Lane, Droylsden, Lancashire. She was still living there at the time of her death at Ancoats Hospital, Manchester. They had four children – William Stanfield (1889–1970), Alice Stanfield (1890–1941), Emily Stanfield (1892–1951) and Lucy Stanfield (1895–96).
- Joseph Kirk (3rd–19th September 1875).

Margaret married John Abbott (1833–1914), a carpenter born at Scothern, Lincolnshire, at St Clement's, Broughton, Salford in 1887. John had married Betsy (also seen as Betsey or Betty) Sharples née Lunn (c.1816–April 1887), born at Netherton, Yorkshire, on 3rd January 1860 registered at Ashton-under-Lyne. Betsy had an illegitimate son, Henry Lunn (13th February 1842–1907) who changed his surname to Sharples. John and Betsy were living at 45 Winton Street, Ashton-under-Lyne in 1861 and at 428 Manchester Road, Hollinwood, Oldham, Lancashire in

Horwich is in the Metropolitan Borough of Bolton in Greater Manchester, although historically it was in Lancashire. After the Norman Conquest, Horwich was held by Albert de Gresle and became a hunting chase. After the Reformation land ownership shifted from Church to Crown and new owners transformed the town into an agricultural economy. By the 17th century Horwich Forest had been much reduced by house building and for fuel. Horwich Moor was enclosed between 1815 and 1818. The cotton industry was at least a secondary occupation in many households, weaving being a widespread occupation. During the early Industrial Revolution, the streams flowing from the nearby moors were harnessed to provide power for bleachworks, dying and paper making. Textile mills became a major employer. After 1884, when the Lancashire & Yorkshire Railway workshops were established, there was a major rise in the population. In 1881 the population was 3,761 but just ten years later had risen to 12,850. The first Horwich built locomotive, No.1008, left the works in 1887 and can be seen at the National Railway Museum. During the two world wars, the works also manufactured munitions and tanks. The last steam locomotive was built at Horwich Works in November 1957, after which it produced shunting diesel trains until December 1962, and then repaired engines and railway wagons. Horwich Works closed on 23rd December 1983 after ninety-seven years. Other industries included quarrying, small collieries, firebrick and tile works and pipeworks. In 1937 the de Havilland Aircraft Co built a factory. It was targeted by the Luftwaffe in July 1942, but the raid failed due to low cloud. The late 20th century saw the demise of the old industries, with high unemployment. These were eventually replaced by small and medium scale enterprises.

1871. Betsy had married John Sharples (c.1805–56), a labourer born at Chorlton, on 13th April 1842 at the Cathedral and Collegiate Church of St Mary, St Denys and St George, Manchester. They were living at 4 Astley Street, Dukinfield, Cheshire in 1851. They had four children – Frances Sharples (1844), Jane Sharples (1846–54), James Sharples (1848–62) and John Sharples (1851). John Abbott married thirdly Mary Ogden née McClelland (c.1841–1919) on 24th January 1899 at St Mary's Church, Moston, Lancashire. They were both living at 2 Buckley Street, off St Mary's Road, Moston and at the time of the 1901 and 1911 Censuses. Mary had married Abraham Ogden (c.1827–97) in 1874 at Manchester. He was an agricultural labourer in 1851, living with his widowed mother at 28 Denton Lane, Chadderton. By 1861 he was a gas fitter and, by 1881, a labourer in a sawmill, when they were living at 254 Oldham Road, Newton, Manchester. By 1891 they were living at 40 Lamb Lane, Newton, when he was a general labourer and she was a tobacconist. Abraham had married Mary Ann Deberex (c.1831–1872) on 11th August 1862 at Ashton-under-Lyne. He was a railway pointsman in 1871, when they were living at Hercules Green, Chadderton.

His maternal grandfather, James Simpson (c.1834–94), born at Hurdsfield, Cheshire, married Betty née Rushton (c.1836–93), also born at Hurdsfield, in 1857 registered at Macclesfield, Cheshire. James was a silk finisher in 1863 and later a domestic servant. He was not with the family at the time of the 1871 Census, when they were living at 293 Droylsden Road, Newton Heath, Lancashire. By 1891 they had moved to 299 Droylsden Road. Their deaths were registered at Prestwich. In addition to Rachel they had five other children:

293 Droylsden Road on the right.

- William Simpson (1858–1929), born at Hurdsfield, Cheshire, was a labourer in a printing works in 1871, living with his mother. He married Elizabeth Longworth (1858–1931), born at Newton Heath, in 1878. She was a box maker in 1871, living with her parents at 21 Mitchell Street, Newton, Manchester. He was a stiffener in a bleach work in 1881, when they were living at the back of 335 Droylsden Road, Newton Heath. By 1891 they were living at 279 Droylsden Road and at 299 Droylsden Road in 1901. He was a worker in a calico bleaching works in 1911, when they were living at 275 Droylsden Road. They had seven children, one of whom died as an infant – Edith Simpson 1879, Leah Simpson 1881, William Simpson 1883, Walter Simpson 1885, Bertha Alice Simpson 1887 and Marion Simpson 1892.
- Mary Simpson (1861–2nd March 1936), born at Newton Heath, was a cotton operative in 1871, living with her mother and a linen winder in 1881, living with her parents. She married Joseph Hilton (1862–1st June 1934), a warehouseman born at Newton Heath, in 1888 at Prestwich. They were living at 14 Hope Street, Newton Heath in 1901. Also living with them was Mary's sister, Amelia. By 1911 they had moved to 15 Oak Terrace, Bury Brow, Newton Heath. He was living at 16 Windsor Street, Newton Heath at the time of his death at 123 Crescent Road, Crumpsall, Manchester. Mary was living at 647 Oldham Road, Newton Heath at the time of her death there. They had two daughters – Edna Hilton (24th August 1889–4th May 1958), who was with the ARP ambulance service in 1939, and Mary Elizabeth Hilton (15th October 1896–1988).
- Walter Simpson (1863–1910) was a damper in a bleach works in 1881, living with his parents. He married Alice Wild (10th October 1865–1950), born at Woodhouses, Ashton-under-Lyne, in 1888. Walter was a beer retailer in a public house in 1901, when they were living at 259 Droylsden Road, Newton Heath (now the Horseshoe public house). Alice was the landlady in a beer house in 1911, still living at 259 Droylsden Road. She was living with her son, James, a storekeeper (tool and jig store), at 273 Droylsden Road in 1939. They had six children, two of whom died in infancy – James Edmund Simpson (28th May 1889), Fred Simpson (1890), Gertrude Alice Simpson (3rd August 1892–1975) married Thomas Godden in 1922, and Arthur Simpson (1894).

- Amelia Simpson (1867–1909) was a linen/cotton winder in 1881 and 1891 living with her parents. She died unmarried.
- James Simpson (1873–1902), was a packer in a factory in 1891, living with his parents. He married Martha Jane Haslam (23rd February 1870–1944), born at Newton Heath, in 1895 at Prestwich. She was living with her parents at 14 Church Street, Newton in 1871. James and Martha were living at 41 Briscoe Lane, Newton Heath in 1901, when he was a weave maker up and she was a cotton weaver. Martha and her daughter, Ethel (26th July 1896–1945), were living with her widowed mother at 8 Hutchinson Street, Newton Heath in 1911. Martha was a weaver and Ethel was an apprentice corset maker. Martha was living with her daughter, Ethel Cooke, and son-in-law, James Arthur Cooke (5th June 1896–30th May 1964), a tailor's cutter and shop manager, at 2 Claremont Avenue, Maghull, Lancashire in 1939. Arthur, as he was known, was also a special constable in the Lancashire Special Constabulary. Arthur and Ethel had married in 1920. Martha's death was registered at Ormskirk, Lancashire. Martha and James had one other child, who died as an infant.

The British had raised the Somaliland Camel Corps in 1912. The Imperial Camel Corps began with four companies of Australians returning from Gallipoli, to conduct long-range patrols around the Suez Canal and into the Sinai Desert in January 1916. A more active combat role followed in August and each company of about 130 men had a machine gun section of fifteen men and three Lewis guns added. With an expanded company headquarters the strength rose to 184 men. The concept was to travel by camel but dismount to fight as infantry. In March 1916 six new companies were raised from British yeomanry regiments and in June another four Australian companies. Reinforcements intended for the New Zealand Mounted Rifles Brigade formed two companies, one in August and another in November. The Imperial Camel Brigade was formed on 19th December 1916, commanded by Brigadier General Clement Leslie Smith VC. It comprised 1st (Australian), 2nd (British), and 3rd (Australian) Battalions, plus supporting units. Battalions comprised four companies and had an authorised strength of 770 men and 922 camels. The 4th (ANZAC) Battalion was raised in May 1917. However, one battalion was always resting and refitting, so only three battalions served at the front at any time. The Brigade received other units – 265th (Camel) Machine Gun Squadron (eight Vickers machine guns), Hong Kong and Singapore (Mountain) Battery (six 2.75″ Mountain Guns), 10th (Camel) Field Troop RE, a signal section, Australian (Camel) Field Ambulance, 97th Australian Dental Unit, Mobile Veterinary Section, Brigade Ammunition Column and Brigade Train, with supplies for five days. The total strength was 4,150 men and 4,800 camels. The Brigade became part of the Egyptian Expeditionary Force and fought in the Senussi Campaign, in Sinai and Palestine and during the Arab Revolt. In June 1918 the Australian troops formed 14th and 15th Light Horse Regiments and the New Zealand troops formed 2nd New Zealand Machine Gun Squadron. All three units became part of 5th Light Horse Brigade. The British remained part of the ICC and two companies fought with TE Lawrence, carrying out sabotage operations along the Hejaz railway. The residual ICC was disbanded in May 1919, having had 240 men killed or died of wounds. A memorial was dedicated on 22nd July 1921 on the Thames Embankment in London.

Kinmel Park Camp was built in 1915 in the grounds of Kinmel Hall, near Abergele, to train recruits for the Great War. Small shops opened nearby in what became known as Tintown. A railway served the camp and was later used for a nearby quarry until it closed in 1964. The poet Robert Graves commanded an officer cadet battalion at Kinmel Park in 1917, while recovering from wounds. After the war the camp housed Canadian troops awaiting repatriation. A riot broke out in March 1919, resulting in the deaths of five soldiers. They were frustrated by basic living conditions and delays in travelling home due to a shortage of shipping. The camp was later reduced to around half its original size and continues as a military training facility.

James was educated at Miss Chadwick's School, Cheadle Hulme, Cheshire, at Brentall Street School, Stockport, Cheshire and at North Road United Methodist School, Clayton, Manchester. He was an apprentice blouse maker in 1911 and later a clerk for Ogden & Madeley's Warehouse in Manchester. James was a keen sportsman, playing centre-half for Seymour Old Boys' Association Football Team, and was honorary secretary in the 1912–13 season, during which the team was undefeated. He was also a member of the Edge Lane Cricket Club.

James enlisted in 2/6th Manchester on 10th October 1914 (3117 & 250806) and trained at Southport, Lancashire and Crowborough, Sussex. He went overseas on 2nd August 1915 and served at Gallipoli from 17th August, probably with 1/6th Battalion. He was promoted lance corporal on 3rd November and was evacuated to Cairo, Egypt with frostbite. He was in hospital throughout December and joined the Imperial Camel Corps following recovery. He was appointed quartermaster sergeant on 5th January 1916 and remained with the Camel Corps until January 1917. He rejoined the Manchester Regiment and went to France in February. He was promoted sergeant in April and returned to Britain on 26th December, recommended for a commission. James trained at 17th Officer Cadet Battalion, Kinmel Park, Rhyl, North Wales from 18th February 1918 and was commissioned on 26th June. He returned to France on 8th October and joined 2nd Battalion on 13th October. **Awarded the VC for his actions at the Sambre-Oise Canal, north of Ors, France on 4th November 1918, LG 6th January 1919.** The VC was presented to his parents by the King in the ballroom at Buckingham Palace on 1st March 1919.

James was killed during his VC action on 4th November 1918. He is buried close to Lieutenant Colonel JN Marshall VC and Lieutenant Wilfred Owen MC, 2nd Manchester, the war poet, in Ors Communal Cemetery, France (A22). He was engaged at the time of his death. James is commemorated in a number of other places:

Wilfred Edward Salter Owen MC (18th March 1893 – 4th November 1918) was one of the leading poets of the Great War, influenced by Siegfried Sassoon. He enlisted on 21st October 1915 in the Artists Rifles and was commissioned on 4th June 1916 in the Manchester Regiment. The blast of a mortar shell left him unconscious for several days. Soon afterward he was diagnosed with neurasthenia (shell shock) and was treated at Craiglockhart War Hospital, Edinburgh. While there he met fellow poet Siegfried Sassoon. He also made friends in Edinburgh's artistic and literary circles and taught in a poor area of the city. In November 1917 he was discharged to light regimental duties at Scarborough, Yorkshire and in March 1918 to the Northern Command Depot at Ripon. In July 1918 he returned to active service in France. On 1st October he led an attack on enemy strongpoints on the Fonsomme Line near Joncourt for which he was awarded the MC, although it was not gazetted until 15th February 1919. Wilfred Owen was killed on 4th November 1918. His mother received the telegram on Armistice Day as the church bells in Shrewsbury rang out in celebration. He is buried in Ors Communal Cemetery (A3). On 11th November 1985, he was one of sixteen Great War poets commemorated on a slate stone unveiled in Westminster Abbey's Poet's Corner. The forester's house in Ors, Maison forestière de l'Ermitage, where he spent his last night, has been transformed into an art installation and permanent memorial to Owen and his poetry. It opened to the public on 1st October 2011.

- A Tameside Metropolitan Borough Blue Plaque attached to 530 Edge Lane, Droylsden, Lancashire.
- Named on a Blue Plaque to all Tameside VCs at the main entrance to Ashton Town Hall, Manchester unveiled on 20th April 1995.
- Named in the Book of Remembrance of the Manchester and King's Regiments in Manchester Cathedral.
- Named on Cheadle Hulme War Memorial at the junction of Ravenoak Road and Manor Road, Cheadle Hulme, Greater Manchester.

The Tameside VCs Blue Plaque at Ashton Town Hall.

Cheadle Hulme War Memorial.

Oldham War Memorial.

The Department for Communities and Local Government commemorative paving stone at Cheadle Hulme War Memorial.

James Kirk's grave in Ors Communal Cemetery. Lieutenant Colonel JN Marshall VC is buried separately to the right and Lieutenant Wilfred Owen MC is in the same row as Kirk some distance to the left.

- A Department for Communities and Local Government commemorative paving stone was dedicated at Cheadle Hulme War Memorial on 4th November 2018.
- Named on The Ring of Remembrance (L'Anneau de la Mémoire or Ring of Memory) at Ablain-Saint-Nazaire, France, inaugurated on 11th November 2014. The Ring commemorates the 576,606 soldiers of forty nationalities who died in Nord-Pas-de-Calais in the Great War.

The Ring of Remembrance (L'Anneau de la Mémoire), designed by Philippe Prost, was inaugurated on 11th November 2014 by French President Hollande, Nord-Pas-de-Calais région président, Daniel Percheron, and German Minister of Defense, Ursula von der Leyen. The inspiration is a human ring holding hands, a sign of fellowship and unity among countries that were enemies. It commemorates 576,606 soldiers of forty nations who died in Nord-Pas-de-Calais in the Great War. It is co-located with the largest French national cemetery of Notre-Dame-de-Lorette, which can be seen in the background. The Ring is a 345m ellipse, including a raised section of sixty-one metres. Although the ring is a symbol of peace in Europe, the overhang reminds visitors that peace is not guaranteed and conflict can return at any time. Within the Ring are 500 stainless steel panels facing inwards arranged like the pages of a book. Each is three metres tall and has c.1,200 names listed alphabetically by surname regardless of nationality, gender, religion or rank. The first name is 'A' and the last is 'Zschiesche'. The 500th panel is blank for newly discovered names. There are four panels of Smiths alone.

The United Reformed Church War Memorial, Cheadle Hulme.

448 N San Pedro Street, San Jose, California, the former Military Medal Museum and Research Center.

- Named on the War Memorial, Church Terrace, Oldham, Greater Manchester.
- Named on the War Memorial, United Reformed Church, Swann Lane, Cheadle Hulme, Cheshire.

In addition to the VC he was awarded the 1914–15 Star, British War Medal 1914–20 and Victory Medal 1914–19. The VC was bought by an American collector, John Langton, at Spink's in 1959 and was displayed in the Military Medal Museum and Research Center, 448 N San Pedro Street, San Jose, California, USA. The Museum closed after Langton's death and the entire collection was placed in storage.

LIEUTENANT COLONEL JAMES NEVILLE MARSHALL
Irish Guards, attached 16th Battalion, The Lancashire Fusiliers

James Marshall was born on 12th June 1886 at 2 Crosby Place, Steven Street, Stretford, Manchester, Lancashire and was baptised on 30th July 1887 at All Saints, Wigan, Lancashire. However, his birth was not registered until the 3rd quarter of 1887. His father, James Henry Marshall (c.1847–27th May 1910), a small ware buyer born in Co Fermanagh, Ireland, had moved to Manchester by 1880. He married Mary Ann née Walmsley (11th August 1862–1950), born at Portland Street, Southport, Lancashire, on 15th September 1880 at St Philip's, Manchester. They were living at

All Saints' Church in Wallgate, Wigan is Grade II* listed. The oldest parts date from the late 13th century and the belfry is probably 16th century. Major rebuilding took place 1845–50 and the church was restored in 1922. A Roman altar is built into the splay of a north window.

St Philip's Church in Wilton Place, off Chapel Street in Salford, Greater Manchester, is Grade II* listed. It was partly subsidised by the Church Building Commission and the architect, Sir Robert Smirke, reused his design for St Mary's Church, Bryanston Square, London. The church was completed in 1824 and the inside was reorganised in 1895. The neighbouring church of St Stephen closed in 1962, and the two parishes amalgamated to form St Philip with St Stephen.

33 Great Clowes Street, Broughton in Salford, Lancashire in 1881, at 2 Crosby Place, Stretford in 1886, at 64 Steven Street, Stretford, Lancashire in 1891, at Broad Road, Acocks Green, Warwickshire around 1892 and Melrose, Clifton Road, Balsall Heath by 1901, by when he was a haberdasher. James senior hanged himself and the death was registered at Solihull. In 1911 Mary was living with her children at Eastbourne House, Warwick Road, Acocks Green, Solihull, Warwickshire, where she ran a private school, assisted by her unmarried daughters, Mary and Nannie. James junior had five siblings:

- Klein Marshall (23rd October 1892–4th June 1973), born at Broad Road, Acocks Green, was a clerk in 1911, living with his mother. He served in the Royal Army Medical Corps (Territorial) (S51) and transferred to the Wiltshire Regiment (209142). He was on active service at Gallipoli from 4th September 1915. Klein married Elizabeth Jones (13th April 1893–11th July 1972) in 1930 at Birmingham. He was a motor engineer and a volunteer ambulance driver and she was a nurse in 1939, when they were living at Homelea, Worcester Street, Bromsgrove. They were both living at 132 Worcester Road, Bromsgrove at the time of their deaths there.
- Mary Louisa Marshall (21st October 1881–19th June 1933), born at Salford, Lancashire, was a commercial bookkeeper in 1901. She never married and was living at Eastbourne House, Acocks Green at the time of her death there.

Great Clowes Street.

Broad Road, Acocks Green.

- Nanny 'Nannie' Constance Marshall (9th June 1883–20th August 1968) also appears as Nancy. She was a pianoforte teacher, living at 12 Heaton Road, Solihull, Warwickshire in 1939. She never married and subsequently died there.
- May Marshall (15th May 1885–30th January 1969) married Charles Lockwood Beckett (30th December 1878–28th October 1962), a laundry proprietor, in 1933 at Birmingham. His birth was registered at Ecclesall Bierlow, Yorkshire. They separated before 1939, when May was living with her sister, Nannie, at 12 Heaton Road, Solihull, where she later died. Charles was living at 111 Yardley Road, Birmingham in 1939 with his sister, Beatrice Mary Beckett (1877–1970), and two children from his first marriage, Joan and Paul. Charles was living at 1 Wake Green Road, Moseley, Birmingham at the time of his death. Charles had married Mabel Violet Turner (1887–31st March 1920) in 1913 at Birmingham. Her birth was registered at King's Norton, Warwickshire. She was a cookery teacher with the Smethwick Education Committee in 1911, living with her parents at 143 Rotton Park Road, Birmingham. Charles and Mabel were living at Berry Brow, Avenue Road, Dorridge, Solihull at the time of her death there. Charles and Mabel had two children:
    - Joan Lockwood Beckett (1913–10th January 2011) was assisting her father in the family dry cleaning business in 1939. She married Stanley G Jones in 1947 at Birmingham. She died at Wishmoor Rest Home, Malvern, Worcestershire. They had a son, David L Jones 1960.
    - Paul Lockwood Beckett (30th July 1917–29th February 1980) was serving as a private in 5th Field Park RAOC in 1939, living with his father. He married Marian Ellen Wilson (7th April 1916–16th October 1988), born at Aston, Warwickshire, in 1942 at Birmingham. She was living with her parents at 12 Miall Park Road, Solihull in 1939, when she was a Dictaphone typist. They were living at 25 College Close, Buckleigh, Westward Ho!, Bideford, Devon at the time of their deaths there. They had a son, Anthony CL Beckett 1947.
- Dorothy Marshall (17th June 1890–21st April 1974), born at 64 Steven Street, Manchester, was university educated (MA). She married Aleck 'Alec' Martin

Wellington (28th April 1890–13th November 1978), born at St Peters, Coleshill, Warwickshire, at Aston, Warwickshire in 1914. He was a civil engineer and in 1919 was Superintendent of the São Paulo Railway in Brazil. The marriage ended in divorce. They had two children:

- Alec Ian Gordon Wellington (1915–25th February 1929), born at Medway, Kent, spent his early childhood in Brazil and returned to England to Bigshotte School, Wokingham, Berkshire. While skating there he fell and was taken to hospital but died there.
- Richard Anthony 'Wimpy' or 'Tony' Wellington (6th July 1919–7th April 1992), born at Moseley, Birmingham, also spent his early childhood in Brazil and became fluent in Portuguese. He was educated at Bigshotte School and at Harrow School 1933–36. He returned to Brazil to farm the family property near Atibaia. In November 1940 he returned to Britain and was commissioned as a pilot officer on probation in the RAFVR on 6th September 1941 (106238). He was promoted flying officer on 6th September 1942 and was posted to No.106 Squadron RAF under Wing Commander Guy Penrose Gibson, who was later awarded the VC. Richard took part in many sorties against the Ruhr and his aircraft was damaged on several occasions. In July 1942 over Wilhelmshaven his aircraft was heavily engaged by anti-aircraft fire and was attacked by an enemy fighter. His bomber sustained severe damage but he managed to fly it back to base. Awarded the DFC, LG 12th March 1943. After completing thirty-four sorties, he and his crew were assigned to No.83 Squadron, RAF Wyton, Cambridgeshire, a Pathfinder unit. Awarded the DSO after completing a large number of sorties, including eighteen attacks on the Ruhr, LG 27th July 1943. He was promoted flight lieutenant on 24th June 1943 but his flying career was terminated by a serious ear injury that month, having completed sixty sorties. He served as a Pathfinder Force staff officer and in December was sent on a lecture tour of Brazil to promote the Allied cause. He married Irene Smallbones (born 10th November 1919), an actress born at Stavanger, Norway, in February 1944 at St Paul's Church, São Paolo, Brazil. She was the daughter of Robert Townsend Smallbones CMG MBE (1884–1976), British Consul General in São Paolo, and Inga Gjertson (1890–1988). Robert arranged visas for 48,000 persecuted Jews to escape Nazi Germany before the Second World War, for which he was posthumously awarded the British Hero of the Holocaust Medal in 2013. In August 1944 Tony was appointed Air Attaché at the British Embassy, Lisbon, Portugal and he was promoted squadron leader on 30th November. Before returning to Britain he arranged a football match between the RAF team (including Stanley Matthews) and the Portuguese Army team. Tony gained the Royal Aero Club Aviator's Certificate (21563) on 12th August 1946. He resigned his commission and retained the rank of wing commander on 16th September 1946. He returned to Brazil as representative of the

de Havilland Aircraft Co for Latin America. On termination of his contract in 1948, he went back to farm at Atibaia. In 1951 they returned to England and he joined the Diplomatic Service, serving in Germany until 1953. He resigned and became ships' manager for South Coast Sand & Ballast Co, Southampton. In 1956 he rejoined the Diplomatic Service, serving in London, Germany, Iran and Spain. Tony was a member of the English Polo Team in 1957. He was appointed HM Consul in Brazil for the States of Pernambuco, Alagoas, Paraiba, Rio Grande do Norte, Ceará, Piaui, Maranhao and Para, with the territory of Amapá, whilst residing at Recife (LG 19th July 1963). He transferred to the Embassy, Rio de Janeiro in 1965 as Press Information Officer and on two occasions acted as temporary head of the Embassy in the new capital of Brasilia. He was awarded the Brazilian Order of Rio Branco in 1969 and the OBE, LG 3rd June 1972. The following year he retired from the Diplomatic Service and joined British Caledonian Airways as public relations officer for Brazil. He also worked for a number of publications, writing articles about Brazil. He wrote a number of books including *The Brazilians – How they live and work* 1974 and an autobiography, assisted by his daughter, Sandra, *Pathfinder Pilot. The Wartime Memoirs of Wing Commander RA Wellington*. Richard died at São Silvestre Hospital, Rio de Janeiro. Irene and Tony had six children but four died shortly after birth. A son was born on 18th December 1945 at the British Hospital, Lisbon and Sandra Inga Wellington was born on 21st September 1948 at São Paolo.

Wing Commander Guy Penrose Gibson VC DSO & Bar DFC & Bar (12th August 1918 – 19th September 1944), commanded No.617 Squadron on the Dambusters raid in May 1943, for which he was awarded the VC.

Robert and Inga Townsend Smallbones.

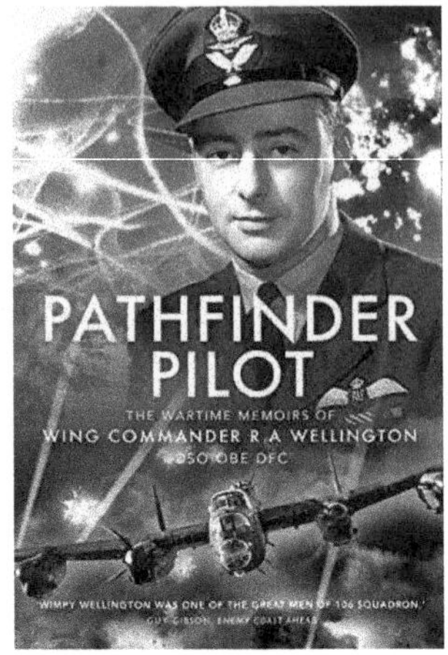

Richard Anthony 'Wimpy' Wellington's autobiography.

Alec married Christina Clow (20th May 1906–14th September 1980) in January 1936 at Rio de Janeiro. They both died at 17 Belvedere Grove, Wimbledon, Surrey. Dorothy married Edward Denys Stevens (13th November 1896–21st November 1940), born at 17 Balaam Street, Plaistow, West Ham, London, at Marrickville, New South Wales, Australia in 1929, where he was a farmer. Edward enlisted in the Inns of Court OTC at 10 Stone Buildings, Lincoln's Inn, London on 8th July 1915 (4684). His next of kin was his father living at 26 Montalt Road, Woodford Green, Essex. He was described as 6′ tall, weighing 140 lbs and his religious denomination was Church of England. Having trained at 2nd Cavalry Cadet School, Kildare, Ireland 1st April–3rd August 1916, he was commissioned in 3/1st Oxfordshire (Queen's Own Oxfordshire Hussars) Yeomanry on 19th August and was attached to 1/1st Lancashire Hussars Yeomanry in France on 10th October. Edward received a gunshot wound to the right arm on 23rd April 1917 and was evacuated to 2nd Stationary Hospital, Abbeville next day. He was attached to 18th (Lancashire Hussars) Battalion, King's Liverpool Regiment on 17th September, when sixteen officers and 290 other ranks of 1/1st Lancashire Hussars Yeomanry joined the Battalion. He was granted leave in Britain 21st October–2nd November and transferred to the RFC on probation as an observer on 22nd November. Edward returned to Britain on 24th November. He attended an Observer course at RFC Artillery & Infantry Cooperation School, Hursley Park Camp, Winchester 16th December–16th January 1918 and a course at No.3 Auxiliary School of Aerial Gunnery, New Romney, Kent 21st January–9th February. Promoted lieutenant on 20th February. On 4th April he was wounded in the leg near St Quentin, while attached to 35 Squadron RAF. He was employed with the RAF in East Lothian 17th March–4th August 1919 and was disembodied at Crystal Palace on 8th August. He resigned his commission, retaining the rank of lieutenant, on 20th July 1920. Edward and Dorothy returned to Britain from Brisbane, Queensland aboard SS *Oronsay*, arriving at Tilbury, London on 3rd December 1936. He was a poultry farmer in 1939, when they were living at Oaktree Farm, Martlesham, Suffolk. Edward was also a member of the RAF Officers Emergency Reserve. He was commissioned as a pilot officer in the RAFVR on 26th September 1939 (74568) and was posted as a flying officer to No.102 Squadron on 26th September 1940. He took part in a raid on Duisburg on the night of 20th/21st November 1940 with four other Whitley bombers. His aircraft did not return. He is commemorated on the Runnymede Memorial, Surrey (Panel 6) with the other four missing members of the crew. Dorothy was living at 9A Sullivan Place, Waldringfield, Suffolk at the time of her death there. They had a daughter:

- Jean Dorothy Stevens (12th August 1930–17th December 2010), born in Australia, married Peter Arthur Sidney Smith (30th November 1926–14th April 2011), born at Hove, Sussex, in 1952, registered at Samford, Suffolk. She died at Petworth, Sussex and he at Chichester, Sussex.

James' paternal grandfather, Edward Marshall, is believed to have been an Inland Revenue Officer in Fermanagh, Ireland. Nothing else is known about him. James' maternal grandfather, William Henry Walmsley (1838–74), born at Chorlton, Lancashire, married Mary Anne née Horton (1838–10th January 1876), born at Manchester, Lancashire, on 1st January 1858 at the Cathedral Parish Church, Manchester. They were both living at 24 Thomas Street, Ardwick, Lancashire at the time. She and her children, Thomas and Jane, were living with her parents at 25 Booth Street, Manchester at the time of the 1861 Census. He was a clerk in 1865, when they were living at 12 Hamilton Terrace, Liverpool, Lancashire. By 1871 he was a book seller's traveller and they were living at 38 Shenstone Street, West Derby, Liverpool. His death was registered at West Derby, Lancashire. She was living at Southport at the time of her death at Southport Infirmary. In addition to Mary they had five other children:

The Air Forces Memorial, or Runnymede Memorial, near Egham, Surrey was dedicated in 1953 to commemorate 20,456 airmen and women who were lost on operations during the Second World War and have no known grave.

Manchester Cathedral, formally the Cathedral and Collegiate Church of St Mary, St Denys and St George, is Grade I listed. It was rebuilt in 1421 and at the end of the 15th century. Its future was uncertain until Elizabeth I granted a new charter in 1578. The Collegiate Church became the Cathedral of the new Diocese of Manchester in 1847. It was extensively restored and extended in Victorian times. Until 1850, the Collegiate Church was the parish church for the whole of Manchester. Within this huge parish were chapels of ease and churches for other denominations but the parish church remained the only place in Manchester where a marriage might legally be contracted. Rather than pay fees for two ceremonies in other churches, couples were married in batches. The Reverend Brookes is believed to have conducted more marriages, funerals and christenings than any English clergyman. In 1838 there were 5,164 christenings, 1,457 funerals, and 2,615 weddings at the church. The Cathedral was damaged during the Blitz and again in the IRA bombing in June 1996. St John the Baptist Chapel is the Regimental Chapel of the Manchester Regiment.

- Thomas Burgess Walmsley (22nd October 1858–24th January 1936), born at Manchester, worked for the Great Western Railway in the Deputy General Manager's Office, Liverpool 14th October 1872–11th October 1874. He emigrated to the USA in 1885 and married Marie Augustine Goddard (28th December 1868–20th February 1926) in 1890 at Manhattan, New York, where she was born. He was an instructor in a trade school in 1910, when they were living at 5206 Cote Brilliante Avenue, St Louis, Missouri. She died at Clearwater, Pinellas Co, Florida and he at Pilot Knob, Missouri. They had three children – Joyce Louise Walmsley (1892–1970), Stephanie E Walmsley (1902) and Godard Thomas Walmsley (1906–77).
- Jane Walmsley (6th September 1860–13th May 1942), born on the Wirral, Cheshire, married John Wall (1849–29th March 1918), a solicitor born at Wigan, Lancashire, in 1885 at Salford, Lancashire. They were living at 127 Wigan Lane, Wigan in 1887, at 40 Bridgeman Terrace, Wigan in 1891, at Laurelton House, Wigan in 1901 and at 146 Wigan Lane, Wigan in 1911. They were living at Freckleton, Wigan at the time of his death there. She was living with her son, John Wall (1886–1944) at 25 Osborne Road, Ainsdale, in 1939.
- Kate Walmsley (28th February 1865–9th June 1927), born at Liverpool St Stephen, was living with her sister, Jane and family, at Wigan in 1891. She never married and was living at the Angel Hotel, Liverpool at the time of her death at Dunoon, Argyllshire, Scotland.
- Fanny Walmsley (1867–1909), born at West Derby, was living at St Elizabeth Institute, East Side, Breckfield Road South, Liverpool in 1881, having been committed there by a magistrate. By 1891 she was living at the Liverpool Royal Infirmary, Mount Pleasant and by 1901 she was a nurse there. She married John Dickinson (born c.1863), an advertising agent, on 21st December 1904 at St Philip's Church, Southport. He was living at 272 Scotland Street and she at 10 Chambres Road there at the time.
- Joyce Thornber Walmsley (13th June 1870–4th February 1951) was living at the New Orphan Houses, Ashley Down, Bristol, Gloucestershire in 1881. She was living with her maternal grandfather at 168a Lord Street, Southport in 1891. Joyce married Joseph Ratcliffe Edisbury (13th May 1859–24th January 1944), birth registered at Wrexham, Denbighshire, but no marriage record has been found. They returned to Liverpool aboard SS *Zaria* on 11th July 1910, having embarked at Grand Canary. He was a hotel manager in 1914. They were living at Erddig, Broad Green Road, Huyton-with-Roby, Lancashire in 1939. Joseph subsequently died there. Joyce was living at 22 Grosvenor Road, Wrexham, Denbighshire at the time of her death there. They had a son, also Joseph Ratcliffe Edisbury (1905–70). Joseph senior had married Minnie Leonora Maria Knight (born 1864), birth registered at Warwick, in 1885 at Chard, Somerset. They were both actors in 1891 living at 34 Northam Road, Hyde, Cheshire. They had at least one daughter, Minnie Leonora Edisbury (born and died 1886).

King Edward VI Camp Hill School for Boys, a selective grammar school, is one of the most academically successful schools in the United Kingdom. It was founded in January 1883 and for two terms was on New Street. That September it opened at its intended site at Camp Hill, near the city centre, and in 1956 moved to its current location on Vicarage Road, adjacent to King's Heath Park, sharing a campus with King Edward VI Camp Hill School for Girls. A former pupil, Clifford Grey, born Percival Davis (1887–1941), was a songwriter, librettist, actor and screenwriter. He wrote for many composers, including Ivor Novello and George Gershwin. Among his best-remembered songs is *If You Were the Only Girl (In the World)*.

James was educated at:

- Wellesbourne House School, Warwick Road, Acocks Green, Warwickshire.
- King Edward VI Grammar School, Camp Hill, Vicarage Road, King's Heath, Birmingham, Warwickshire, having gained a Foundation Scholarship, January 1899–5th March 1902. Known as 'Bogey' by his classmates, he was a useful forward in the rugby team and was also a swimmer and diver.
- Birmingham University for two years in the period 1905–10. He is understood to have studied veterinary science but did not gain a qualification. He served in the OTC.

James was employed as a clerk at the Birmingham and Midland Institute for a year before attending Birmingham University. What happened in the years 1905–10 is unclear. He may have then practiced as a horse doctor at Sawbridgeworth, near Bishop's Stortford, Hertfordshire. After his father's death in 1910, James inherited some of the estate and purchased Bromleys Farm, Latton, Harlow in 1911, where he practised as a vet. In the 1911 Census there he appears as Jasper Neville Marshall, aged thirty-two (he was twenty-four) and claims to have been born at Las Palmas, Grand Canary. He became well known in local agricultural circles, established

The Birmingham and Midland Institute, known as the Midland Institute, promotes education and learning in Birmingham. It was founded in 1854 to pioneer adult scientific and technical education and is a registered charity. The foundation stone of the original building, seen here, next to the Town Hall in Paradise Street, was laid by Prince Albert in November 1855. These premises were demolished in 1965, when the city centre was redeveloped, and the Institute moved to Margaret Street. Past Presidents include – author Charles Dickens 1869, biologist Thomas Huxley 1871, author Charles Kingsley 1872, ornithologist Sir Peter Scott 1977, violinist Yehudi Menuhin 1980 and broadcaster Wynford Vaughan-Thomas 1981.

St Mary the Virgin or St Mary-at-Latton Church, Latton, Harlow is Grade I listed. The Norman church was built in 1087. There is a Norman window in the south wall and the arch of the disused Norman south door is still visible. The West tower had been built by 1234 and the north chapel was completed in 1466. In 1562 the porch was added and in the late 16th century the tower and the west end of the nave were rebuilt. Many changes were made during the 19th century, including restorations and repairs. The church was damaged by a V1 in 1945, which destroyed the stained-glass windows on the south side. In 1964 a fire resulted in the church being completely restored the following year. A vestry was built in 1971 and the tower was restored in 1977. The church contains many monuments to families who owned the nearby Mark Hall Estate.

himself as a point-to-point steeplechaser and took the Boy Scouts camping. He was in the newspapers for crashing his car into a ditch. In 1913 he was convicted for threatening a farmer. The Royal College of Veterinary Surgeons brought an action against him, which he successfully defended because he never claimed to be a veterinary surgeon, describing himself as a 'quack'. When he applied for a commission, he was running a stud farm.

James Marshall married Edith Maud Taylor (born 26th February 1885), born at Ware, Hertfordshire, on 20th September 1911 at St Mary at Latton Church, Harlow, Essex. He recorded a number of falsehoods on the marriage certificate – name James Neville Wellesley Marshall, aged thirty-two although twenty-four, father James Henry Wellesley Arthur Marshall, a soldier instead of a haberdasher, was not recorded as deceased. Edith shared a passion for horses with James and they hunted with the Essex Hounds.

Edith's father, Henry Algernon Taylor (4th May 1855–4th October 1935), a maltster, married Georgiana née Cass (1856–6th July 1939), both born at Ware, Hertfordshire, in 1879 at Kensington, London. They were living at The Grange,

Stanstead Abbotts or Abbots lies three kilometres south-southeast of Ware and six kilometres southeast of Hertford. The village name was recorded as Stanstede at the time of the Domesday Book. In the 12th century the manor passed to the abbot of Waltham Holy Cross and, by the 14th century, the suffix Abbatis, Abbotts or Abbot was part of the parish's name. The abbey continued possession of the manor until the dissolution in 1531. The manor of Stanstead Abbotts was granted to Anne Boleyn. In 1559 Elizabeth I granted it to Edward Baeshe and it remained in the family for several generations. The main entrance to All Nations Christian College was used as the entrance to the school in the *St Trinians* films.

Great Amwell, Hertfordshire in 1880, at Widbury Hill House, Ware in 1891, at Bonningtons, Stanstead Abbots, Hertfordshire in 1901, at Northbrooks, Harlow, Essex in 1911 and later at The Retreat, Hockerill Park, Bishops Stortford, Hertfordshire, where they both subsequently died. When Henry died, he left effects valued at £88,613/14/10 (£7.5M in 2023). In addition to Edith they had other six children:

- Algernon Edward Taylor (7th May 1880–11th February 1918), born at The Grange, Amwell, Ware, was also known as Edward Algernon Taylor. He was a maltster in 1901, living with his parents, and later emigrated to Broken Hill, New South Wales, Australia, where he was a ranch owner raising cattle. He enlisted in 16th Battalion, County of London Regiment (Queen's Westminster Rifles) (5427 & 552416) at 58 Buckingham Gate, London on 22nd January 1916, giving his address as The Retreat, Bishop's Stortford. He was 5′ 9¼″ tall. He applied for a commission on 7th May while serving with 3/16th Battalion at Hazeley Down Camp, Winchester. He transferred to 1/16th Battalion and embarked at Southampton on 5th July, disembarking at Le Havre next day and joined 8th Infantry Base Depot. In his will dated 19th July he left everything to his brother, John Henry Taylor, of Wetheron, Queensland, Australia. Algernon joined the Battalion in the field on 22nd July but returned to Britain for officer training on 15th August, on the strength of the Depot. He joined No.10 Officer Cadet Battalion, Gailes, Scotland on 18th September. Algernon was commissioned in 1st Hertfordshire on 19th December 1916. He went to France on 3rd February 1917. On 11th February 1918 he was on patrol with 266242 Lance Corporal William George Overton in the Gouzeaucourt sector, near Cambrai. Both were shot and killed by a sniper and they are buried in Fins New British Cemetery, Sorel-le-Grand, France (IV B 6 & 7).
- Winifred Taylor (11th October 1882–25th December 1967), born at Ware, married Osmond Robert McMullen (29th August 1865–13th January 1946) on 7th October 1903 at Hertford, where he was born. He was commissioned in 1st (Hertfordshire) Volunteer Battalion, Bedfordshire Regiment on 6th May 1893 and was promoted lieutenant on 6th November 1895 and captain on 25th July 1900. He served in 4th East Anglian Brigade RFA TF from 1st April 1908. Promoted major on 19th May 1908 in 1st Hertfordshire Battery, 4th East Anglian Brigade, RFA. He resigned on 7th July 1911. Awarded the Territorial Decoration, LG 30th August 1912. On 5th August 1914 he was recalled as

Algernon Edward Taylor's grave, on the left, in Fins New British Cemetery alongside William George Overton.

a major with 1st Hertfordshire Battery, 2/4th East Anglian Brigade RFA. Appointed temporary lieutenant colonel on 26th June 1915 and transferred to the Territorial Force Reserve as a major on 4th March 1916. He was appointed CO 1st Fifeshire RGA, B Brigade Heavy Artillery RGA and appointed lieutenant colonel on 10th May 1916. Transferred to E Brigade Heavy Artillery on 7th August and 351st Brigade RGA on 30th November. MID, LG 24th February 1917. Awarded the CMG, LG 1st January 1918. Transferred to 4th East Anglian Brigade as acting lieutenant colonel on 14th February 1918 and also served with No.2 Reserve Brigade. He relinquished his commission due to ill-health on 1st January 1919 and retained the rank of lieutenant colonel. Osmond joined McMullen & Sons Brewery Ltd, Hertford in 1884 and was appointed Managing Director in 1897 and Chairman in 1914. They were living at Rush Green Lodge, Hertford in 1911 before moving to Presdales Hall, Ware, where they were in 1939. He was appointed DL for Hertfordshire, LG 24th July 1936. Osmond died at the County Hospital, Hertford, leaving effects valued at £284,048/1/4 (£14.6M in 2023). Winfred died at Evelyn Nursing Home, Cambridge. They had four children:

McMullen's brewery was founded in Back Street (now Railway Street), Hertford in 1827 by Peter McMullen (1798–1881). It expanded during the second half of the 19th century by purchasing other breweries. The brewery occupied several different sites in Hertford before moving to its current location in 1891, which is now Grade II listed. There were eight breweries in Hertford in 1838 but by 1966 McMullen's was the sole survivor. In 1897, when the brewery became a limited company, it owned ninety pubs. By 1902 this had increased to 131 pubs and by 1966 to 200. A modern brewhouse was built in 1984.

- Osmond James George McMullen (2nd March 1906–3rd December 1994) served as a captain in 135th Field Regiment RA (Hertfordshire Yeomanry) and was taken prisoner in Burma in the Second World War. He was a director of McMullens until his death.
- Elizabeth Josephine McMullen (1908–79).
- Robert Peter McMullen (18th February 1914–15th October 1983) was commissioned in the Bedfordshire and Hertfordshire Regiment (TA) and was promoted lieutenant on 5th November 1935. He was awarded the MBE (LG 9th June 1938) and was promoted captain on 9th November 1938 (53905). Awarded the DSO, LG 31st August 1944. He was attached to No.1 Special Force, HQ Special Operations (Mediterranean), Central Mediterranean Force and was parachuted into northern Italy near Genoa on 18th January 1945 to work with partisans until the liberation. Awarded the US Bronze Star Medal, LG 20th March 1947, a Bar to the DSO, and

the TD, LG 21st April 1950. He ran the family brewing business 1946–80 and was appointed Sheriff in the Queen's Bench Division of the High Court of Justice on 12th November 1952. He was appointed DL for the County of Hertfordshire on 28th October 1959. He retired from the Territorial Army Reserve of Officers as an honorary lieutenant colonel, having exceeded the age limit, on 26th February 1964.

    - Rosemary HW McMullen (born 4th June 1917).

Robert Peter McMullen.

- Helen Margaret Taylor (11th August 1886–14th December 1957) was living at 10A Roderick Lane, Harlow, Hertfordshire in 1939. She never married and was living at Broxbourne Nursing Home, Broxbourne, Hertfordshire at the time of her death.
- Ernest George Taylor (22nd October 1887–2nd May 1915) was living at Penbeagle, St Ives, Cornwall when he applied for a commission on 15th August 1914. He was commissioned in 3rd King's Own (Royal Lancaster Regiment) on 10th October 1914. He was killed in action on 2nd May 1915 and on 8th July the Military Secretary's office informed Ernest's father that he had been 'buried about two miles North East of Ypres'. However, after the war his remains could not be identified and he is commemorated on the Ypres (Menin Gate) Memorial, Belgium (Panel 12).
- John Henry Tuke Taylor (1888–21st July 1977) emigrated to Australia to visit his brother Edward. He settled in Queensland, purchasing Wetheron, a property near Gayndah and became a grazier. He married Evelyn Flossie Walker (27th March 1894–8th May 1991), born at Boggabri, Barcaldine, Queensland, on 31st December 1919. He was living at Widbury, Eidsvold in 1920 when his brother Ernest's estate was being sorted out. John purchased an additional block of land named Connaught in 1939 and built a homestead there the following year. He renamed the property Widbury, after the estate where he was raised in England. He formed the Widbury Pastoral Co, which passed to his daughter, Barbara. He also purchased Mooroongie, an adjoining property, in 1969, and ran it in partnership with three

Ernest George Taylor is commemorated on the Ypres (Menin Gate) Memorial, seen here at the beginning of the renovations that commenced in 2023.

of his daughters, Edith, Diana and Barbara. John and Evelyn both subsequently died there. Barbara bought out her sisters after their father's death and managed all the properties. They had five children – Joan Odette Taylor (1921–19th August 1944), Edith Pamela Taylor (7th February 1923–29th December 2015), Donald Dobede Taylor (10th September 1924–27th October 2012), Diana May Taylor (11th March 1926–20th February 2013) and Barbara Evelyn Taylor (15th June 1927–25th June 2019).
- Marion Taylor (28th February 1894–29th January 1989), died at St George's Nursing Home, Royston, Hertfordshire.

James offered his services to Belgium at the outbreak of war and joined 1st Regiment d'Artillerie, 1st Division d'Armie as a first lieutenant on 13th September 1914. The Belgian Army appears to have believed that he was a doctor and he performed this function. He was at Antwerp and was wounded on 28th September and 18th October. On the latter occasion he was severely wounded in the lung and leg and in January 1915 was sent on two months sick leave to England. He never returned to the Belgian Army. Awarded Officer of the Order of Leopold on 6th December 1914 for gallant conduct. The medal was presented by King Albert of Belgium on 11th January 1915 (LG 21st April 1917, downgraded to Chevalier, LG 26th July 1917).

In 1915 James changed his first name to John for no apparent reason. He joined the British Army but spent most of 1915 recovering from his wounds and suffered periodic haemorrhages from the lung wound. Claims that he joined the Army Veterinary Corps at Melton Mowbray in August 1915 and was employed by War Office Remounts Department buying horses from Argentina, have no hard evidence. When James enlisted, he made a number of false statements:

- He had studied to be a vet at Rush College, Chicago for which there is no record.
- He fought with the Cape Mounted Rifles in the Boer War 1900–02 and was wounded twice in the jaw and arm. He would only have been thirteen or fourteen at the time.

The Order of Leopold, the oldest and highest Belgian order, named in honour of its founder, King Leopold I, consists of military, maritime and civil divisions. It was established on 11th July 1832 and equates to the British Order of the Bath. The Order has five classes – Grand Cordon, Grand Officier, Commandeur, Officier and Chevalier (seen here). No membership can be granted to a person under the age of forty-two, except in the military division. The Belgian King chairs the Order as Grand Maître. Amongst the famous foreigners to be awarded the order are French President Raymond Poincaré, explorer Henry Morton Stanley, aviator Charles Lindbergh, General George S Patton, Field Marshal Bernard Montgomery, Sir Winston Churchill, General Dwight Eisenhower and French President Charles de Gaulle.

- He fought in the Spanish Moroccan War 1908 which, although unlikely, is more difficult to disprove since this is during the unknown years of his life.

James was commissioned in the Supplementary Reserve of the Irish Guards on 8th December 1915 and joined the 3rd Battalion. He was promoted lieutenant, backdated to 8th December 1915, and went to France on 13th May 1916 to join an entrenching battalion near Albert. He transferred to 1st Irish Guards near Ypres on 15th June. On 19th June he was shot in the arm by a sniper, while on a working party, but finished the task. He spent ten days in hospital. On 14th July, between Buff Road and Forward Cottage, near Wieltje, north of Ypres, he led a patrol to investigate an enemy sap and was wounded by a shrapnel ball in the side (pelvis) as he left the trench. **Awarded the Belgian Croix de Guerre on 20th July 1916, LG 6th February 1922.**

The next month was spent on light duties but eventually he had to go to hospital on 8th August and was evacuated from Boulogne aboard HMHS *St David* on 8th September, arriving at Dover the same day. He was treated at Mason's Hospital, probably Lady Evelyn Mason's Hospital, 16 Bruton Street, London. A medical board at Caxton Hall, London on 21st September found him unfit for General Service for three months, Home Service for two months and light duties for one month. His leave was extended until 20th October. A medical board at 3rd Southern General Hospital, Oxford on 31st October found him unfit for General and Home Service for two months but fit for light duties and he reported to 3rd (Reserve)

King Albert I (8th April 1875 – 17th February 1934) was King of the Belgians from 23rd December 1909. He married Elisabeth of Bavaria and they had three children. His reign coincided with a period of huge turbulence and change, which included the Great War, during which most of the country was occupied by the Germans. Albert died in a mountaineering accident and was succeeded by his son, King Leopold II, who reigned until 1951.

The Belgium Croix de Guerre was established on 25th October 1915, primarily to recognise individual bravery or other military virtue on the battlefield. It could also be awarded for three years or more service on the front line, for good conduct on the battlefield, to volunteers aged over forty or younger than sixteen after a minimum of eighteen months service, to escaped prisoners of war rejoining the armed forces, and to military personnel placed on inactive duty because of injury. It was re-established on 20th July 1940 by the Belgian government in exile. The post-1940 decoration could also be awarded to units. The decoration was again re-established on 3rd April 1954 but has yet to be awarded.

Battalion, Irish Guards on 6th November. However, a medical board at Caxton Hall on 2nd December found him unfit for General and Home Service for six weeks and light duties for one month. His leave was extended until 2nd January 1917.

Awarded the MC in the New Years Honours for his work in the period June-August 1916, LG 1st January 1917. A medical board at Caxton Hall on 23rd January found him unfit for General Service for three months, Home Service for two months and light duties for one month. His leave was extended until 22nd February. A medical board at Warwick Military Hospital on 23rd March found him fit for General Service and he returned to France on 30th March to join 2nd Irish Guards. It is believed that the Belgian Croix de Guerre was presented by King Albert of Belgium on 15th May 1917.

James was appointed Second-in-Command, 1/6th Lancashire Fusiliers on 25th May. However, he suffered from haematemesis and a duodenal ulcer, the after-effects of an old abdominal gunshot wound, and left the unit on 9th August. A medical board at 2nd Red Cross Hospital, Rouen on 21st August found him unfit for General Service for three weeks. James returned to Britain on 24th August from Le Havre aboard SS *Hautonia*, arriving at Southampton next day. Sick leave was granted until 14th September. A medical board at Colchester on 19th September found him fit for General Service and he returned to France about 25th September. On 12th October James was appointed acting major and he received a stab wound to the face on 20th October but remained at duty. He gave up being Second-in-Command when 1/6th and 2/6th Battalions amalgamated on 12th February 1918. He was wounded on 14th February but remained at duty. **Mentioned in Field Marshal Sir Douglas Haig's Despatch of 7th April 1918, LG 23rd May 1918.**

James worked in HQ 125th Brigade until 7th May, when he rejoined 2nd Irish Guards. He had been wounded on 6th May but remained at duty. On 1st June he joined 2nd Manchester as Second-in-Command and was appointed acting major on 17th June. **Awarded a Bar to the MC for his actions on 10th August in an attack on Parvillers and Damery Woods. He was ordered to take a company and two platoons to fill a gap and capture a position held by the enemy, which he succeeded in doing. He advanced further than the unit on his left, formed a defensive line and beat off an attack during which he was wounded, LG 7th November 1918.** He had returned to duty by 19th August.

On 12th October James was promoted lieutenant colonel and assumed command of 16th Lancashire Fusiliers. **Awarded the VC for his actions at the Sambre-Oise Canal, near Catillon, France on 4th November 1918, LG 13th February 1919.** James was killed during the VC action on 4th November 1918 and is buried in Ors Communal Cemetery, France (in line with A22). The posthumous VC was presented to his widow by the King in the ballroom at Buckingham Palace on 12th April 1919. At the time of his death James was wearing ten wound stripes, although there is only evidence to support six. Although during his life he invented and inflated facts, he was a fine soldier who was well respected and held in the highest regard by all who came into contact with him. James is commemorated in a number of other places:

- Old Harlow, Essex
    - War Memorial, St Mary's Church, Churchgate Street and also on the roll of honour inside the church.
    - Named on the War Memorial, Old Harlow Baptist Church, Fore Street.
    - Potter Street, Latton and Surrounding District Memorial Cross.
- Named on the war memorial at King Edward VI's Camp Hill School, Vicarage Road, King's Heath, Birmingham.
- Named on the Great War Memorial, Aston Webb Great Hall, University of Birmingham.
- Named on The Household Division (Foot Guards) VC Honour Roll in the Sergeants' Mess, Guards Depot, Wellington Barracks, London.
- Named on The Ring of Remembrance (L'Anneau de la Mémoire or Ring of Memory) at Ablain-Saint-Nazaire, France, inaugurated on 11th November 2014. The Ring commemorates the 576,606 soldiers of forty nationalities who died in Nord-Pas-de-Calais in the Great War.
- Department for Communities and Local Government commemorative paving stones were dedicated at the Walk of Heroes, Hall of Memory, Centenary Square,

James Marshall's grave in Ors Communal Cemetery. It is on its own in a corner but is in line with the row that includes the graves of James Kirk VC and Wilfred Owen MC.

Old Harlow War Memorial, outside St Mary's Church. James Marshall's name and details are rather worn but are still readable.

King Edward VI's Camp Hill School war memorial.

Birmingham on 7th December 2015, by the Duke of Cambridge, and at Trafford Town Hall, Sunken Gardens, Talbot Road, Stretford, London on 4th November 2018.

- Blue Plaque dedicated at Stretford Public Hall on 4th November 2018.

Edith lived at Lascelles Lodge, Matching Green, near Harlow, Essex after her husband's death, which had been purchased by her father in 1922 and bequeathed to Edith. About 1928 she went to live in Kenya with one of her sisters and bred polo ponies. She returned to England and was living with her sister, Winifred and brother-in-law Osmond McMullen, at Presdales, Ware in 1939.

In addition to the VC and MC and Bar he was awarded the British War Medal 1914–20, Victory Medal 1914–19 with Mentioned-in-Despatches Oakleaf, Belgian Chevalier of the Order of Leopold and the Belgian Croix de Guerre 1914–18. The medals were presented to the Irish Guards by his sister, Dorothy Stevens, on 17th December 1970, with his brother, Klein Marshall, in attendance. The VC is held by the Guards Regimental Headquarters, Wellington Barracks, Birdcage Walk, London.

Lascelles is a 14th century hall house with two jettied crosswings.

17324 PRIVATE FRANCIS GEORGE MILES
1/5th Battalion, The Gloucestershire Regiment

Francis Miles was born on 9th July 1896 at Clearwell, near Coleford, Gloucestershire. His father, Christopher George Miles (1870–1917), born at Broad Town, near Wooton Bassett (now Royal Wooton Bassett), Wiltshire, was an orphan in 1881 at the New Orphan Houses, Ashley Down, Bristol, Gloucestershire. By 1891 he was a general labourer, living with his uncle, John Miles, and aunt, Elizabeth Miles at Tannery, Newland, Clearwell. He married Annie Jane née Perkins (8th November 1874–1942) on 30th September 1895, registered, as was her birth, at Monmouth. By 1901 Christopher was a farm carter, living at Victoria Street, East Dean, Gloucestershire in the employ of Alfred E Dykins, auctioneer and income tax collector, and was still there in 1911, by when he was a servant. The marriage is believed to have broken up shortly after the birth of Francis. Christopher's death was registered at Westbury-on-Severn, Gloucestershire. At the time of the 1901 Census Annie was described as a married general servant at the Swan Hotel, Lydney, Gloucestershire.

Clearwell, originally Clower-Wall, is a village in the Forest of Dean area of Gloucestershire. The mining of ochre there dates back to 5,000 BC. The Romans mined iron ore and iron production expanded in medieval times to a peak in the 16th and 17th centuries. The former Old Ham ore mine was developed as Clearwell Caves, a mining museum, and has been used as a film location, including for the television series *Merlin* and *Dr Who*. Most buildings in the village were replaced by stone cottages from the late 18th century onwards, although several older buildings survive, including the Wyndham Arms. The prominent cross in the centre of the village was erected in the 14th century. The first manor house was probably built by Robert Greyndour, who died in 1443. Various families inherited it thereafter. Thomas Wyndham demolished the old house and in 1728 replaced it with the present neo-Gothic mock-castle, known as Clearwell Castle from 1908. The interior was refurbished by Caroline, Countess of Dunraven, who held Clearwell from 1814 to her death in 1870. During Colonel Charles Vereker's ownership there was a major fire in 1929 but the house was restored. After his death in 1947, the property was purchased by Gloucestershire County Council and it was sold to a demolition contractor who removed the lead roof, floors and fittings. However, in 1952 it was bought by Frank Yeates, who restored it. In the 1970s it was used as a recording studio by a number of major rock bands, including *Led Zeppelin*, *Deep Purple*, *Black Sabbath* and *Queen*. The Castle was sold in the early 1980s and became a hotel. In 1830 a chapel was built in the village but was replaced in 1866 by a church by the Countess of Dunraven. She also built the village school in 1859 and a cottage hospital in 1869.

Coleford, a market town close to the Welsh border, is the administrative centre of the Forest of Dean. The settlement originated at a ford used to transport charcoal and iron ore. In 1642 the Parliamentary garrison during the English Civil War established a market, because the nearest chartered market was in Monmouth under Royalist control. On 20th February 1643, a Royalist force under Lord Herbert marched through Coleford heading for Gloucester. They were resisted by a troop of Parliamentarians and a disorderly group of country people. In the skirmish the market house was burned down and Major General Lawday and two other officers were killed. The Royalists forced their way through, and the Parliamentarians fled. After the Restoration a market was granted in 1661 and a new market house was built in 1679. In the late 18th and early 19th centuries, the town expanded and most of the older houses were rebuilt. There was a place of worship in the town by 1489. The church was rebuilt in 1820 but it was too small for the growing congregation and was demolished in 1882. A larger church, St John the Evangelist's, was built overlooking the town. Iron production in Coleford dates back to the Middle Ages and coalmining from the 16th century. Limestone was quarried and lime kilns in the area supplied much of Monmouthshire. In 1812 a tramway opened to link mines in the Forest of Dean with the River Wye. The track was lifted in the late 1870s. The first railway, opened by the Severn & Wye Railway Co, reached Coleford in 1875. A second railway opened in 1883, the Coleford Railway from Monmouth, using parts of the old tramway. The Severn and Wye line ceased passenger services in 1929 and closed in 1967.
Mary Howitt née Botham, author of the famous poem *The Spider and the Fly*, was born at Coleford. She married William Howitt in 1821 and wrote many works with him.

Annie married Fred Clack (5th November 1884–12th May 1940), a farm labourer born at Painswick, Gloucestershire, on 26th April 1905 at Monmouth Register Office. She was recorded under her maiden name. They were living at High Nash, Coleford, Gloucestershire in 1911. Fred was a collier when he enlisted in the Gloucestershire Regiment on 28th December 1914 and joined the Depot at Horfield Barracks, Bristol (9/17328) on 30th December. He was 5′ 3¾″ tall and joined 9th Battalion on 1st January 1915. Fred went to France on 20th September and joined the Mediterranean Expeditionary Force on 11th November. He was

Newerne Street, Lydney. Lydney is on the west bank of the River Severn in the Forest of Dean, southwest of Gloucester. In the Iron Age a fort was established at what is now Lydney Park, which was later used for iron ore mining. The Romans built a temple on the site of the fort. The town is mentioned in the 1086 Domesday Book. In 1588 Sir William Winter, Vice Admiral of England, was granted the manor of Lydney in recognition of his services against the Spanish Armada. Charles Bathurst, 1st Viscount Bledisloe GCMG KBE PC (1867–1958) was born in London, second son of Charles Bathurst, of Lydney Park. He was educated at Sherborne, Eton and University College, Oxford. He was admitted to the Inner Temple in 1892 and was later called to the bar. Having been a Conservative politician, he was Governor General of New Zealand 1930–35. At the end of that appointment he was created Viscount Bledisloe of Lydney and inherited Lydney Park on the death of his elder brother.

The New Orphan Houses, Ashley Down, also known as Muller Homes, were built by the Prussian evangelist George Müller (1805–98). He and his wife opened their own home at 6 Wilson Street, Bristol for thirty girls in 1836. Müller held a public meeting at which he announced that he would not appeal for funds but would pray for support. By June 1837, £1,000 had been received and a new home was opened. A second and a third house, the latter for boys, followed. A fourth house opened in 1843. However, in 1845 neighbours complained about the inconvenience caused by so many children. Müller prayed for funds to build a new orphanage for 300 children. By late January 1847 he had the £10,000 required. Seven acres were purchased at Ashley Down and the cornerstone of The New Orphan House was laid on 19th August 1847. In June 1849, 118 orphans transferred to the new building. A month later 170 new children were admitted. There were eventually five houses, accommodating up to 2,050 children. About 17,000 children passed through them before they were sold in 1958. The five houses were built between 1849 and 1870:

No.1 House opened in 1849 for 300 children.
No.2 House opened in 1857 for 400 children.
Nos.3, 4 and 5 Houses opened in 1862, 1868 and 1870 respectively, each for 450 children.

The author, Charles Dickens, arrived unannounced and, on returning to London, wrote a positive report on the orphan houses in his publication 'Household Words'. Dr Barnardo also visited. From 1901 destitute children, born in wedlock, who had lost one parent were admitted. A swimming pool was added in 1910 and a laundry. A nursery was opened but the number of orphans declined as social conditions improved. By 1921 it was difficult to obtain jobs for boys and some were sent to farms in Canada. By late 1938, No.2 House was empty and was loaned to the City of Bristol. No.4 House was requisitioned by the Royal Navy as HMS *Bristol*. In 1940 the Government requisitioned No.5 House as billets, which were later used by American troops. On 2nd December, a German aircraft dropped bombs over Ashley Down but the only casualties were 400 windows. By 1946 the area around Ashley Down had been built over. An estate of 400 acres was acquired at Backwell Hill to convert an existing house and build new orphan houses. However, rising costs made the development unfeasible and instead it was decided to purchase houses to hold fifteen children each within a thirty kilometres radius. In 1951 responsibility for education passed to Bristol Education Committee. By then only No.3 House was in full use and No.5 partly. In 1957 the orphanage disposed of Backwell and the children were dispersed to the Scattered Homes, as they were known. In spring 1958 the final residents of No.3 House left Ashley Down, ending 109 years of childcare on the site. Nos.4 and 5 Houses are owned by the City of Bristol College. Nos.1 and 3 Houses have been converted into private flats. No.2 House was sold for redevelopment in 2016. Some of the Houses have been Grade II listed.

appointed unpaid lance corporal on 22nd January 1917. Having contracted malaria, he was aboard ship from 19th March until 20th April 1918, joined the Depot next day and 3rd Battalion on 25th May. He transferred to the Class Z Army Reserve on 11th July 1918 and was discharged on 23rd January 1919.

Annie and Fred were living at Lower Clearwell, Gloucestershire in 1939. On the evening of 11th May 1940 Fred was with a group of friends near his home after a night out at the Lamb Inn, Clearwell. There was a total blackout. He suddenly stepped into the road in the path of a car and was knocked into the gutter. The car was driven by Private Samuel Fender, who had been drinking with his colleagues at the Crown Hotel, St Briavels. Fred was rushed to Monmouth Hospital, where he died the following day, as a result of compound fractures of the left tibia and fibula

The Lamb Inn at Clearwell, outside which Fred Clack was knocked down and fatally injured. The inn is a former iron miners' pub and is over 200 years old.

Painswick, in the Stroud District of Gloucestershire, originated through the wool trade. Nearby is an Iron Age hill fort on Painswick Beacon and an 11th century monastery, Prinknash Abbey. Painswick first appears in historical records in the 1086 Domesday Book. On 5th September 1643, during the English Civil War, the Royalist army camped overnight at Painswick and the King stayed at Court House. Thomas Twining (1675–1741), founder of the tea company, Twining's of London, was born at Painswick.

and the vault of the skull. An inquest at the Shire Hall, Monmouth on 15th May concluded that the death was the result of an accident with no blame attached to anyone.

Francis had at least seven siblings:

- John Miles (18th January 1902–1982) born at Clearwell, near Coleford, married Lizzie Witts (7th October 1902–1978) in 1923 at Monmouth, where her birth was registered. He was a colliery hewer in 1939, when they were living at Broadwell, Coleford. They a daughter:
    - Muriel Miles (10th January 1928–8th February 2001) married Raymond Philip Nash (8th September 1925–February 1998) on 11th November 1946. They had three children – Michael J Nash 1947, Anthony P Nash 1951 and Robert Nash 1956.
- Hannah Mary Clack (10th September 1905–1993) married Stanley John Parry (24th December 1905–1984), born at Palmers Flat, West Dean, Gloucestershire, on 26th December 1931 at St Peter's Parish Church, Church Road, Clearwell. He was a builder's labourer in 1939, when they were living at Broadwell, Coleford. They had three children:
    - Myrtle J Parry (born 1934) married Ralph Ashley Powell (16th September 1930–27th January 2003), born at Westbury-on-Severn, Gloucestershire, in 1955. He was living with his parents at 10 Victoria Street, Cinderford, Gloucestershire in 1939.

  - Beryl J Parry (born 1937) married Mervyn V Watkins (born 1935) in 1956. He was living with his parents at Berry Hill Road, West Dean in 1939. Beryl and Mervyn had at least four children – Brian J Watkins 1956, Gillian Watkins 1959, Alan Watkins 1960 and Colin V Watkins 1961.
  - Kathleen Mary Parry (born 20th July 1939) married Colin Manfield (born 1937), born at Gloucester, on 3rd June 1971. He was living with his parents at Honeysuckle Cottage, Scowles, Coleford in 1939. They had two daughters – Tracy Anne Manfield 1971 and Nicola Jane Manfield 1974.
- Nellie Elizabeth Clack (1st November 1906–1974), born at Crumlin, Monmouthshire, married Harold Frank Jones (25th September 1901–1970) in 1933 at Monmouth. He was a farm labourer in 1939, when they were living at 9 Lower Clearwell, West Dean.
- Alfred Martin Clack (8th November 1907–13th August 1975), a collier, married Gladys Emma Worgan (22nd October 1909–13th December 2004) on 9th September 1933 at St Mary the Virgin, St Briavels, Gloucestershire. He was a general labourer with Gloucestershire County Council in 1939, when they were living at East View, St Briavels. They had moved to Pleasant View, St Briavels by 1953 and to 23 Smithville Close, St Briavels at the time of their deaths there. They had two children:
  - Terence Alfred Clack (20th March 1935–1965), birth registered at Chepstow, Monmouthshire, married Pamela D Mould (born 1943) in 1962. They had a daughter – Elaine J Clack in 1965.
  - Patrick M Clack (born 1946) married Pamela J Nicholson (born 1948), born at Chepstow, in 1970 at Caerleon, Monmouthshire. They had two children – Christopher Terence Clack 1973 and Karen Julia Clack 1976.
- Florence Annie Clack (6th August 1911–19th October 1984) was incapacitated in 1939, living with her parents at Lower Clearwell, Clearwell. She never married and died there.
- Beatrice Olive Clack (26th October 1913–26th May 1995), born at Coleford, married Frank Ernest Amos (22nd June 1912–3rd February 1990), birth registered at Weobley, Herefordshire, in 1937 at Wantage. He was a gardener, groom, handyman and a volunteer with the British Red Cross Society, Berkshire Branch in 1939, when they were living at Cairnsmore, Hermitage, Berkshire. They were living at 66 Goldwire Lane, Monmouth, Gwent at the time of his death there. She was living at Marsden House, Whitchurch, Ross-on-Wye, Herefordshire at the time of her death there. They had two children:
  - Brian F Amos (born 1944) married Elizabeth Prynne (born 1949) in 1973, registered at East Glamorgan. They had at least one daughter – Katherine Elizabeth Amos in 1979.
  - Alison C Amos (born 1956), born at Caerleon, married Adrian L Walby (born 1955), born at Hereford, in 1977 at Ross-on-Wye, Herefordshire. They had at least one son – Thomas Adrian Walby in 1981.

The village of Clyffe Pypard, five kilometres south of Royal Wootton Bassett, was known as White Cleeve (Clive in the Domesday Book). The ancient parish had five tithings – Clyffe Pypard, Broad Town, Bushton, Thornhill and Woodhill, the latter including Bupton. In 1884, Broad Town and Thornhill transferred to the newly created Broad Town civil parish. A Free School was established at Thornhill in 1782 and continued until 1875. A National School, built in 1850, became a voluntary controlled school in 1954 and closed in 1978. Woodhill Park, a Georgian country house, was built in the 18th century, with additions in 1804. Nearby is the site of the medieval village, including a moated manor house. There has been a church at Clyffe Pypard since the 13th century. The present nave and west tower of the Church of St Peter were constructed in the 15th century. The chancel and aisles were rebuilt in 1860. The church is Grade I listed. RAF Clyffe Pypard, under Flying Training Command, opened in 1941 with grass runways. It closed in 1947 but continued to be used by RAF Lyneham for accommodation and by the Army for exercises until 1961. Most of the airfield has returned to farmland but a small number of buildings remain.

St Mary Redcliffe, a Grade I listed building, is renowned for its Gothic architecture. Queen Elizabeth I described it as 'the fairest, goodliest, and most famous parish church in England'. Today St Mary Redcliffe is one of the largest parish churches in England and some sources believe that it is the largest. The first church was Saxon. In medieval times, sitting on a red cliff above the Avon, it was a sign to seafarers, who prayed there before departure and gave thanks upon their return. Little remains of the early churches and much of the current building dates from the late 13th and 14th centuries. The upper part of the spire, which was destroyed by lightning in 1446, was not rebuilt until 1872. Until 2020 the spire was the tallest structure in the city. Most of the original stained glass was damaged during the English Civil War and most of the new glass was added by the Victorians. During the Second World War a bomb exploded in a nearby street, throwing a tramway rail over the houses. It embedded itself in the churchyard and was left there as a monument to how narrowly the church escaped destruction. The church contains many monuments to individuals from the city, including Sir William Penn, the father of William Penn, founder of Pennsylvania. There is also the rib of a whale brought back from one of his voyages by John Cabot. The stained-glass window commemorating the 17th century Royal African Co magnate Edward Colston was removed in June 2020, following the toppling of his statue by anti-slavery protesters. *Sealing the Tomb*, an altarpiece by William Hogarth, was commissioned in 1756 to fill the east end of the chancel. The altarpiece was removed in the mid-Victorian era and was later displayed at Bristol City Museum and Art Gallery. It is now in the church of St Nicholas, Bristol.

- Frederick Walter Clack (1st April 1916–1968) was a steel worker's labourer in 1939, living with his parents. He was an engineer in 1962.

Francis' paternal grandfather, Edmund Miles (born c.1833), born at Cliffe Pypard, Wiltshire, was a carpenter in 1851 living with his parents at Broadtown Road, Cliffe Pypard. He was a carpenter and miller in 1861, lodging with John and Elizabeth Miles (probably his brother and sister-in-law) at Snowhill, Broad Hinton, Wiltshire. Edmund married Ellen née Chesterman (born 1838), born at Broad Town, Cliffe Pypard, on 31st August 1863 at St Mary Redcliffe Church, Bristol, Gloucestershire. They were both living at 10 Rowley Place, Bristol at the time. They were living at Cliffe Pypard, next door to his parents, in 1871. Neither Edmund nor Ellen have been found in any census after 1871. In addition to Christopher they had four other children:

- Mary Amelia Miles (c.1865–February 1870) was baptised on 19th March 1865 at Broad Town, Wiltshire.
- Clara Ellen Miles (possibly 10th November 1866–1956), birth registered at Cricklade, Wiltshire, was baptised at Broad Town on 30th December 1866. She married Hubert Kear (6th January 1874–21st January 1962), a collier born at West Dean, on 21st October 1916 at St James' Parish Church, Bream, Gloucestershire. They were both living at Clements End Green, Coleford, Gloucestershire. She died at Clements End. He was living at Rose Cottage, Clements End Green at the time of his death at Rosslyn, Sling, near Coleford. Hubert had married Emily Haynes (1879–March 1913) in 1904, registered at Monmouth, as was her birth. They were living at Clements End Green in 1911. She died at Clements Tump. There were no children.
- Edwin Robert Miles (born 1868), born at Wootton Bassett, Wiltshire, was baptised at Broad Town on 15th November 1868. He was being cared for, with his brother Christopher, at The New Orphan Houses, Bristol, Gloucestershire in 1881. He was a general labourer in 1891, living with his uncle, John Miles, and aunt, Elizabeth Miles, at Tannery, Newland, Clearwell. Edwin married Ann 'Annie' Mountjoy née Hill (1844–1925), born at West Dean, in 1904 registered at Westbury-on-Severn, Gloucestershire. Ann was a laundress and Edwin was a newsvendor in 1911, when they were living at Lamb Lane, Cinderford, Gloucestershire. Ann had married Thomas Mountjoy (1844–1902), born at West Dean, on 1st August 1868 St James' Parish Church, Bream. She was a servant, living at Clements Tump and he was a coalminer, living at Clearwell at the time. They were living at Clearwell in 1901. They had at least two sons:
    - Harry Landers Mountjoy (1882–1954), a miner living with his parents in 1901, married Florence Watts in 1911. They had five children – Cyril R Mountjoy 1912, Eunice IA Mountjoy 1913, twins Dorrien H and Gilbert D Mountjoy 1915 and Grenville T Mountjoy 1919.

    - Arthur Mountjoy (born 1883) was a miner living with his parents in 1901.
- Edith Emily Miles (possibly 1st May 1871–1944), born at Broad Town, Wiltshire, was baptised there on 30th July 1871. She was being cared for by her uncle, John Miles, a retired carpenter, and aunt, Elizabeth living at Clearwell Road, Newland, Gloucestershire in 1881. She was still living with her uncle and aunt in 1891, by when they had moved to Tannery, Newland, Clearwell. Edith married William Addis (18th August 1872–June 1949), an iron ore miner born at Clearwell, in 1894, registered at Monmouth. They were living at Clearwell in 1911 and at High Street, West Dean in 1939. He was living on Buckshaft Road, Ruspidge, Cinderford at the time of his death. They had eight children:
    - Amelia Elizabeth Addis (21st July 1894–2000) married Barnabus Harris in 1920. They had two sons – Donald WG Harris 1921 and Horace R Harris 1929.
    - Florence Annie Addis (born and died 1896).
    - Edith Annie Addis (24th April 1898–1986) married Ernest Gane (1882–1938) in 1916. They had a son, Ernest W Gane in 1917. Edith married George Holt in 1940.
    - Hilda Addis (4 June 1900–2000) married William H Driver in 1922 and they had two children – Cicely D Driver 1922 and June M Driver 1929.
    - Ethel Blanch Addis (1902–47).
    - William John Henry Addis (13th February 1905–1982) married Eileen D Powell in 1935. They had three children – Trixie D Addis 1935, Barrie WJ Addis 1940 and Michael WJ Addis 1944.
    - Dorothy May Addis (30th April 1908–1976) married Ernest M Hewlett (1902–61) in 1927. They had two children – Ruby M Hewlett 1927 and Colin E Hewlett 1944.
    - Enid Addis (1912–2006) married Arthur G King (1899–1966) in 1937.

The Grade 1 listed St Peter's Church opened in 1866. The building was commissioned by the Dowager Countess of Dunraven of Clearwell Castle in 1855 and was built in French Gothic style with coloured stonework, stained glass and stencilled roof. It replaced a church built in 1828 on the site of the Cemetery Chapel in Clearwell.

His maternal grandfather, Francis Perkins (born 1851), born at Newland, Gloucestershire, married Mary Ann née Williams (born 1852), born at Chepstow, Monmouthshire, on 3rd June 1872 at St Peter's Church, Clearwell, Gloucestershire. She was living with her parents at the Travellers Rest public house, Newland in 1871. Francis was a farm labourer in 1881, when they were living at Clearwell. By 1901 he was a stone quarry worker still living at Clearwell. In addition to Annie they had three other children:

- John Perkins (1872–1905) was a farm labourer in 1901.
- Sarah Perkins (15th January 1877–30th September 1962) was a charwoman in 1939, living with her sister, Annie Clack, and family at Lower Clearwell. Sarah never married and subsequently died there.
- Beatrice 'Beaty' Mary Perkins (25th September 1892–November 1980) was a general servant living with her sister, Annie and husband Fred Clack, in 1911. She married Tom Yearsley (25th April 1890–1949), born at Bream, in 1915. He was a collier filler in a pit in 1911, living with his parents at Clements End in 1911. He was a colliery roadman underground in 1939, when they were living at Clements End, near Coleford. She died at Dilke Memorial Hospital, Cinderford. They had five children:
    - Tom Yearsley (23rd August 1920–August 1995) married Beatrice S Sutton née Aston (born 1921) in 1953. She had married Maurice E Sutton in 1943, registered at Alton, Hampshire. They had a son, Maurice K Sutton, in 1944.
    - Annie Yearsley (born and died 1922).
    - George Yearsley (25th August 1923–December 1998).
    - Bessie Yearsley (1926–27).
    - Royston John Yearsley (9th September 1930–1947).

Francis married May Elizabeth/Elizabeth May Elwick (1st May 1891–21st February 1974) in 1932. She was born at South Bourne, Surrey and was working as a domestic servant for the family of Major (Ret'd) Arthur Bostock AVC at 18 Ramillies Road, Acton Green, Middlesex in 1911. Francis and May lived at Cemetery House, Clearwell, Coleford. She died at Cinderford. They had one child:

- Christopher Victor Colin Miles (22nd September 1932–6th January 2005) lived at Cemetery House, Clearwell.

May Elizabeth Elwick had married Thomas Taylor in 1911 at Brentford, Middlesex. They had eight children:

- Frances B Taylor (born 19th November 1914) married Donald J Russell (22nd May 1913–1955), born at Hackney, London, in 1934. He was a labourer in a mine in 1939, when they were living at Glendale, Lower Milkwall, West Dean, Gloucestershire. They had two sons – William H Russell 1934 and Terence F Russell 1940. Frances married George Bartlett in 1956 and Sydney Desmond Hale (born 1st September 1921) on 20th August 1980. Sydney was a coalminer, rope rider, in 1939, living with his parents at Broadwell, Coleford. Sydney had married Eileen M Jennings in 1946 and they were living at 5 Baynham's Walk, Broadwell in 1953 and at 10 Machen Road, Broadwell in 1961. Sydney and Eileen had three children – Alan Desmond Hale 1949, Vivien J Hale 1950 and Stephen J Hale 1953.

- Thomas George H Taylor (21st September 1917–1976), born at Clearwell, married Ivy Nora Allford (26th December 1921–1994) in 1949. She was living with her parents at Stank Cottage, Clearwell in 1939.
- Harold Arthur Taylor (6th January 1920–May 1993) was a labourer in a colour works in 1939, living with his mother. His death was registered at Camden, London.
- Sydney James Taylor (1921–21st January 2008) married Ruby May Arkwell (born 16th April 1919) in 1948. Her birth was registered at Bedwellty, Monmouthshire. She was a domestic worker, living with her parents at Barn House, Broadwell in 1939. Sydney and Ruby lived at Coalway, Coleford. They had a daughter – Rachel M Taylor in 1949.
- Phyllis Dorothy Taylor (20th May 1923–1997) married Dennis Ralph T Martin (28th November 1920–1998) in 1946. He was a lorry driver living with his parents at Sling, West Dean in 1939. They had two children – Brian H Martin 1947 and Sally A Martin 1952.
- Betty A Taylor (born 1925).
- George W Taylor (born 1927) married Eileen Hale (born 1928) in 1948. Her birth was registered at Westbury-on-Severn, Gloucestershire. She was living with her parents at 95 St White's Road, Cinderford, East Dean, Gloucestershire in 1939. They had four children – Robert J Taylor 1948, Christopher G Taylor 1950, Kevin M Taylor 1959 and Shaun I Taylor 1964.
- Doreen Mary Taylor (10th November 1929–2nd January 2015) married John Whiting (11th January 1926–21st October 1997), born at St Donats, Vale of Glamorgan, on 23rd April 1948 at Bridgend, Glamorgan. He was living with his parents at Village House, St Donats, Cowbridge, Glamorgan in 1939. He died at Bridgend and she at Maesteg, Glamorgan. They had a daughter.

May's father, Henry 'Harry' Elwick (18th September 1851–1941), born at Basing, Hampshire, married Ann 'Annie' Elizabeth née Munday (1855–1931), also born at Old Basing, on 22nd March 1874 at the Parish Church Basing. Annie was living with her grandparents, George, a railway labourer, and Mary Munday, in 1861 at Basing. By 1871 she was a servant at the home of Ann Gidge at Basing. Harry was an agricultural labourer in 1891, when they were living at Lower Bourne, Farnham. By 1901 he was a road repair labourer and they were living at Middle Bourne, Farnham. By 1911 he was a jobbing gardener, still living at Middle Bourne. In 1939 Harry was residing at Hall Road County Hospital and Institution, Farnham and subsequently died there. In addition to May they had five other children, all registered at Farnham except for Edith Kate:

- Edith Kate Elwick (21st June 1874–22nd December 1944), birth registered at Basingstoke, married William Andrews (1873–23rd February 1933), born at Aldershot, Hampshire, on 27th February 1897 at St Thomas, Bourne. They were living at 12 Liverpool Terrace, Liverpool Road, Reading, Berkshire when her brother, George, enlisted in 1899. William was a railway engine stoker in 1901, when they were living at 85 Norton Road, Reading. By 1911 he was an engineman with the South Eastern and Chatham Railway Company and they were living at Ash Green Road, Ash and Normandy, near Guildford, Surrey. They were living at Pinecroft, Pirbright Road, Normandy at the time of his death there. Edith was still living there in 1939, with her daughter, Edith, her husband, Richard Anthony Atkins (born 1910), and grandson, William J Andrews (born 1923). Edith later died there. Edith and William had five children – Dorothy May Andrews 1899, William James Andrews 1900, Richard Frederick Andrews 1904, Cecil Henry Andrews 1908 and Edith Alice Andrews 1909.
- Sarah Jane Elwick (born 1st January 1878–10th May 1951), known as Jane, married Edmund Binfield (26th September 1875–11th November 1956) on 14th June 1896 at St Andrew, Farnham. He was a labourer in 1901, when they were living at The Mount, Lodge Hill Road, Farnham. By 1911 he was domestic gardener and they had moved to Middle Bourne, Farnham. They were living at Strawberry Bank Cottage, Middle Bourne Lane, Farnham in 1939 with their son, George. Sarah later died there. Edmund was still living there at the time of his death at Farnham Hospital. They had five children:
    - Unnamed male (born and died 1896).
    - Edmund Joseph Binfield (born and died 1897).
    - George Binfield (born and died 1898).
    - Dorothy May Binfield (10th January 1903–1986) married Frederick W Trusler (16th May 1897–1972) in 1927, registered at Farnham. They had a daughter, Anne D Trusler, in 1932.
    - George Maurice Binfield (23rd March 1907–1986) was a gas fitter in 1939, living with his parents.
- George Henry Elwick (born 1880), enlisted as a driver in the Army Service Corps (15231) on 31st October 1899 at Aldershot, Hampshire. He was described as a labourer, twenty-one years and three months old, 5′ 3½″ tall, weighing 127 lbs, with fresh complexion, brown eyes, dark brown hair and his religious denomination was Church of England. He was living at 12 Liverpool Terrace, Liverpool Road, Reading, Berkshire. A George Elwick deserted from 4th Oxfordshire Light Infantry (5168) at Oxford on 1st May 1900. George Elwick in the ASC was placed in custody in a civil prison on 27th August 1900 and returned to duty on 11th September. It is not known if the man who deserted on 1st May was the same man who enlisted in the ASC. No reason is given in his service record why he was imprisoned on 27th August. He deserted from Southampton on 13th September until 30th December, when he was charged with desertion and loss of

kit. On 22nd January 1901 he was convicted and imprisoned until 19th February. He also forfeited all previous service. He deserted again on 23rd March and was arrested the following day. He was convicted of desertion, loss of kit and stealing goods from a comrade. As a result he was imprisoned on 6th April, forfeiting all prior service. At the time of the 1901 Census he was a patient at the Royal Victoria Hospital, Netley, Hampshire and was discharged from the Army with

Construction of the Royal Victoria Hospital, Netley commenced in 1856 at the suggestion of Queen Victoria. It resulted from the poor conditions found in military hospitals in the Crimea, that contributed to the fall of the government in 1855. The foundation stone was laid by the Queen on 19th May 1856, beneath which were placed a copy of the plans, the first Victoria Cross, a Crimea Medal and coins of the realm. The hospital opened for patients on 11th March 1863. The design was controversial and attracted criticism from Florence Nightingale when she returned, too late to influence the layout. Prime Minister Lord Palmerston believed that what was best for the comfort and recovery of patients, had been sacrificed to the vanity of the architect. The building was neither convenient nor practical. Corridors on the sea-facing front of the building resulted in the wards, which faced the inner courtyard, having little light and air. Ventilation was poor and unpleasant smells lingered. The main building was the world's longest at 435m when it was completed. The hospital had 138 wards with 1,000 beds. It cost £350,000 (£44.8M in 2023) to build and was late and over budget. Supporting infrastructure included a reservoir and a gasworks and, in 1903, an electricity generating station. To bring the sick and wounded directly to the hospital, a 170m long cast iron pier was built into Southampton Water in 1865. However, it did not reach deep water and was not used after 1901 for patient transfer. It was used by Queen Victoria for her frequent visits from Osborne House on the Isle of Wight. During these visits she presented three VCs to patients. A railway connected Netley to Southampton Docks in 1866 and, at Queen Victoria's suggestion, it was extended a short distance into the hospital grounds in 1900. However, the station behind the hospital was difficult to operate, with gradients that were challenging for the locomotives of the time. Some trains had to have a locomotive at each end to travel just 1,200m. Netley Hospital was the home of the Army Medical School until 1902, training civilian doctors for service with the army. During the Great War a Red Cross hutted hospital at the rear of the site expanded accommodation to 2,500 beds. About 50,000 patients were treated during the war. During the Second World War about 68,000 casualties were treated. A break was made in the pier to prevent it being used by the Germans during an invasion. It was never repaired and was demolished by 1955. The hospital became the 28th US General Hospital during the invasion of Europe in 1944–45. After the war, the hospital continued to care for some casualties. However, the high cost of maintenance saw it fall into disuse and the main site closed in 1958. A large fire damaged much of the building in 1963. Jonathan Miller filmed *Alice in Wonderland* there just before it was demolished in 1966, with only the chapel being retained (Grade II listed in 1974). At the rear of the site, D Block (Victoria House) and E Block (Albert House) continued as a psychiatric hospital until 1978, when the Joint Armed Services Psychiatric Unit moved to Queen Elizabeth Military Hospital, Woolwich. The site is now the Royal Victoria Country Park. Some buildings at the rear of the site are used by Hampshire Police for training.

ignominy on 21st September 1901. He married Margaret Munday (6th January 1879–1962), born at Croydon, Surrey, in 1903 registered at Reading, Berkshire. She was living with her parents at Oakfield House, Camberwell, London in 1881. In 1901 she was a general domestic servant, residing at Epsom District Union Workhouse. By 1911 she was a domestic cook at the home of the Reverend Henry Keable and his wife, Constance Mary, at Wrecclesham Vicarage, Farnham. In 1939 she was a widow and domestic servant in the home of Alice Andrews, widow, at Lynton, Firgrove Hill, Farnham. It is not known what became of George after 1903.

- Mary Ellen Elwick (1884–86).
- Mary Annie Elwick (born 5th June 1886), known as Annie, married Thomas Reeves (born 24th March 1887), a labourer, in 1909 at Farnham. They were living with her parents in 1911. They were living at Southwark Cottages, Farnham in 1939, by when he was a house decorator. They had four children – Thomas George H Reeves 1911, Ethel M Reeves 1921, Mildred B Reeves 1926 and Peter J Reeves 1928.

Clearwell Church of England School opposite St Peter's Church.

Francis was living with his maternal grandparents at Clearwell in 1901. He was educated at Clearwell Church of England School, near Coleford. In 1911 he was a farm labourer, living with his mother and stepfather at High Nash, Coleford, and was later employed as a miner by the Princess Royal Colliery Company at Bream. Whilst employed at the colliery he also attended evening classes run by Mr S Evans.

Francis enlisted with his stepfather, Fred Clack, in 9th Gloucestershire on 28th December 1914, described as 5′ 4″ tall. He carried out training at Cheltenham, Gloucestershire and Fovant, near Salisbury, Wiltshire. On 20th September 1915 he went to France but suffered a poisoned foot. Whilst in hospital the Battalion transferred to Salonika in November. On his release he was attached to 8th Gloucestershire (57th Brigade, 19th Division), and was attached to the Royal Engineers, where his skills as a miner were put to good use. He was wounded in the right thigh

Princess Royal Colliery, also known as Park Gutter, just before it closed in 1962. The Princess Royal Colliery Co formed in 1891 to run Park Gutter and Flourmill Collieries. A branch line of the Severn and Wye Railway was extended to reach Park Gutter. The shaft was 187m deep and eventually sloped downwards to 457m. In the 1930's the annual output was 300,000 tons. About twenty tons of water had to be pumped out for every ton of coal extracted. At its peak, Princess Royal employed 1,300 men.

St Luke's Hospital at Skircoat, Halifax, West Yorkshire, during the Great War. St Luke's opened in 1901 as the Halifax Union Workhouse Infirmary. During the Great War St Luke's Military Hospital treated soldiers sent back from Flanders and other theatres. Marquees in the hospital grounds added 302 beds and the hospital was able to accommodate 800–900 patients. In the 1920s the Poor Laws were finally abolished and the hospital was transferred to the local Council. In 1929 there were 400 beds, with an average occupancy of 367. After the formation of the National Health Service in 1948 it became Halifax General Hospital. In 2004 a large new Calderdale Royal Hospital was built alongside the old building, which is now an administrative wing.

on 24th July 1917, possibly in a mine explosion. He was evacuated to Britain and was treated at St Luke's Military Hospital, Halifax, Yorkshire. When he recovered he was posted to 5th Gloucestershire (145th Brigade, 48th Division) in Italy in November, where he remained until August/September 1918, when the Battalion moved to France to join 25th Division.

Awarded the VC for his actions at Moulin Jacques, near Bois-l'Évêque, France on 23rd October 1918, LG 6th January 1919. He was the only other rank in the Gloucestershire Regiment to receive the VC. The VC was presented by the King in the quadrangle of Buckingham Palace on 29th May 1919. On his return he was welcomed by the Mayor and Mayoress of Gloucester, and the City's High Sheriff, to be presented with a gold watch. Francis was transferred to the Army Reserve on 11th July 1919. He returned to mining until November 1948. As a mark of respect his wage packets were always marked FG Miles VC. Francis served with the Monmouthshire Regiment (Territorial Army) 16th December 1922–15th December 1926 and with 8th (Home Defence) Battalion, Gloucestershire Regiment (D/23826) 23rd September 1939–30th June 1940, when he was discharged as 'permanently unfit for any form of military service'. Despite this he may have served thereafter in 17th Gloucestershire (Wye Valley) Battalion, Home Guard, which was commanded by former Vice Admiral AFB Carpenter, who was awarded the VC for his part in the raid on Zeebrugge on 22nd/23rd April 1918.

The Lydney and District Hospital was founded in 1882 in a converted cottage in Aylburton. A new hospital was built between 1907–09. During the Great War the hospital was used by the Red Cross for war wounded. Extensions were added in 1932 and, after transfer to the South Western Regional Hospital Board in 1948, again in 1958–63.

Francis, on the left, with his stepfather, Fred Clack.

Francis attended a number of VC Reunions – the VC Garden Party at Buckingham Palace on 26th June 1920, the Victory Day Celebration Dinner & Reception at The Dorchester, London on 8th June 1946 and the VC Centenary Celebrations at Hyde Park, London on 26th June 1956. Although he attended the latter event, he was reported missing from the parade when the Queen arrived. Two Guardsmen found him in a public house.

On 23rd September 1953 Francis was declared to be one hundred percent disabled, suffering from deafness, emphysema and arteriosclerosis. He died at Lydney & District Hospital, Gloucestershire on 8th November 1961. He is buried in St Peter's Parish Churchyard, Clearwell. The Gloucestershire Regimental Association erected a headstone over his grave on 22nd May 2004. Each year on the Sunday before Armistice a short service is held at his graveside. He is commemorated in a number of other places:

Francis Miles' grave in St Peter's Parish Churchyard, Clearwell. The headstone is the replacement provided by the Gloucestershire Regimental Association in 2004.

- Clearwell, Gloucestershire
    - Memorial plaque on the house where he was born, unveiled by Major General Robin Digby Grist OBE DL, Colonel of the Regiment.
    - Memorial plaque in St Peter's Church.
    - A Department for Communities and Local Government commemorative paving stone was dedicated at Clearwell Church Cemetery, High Street on 23rd October 2018.

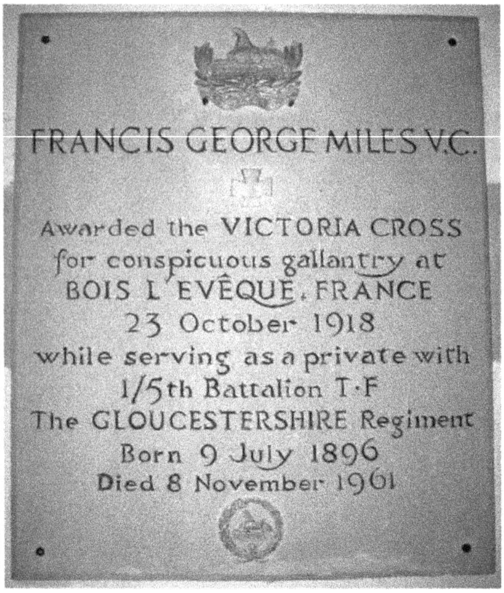

The memorial plaque in St Peter's Church.

The War Medal 1939–45 was instituted on 16th August 1945 and was awarded to all full-time personnel of the armed forces and Merchant Navy for serving for twenty-eight days, irrespective of where they were serving, between 3rd September 1939 and 2nd September 1945.

- An armoury block named after him at Catterick Camp, North Yorkshire.
- A painting of the VC action by David Rowlands.

In addition to the VC he was awarded the 1914–15 Star, British War Medal 1914–20, Victory Medal 1914–19 with Mentioned-in-Despatches Oakleaf, War Medal 1939–45 and George VI Coronation Medal 1937. He was entitled to the Elizabeth II Coronation Medal 1953 but it is not with his medal group. There is a MID Oakleaf on the Victory Medal ribbon but no London Gazette entry has been found. His medals were sold for £72,000 to Lord Ashcroft at Morton & Eden on 25th May 2005. The VC is held by the Michael Ashcroft Trust, the holding institution for the Lord Ashcroft Victoria Cross Collection and is displayed in the Imperial War Museum's Lord Ashcroft Gallery.

MAJOR ARNOLD HORACE SANTO WATERS
218th Field Company, Royal Engineers

Arnold Waters was born on 23rd September 1886 at 2 Mildmay Place, Plymouth, Devon. His father, Richard Waters (26th April 1852–14th March 1906), born at Crowan, Cornwall, worked in an iron mine. He was an engine driver to an iron mine in 1861, living with his parents. Richard married Abigail née Santo (8th March

1850–1st February 1941), born at Bridge End, St Winnow, Lostwithiel, Cornwall, on 13th August 1879 at the United Methodist Free Church, Lostwithiel. He became a United Methodist Free Church Minister and served for twenty-six years at the Hope United Methodist Free Church, Ebrington Street, Plymouth. They were living at 3 Green Bank Terrace, Charles the Martyr, Plymouth in 1881 and at 29 Mildmay Street, Plymouth in 1901. Richard built up the congregation and raised a new church until 1905, when he moved to a less demanding ministry at Scarborough, Yorkshire. He was living there at 45 Trafalgar Square at the time of his death. Abigail was living with her daughters, Alice and Gladys, at 48 Chesilton Road, Fulham, London in 1911. She was living with her daughter, Gladys, at 15 Bayham Road, Sevenoaks, Kent in 1939 and at Lynwood, Restormel Road, Lostwithiel, Cornwall at the time of her death there. Arnold had three siblings:

- John Richard Norman Waters (27th December 1881–23rd May 1970), born at 3 Greenbank Terrace, Plymouth, was known as Norman. He married his cousin, May Crowle (31st October 1876–4th November 1971), birth registered at St George, Hanover Square, London, on 29th July 1908 at Warwick Gardens Methodist Church, Kensington, London. They were living at 58 Addison Road, Kensington in 1911 but soon afterwards moved to Fawke Farm House, Sevenoaks, Kent. John was an Air Raid Precautions

2 Mildmay Place, Plymouth, where Arnold was born.

Bridge End, St Winnow, Lostwithiel, where Arnold's mother was born. Lostwithiel lies at the head of the Fowey estuary. It was founded in the early 12th century by the Normans, who built Restormel Castle nearby, and received its town charter in 1189. At the Battle of Lostwithiel, 21st August–2nd September 1644, Parliamentarian forces were defeated by the Royalists in their worst defeat of the war. Despite the Parliamentarians eventually winning the war, Cornwall remained under Royalist control until 1646. Lostwithiel elected two members to Parliament but was disenfranchised by the 1832 Reform Act.

Arnold's parents married at Lostwithiel United Free Methodist Church, constructed in 1835 on The Bank (Albert Terrace from 1846 after the visit of Queen Victoria and Prince Albert). It was known as Bank Methodist Chapel. The original chapel, which held 400 people, was rebuilt in the late 1890's and reopened in 1900. It closed as a chapel in 1987 and was converted into apartments. The building is Grade II Listed. (Eirian Evans)

Warden with Sevenoaks Rural District in 1939. They moved to Moor Down, Winkleigh, Devon in the 1950s. John was a director of numerous companies of provision merchants, restaurants and hotels. John and May both died at Moor Down, Winkleigh. They had four children:

- Richard 'Dick' Graham Waters (16th April 1909–3rd July 1993), born at Kensington, London, married Alice Volum (26th September 1912–15th November 1990), born in Ceylon, on 19th August 1936 registered at Sevenoaks, Kent. She was the daughter of Andrew James Volum (1871–1957), a tea planter and Violet Gray (1874–1960). Alice and her daughter, Dorothy, were living with her parents at Whyteladies, Wildernesse Avenue, Sevenoaks in 1939. Richard and Alice were living at Flat 2, Vine Lodge, Sevenoaks at the time of her death there. Richard was living at Thornton Park, Hurrell Lane, Thornton-le-Dale, North Yorkshire at the time of his death there. They had three children – unnamed male 1937, Dorothy Elizabeth Waters 1939 and Alison B Waters 1946.
- Arnold John 'Jack' Waters (8th April 1911–2nd March 2005) married Betty Durtnell (6th April 1909–24th February 2004), born at Sevenoaks, at Kensington on 20th June 1934. He qualified as a solicitor in 1931 and served in The Artist's Rifles. He was commissioned in 6th Queen's Own Royal West Kent Regiment on 19th November 1939 (105482). Betty and her daughter,

The Reverend Richard Waters was living at 45 Trafalgar Square, Scarborough when he died in 1906.

Lynwood, Restormel Road, Lostwithiel, where Arnold's mother died in 1941.

Spangenberg Castle has been a medieval castle, fortress, hunting lodge, prison and forestry school. The castle guarded the important trading route from Frankfurt to Leipzig and the road was an important factor in the development of the settlement below the castle, which was granted town rights in 1309. The first recorded owner of the castle and town was Lord Hermann of Treffurt in 1235. Since that time the Lords of Treffurt were also the Lords of Spangenberg. The Treffurts were robber barons who caused much unrest in Thuringia. There was a decline in their fortunes due to their violent behaviour. In 1350 Lord Hermann IX sold the castle, title and estate to Hesse II and thereafter Spangenberg was Hessian. The castle became a residence and hunting lodge for two centuries. With the advent of firearms, the castle was strengthened significantly and again during the Seven Years' War (1756–63). However, it was captured by the French in a surprise attack in 1758. From 1763 the fortress became a state prison. It closed in 1860 when Hesse was annexed by Prussia. However, during the Franco-Prussian War (1870–71) French prisoners were held there. In 1907–08 the castle became a school of forestry, requiring major reconstruction but an effort was made to preserve the original character. Kaiser Wilhelm II visited on 15th June 1913. During the Second World War the castle was a prisoner-of-war camp (Oflag IX-A/H) for officers, opening in October 1939. The first escapee was Flight Lieutenant Howard Wardle in August 1940. He was recaptured and sent to Colditz. The castle had a bad reputation. In his autobiography Eric Foster, who was transferred there from Dulag Luft, commented *Dulag Luft had been described as the best camp in Germany... Spangenberg was described as the end of hope*. There were foul smells from pigs in the moat, the guards were rough and unpleasant, and discipline was severe. The Germans marched the prisoners eastwards on 29th March 1945 and twenty-five escaped as they left the castle. The Americans liberated the camp's inmates on 4th April. A number of well-known prisoners were held there:

- Pilot Officer Anthony Barber, No.1 Photographic Reconnaissance Unit RAF, future Chancellor of the Exchequer.
- Colditz escapees – Dominic Bruce, Airey Neave, Brian Paddon, Peter Tunstell and Howard Wardle.
- Wing Commander Harry Day, a Great Escape survivor.
- Lieutenant Colonel John Frost, CO 2nd Battalion, The Parachute Regiment, captured at Arnhem.
- Major General Victor Fortune, GOC 51st (Highland) Division, captured at St Valery in June 1940, who was the senior British POW in Germany. He was knighted after his release for promoting the welfare of British prisoners.
- Flying Officer Oliver Philpot, one of the Wooden Horse escapees.
- Major Bruce Shand, father of Camilla, Queen Consort of King Charles III.
- Wing Commander Robert Stanford Tuck, Battle of Britain ace.
- St Nazaire Raiders – Lieutenant Colonel Charles Newman VC, Bill 'Tiger' Watson, Bill Copland DSO, Bob Montgomery MC, Corran Purdon MC (escaped and sent to Colditz), Micky Burn MC and Donald 'The Laird' Roy DSO.

Shortly after the prisoners departed, the castle was destroyed in an American air raid. It was reconstructed by the State of Hesse in the 1950s. Today the castle is a hotel and restaurant with conference rooms.

Jennifer, were living with her father at 80 St John's Road, Sevenoaks in 1939. Jack was in action at Doullens on the evening of 20th May 1940, with 36th Infantry Brigade under Brigadier George Patrick Rowland Roupell VC. His position was overrun and he was ordered to evacuate his platoon under cover of darkness and try to get to the coast. He kept his men together for ten days, fighting minor skirmishes against enemy patrols, and led them through occupied country to the coast near the mouth of the Somme. Jack and his men pooled their cash and arranged to purchase a boat from a fisherman. When they went to collect it after dark German searchlights spotted them and they were surrounded and captured. Jack spent the remainder of the war in Oflag IX-A/H, Schloss Spangenberg, Hesse, Germany (POW No.682). Promoted War substantive lieutenant on 19th May 1941. He was released by American troops in April 1945. For his gallantry in 1940 he was awarded the MC, 29th November 1945. He had been released from full time service by the time of the January–March 1946 Army List as an honorary lieutenant. Awarded the Efficiency Medal (Territorial), LG 19th July 1949. Arnold returned to the family legal practice, Turner & Co, in the City of London and became the senior partner until he retired in 1986. Betty and Arnold both died at Liphook, Surrey. They had two daughters – Jennifer G Waters 1937 and Elizabeth A Waters 1951.

- Hugh Percival Norman 'Tim' Waters (27th September 1914–7th March 1957), born at Parkside, The Common, Sevenoaks, married Joan Margaret Lovell Morris (4th February 1914–20th February 1993), born at Felling, Co Durham, on 3rd September 1938 at Holy Trinity Church, Roehampton, London. They lived at Mare Reeds, Fawke Common, Sevenoaks. He was manager of a meat and poultry provision business in 1939. He served as a corporal in the Royal Air Force (1186414) during the Second World War and was discharged due to contracting tuberculosis on 16th February 1945. Tim was a building surveyor with Messrs Montagu Evans & Partners in London. They were living at Fawke, Upton Way, Broadstone, Bournemouth, Hampshire at the time of his death at The Royal National Sanatorium, Bournemouth. Joan was living at Holly Tree Cottage, Broomhill, Wimborne, Dorset at the time of her death at The Red House, Eye, Suffolk. They had two children – Jeremy David Waters 1939 and Susan Lovell Waters 1944.
- Barbara Joan Waters (11th May 1917–17th May 1995) was educated at Roedean School, Brighton, Sussex and played lacrosse for England. She was a lacrosse teacher living with her parents in 1939. During the Second World War she served in the Auxiliary Fire Service, Sevenoaks Urban District and the Navy, Army and Air Force Institutes. Barbara founded Sevenoaks Riding Club in October 1948, one of the first riding clubs under the British Horse Society, which formed in 1947. By 1954 the Sevenoaks Riding Club was one of the leading clubs in the country. She never married and was living at Aalen House Nursing Home, 12 Parklands, Okehampton, Devon at the time of her death there.

- Alice Gertrude Waters (31st January 1884–7th January 1938), born at 2 Mildmay Place, Plymouth. She was a clerk and shorthand typist for the Baptist Missionary

Illogan lies three kilometres northwest of Redruth. Originally a farming and agricultural settlement, it shared in the prosperity brought by the mining boom. The ruins of a Roman villa were discovered at Magor Farm in 1931. A church was known to be there in 1235. By 1844 the then church had become too small to serve the increasing population, so a new church was built and came into use on 4th November 1846. The bell tower is all that remains of the old church. It was retained at the insistence of Trinity House as a landmark for shipping. There are fifty-two CWGC burials in the churchyard. Demelza Carne in the *Poldark* novels by Winston Graham was born at Illogan.

St Crewanna Parish Church, Crowan, where Arnold's paternal grandparents married in 1851. St Crewenna was possibly an Irish saint, who accompanied Saints Germoe and Breaca. Crowan church was given by William, Earl of Gloucester to St James' Priory, Bristol, a dependency of the Benedictine Abbey of Tewkesbury. The present church is 15th century, with parts dating to the 11th century, and was substantially restored in 1872. It contains many monuments to members of the St Aubyn family.

Society in 1911, living with her mother. She was a spinster living at 895a Fulham Road, London at the time of her death there.

- Gladys Waters (21st May 1889–28th May 1990) lived with and cared for her mother until her death. She was a spinster living at Halwill Manor Nursing Home, Beaworthy, Devon at the time of her death there.

Arnold's paternal grandfather, Joseph Waters/Watters (30th September 1826–30th August 1875), born at Crowan, Cornwall, married Elizabeth White Harris née Craze (1829–14th December 1907), born at Illogan, Cornwall, on 8th June 1851 at St Crewanna Parish Church, Crowan, Cornwall. He was an engine driver in an iron mine in 1861, when they were living at Halfway House, St Issey, Cornwall. By the time of the 1871 Census, he was debilitated and unemployed, living with his family at Water Style, Camborne, Cornwall. They both died at Camborne. In addition to Richard they had six other children:

- Elizabeth Jane Waters (born 1853), born at Illogan, registered as Watters at Redruth, married John Hendra (born 1860), a tin miner, in 1883 at Redruth, where he was born. They were living at Pool, Illogan in 1891. They may have emigrated to Australia in 1900 aboard the *Ormwy*, departing Plymouth on 3rd February 1900 and disembarking at Adelaide, South Australia seventy-five days later. A John Hendra of unknown age died at Adelaide in 1918.

- Eliza Ann White Waters (14th December 1857–26th July 1935), born at Breage, Cornwall, married William Henry Bosanko (1863–7th April 1933), an iron ore miner, in 1883, registered at Redruth. His birth was registered at Helston. They were living at 19 Bankfield Road, Millom, Cumberland in 1891, at 21 Concrete Square, Haverigg, near Millom in 1901 and 18 Concrete Square in 1911. They were still there at the time of his death at Hodbarrow Hospital, Millom. She was still living there at the time of her death. They had six children, all registered at Bootle, Cumberland, including:
    - Richard Henry Bosanko (1886–1953) married Catherine Gill (15th December 1895–1983), birth registered at Chorlton, Lancashire, in 1916 registered at Wigan, Lancashire. They had a son, Bernard Bosanko (6th September 1918–1992), who married Mary Cowan in 1947 and they had two children – Robert B Bosanko 1948 and Peter Bosanko 1951. Both Richard's and Catherine's deaths were registered at Stockport, Cheshire (Greater Manchester from 1974).
    - Edith Annie Bosanko (1890–1965) married William T Metcalf in 1915. They had three children – Amy Metcalf 1925, Stanley Metcalf 1927 and Melbourne Metcalf 1929. Edith's death was registered at St Albans, Hertfordshire.
    - Albert Victor Clarence Bosanko (1892–22nd January 1932) married Annie M Singleton (1892–1964) in 1919. They had seven children – Dorothy Bosanko 1921, twins May and Ronald Bosanko (both born and died 1923), Norman Bosanko 1924, Arnold Bosanko 1926, Thomas W Bosanko 1929 and Melville Bosanko 1930.
    - William Ernest Bosanko (1895–24th December 1958).
    - Elizabeth May Bosanko (1897–1987).
- Annes (also seen as Annis and Annie) Grace White Waters (21st April 1858–2nd August 1937), born at Crowan, followed her fiancée, Edward Quintrell (also seen as Quentrall) (1857–25th May 1914), a tin miner born at Camborne, Cornwall, to Australia. They married at Cross Roads, Moonta, South Australia on 26th September 1881. He died at Cross Roads and she at her daughter Ruby's home at 23 Alexander Street, Wallaroo, SA. They had eight children:
    - Joseph Henry Quintrell (20th December 1882–22nd October 1899).
    - Richard Ernest Quintrell (5th December 1886–22nd May 1945).
    - Stanley Quintrell (23rd March 1889–31st October 1957) enlisted in 2nd Depot Battalion AIF at Kadina, SA on 13th April 1916 (7065), described as a miner, 5′ 6½″ tall, weighing 150 lbs, with fair complexion, grey eyes, light brown hair and his religious denomination was Methodist. He joined A Company, 2nd Depot Battalion on 1st May, the Engineers Base on 16th May, Miners Reinforcements, Seymour on 27th June and Langwarrin on 29th September. He joined Reinforcements Tunnelling Companies on 27th February 1917 and embarked aboard HMAT A9

Moonta, on the Yorke Peninsula in South Australia is one hundred kilometres north-northwest of the state capital of Adelaide. It is one of three towns known as the Copper Coast or Little Cornwall because of their shared copper mining history. There are eleven suburbs including Cross Roads. The coast of the Yorke Peninsula was separately navigated by Matthew Flinders and Nicolas Baudin in 1802. In 1840 John Hill and Thomas Burr landed fifteen kilometres south of Point Riley, near Moonta Bay. They made their way back to Adelaide on horseback, reporting *a very excellent tract of country*. A few British settlers arrived in the area in the 1840s, but there was no significant development until rich deposits of copper were discovered in 1861. A horse tramway from Moonta to the port at Wallaroo opened in July 1866 and in the 1880s was converted to a steam locomotive railway. Cornish miners began arriving in large numbers and Moonta became a Corporate Town in 1872. The mines were the richest in South Australia by 1917, exceeding the total wealth created by all other mines since 1836. The population of Moonta in 1875 had risen to 12,000. The main copper mining operations ceased in 1923, although a number of small mines continued for some years. Smaller-scale operations recommenced in the late 1980s but had closed by the mid-1990s. Post-copper mining, the district successfully switched to dry land farming, growing barley, wheat and legumes. Tourism is also significant.

Shropshire at Melbourne on 11th May. He disembarked at Plymouth, Devon on 19th July and joined 1 & 3 Camp Details, Parkhouse Camp, Salisbury Plain next day. On 18th August he went to France via Southampton, joined the Australian General Base Depot, Rouelles next day and 1st Australian Engineer Battalion on 5th September. Stanley received a gunshot wound to the right knee on 14th September and was admitted to 1st Australian Field Ambulance and a casualty clearing station next day. On 24th September he was evacuated to England from 83rd General Hospital, Boulogne and was admitted to Bevan Military Hospital, Sandgate, Kent. He was transferred to 3rd Australian Auxiliary Hospital, Dartford on 10th October and was discharged to furlough on 13th October, to report to No.3 Command Depot, Hurdcott, Wiltshire on 27th October. He was classified B1A3 on 12th December and A3 on 2nd January 1918. Stanley joined the Overseas Training Brigade, Longbridge Deverill, Wiltshire on 5th January and went to France via Southampton on 8th February, joining the Australian General Base Depot, Rouelles next day. He joined the Australian Corps Depot on 11th March and 2nd Australian Tunnelling Company from Tunnelling Reinforcements, Australian Corps Depot on 15th March. He was granted leave in Paris 31st October–10th November and Britain 20th January–12th February 1919. He returned to England from the Australian Base Depot on 26th April and joined No.2 Group next day. Stanley returned to Australia aboard HT *Mahia*, departing London on 5th June and disembarked in 3rd for 4th Military District on 17th July. He was discharged from 4th Military District on 17th August 1919. Stanley married Gladys Irene

Pearl Jacka (1898–1963) at Adelaide, SA in 1921. They had at least one child, Glen Morris Quintrell, in 1922.

- Percy Quintrell (17th June 1891–17th December 1919) enlisted at Kadina, SA in 2nd Depot Battalion AIF on 19th April 1916 (5813), described as a miner, single, 5′ 9″ tall, weighing 154 lbs, with dark complexion, brown eyes, dark brown hair and his religious denomination was Methodist. His mother was his next of kin but one document says it was his daughter, Phyllis May Quintrell, living at Cross Roads, Moonta. He joined A Company on 4th May, Base Engineers on 16th May and Miners Reinforcements, Seymour on 27th June. Percy embarked aboard HMAT A38 *Ulysses* at Melbourne on 25th October and disembarked at Plymouth, Devon on 28th December. He joined the Australian Details Camp, Perham Down, Salisbury Plain on 29th December. He went to France from Folkestone aboard SS *Onward* on 28th January 1917 and joined the Australian General Base Depot next day. Percy joined 3rd Tunnelling Company from Reinforcements Tunnelling Companies on 6th February. On 15th March he was awarded twenty-one days Field Punishment No.1 and forfeited seven days' pay for being in an estaminet during prohibited hours and giving a false name to the Provost Corporal on 11th March. He received a gunshot wound to the right leg on 3rd May and was admitted to a field ambulance and No.58 Casualty Clearing Station, Lillers. He was transferred to 7th General Hospital, St Omer on 5th May, joined Base Details on 10th June and rejoined his unit next day. On 28th July he was gassed and was evacuated to No.18 Casualty Clearing Station, Lapugnoy next day. He was transferred to 7th General Hospital, St Omer on 31st July, to 7th Convalescent Depot, St Omer on 9th August and was discharged to Base Details on 14th August. He joined the Australian General Base Depot, Rouelles on 17th August and rejoined his unit on 30th August. On 31st March 1918 he was admitted to 10th Australian Field Ambulance and No.33 Casualty Clearing Station, Haverskerque with bronchitis. He was transferred to 7th Canadian Stationary Hospital, Le Havre on 4th April, to 1st Australian Convalescent Depot, Boulogne on 8th April and was discharged to the Australian General Base Depot, Le Havre on 15th May. He forfeited three days' pay for being absent without leave from Rouelles from 9.30 p.m. until accosted by the Military Police at 10.00 p.m. on 5th June. Percy returned to Britain on 10th June, joined No.2 Command Depot, Weymouth next day and transferred to No.4 Command Depot, Hurdcott on 19th June. He was absent without leave from Hurdcott from 10.00 p.m. on 2nd August until 8.00 a.m. on 11th August, but the charge was dismissed. On 2nd September he joined the Overseas Training Brigade, Longbridge Deverill and went to France via Southampton on 23rd September. He joined the Australian General Base Depot, Rouelles next day and his unit on 29th September. On 27th March 1919 he joined

the Australian Infantry Base Depot and returned to Britain on 2nd April, joining No.3 Group, Codford next day. He forfeited a day's pay for being absent from Codford from 11.59 p.m. on 21st April until 9.50 a.m. on 22nd April. Percy departed London aboard HT *Borda* on 11th May, arrived in 4th Military District, Australia on 23rd June and was discharged on 1st August. He died shortly thereafter.
    - Ruby Quintrell (13th August 1893–1970) married William Lanyon (born 1897) at Daly, SA in 1920.
    - Edith Venetta Quintrell (6th January 1896–18th September 1968) married Edgar Hartley Magor (1896–1973) at Adelaide, SA in 1921. They had at least one child, Kenneth Edward Magor, in 1921.
    - Albert Roy Quintrell (1899–1987).
    - Leonard Quintrell (c.1902–23rd September 1976).
- Joseph Henry Waters (1861–24th December 1880), birth registered as Watters.
- Frances Ellen Waters (1st June 1865–20th December 1945) married John Charles Smitheram (27th June 1865–26th December 1937), born at Centenary Row, Camborne, on 10th January 1902 at the United Methodist Chapel, Camborne. He was a labourer at an iron foundry in 1891 living with his parents. He was a police constable in the Cornwall Constabulary in 1901, living alone at Chyandour, Madron, Cornwall. They were living at Kilkhampton, Cornwall in 1911, before moving to 47 Dolcoath Road, Camborne, where they both subsequently died.
- Edith Waters (30th April 1870–26th December 1953) married Alfred Rickard (19th December 1871–19th April 1944) in 1898. He was a blacksmith in a tin mine in 1901, when they were living at 2 North Road, Camborne. He was an assistant superintendent of an insurance company in 1911, when they were living at 47 Dolcoath Road, Camborne. They were living at 1 Vyvyan Street, Camborne in 1939, where they both subsequently died. They had four children including:
    - Alfred Garfield Rickard (1900–02).
    - Gwendoline May Rickard (1905–3rd June 1963) married Redvers Emmett (5th January 1903–1973) in 1929. They had a son, David R Emmett, in 1930.
    - Alfred Leonard Rickard (18th December 1909–15th October 1966) married Elsie M Edwards (1915–39) in 1935. They had two sons – Alfred E Rickard 1936 and Brian Rickard 1939. Alfred was a widower and maintenance bricklayer/mason with Great Western Railway, living with his parents in 1939. He married Violetta Farrell née Carlyon (1897–1958) in 1950. Violetta had married John Farrell (c.1906–44) in 1937. Alfred married Violet Jane Symons (2nd June 1911–1984) in 1961. Alfred was living at 1 Vyvyan Street, Camborne when he died.

His maternal grandfather, Hugh Santo (1812–23rd December 1874), born at Boconnoc, Cornwall, married Jane née Hoar (17th February 1811–30th April 1887), born at St Austell, Cornwall, on 6th October 1835 at Lanlivery Rural, Cornwall.

St Austell, sixteen kilometres south of Bodmin, is one of the largest towns in Cornwall. It was a village until the advent of tin mining. The town is named after the 6th century Cornish St Austol, who is recorded in a 10th century Vatican manuscript. St Austell is not mentioned in the Domesday Book of 1086. A church was dedicated on 9th October 1262 and other records show a church there in 1169, dedicated to Sanctus Austolus. The current church dates from the 13th/14th centuries and was extended in 1498–99. In the 18th century the nearby Polgooth Mine was the greatest tin mine in the world. The discovery of china clay nearby, combined with tin mining, contributed to St Austell growing in prominence. China clay took over from tin and copper mining in the mid 19th to early 20th centuries. The town was a centre of Methodism with thirty-seven chapels there by 1839. The station on the Cornwall Railway opened on 4th May 1859 and two branch lines opened later to serve the china clay industry.

He was a butcher and farmer in 1841, when they were living at Bridgend, St Winnow, Cornwall. They both died at Lostwithiel, Cornwall. In addition to Abigail they had four other children:

Lanlivery is eight kilometres south of Bodmin. The parish church is dedicated to St Brevita or Bryvyth, about whom nothing is known. The building was enlarged in the 15th century by the addition of a tower and south aisle. It is *one of the great churches of Cornwall* according to John Betjeman. There is a holy well dedicated to St Bryvyth just outside the village and there are four stone crosses in the parish.

- John Santo (c.1835–5th April 1918), born at Lostwithiel, was an assistant to his father in 1851. He was also a butcher and a farmer, who served as JP for Cornwall and was Mayor of Lostwithiel on three occasions. He married Martha Billing (c.1834–8th October 1870) on 6th January 1866 at St Winnow, Cornwall. He married Amelia West (1850–25th December 1916) in 1876, registered at Bodmin, as was her birth. They were living at Hillyar Cottage, Lostwithiel in 1911, where they both subsequently died. John had nine children from his two marriages including:
    - Emily Santo (born 1867).
    - Bertha Santo (born 1868).
    - Ada Santo (born 1869).
    - Martha Santo (1877–24th January 1890).
    - Ethel Santo (1st October 1878–1971) married William Bartholomew Lee (2nd February 1896–1980) at Plymouth, Devon in 1915. Her death was registered at Warwick and his at Plymouth.

  - Reginald Santo (1881–5th March 1963) was a meat purveyor living with his parents in 1911. He married Emily Trembath (1880–1967) in 1911. Their deaths were registered at St Austell. They had three children – Sylvia Santo 1912, Beryl Santo 1918 and Brian Santo 1922.
  - Hugh Santo (1884–25th August 1966) was a farmer living with his parents in 1911. He married Mabel Jessie Clements (16th November 1884–1977), born at Stoke Damerel, Devon, in 1916 registered at Frome, Somerset. They had two children – Ruth Santo 1917 and John C Santo 1920. Mabel's death was registered at Paddington, London.
  - Possibly John Santo (1885–86).
  - Hilda Santo (born 1887).
- Mary Jane Santo (13th September 1840–4th August 1917), born at Bridgend, Lostwithiel, married Philip Brewer Liddicoat (1836–4th January 1918), a farmer and butcher born St Columb, in 1865. They were living at Mount Pleasant, St Winnow in 1891 and at Bridgend, St Winnow in 1901, where they both subsequently died. They had six children:
  - Arthur Santo Liddicoat (11th June 1866–3rd May 1942) married Harriett 'Hettie' Reed (1867–1935) in 1890. He was living at Tredethick Farm with his spinster daughters, Gladys and Winifred, in 1939. He was living at Tredethick Street, St Winnow, Lostwithiel when he died. They had four children – Florence Liddicoat (4th January 1891–26th February 1977), Gladys Liddicoat (14th February 1895–1973), Winifred Maude Liddicoat (26th March 1899–1964) and Harold Arthur Liddicoat (1902–99).
  - Charles Liddicoat (29th March 1868–20th October 1958) married Elizabeth Barnes (26th April 1864–1955) in 1895 at Hackney, London. They were living at 3 The Terrace, Lostwithiel in 1939. They had four sons, births registered at Bodmin – Lancelot Wilfred Liddicoat (1896–1976), Ralph Oliver Liddicoat (1897–1988), Eric Liddicoat (1899–1964) and Arnold Liddicoat (1903–89).
  - John Liddicoat (1869–20th May 1937) was a farmer and butcher in 1911 at Tremaine Pelynt, Duloe. He employed four people, including Frances Emma Hoar (1871–26th August 1946), his cousin and housekeeper. They married in 1923. They were living at Fernleigh, Avery Terrace, Lostwithiel when they died.
  - Ernest Hugh Liddicoat (1871–5th May 1872).
  - Alfred Liddicoat (1874–24th November 1875).
  - Marianne 'Annie' Liddicoat (27th September 1876–7th September 1958) never married. She was living at Mount Pleasant, 27 Grenville Road, Lostwithiel with her niece, Florence Liddicoat, a butcher's shop accountant, in 1939, and when she died at Polmenna, Lostwithiel.
- Ann Santo (1843–31st January 1923), born at St Winnow, married John Crowle (12th February 1841–12th June 1906), a master butcher born at Charleston,

Slaters Ltd at 18–20 High Street, Kensington. This shop was replaced by another in 1909, when the north side of the High Street was redeveloped.

Sannah's Post, Bloemfontein, South Africa.

Cornwall, on 3rd August 1866 at St Winnow. They were living at 302 Clapham Road, Lambeth, London in 1871. By 1881 they had moved to 18 & 20 High Street, Kensington, London. He was employing thirteen men at Slaters Ltd, butchers and provision merchants with Royal Warrants to supply Kensington Palace. By 1891 he was Managing Director of Slaters Ltd and they had moved to 36 Phillimore Gardens, Kensington. He subsequently died there, leaving effects valued at £442,696/2/5 (resworn £345,190/19/8 – £50M in 2023). Ann was still living at 36 Phillimore Gardens in 1911 and at Albert House, Milton Road, Westcliff-on-Sea, Essex at the time of her death. They had six children:

- Emily Beatrice Santo Crowle (12th August 1867–18th June 1942) married John William Reacher (c.1860–1921) at Kensington in 1890.
- Harriet 'Hetty' Crowle (31st July 1868–1923).
- Annie Crowle (21st February 1870–23rd April 1940).
- Percival Hugh Santo Crowle (1st September 1871–31st March 1900) was educated at Manor House, Clapham, and Downing College, Cambridge. He was a law student in 1891, living with his parents, and qualified as a solicitor in 1894. He was at Sydney, Australia when the Second Boer War broke out in 1899 and hurried to Cape Town, South Africa where he volunteered for service with Roberts' Horse. He was present at the relief of Kimberley and was instrumental in capturing a Boer convoy, including General Botha's wagon. Percival was killed in action as a lieutenant at Sannah's Post, Bloemfontein.
- Ernest Crowle (10th July 1873–12th April 1875).
- May Crowle (31st October 1876–8th November 1971).

• Elizabeth Santo (1847–30th March 1932), birth registered at Bodmin, married Edwin Henwood (1837–3rd February 1919), a miller born at Trevance, St Issey, at Bodmin in 1868. They were living at Polmorla, St Breock in 1871. He was a miller and a farmer of twenty-five acres at St Breock, Cornwall in 1881, before moving to Tresloggett Farm, St Mabyn, Cornwall, where he subsequently died. Elizabeth died at St Breock. They had two daughters:

- Mabel Santo Henwood (1872–6th May 1953) married Richard Hawken in 1926 registered at St Columb.
- Abigail Santo Henwood (1879–26th February 1926) never married.

The Hoe Grammar School was started in 1867 at 6 Lockyer Street, The Hoe, Plymouth. By 1889 there were thirty-six boys. The premises were extended to include 7 and 8 Lockyer Street and eventually 2 Alfred Street. By 1893 there were four classes. The School was destroyed by fire during an air raid in the Second World War. The remains were demolished in 1959. A plaque commemorating the existence of Hoe Grammar School was dedicated on the site on 11th June 1966.

Arnold was educated at Hoe Grammar School, Plymouth and University Tutorial College, London, where he trained as an engineer, qualifying in 1910. He worked on projects in Plymouth for Cattewater Harbour Commissioners 1902–05 while articled to Henry Victor Prigg, civil engineer, for a fee of £150. Arnold worked for a contractor in London from 1906 on various tasks for the Metropolitan Water Board. He was then employed by Messrs Wilcox and Raikes, Consulting Engineers, of Birmingham and Westminster and moved to Birmingham to work on the Rhymney and Eastern Valleys water project in South Wales. He was living at the Alexandra Hotel, Queen Street, Cardiff at the time of the 1911 Census. Whilst in Birmingham he shared accommodation with his friend, Cecil Leonard Knox, who was also awarded the VC during the Great War (see the sixth book in this series – *Victoria Crosses on the Western Front, Cambrai to the German Spring Offensive, November 1917–March 1918*.

Arnold was commissioned in the Royal Engineers on 30th January 1915. He spent the early days of the war supervising the construction of water supplies in the new camps being built on Salisbury Plain. He went to France on 19th May 1915 with 90th Field Company (9th (Scottish) Division). He was promoted lieutenant on 8th December and later transferred to 218th Field Company. **Awarded the MC for his actions on the night of 30th June/1st July 1917 at Nieuport, Belgium. He volunteered to lead a Bangalore torpedo party to allow a raiding party of 2nd Manchester to enter the enemy trenches. Two belts of wire close to the enemy parapet required four torpedoes to be positioned, each almost three metres long. While one was being pushed through the wire, a seven-man enemy patrol approached and opened fire before returning to their trench. Surprise was lost but Arnold continued and, after forty-five minutes, succeeded in blowing gaps in both belts of wire. The raiding party was**

One of the many camps built on Salisbury Plain early in the Great War was at Larkhill. Before the war it had been used for exercises with troops being accommodated in temporary tented camps. However, once hostilities commenced it became clear that more permanent quarters were required. Thirty-four battalion sized camps were constructed at Larkhill, an enormous undertaking. This picture shows Rollestone Camp, with the railway that connected the camps to the mainline station at Amesbury in the foreground. Rollestone was on the west side of the main Larkhill camp area and there is still a training camp there.

then able to advance and the success of the operation was entirely due to his coolness, skill and courage under very trying and dangerous conditions, LG 26th September 1917.

Arnold was appointed acting major on 24th July 1917 and was promoted captain on 18th September. He was regarded as an officer of exceptional ability and powers of leadership, a good administrator and organiser with a very good knowledge of his profession. **He was mentioned in Field Marshal Sir Douglas Haig's Despatch of 7th April 1918, LG 21st May 1918. Awarded the DSO, LG 3rd June 1918.** Arnold was promoted major on 1st October. **Awarded the VC for his actions on the Sambre-Oise Canal, near Ors, France on 4th November 1918, LG 13th February 1919.** The 218th Field Company war diary records the award of a Bar to his DSO in December 1918. This was subsequently upgraded to the VC. He was a very modest man and later claimed that he was protected by the bodies of sappers and infantry casualties around him. The VC was presented by the King at Buckingham Palace on 15th March 1919. He was demobilised on 12th April 1919 and last appears in the Army List in June 1920.

Arnold was introduced to Edward, Prince of Wales, at a review of 6,000 Boy Scouts and schoolchildren at Plymouth Hoe, Devon in June 1919. He was presented with an inscribed ceremonial sword and illuminated address by the Mayor of Plymouth at the Guildhall in November 1919. He was one of the Honour Guard at the burial of the Unknown Warrior at Westminster Abbey on 11th November 1920.

After the Great War Arnold returned to civil engineering and eventually set up his own consulting civil engineer business in Birmingham, AHS Waters & Partners, dealing with water supply and sewage disposal. He was often called as an expert witness at public enquiries, twice giving evidence in the House of Lords. Despite living a full and successful life after the Great War, he suffered periods of depression and felt the loss of his comrades deeply. Many of his appointments were honorary, undertaken without remuneration. He championed the war disabled and became Chairman of the Birmingham and Sutton Coldfield War Pensions Committee. He joined the British Legion and wrote a paper in April 1922 entitled, *Why am I a Member of the Legion? – Rank Carries No Privilege or Distinction.* He held a number of other appointments:

President of the Birmingham and Midland Limbless Ex-Servicemen's Association.
Justice of the Peace from 1930 and Chairman of the Sutton Coldfield Magistrates.
Treasurer of the Boys' Brigade (Birmingham Battalion) 1935–72 and was an Honorary Vice President at the time of his death.
Divisional Food Officer for the West Midlands 1939–45.
Chairman of the Planning Ministry's Advisory Committee on Sand and Gravel Workings for seven years. **Appointed CBE, LG 9th June 1949.**
Chairman of the South Staffordshire Waterworks Co 1946–59. **Knight Bachelor for services to the Ministry of Housing and Local Government on 6th July 1954, LG 9th July 1954.**
Life Governor of Birmingham University.
Deputy Lieutenant for Warwickshire from 10th January 1957, LG 18th January 1957.

He was a member of a number of institutions/societies:

Institution of Civil Engineers.
Institution of Mechanical Engineers.
Institution of Water Engineers
Institution of Structural Engineers from 1926 and President 1933–34 and 1943–44, the only person to have serve in the appointment twice.
Institution of Public Health Engineers (Honorary Fellow).
Institution of Radio Engineers (Honorary Member).
Royal Geographical Society (Fellow).
Royal Engineers Association.

Arnold married Gladys Eveline/Evelyne Maud Barriball (21st September 1900–17th August 1988), born at Penzance, Cornwall, on 27th October 1924 registered at Birmingham North, Warwickshire. The best man was Cecil Leonard Knox VC. They lived at Holly Cottage, Birmingham Road, Sutton Coldfield, Warwickshire

Penzance is the most westerly major town in Cornwall. The earliest evidence of settlement is from the Bronze Age and Lescudjack Castle is almost certainly Iron Age. In 1066 the Manor of Alwarton was owned by Alward, who was dispossessed by Robert, Count of Mortain, half-brother of William the Conqueror, but Penzance is not mentioned in the 1086 Domesday Book. The first mention of the name Pensans is in the Assize Roll of 1284. A market was granted by Edward III on 25th April 1332 and two fairs were also granted. Henry IV granted three more fairs on 8th April 1404. In medieval times the town was raided frequently by Barbary Corsairs. The plague hit Penzance in the summer of 1578 and deaths increased from twelve the previous year to 155, about 10% of the population. On 23rd July 1595 four Spanish galleys landed troops in Cornwall and the militias fled in panic. Penzance and surrounding villages were sacked. In 1614 James I granted the town Borough status. During the English Civil War Penzance was sacked by Parliamentarian forces under Sir Thomas Fairfax. The plague returned in 1647 and deaths increased from twenty-two to 217 in one year. In 1512 Henry VIII granted the right to charge harbour dues and by then the first pier had been built. The southern arm was built in 1766 and extended in 1785. The pier was extended again in 1812 and a small dry dock was added in 1814. Albert Pier was completed in 1853 to provide better shelter. At the same time the Old Pier was extended and a lighthouse was commissioned on it in 1855. It remains operational and is visible up to thirty-one kilometres out to sea. The Scilly Isles Steam Navigation Co was founded in 1858 and in 1870 the West Cornwall Steam Ship Co also joined the route, taking over the Scilly Isles Co the following year. A larger dry dock was built in 1880 and a floating harbour in 1884. Penzance became the western depot for Trinity House to service lighthouses and lightships from Start Point to Trevose Head. The Buoy Store became the Trinity House National Lighthouse Museum until it closed in 2005. New workshops were built in the 1930s and were used by the Scilly Isles ferries, merchant ships, Trinity House, Royal Navy and Royal Maritime Auxiliary Service. The first lifeboat in Cornwall, bought by Penzance in 1803, lasted until 1812. In 1853 the RNLI stationed a boat in the town and maintained a station there until 1908, when it was transferred to Newlyn. A submarine mine, Wheal Wherry Mine, was worked 1778–98 and 1836–40. During the 19th century and until 1912 Penzance had the largest tin smelting house in Cornwall. The Penzance Mining and Science School, founded in 1890, amalgamated with Camborne and Redruth Mining School to form the School of Metalliferous Mining at Camborne in 1910. This was later the Camborne School of Mines, which moved to the Combined Universities of Cornwall campus at Falmouth. Penzance railway station, the terminus of the West Cornwall Railway, opened on 11th March 1852. In August the line was extended to Truro and the link to Plymouth opened in May 1859. The line was sold to the Great Western Railway in 1866 and through passenger trains ran from London Paddington from March 1867. This allowed fresh produce to be carried to distant markets and made it easier for tourists to get to Penzance. Land was reclaimed beside Albert Pier in the 1930s to allow the railway station to be enlarged. The economy of Penzance suffered from the decline of fishing, mining and agriculture and now has a mixed economy of light industry, tourism and retail. Penzance was the birthplace of Sir Humphry Davy (1778–1829), President of the Royal Society, inventor of the process of electrolysis, the first person to isolate sodium and the first to discover nitrous oxide. With Michael Faraday, he discovered that diamonds are made of pure carbon. However, he is best known as the inventor of the miners' Davy Safety Lamp. John Divane VC (1823–88), born in Carrabane, Co Galway, was serving in 1st Battalion, 60th Rifles when he was awarded the VC for his actions on 10th September 1857 at Dehli during the Indian Mutiny. He died at 1 New Street, Penzance and is buried in Penzance Cemetery. The Admiral Benbow pub, home of a smuggling gang in the 1800s, is possibly the inspiration for *Treasure Island*'s Admiral Benbow Inn. Penzance was a peaceful resort town and the idea of it being overrun by pirates in Gilbert & Sullivan's 1879 comic opera, *The Pirates of Penzance*, was amusing to contemporaries.

and at St Winnow, Bracebridge Road, Four Oaks, Sutton Coldfield. Gladys was living at 21 Bracebridge Road at the time of her death there. They had three sons:

Holly Cottage, Birmingham Road, Sutton Coldfield.

- Antony 'Tim' John Waters (4th February 1926–18th April 2022), birth registered at Tamworth, Staffordshire. He attended The Leys School, Cambridge and was evacuated with it to Pitlochry, Perthshire, Scotland at the start of the autumn term in 1940. He boarded in one of the towers at Atholl Palace Hotel. Antony intended joining the Royal Engineers but his National Registration number classified him as a Bevin Boy, requiring him to either work in the mines or go to university. He studied mechanical engineering at Birmingham University (1st Class Honours), sponsored by the Royal Electrical and Mechanical Engineers. He joined his father as a consulting engineer and was a founding partner of AHS Waters & Partners in 1955. The firm joined Mott, Hay & Anderson (later Mott MacDonald) in 1985. He was a director of the combined firm until retirement but continued as a consultant until 1996. Antony married Ann Jewiss (born 18th October 1935), born at Surbiton, Surrey, on 10th October 1957 at Erdington, Warwickshire. They had three daughters, all registered at Birmingham – Sarah J Waters 1960, Lucy A Waters 1962 and Susannah Mary Waters 1964.
- Roger Norman Waters (20th October 1931–4th September 2018) married Pamela Jean Macferson (born 1938) in 1962 at Birmingham, where she was born. Roger died at Aspen Court Nursing Home, Taunton, Somerset. They had two children both registered at Sutton Coldfield – David Jamieson 'Jamie' Waters 1963 and Anne Marie Waters 1965.
- Andrew Arnold Waters (13th January 1937–11th September 2020), birth registered at Sutton Coldfield, married Diana Mathieson (born 1939) in 1963. Her parents were living at 43 Maxstoke Road, Sutton Coldfield in 1939. Diana and Andrew had two sons – John Macdonald Waters 1965, registered at Lichfield, Staffordshire, and Arnold Richard Waters 1968, registered at Sutton Coldfield.

Gladys' father, the Reverend Charles Daniel Barriball (5th March 1873–10th September 1953), born at Ridgeway, Devon, married Bessie Louisa née Bate (1870–30th December 1927), in 1899 at Launceston, Devon, where she was born. Charles was a United Methodist Minister by 1901, when they were living at 4 Penlee View, Penzance, Cornwall. By 1911 they had moved to Egloskerry, 91 Compton Road, Gravelly Hill, Birmingham, Warwickshire. Bessie died there. Charles married

Isabella Wilson Swan (9th December 1884–1946), born at Glasgow, Lanarkshire, on 29th September 1930 at Redland Grove Methodist Church, Redland, Bristol, Gloucestershire. He was living at Fernbank Road, Redland and she at the Royal Hotel, College Green at the time. They were living at 3 Welsford Road, Bristol in 1939. Her death was registered at Camelford, Cornwall. He was living at Trevean, Tintagel at the time of his death there. In addition to Gladys, Bessie and Charles had a son:

Redland Grove Methodist Church, Fairview Drive, Bristol was founded in 1876 and closed as a place of worship in 1941. The premises are now offices.

- Charles Newall Barriball (19th May 1904–7th November 1964), born at Aston, Warwickshire, married Kathleen May Brown (May 1899–23rd October 1978) in 1931 at Weymouth, Dorset. He was a commercial traveller for Cadburys in 1939, when they were living at 9 Weymouth Bay Avenue, Weymouth. He was also a volunteer in the Auxiliary Fire Service and she was with the Women's Voluntary Service (Soldiers, Sailors, Airmens and Families Association). Charles was living at 12 Weymouth Bay Avenue, Weymouth at the time of his death at the Chest Hospital, Southampton, Hampshire. Kathleen died at 12 Weymouth Bay Avenue. They had a son:

  - Charles Richard Barriball (28th January 1932–25th February 2012) married Jennifer R Maggs (born 1935) at Weymouth in 1956. They had two daughters – Amanda Barriball 1958 and Nicola Barriball 1960.

Arnold applied for service during the Second World War but was turned down because of his age. He was appointed Honorary Colonel of 127th Construction Regiment RE TA 1952–58. He attended a number of VC Reunions – the VC Garden Party at Buckingham Palace on 26th June 1920, the VC Dinner at the Royal Gallery of the House of Lords, London on 9th November 1929, the VC Centenary Celebrations at Hyde Park, London on 26th June 1956 and the third VC & GC Association Reunion at the Café Royal, London on 18th July 1962.

Arnold Waters died at his home at St Winnow, 22 Ladywood Road (the Grade II Listed building was destroyed by fire in 2015), Four Oaks, Sutton Coldfield, Warwickshire on 22nd January 1981. He was cremated at Sutton Coldfield Crematorium and his name is recorded in the Book of Remembrance there. His ashes were laid to rest in the Garden of Remembrance at All Saints Churchyard, Foley Road East, Streetly, Warwickshire. A memorial service was held on 17th February 1981 at Four Oaks Methodist Church, Sutton Coldfield. He left effects valued at £28,379. He is commemorated in a number of other places:

All Saints Churchyard, Foley Road East, Streetly, Warwickshire, where Arnold's ashes were laid to rest. (*Memorials to Valour*)

The For Valour board at the Royal Engineers Museum. Arnold's name is sixth from the bottom on the right side. (*Memorials to Valour*)

The Queen Elizabeth II Silver Jubilee Medal was created in 1977 to mark the 25th anniversary of the Queen's accession in the United Kingdom, Canada, Australia and New Zealand. Until 1977 the United Kingdom authorities decided on a total number for coronation and jubilee medals, which were then allocated to Empire, Dominion and Commonwealth countries. From 1977 the award was at the discretion of each national government – 30,000 in Britain, 1,507 in New Zealand, 6,870 in Australia and 30,000 in Canada.

- Named on the For Valour board at the Royal Engineers Museum, Gillingham, Kent.
- A Department for Communities and Local Government commemorative paving stone was dedicated at the War Memorial, Plymouth Hoe, Devon on 3rd November 2018.
- A painting of the Waters and Archibald VC action is held by the Royal Engineers Museum, Gillingham.
- Named on the Foundation Stone of Northgate Methodist Church, Barrack Street, Warwick, Warwickshire, which he laid on 3rd December 1960.

In addition to the VC, OBE, DSO and MC he was awarded the 1914–15 Star, British War Medal 1914–20, Victory Medal 1914–19 with Mentioned-in-Despatches Oakleaf, George VI Coronation Medal 1937, Elizabeth II Coronation Medal 1953 and Elizabeth II Silver Jubilee Medal 1977. The VC group was presented by Lady Waters to the Royal Engineers Museum soon after her husband's death and remains there.

43839 PRIVATE ALFRED ROBERT WILKINSON
1/5th Battalion, The Manchester Regiment

Alfred Wilkinson was born on 5th December 1896 at 27 Brideoake Street, Leigh, Lancashire. His father, also Alfred Robert Wilkinson (8th January 1866–19th January 1916), a yarn piecer for a cotton spinner, was born at Bedford, near Leigh. He was living with his mother and her husband, James Grimshaw, at Turner Street, Bedford, Leigh in 1881. By 1891 he was living with them at 35 Battersby Street, Bedford, by when he was a cotton spinner. He married Sarah née Swift (3rd March 1872–4th June 1949), also born at Bedford, near Leigh, in 1893 at Leigh. Alfred senior worked as a self-acting

Brideoake Street in Leigh, where Alfred was born. Leigh was historically in Lancashire. The three townships of Pennington, Westleigh and Bedford merged in 1875 to form the Leigh Local Board District. The town became an urban district in 1894 and a municipal borough in 1899. In 1972 it became part of the Metropolitan Borough of Wigan in Greater Manchester. Neolithic and Bronze Age remains have been found in the area. There is evidence for a Saxon presence around Leigh due to local place names such as Leigh, Tyldesley, Shakerley and Astley. In the 12th century Leigh was made up of six townships. Weekly markets were held and a cattle fair twice-yearly. During the English Civil War Leigh's population was divided in its support for the Royalists and the Parliamentarians. There was a battle in the town on 2nd December 1642, in which the Cavalier troops were routed. The economy of the area was mainly agricultural and dairy, particularly the production of Leigh cheese, until late in the 16th century, when spinning and weaving began to develop and grew in importance. There is a tradition in Leigh that it was a local man, Thomas Highs, who invented the spinning jenny and the water frame in the 1760s, but the latter was pirated by Richard Arkwright, who subsequently made a fortune from the patent. Whatever the truth, improvements to the spinning process led to the introduction of power looms in Manchester. This resulted in less work for the Leigh spinners and serious unemployment in the town. In 1827 silk weaving began in Leigh and several cotton mills were also built. On 14th August 1839 a mob gathered in Leigh in response to the Chartists' call for a strike at a time of high unemployment and cost of living. Workers threatened to burn down Hayes Mill and troops and special constables were brought in. The Riot Act was read, and the mob dispersed but reassembled later and there were many injuries in the fighting that followed. Eventually multi-storey spinning mills were built in Leigh and five survive today. By 1911 more than 6,000 people were employed in textiles. Drift mines had existed since the 12th century but in the second half of the 19th century deep mines were sunk. The last was Parsonage Colliery, one of the deepest in the country, with a depth of over 900m. There were a number of mining disasters in Leigh, including an explosion that caused the deaths of thirty-eight miners at Bedford Colliery on 13th August 1886. The Bridgewater Canal reached Leigh in 1795 and the Leigh Branch of the Leeds and Liverpool Canal in 1820. The Bolton and Leigh Railway opened for freight on 1st August 1828. It closed to passengers in March 1954 and later closed completely. In 1861 the London and North Western Railway built a branch on the Liverpool to Manchester Line via Leigh and Pennington. It closed in May 1969, leaving the town without a railway. Amongst the famous people associated with Leigh are:

- Roger Hunt MBE (20th July 1938 – 27th September 2021), born at nearby Glazebury and educated at Leigh Grammar School, played for Liverpool FC. He is the club's leading league goal scorer with 244 goals and was in the team that won two league titles and an FA Cup. In August 1964 he scored the first goal seen on the BBC's Match of the Day. In 1966 he was a member of the England team that won the World Cup, playing in all six England games and scoring three times.
- Georgie Fame (born 26th June 1943), the rhythm and blues singer and musician, was born in Leigh. He is the only British music act to have three number one hits from three Top 10 chart entries – *Yeh, Yeh* 1964, *Get Away* 1966 and *The Ballad of Bonnie and Clyde* 1967.
- Thomas Aspinall Burke (2nd March 1890 – 13th September 1969) attended St Joseph's School but, being six years older than Alfred, had probably left the School before he started in 1903. Thomas was from a poor family, who at one time lived at 7 Mather Lane, close to Alfred's grandmother. He left school aged twelve to work at Courtauld's Silk Mill before working in a coal mine from the age of fourteen. Thomas was first cornet player in Leigh Borough Brass Band, which competed at the Crystal Palace, where he won the silver medal for the best cornet soloist. He also sang in the church choir. When a local music society was performing the Messiah, the tenor fell ill and Thomas substituted, for which he received a good review. He attended the Manchester College of Music and in 1913 was contracted to study under Edgardo Levi at the Royal Academy of Music, whilst also carrying out singing engagements at various venues. Thomas went to Italy to continue his studies. In Milan he debuted as the Duke in *Rigoletto* but was recalled under conscription soon afterwards. He did not join the services but instead gave a series of charity concerts. In 1919 he debuted at the Royal Opera House, Covent Garden before the King as Rodolfo to Nellie Melba's Mimi in *La bohème*. He went on to sing various other parts at the Royal Opera House before commencing a North American career in 1920. He performed at the National Theatre in Washington DC and a number of other locations across the country, including Keith's Theatre, Washington DC 1923–27, where he often topped the bill. He returned to the Royal Opera House in operatic roles in 1927 but also continued with non-opera performances, including in Leigh in November 1927 and January 1928. In the late 1920s and early 1930s he also had a recording career and between 1932 and 1938 he appeared in four films. Thomas was married twice and had two daughters. One was the actress Patricia Burke (1917–2003). He is remembered in Leigh when the former Leigh Grand Theatre and Hippodrome was converted into a public house and was named after him.
- James Hilton (9th September 1900 – 20th December 1954) the novelist was born in Leigh. He is best known for *Lost Horizon* and *Goodbye, Mr Chips*.

Bedford is one of the three ancient townships that merged in 1875 to form the town of Leigh. It was a rural area with a small settlement where the road to Warrington branched from the Leigh to Manchester road. There were several inns near the junction and a corn mill was built by the Breaston Brook. Similar to Leigh, agriculture gave way to silk and cotton weaving and mining. Corn mills powered by steam were built at the canal basin to process wheat imported from the USA. Bedford Colliery was sunk after the London and North Western Railway line was built.

minder (cotton) at the Mather Lane Spinning Co, Brideoake Street, Leigh. They were living at 1 Brideoake Street by 1901 and had moved to 10 Rothsay Street, Bedford, Leigh by 1911. Sarah was a shopkeeper selling sweets and tobacco in 1939, living at 59 Bradshawgate, Leigh. She was living at 34 Allenby Street, Atherton, Lancashire at the time of her death there. Alfred junior had six siblings, all born at Leigh:

The Mather Lane Mills complex was built alongside the Bridgewater Canal. The No.2 Mill and its warehouse are Grade II listed. The Mather Lane Company was formed at a meeting in the Black Horse pub in Leigh. Thomas Smith was voted to the chair and Richard Thomas Marsh became its managing director until 1920. The mill became operational in 1878, a second opened in 1883 and a third in 1891 on the opposite (south) side of the Canal, seen here. Alfred Wilkinson VC also worked at No.3 Mill. In the 1920s the company was merged into Combined Egyptian Mills Ltd.

- John Wilkinson (4th October 1893–June 1894).
- Beatrice Wilkinson (10th October 1894–11th May 1989) was a cotton operative (weaver) in 1911. She married Joseph Harold Lythgoe (17th December 1896–26th January 1977) in 1922 at Leigh. He was a cotton operative living at 21 Mayfield Street, Atherton when he enlisted in the Royal Field Artillery on 20th May 1915 at Leigh (L24526). He joined at St Anne's on the Sea on 22nd May and was described as 5′ 10½″ tall. He joined 171st (Howitzer) Brigade RFA and transferred to 38th Divisional Ammunition Column on 8th October. The unit became 31st Divisional Ammunition Column on 20th December. He joined the Mediterranean Expeditionary Force on 11th January 1916 and transferred to 56th Brigade RFA in 13th and later 52nd Divisions on 8th February. He served in Mesopotamia from 18th February and was promoted lance bombardier. He served in Egypt 14th January–2nd April 1918 and transferred to France 3rd-11th April. On 28th June he reverted to the ranks at his own request. Posted to 52nd Divisional Ammunition Column on 11th September and was granted leave in Britain 1st-14th October. Joseph returned to Britain on 31st January 1919 and was posted to Prees Heath, near Whitchurch, Shropshire. He transferred to the Class Z Army Reserve on 2nd March 1919. He was a police sergeant in 1939, when they were living at 19 Towers Avenue, Bolton, Lancashire. They were living at 10 Westbourne Road, Knott End, Blackpool, Lancashire at the time of his death there. She was living at Nazareth House Care Home, Ashton Road, Lancaster, Lancashire at the time of her death there. They had a son, Francis Lythgoe (born 1st January 1925).

Bradshawgate, Leigh.

- Henry 'Harry' Wilkinson (11th March 1899–24th June 1977) served in the South Lancashire Regiment during the Great War. He was a wireless (radio) repairman at the time of the 1939 Register, living with his mother at 59 Bradshawgate, Leigh. Harry took over the confectionary shop on Leigh Road previously run by his brother Alfred. He married Anastasia Boardman (12th August 1910–1974), born at Leigh, on 16th October 1940. She was living with her parents at 23 Sidney Street, Leigh in 1911. In 1939 she was a shop assistant and tailoress, living with her parents at 39 Bond Street, Leigh. Harry was a poultry farmer in 1949 and they later moved to Lillisford Farm, Littlehempston, Totnes, Devon. They had four children all born at Leigh:
  - Josephine A Wilkinson (born 1941) married Sydney/Sidney D Higman (born 1943) in 1968, registered at Totnes. They had a daughter Charlotte Anne Higman in 1969. The marriage ended in divorce. Josephine married William R Donaldson (born 1953) registered at Torbay in April 1991.
  - Alan H Wilkinson (born 1943) married Margaret A Curwood (born 1949) in 1969, registered at Newton Abbot. They had three children – Sarah Elizabeth Wilkinson 1972, Isabella Margaret Wilkinson 1973 and Henry John Wilkinson 1981.
  - John P Wilkinson (born 1945) married Anne Backwell (born 1947) in 1968, registered at Torbay. They had two children – Daniel John Wilkinson 1970 and Mark John Wilkinson 1972.
  - Anthea E Wilkinson (born 1949) married Michael H Jewell (born 1948) in 1970, registered at Newton Abbot. They had two children – Nicola Helen Jewell 1975 and Paul Michael Jewell 1976.
- Alice Wilkinson (13th April 1901–July 1987) was manageress of the family sweet and tobacco shop in 1939, when she was living with her mother at 59 Bradshawgate, Leigh. Alice married Stanley Hawkins in 1942.
- Agnes Wilkinson (22nd December 1903–1981) was the manageress of a wallpaper store in 1939, when she was living with her mother at 59 Bradshawgate, Leigh. Agnes married Eric William McGowan (12th February 1899–11th July 1944), a bank cashier born at Wigan, Lancashire, at St Joseph's Catholic Church, Chapel Street, Leigh on 5th October 1942. He was living with his parents at Round Houses, Wigan in 1901, with his widowed father and siblings at 24 Wallace Lane, Wigan in 1911 and with his father at 34 Allenby Street, Atherton in 1939. Eric was still living there at the time of his death at High Carley Sanatorium, Ulverston, Lancashire. Agnes' death was registered at Garstang, Lancashire. Eric had married Margaret Hooton in 1920 at Wigan and they had two children:
  - James Ronald McGowan (20th February 1921–24th April 2013), born at Wigan and died at Worksop, Nottinghamshire.
  - Audrey Margaret McGowan (18th July 1923–21st January 1995), born at Bolton, Lancashire, married Arthur Birtwistle (25th March 1918–27th November 2013), born at Bury, in 1945. He was a student in 1939,

living with his parents at 49 Ramsey Grove, Bury. Audrey and Arthur lived at 16 Ash Grove, Bowdon, Altrincham, Cheshire. They had three children – Peter E Birtwistle 1947, Philip T Birtwistle 1951 and Patricia J Birtwistle 1959.

- Francis 'Frank' Wilkinson (4th January 1905–1st October 1976) married Agnes Holden (31st August 1905–22nd February 1998) in 1935. He was a motor body builder and wheelwright with his own coach-building business and Agnes was an elementary school teacher in 1939, when they were living at 127 Platt Fold Road, Leigh. He was living at 38 Arundel Road, Birkdale, Lancashire at the time of his death there. Her death was registered at Sefton North, Merseyside, Lancashire.

Alfred's paternal grandfather is not known but is understood to have been a Haythornthwaite. His paternal grandmother, Sophia Wilkinson (1845–1912), born at Bedford, near Leigh, married James Grimshaw (1844–1901) there in 1871. He was a cotton spinner and she was a silk weaver, living at 7 Back King Street, Pennington, Lancashire, in 1871, at Turner Street, Bedford, near Leigh by 1881, at 35 Battersby Street, Bedford by 1891 and at 34 Clifford Street, Leigh by 1901. Sophia was living with her daughter Sarah and family at 23 Mather Lane, Leigh in 1911. They had at least four children:

34 Clifford Street, Leigh. (*The Move Market*)

- Sarah Grimshaw (1872–1929), born at Atherton, Lancashire, was a silk winder in 1891. She married Francis Smith (1868–11th January 1921), a spinning overlooker, in 1895 at Leigh. They were living at 23 Mather Lane in 1911 and at 91 Bold Street, Leigh at the time of his death there. They had four children – Edward Smith (c.1896) was a cotton spinner piecer in 1911 living with his parents, Wilfred Smith (1899), Winifred Smith (c.1907) and Agnes Smith (c.1909).
- Margaret Grimshaw (1877–4th January 1946), born at Bedford, Leigh, was a cotton weaver in 1891. She married Henry Warhurst (1875-3rd September 1955), an iron dresser in an agricultural implement foundry, in 1896. They were living at 12 Hartley, Glazebury, Lancashire in 1911 and emigrated to Adelaide, South Australia in 1914. They were living at Glen Osmond, Adelaide in 1915. They had seven children:
    - Alfred Warhurst (1896–3rd December 1954), an iron turner in a brickmaking machine makers in 1911. He was a fitter and turner, apprenticed for four years to Sutcliffe & Speakman Engineers at Leigh, when he enlisted in the AIF

at Keswick, SA (3519A) on 26th July 1915. His place of birth was recorded incorrectly as Leeds, Lancashire. He was described as 5′ 9″ tall, weighing 137 lbs, with fresh complexion, blue eyes, brown hair and his religious denomination was Church of England. On 16th August he transferred to A Company, 3rd Depot Battalion and embarked aboard HMAT A24 *Benalla* at Adelaide on 27th October. He disembarked at Suez on 24th November, embarked at Alexandria on 29th March 1916 and disembarked at Marseille, France on 4th April. He was at 1st Australian Division Base Depot, Étaples when he was attached to the HQ 3rd Australian Brigade Band on 13th December. Alfred joined HQ 3rd Australian Brigade on 10th January 1917 and was taken on the strength of 10th Battalion on 28th November. He transferred to 11th Battalion on 12th December and was wounded on 1st January 1918. He was admitted to 2nd Australian Field Hospital and No.20 Casualty Clearing Station with appendicitis on 8th August and was transferred by Ambulance Train 23 to 2nd Canadian Stationary Hospital, Outreau. On 23rd August he was evacuated to Britain and was admitted to 2/1st Southern General Hospital, Dudley Road, Birmingham next day. He transferred to 1st Australian Auxiliary Hospital, Harefield, Middlesex on 17th September. He was discharged to No.2 Command Depot, Weymouth on 19th September and transferred to No.1 Command Depot, Sutton Veny on 15th October. Alfred was absent without leave from No.1 Command Depot from 11.59 p.m. on 10th January until 7.50 a.m. on 13th January for which he forfeited five days' pay. He embarked aboard HT *Armagh* at Devonport for return to Australia on 5th April 1919. At Durban, South Africa on 29th April he absented himself from guard mounting for which he was awarded fourteen days Field Punishment No.2 and forfeited fourteen days' pay. He disembarked in 4th Military District on 16th May and was discharged on 8th July. Alfred was an industrial trainee when he applied to the Repatriation Commission in Melbourne for assistance in August 1921. He had previously been granted £4/4/- for sustenance whilst awaiting training, £9/6/2 for tools and £158/9/4 for a course of mechanical drawing at the School of Mines, including sustenance during training, which commenced on 11th August 1919. He applied for further assistance for an extension of training and £12/14/- was granted for six months from 11th August 1921. Alfred married Margaret O'Donoghue (possible died 1946) at Adelaide in 1921. They had three children – Aileen Joyce Warhurst 1922, Beryl Dawn Warhurst 1925 and Audrey May Warhurst 1928.

- Eliza Warhurst (born and died 1898).
- Eliza Warhurst (born 1900) married Arthur Maudlock Taylor (died 1964) at Adelaide in 1920. They had four children – John David Taylor 1921, Trixie Maudlock Taylor 1923, Ellen Margaret Taylor 1925 and Joan Taylor 1927.

    - James Warhurst (1903–68) married Ellen Melville (1904–95) at Adelaide in 1928.
    - John Warhurst (born 1906).
    - Abel Warhurst (born 1908).
    - Joseph Edward 'Eddie' Warhurst (1914–94), born at Norwood, SA, married Eva Audrey Vowles (1919–93) in 1939.
- Elizabeth Grimshaw (born 1880) was a cotton winder living with her parents in 1901.
- James Grimshaw (3rd August 1884–7th July 1947) was a grocer's assistant living with his parents in 1901. He married Nancy Littler (19th August 1885–11th December 1976), born at Abram, Lancashire, in 1907 at Wigan, Lancashire. She was living with her parents at 32 Bickershaw Lane, Abram in 1891. James was a grocery manager at a cooperative society in 1911, when they were living at 149 Warrington Road, Culcheth and Glazebury, Lancashire. He was licensee of the Farmyard Hotel, Leigh Road, Hindley, Lancashire in 1939 and was also a part time Air Raid Precautions warden. He died at the Cross Keys Hotel, Bridge Street, Hindley. Nancy was living at 18 Langholme Street, Nelson, Lancashire at the time of her death there. They had three children:
    - Annie Maud Grimshaw (19th October 1907–13th December 1983), a schoolteacher, married John Hurst at Ince, Lancashire in 1939. Her death was registered at Blackpool, Lancashire.
    - Dora Grimshaw (13 February 1909–1996) was a schoolteacher in 1939.
    - Joseph Grimshaw (21st May 1914–1988).

His maternal grandfather, George Swift (1845–1919), an iron moulder born at Bolton, Lancashire, was living with his widowed grandmother at 9 Britain Street, Little Bolton in 1851. He married Ann née Eaton (1844–1920), a card room operative in a cotton mill born at Bedford, near Leigh, in 1867. They were living at 1 Back Foundry Street, Leigh in 1871, at 7 Chapmans Road, Bedford, near Leigh in

Bolton was historically in Lancashire. In 1838 it became a municipal borough and in 1889 a county borough. In 1974 it became part of the Metropolitan Borough of Bolton in Greater Manchester. Evidence of settlement dates back to the Bronze Age. Roman roads passed nearby and there was a Saxon settlement in the area of the parish church. A charter to hold a market was granted in 1251 by King Henry III and continued until the 18th century. In 1337 Flemish weavers settled in Bolton and introduced woollen cloth manufacturing. More Flemish weavers arrived in the 17th century producing fustian, a rough cloth of linen and cotton. The digging of sea coal

is recorded in 1374 and deep mining was developed in the 19th century. During the English Civil War the parliamentary garrison was attacked twice without success. However, on 28th May 1644 the Royalists, under the Earl of Derby, attacked again in what became known as the Bolton Massacre, in which 1,500 died, 700 were taken prisoner and the town was plundered. After the war, Lord Derby was executed for his part in the massacre outside Ye Olde Man & Scythe Inn on 15th October 1651. The town expanded with the introduction of textile manufacturing during the Industrial Revolution. Improvements to spinning technology by local inventors Richard Arkwright and Samuel Crompton led to a rapid growth of the textile industry in the 19th century. The availability of coal in the area and the advent of steam power led to the construction of large multi-storey mills. Important transport links contributed to the growth of the town and the textile industry. The Manchester Bolton & Bury Canal was constructed in 1791. The oldest railway in Lancashire, the Bolton and Leigh Railway, opened for goods traffic in 1828 and passengers in 1831. The railway connected Bolton to the Leeds and Liverpool Canal in Leigh, an important link to Liverpool for the import of cotton. By 1911 the textile industry in Bolton employed about 36,000 people. By 1929 there were 216 cotton mills, plus other associated works, making Bolton the largest centre for cotton spinning in the world. However, the industry declined after the Great War and by the 1980s cotton manufacture had virtually ceased. On the night of 26th September 1916, Zeppelin L21 dropped twenty-one bombs on the town, killing thirteen people and destroying six houses. Bolton Wanderers FC was formed in 1874 and has won the FA Cup four times. The club holds the dubious record of spending seventy-three seasons in the top division of the English League without ever being league champions. Amongst the famous people associated with Bolton are:

- Hylda Baker (1905–86) actress, comedienne and music hall star.
- Alan Ball (1945–2007) member of the England 1966 Football World Cup winning team.
- Daniel Francis Boyle (born 20th October 1956) director and producer, best known for his films *Trainspotting*, *Slumdog Millionaire* and *Yesterday*. He has won numerous BAFTA, Academy and Golden Globe awards. In 2012 he was the artistic director for the opening ceremony of the Summer Olympic Games in London.
- Fred Dibnah MBE (1938–2004), steeplejack, came to public notice when he repaired Bolton parish church. In 1978 he was filmed while making repairs to Bolton Town Hall. The BBC commissioned a documentary about his work on chimneys and his gentle philosophical outlook proved popular with viewers. In 1998 he presented a programme on Britain's industrial history and went on to present a number of series concerned with the Industrial Revolution.
- Amir Iqbal Khan (born 8th December 1986) professional boxer from 2005 to 2022, who held numerous world titles. He was the light-welterweight world championship 2009–12 and the Commonwealth lightweight champion 2007–08.
- Sir Jason Francis Kenny CBE (born 23rd March 1988) track cyclist and holder of the most Olympic gold medals. His wife, Laura, holds the same record on the female side. Together they are the most successful married couple in Summer Olympic history.
- Lever Brothers was founded in 1885 by William Hesketh Lever, 1st Viscount Leverhulme (1851–1925), and James Darcy Lever (1854–1916). Lever Brothers was one of several British companies that took an interest in the welfare of its employees. Its brands included Lifebuoy, Lux and Vim. The company merged with Margarine Unie in 1929 to form Unilever.
- Clive Myrie (born 25th August 1964) BBC journalist, newsreader and presenter.
- By coincidence two sea captains involved in the response to the *Titantic* disaster in April 1912 came from Bolton. Sir Arthur Henry Rostron KBE (1869–1940) worked for Cunard and was captain of RMS *Carpathia* when it rescued hundreds of survivors from RMS *Titanic*. He was widely praised for his efforts to reach *Titanic* before she sank and for his efficient preparations for and conduct of the rescue. He was awarded a US Congressional Gold Medal and in 1926 was appointed KBE. He rose to Commodore of the Cunard fleet and retired in 1931. By contrast, Stanley Phillip Lord (1877–1962) was captain of SS *Californian*, the closest ship to *Titanic* on the night that she sank. Lord was criticised for not rendering timely assistance despite being relatively close by. Two official inquiries were critical of Lord but did not recommend criminal charges.

1881, at 222 Chapel Street, Bedford by 1891 and at 45 Mill Lane, Culcheth, Leigh, Lancashire by 1901. In addition to Sarah, Ann had a daughter before she married and three other children with George:

- Mary Alice Eaton (3rd June 1867–30th August 1950), registered at birth as Heaton, later changed her name to Swift. She was a cotton weaver in 1881. She married Albert John Maggs (28th June 1864–5th August 1945), an iron fitter in an agricultural implement works born at Bristol, Gloucestershire, in 1890. They were living at 18 Severn Street, Leigh in 1911 and at 135 Walmesley Road, Leigh in 1939, where they both subsequently died. They had eleven children:
    - Albert George Maggs (10th August 1890–5th June 1971) was an iron fitter in an agricultural implement works in 1911, living with his parents. He married Nancy Talbot (1892–1965) in 1913 and they had four children – Edna A Maggs 1913, Minnie Maggs 1915, Harold Maggs 1919 and Albert J Maggs 1923.
    - Frances Florence Maggs (2nd March 1892–19th December 1962) was a cotton cloth weaver living with her parents in 1911 and a silk weaver in 1939.
    - Walter John Maggs (18th October 1893–1973) was a moulder in an agricultural implement works in 1911, living with his parents. He married Florence Wood (1895–1966) in 1916. They had a son, Normans S Maggs, in 1917.
    - Frederick James Maggs (8th August 1895–1969) was a cotton spinner piecer in 1911, living with his parents. He married Annie Collier (9th February 1898–1971) in 1915 and they had two children – Doris Maggs 1915 and Ernest W Maggs 1937.
    - Wilfred Ethelbert Maggs (21st October 1897–30th March 1976) was a cotton spinner piecer in 1911, living with his parents. He married Annie Agar (9th February 1898–1971) in 1923.
    - Clifford Sylvester Maggs (1900–04).
    - Beatrice May Maggs (1902–03).
    - Edna Alice Maggs (1903–04).
    - Clifford Sylvester Maggs (10th January 1905–8th August 1985) married Lizzie Holdbrook (9th October 1904–1986) in 1928.
    - Sydney Cyril Maggs (25th April 1907–31st January 1994) married Nellie Goodall (born 1909) in 1931. They had a son, Albert J Maggs, later that year.
    - Norman Stanley Maggs (1909–15).
- John Swift (1874–1953), an operative cotton spinner, married Zoa Ann Tyldesley (1874–1957) in 1898 at Leigh. She was living with her parents at 7 Mather Lane, Bedford in 1881. By 1891 she was a cotton weaver living with her widowed father and siblings at 13 Mather Lane. John and Zoa were living at 135 Sandy Lane, Lowton, Lancashire in 1911. They had a daughter, Margaret Doris Swift (22nd July 1898–1976).

- Elizabeth Ann Swift (20th March 1877–1951) married Ellis Clare (2nd March 1875–28th April 1955) in 1903. He was a labourer in an agricultural implement foundry works and Elizabeth was a beer seller in 1911, when they were living at 222 Chapel Street, Leigh. Ellis was the licensee of the Royal Oak Inn, Leigh in 1939. They had two children:
    - Ellis Clare (27th May 1910–1964) was a domestic gasfitter in 1939 living with his parents. He married Doris Leonard in 1958.
    - George Swift Clare (24th August 1912–27th May 1966) was a chemical engineer specialist in solvent recovery plants using activated carbon. He was also a member of the AFS in 1939 living with his parents. He married Helen Clare (sic) in 1949.
- Martha Alice Swift (12th August 1881–15th March 1964), a silk weaver, married Anthony Ward (6th January 1878–5th December 1952) in 1904. He was a mechanic in a cotton mill in 1911, when they were living at 25 Bedford Square, Leigh. He was a grocer and cooked meals dealer in 1939, when they were living at 5 Wren Street, Coventry, Warwickshire. They were still living there at the time of his death at The Coventry and Warwickshire Hospital, Keresley and her death at Gulson Hospital, Coventry. They had a son:
    - Clifford Anthony Ward (23rd March 1905–January 1987) married Mary M Eld (born 10th October 1904) in 1933. He was an assistant technical engineer and she was a private secretary to the managing director of Austin Engineering in 1939, when they were living at 353 Green Lane, Warwick.

Alfred was educated at St Joseph's Roman Catholic Day School, Leigh and the Junior School, Leigh 1st May 1903–3rd December 1909. He worked as a piecer at the Mather Lane Spinning Company's No.3 Mill, Leigh and was described as a cotton operative little piecer scavenger in the 1911 Census. He was a member of the St Joseph's Boys' and Young Mens' Sodality at the church.

Alfred enlisted in 2/5th Battalion, The Manchester Regiment at Atherton, Manchester, Lancashire on 14th December 1914 (3120), giving his age as eighteen years and eleven months. He was 5′ 7½″ tall. On 27th July 1916 he transferred to 18th Battalion (43839) and went to France on 29th July 1916. He was admitted to 98th Field Ambulance and No.43 Casualty Clearing Station, Warlencourt with a sprained ankle on 8th November and was transferred to 16th General Hospital, Étaples on 13th November. Alfred rejoined the Battalion on 23rd December and took part in the Battle of Arras in April 1917 and the Third Battle of Ypres. The

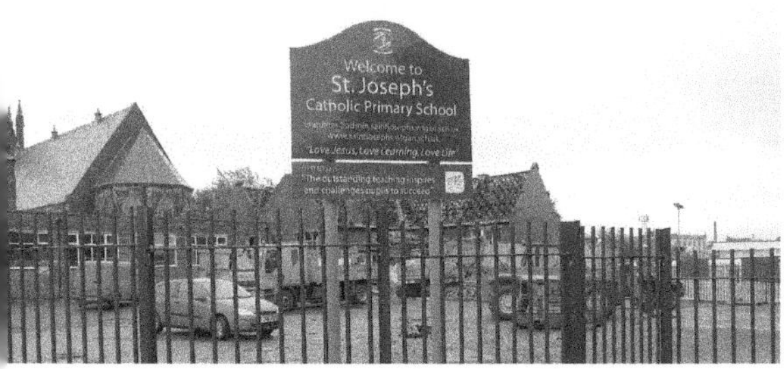

St Joseph's Roman Catholic Day School (now St Joseph's Catholic Primary School) with St Joseph's Church behind.

18th Battalion was disbanded on 20th February 1918 and it is believed that Alfred transferred to 1/5th Manchester about that time. **Awarded the VC for his actions at Marou, near Solesmes, France on 20th October 1918, LG 6th January 1919.** He wrote to his mother after hearing of the award of the VC:

> *Dear Mother, I have got some good news for you this time. It is quite true about my decoration. I have been awarded the V.C. I feel too glad to write now, as I have just had it* (the ribbon) *pinned on my breast by my officer. He is more proud of me than I am, nearly. I had a telegram from the Colonel yesterday to congratulate me. I will be alright now, for I shall be coming home on a month's leave as soon as I get back to the Battalion, and I will get £50 a year for life now. This is all now, so I will wish you a Merry Christmas and a Happy New Year.'*

Alfred was promoted lance corporal and was granted fourteen days special leave at home from 8th February 1919. This was extended by the War Office to 25th February and later to 1st March. At Leigh railway station he was met by his family, the Mayor and many other people. He was driven in an open landau to the Town Hall, escorted by mounted and foot police, military guards from Leigh prisoner-of-war camp, Boy Scouts, St John's brass band and discharged soldiers and sailors. At the reception he was presented with an illuminated address, 500 War Savings certificates and £50 in cash. Subsequently he received other gifts, including a gold watch from members of St Joseph's Boys' and Young Men's Sodality, an illuminated address from the directors of the Mather Lane Spinning Company and £442/10/6 raised by public subscription. The VC was presented by the King in the ballroom at Buckingham Palace on 22nd February.

SS *Sicilian* (6,224 tons) was built for the Allan Line by Workman, Clark & Co Ltd in Belfast and was launched in August 1899. That November she was chartered as a transport for the Boer War. Her first commercial voyage was from Liverpool, Lancashire to Portland, Maine, USA. There were berths for fifty first, 150 second and 400 third class passengers. A refit in 1906 increased passenger accommodation to 1,180 berths and a second refit in 1908 increased her tonnage to 7,328 tons. The Allan Line was taken over by Canadian Pacific Line in 1917. *Sicilian* was renamed *Bruton* in 1923 and was converted to carry freight. She was scrapped in Italy in 1925.

Alfred rejoined his unit in Belgium. On 28th March, the cadre of 1/5th Manchester left Charleroi with six officers and fifty other ranks. They arrived at Antwerp next day in a snowstorm and spent the night in a rest camp. On 1st April they embarked aboard SS *Sicilian* and anchored off the Hook of Holland for the night because transports were not allowed to pass

The Victory Parade on 19th July 1919 followed a route of over eleven kilometres through central London. On the Thames warships formed a Naval Pageant and in Hyde Park there was a variety of festivities, together with numerous other events around the country. However, the organisation of the event did not have a smooth ride. Some objected to it because of the huge sacrifices that had been made to achieve the victory. The date of the Parade was constantly in doubt because it was not possible to predict when the signing of the peace with Germany would happen. The organisation committee was chaired by Lord Curzon, a member of the War Cabinet, who had created the vast and spectacular Delhi Durbar of 1903. The committee included the Home Secretary, First Commissioner of Work, and representatives of the Admiralty, War Office and Colonial Office but not the ex-service organisations. On 28th June, the Treaty of Versailles was signed, and the War Cabinet met two days later with 'Peace Celebrations' at the top of the agenda. The parade route commenced at the Albert Gate to Hyde Park, turned south to cross the river and wound through London south of the Thames. It then crossed Westminster Bridge, went past Parliament and Big Ben and turned into Whitehall, where the temporary Cenotaph had just been unveiled. On into Trafalgar Square and onto the Mall, past the Victoria Memorial, where the King and royal party took the salute, then along Constitution Hill to finish back in Hyde Park. Veterans who were too disabled to march were given prime spots at the front of the crowds, while a large part of the seating on Constitution Hill was reserved for the 'mothers, widows and children of the soldiers who never returned'. The parade of 20,000 men and women began at 10.00 a.m. and was led off by US General Pershing on a great brown horse. In Whitehall every contingent saluted the Cenotaph. There were contingents from Belgium, China, Czecho-Slavs, France, including Marshal Foch on a black charger, Greece, Italy, Japan, Poland, Portugal, Rumania, Serbia and Siam. Then followed the British contingents, led by Admiral Beatty and of all ranks from the Royal Navy plus naval nurses, WRNSs and members of the mercantile marine. Field Marshal Haig led the soldiers with many of his generals, ahead of officers and men of the 'Old Contemptibles'. They were followed by groups from every part of the British Army – Guards, Regulars, Territorials and Yeomanry, including artillery with their guns, engineers, infantry and machine-gunners. Then it was the turn of the Dominions, the Labour Corps, Women's Legion, doctors, nurses, VADs, chaplains, and WAACs. The parade was completed by the youngest service, the Royal Air Force. The procession took more than two hours to pass each point along the route. The celebrations culminated in a huge night-time firework display of eighty-four spectacular set-pieces. A line of bonfires and beacons was lit from the Channel to the Cromarty Firth.

through the mine-swept passage in the dark. They disembarked at Southampton on 3rd April and travelled by train to Oswestry, where transport and equipment were handed in. On 7th April the cadre, complete with the Colours, arrived at Wigan to be welcomed by the Mayor and townspeople. Many old comrades were present, as were members of the Boy Scouts and the Church Lads Brigade. The cadre marched through the town and, following a hot-pot meal at Wigan drill hall, the soldiers dispersed to their homes and families.

Alfred was discharged on 19th July 1919 after being part of the Battalion Colour Party that took part in the Victory Parade that day. The other members of the Colour Party were Captain Colin Philip Brown, Lieutenant Holmes and RQMS William Henry Christy DCM. Alfred returned to work with the Leigh Operating Spinners Association at the Mather Lane Spinning Company. In the early 1930s he

Looking along Plank Lane towards Bickershaw Colliery from the canal bank.

Bickershaw Colliery necessitated the sinking of deep shafts to access the coal. However, the proximity to the Leeds and Liverpool Canal at Plank Lane made distribution relatively easy. The first shaft was sunk in 1830. A tramway connected the pit to the canal and was used to transport coal until 1972 when road transport took over. In 1872 work started on two new shafts – No.1 (447m) and No.2 (450m) at Plank Lane beside the canal. In 1877 No.3 and No.4 (both 630m) were sunk and No.5 was completed before the Great War. On 10th October 1932 a mine-shaft elevator carrying twenty people fell, killing all but one. Bickershaw and Abram Collieries amalgamated in 1933 but operations at the Abram Pits ceased in the late 1930s, except for Abram Nos.1 and 2, which were taken over by Albert Longworth, and were known as Albert Pit. It closed in 1965. Opencast mining extracted from the area previously worked by Abram No.1 and 2 until 1985. Following the consolidation of Bickershaw and Abram, Nos.3 and 4 shafts were deepened to 712m and 720m respectively. The advent of the National Coal Board led to a reorganisation of the pits in the area. No.5 shaft was abandoned in 1950 and the following year two horizontal tunnels were driven 2,510m southwards from Nos.3 and 4 shafts. In 1960 these tunnels intersected the Crombouke seam, allowing two more faces to be opened for production. Two similar tunnels were driven 1,400m westwards to access to White and Black seam. In 1967 all production and coal winding was concentrated in Nos.3 and 4 shafts, leaving Nos.1 and 2 shafts for ventilation. In 1973 development started to link Bickershaw underground with Parsonage and Golborne Collieries, including the installation of eleven kilometres of underground conveyor belt to consolidate coal extraction to the surface at Bickershaw. Parsonage became fully integrated with Bickershaw in January 1983 with an underground workforce of 550 men. The changes resulted in the ability to process one million tons of coal annually. Ninety percent went for electricity generation and a rapid loading system at Bickershaw enabled a train of forty-five wagons, each holding thirty tons, to be loaded in less than ninety minutes. Golborne Colliery closed in 1989 and Bickershaw and Parsonage Collieries in March 1992. The derelict site became part of the National Coalfields Programme in 1996 and was included in the Government's Carbon Challenge initiative, since when it has been redeveloped for housing, a marina and a nature reserve.

opened a tobacconist and sweet shop run by his wife on Leigh Road. Just before the Second World War he started working as a clerk in the mine surveyor's laboratory at Bickershaw Colliery, Planks Lane, Leigh.

Alfred Wilkinson married Grace Davies (7th April 1906–July 2001), born at Wem, Shropshire, on 22nd October 1932 at the Church of the Twelve Apostles, Westleigh, Lancashire. She was living at 2 Hazel Grove, Leigh at the time. Alfred's sister, Alice, was a bridesmaid and his brother, Henry, was the best man. They honeymooned at Blackpool, Lancashire. They were living at 34 Leigh Road, Leigh in 1939, by when she was a sweet and tobacco shopkeeper. They were living at 113 Etherstone Street, Leigh at the time of Alfred's death. They had two children born at Leigh:

- Henry Joseph Wilkinson (1933–4th January 2004), married Mary Catherine Frawley (23rd April 1920–2nd January 1997) in 1953. She was a clerk at a grocery

Wem was an Iron Age settlement before the Roman conquest. Later it was an Anglo-Saxon estate and Norman town with a motte and bailey castle. The town is recorded in the Domesday Book. It was burned by Welsh rebels in 1412. Although it is believed that there was a market previously, King John granted a charter in 1202 for a Sunday market. This was revised in 1351 to a Thursday, which remains Wem's market day. The manor was held by some great baronial families, including the Earls of Arundel and Lords Dacre, Bradford and Barnard, although they were not resident after the 14th century. Traditionally the economy was based on agriculture and forestry. During the English Civil War a force of just forty Parliamentarians held off a vastly superior Royalist force, under Lord Capel, inflicting heavy casualties upon them. The defences of Wem were not complete and local women in red coats positioning themselves to mislead the Royalists, who were so confident that they only attacked one side of the town – 'The women of Wem and a few musketeers, Beat the Lord Capel and all his Cavaliers'. On 3rd March 1677 a great fire destroyed many of the wooden buildings in the town. Judge Jeffreys (1645–89), known for his willingness to impose capital punishment after the Monmouth Rebellion, had his seat at Lowe Hall, Wem and in 1685 he was made Baron Jeffreys of Wem. The town was served by two stagecoaches and in 1858 the Crewe and Shrewsbury Railway arrived. The sweet pea was first cultivated commercially in the town as Eckford Sweet Pea, after its creator, Henry Eckford, who set up in Wem in 1888. During the Second World War, Anna Essinger (1879–1960), a German Jew, evacuated her boarding school from Kent to Trench Hall, near Wem. The Americans had a storage facility at Aston Park from December 1942, which was later converted into a prisoner of war camp. Wem was the childhood home of the essayist and critic, William Hazlitt (1778–1830).

The Church of the Twelve Apostles, Westleigh. The population grew rapidly during the late 19th century due to an influx of people working in the coalmine and cotton mills, many of whom were Irish Catholics. A school at Twelve Apostles opened in November 1879 and was used for Mass at weekends, until a corrugated iron church was built. The foundation stone for the present church was laid in 1927 and it opened in 1929. The infant school moved to a new site in 1976 and in 1978 the juniors followed. The final mass at the Church of the Twelve Apostles was held on 30th August 2019.

warehouse in 1939, living with her parents at 15 Mill Lane, Leigh. They had a son, James Wilkinson, in 1958.

- Grace Mary Wilkinson (2nd May 1936–June 1999) married Harold Glover (18th December 1933–5th January 2013) in 1955. They had a daughter, Jacqueline M Glover, in 1958. Grace married John Bergin in 1990.

Grace's father, Thomas Forgham Davies (1869–July 1907), a master saddler born at Wem, near Shrewsbury, Shropshire, married Katherine 'Kate' née Box (1866–1955), born at Dudley, Staffordshire, on 20th July 1890 at Wem. She was a domestic

25 Bell Vue Road, Shrewsbury, where Grace's mother was working as a domestic nurse in 1881. (*The Move Market*)

There is still a shop at 34 Leigh Road, Leigh, although the type of commercial activity there seems to change fairly regularly. (*MoveHut*)

nurse in 1881 at the home of the Bowdler family at 25 Bell Vue Road, Shrewsbury. When they married she was registered as Catherine. They were living at 16 Noble Street, Wem in 1891 and at 12 Barnard Street, Wem in 1901. She was living with her children, Charles, Marjorie and Grace, at 16 Shrewsbury Street, Hodnet, Shropshire in 1911 and at 55 Henrietta Street, Leigh in 1917. According to the 1911 Census, in addition to Grace they had eight other children, including:

- Gertrude Helena Davies (27th June 1891–1977) married Charles Henry Powis (18th December 1884–1963), birth registered at Atcham, Shropshire, in 1917. He was a road foreman in 1939, when they were living at 3 Brooklyn Avenue, Littleborough, Lancashire.
- Charles Forgham Davies (31st March 1893–12th October 1967) was a domestic groom in 1911, living with his mother. He married Edith Maud Mitchell (15th December 1895–17th August 1993) in 1923. She was living with her parents at 5 Sephton Street, Leigh in 1901. By 1911 she was an apprentice to a stationary salesman, living with her parents at 2 Brook Villas, Henrietta Street, Leigh. Charles was a traveller in wine and spirits in 1939, when they were living at 4 Brooklands Avenue, Leigh. They were still living there at the time of his death. She was living at 40 Warren Drive, Deganwy, Gwynedd, North Wales at the time of her death there. They had two children:
    - Kathleen Ann Davies (1st April 1926–2005).
    - Frank Forgham Davies (19th January 1928–5th December 1980) was living at 101 Sydney Avenue, Leigh when he died.
- Francis Thomas Davies (2nd June 1894–1968) married Martha Green (31st July 1894), born at Loppington, Shropshire, in 1914 at Wem. She was living with her

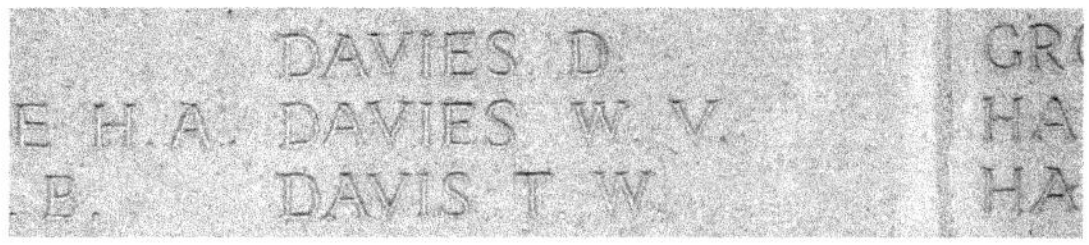

William Victor Davies' name on the Arras Memorial.

parents at Noneley Village, Loppington in 1901 and was a domestic servant at Noneley in 1911. Francis was a cowman on a farm in 1939, when they were living at 2 Hall Cottages, Wem. They had four children:
    - Sidney Davies (1st February 1916).
    - Katherine G Davies (1919).
    - Joan Evelyn Davies (9th September 1926) married John J Edwards in 1948, registered at Whitchurch.
    - Francis C Davies (1928).
- Jessie Davies (born 25th October 1895) was a housemaid to Edward Augustus Harbord at 15 Titchfield Terrace, Regent's Park, London in 1911.
- William Victor Davies (28th April 1897–28th April 1917) was living in London when he enlisted at Chelsea in 17th Middlesex (F/1169). He was killed in action and his body was never recovered (Arras Memorial Bay 7).
- Doris Kate Davies (14th February 1900–9th November 1974) married Alfred Clarence Bessant (28th April 1900–9th January 1968), born at Mynyddislwyn, Monmouthshire, on 9th October 1927 at St Barnabas, Shore, Lancashire. He was the headmaster of an elementary school in 1939, when they were living at 20 Greenway Close, Sale, Cheshire. They were living at 7 Braemar Avenue, Thornton-Cleveleys, Lancashire at the time of his death there. She was living at 40 Grosvenor House, Grosvenor Square, Sale at the time of her death there. They had two children:
    - Pauline K Bessant (1930) married John F Brady in 1951 registered at Bucklow. They had three children – Philip D Brady 1953, Kathryn L Brady 1958 and Andrew J Brady 1959.
    - Glynne Bessant (1933–24th June 1955) was serving as a lance corporal in 1st Somerset Light Infantry (23084650) when he died on active service during the Malayan Emergency at Kuala Lumpur, Malaysia (Kuala Lumpur (Cheras Road) Civil Cemetery – Row 22, Grave 1164).
- Margery Ella Davies (6th December 1903–8th April 1972) married Fred Lee (13th October 1902–2nd April 1978), a company secretary born at Atherton, Lancashire, at Christ Church, Pennington, Lancashire on 15th February 1928. She was living at 55 Henrietta Street, Leigh and he at 39 Crawford Avenue, Tyldersley at the time. He was a chief clerk at a cotton mill in 1939, when they were living at 259 New Brook Road, Westhoughton, Lancashire. Her death was

registered at Bucklow, Cheshire. He was living at 15 Ashlawn Drive, Boston, Lincolnshire at the time of his death there. They had two daughters – Joan C Lee (1928) and Sheila P Davies (4th July 1932).

Glynne Bessant's grave in Kuala Lumpur (Cheras Road) Civil Cemetery, Malaysia. The Cemetery also contains the grave of Sir Henry Gurney, High Commissioner for Federated Malaya, who was assassinated in 1951. There are 137 Commonwealth burials from 1939–45 and more than 600 non world war burials of servicemen and dependants, many from the Malayan Emergency. (*Roll of Honour*)

Alfred attended two VC reunions – the VC Garden Party at Buckingham Palace on 26th June 1920 and the VC Dinner at the Royal Gallery of the House of Lords, London on 9th November 1929. His pay was docked when he attended the latter. However, the local press learned of this and his employers were quick to reimburse him. Alfred went to Lourdes, France, as part of an ex-servicemen's pilgrimage on 19th September 1934. Whilst there an Irishman from Sligo named Carroll died suddenly and his pall bearers were seven VCs, including Alfred. The six other VCs were John Caffrey, Robert Downie, Martin Moffatt, Michael O'Leary, John O'Neill and John Ormsby. Alfred was presented to the King and Queen when they visited Leigh in May 1938.

Alfred was a Special Constable in the Leigh Constabulary at the time of the 1939 Register. He joined the Local Defence Volunteers/Home Guard after the outbreak of the Second World War. On 17th October 1940 he received confirmation of his appointment to a commission in the Pioneer Corps.

The following day he went to work at Bickershaw Colliery and later complained to a colleague that he was feeling unwell. He took a seat in his office at the Surveyor's Laboratory and was found dead there at lunchtime. A sparrow had become lodged in a ventilation pipe and this may have contributed to his death by carbon monoxide poisoning. A large congregation attended a requiem mass at St Joseph's Church and the route to the cemetery was lined by crowds of people. At the head of the

St Joseph's Church is Grade II listed. After the Reformation several families in Leigh kept the Catholic faith, with Mass being heard in secret at various locations. A chapel was built in 1778 and a school followed in the 1830s. The chapel was replaced by St Joseph's Church in 1855 and the tower was completed in 1878.

procession was former CSM Gill, who had been Alfred's sergeant major during the VC action. Alfred was buried with full military honours provided by the Home Guard and British Legion in the family plot at Leigh Borough Cemetery (R/C 1-U-99). The headstone fell into disrepair until veteran Bert Paxford, on behalf of the Manchester Regiment Old Comrade's Association, called on Wigan Council to restore the grave, which was done at a cost of £250. Alfred is commemorated in a number of other places:

The restored family gravestone in Leigh Borough Cemetery.

- Leigh, Lancashire
    - Wilkinson Park Drive, Pennington Wharf on the site of the former Bickershaw Colliery.
    - A Department for Communities and Local Government commemorative paving stone was dedicated at Pennington Wharf Community Centre, Plank Lane on 26th October 2018.
    - Memorial plaque and framed photograph in the Town Hall unveiled on 27th January 2005.
    - Life-size statue by Andrew Burgess in the centre of the circular Wilkinson Park Drive at Pennington Wharf, unveiled on 26th October 2018.
    - A street mural in Twist Lane, which was completed by Remembrance Sunday on 13th November 2021.
- Named in the Book of Remembrance of the Manchester and King's Regiments in Manchester Cathedral.
- Memorial Plaque at Wigan Town Hall, Lancashire,

The statue at Pennington Wharf.

In addition to the VC he was awarded the British War Medal 1914–20, Victory Medal 1914–19 and George VI Coronation

The British War Medal was instituted on 26th July 1919 for all ranks who served for twenty-eight days in an operational theatre between 5th August 1914 and 11th November 1918, or who died on active service before completing twenty-eight days. Eligibility was extended in 1919–20 to mine-clearing at sea and operations in North and South Russia, eastern Baltic, Siberia, Black Sea and Caspian Sea. Many veterans were awarded the 1914–15 Star, British War Medal and Victory Medal. They became known as Pip, Squeak and Wilfred after a strip cartoon published in the *Daily Mirror* from 1919 to 1956.

The King George VI Coronation Medal was awarded to the Royal Family, selected officers of state, officials, servants of the Royal Household, ministers, government and local government officials, mayors, public servants, members of the armed forces and police in Britain, the colonies and Dominions. A total of 90,279 medals were awarded.

Medal 1937. The VC was listed for £1,850 by JB Hayward in March 1973. His medal group was sold to Lord Ashcroft for £110,000 at a Dix Noonan Webb auction on 29th June 2006. The VC is held by the Michael Ashcroft Trust, the holding institution for the Lord Ashcroft Victoria Cross Collection and is displayed in the Imperial War Museum's Lord Ashcroft Gallery.

Grace married Thomas Crusham (24th January 1909–1985) in 1951. He died at Leigh and she in Denbighshire North, Clwyd, Wales. Thomas had married Doris Prescott (born 21st February 1912) in 1936 at Leigh. He was a packer for a cable manufacturer in 1939, when they were living at her mother's home at 3 Poplar Street, Leigh. Her mother was an office cleaner at the time of the 1939 Register. The marriage ended in divorce.

Reflections

The land forces of the BEF on the Western Front were awarded 492 VCs (including Noel Chavasse twice), of which 135 were posthumous. The first is considered to be Maurice Dease on 23rd August 1914 (LG 16th November 1914), in the first major clash between British and German forces. The last was to Brett Cloutman on 6th November 1918 (LG 31st January 1919), five days before hostilities ended.

In the four years and eighty days between those two events the nature of warfare changed considerably. In the early days of the conflict operations were mobile and large distances were covered by the opposing forces. Then the grip of technology was felt as a combination of entrenchments, barbed wire, machine guns and artillery saw defence in the ascendency. A whole new style of combat then evolved, trench warfare, aspects of which harked back to the siege warfare of the Middle Ages. Increasingly sophisticated lines of defence were developed, culminating in the German Hindenburg and other lines. Gradually means of overcoming these immensely strong defences were developed – gas, tanks, new infantry weapons, improved communications, new tactics and, in particular, the spectacular advances made in the control and accuracy of artillery fire. In 1914 the field artillery operated much as it had at Waterloo a century earlier, albeit with breach loaders and increased range. In general, only targets that could be seen were engaged. Heavier guns were introduced, as were technological and scientific developments, including the measurement of barrel wear and atmospheric conditions, flash spotting, sound ranging, improved survey and predicted fire.

The high-water mark of the defensive came in 1917. Thereafter the offensive gradually took over. By November 1918 the BEF had refined the all-arms battle to devastating effect. The lessons of the final Hundred Days were not lost on the defeated German Army, which developed those techniques and equipment into the Blitzkrieg unleashed in 1939–41.

The BEF was not organised to fight a major continental war in 1914. Its infantry divisional structure had been developed to fight colonial wars and resulted from the reforms introduced after the Second Boer War. It was a very good organisation for its purpose and the regular divisions were well equipped and trained. With some developments the divisional organisation served the Army well throughout the conflict. However, there were weaknesses, particularly the lack of heavy artillery, without which deeply entrenched positions could not be reduced. This and other capability gaps took time to fill. By the end of the war each division had lost three infantry battalions (a manpower saving measure rather than a desirable tactical change) but gained a pioneer battalion to undertake the vast amount of labouring tasks. The divisional artillery was reduced from seventy-six guns to forty-eight. However, it would invariably be reinforced by army field brigades and heavy artillery assets for specific operations. As a result, the artillery firepower available to the division was increased, although the number of embedded artillery pieces was reduced. Despite these reductions, overall the division's organic firepower increased enormously. By 1918 there were 336 Lewis guns where none had existed in 1914. An extra forty Vickers machine guns were added to the twenty-four on the 1914 establishment. There were also thirty-six mortars, mainly Stokes 3″ mortars.

Tactically the infantry had also come a long way. By 1917 the sixteen platoons in each infantry battalion were able to operate independently to some extent, with their own integral supporting firepower of Lewis guns, rifle grenades and bombers.

The expansion of the BEF resulted in a tenfold increase in the size of the land forces. Clearly this caused massive supply issues for weapons, ammunition and other equipment in the early years. There was also a dearth of experience on which to build the new armies, not only in Britain but across the Dominions. There was plenty of manpower, but where were the generals, officers and NCOs to be found? The volunteers had to learn their craft 'on the job', at the same time as coming to terms with the constantly changing tactical and technological conditions. It has been compared to changing the wheels on an express train in mid journey. It should, therefore, not be a great surprise that gallantry often had to try to make up for skill, expertise and equipment deficiencies.

While researching the various VC actions, it proved quite difficult in some early actions to locate precise locations. Maps were poor and generally large scale (1:40,000 and upwards). Units were moving rapidly and record keeping in many cases was rudimentary. During 1915 trench maps appeared with outstanding accuracy and detail. Tracing VC actions until the middle of 1918 then became relatively simple, although there were sometimes inevitably discrepancies between accounts. The brigade HQ war diaries were usually the best kept and have a wider perspective. They generally contain operation orders, marked maps and post-operation reports, as well as the usual minute by minute narrative of events. Brigade diaries also often contain the battalion reports. Accessing divisional, and sometimes corps and army, level archives was often necessary to gain better granularity of information. However, much of this was swept away in 1918, particularly in the Hundred Days, when the trench map coverage was left behind and the speed of movement once again resulted in reduced detail about where events took place.

The casualties (killed, died of wounds, wounded, prisoners or missing) for British forces on the Western Front are known month by month. However, finding accurate monthly casualty figures for Dominion and Empire forces has proved more difficult. What follows is therefore based upon the British casualties and VCs only.

Total casualties on the Western Front were 2,706,154 and 358 VCs were awarded to land forces there. On average there were 52,041 casualties and 6.9 VCs per month, which equates to one VC for every 7,542 casualties. At **Table 1** (at the end) are the monthly casualties and VCs awarded, followed in brackets by the number of casualties per VC. Huge disparities are apparent between months. No VCs were awarded in seven of the months. The lowest monthly casualty total was 6,542 in January 1915. The highest monthly casualty total was 196,081 in July 1916. The average monthly casualty rate increased every year. However, the number of VCs and casualties per award did not rise commensurately. In 1914 the casualty to VC ratio was relatively low at 2,453 but rose to 12,182 by 1916, before reducing again. However, by the end of the war it still stood at 7,037, almost thrice the figure for 1914:

1914–19,131–7.8 VCs (2,453).
1915–24,717–4.8 VCs (5,149).
1916–53,603–4.4 VCs (12,182).
1917–68,149–8.1 VCs (8,413).
1918–71,071–10.1 VCs (7,037).

The bloodiest year was 1918 and hostilities ended fifty days before the end of the year. Had the war gone on until 31st December, and the average casualty rate had remained the same, the total casualties for 1918 would have been 988,235 and the total of VCs awarded would have been 128.

Of the 492 VCs awarded to BEF land forces, half (246) were for the thirty-six months between August 1914 and August 1917. The other 246 VCs were earned in just under sixteen months. This reflects the growing strength of the BEF, the number of troops employed and the volume of combat involved, which increased year on year. The halfway point for casualties was almost the same in June 1917.

Despite there being 491 VC recipients and 365/6 days in a year, there were, rather surprisingly, ninety-nine dates on which none had birthdays, including 29th February. Six VCs were born on two dates. On 27th January, by coincidence, all six were wartime volunteers born in the United Kingdom. On 29th September all six attended normal schools and all survived their VC actions.

With twelve star-signs and 491 individuals, it was expected that each star-sign would have about forty-one VCs. However, some were above the average and some below:

Libra – 48
Aquarius – 46
Sagittarius – 45
Aries – 44
Scorpio – 41
Taurus – 41

Virgo – 40
Gemini – 39
Leo – 37
Pisces – 36
Cancer – 36
Capricorn – 35

The table below breaks down the number of VCs by country of birth and service. The variations in the distribution of VC birthplaces and the countries with which they served, reflects partly the effects of migration from the United Kingdom in the years prior to the Great War:

	Birth	Service
Australia	43	53
Belgium	1	
Canada	25	60
Ceylon	2	
China	1	
Denmark	2	
Germany	1	
India	10	9
Japan	1	
Nepal	1	
Netherlands	1	

	Birth	Service
New Zealand	10	10
Newfoundland	2	1
South Africa	4	2
Ukraine	1	
United Kingdom	381	356
England Ireland Scotland Wales	283 26 61 11	
United States	4	
Unknown	1	

The majority of birthplaces were in the United Kingdom, where 382 were born. In England thirty-seven counties are represented but of the 283 births, 119 (42%) were in just three counties (Lancashire 44, London 49 and Yorkshire 26). This is to be expected as these were the main centres of population. In Scotland nineteen counties are represented, with thirty-one (51%) of the sixty-one births being in the main population centres (Clackmannanshire 6, Fife 5, Lanarkshire 12 and Midlothian 8). The majority (79%) of the forty-three Australian births were in New South Wales (12), Tasmania (9) and Victoria (13). In Canada most (64%) of the twenty-five births were in Ontario (10) and Québec (6). A full breakdown of known birthplaces is in **Table 2** at the end.

The highest level of education attained was:

University	29	All officers except three
College	2	Both officers
Public School or similar	74	All officers except one
Privately	8	All officers
Grammar School or equivalent	56	All officers except ten
Technical College or similar	10	Three were officers
Normal state provided education	279	Only 28 were officers
None	2	
Unknown	30	Two were officers

The average age for a VC on the day of their actions was twenty-seven years and seven months. The average age reduced each year from 1914 to 1917 and then rose again by one year in 1918. The average ages for each year of the war were:

1914 – 29.2
1915 – 27.2
1916 – 27.0
1917 – 26.8
1918 – 27.8

The ranks held at the time of the VC actions were:

Private – 123
Lance Corporal – 38
Corporal – 47
Lance Sergeant – 11
Sergeant – 69
Colour Sergeant – 2
Warrant Officer 2 – 11
Total other ranks = 301

Second Lieutenant – 45
Lieutenant – 56
Captain – 49
Major – 12
Lieutenant Colonel – 26
Brigadier General – 2
Total officers = 190

There were far fewer officers than other ranks, so it seems that awards to junior officers are out of proportion. Similarly, the number of awards to sergeants also seems to be excessive, compared to the most common rank of private. However, when things go wrong, as they frequently do on the battlefield, it is the junior officers and sergeants who are the most forward and have to grip the situation and take drastic action. It is therefore not surprising that 219 VCs (44.5%) were awarded to junior officers and sergeants.

Of the 491 recipients, 305 (62%) had previous military experience of various kinds:

Regular – 94.
Regular & Special Reserve – 43.
Territorial Force and equivalent – 28.
Territorial Force Reserve – 13.
Militia – 47.
Belgian Army – 1.
Russian Army – 1.
Boer War – 6.
South African Constabulary – 1.
Royal Navy – 2.
School or other youth cadet forces – 54.
UOTC & equivalent – 15.

The remainder were:

Wartime volunteers (Kitchener, AIF, CEF, NZEF etc) – 173.
Conscripts – 13 – it is interesting to note that, despite conscription being introduced by the British in 1916, and other nations later, conscripts received very few awards.

At least the following numbers of VCs were members of various societies and organisations:

Freemasons – 69, mostly post their VC award. Almost 20% of those who survived their VC action became Freemasons.
Church Lads' Brigade – 14.
Boys' Brigade – 11.
Boy Scouts – 16.
Red Cross – 1.
YMCA – 1.

There is no such thing as a routine VC. However, amongst the 492 on the Western Front some stick out more than others. For example:

Adrian Carton de Wiart, with his eye patch and a hook for a left hand.

William Hackett's cold decision to remain entombed rather than leave a comrade.

Bill Coltman, the most decorated other rank of the Great War (VC, DCM & Bar, MM & Bar), who never harmed anyone.

Noel Chavasse, the only double VC of the Great War, and one of only three men to receive a Bar ever.

Other interesting facts:

The youngest at the time of his VC action was Thomas Ricketts, aged seventeen years and six months, and the oldest was Theodore Hardy, aged fifty-four years and six months.

The longest period between VC actions was after Walter Mills on 11th December 1917, when there was a gap of eighty-eight days, until Charles Graham Robertson on 9th March 1918.

The most VCs awarded for a single day was thirteen on 2nd September 1918. The most VCs in a month was forty-five in September 1918.

The longest period between a VC action and the announcement of the award in the London Gazette was for William Bruce. His VC action was on 19th December 1914 and the LG date was 4th September 1919. The shortest period was for John Dimmer, 12th–19th November 1914.

Noel Chavasse, the only Great War double VC, was related by marriage to Charles Upham, the only Second World War double VC. When Chavasse was mortally wounded during his second VC action, he was taken to No.32 Casualty Clearing Station at Brandhoek where the only other double VC, Arthur Martin-Leake, was the CO.

Billy Congreve was the first officer in the Great War to gain all three gallantry decorations – VC, DSO and MC. His father was also awarded the VC in the Second Boer War. Billy was distantly related to three other VCs – Fenton John Aylmer VC KCB, John Augustus Conolly VC and Frederick Francis Maude VC.

Arthur Cross's VC appeared in the film *Carrington VC*, worn by the star, David Niven.

John Dimmer was in the first listing for the newly introduced MC, thus making him the first VC and MC.

Mir Dast's brother, Jemadar Mir Mast, fought for the British at the outbreak of the Great War and defected to the Germans in France in March 1915. He was later awarded the Iron Cross. Mir Dast was also awarded the Indian Order of Merit, and the combination of VC and IOM is unique.

Philip Neame took part in the Paris Olympic Games in 1924, winning gold with the Running Deer team.

Job Drain and Frederick Luke received their VCs from the King at Locon, near Bethune, France on 1st December 1914, the first time that the King had presented the VC in the field.

George Prowse's was the last VC awarded with the blue Royal Navy ribbon.

Corporal John Thomas Davies's VC is the only posthumous award made to a living recipient. He was taken prisoner but listed as 'missing presumed killed'.

William Gregg was the first of eight men in the Great War to be awarded the VC, DCM and MM. Reginald Judson, one of the eight, achieving all three medals in just thirty-four days, an extraordinary achievement.

Harcus Strachan died aged ninety-seven years and 175 days and was the longest-lived VC holder.

Charles Rutherford was the last surviving VC of the Great War, holding the award for the longest, a total of seventy years and ten months.

Table 1: British Monthly and Yearly Casualties and VC Awards

1914 – 95,654 casualties and 39 VCs – average 19,131 casualties and 7.8 VCs per month (2,453):

Aug – 14,409 – 13 (1,108)
Sep – 15,189 – 10 (1,519)
Oct – 30,192 – 6 (5,032)
Nov – 24,785 – 5 (4,957)
Dec – 11,079 – 5 (2,215)

1915 – 296,603 casualties and 58 VCs – average 24,717 casualties and 4.8 VCs per month (5,149):

Jan – 6,542 – 0
Feb – 9,195 – 1 (9,195)
Mar – 24,483 – 9 (2,720)
Apr – 31,264 – 6 (5,211)
May – 65,730 – 11 (5,975)
Jun – 22,563 – 1 (22,563)
Jul – 16,315 – 1 (16,315)
Aug – 14,587 – 1 (14,587)
Sep – 59,615 – 18 (3,312)
Oct – 25,909 – 5 (5,018)
Nov – 9,263 – 4 (2,316)
Dec – 11,117 – 1 (11,117)

1916 – 643,246 casualties and 53 VCs – average 53,603 casualties and 4.4 VCs per month (12,182):

Jan – 10,975 – 0
Feb – 13,014 – 1 (13,014)
Mar – 18,949 – 2 (9,475)
Apr – 22,409 – 1 (22,409)
May – 24,661 – 1 (24,661)
Jun – 39,959 – 7 (5,708)
Jul – 196,081 – 21 (9,337)
Aug – 75,249 – 3 (25,083)
Sep – 115,056 – 11 (10,460)
Oct – 66,852 – 3 (22,284)
Nov – 46,238 – 3 (15,413)
Dec – 13,803 – 0

1917 – 817,790 casualties and 97 VCs – average 68,149 casualties and 8.1 VCs per month (8,413):

Jan – 15,289 – 1 (15,289)	Jul – 84,695 – 15 (5,646)
Feb – 26,140 – 1 (26,140)	Aug – 81,080 – 9 (9,009)
Mar – 25,788 – 2 (12,894)	Sep – 81,249 – 10 (8,125)
Apr – 120,070 – 17 (7,063)	Oct – 119,808 – 14 (8,558)
May – 76,040 – 5 (15,208)	Nov – 73,888 – 15 (4,926)
Jun – 75,123 – 4 (18,780)	Dec – 38,620 – 4 (9,655)

1918 – 852,861 casualties and 111 VCs – average 71,071 casualties and 10.1 VCs per month (7,037):

Jan – 13,042 – 0	Jul – 32,562 – 0
Feb – 9,809 – 0	Aug – 122,272 – 11 (11,116)
Mar – 173,721 – 27 (6,434)	Sep – 114,831 – 25 (4,593)
Apr – 143,168 – 12 (11,931)	Oct – 121,046 – 23 (5,263)
May – 69,049 – 4 (17,262)	Nov – 20,925 – 9 (2,325)
Jun – 32,436 – 0	

Table 2: Birthplaces

Australia – 43
- New South Wales – 12
- Queensland – 3
- South Australia – 5
- Tasmania – 9
- Victoria – 13
- Western Australia – 1

Belgium – 1

Canada – 25
- Manitoba – 3
- New Brunswick – 3
- Nova Scotia – 3
- Ontario – 10
- Québec – 6

Ceylon – 2

China – 1

Denmark – 2

Germany – 1

India – 10

Japan – 1

Nepal – 1

Netherlands – 1

New Zealand – 10

Newfoundland – 2

South Africa – 4

Ukraine – 1

United Kingdom – 381
- England – 283
- Bedfordshire – 1
- Berkshire – 3
- Buckinghamshire – 2
- Cheshire – 9
- Cornwall – 1
- Cumberland – 5
- Derbyshire – 4
- Devon – 7
- Dorset – 1
- Durham – 9
- Essex – 2
- Gloucestershire – 10
- Hampshire – 10
- Herefordshire – 1
- Hertfordshire – 8
- Huntingdonshire – 2
- Kent – 6
- Lancashire – 44
- Leicestershire – 2
- Lincolnshire – 5
- London – 49
- Middlesex – 5
- Norfolk – 7
- Northamptonshire – 2
- Northumberland – 4
- Nottinghamshire – 5
- Oxfordshire – 1
- Shropshire – 1
- Somerset – 1
- Staffordshire – 8
- Suffolk – 4
- Surrey – 9
- Sussex – 10
- Warwickshire – 12
- Wiltshire – 2
- Worcestershire – 5
- Yorkshire – 26

Ireland – 26
- Antrim – 2
- Armagh – 1
- Cork – 2
- Down – 2
- Fermanagh – 1
- Kildare – 1
- Kilkenny – 1
- Laois – 1
- Limerick – 1
- Louth – 2
- Meath – 1
- Monaghan – 2
- Offaly – 1
- Sligo – 1
- Tipperary – 3
- Tyrone – 1
- Westmeath – 2
- Wexford – 1

Scotland – 61
- Aberdeenshire – 4
- Argyllshire – 2
- Ayrshire – 2
- Banffshire – 3
- Clackmannanshire – 6
- Dumfriesshire – 2
- Dunbartonshire – 3
- Fife – 5
- Kirkcudbrightshire – 1
- Lanarkshire – 12
- Midlothian – 8
- Morayshire – 2
- Nairnshire – 1
- Perthshire – 2
- Renfrewshire – 2
- Roxburghshire – 1
- Stirlingshire – 1
- West Lothian – 2
- Wigtownshire – 2

Wales – 11
- Cardiganshire – 1
- Carmarthenshire – 2
- Flintshire – 1
- Glamorganshire – 5
- Monmouthshire – 1
- Montgomeryshire – 1

United States – 4
- Illinois – 1
- Maine – 1
- Minnesota – 1
- Oregon – 1

Sources

Regimental Museums

The following Museums and Regimental Headquarters kindly provided information:

Royal Warwickshire Regiment Museum, Warwick; Light Infantry Office (Yorkshire), Pontefract; RHQ The Argyll & Sutherland Highlanders, Stirling; The Cameronians Regimental Museum, Hamilton; Royal Engineers Museum, Chatham; Museum of the Manchesters, Ashton-under-Lyne; RHQ King's Own Scottish Borderers, Berwick-upon-Tweed; South Wales Borderers and Monmouthshire Regimental Museum, Brecon; Royal Inniskilling Fusiliers Regimental Association, Enniskillen, Co Fermanagh, Northern Ireland; York & Lancaster Regiment Museum, Rotherham; Canadian War Museum, Ottawa; Royal Artillery Historical Trust; The Royal Sussex Regiment Museum.

Individuals

The following individuals provided information and assistance:

Doug and Richard Arman, Alan Baynham-Jones, Rob Gorle, David Harvey, Sue Hedges, Terry Hissey, Derek Hunt, Alastair Jack, Tom Johnson, Anne C Johnston, Alan Jordan, David Harvey, Mary A Kelly, Cynthia List, Robert Mansell, Jeffrey Marshall, Eddie McGuffie, Col (Ret'd) Gerald Napier, Sue Overton, Charles Snape, Vic Tambling, Antony J Waters, Tim West, Lt Col Les Wilson MBE.

Divisional Histories

Listed in numerical order:

The Fifth Division in the Great War. Brig Gen A H Hussey and Maj D S Inman. Nisbet 1920.

The History of the 9th (Scottish) Division 1914–19. J Ewing. Murray 1921.

The 18th Division in the Great War. Capt GHF Nicholls. Blackwood 1922.

The History of the 20th (Light) Division. Capt VE Inglefield. Nisbet 1921.

The 25th Division in France and Flanders. Lt Col M Kincaid-Smith. Harrison 1919.

The Story of the 29th Division – A Record of Gallant Deeds. Capt S Gillon. Nelson 1925.

The Thirty-Fourth Division 1915–19 – The Story of its Career from Ripon to the Rhine. Lt Col J Shakespear. Witherby 1921.

The History of the 36th (Ulster) Division. C Falls. Linenhall Press 1922.

The History of the 51st (Highland) Division 1914–18. Maj FW Bewsher. Blackwood 1921.

Brigade Histories

The 54th Infantry Brigade 1914–18 – Some Records of Battle and Laughter in France. Gale & Polden 1919.

Regimental/Unit Histories

Works appear by Regiment in precedence order:

Royal Artillery

The Royal Artillery War Commemoration Book. Anon. G Bell 1970.

History of the Royal Regiment of Artillery, Western Front, 1914–18. Gen Sir Martin Farndale. Dorset Press 1986.

ARTYVICS – The Victoria Cross and the Royal Regiment of Artillery. Marc J Sherriff. Witherbys, Aylesbury St, London.

Royal Engineers

History of the Corps of Royal Engineers, Volume V, The Home Front, France, Flanders and Italy in the First World War. Institute of the Royal Engineers 1952.

Scots Guards

The Scots Guards in the Great War 1914–18. F Loraine Petre, W Ewart and Maj Gen Sir C Lowther. Murray 1925.

Irish Guards

The Irish Guards in the Great War. R Kipling. MacMillan 1923.

The Micks, The Story of the Irish Guards. P Verney. Peter Davies 1970.

The Royal Scots

The Royal Scots 1914–19. Maj J Ewing. Oliver & Boyd 1925. Two volumes.

The Royal Warwickshire Regiment

The Story of the Royal Warwickshire Regiment. CL Kingsford. Country Life 1921.

The Bedfordshire Regiment

The 16th Foot, A History of the Bedfordshire and Hertfordshire. Maj Gen Sir F Maurice. Constable 1931.

The Story of the Bedfordshire and Hertfordshire Volume II – 1914–58 Bedfordshire and Hertfordshire. Compiled by Lt Col TJ Barrow DSO, Maj VA French and J Seabrook Esq. Published privately Bedfordshire and Hertfordshire 1986.

The Lancashire Fusiliers

The History of the Lancashire Fusiliers 1914–18, Volumes I and II. Maj Gen JC Latter. Gale & Polden 1949.

Salford Pals – 15th, 16th, 19th and 20th (Service) Battalions Lancashire Fusiliers. M Stedman. Leo Cooper 1993.

The Lancashire Fusiliers Annual No.28 – 1918. Editor Maj B Smyth. Sackville Press 1919.

The History of the South Wales Borderers 1914–18. CT Atkinson. Medici Society 1931.

The King's Own Scottish Borderers

The King's Own Scottish Borderers in the Great War. Capt Stair Gillon. Nelson 1930.

The Cameronians (Scottish Rifles)

A Short History of the Cameronians (Scottish Rifles). Col HC Wylly. Gale & Polden 1924.

History of the Cameronians (Scottish Rifles), Volume II 1910–22. Col HH Story. Published 1961.

The Royal Inniskilling Fusiliers

The Royal Inniskilling Fusiliers in the Great War. Sir F Fox. Constable 1928.

The Gloucestershire Regiment

The Gloucestershire Regiment in the Great War 1914–18. E Wyrell. Methuen 1931.

The Slasher. A New Short History of the Gloucestershire Regiment 1694–1965. Anon.

The Royal Sussex Regiment

A History of the Royal Sussex Regiment 1701–1953. GD Martineau. Moore & Taylor 1955.

A Short History of the Royal Sussex Regiment 1701–1926. Anon. Gale & Polden 19527.

The Northamptonshire Regiment

The Northamptonshire Regiment 1914–18. Regimental Committee. Gale & Polden.

Four VCs in Forty Months. The Proud Record in World War One of the 6th (Service) Battalion The Northamptonshire Regiment. G Moore. G Moore 1979.

The King's Own (Yorkshire Light Infantry)

History of the King's Own Yorkshire Light Infantry in the Great War. Lt Col RC Bond. Percy Lund, Humphries 1930.

The King's Own Yorkshire Light Infantry, Register of Officers 1755–1945. CP Deedes.

The Manchester Regiment

History of the Manchester Regiment, Volume II 1883–1922. Col HC Wylly. Forster Groom 1925.

The York & Lancaster Regiment

The York & Lancaster Regiment 1758–1919. Col HC Wylly. Butler & Tanner 1920. Two volumes.

Princess Louise's (Argyll & Sutherland Highlanders)

Argyllshire Highlanders 1860–1960. Lt Col GI Malcolm. Halberd Press.

Fighting Highlanders – The History of the Argyll & Sutherland Highlanders. PJR Mileham. Arms and Armour Press 1993.

Machine Gun Corps

Machine Guns, Their History and Tactical Employment (Being also a History of the Machine Gun Corps 1916–22). Lt Col GS Hutchinson. MacMillan 1938.

Canadian Expeditionary Force

Official History of the Canadian Army in the First World War – Canadian Expeditionary Force 1914–19. Col GWL Nicholson 1962.

General Works

A Bibliography of Regimental Histories of the British Army. Compiler A S White. Society for Army Historical Research 1965.

A Military Atlas of the First World War. A Banks & A Palmer. Purnell 1975.

Topography of Armageddon, A British Trench Map Atlas of the Western Front 1914–18. P Chasseaud. Mapbooks 1991.

Before Endeavours Fade. R E B Coombs. Battle of Britain Prints 1976.

British Regiments 1914–18. Brig E A James. Samson 1978.

Orange, Green and Khaki, The Story of the Irish Regiments in the Great War 1914–18. T Johnstone. 1992.

The Story of the Fourth Army in the Battles of the Hundred Days, August 8th to November 11th, 1918. Major General Sir Archibald Montgomery KCMG CB General Staff Fourth Army. Hodder and Stoughton Limited, London.

Biographical/Autobiographical

The Dictionary of National Biography 1901–85. Various volumes. Oxford University Press.

The Cross of Sacrifice, Officers Who Died in the Service of the British, Indian and East African Regiments and Corps 1914–19. S D and D B Jarvis. Roberts Medals 1993.

Australian Dictionary of Biography.

Dictionary of Canadian Biography.

Valiant Hearts. Atlantic Canada and the Victoria Cross. John Boileau. Nimbus Publishing, Halifax, Nova Scotia 2005.

Specific Works on the Victoria Cross

The Register of the Victoria Cross. This England 1981 and 1988.

The Story of the Victoria Cross 1856–1963. Brig Sir J Smyth. Frederick Muller 1963.

The Evolution of the Victoria Cross, A Study in Administrative History. M J Crook. Midas 1975.

The Victoria Cross and the George Cross. IWM 1970.

The Victoria Cross, The Empire's Roll of Valour. Lt Col R Stewart. Hutchinson 1928.

The Victoria Cross 1856–1920. Sir O'Moore Creagh and E M Humphris. Standard Art Book Company, London 1920.
Victoria Cross – Awards to Irish Servicemen. B Clark. Published in The Irish Sword summer 1986.
Heart of a Dragon, VCs of Wales and the Welsh Regiments 1914–82. W Alister Williams. Bridge Books 2006.
Devotion to Duty, Tributes to a Region's VCs. James W Bancroft. Aim High 1990.
For Valour, The Victoria Cross, Courage in Action. J Percival. Thames Methuen 1985.
VC Locator. D Pillinger & A Staunton. Highland Press, Queanbeyan, New South Wales, Australia 1991.
Black Country VCs. Barry Harris. Black Country Society 1985.
The VC Roll of Honour. J W Bancroft. Aim High 1989.
A Bibliography of the Victoria Cross. W James McDonald. W J Mcdonald, Nova Scotia 1994.
Canon Lummis VC Files held in the National Army Museum, Chelsea.
Recipients of the Victoria Cross in the Care of the Commonwealth War Graves Commission. CWGC 1997.
Victoria Cross Heroes. Michael Ashcroft. Headline Review 2006
Monuments to Courage. David Harvey. 1999.
The Sapper VCs. Gerald Napier. The Stationery Office, London 1998.
Irish Winners of the Victoria Cross. Richard Doherty & David Truesdale. Four Courts Press, Dublin, Ireland 2000.
The Victoria Crosses and George Crosses of the Honourable East India Company & Indian Army 1856–1945. National Army Museum 1962.
Our Bravest and our Best. The Stories of Canada's Victoria Cross Winners. Arthur Bishop 1995.

Works on Other Honours and Awards

Distinguished Conduct Medal 1914–18, Citations of Recipients. London Stamp Exchange 1983.
Recipients of Bars to the Military Cross 1916–20. JV Webb 1988.
The Distinguished Service Order 1886–1923 (in 2 volumes). Sir O'Moore Creagh and E M Humphris. J B Hayward 1978 (originally published 1924).
Orders and Medals Society Journal (various articles).
South African War – Honours and Awards 1899–1902. Lionel Leventhal Ltd.

Official Publications and Sources

History of the Great War, Order of Battle of Divisions. Compiler Maj A F Becke. HMSO.
History of the Great War, Military Operations, France and Belgium. Compiler Brig Gen Sir J E Edmonds. HMSO. Published in 14 volumes of text, with 7 map volumes and 2 separate Appendices between 1923 and 1948.
Unit War Diaries in the National Archives under WO 95
Military maps in the National Archives under WO 297.

Medal Cards and Medal Rolls in the National Archives under WO 329 and ADM 171.
Soldiers' Service Records in the National Archives under WO 97, 363 and 364.
Officers' Records in the National Archives under WO 25, 76, 339 and 374.
Army Lists
Location of Hospitals and Casualty Clearing Stations, BEF 1914–19. Ministry of Pensions 1923.
London Gazettes
Census returns, particularly for 1881, 1891 and 1901.
Births, Marriages and Deaths records in the Family Records Centre, Islington, London.
Service records from the Library and Archives of Canada.
Officers and Soldiers Died in the Great War.

Reference Publications

Who's Who and Who Was Who.
The Times 1914 onwards.
The Daily Telegraph 1914 onwards.
Kelly's Handbook to the Titled, Landed and Official Classes.
Burke's Peerage.
Debrett's.
The Landed Gentry of Ireland 1958.

Internet Websites

History of the Victoria Cross – www.victoriacross.org.uk – Iain Stewart.
Commonwealth War Graves Commission – www.cwgc.org
Free Births, Marriages and Deaths – www.freebmd.org.uk
Memorials to Valour – http://www.memorialstovalour.co.uk
Scotland's People – www.scotlandspeople.gov.uk

Periodicals

This England magazine – various editions.
Coin and Medal News – various editions.
Journal of The Victoria Cross Society – no longer published
Stand To – journal of the Western Front Association.

Useful Information

(Some details may be affected by Brexit)

Accommodation – there is a wide variety of accommodation available in France and Belgium. Search online for your requirements. There are also numerous campsites, but many close for the winter from late September.

Clothing and Kit – consider taking:

Waterproofs.
Headwear and gloves.
Walking shoes/boots.
Shades and sunscreen.
Binoculars and camera.
Snacks and drinks.

Customs/Behaviour – local people are generally tolerant of battlefield visitors but please respect their property and address them respectfully. The French are less inclined to switch to English than other Europeans. If you try some basic French, it will be appreciated.

Driving – rules of the road are similar to UK, apart from having to drive on the right. If in doubt about priorities at junctions, always be prepared to give way to the right, particularly in France. In many areas, particularly rural, you usually have to give way to vehicles coming in from the right, even from apparently minor roads onto major routes. Obey laws and road signs – police impose harsh on-the-spot fines. Penalties for drinking and driving are heavy and the legal limit is lower than UK (50mg rather than 80mg). Most Autoroutes in France are toll roads. In rural areas covered in this book the speed limit is 80kph but in many places the old 90kph signs remain. The red-framed name board at the entrance to a village or town automatically imposes a 50kph speed limit.

Fuel – petrol stations are only open 24 hours on major routes and larger supermarkets. Payment by credit/debit card in automatic tellers is increasingly becoming the norm. The cheapest fuel is generally at hypermarkets.

Mandatory Requirements – if taking your own car you need:
Full driving licence.
Vehicle registration document.
Comprehensive motor insurance valid in Europe (Green Card).
European breakdown and recovery cover.
Letter of authorisation from the owner if the vehicle is not yours.
Spare set of bulbs, headlight beam adjusters, warning triangle, GB sticker and high visibility vest. Requirements do vary, so check before departing.
An emission quality sticker (Crit'Air) is required if driving in Paris or certain other cities/areas.

Emergency – keep details required in an emergency separate from your wallet or handbag:
Photocopy passport, insurance documents and EHIC/GHIC (see Health below).
Mobile phone details.
Credit/debit card numbers and cancellation telephone contacts.
Travel insurance company contact number.
Who to contact in an emergency.

Ferries – the closest ports are Boulogne, Calais and Dunkirk. The Shuttle is quicker, but usually more expensive.

Health

European Health Insurance Card – entitles the holder to medical treatment at local rates. Apply online at www.ehic.org.uk/Internet/startApplication.do. It is issued free and is valid for five years. You are only covered if you have the EHIC with you when you go for treatment. Since Brexit, EHIC is being gradually replaced by a Global Health Insurance Card (GHIC).

Travel Insurance – you are also strongly advised to have travel insurance. If you receive treatment get a statement by the doctor (*feuille de soins*) and a receipt to make a claim on return.

Personal Medical Kit – treating minor ailments saves time and money. Pack sufficient prescription medicine for the trip.

Chemist (*Pharmacie*) – look for the green cross. They provide some treatment and if unable to help will direct you to a doctor. Most open 0900–1900 except Sundays. Out of hours services (*pharmacie de garde*) are advertised in Pharmacie windows.

Doctor and Dentist – hotel receptions have details of local practices. Beware private doctors/hospitals, as extra charges cannot be reclaimed – the French national health service is known as *conventionné*.

Rabies – contact with infected animals is very rare, but if bitten by any animal, get the wound examined professionally immediately.

Money

ATMs – at most banks and post offices with instructions in English. Check your card can be used in France and what charges apply. Some banks limit how much can be withdrawn. Let your bank know you will be away, as some block cards if transactions take place unexpectedly.

Credit/Debit Cards – major cards are usually accepted, but some have different names – Visa is Carte Bleue and Mastercard is Eurocard.

Exchange – beware 0% commission, as the rate may be poor. The Post Office takes back unused currency at the same rate, which may or may not be advantageous. Since the Euro, currency exchange facilities are scarce.

Local Taxes – if you buy high value items you can reclaim tax. Get the forms completed by the shop, have them stamped by Customs, post them to the shop and they will refund about 12%. Brexit may change this.

Passport – a valid passport is required.

Post – postcard stamps are often available from vendors, newsagents and tabacs.

Public Holidays – just about everything closes and banks can close early the day before. Transport may be affected, but tourist attractions in high season are unlikely to be. The following dates/days are public holidays:

1 January
Easter Monday
1 May
8 May
Ascension Day
Whit Monday
14 July
15 August
1 & 11 November
25 December

In France many businesses and restaurants close for the majority of August.

Radio – if you want to pick up the news from home, try BBC Radio 4 on 198 kHz long wave. BBC Five Live on 909 kHz medium wave can sometimes be received. There are numerous internet options for keeping up with the news.

Shops – in large towns and tourist areas they tend to open all day. In more remote places they may close for lunch. Some bakers open Sunday a.m. and during the week take later lunch breaks. In general shops do not open on Sundays and those that do have limited hours.

Telephone

To UK – 0044, then delete the initial 0 and dial the rest of the number.
Local Calls – dial the full number even if within the same zone.
Mobiles – check yours will work in France and the charges.
Emergencies – dial 112 for medical, fire and police anywhere in Europe from any landline, pay phone or mobile. Calls are free.
British Embassy (Paris) – 01 44 51 31 00.

Time Zone – one hour ahead of UK.

Tipping – a small tip is expected by cloakroom and lavatory attendants and porters. Not required in restaurants when a service charge is included.

Toilets – the best are in museums and the main tourist attractions. Towns usually have public toilets where markets are held; some are coin operated. Otherwise on the battlefields facilities are sparse. Finding a local café may be the best option, although they are closing as rapidly as British pubs.

Index

Notes:

1. Not every person or location is included. Most family members named in the Biographies are not.
2. Armed forces units, establishments, etc are grouped under the respective country, except for Britain's, which appear under the three services – British Army, Royal Air Force and Royal Navy. Royal Naval Division units appear under British Army for convenience.
3. Newfoundland appears under Canada although not part of it at the time.
4. Cemeteries/Crematoria, Cathedrals, Churches, Hospitals, Museums, Schools, Ships, Trenches, Universities and Commonwealth War Graves Commission appear under those group headings.
5. All orders, medals and decorations appear under Orders.
6. Belgium, Britain, France and Germany are not indexed in the accounts of the VC actions, as there are too many mentions. Similarly, England, Britain and United Kingdom are not indexed in the biographies.